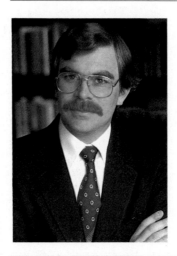

E. Jerome McCarthy received his Ph.D. from the University of Minnesota in 1958. Since then he has taught at the Universities of Oregon, Notre Dame, and Michigan State. He has been deeply involved in teaching and developing new teaching materials. Besides writing various articles and monographs, he is the author of textbooks on data processing and social issues in marketing.

Now 56 years old, Dr. McCarthy is active in making presentations to academic conferences and business meetings. He has worked with groups of teachers throughout the country and has addressed international conferences in South America, Africa, and India.

Dr. McCarthy was voted one of the "top five" leaders in Marketing Thought in 1975 by marketing educators. He was also a Ford Foundation Fellow in 1963–64 doing independent research on the role of marketing in economic development. In 1959–60 he was a Ford Foundation Fellow at the Harvard Business School—working on mathematical methods in marketing.

Besides his academic interests, Dr. McCarthy is involved in consulting for, and guiding the growth of, several businesses. He has worked with executives from Dow-Corning, Lear-Siegler, 3M, Cordemex, Grupo Industrial Alfa, and many smaller companies. He is director of several for-profit and not-for-profit organizations. His primary interests, however, are in (1) "converting" students to marketing and marketing strategy planning and (2) preparing teaching materials to help others do the same. This is why he has continued to spend a large part of his time revising and improving marketing texts. This is a continuing process, and this edition incorporates the latest thinking in the field.

William D. Perreault, Jr., received his Ph.D. from the University of North Carolina, Chapel Hill in 1973. Currently, he is Hanes Professor at the School of Business at the University of North Carolina at Chapel Hill—where he is deeply involved in teaching in each of the School's degree programs. In 1978 he was the first recipient of the School's Rendleman Award for teaching excellence. He has been teaching the introductory course in marketing for more than a decade—as well as courses in sales management, marketing strategy, consumer behavior, industrial marketing, advertising, marketing channels, physical distribution and marketing research. He has worked in evaluating educational programs for the U.S. Department of HEW and the Venezuelan Ministry of Education, and is coauthor with E. J. McCarthy of *Basic Marketing: A Managerial Approach.*

In 1982, at age 34, Dr. Perreault started a three-year term as editor of the *Journal of Marketing Research.* He has also served as an associate editor of *Management Science* and is on the review board of the *Journal of Marketing* and other publications. He is a well-known author—and his ideas about marketing management and marketing research have been published in scores of journals.

Dr. Perreault was a founding Director of the Triangle Chapter of the American Marketing Association and is a member of the AMA Advisory Committee to the U.S. Bureau of the Census. He has served as a marketing consultant to many organizations, including Libby-Owens-Ford, Whirlpool, Owens Corning Fiberglass, General Electric, and the Federal Trade Commission, as well as a variety of wholesale and retail firms.

The Irwin Series in Marketing

Consulting Editor
Gilbert A. Churchill, Jr.
University of Wisconsin,
Madison

Essentials of Marketing

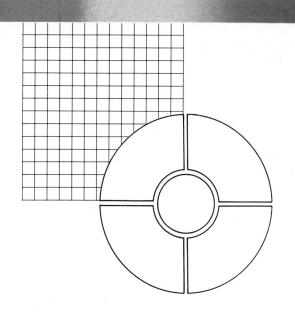

Third Edition

E. Jerome McCarthy, Ph.D.
Michigan State University

William D. Perreault, Jr., Ph.D.
University of North Carolina

 1985

RICHARD D. IRWIN, INC.
Homewood, Illinois 60430

ISBN 0-256-03300-5

Library of Congress Catalog Card No. 84 – 62328

Printed in the United States of America

1 2 3 4 5 6 7 8 9 0 D 2 1 0 9 8 7 6 5

■ Preface

This book presents the "essentials" of marketing. A basic objective was to make it easy for students to grasp these very important "essentials"— "accessibility" was a key goal.

Essentials of Marketing is a shortened version of *Basic Marketing*—a book that has been widely used in the first marketing course. While cutting the material down to the *Essentials,* much time and effort was spent on carefully defining terms and finding the "right" word to speed understanding. Similarly, figures, pictures, and illustrations were selected to help today's more visual student "see" the material better.

Twenty-four years ago, the first edition of *Basic Marketing* pioneered an innovative structure—using the "4 Ps" with a managerial approach—for the introductory marketing course. Since then, the book has been continually improved and refined. The response of both teachers and students has been gratifying. *Basic Marketing* and *Essentials of Marketing*—and the supporting materials—have been more widely used than any other teaching materials for introductory marketing. The "4 Ps" has proved to be an organizing structure that has worked for millions of students and teachers.

Now, about 50 introductory marketing texts are available—and almost all of them have, in varying degrees, tried to copy the content, structure, and managerial emphasis of *Basic Marketing* and *Essentials of Marketing*. Imitation, they say, is the sincerest form of flattery. But we have responded to this form of "flattery" with an effort and commitment to excellence that should set a new target for the imitators.

We are trying to offer the highest quality teaching resource ever available for the introductory course. We have worked together closely to enhance the best and proven elements of the earlier editions—while blending in new perspectives from our teaching, research, and business experiences.

v

The whole text has been critically revised, updated, and rewritten. Clear and interesting communication has been a priority—as in past editions. Careful explanations—coupled with a focus on the important "essentials"—motivate learning. Hundreds of new examples—carefully integrated with the text discussion—bring the concepts alive to heighten your interest. Special attention was given to new teaching aids—graphs, figures, and photographs—that reinforce key points. The contemporary design of the text accents the "state-of-the-art" treatment of topics. Our publisher, too, shared in our commitment: a five-color book offered exciting new possibilities for communicating important ideas.

The aim of all this revising, refining, editing, and illustrating was to try to make sure that each student really does get a good feel for a market-directed system and how he or she can help it—and some company—run better. We believe marketing is important and interesting—and we want every student who reads *Essentials of Marketing* to share our enthusiasm.

The emphasis of *Essentials of Marketing* is on marketing strategy planning. Twenty chapters introduce the important concepts in marketing management—and the student sees marketing through the eyes of the marketing manager. The organization of the chapters and topics was carefully planned. But we took special care in writing so that it is possible to rearrange and use the chapters in many ways—to fit various needs.

The first two chapters deal with the nature of marketing—focusing both on its macro role in society and its micro role in businesses—and other organizations. Next, a chapter on marketing opportunity analysis introduces a strategic planning view of how managers can identify opportunities and segment markets. This strategic view alerts the student to the importance of understanding the external environments affecting marketing—which are discussed in Chapter 4. Chapter 5 is a contemporary view of getting information—from marketing research and information systems—for marketing management planning. The next two chapters study the behavioral features of the consumer market and how intermediate customers—like manufacturers, channel members, and government purchasers—are similar to and different from final consumers. Chapter 8 discusses market segmentation in more detail—and helps the student see how to forecast the size of a market segment.

The next group of chapters—Chapters 9–18—is concerned with developing a marketing mix—out of the four Ps: Product, Place (involving channels of distribution and customer service levels), Promotion, and Price. These chapters are concerned with developing the "right" Product and making it available at the "right" Place with the "right" Promotion and the "right" Price—to satisfy target customers and still meet the objectives of the business. These chapters are presented in an integrated, analytical way, so there is a logical development of a student's thinking about planning marketing strategies.

Chapter 19 applies the principles of the text to international marketing. While there is a multinational emphasis throughout the text, this separate chapter is provided for those wishing special emphasis on international marketing.

The final chapter considers how efficient the marketing process is. Here we discuss many criticisms of marketing and evaluate the effectiveness of both micro and macro marketing—considering whether changes are needed. After this chapter, the student might want to look at Appendix C—about career opportunities in marketing.

Some textbooks treat "special" topics—like social marketing, consumerism, industrial marketing, services marketing, and marketing for nonprofit organizations—in separate chapters. We have not done this because we are convinced that treating such materials as separate topics leads to an unfortunate "compartmentalization" of ideas. We think they are too important to be isolated in that way. Instead, they are interwoven and illustrated throughout the text—to emphasize that marketing thinking is crucial in all aspects of our society and economy.

Really understanding marketing and how to plan marketing strategies can build self-confidence—and make a student more ready to take an active part in the business world. To move students in this direction, we deliberately include a variety of frameworks, models, classification systems, and "how-to-do-it" techniques which should speed the development of "marketing sense"—and enable the student to analyze marketing situations in a confident and meaningful way. Taken seriously, they are practical and they work. By making these materials more interesting and understandable, we hope to help students see marketing as the challenging and rewarding area it is.

Essentials of Marketing can be studied and used in many ways—because the *Essentials of Marketing* "text material" is only the central component of a *Professional Learning Units* System (our *PLUS*) for students and teachers. Many combinations of components are possible—depending on course objectives.

To help the student see what is coming in each *Essentials of Marketing* chapter, behavioral objectives are included on the first page of each chapter. And to speed student understanding, important new terms are shown in red and defined immediately. They are also listed in the separate *Student Aid*—with page numbers for convenient reference. Further, a glossary of these terms is presented at the end of the book. These aids help the student understand important concepts—and speed review before exams.

Understanding of the "text material" can be deepened by discussion of the cases suggested at the end of each chapter. In addition, end-of-chapter questions can be used to encourage students to investigate the marketing process and develop their own ways of thinking about it.

There are more components, too. A separate unit, *Readings and Cases in Basic Marketing,* provides carefully selected complementary materials. The readings are thought-provoking—and illustrate concepts from the text. End-of-reading questions can start the discussion. The longer cases in this book can be used for detailed student analysis—or for instructor presentation. Finally, a separate *Student Aid* contains several more components of the PLUS system—and offers further opportunities to obtain a deeper understanding of the material. This *Student Aid* can be used by the student alone or with teacher direction. It includes a brief introduction to each chapter, a list of the important new terms (with page numbers), true-false questions (with answers and page numbers) which cover *all* the important terms and concepts, and multiple-choice questions (with answers) which illustrate the kinds of questions that may appear in the examinations. Finally, the *Student Aid* has cases, exercises, and problems—with instructions and blanks to fill in. They can be used as classwork or homework—to drill on certain topics—and to deepen understanding of others by forcing application and then discussion. In fact, reading *Essentials of Marketing* and working with the *Student Aid* can be the basic activity of the course.

Finally, feedback—from both students and teachers—is encouraged. We want to prepare the best teaching materials available anywhere. Any suggestions for improving the learning process in the marketing area will be greatly appreciated.

E. Jerome McCarthy
William D. Perreault, Jr.

■ Acknowledgments

Preparing the current revisions of *Basic Marketing* and *Essentials of Marketing* has been a consuming, four-year effort. The resulting texts represent a blending of our career-long experiences—and they have been influenced and improved by the inputs of more people than it is possible to list.

Faculty and students at our current and past academic institutions—Michigan State University, University of North Carolina, Notre Dame, University of Georgia, Northwestern University, University of Oregon, and University of Minnesota—have significantly shaped the book. Faculty at Notre Dame had a profound effect when the first editions of the book were developed. Professor Yusaku Furuhashi has continued to provide suggestions and counsel on the multinational emphasis. Similarly, Professor Andrew A. Brogowicz of Western Michigan University has contributed many fine ideas. We are especially grateful to our many students who have criticized and made comments about materials in *Basic Marketing* and *Essentials of Marketing*. Indeed, in many ways, our students have been our best teachers.

Many improvements in the current editions were stimulated by comprehensive reviews prepared by Barton Weitz at the University of Pennsylvania and Gilbert A. Churchill, Jr., at the University of Wisconsin. Bixby Cooper at Michigan State, Nicholas Didow at the University of North Carolina, and Donna Hoffman at Columbia University provided many constructive suggestions incorporated in the current editions. Barbara McCuen of the University of Nebraska at Omaha provided input on the visual aspects of the texts.

The designers, artists, editors, and production people at Richard D. Irwin,

Inc., who worked with us on these editions warrant special recognition. Each has shared our commitment to excellence and brought their own individual creativity to the project.

Helpful criticisms and comments on earlier editions were made by David Rink, Homer M. Dalbey, J. H. Faricy, David Lambert, Walter Gross, and Guy R. Banville. Barbara Bart, Robert C. Stephens III, Harry Summers, Gerald Waddell, Donna Rich, Carmen C. Reagan, Dean Almon, Antonio Chriscolo, Chauncy Elkins, Rosann Spiro, John Langly, and Dave Sparks participated in focus group discussions at Southern Marketing Association meetings. Many improvements have been incorporated in response to suggestions from these people.

Our families have been patient and consistent supporters through all phases. The support has been direct and substantive. Joanne McCarthy and Pam Perreault provided invaluable editorial assistance—and many fresh ideas—through each draft and revision. The quality of their inputs is matched only by their energy and enthusiasm. Carol McCarthy helped in research and reorienting the "Career Planning in Marketing" appendix—reflecting her needs and experiences as a college student looking for a career in advertising.

We are indebted to all the firms which allowed us to reproduce their proprietary materials here. Similarly, we are grateful to associates from our business experiences who have shared their perspectives, and enhanced our sensitivity to the key challenges of marketing management.

A textbook must capsulize existing knowledge—while bringing new perspectives and organization to enhance it. Our thinking has been shaped by the writings of literally thousands of marketing scholars and practitioners. In some cases it is impossible to give unique credit for a particular idea or concept—because so many people have played important roles in anticipating, suggesting, shaping, and developing an area. We gratefully acknowledge these contributors—from the early thought-leaders to contemporary authors—who have shared their creative ideas. We respect their impact on the development of marketing and more specifically this book.

To all of these persons—and to the many publishers who graciously granted permission to use their materials—we are deeply grateful. Responsibility for any errors or omissions is certainly ours, but the book would not have been possible without the assistance of many others. Our sincere appreciation goes to everyone who helped in their own special way.

E. Jerome McCarthy
William D. Perreault, Jr.

Contents

9 Elements of product planning, 208

10 Product management and new-product development, 238

11 Place and physical distribution, 258

12 Retailing, 284

13 Wholesaling, 306

14 Promotion—introduction, 324

15 Personal selling, 346

16 Mass selling, 368

17 Pricing objectives and policies, 390

Appendix B ■ Marketing arithmetic, 412

18 Price setting in the real world, 426

19 Marketing strategy planning for international markets, 448

20 Marketing in a consumer-oriented
society: Appraisal and challenges,
472

Appendix C ■ Career planning in marketing,
490

Cases ■

Essentials of Marketing

Chapter 1 ■ Marketing's role in society

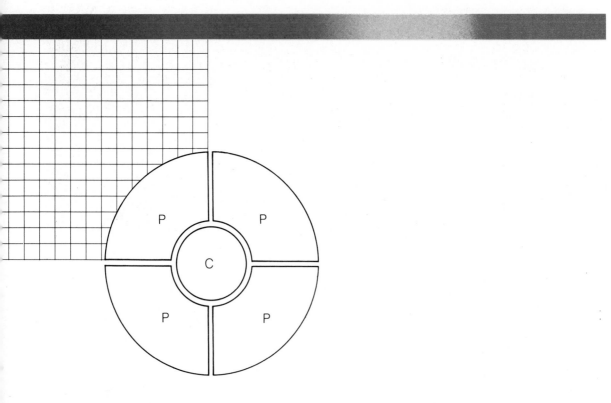

When you finish this chapter, you should:

1. Know what marketing is and why you should learn about it.

2. Know why and how macro-marketing systems develop.

3. Know why marketing specialists—including middlemen and facilitators—develop.

4. Know the marketing functions and who performs them.

5. Recognize the important new terms (shown in red).

Marketing affects almost every aspect of your daily life.

Some students take an introductory marketing course because friends tell them it's really interesting. Some students study marketing because they've heard good jobs are available in marketing. Others take it because it's a required subject.

No matter why you're taking this course, it's a pretty safe bet that you have little—if any—idea of what marketing is all about. Don't worry—you're not alone! Most Americans—even some business managers—have a hard time giving an exact definition of marketing.

Before defining marketing, we will give you a general idea of what marketing is all about—and how it can help you in your career plans.

MARKETING—WHAT'S IT ALL ABOUT?

Marketing Is More Than Selling or Advertising

If forced to define marketing, most people say that marketing means "selling" or "advertising." It's true that these are parts of marketing. But it's very important for you to see that *marketing is much more than selling and advertising.*

How Did All Those Tennis Rackets Get Here?

Let's think about the marketing of tennis rackets. Most of us weren't born with a tennis racket in our hand. Nor do most of us make our own tennis rackets. Instead, they are made by firms such as Wilson, Spaulding, Davis, Head, and Prince.

Most tennis rackets look pretty much alike. All are intended to do the same thing—hit the ball over the net. But a tennis player can choose from a wide assortment of rackets. There are different shapes, materials, weights, handle sizes, and types of strings. You can buy a prestrung racket for less than $15. Or you can spend more than $200 just for a frame!

This variety in sizes and materials complicates the production and sale of tennis rackets. The following list shows some of the many things a firm should do *before* and *after* it decides to manufacture tennis rackets.

1. Estimate how many people will be playing tennis over the next several years—and how many tennis rackets they will buy.
2. Predict exactly when players will want to buy tennis rackets.
3. Find out what types of rackets—handle sizes, shapes, weights, and materials—people will want and how many of each.
4. Estimate what price the different tennis players will be willing to pay for their rackets.
5. Determine where these tennis players will be—and how to get the firm's rackets to them.
6. Decide which kinds of promotion should be used to tell potential customers about the firm's tennis rackets.
7. Estimate how many other firms will be manufacturing tennis rackets, how many rackets they will produce, what kind, at what prices, and so on.

The above activities are *not* part of **manufacturing**—actually *producing* goods and services. Rather, they are part of a larger process—called marketing—which can provide needed direction for manufacturing—and help make sure that the right products are produced and find their way to consumers.

As our tennis racket example shows, marketing includes much more than selling or advertising. We will describe these activities in the next chapter—and you'll learn much more about them before you finish this book. For now, it's important to see that marketing plays a necessary role in providing consumers with goods and services that satisfy their needs.

HOW MARKETING RELATES TO MANUFACTURING

Manufacturing is a very important economic activity. Whether for lack of skill and resources—or just lack of time—most people don't make most of the products they use. Picture yourself, for example, building a 10-speed bicycle, a stereo system, or a digital watch—starting from scratch! Clearly, the high standard of living that most Americans enjoy is not possible without modern manufacturing.

All tennis racquets can hit the ball over the net—but there are many variations to meet the needs of different people.

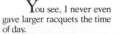
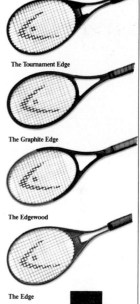
Tennis Rackets, Like Mousetraps, Don't Sell Themselves

Although manufacturing is a necessary economic activity, some people overrate its importance in relation to marketing. Their attitude is reflected in the old saying: "If a man . . . makes a better mousetrap . . . the world will beat a path to his door." In other words, they think that if you make a good product, customers will line up at your factory door.

The mousetrap idea probably wasn't true in Grandpa's time—and it certainly isn't true today. In modern economies, the grass grows high on the path to the Better Mousetrap Factory—if the new mousetrap is *not* properly marketed. We have already seen, for example, that there's a lot more to selling tennis rackets than just manufacturing them. This is true for most products.

The point is that manufacturing and marketing are both important parts of a total business system—aimed at providing consumers with need-satisfying goods and services. Together, manufacturing and marketing provide the four basic economic utilities—form, time, place, and possession utilities—which are needed to provide consumer satisfaction. Here, **utility** means the power to satisfy human needs.

Tennis Rackets Do Not Automatically Provide Utility

Form utility is provided when a manufacturer makes something—for instance, a tennis racket—out of other materials. But just producing tennis rackets doesn't result in consumer satisfaction. Time, place, and possession utility must also be provided. **Time utility** means having the product available *when* the customer wants it. And **place utility** means having the product available *where* the customer wants it. For example, how much satisfaction does a tennis player in California get from a tennis racket in a manufacturer's warehouse in Pennsylvania? That tennis racket won't win any games unless it is available *when* (time utility) and *where* (place utility) the tennis player wants it. Further, to have the legal right to use the racket, the tennis player has to pay for it before enjoying possession utility. **Possession utility** means gaining possession so that one has the right to use a product.

Stated simply, manufacturing creates form utility, and marketing provides time, place, and possession utility. We'll look at how marketing does this later in this chapter. First, we want to tell you why you should study marketing—and then we'll define marketing.

MARKETING AND YOU

Why You Should Study Marketing

One reason for studying marketing is that you—as a consumer—pay for marketing. It's estimated that marketing costs about 50 cents of each consumer's dollar.[1]

Another important reason for learning about marketing is that marketing *affects your daily life.* The products you buy. The stores where you shop. All that advertising you see and hear. They are all part of marketing. Even your job resumé is part of a marketing campaign to sell yourself to some employer! Some courses are interesting when you take them—but never relevant again once they're over. Not so with marketing—you will be a consumer dealing with marketing for the rest of your life.

Still another reason for studying marketing is that there are many exciting and rewarding *career opportunities in marketing.* Marketing is often the route to the top. At several places in this book, you find information about opportunities in different areas of marketing. (Also, see Appendix C on "career planning.")

Even if you're looking for a non-marketing job, you will have to work with marketing people. Knowing something about marketing will help you understand them better. It will also help you do your own job better. Remember, a

company that can't successfully market its products won't need accountants, computer programmers, financial managers, personnel managers, production managers, traffic managers, or credit managers. It's often said: "Nothing happens unless the cash register rings."

Even if you're not planning a business career, marketing concepts and techniques have broad *application for non-profit organizations,* too. The same approaches used to sell soap are used to "sell" ideas, politicians, mass transportation, health care services, energy conservation, and museums.[2]

A final and even more basic reason for studying marketing is that *marketing plays a big part in economic growth and development.* Marketing stimulates research and new ideas—resulting in new products. If these products satisfy customers—this can lead to fuller employment, higher incomes, and a higher standard of living. An effective marketing system is important, therefore, to the future of our nation—and all nations.

HOW SHOULD WE DEFINE MARKETING?

As we said earlier, some people define marketing too narrowly as selling and advertising. On the other hand, one marketing expert defined marketing as "the creation and delivery of a standard of living."[3]

Micro- or Macro-Marketing?

There is a big difference between these two definitions. The first definition focuses on micro-marketing—the activities of individual business firms. The second focuses on macro-marketing—the economic welfare of a whole society.

Which view is correct? Is marketing a set of activities done by individual firms or organizations? Or is it a social process?

To answer this question, let's go back to our tennis racket example. We saw that a manufacturer of tennis rackets has to perform several customer-related activities besides just producing rackets. The same is true for an art museum or a family service agency. This supports the idea of marketing as a set of activities done by individual organizations.

On the other hand, people can't live on tennis rackets and art museums alone! In an advanced economy like ours, it takes thousands of goods and services to satisfy the many needs of society. A large supermarket may handle as many as 20,000 products. And a typical K mart stocks 15,000 different items.[4] A society needs some sort of marketing system to organize producers to satisfy the needs of all its citizens. So it appears that marketing is an important social process.

It seems that the answer to our question is that *marketing is both a set of activities performed by organizations* **and** *a social process.* In other words, marketing exists at both the micro and macro levels. Therefore, we will use two definitions of marketing—one for *micro*-marketing and another for *macro*-marketing. The first looks at customers and the organizations that serve them. The second takes a broad view of our whole production-distribution system.

A society needs some sort of marketing system to organize the efforts of producers to satisfy the needs of different customers.

MICRO—MARKETING DEFINED

Micro-marketing is the performance of activities which seek to accomplish an organization's objectives by anticipating customer or client needs and directing a flow of need-satisfying goods and services from producer to customer or client.

Let's look at this definition.

Applies to Profit and Non-Profit Organizations

To begin with, this definition applies to both profit and non-profit organizations. Their customers or clients may be individual consumers, business firms, non-profit organizations, government agencies, or even foreign nations. While most customers and clients pay for the goods and services they receive, others may receive them free of charge or at a reduced cost—through private or government subsidies.

More Than Just Persuading Customers

You already know that micro-marketing is not just selling and advertising. Unfortunately, many executives still think this is true. They feel that the job of marketing is to "get rid of" whatever the company happens to produce. This view of marketing should be rejected. As noted management consultant Peter Drucker has stated:

> There will always, one can assume, be a need for some selling. But the aim of marketing is to make selling superfluous. The aim of marketing is to know and understand the customer so well that the product or service sells itself. Ideally, marketing should result in a customer who is *ready* to buy.[5]

Thus, when we defined micro-marketing as those activities which anticipate customer or client needs and direct a flow of need-satisfying goods and services, we meant just that—*anticipate* and *direct*.

Marketing is concerned with supplying need-satisfying goods and services.

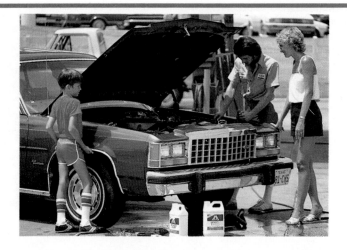

Begins with Customer Needs

Marketing should begin with potential customer needs—not with the production process. Marketing should try to anticipate needs. And then marketing, rather than production, should determine what products are to be made—including decisions about product development, product design, and packaging; what prices or fees are to be charged; credit and collection policies; transporting and storing policies; when and how the products are to be advertised and sold; and after the sale—warranty, service, and perhaps even disposal policies.

Marketing Does Not Do It Alone

This does *not* mean that marketing should try to take over production, accounting, and financial activities. Rather, it means that marketing—by interpreting customers' needs—should provide direction for these activities and try to coordinate them. After all, the purpose of a business or non-profit organization is to satisfy customer or client needs. It is *not* to supply goods or services which are *convenient* to produce—and which *might* sell or be accepted free.

THE FOCUS OF THIS TEXT— MANAGEMENT–ORIENTED MICRO–MARKETING

Assuming that most of you are preparing for a career in business, the main focus of this text will be on micro-marketing. We will see marketing through the eyes of the marketing manager. But most of this material will also be useful for those who plan to work for non-profit organizations.

It is very important, however, that marketing managers never forget that their organizations are just small parts of a larger macro-marketing system. Therefore, the rest of this chapter will look at the macro—or "big picture"— view of marketing. Let's begin by defining macro-marketing—and then review some basic ideas.

What is "good" for some producers and consumers can create problems for society as a whole.

MACRO–MARKETING DEFINED

Macro-marketing is a social process which directs an economy's flow of goods and services from producers to consumers in a way which effectively matches supply and demand and accomplishes the objectives of society.

Emphasis Is on Whole System

Like micro-marketing, macro-marketing is concerned with the flow of need-satisfying goods and services from producer to consumer. However, when we talk about macro-marketing the emphasis is not on the activities of *individual* organizations. Instead, the focus is on *how the whole system works.*[6]

Every Society Needs an Economic System

All societies must provide for the needs of their members. Therefore, every society needs some sort of **economic system**—the way an economy is organized (with or without the use of money) to use *scarce* productive resources (which could have alternative uses) to produce goods and services and distribute them for consumption—now and in the future—among various people and groups in the society.

How an economic system operates depends on a society's objectives and its political system.[7] But all economic systems must decide *what and how much* is to be produced and distributed *by whom, when, and to whom. How* these decisions are made varies from nation to nation—but the macro-level objectives are basically the same: to create goods and services and make them available when and where they are needed—to maintain or improve each nation's standard of living.

HOW ECONOMIC DECISIONS ARE MADE

There are two basic kinds of economic systems: planned systems and market-directed systems. Actually, no economy is *entirely* planned or market-directed. Most are a mixture of the two extremes.

Government Planners May Make the Decisions

A **planned economic system** is one in which government planners decide what and how much is to be produced and distributed by whom, when, and to whom. Producers generally have little choice about product design. Their main task is to meet their assigned production quotas. Prices are set by government planners and tend to be very rigid—not changing according to supply and demand. Consumers usually have *some* freedom of choice—because it is impossible to control every single detail! But the assortment of goods and services may be quite limited. Activities such as market research, branding, and advertising usually are neglected. Sometimes they aren't done at all.

Government planning may work fairly well as long as an economy is simple—and the variety of goods and services is small. It may even be necessary under certain conditions—during wartime, for example. However, as economies become more complex, government planning becomes more difficult. It may even break down. Planners may face too many complex decisions. And consumers may lose patience if the planners don't meet their needs. To try to reduce consumer dissatisfaction, planners in the Soviet Union and other socialist countries have put more emphasis on marketing (branding, advertising, and market research) in recent years.[8]

A Market-Directed Economy Adjusts Itself

A **market-directed economic system** is one in which the individual decisions of the many producers and consumers make the macro-level decisions for the whole economy.

Price is a measure of value

In a pure market-directed economy, consumers make a society's production decisions when they make their choices in the marketplace. They decide what is to be produced and by whom—through their dollar "votes." Prices in the marketplace are a rough measure of how society values particular goods or services. If consumers are willing to pay the market prices, then apparently they feel they are getting at least their money's worth.

Where a new consumer need arises, an opportunity is created for some profit-minded business. All consumer needs that can be served profitably will encourage producers to try to meet those needs. Ideally, the control of the economy is completely democratic. Power is spread throughout the economy.

Greatest freedom of choice

Consumers in a market-directed economy enjoy maximum freedom of choice. They are not forced to buy any goods or services, except those that must be provided for the good of society—things such as national defense. schools, police and fire protection, mass transportation, and public health services. These are provided by the community—and citizens are taxed to pay for them.

Similarly, producers are free to do whatever they wish—provided that they stay within the rules of the game set by government *and* receive enough dollar "votes" from consumers. If they do their job well—they earn a profit and stay in business. But profit, survival, and growth are not guaranteed.

The role of government

The American economy is mainly—but not completely—market-directed. For example, besides setting and enforcing the "rules of the game," the federal government controls interest rates and the supply of money. It also sets import and export rules, regulates radio and TV broadcasting, sometimes controls wages and prices, etc. Government also tries to be sure that property is protected, contracts are enforced, individuals are not exploited, no group unfairly monopolizes markets, and that producers deliver the kinds and quality of goods they claim to be offering.

You can see that some of these government activities are needed to achieve short-run objectives—and make sure the economy runs smoothly. However, some observers worry that increasing government interference is a growing threat to the survival of our market-directed system—and the economic and political freedom that goes with it.[9]

ALL ECONOMIES NEED MACRO– MARKETING SYSTEMS

At this point, you may be saying to yourself: All this sounds like economics—where does *marketing* fit in? Studying a *macro-marketing system* is a lot like studying an economic system—except more detailed attention is given to the "marketing" components of the system—including consumers and other customers, middlemen, and marketing specialists. The focus is on the activities they perform—and how the interaction of the components affects the effectiveness and fairness of a particular system.

In general, we can say that no economic system—whether centrally planned or market-directed—can achieve its objectives without an effective macro-marketing system. To see why this is true, we will look at the role of marketing in primitive economies. Then we will see how macro-marketing tends to become more and more complex in advanced economic systems.

Marketing Involves Exchange

In a **pure subsistence economy**—each family unit produces all the goods it needs. There is no need to exchange goods and services. Each producer-consumer unit is totally self-sufficient. No marketing takes place—because *marketing doesn't take place unless there are two or more parties who want to exchange something for something else.*

What Is a Market?

The term "marketing" comes from the word **market**—which is a group of sellers and buyers bargaining the terms of exchange for goods and/or services. This can be done face-to-face at some physical location (for example, a farmers' market). Or it can be done indirectly—through a complex network of middlemen who link buyers and sellers who are far apart.

In primitive economies, exchanges tend to occur in central markets. **Central markets** are convenient places where buyers and sellers can meet face-to-

■ FIGURE 1–1   Ten exchanges required when a central market is not used

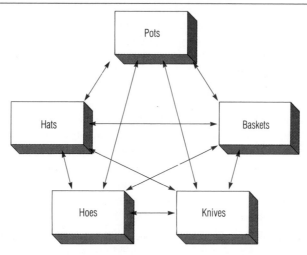

Source: Wroe Alderson, "Factors Governing the Development of Marketing
Channels," in *Marketing Channels for Manufactured Products,* ed. Richard M.
Clewett (Homewood, Ill.: Richard D. Irwin, 1954), p. 7.

face to exchange goods and services. We can understand macro-marketing
better by seeing how and why central markets develop.

**Central Markets Help
Exchange**

Imagine a small village of five families—each with some special skill for
producing some need-satisfying product. After meeting basic needs, each
family decides to specialize. It's easier for one family to make two pots and
another to make two baskets than it is for each one to make one pot and one
basket. Specialization makes labor more efficient and more productive. It can
increase the total amount of form utility created.

If these five families specialize in one product each, they will have to trade
with each other. As Figure 1–1 shows, it will take the five families 10 separate
exchanges to obtain some of each of the products. If the families live near
each other, the exchange process is relatively simple. But if they are far apart,
travel back and forth will take time. And who will do the traveling—and when?[10]

Faced with this problem, the families may agree to come to a central
market and trade on a certain day. Then each family needs to make only one
trip to the market to trade with all the others. This would reduce the total
number of trips to five. This makes exchange easier, leaves more time for
production and consumption, and also provides for social gatherings. In total,
much more time, place, possession, and even form utility is enjoyed by each
of the five families.

**Money System Speeds
Trading**

While a central meeting place simplifies exchange, the individual bartering
transactions would still take much time. Bartering only works when someone
else wants what you have—and vice versa. Each trader must find others who

have products of about equal value. After trading with one group, a family may find itself with extra baskets, knives, and pots. Then it has to find others willing to trade for these products.

A money system changes all of this. A seller only has to find a buyer who wants his products, agree on the price, and be free to spend his money to buy whatever he wants.

Middlemen Help Exchange Even More

The development of a central market and a money system simplifies the exchange process among the five families in our imaginary village. But a total of 10 separate transactions are still required. Thus, it still takes much time and effort to carry out exchange among the five families.

This clumsy exchange process can be made much simpler by the appearance of a **middleman**—someone who specializes in trade rather than production. A middleman is willing to buy each family's goods—and then sell each family whatever it needs. He charges for the service, of course. But this charge may be more than offset by savings in time and effort.

In our simple example, using the services of a middleman at a central market reduces the necessary number of exchanges for all five families from 10 to 5. See Figure 1–2. Each family has more time for production, consumption, and visits with other families. Also, each family can specialize in production—creating more form utility. Meanwhile, by specializing in trade, the middleman provides additional time, place, and possession utility. In total, all the villagers may enjoy greater economic utility—and greater consumer satisfaction—by using a middleman in the central market.

Note that the reduction in transactions that results from using a middleman

■ FIGURE 1–2   Only five exchanges are required when a middleman in a central market is used

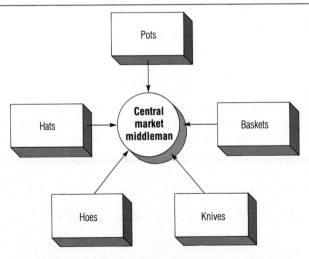

Source: Adapted from Wroe Alderson, "Factors Governing the Development of Marketing Channels," in *Marketing Channels for Manufactured Products*, ed. Richard M. Clewett (Homewood, Ill.: Richard D. Irwin, 1954), p. 7.

in a central market becomes more important as the number of families increases. For example, if the population of our imaginary village increases from 5 to 10 families, 45 transactions are needed without a middleman. Using a middleman reduces the necessary number of transactions to 10—1 for each family.

Today such middlemen—offering permanent trading facilities—are known as *wholesalers* and *retailers.* The advantages of working with middlemen increase as the number of producers and consumers, their distance from each other, and the number and variety of competing products increase. That is why there are so many wholesalers and retailers in modern economies.

THE ROLE OF MARKETING IN ECONOMIC DEVELOPMENT

Modern economies have advanced well beyond the five-family village—but the same ideas still apply. The main purpose of markets and middlemen is to make exchange easier and allow greater time for production, consumption, and other activities—including recreation.

Effective Marketing System Is Necessary

Although it is tempting to decide that more effective macro-marketing systems are the result of greater economic development, just the opposite is true. *An effective macro-marketing system is necessary for economic development.* Improved marketing may be the *key* to growth in less-developed nations.

Breaking the Vicious Circle of Poverty

Without an effective macro-marketing system, the less-developed nations may not be able to escape the "vicious circle of poverty." They can't leave their subsistence way of life to produce for the market, because there are no buyers for the goods they produce. And there are no buyers because everyone else is producing for their own needs.[11]

Breaking this vicious circle of poverty may require a major change in the micro- and macro-marketing systems that are typical in the less-developed nations.[12]

Without an effective macro-marketing system, people will not leave their subsistence way of life to produce for the market.

CAN MASS PRODUCTION SATISFY A SOCIETY'S CONSUMPTION NEEDS?

The growth of cities brings together large numbers of people. They must depend on others to produce most of the goods and services they need to satisfy their basic needs. Also, many consumers have higher incomes. They can afford to satisfy higher-level needs as well. A modern economy faces a real challenge to satisfy all these needs.

Economies of Scale Mean Lower Cost

Fortunately, advanced economies can take advantage of mass production with its **economies of scale**—which means that as a company produces larger numbers of a particular product, the cost for each of these products goes down. For example, a one-of-a-kind, custom-built car would cost *much* more than a mass-produced standard model.

Modern manufacturing skills can help produce great quantities of goods and services to satisfy large numbers of consumers. But mass production alone can't solve the problem of satisfying consumers' needs. Effective marketing is also needed.

Effective Marketing Is Needed to Link Producers and Consumers

Effective marketing means delivering the goods and services that consumers want and need. It means getting the goods to them at the right time, in the right place, and at a price they're willing to pay. That's not an easy job, especially if you think about the big variety of goods a highly developed economy can produce—and the many kinds of goods and services consumers want.

Effective marketing in an advanced economy is more difficult because producers and consumers are separated in several ways—as Figure 1–3 shows. It is also complicated by "discrepancies of quantity" and "discrepancies of assortment" between producers and consumers. This means that individual producers specialize in producing and selling large amounts of a narrow

Marketing helps adjust the discrepancies between the quantity and assortment of goods produced and what is desired by customers.

■ FIGURE 1–3   Marketing facilitates production and consumption

Production sector

Specialization and division of labor result in heterogeneous supply capabilities

MARKETING Needed to overcome	SPATIAL SEPARATION	Producers and consumers are separated geographically. Producers tend to cluster together by industry in a few concentrated locations, while consumers are located in many scattered locations.
	SEPARATION IN TIME	Consumers may not want to consume goods at the time they are produced, and time may be required to transport goods from producer to consumer.
	SEPARATION OF INFORMATION	Producers do not know who needs what, where, when and at what price. Consumers do not know what is available from whom, where, when, and at what price.
	SEPARATION IN VALUES	Producers value goods and services in terms of costs and competitive prices. Consumers value goods and services in terms of economic utility and ability to pay.
	SEPARATION OF OWNERSHIP	Producers hold title to goods and services which they themselves do not want to consume. Consumers want to consume goods and services which they do not own.
	DISCREPANCIES OF QUANTITY	Producers prefer to produce and sell in large quantities. Consumers prefer to buy and consume in small quantities.
	DISCREPANCIES OF ASSORTMENT	Producers specialize in producing a narrow assortment of goods and services. Consumers need a broad assortment.

Consumption sector

Heterogeneous demand for form, time, place, and possession utility to satisfy needs and wants

Source: Adapted from William McInnes, "A Conceptual Approach to Marketing," in *Theory in Marketing*, 2d ser., ed. Reavis Cox, Wroe Alderson, and Stanley J. Shapiro (Homewood, Ill.: Richard D. Irwin, 1964), pp. 51–67.

assortment of goods and services, but each consumer wants only small quantities of a wide variety of goods and services.[13]

Universal Marketing Functions Must Be Performed

The purpose of a macro-marketing system is to overcome these separations and discrepancies. The "universal functions of marketing" do this.

The **universal functions of marketing** are: buying, selling, transporting, storing, standardization and grading, financing, risk taking, and market information. They are *universal* in the sense that they must be performed in *all* macro-marketing systems. *How* these functions are performed—and by *whom*—may differ among nations and economic systems. But they are needed in any macro-marketing system. Let's take a closer look at them now.

The **buying function** means looking for and evaluating goods and services. The **selling function** involves promoting the product. It includes the use of personal selling, advertising, and other mass selling methods. This is probably the best known function of marketing.

The **transporting function** means the movement of goods from one place to another. The **storing function** involves holding goods until customers need them.

Standardization and **grading** involve sorting products according to size and quality. This makes buying and selling easier—because it reduces the need for inspection and sampling. **Financing** provides the necessary cash and credit to manufacture, transport, store, promote, sell, and buy products. **Risk taking** involves bearing the uncertainties that are part of the marketing process. A firm can never be sure that customers will want to buy its products. Products can also be damaged, stolen, or outdated. The **market information function** involves the collection, analysis, and distribution of all the information needed to plan, carry out, and control marketing activities.

WHO PERFORMS MARKETING FUNCTIONS?

Producers, Consumers, and Marketing Specialists

From a macro-level viewpoint, these marketing functions are all part of the marketing process—and must be done by someone. *None* of them can be eliminated. In a planned economy, some of the functions may be performed by government agencies. Others may be left to individual producers and consumers. In a market-directed economy, marketing functions are performed by producers, consumers, and a variety of marketing specialists. See Figure 1–4.

Earlier in this chapter, we saw that adding a middleman to a simple five-family village of producers and consumers made exchange easier—and increased the total amount of economic utility. We said that this effect is even greater in a large, complex economy. This helps explain why most products for consumers are distributed through wholesalers and retailers—instead of directly from producers to consumers.

You saw how producers and consumers benefited when marketing specialists (middlemen) took over some buying and selling. Producers and consumers also benefit when marketing specialists perform the other marketing functions. So we find marketing functions being performed not only by marketing middlemen—but also by a variety of other **facilitators**—firms which provide one or more of the marketing functions *other than buying or selling.* These include advertising agencies, marketing research firms, independent product-testing laboratories, public warehouses, transporting firms, and financial institutions (including banks). Through specialization and economies of scale, marketing middlemen and facilitators are often able to perform the marketing functions better—and at a lower cost—than producers or consumers can. This

■ FIGURE 1–4   Model of U.S. macro-marketing system*

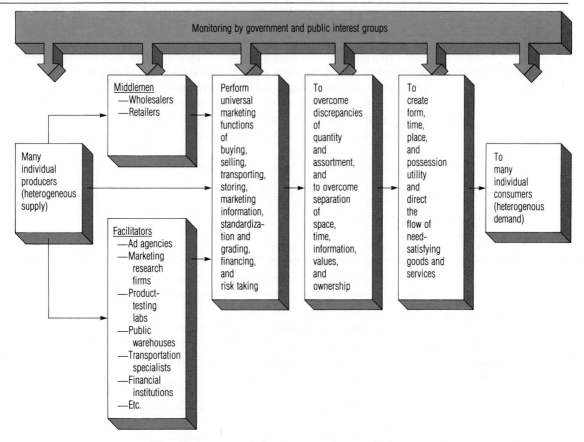

*Our nation's macro-marketing system must interact with the macro-marketing systems of many other nations.

Source: This model was suggested by Professor A. A. Brogowicz of Western Michigan University.

allows producers and consumers to spend more time on production and consumption.

Functions Can Be Shifted and Shared

From a macro viewpoint, all of the marketing functions must be performed by someone. But, *from a micro viewpoint, not every firm must perform all of the functions.* Some marketing specialists perform all the functions. Others specialize in only one or two. Marketing research firms, for example, specialize only in the market information function.

Sometimes several middlemen or facilitators are used between producer and consumer. Then some of the marketing functions may be performed several times. But the important idea to remember is this: *Responsibility for performing the marketing functions can be shifted and shared in a variety of ways, but no function can be completely eliminated!*

HOW WELL DOES OUR MACRO–MARKETING SYSTEM WORK?

It Connects Remote Producers and Consumers

A macro-marketing system does more than just deliver goods and services to consumers—it allows mass production with its economies of scale. Also, mass communication and mass transportation allow products to be shipped where they're needed. Oranges from California are found in Minnesota stores—even in December—and electronic parts made in New York State are used in making products all over the country.[14]

It Encourages Growth and Innovation

In addition to making mass production possible, our market-directed, macro-marketing system encourages innovation—the development and spread of new ideas and products. Competition for consumers' dollars forces firms to think of new and better ways of satisfying consumer needs.

It Has Its Critics

In explaining marketing's role in society, we described some of the benefits of our macro-marketing system. We feel this approach is right because our macro-marketing system has provided us with one of the highest standards of living in the world. We must admit, however, that marketing—as we know it in the United States—has many critics! Marketing activity is especially open to criticism—because it is the part of business most visible to the public. There is nothing like a pocketbook issue for getting consumers excited!

Typical complaints about marketing include:

Advertising is too often annoying, deceptive, and wasteful.

Products are not safe—or the quality is poor.

Marketing makes people too materialistic—it motivates them toward the "almighty dollar" instead of social needs.

Easy consumer credit makes people buy things they don't need—and really can't afford.

Packaging and labeling are often confusing and deceptive.

Middlemen add to the cost of distribution—and raise prices without providing anything in return.

Marketing creates interest in products that pollute the environment.

Too many unnecessary products are offered.

Marketing serves the rich—and exploits the poor.

Consumer Complaints Should Be Taken Seriously

Such complaints cannot and should not be taken lightly.[15] They show that many Americans aren't happy with some parts of our marketing system. Certainly, the strong public support that consumer protection laws have received proves that not all consumers feel they are being treated like kings and queens. But some of the complaints are because people don't understand what marketing is all about. As you go through this book, we will try to answer some of these criticisms—to help you understand marketing better.

Some critics argue that marketing serves the rich and exploits the poor.

■ CONCLUSION

In this chapter, we defined two levels of marketing: micro-marketing and macro-marketing. Macro-marketing is concerned with the way the whole economy works. Micro-marketing focuses on the activities of individual firms. We discussed the role of marketing in economic development—and talked about the functions of marketing and who performs them. We ended by raising some of the criticisms of marketing—both of the whole macro system and of the way individual firms work.

We discussed macro-marketing in this chapter, but the emphasis of this book is on *micro*-marketing. We believe that most criticism of marketing

results from ineffective decision making at the micro level. Therefore, the best way to answer some of this criticism is to educate future business people. This will help improve the way individual organizations work. Eventually, it will help our macro-marketing system work better.

The effect of micro-level decisions on society will be discussed throughout the text. Then—in Chapter 20—after you have begun to understand how and why producers and consumers think and behave the way they do—we will look at macro-marketing again. We will try to evaluate how well both micro-marketing and macro-marketing perform in our market-directed economic system.

■ QUESTIONS AND PROBLEMS

1. It is fairly easy to see why people do not beat a path to the mousetrap manufacturer's door, but would they be similarly indifferent if some food processor developed a revolutionary new food product which would provide all necessary nutrients in small pills for about $100 per year per person?

2. Distinguish between macro- and micro-marketing. Then explain how they are interrelated, if they are.

3. Distinguish between how economic decisions are made in a planned economic system and in a market-directed economy.

4. Explain (*a*) how a central market facilitates exchange and (*b*) how the addition of a middleman facilitates exchange even more.

5. Identify a "central market" in your city and explain how it facilitates exchange.

6. Discuss the nature of marketing in a socialist economy. Would the functions which must be provided and the development of wholesaling and retailing systems be any different?

7. Describe a recent purchase you have made and indicate why that particular product was available at a store and, in particular, at that store.

8. Define the functions of marketing in your own words. Using an example, explain how they can be shifted and shared.

9. Explain, in your own words, why the emphasis in this text is on micro-marketing.

10. Why is satisfying customers or clients considered equally as important as satisfying an organization's objectives—in the text's definition of micro-marketing?

■ SUGGESTED CASES

2. Borman Cleaning Company

28. Servo, Inc.

Chapter 2 ■ Marketing's role within the firm

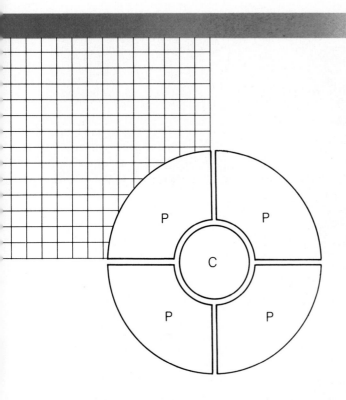

When you finish this chapter, you should:

1. Know what the marketing concept is—and how it should affect a firm's strategy planning.

2. Understand what a marketing manager does.

3. Know what marketing strategy planning is—and why it will be the focus of this book.

4. Understand target marketing.

5. Be familiar with the four Ps in a marketing mix.

6. Know the difference between a marketing strategy, a marketing plan, and a marketing program.

7. Recognize the important new terms (shown in red).

"A master plan to hit the target" is not a Star Wars *story line—but the objective of a good marketing manager.*

Marketing and marketing management are important in our society—and in business firms. As you saw in Chapter 1, marketing is concerned with anticipating needs and directing the flow of goods and services from producers to consumers. This is done to satisfy the needs of consumers—and achieve the objectives of the firm (the micro view) and of society as a whole (the macro view).

To get a better understanding of marketing, we're going to look at things through the eyes of the marketing manager—the one who makes a company's important marketing decisions. Let's look at just a few decisions marketing managers for Coca-Cola had to make when developing some new soft drinks.

In 1970, the Coca-Cola Company started a catchy advertising campaign that described Coke as "the real thing." For nearly 100 years, a Coca-Cola was very clearly only one thing—and everyone knew what it was. But by 1983, marketing research showed that many soft drink customers—especially in the large market of middle-age consumers—wanted something different. Some wanted low calories for slimmer waistlines. Others wanted less sugar. Others

wanted to avoid caffeine. So the Coca-Cola Company decided to introduce Diet Coke and Caffeine Free Coke. To get these products to the market, however, many decisions had to be made.

The company had to develop and test each product—to make sure people liked the taste. They had to decide whether to use the familiar "Coke" name and label design—or design a new one, as they did with "Sprite." Marketing managers also had to pick a theme for the advertising campaign—and decide how much to spend on advertising and where to spend it. They also had to decide how to promote the idea to their independent bottlers—the "middlemen" who actually get the products to places where customers can buy them. They had to decide if the price of the new drinks would be the same as for their old "standard"—and whether to set a special low price during the introductory period. They had to decide whether to "test market" the products in a few selected areas—to see how they sold—or distribute them in as many places as possible all at once.

These are just a few of the many important decisions Coke's marketing managers had to make—and you can see that each of the decisions affects the others. Making effective marketing decisions is never easy—but it helps to know what basic decision areas must be considered. This chapter will get you started—giving you a framework to think about all the marketing management decision areas—which is what the rest of this book is all about.

MARKETING'S ROLE HAS CHANGED A LOT OVER THE YEARS

In our Coca-Cola example, it's clear that marketing management is very important. But this hasn't always been true. In fact, it's only in the last 20 years or so that more and more producers, wholesalers, and retailers have adopted modern marketing thinking. These companies used to think mainly of just making a product. Now they focus on customers—and try to aim the company's total effort toward satisfying them.

We're going to discuss fives stages in this marketing evolution: (1) the simple trade era, (2) the production era, (3) the sales era, (4) the marketing department era, and (5) the marketing company era.[1] We'll talk about these eras as if all firms are now marketing-oriented—but keep in mind that some managers haven't made it to the final stages. They're still stuck in the past.

Specialization Permitted Trade—And Middlemen Met the Need

When societies first moved toward some specialization of production, traders played an important role. Early producers made products needed by themselves and their neighbors. As trading became harder, they moved into the **simple trade era**—a time when families traded or sold their "surplus" output to local middlemen, who then sold these goods to other consumers or distant middlemen. This was the early role of marketing—and it didn't change much until the Industrial Revolution, just over a hundred years ago.

**From the Production
to the Sales Era**

From the Industrial Revolution until the 1920s, most companies were in the production era. The **production era** is a time when a company focuses on production—perhaps because few products are available in the market.

By 1930, new machines made it possible to produce more than ever before. Now the problem wasn't just to produce—but to beat competition and win customers. This led many firms to enter the sales era. The **sales era** is a time when a company emphasizes selling—because of increased competition.

**To the Marketing
Department Era**

For most firms, the sales era continued until about 1950. By then, sales were growing rapidly. Someone had to tie together the efforts of research, purchasing, production, and sales. The sales era was replaced by the marketing department era. The **marketing department era** is a time when all marketing activities are brought under the control of one department—to improve short-run policy planning—and to try to tie together the firm's activities.

**To the Marketing
Company Era**

Since 1960, many firms have developed at least some staff with a marketing management outlook. Some have moved all the way to the marketing company era. The **marketing company era** is a time when—in addition to short-run marketing planning—marketing people develop long-range plans— and the whole company effort is guided by the marketing concept.

WHAT DOES THE MARKETING CONCEPT MEAN?

The **marketing concept** means that a firm aims *all* its efforts at satisfying its *customers*—at a *profit.*

It isn't really a new idea in business—it's been around a long time. But some managers act as if they're stuck at the beginning of the production era.

As part of its customer orientation, Ford set up a special group to try to solve consumers' problems.

They still have a **production orientation**—making products which are easy to produce and *then* trying to sell them.

In well-managed firms, this production orientation has been replaced with a marketing orientation. A **marketing orientation** means trying to carry out the marketing concept. Instead of just trying to get customers to buy what the firm has produced, a marketing-oriented firm tries to produce what customers need.

Three basic ideas are included in the definition of the marketing concept:

1. A customer orientation.
2. A total company effort.
3. Profit—not just sales—as an objective.

These three ideas deserve more discussion.

A Customer Orientation Guides the Whole System

"Give the customers what they need"—may seem so obvious that it's hard for you to understand why the marketing concept is worth special attention. However, people don't always do the logical and obvious. Twenty years ago—in a typical company—production managers thought mainly about getting out the product. Accountants were interested only in balancing the books. Financial people looked after the company's cash position. And salespeople were mainly concerned with getting orders. Each department thought of its own activity as the center of the business—with others working around it. No one was concerned with the whole system. As long as the company made a profit, each department went merrily on—"doing its own thing." Unfortunately, this is still true in many companies today.

Work Together . . . Do a Better Job

Ideally, all managers should work together—because the output from one department may be the input to another. But managers tend to build "fences" around their own departments—as seen in Figure 2–1A. Each department

---

FIGURE 2-1

A. A business as a box
    (most departments have high fences)

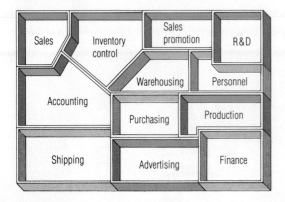

B. Total system view of a
    business (implementing marketing concept;
    still have departments but all guided by
    what customers want)

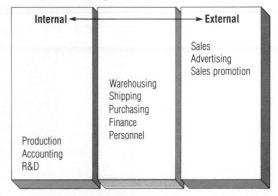

Marketing's role within the firm **29**

runs its own affairs for its own benefit. There may be meetings to try to get them to work together—but usually each department head comes to such meetings with the idea of protecting his own department's interests.

We use the term "production orientation" to describe this lack of a central focus in a business firm. But keep in mind that this problem is also seen in sales-oriented sales representatives, advertising-oriented agency people, finance-oriented finance people, and so on.

In a firm that has accepted the marketing concept, however, the fences come down. There are still departments, of course, because there are efficiencies in specialization. But the total system's effort is guided by what customers want—instead of what each department would like to do.

In such a firm, it is more realistic to view the business as a box with both internal and external activities. See Figure 2–1B. Some internal departments—production, accounting, and research and development (R&D)—are mainly concerned with affairs inside the firm. And the external departments are concerned with outside matters—sales, advertising, and sales promotion. Finally, some departments work with both inside and outside problems—warehousing, shipping, purchasing, finance, and personnel.

The important point is having a guiding focus that all departments adopt. It helps the organization work as a total system—rather than a lot of separate parts. Further, the marketing concept is more complete than many systems-oriented ideas. It actually specifies a "high-level" objective—customer satisfaction—that makes sense for all parts of the system. It also specifies a profit objective—which is necessary for the system's survival.

It's Easy to Slip into a Production Orientation

It's very easy to slip into a production-oriented way of thinking. For example, a retailer might prefer only weekday hours—avoiding nights, Saturdays, and Sundays—when many customers would like to shop. Or a company might rush to produce a clever new product developed in its laboratory—rather than first finding out if it fills a need.

Take a look at Figure 2–2. It shows some differences in outlook between adopters of the marketing concept and typical production-oriented managers. As this suggests, the marketing concept is really very powerful—if taken seriously. It forces the company to think through what it is doing—and why. And it also forces the company to develop plans for reaching its objectives.

ADOPTION OF THE MARKETING CONCEPT HAS NOT BEEN EASY OR UNIVERSAL

The marketing concept seems so logical that you might think it would have been quickly adopted by most firms. In fact, it was not. The majority of firms are either production-oriented—or regularly slip back that way—and must consciously bring the customers' interests into their planning.

The marketing concept was first accepted by consumer goods companies—such as General Electric and Procter & Gamble. Competition was intense in

■ FIGURE 2–2   Some differences in outlook between adopters of the marketing concept and the typical production-oriented managers

Marketing orientation	Attitudes and procedures	Production orientation
Customer needs determine company plans	←———— Attitudes toward customers ————→	They should be glad we exist, trying to cut costs and bring out better products.
Company makes what it can sell	←———— Product offering ————→	Company sells what it can make
To determine customer needs and how well company is satisfying them	←———— Role of marketing research ————→	To determine customer reaction, if used at all
Focus on locating new opportunities	←———— Interest in innovation ————→	Focus is on technology and cost cutting
A critical objective	←———— Importance of profit ————→	A residual, what's left after all costs are covered
Seen as a customer service	←———— Role of customer credit ————→	Seen as a necessary evil
Designed for customer convenience and as a selling tool	←———— Role of packaging ————→	Seen merely as protection for the product
Set with customer requirements and costs in mind	←———— Inventory levels ————→	Set with production requirements in mind
Seen as a customer service	←———— Transportation arrangements ————→	Seen as an extension of production and storage activities, with emphasis on cost minimization
Need-satisfying benefits of products and services	←———— Focus of advertising ————→	Product features and quality, maybe how products are made
Help the customer to buy if the product fits his needs, while coordinating with rest of firm—including production, inventory control, advertising, etc.	←———— Role of sales force ————→	Sell the customer, don't worry about coordination with other promotion efforts or rest of firm.

Source: Adapted from R. F. Vizza, T. E. Chambers, and E. J. Cook, *Adoption of the Marketing Concept—Fact or Fiction* (New York: Sales Executive Club, 1967), pp. 13–15.

some of their markets—and trying to satisfy customers' needs better was a way to win in this competition.[2]

Producers of industrial commodities—steel, coal, paper, glass, chemicals—have accepted the marketing concept more slowly—if at all—Similarly, many retailers have been slow to accept the marketing concept—in part because they are so close to final consumers that they feel that they really know their customers.

Service Industries Are Catching on Fast

In the last 10 years or so, many service industries—including airlines, lawyers, physicians, accountants, and insurance companies—have begun to apply the marketing concept.

Of course, acceptance of the marketing concept varies widely in these industries. But the government has stimulated more emphasis on marketing—by encouraging advertising and price competition among lawyers, accountants,

Many service industries have begun to apply the marketing concept.

and other professional groups. This has led many of these professionals to pay more attention to their customers' needs. Some have been forced into it by aggressive competitors who are advertising and using price to attract new customers—contrary to long-accepted professional practice.

Marketing Concept Applies Directly to Non-Profit Organizations

The same ideas apply directly to non-profit organizations. The objectives are different—but the marketing concept works here, too. The Red Cross, art museums, and opera companies are all trying to satisfy some groups of consumers.[3]

Through this text, we'll be talking about applying the marketing concept. Usually we'll just say "in a firm" or "in a business"—but you should keep in mind that most of the ideas discussed in the book can be applied in *any* type of organization.

THE MANAGEMENT JOB IN MARKETING

We've discussed the marketing concept as a guide for the whole firm. Now let's look more closely at how a marketing manager helps a firm reach its objectives—using the *marketing management process.*

The **marketing management process** is the process of (1) *planning* marketing activities, (2) directing the *implementation* of the plans, and (3) *controlling* these plans. See Figure 2–3.

In Figure 2–3, all the steps are connected to show that the marketing management process is continuous. The planning job sets guidelines for implementing the plans—and specifies expected results. These expected results are compared in the control job—to see if everything has worked out as planned. This feedback is especially important. It can lead to changing the plans.

Marketing is increasingly being used by non-business organizations.

■   FIGURE 2–3   The marketing management process

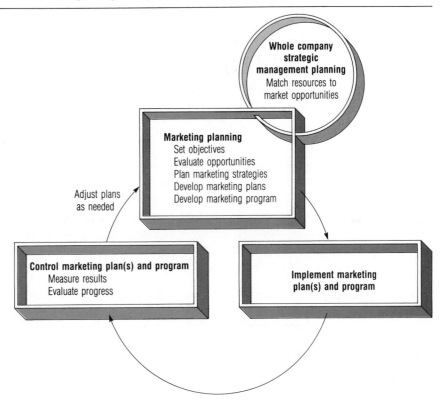

Whole company
strategic
management planning
Match resources to
market opportunities

Marketing planning
Set objectives
Evaluate opportunities
Plan marketing strategies
Develop marketing plans
Develop marketing program

Adjust plans
as needed

Control marketing plan(s) and program
Measure results
Evaluate progress

Implement marketing
plan(s) and program

**Marketing Managers
Should Seek New
Opportunities**

A marketing manager is not concerned only with present plans. He must always be looking for attractive new opportunities—and making plans for new strategies.

**Strategic Management
Planning Concerns
the Whole Firm**

The job of planning strategies to guide a *whole company* is called **strategic (management) planning**—the managerial process of developing and maintaining a match between the resources of an organization and its market opportunities. This is a big job that includes not only marketing activities but also planning for production, research and development, and other functional areas.

We won't get into such detail in this text—and it is important to see that the marketing department's plans are not whole company plans. On the other hand, company plans should be market-oriented—and the marketing department's plans can help set the tone and direction for the whole company. If the marketing department applies the marketing concept, this can lead the whole company to follow. So for our purposes, "strategy planning" and "marketing strategy planning" mean the same thing.[4]

■   FIGURE 2–4   A marketing strategy

WHAT IS MARKETING STRATEGY PLANNING?

Marketing strategy planning means finding attractive opportunities—and developing profitable marketing strategies and plans. But what is a "marketing strategy" and a "marketing plan?" We have used these words rather casually so far. Now let's see what they really mean.

What Is a Marketing Strategy?

A **marketing strategy** is a target market and a related marketing mix. It is a "big picture" of what a firm will do in some market. Two interrelated parts are needed:

1. A **target market**—a fairly homogeneous (similar) group of customers to whom a company wishes to appeal.
2. A **marketing mix**—the controllable variables which the company puts together to satisfy this target group.

The importance of target customers in this process can be seen in Figure 2–4, where the customer—the "C"—at the center of the diagram—is surrounded by the controllable variables which we call the "marketing mix." A typical marketing mix would include some product, offered at a price, with some promotion to tell potential customers about the product, and a way to reach the customer's place.

Hanes Corporation's strategy for L'eggs hosiery is to aim at convenience-oriented young women in urban areas with a dependable product that comes in a distinctive package. The product is made conveniently available at as many grocery and drug stores as possible. Its pricing is more or less competitive. And Hanes supports the whole effort with a great deal of promotion.

SELECTING A MARKET–ORIENTED STRATEGY IS TARGET MARKETING

Target Marketing Is Not Mass Marketing

Note that a marketing strategy specifies some *particular* target customers. This approach is called "target marketing" to distinguish it from "mass marketing." **Target marketing** aims at some specific target customers. **Mass market-**

L'eggs made its distinctive package conveniently available.

ing—the typical production-oriented approach—aims at "everyone" with the same marketing mix. Mass marketing assumes that everyone is the same—and that everyone is a potential customer. See Figure 2–5.

"Mass Marketers" May Do Target Marketing

Commonly used terms can be confusing here. The terms "mass market*ing*" and "mass market*ers*" do not mean the same thing. Far from it! "Mass marketing" means trying to sell to "everyone," as we explained above—while "mass

■ FIGURE 2–5   Production-oriented and marketing-oriented managers have different views of the market

Production-oriented manager sees everyone as basically similar and practices "mass marketing"

Marketing-oriented manager sees everyone as different and practices "target marketing"

marketers" like General Foods and Sears, are not aiming at "everyone." They do aim at clearly defined target markets. The confusion with "mass marketing" occurs because their target markets usually are large and spread out.

Target Marketing—Can Mean Big Markets and Profits

Remember that target marketing is not limited to small market segments—only to fairly homogeneous ones. A very large market—even what is sometimes called the "mass market"—may be fairly homogeneous in some cases—and a target marketer will deliberately aim at it.

The reason for this focus on some specific target customers is to gain a competitive advantage—by developing a more satisfying marketing mix—which should also be more profitable for the firm.

DEVELOPING MARKETING MIXES FOR TARGET MARKETS

There Are Many Marketing Mix Variables

There are many possible ways to satisfy the needs of target customers. A product can have many different features and colors. The package can be of various sizes, colors, or materials. The brand names and trademarks can be changed. Various advertising media—newspapers, magazines, radio, television, billboards—may be used. A company's own sales force or other sales specialists can be used. Different prices can be charged—and so on. With so many variables available, the question is: Is there any way of simplifying the selection of marketing mixes? And the answer is: Yes.

The Four "Ps" Make Up a Marketing Mix

It is useful to reduce the number of variables in the marketing mix to four basic ones:

Product.
Place.
Promotion.
Price.

It helps to think of the four major parts of a marketing mix as the "four Ps." Figure 2–6 emphasizes their relationship—and their focus on the customer—"C."

Customer is not part of the marketing mix

The customer is shown surrounded by the four Ps in Figure 2–6. Some students assume that the customer is part of the marketing mix—but this isn't so. The customer should be the *target* of all marketing efforts. The customer is placed in the center of the diagram to show this—the "C" stands for the target market.

Table 2–1 shows some of the variables in the four Ps—which will be discussed in later chapters. For now, let's just describe each P briefly.

■ FIGURE 2–6   A marketing strategy—showing the 4 Ps of a marketing mix

Product—the Right One for the Target

The Product area is concerned with developing the right "product" for the target market. This product may involve a physical good and/or service. The product of a taxi company is a ride to your destination. The important thing to remember in the Product area is that your good—and/or service—should satisfy some customers' needs.

Along with other Product decisions, we'll talk about developing new products and whole product lines. We will also discuss the characteristics of various kinds of products—so that you will be able to make generalizations about product classes. This will help you to develop whole marketing mixes more quickly.

Place—Reaching the Target

Place is concerned with getting the right product to the target market's place. A product isn't much good to a customer if it isn't available when and where it's wanted.

■ TABLE 2–1   Strategic decision areas

Product	Place	Promotion	Price
Features	Objectives	Objectives	Objectives
Accessories	Channel type	Promotion blend	Flexibility
Installation	Market exposure	Salespeople	Level over product
Instructions	Kinds of middlemen	Kind	life cycle
Service	Kinds and locations	Number	Geographic terms
Warranty	of stores	Selection	Discounts
Product lines	Who handles	Training	Allowances
Packaging	transporting	Motivation	
Branding	and storing	Advertising	
	Service levels	Targets	
	Recruiting	Kind of ads	
	middlemen	Media type	
	Managing	Copy thrust	
	channels	Prepared by whom	
		Sales promotion	
		Publicity	

Goods and services often move to customers through channels of distribution. A **channel of distribution** is any series of firms (or individuals) from producer to final user or consumer. A channel can include several kinds of middlemen and specialists. Marketing managers work with these channels. So our study of Place is very important to marketing strategy planning.

Sometimes a channel system is quite short. It may run directly from a producer to a final user or consumer. Usually, it is more complex—involving many different kinds of middlemen and specialists. And if a marketing manager has several different target markets, several channels of distribution might be needed. See Figure 2–7.

Promotion—Telling and Selling the Customer

The third P—Promotion—is concerned with telling the target market about the "right" product. Promotion includes personal selling, mass selling, and sales promotion. It is the marketing manager's job to blend these methods.

Personal selling involves direct face-to-face communication between sellers and potential customers. Personal selling lets the salesperson adapt the firm's marketing mix to each potential customer. But this individual attention comes at a price. Personal selling can be very expensive. Often this personal effort has to be blended with mass selling and sales promotion.

Mass selling is communicating with large numbers of potential customers at the same time. **Advertising** is any paid form of non-personal presentation of ideas, goods, or services by an identified sponsor. It is the main form of mass selling. **Publicity** is any *unpaid* form of non-personal presentation of ideas, goods, or services.

Sales promotion refers to those promotion activities—other than advertising, publicity, and personal selling—which stimulate interest, trial, or purchase

■ FIGURE 2–7   Four possible (basic) channels of distribution for consumer goods

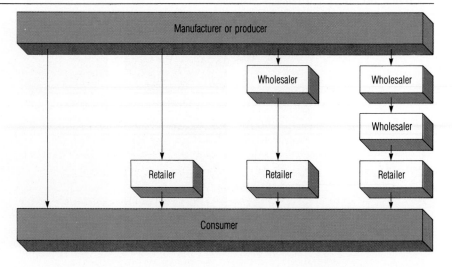

by final customers or others in the channel. Sales promotion people try to help the personal selling and mass selling specialists.

Price—Making It Right

In addition to developing the right Product, Place, and Promotion, marketing managers must also decide the right Price. In setting a price, they must consider the kind of competition in the target market. They must also try to estimate customer reaction to possible prices.

If customers won't accept the Price, all of the planning effort will be wasted. So you can see that Price is an important area for the marketing manager.

Each of the Four Ps Contributes to the Whole

All four Ps are needed in a marketing mix. In fact, they should all be tied together. But is any one more important than the others? Generally speaking, the answer is *no*. When a marketing mix is being developed, all decisions about the Ps should be made at the same time. That's why the four Ps are arranged around the customer (C) in a circle—to show that they all are equally important.

Strategy Guides Implementing

Let's sum up our discussion of marketing mix planning so far. We develop a *Product* that we feel will satisfy the target customers. We find a way—*Place*—to get our product to our target customer's place. *Promotion* tells the target customers about the availability of the product that has been designed for them. Then the *Price* is set—after estimating expected customer reaction to the total offering and the costs of getting it to them.

Both jobs must be done together

It is important to stress—*it cannot be overemphasized*—that selecting a target market and developing a marketing mix are interrelated. A marketing manager cannot do one step and then another. Both steps must be done together. It is *strategies* which must be evaluated against the company's objectives—not alternative target markets or alternative marketing mixes.

These ideas can be seen more clearly with an example in the home decorating market.

A British paint manufacturer looks at the home decorating market

The experience of a paint manufacturer in England illustrates the strategy planning process—and how strategic decisions help decide how the plan is carried out.

First, this paint manufacturer's marketing manager interviewed many potential customers and studied their needs for the products he could offer. By combining several kinds of customer needs and some available demographic data, he came up with the view of the market shown in Figure 2–8. In the following description of these markets, note that useful marketing mixes come to mind immediately.

There turned out to be a large market for "general-purpose paint" products. The manufacturer didn't consider this market—because he didn't want to compete "head-on" with the many companies already in this market. The other four markets—which were placed in the four corners of a market diagram just

■ FIGURE 2–8   The home decorating market (paint area) in England

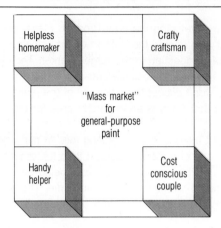

to show that they were different markets—he called Helpless Homemaker, Handy Helper, Crafty Craftsman, and Cost-Conscious Couple.

The *Helpless Homemaker*—the manufacturer found—really didn't know much about home painting or specific products. This customer needed a helpful paint retailer who could supply not only paint and other supplies—but also much advice. And the retailer who sold the paint would want it to be of fairly good quality—so that the homemaker would be satisfied with the results.

The *Handy Helper* was a jack-of-all-trades who knew a lot about paint and painting. He wanted a good-quality product and liked to buy from an old-fashioned hardware store or lumber yard—which usually sells mainly to men. The *Crafty Craftsman* had similar needs. But these older men didn't want to buy paint at all. They wanted pigments, oils, and other things to mix their own paint.

Finally, the *Cost-Conscious Couple* was young, had low income, and lived in an apartment. In England, an apartment renter must paint the apartment during the course of the lease. This is an important factor for some tenants as they choose their paint. If you were a young apartment renter with limited income, what sort of paint would you want? Some couples in England—the manufacturer found—didn't want very good paint! In fact, something not much better than whitewash would do fine.

The paint manufacturer decided to cater to "Cost-Conscious Couples" with a marketing mix flowing from the description of that market. That is, knowing what he did about them, he offered a low-quality paint (Product), made it conveniently available in lower-income apartment neighborhoods (Place), aimed his price-oriented ads at these areas (Promotion), and, of course, offered an attractive low price (Price). The manufacturer has been extremely successful with this strategy—giving his customers what they really want—even though the product is of low quality.

A MARKETING PLAN IS A GUIDE TO IMPLEMENTATION AND CONTROL

We have been talking about marketing strategy planning. Now let's return to our discussion of the marketing management process. You will see how a marketing strategy leads to a marketing plan and—finally—to implementation and control. (See Figure 2–3).

Marketing Plan Fills Out Marketing Strategy

A marketing strategy is a "big picture" of what a firm will do in some market. A marketing plan goes farther. A marketing plan is a written statement of a marketing strategy *and* the time-related details for carrying out the strategy. It should spell out the following—in detail: (1) what marketing mix is to be offered to whom (that is, the target market) and for how long; (2) what company resources (shown as costs) will be needed—at what rate (month by month perhaps); and (3) what results are expected (sales and profits—perhaps monthly or quarterly). It should also include some control procedures—so that whoever is to carry out the plan will know when things are going wrong. This might be something as simple as comparing actual sales against expected sales—with a "warning flag" to be raised whenever total sales fall below a certain level. See Figure 2–9.

Implementation Puts Strategies and Marketing Plans to Work

After a marketing strategy and related plan is developed, a marketing manager is concerned with implementation—that is, with putting the marketing plan into operation. For the marketing manager, this may involve personnel selection; salary administration; middlemen selection; setting commission rates; selection of promotion materials; organizing, storing and transporting; and so on.

Often implementation will take up more of the manager's time than marketing strategy planning. But implementation is not the major concern of this text. The details of implementation must be left for advanced texts and courses in marketing—after you have learned about planning marketing strategies. Of course, as you learn more about each of the Ps—Product, Place, Promotion, and Price—you will also be learning what managers need to know to implement a strategy.[5]

Several Plans Make a Whole Marketing Program

Most companies have more than one marketing strategy at the same time. They may have a whole line of products—some of them quite different—designed to appeal to different target markets. The other elements of the marketing mix might vary, too. A Bic pen, a Bic windsurfer, and a Bic razor all involve different target markets and different marketing mixes, but the strategies for each must be implemented by Bic at the same time. A marketing program blends all of a firm's marketing plans into one "big" plan. See Figure 2–10. This program, then, is the responsibility of the whole company. Typically, the whole *marketing program* will be an integrated part of the whole-company strategic plans we discussed earlier.

■ FIGURE 2–9   Forms to plan and control each of a firm's marketing plans—with illustrative comments and numbers for first two pages (one set of forms for each plan, number of time periods depending on length of plan)

Time period ___July___

	Forecast	Actual	Difference	Cumulative difference
Sales	$ 0	$ 0	$ 0	$ 0
Costs (direct)	700	500	−200	−200
Overhead	$ 3,000	$ 3,000	0	0
Profit (loss)	$ (3,700)	$ (3,500)	$ (200)	$ (200)
Investment	$30,000	$32,000	$ 2,000	$ 2,000

Tasks to be done

PRODUCT   Be sure that all elements of package are meeting production schedule

PLACE

PROMOTION   Prepare copy for direct mail pieces.
Prepare journal ad copy.
Prepare sales training materials.

PRICE   Set tentative price for text and other package elements.

Product Identification   McCarthy and Perreault, ESSENTIALS of MARKETING, 3rd ed. (and related materials)
Target Market   Instructors of first marketing course who want to use a "short" book
PRODUCT-MARKET DEFINITION:
Product type   "Short" textbook (and related materials)
Functional needs   To aid teaching and learning
Customer types   College-level instructors interested in an integrated, analytical, management-oriented approach to marketing—i.e., logical, organized, pragmatic instructors
Geographic area   English language instructors world-wide, except Canada
Competition   Other "short book" publishers (actual names used in real situations)
Nature of competition   Monopolistic competition
Product life cycle   Market maturity

MARKETING MIX

PRODUCT
Type   New (revised) component part for instructor (and specialty good to students)
Total product   Package of teaching materials and aids
Brand familiarity   Recognition to insistence

PLACE
Type of channel   Direct to retail book stores
Degree of market exposure   Exclusive OK
Pulling or pushing   Push to instructors, contact retailers
Physical distribution service level   Immediate delivery to book stores

PROMOTION
Blend type   Heavy on personal selling with some ads, and exhibits at teachers' meetings
Type of salespeople   Order getting and taking
Message emphasis   "Short" book with integrated, analytical, etc., package
Media emphasis   Direct mail and professional journals

PRICE
Flexibility   One price
Level   Meet competition
Geographic   F.O.B. shipping point
Discounts and allowances   20 percent off retail selling price, restricted returns

Most companies offer several different products to appeal to different target markets.

Some people think that planning and control are of concern only to top-level executives of large companies. This isn't true. All organizations—even the smallest farmer, retailer, or wholesaler—should have plans—and some kind of control procedures.

This means that marketing strategy planning will be very important to you—soon—perhaps in your present job or college activities. In Appendix C—on marketing careers—some strategy planning ideas for getting a marketing job are presented.

THE IMPORTANCE OF MARKETING STRATEGY PLANNING

Most of our emphasis in this book will be on the planning part of the marketing manager's job—for a good reason. Success or failure—for a firm—can

■   FIGURE 2–10   Elements of a firm's marketing program

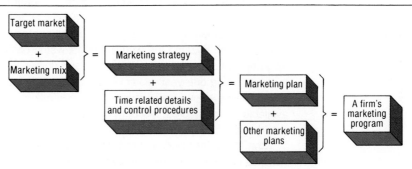

depend on "one-time" strategy decisions—the decisions that decide what business the company is in and the strategies it will follow. An extremely good plan—carried out badly—might still be profitable. A poor plan—even if well-implemented—can lose money. The examples that follow show the importance of planning—and why we're going to emphasize marketing strategy planning in this text.

Henry Ford's Strategy Worked—Until General Motors Caught Up

Henry Ford is remembered for developing the mass production techniques that produced a car for the masses. His own view of his approach, however, was that mass production developed *because* of his basic decision to build a car for the masses. Cars then were almost custom-built for wealthy buyers. Ford decided on a different strategy. He wanted to make a car that could appeal to most potential buyers.

Certainly, new production ideas were needed to carry out Ford's strategy. But the really important decision was the initial market-oriented decision that there was a market for millions of cars in the $500 price range. Much of what followed was just carrying out his decision. Ford's strategy to offer a low-priced car was an outstanding success—and millions of Model Ts were sold during the 1910s and 1920s. But there was a defect in his strategy. To keep the price down, a very basic car was offered in "any color you want as long as it's black."

In the 1920s, General Motors felt there was room for a new strategy. They hit on the idea of looking at the market as having several segments (based on price and quality). They decided to offer a full line of cars with different styles and colors in each price range. The GM strategy was not an immediate success. But they stuck with it and slowly caught up with Ford. In 1927, Ford finally closed down his assembly line for 18 months—switched his strategy—and introduced the more market-oriented Model A to meet the new competition. But GM was already well on its way to the strong market position it still holds.[6]

The Watch Industry Sees New Strategies

The conventional watch makers—both domestic and foreign—had always aimed at customers who thought of watches as high-priced, high-quality symbols to mark special events—like graduations or retirement. Advertising was concentrated around Christmas and graduation time—and stressed a watch's symbolic appeal. Jewelry stores were the main retail outlets—with big markups.

This strategy of the major watch companies ignored people who just wanted to tell the time—and were interested in a reliable, low-priced watch. So the U.S. Time Company developed a successful strategy around its Timex watches—and became the world's largest watch company. Timex completely upset the watch industry—both foreign and domestic—by offering a good product (with a one-year repair or replace guarantee) at a lower price, and also using new, lower-cost channels of distribution. Its watches were widely available in drug stores, discount houses, and nearly any other retail store that would carry them.

Now Timex faces competition from new competitors. And digital and quartz watches coming from new sources have forced some of the traditional watch makers—like the once famous Swiss—to close their factories. Here, technological improvements—combined with modern marketing strategy planning—may completely change this whole industry in only a few years.[7]

Creative Strategy Planning Needed for Survival

Such dramatic shifts in strategy may surprise conventional, production-oriented managers. But such changes are becoming much more common—especially in industries where some of the firms have accepted the marketing concept.

Creative strategy planning is becoming even more important—because profits no longer can be won just by spending more money on plant and equipment. Also, domestic and foreign competition threatens those who can't create more satisfying goods and services. New markets, new customers, and new ways of doing things must be found if companies are to operate profitably in the future—and contribute to our macro-marketing system.

Timex pioneered new ways to market watches, but now faces tough competition from other makers of watches.

Timex:
The Beautiful Quartz

Timex believes these are the most beautiful quartz watches available to you, at any price. The design is handsome. Rich. Gleaming in the look of silver or gold. With accuracy to within 30 seconds a month. From $29.95 to $79.95 (suggested retail prices). Great design and great beauty are not expensive. Just rare.

TIMEX®
We make technology beautiful

MARKET–ORIENTED STRATEGY PLANNING HELPS NON–MARKETING PEOPLE, TOO

While market-oriented strategy planning is helpful to marketers, it's also needed by accountants, production and personnel people—and all other specialists. A market-oriented plan lets everybody in the firm know what "ballpark" they are playing in. It gives direction to the whole business effort. For example, an accountant can't set budgets without a plan. And a financial manager can't estimate cash needs without some idea of expected sales to some customers—and the costs of satisfying them.

We will use the term "marketing manager" for convenience. But when we talk about marketing strategy planning, we're talking about the planning that a market-oriented manager should do when developing a firm's strategic plans. This kind of thinking should be understood by everyone in an organization who is responsible for planning—and this means even the lowest-level salesperson, production supervisor, retail buyer, or personnel counselor.

■ CONCLUSION

Marketing's role within a marketing-oriented firm is to tie the company effort together. The marketing concept provides direction. It stresses that the firm's efforts should be focused on satisfying some target customers—at a profit. Production-oriented firms forget this. Often the various departments within such a firm let their natural conflicts of interest lead them to building "fences" around their areas.

The job of marketing management is one of continuous planning, implementing, and control. The marketing manager must constantly study the environment—seeking attractive opportunities. And new strategies must be planned continually. Potential target markets must be matched with marketing mixes that the firm can offer. Then,

attractive strategies—really, whole marketing plans—are chosen for implementation. Controls are needed to be sure that the plans are carried out successfully. If anything goes wrong along the way, this continual feedback should cause the process to be started over again—with the marketing manager planning more attractive marketing strategies.

A marketing mix has four variables—the four Ps—Product, Place, Promotion, and Price. Most of this text is concerned with developing profitable marketing mixes for clearly defined target markets. So after several chapters on selecting target markets, we will discuss the four Ps in greater detail.

■ QUESTIONS AND PROBLEMS

1. Define the marketing concept in your own words and then explain why the notion of profit is usually included in this definition.

2. Define the marketing concept in your own words and then suggest how acceptance of this concept might affect the organization and operation of your college.

3. Distinguish between "production orientation" and "marketing orientation" illustrating with local examples.

4. Explain why a firm should view its internal activities as part of a "total system." Illustrate your answer for (a) a large grocery products manufacturer, (b) a plumbing wholesaler, and (c) a department store chain.

5. Does the acceptance of the marketing concept almost require that a firm view itself as a "total system?"

6. Distinguish clearly between a marketing strategy and a marketing mix. Use an example.

7. Distinguish clearly between mass marketing and target marketing. Use an example.

8. Why is the customer placed in the center of the four Ps in the text diagram of a marketing strategy? Explain, using a specific example from your own experience.

9. Explain, in your own words, what each of the four Ps involves.

10. Evaluate the text's statement, "Strategy guides implementing."

11. Distinguish between a marketing strategy, a marketing plan, and a marketing program—illustrating for a local retailer.

12. Outline a marketing strategy for each of the following new products: (a) a radically new design for a hair comb, (b) a new fishing reel, (c) a new "wonder drug," (d) a new industrial stapling machine.

13. Provide a specific illustration of why marketing strategy planning is important for all business people, not just for those in the marketing department.

■ **SUGGESTED CASES**

1. Foodco, Inc.

3. Apex Chemical Company

29. Tower Manufacturing Company

Appendix A ■ Economics fundamentals

A good marketing manager should be an expert on markets—and the nature of competition in markets. The economist's traditional demand and supply analysis are useful tools for analyzing the nature of demand. In particular, you should master the concepts of a demand curve and demand elasticity. A firm's demand curve shows how the target customers view the firm's Product—really its whole marketing mix. And the interaction of demand and supply curves helps set the size of the market—and the market price. These ideas are discussed more fully in the following sections.

PRODUCTS AND MARKETS AS SEEN BY CUSTOMERS AND POTENTIAL CUSTOMERS

Economists Provide Useful Insights

How potential customers (not the firm) see a firm's product (marketing mix) affects how much they are willing to pay for it, where it should be made available, and how eager they are to obtain it—if at all. In other words, it has a very direct bearing on marketing strategy planning.

Economists have been concerned with these basic problems for years. Their analytical tools can be quite helpful in summarizing how customers view products—and how markets behave.

Economists See Individual Customers Choosing among Alternatives

Economics is sometimes called the "dismal" science—because it says that customers simply cannot buy everything they want. Since most customers have a limited income over any period of time, they must balance their needs and the prices of various products.

Economists usually assume that customers have a fairly definite set of preferences—and that they evaluate alternatives in terms of whether they will make them feel better (or worse)—or in some way improve (or change) their situation.

But what exactly is the nature of a customer's desire for a particular product?

Usually the argument is given in terms of the extra utility the customer can obtain by buying more of a particular product—or how much utility would be lost were the customer to have less of the product. (Students who wish further discussion of this approach should refer to indifference curve analysis in any standard economics text.)

It may be easier to understand the idea of utility if we look at what happens when the price of one of the customer's usual purchases changes.

The Law of Diminishing Demand

Suppose that a consumer buys potatoes in 10-pound bags at the same time he buys other foods—such as meat and vegetables. If the consumer is mainly interested in buying a certain amount of foodstuffs—and the price of the potatoes drops—it seems reasonable to expect that he will switch some of his food money to potatoes—and away from some other foods. But if the price of potatoes rises, you expect our consumer to buy fewer potatoes—and more of other foods.

The general interaction of price and quantity illustrated by this example is called the **law of diminishing demand**—which says that if the price of a product is raised, a smaller quantity will be demanded—and if the price of a product is lowered, a greater quantity will be demanded.

A Group of Customers Makes a Market

When our hypothetical consumers are considered as a group, we have a "market." It seems reasonable that many consumers in a market will behave in a similar way—that is, if price declines, the total quantity demanded will increase—and if price rises, the quantity demanded will decrease. Experience supports this reasoning—especially for broad product categories, or commodities such as potatoes.

The relationship between price and quantity demanded in a market is shown in Table A–1. It is an example of what economists call a "demand schedule." Note that as the price drops, the quantity demanded increases. In the third column, total dollar sales—total revenue of the potato market—is shown. Note, however, that as prices go lower, the total *unit* quantity increases, yet the total *revenue* decreases. It is suggested that you fill in the missing blanks and observe the behavior of total revenue—an important

■ TABLE A–1 Demand schedule for potatoes

Point	(1) Price of potatoes per bag (P)	(2) Quantity demanded (bags per month) (Q)	(3) Total revenue per month (P × Q = TR)
A	$0.80	8,000,000	$6,400,000
B	0.65	9,000,000	
C	0.50	11,000,000	5,500,000
D	0.35	14,000,000	
E	0.20	19,000,000	

number for the marketing manager. We will explain what you should have noticed—and why—a little later.

The Demand Curve—Usually Down-Sloping

If your only interest is seeing at which price customers will be willing to pay the greatest total revenue, the demand schedule may be adequate. But a demand curve "shows" more. A **demand curve** is a "picture" of the relationship between price and quantity demanded in a market—assuming that all other things stay the same. It is a graph of the demand schedule. Figure A–1 shows the demand curve for potatoes—really just a plotting of the demand schedule. It shows how many potatoes would be demanded by potential customers at various possible prices. This is a "down-sloping demand curve."

Most demand curves are down-sloping. This just means that if prices are decreased, the quantity that customers will demand will increase.

Note that the demand curve only shows how customers will react to various prices. In a market, we see only one price at a time—not all of these prices. The curve, however, shows what quantities will be demanded—depending on

■ FIGURE A–1 Demand curve for potatoes (10-pound bags)

■ TABLE A–2 Demand schedule for refrigerators

Point	(1) Price per refrigerator (P)	(2) Quantity de- manded per year (Q)	(3) Total revenue per year (P × Q = TR)
A	$300	20,000	$ 6,000,000
B	250	70,000	17,500,000
C	200	130,000	26,000,000
D	150	210,000	31,500,000
E	100	310,000	31,000,000

what price is set. It would seem that most business people would like to see the price set at the point where the resulting revenue would be large.

Before discussing this, however, we should consider the demand schedule and curve for another product—to get a more complete picture of what is involved in demand-curve analysis.

A Refrigerator Demand Curve Looks Different

A different demand schedule is the one for refrigerators shown in Table A–2. Column (3) shows the total revenue that will be obtained at various possible prices and quantities. Again, as the price of refrigerators goes down, the quantity demanded goes up. But here, unlike the potato example, total revenue increases—at least until the price drops to $150.

Every Market Has a Demand Curve—For Some Time Period

These general demand relationships are typical for all products—but each product has its own demand schedule and curve in each potential market—no matter how small the market. In other words, a particular demand curve has meaning only for a particular market. We can think of demand curves for individuals, regions, and even countries. And the time period covered really should be specified—although this is often neglected, as we usually think of monthly or yearly periods.

The Difference between Elastic and Inelastic

The demand curve for refrigerators (see Figure A–2) is down-sloping—but note that it is flatter than the curve for potatoes. It is quite important that we understand what this flatness means.

We will consider the flatness in terms of total revenue—since this is what interests business managers.*

When you filled in the total revenue column for potatoes, you should have noticed that total revenue drops continually if the price is reduced. This looks undesirable from a manager's point of view—and illustrates inelastic demand. Inelastic demand means that although the quantity demanded increases if the price is decreased, the quantity demanded will not "stretch" enough—that is, it is not elastic enough—to avoid a decrease in total revenue.

---

*Strictly speaking, two curves should not be compared for flatness if the graph scales are different, but for our purposes now, we will do so to illustrate the idea of "elasticity of demand." Actually, it would be more correct to compare two curves for one product—on the same graph. Then both the shape of the demand curve and its position on the graph would be important.

■ FIGURE A–2   Demand curve for refrigerators

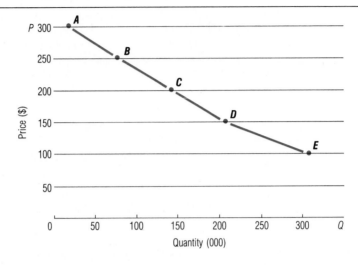

In contrast, **elastic demand** means that if prices are dropped, the quantity demanded will stretch enough to increase total revenue. The upper part of the refrigerator demand curve is an example of elastic demand.

But note that if the refrigerator price is dropped from $150 to $100, total revenue will decrease. We can say, therefore, that between $150 and $100, demand is inelastic—that is, total revenue will decrease if price is lowered to $100.

Thus, elasticity can be defined in terms of changes in total revenue. *If total revenue will increase if price is lowered, then demand is elastic. If total revenue will decrease if price is lowered, then demand is inelastic.*

Total revenue may decrease if price is raised

A point that is often missed in discussions of demand is what happens when prices are raised instead of lowered. With elastic demand, total revenue will *decrease* if the price is *raised*. If total revenue remains the same when prices change, then we have a special case known as "unitary elasticity of demand."

The possibility of raising price and increasing revenue at the same time is of special interest to managers. This only occurs if the demand curve is inelastic. If this is the case, it is obviously an attractive situation. Total revenue will increase if price is raised, but costs probably will not increase—and may actually go down. So profits will increase as price is increased.

The ways total revenue changes as prices are raised are shown in Figure A–3. Here, total revenue is the rectangular area formed by a price and its related quantity.

P_1 is the original price here—and the total potential revenue with this original price is shown by the area with the diagonal lines slanted down from the left. The total revenue area with the new price, P_2, is shaded with lines running diagonally upward from the left. In both cases, there is some overlap—so the important areas are those with only a single shading. Note that in the left-hand figure—where demand is elastic—the revenue added when the price is increased is less than the revenue lost (compare only the single-shaded areas). When demand is inelastic, however, only a small single-shaded revenue area is given up for a much larger one when price is raised.

An Entire Curve Is Not Elastic or Inelastic

It is important to see that it is *wrong to refer to a whole demand curve as elastic or inelastic.* Rather, elasticity for a particular curve refers to the change in total revenue between two points on a curve—and not along the whole curve. The change from elasticity to inelasticity can be seen in the refrigerator example. Generally, however, nearby points are either elastic or inelastic—so it is common to refer to a whole curve by the degree of elasticity of the curve in the price range that normally is of interest—the *relevant range.*

Demand Elasticities Affected by Availability of Substitutes and Urgency of Need

At first, it may be difficult to see why one product has an elastic demand and another an inelastic demand. Many factors affect elasticity—such as the availability of substitutes, the importance of the item in the customer's budget, and the urgency of the customer's need and its relation to other needs. By looking at one of these factors—the availability of substitutes—we should better understand why demand elasticities vary.

■ FIGURE A–3   Changes in total revenue as prices increase

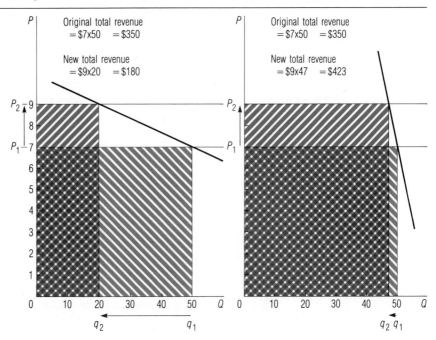

■ FIGURE A-4   Demand curve for hamburger (a product with many substitutes)

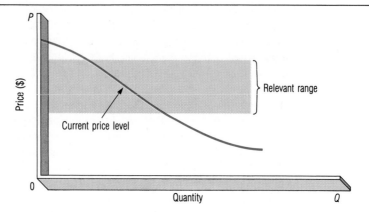

Substitutes are goods and/or services that offer a choice to the buyer. The greater the number of "good" substitutes available, the greater will be the elasticity of demand—"good" here referring to the degree of similarity—or homogeneity—that customers see. If they see a product as extremely different—or heterogeneous—then a particular need cannot easily be satisfied by substitutes—and the demand for the most satisfactory product may be quite inelastic.

As an example, if the price of hamburger is lowered (and other prices stay the same), the quantity demanded will increase a lot—as will total revenue. The reason is that not only will regular hamburger users buy more hamburger, but those consumers who formerly bought hot dogs, steaks, or bacon probably will buy hamburger, too. But if the price of hamburger rises, the quantity demanded will decrease—perhaps sharply. Consumers will still purchase some hamburger—depending on how much the price has risen, their individual tastes, and what their guests expect (see Figure A-4).

■ FIGURE A-5   Demand curve for salt (a product with few substitutes)

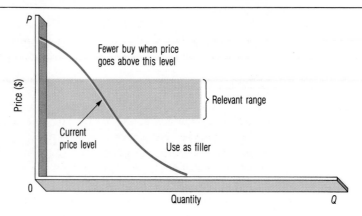

In contrast to a product which has many "substitutes"—such as hamburger—consider a product with few or no substitutes. Its demand curve will tend to be inelastic. Salt is a good example. Salt is needed to flavor food. Yet no one person or family uses great quantities of salt. And even with price changes *within a reasonable range,* it is not likely that the quantity of salt purchased will change much. Of course, if the price is dropped to an extremely low level, manufacturers may buy more—say, for low-cost filler, instead of clay or sand (Figure A–5). Or, if the price is raised to a staggering figure, many people will have to do without. But these extremes are outside the relevant range.

MARKETS AS SEEN BY SUPPLIERS

Demand curves are introduced here because the degree of elasticity of demand shows how potential customers feel about a product—and especially whether there are substitutes for the product. But to get a better understanding of markets, we must extend this economic analysis.

Customers may want some product—but if suppliers are not willing to supply it, then there is no market. So we will study the economist's analysis of supply—and then bring supply and demand together for a more complete understanding of markets.

Economists often use the kind of analysis we are discussing here to explain pricing in the marketplace. This is *not* our intention. Here we are interested in how and why markets work—and the interaction of customers and potential suppliers. The discussion in this appendix does *not* explain how individual firms set prices—or should set prices. That will come in Chapters 16 and 17.

Supply Curves Reflect Supplier Thinking

Generally speaking, suppliers' costs affect the quantity of products they are willing to offer in a market during any period. In other words, their costs affect their supply schedules and supply curves. While a demand curve shows the quantity of products customers will be willing to buy at various prices, a **supply curve** shows the quantity of products that will be supplied at various possible prices. Eventually, only one quantity of goods will be offered and purchased—so a supply curve is really a hypothetical description of what will be offered at various prices. It is, however, a very important curve. Together with a demand curve, it summarizes the attitudes and probable behavior of buyers and sellers about a particular product in a particular market—i.e., in a product-market.

Some Supply Curves Are Vertical

We usually assume that supply curves tend to slope upward—that is, suppliers will be willing to offer greater quantities at higher prices. If a product's market price is very high, it seems only reasonable that producers will be anxious to produce more of the product—and even put workers on overtime or perhaps hire more workers to increase the quantity they can offer. Going further, it seems likely that producers of other products will switch their resources

■ TABLE A–3   Supply schedule for potatoes

Point	Possible market price per 10-lb. bag	Number of bags sellers will supply per month at each possible market place
A	$0.80	17,000,000
B	0.65	14,000,000
C	0.50	11,000,000
D	0.35	8,000,000
E	0.20	3,000,000

Note: This supply curve is for a month to emphasize that farmers might have some control over when they deliver their potatoes. There would be a different curve for each month.

(farms, factories, labor, or retail facilities) to the product that is in great demand.

On the other hand, if a very low price is being offered for a particular product, it's reasonable to expect that producers will switch to other products—reducing supply. A supply schedule (Table A–3) and a supply curve (Figure A–6) for potatoes illustrate these ideas. This supply curve shows how many potatoes would be produced and offered for sale at each possible market price in a given month.

In the very short run (say, over a few hours, a day, or a week), a supplier may not be able to increase the supply at all. In this situation, we would see a vertical supply curve. This situation is often relevant in the market for fresh produce. Fresh strawberries, for example, continue to ripen, and a supplier wants to sell them quickly—preferably at a higher price—but in any case, he wants to sell them. For less perishable products, he may set a minimum price and, if necessary, store them until market conditions are better.

■ FIGURE A–6   Supply curve for potatoes (10-pound bags)

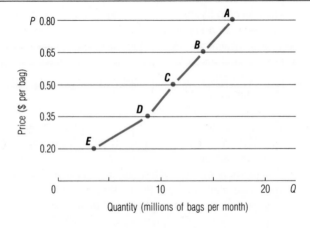

Quantity (millions of bags per month)

If the product is a service, it may not be easy to expand the supply in the short run—and there is no way to store it either. Additional barbers or medical doctors are not quickly trained and licensed—and they only have so much time to give each day. When the day is done, the unused "supply" is lost. Further, the prospect of much higher prices in the near future cannot easily expand the supply of many services. For example, a good play or an "in" restaurant or nightclub is limited in the amount of "product" it can offer at a particular time.

Elasticity of Supply

The term *elasticity* also is used to describe supply curves. An extremely steep or almost vertical supply curve—often found in the short run—is called inelastic supply because the quantity supplied does not stretch much (if at all) if the price is raised. A flatter curve is called elastic supply because the quantity supplied does stretch more if the price is raised. A slightly up-sloping supply curve is typical in longer-run market situations. Given more time, suppliers have a chance to adjust their offerings—and competitors may enter or leave the market.

DEMAND AND SUPPLY INTERACT TO DETERMINE THE SIZE OF THE MARKET AND PRICE LEVEL

We have treated market demand and supply forces separately. Now we must bring them together to show their interaction. The *intersection* of these two forces determines the size of the market and the market price—at which point (price and quantity) the market is said to be in *equilibrium.*

The intersection of demand and supply is shown for the potato data discussed above. The demand curve for potatoes is now graphed against the supply curve in Figure A–6—see Figure A–7.

■ **FIGURE A–7**   Equilibrium of supply and demand for potatoes

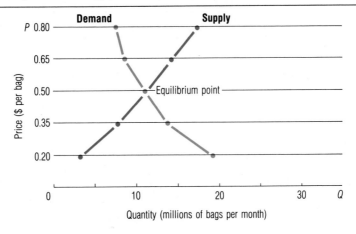

In this potato market, demand is inelastic—the total revenue of all the potato producers would be greater at higher prices. But the market price is at the **equilibrium point**—where the quantity and the price sellers are willing to offer are equal to the quantity and price that buyers are willing to accept. The $0.50 equilibrium price for potatoes yields a smaller *total revenue* to potato producers than a higher price would. This lower equilibrium price comes about because the many producers are willing to supply enough potatoes at the lower price. *Demand is not the only determiner of price level. Cost also must be considered—via the supply curve.*

Some Consumers Get a Surplus

It is important to note that not everyone gets *only* his money's worth in a sales transaction. Presumably, a sale takes place *only* if both buyer and seller feel they will be better off after the sale. But sometimes the price is better than "right."

The price we are talking about is the market price set by demand and supply forces. Typically, demand curves are down-sloping, and some of the demand curve is above the equilibrium price. This is simply a graphic way of showing that some customers are willing to pay more than the equilibrium price if they have to. In effect, some of them are getting a "bargain" by being able to buy at the equilibrium price. Economists have traditionally called these bargains the **consumer surplus**—that is, the difference to consumers between the value of a purchase and the price they pay.

It is important to see that there is such a surplus—because some business critics assume that consumers do badly in any business transaction. In fact, a sale takes place only if the consumer feels he is at least "getting his money's worth." As we can see here, some are willing to pay much more than the market price.

DEMAND AND SUPPLY HELP US UNDERSTAND THE NATURE OF COMPETITION

The elasticity of demand and supply curves—and their interaction—help predict the nature of competition a marketing manager is likely to face. For example, an extremely inelastic demand curve together with the usual up-sloping supply curve means that the firm will have much choice in its strategy planning—and especially its price setting. Apparently customers like the product and see few substitutes—they are willing to pay higher prices before cutting back much on their purchases.

Clearly, the elasticity of a firm's demand curves makes a big difference in strategy planning—but there are other factors which affect the nature of competition. Among these are the number and size of competitors—and the uniqueness of each firm's marketing mix. These ideas are discussed more fully in Chapters 3 and 4. Those discussions presume a real understanding of the contents of this appendix—so now you should be ready to handle that—and later material involving demand and supply analysis (especially Chapters 16 and 17).

■ CONCLUSION

The economist's traditional demand and supply analysis provides useful tools for analyzing the nature of demand and competition. It is especially important that you master the concepts of a demand curve and demand elasticity. How demand and supply interact helps determine the size of a market—and its price level. It also helps explain the nature of competition in different market situations. These ideas are discussed in Chapters 3 and 4—and then built upon throughout the text. So careful study of this appendix will build a good foundation for later work.

■ QUESTIONS AND PROBLEMS

1. Explain in your own words how economists look at markets—and arrive at the "law of diminishing demand."

2. Explain what a demand curve is—and why it is usually down-sloping.

3. What is the length of life of the typical demand curve? Illustrate your answer.

4. If the general market demand for men's shoes is fairly elastic, how does the demand for men's dress shoes compare to it? How does the demand curve for women's shoes compare to the demand curve for men's shoes?

5. If the demand for fountain pens is inelastic above and below the present price, should the price be raised? Why or why not?

6. If the demand for steak is highly elastic below the present price, should the price be lowered?

7. Discuss what factors lead to inelastic demand and supply curves. Are they likely to be found together in the same situation?

Chapter 3 ■ Finding attractive marketing opportunities

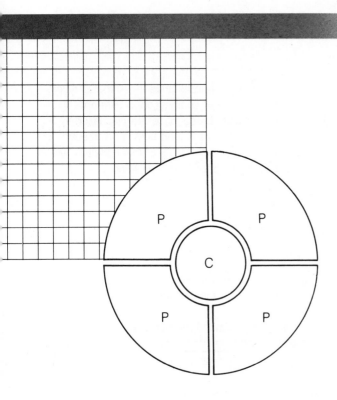

When you finish this chapter, you should:

1. Understand how to find marketing opportunities.

2. Know about defining relevant markets, generic markets, and product-markets.

3. Know about the different kinds of marketing opportunities.

4. Understand how the resources and objectives of a firm can help in the search for opportunities.

5. Understand why a firm should match its opportunities to its resources and objectives.

6. Understand how to screen and evaluate opportunities.

7. Recognize the important new terms (shown in red).

Finding attractive opportunities is part of marketing strategy planning.

The main focus of this book is on marketing strategy planning—an important part of which is finding attractive opportunities. But what are "attractive opportunities?" Should U.S. auto makers—for example—consider making computers? Or should the owner of a small gift shop convert to a computer store—to sell both hardware and software?

Let's define what we mean by "attractive opportunities"—and then see how a company's objectives and resources can affect the search for such opportunities. Remember, strategy planning tries to match a firm's resources—what it can do—to its market opportunities. Thus, we'll discuss not only finding opportunities but also how to evaluate them. This chapter is important—because attractive opportunities make the rest of marketing strategy planning easier.

WHAT ARE ATTRACTIVE OPPORTUNITIES?

Optimists see opportunities everywhere. Should a marketing manager go after all of the possibilities? Is every one really an attractive opportunity for his firm? The answer, in general, is *no!* Attractive opportunities for a particular firm are those which the firm has some chance of doing something about—given its resources and objectives. Usually, attractive opportunities are fairly close to markets the firm already knows. It makes sense to build on a firm's strengths— and avoid its weaknesses.

How many opportunities a firm "sees" depends on the thinking of top management—and the objectives of the firm. Some want to be innovators—and eagerly search out new opportunities. Others are willing to be creative imitators of the leaders. And others are risk-avoiding "me-too" marketers.

Kodak tries to identify breakthrough opportunities—ones which competitors can't copy quickly.

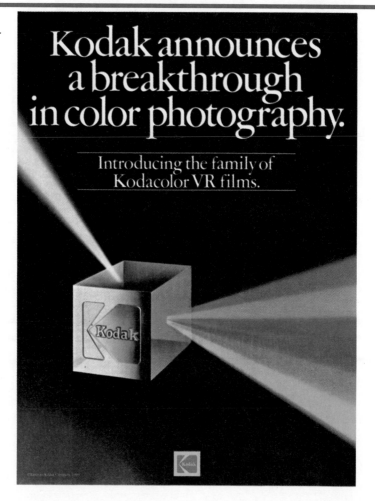

■ FIGURE 3–1   Finding and evaluating opportunities

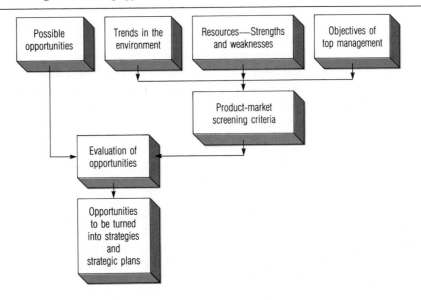

Figure 3–1 shows the process we will be discussing in this chapter—finding possible opportunities and screening them to choose the ones to be turned into strategies and strategic plans. As Figure 3–1 shows, we'll look first at possible opportunities—and then evaluate them against screening criteria. These criteria grow out of analysis of the company's resources, the long-run trends facing the firm, and the objectives of top management.

Breakthrough Opportunities Are Wanted

Throughout this book, we will emphasize finding **breakthrough opportunities**—opportunities which help innovators develop hard-to-copy marketing mixes that will be very profitable for a long time. A breakthrough opportunity can give a firm a "competitive advantage" over other firms—and a monopoly "in its own little market"—at least for awhile.

Finding breakthrough opportunities is important because such opportunities are needed—just to survive—in our increasingly competitive markets. The "me-too" products which production-oriented people like to turn out aren't very profitable anymore.

SEARCH FOR OPPORTUNITIES CAN BEGIN BY NAMING PRESENT MARKETS

When marketing managers really understand their target markets, they may see breakthrough opportunities—as this Eastman Kodak example shows. Eastman Kodak—maker of cameras and photographic supplies—also produces an industrial good, X-ray film. Until a few years ago, Kodak felt all this market wanted was faster X-ray pictures at cheaper prices. But closer study showed that the real need in hospitals and health-care units was saving the radiologist's time. Time was precious—but just giving the radiologist a faster picture wasn't enough. Something more was needed to help do the whole job faster.

Kodak came to see that its business was not just supplying X-ray pictures, but really helping to improve the health care supplied to patients. As a result, Kodak came up with new time-savers for radiologists: a handy cassette film pack—and a special identification camera that records all vital patient data directly on X-ray at the time the X-ray is made. Before, this tagging had to be done in the back room during developing—which took more time and created the risk of error. This was a different marketing mix aimed at satisfying a different need. And it worked very well.

What Is a Company's Market?

What is a company's market is an important—but sticky—question. A **market** is a group of potential customers with similar needs—and sellers offering various products—that is, ways of satisfying those needs.

Companies sometimes avoid the difficulties of naming markets by describing them in terms of products they sell. This production-oriented approach is easy—but it can make the firm miss opportunities. Producers and retailers of Christmas cards, for example, may define their market very narrowly as the "Christmas-card" market. Or, if they think a little broader, they may call their market the "greeting-card" market—including birthday cards, Easter cards, all-occasion cards, and humorous cards. But by taking a more customer-oriented view, the firm could define its market as the "personal-expression" market. This might lead the firm to offer all kinds of products which can be sent as gifts—to express one person's feelings towards another. The possibilities—besides greeting cards—include jewelry, plaques, candles, puzzles, etc. Companies like Hallmark have this bigger view—and they have expanded far beyond just selling standard greeting cards for the major greeting-card days—birthdays and Christmas.

Often there are several ways of satisfying a customer's need.

From Generic Markets to Product-Markets

It is useful to think of two basic types of market—a generic market and a product-market. A **generic market** is a market with *broadly* similar needs—and sellers offering various *often diverse* ways of satisfying those needs. In contrast, a **product-market** is a market with *very* similar needs—and sellers offering various *close substitute* ways of satisfying those needs.[1] A generic market description looks at markets broadly—and from a customer's viewpoint. Status-seekers, for example, have several very different ways to satisfy their status needs. A status-seeker may buy an expensive car, take a luxury cruise, or buy designer clothes at an exclusive shop. See Figure 3–2. Any one of these very different products may satisfy this status need. Sellers in this generic status-seeker market have to focus on the *need(s)* the customers want satisfied—not on how one seller's product (car, vacation, or designer label) is better than that of another producer. By really understanding the people's needs and attitudes, it may be possible for producers of "status symbols" to encourage shifts to their particular product.

The fact that quite different products may compete with each other in the same generic market makes it harder to understand and define the market. But if customers see all these products as substitutes—as competitors in the same generic market—then marketers will have to live with this complication.

Suppose, however, that one of our status seekers decides to satisfy this status need with a new, expensive car. Then—in this *product*-market—Mercedes, Cadillac, and Ferrari may compete with each other for the status-seeker's dollars.

To summarize—in the broad *generic* market for status—cars, designer clothes, and expensive vacations may all be competing with each other. In a narrower *product*-market concerned with cars *and* status (not just personal transportation!)—consumers compare similar products to satisfy their status need (e.g., a Ferrari with a Mercedes or a Cadillac).

Most companies quickly narrow their focus to product-markets—because of

■ FIGURE 3–2   The position of some products in a "status-seeker" market

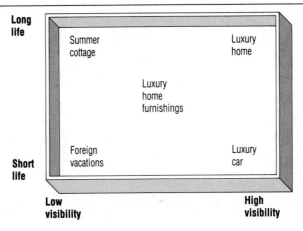

Long life

Summer cottage

Luxury home

Luxury home furnishings

Foreign vacations

Luxury car

Short life

Low visibility

High visibility

the firm's past experience, resources, or management preferences. And we will usually be thinking of product-markets when we refer to markets. But this should be done carefully when looking for opportunities—because it's so easy to miss opportunities—as the Christmas card example showed.

Broaden Market Definitions for Finding Opportunities

Broader market definitions—including broader product-market definitions and generic market definitions—can help in finding opportunities. But deciding how broad to go isn't easy. Too narrow a definition will limit a firm's opportunities—but too broad a definition will make the company's efforts and resources seem worthless.

Our strategy planning process can help to define a firm's relevant market— the market which is suitable for the firm's purpose. Here we are trying to match opportunities to a firm's resources and objectives—so the *relevant market for finding opportunities* should be bigger than the firm's present prod-

Lanier knows that its office machines compete with other alternatives in the same generic market.

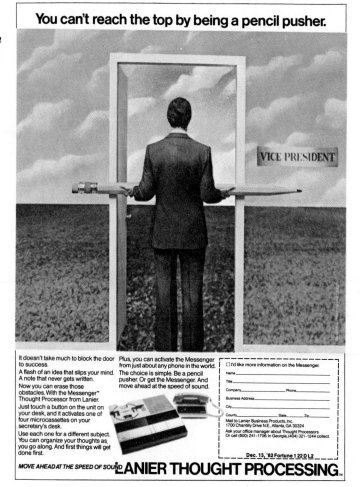

uct-market—but not so big that the firm couldn't expand and be an important competitor. A small manufacturer of screwdrivers, for example, shouldn't define its market as broadly as "the world-wide tool users market" or as narrowly or "our present screwdriver customers." But it may have the production and/or marketing potential to consider "the U.S. handyman's hand tool market." You can see that naming your product-market can help you see possible opportunities.

Naming a Product-Market

A product-market definition should include a four-part description:[2]

What:	1. Product Type
To Meet What:	2. Customer (User) Functional Need
For Whom:	3. Customer Types
Where:	4. Geographic Area

In other words, a product-market description must include some customer-related terms—*not* just product-related terms. Product-related terms are *not*—by themselves—an adequate description of a market.

Note: A generic market description *doesn't include any product-related terms.* It consists of the last three parts of a product-market definition—omitting the product type. This emphasizes the functional needs of the market—for example, the needs for personal expression, or status, or personal transportation. Figure 3–3 shows the relationship between generic market and product-market definitions.

Naming a market is a "common-sense" process—making full use of current knowledge about "substitutes" now being offered in this market area. For example, a U.S. car maker might proceed in the following way. One possible product-market definition might be: cars for transporting done by final consumers in the United States. But on further thought, it probably would become obvious that different product types are being offered to satisfy the different functional needs of various customer types. And this would lead to more specific product-market definitions. It might become clearer, for example, that cars sold to U.S. final consumers must satisfy at least two different transporting needs: (1) the need for economical transportation by consumers who usually carry only one or two people and (2) the need for transporting families or other groups of three to six people and/or bulky parcels. These different needs suggest different products. And different strategies might be needed for these

---

■ **FIGURE 3–3**   Relationship between generic and product-market definitions

| | Product Type |
| Generic Market Definition | + Customer (User) Functional Needs + Customer Types + Geographic Area | Product-Market Definition |

product-markets. So, at the least, a possible product-market name—cars for transporting done by final consumers in the United States—could be split and expanded into two more specific product-markets:

1. Small personal cars for economical "personal" transportation by final consumers in the United States.
2. Station wagons for "family" transportation by final consumers in the United States.

Defining the product-type part of a market definition means using commonly understood product-related terms that will describe all of the product elements which are being offered to a product-market. Typically, the product offering is much more than just a physical product. Installation, warranties, service, etc., may be included.

Somewhere in the description of either product type and/or functional need,

Understanding customers' functional needs helps develop better products.

©1983 CBS INC.   ©WALT DISNEY PRODUCTIONS

Disney Busy Poppin' Pals® Mickey, Pluto, Goofy, Dumbo and Donald keep popping up to help li'l Disney fans improve motor skills 5 different ways. Ages over 1½–3 years.

If it's fun+learning, it's a Child Guidance® toy.

The more kids play with a toy, the more they learn. So we pack a ton of fun into every Child Guidance toy. We create the kinds of shapes, sounds, motions and colors that entertain kids for months—not minutes. And when kids keep coming back for more, there's no limit to what they discover. Child Guidance toys. There's a ton of fun in every one.

CHILD GUIDANCE®

(Portion of Child Guidance ® ad reproduced here)

you must define what the product type does for someone. Sometimes naming the product type gets at the functional need at the same time—for example, caulking products are for caulking. In other cases, naming the functional need requires much thought—because the same product type may solve several functional needs—or even sets of functional needs. Cars, for example, can be for transporting *and* socializing *and* status *and* fun.

Potential customers' needs—and their attitudes toward the products in the general area being considered—can help name the relevant product-market or generic market. If your firm is interested in the transporting market, for example, it should think about why people buy transporting "substitutes." To some degree, the following products are substitutes: airplanes, pickup trucks, cars, motorcycles, bus service—and shoes. If you think about why some of these substitutes are better than others, you can convert these product-related solutions to more specific needs. You can see—for example—that some of these substitutes are better than others with respect to speed, convenience (in all weather), and cost.

Often it's necessary to go beyond "basic" needs—like transporting—to emotive needs, such as for status, fun, excitement, pleasing appearance, etc. Correctly defining functional need(s) and customer types is quite important in naming markets—and requires a good understanding of peoples' needs and wants. These topics are discussed more fully in Chapters 6 to 8.

The geographic area part of a market definition simply means the geographic area in which the firm is now competing—or thinking of competing. Just identifying the current geographic boundaries can suggest new opportunities. A supermarket in Los Angeles is not catering to all consumers in the Los Angeles area—so there may be opportunities to serve unsatisfied customers in that market. Similarly, if a firm is aiming only at the U.S. market, this may suggest world market opportunities.[3]

Creativity Is Needed in Naming Markets

Creative analysis of the needs and attitudes of present and potential target markets—in relation to the benefits being offered by the firm and competitors—will help you see new opportunities. In the next several chapters, we'll study the many possible dimensions of markets. But for now, you should see that markets can be defined in various ways. Defining them only in terms of current *products* is *not* the best way of finding new opportunities—or planning marketing strategies. Instead, you should try to define generic markets and product-markets—with emphasis on the customer-related characteristics, including geographic dimensions—as well as needs and attitudes.

MARKET SEGMENTATION LEADS TO THREE APPROACHES TO TARGET MARKETING

What Is Market Segmentation?

We've talked about getting started on naming product-markets—and finding new opportunities. Marketing managers can use these broad product-market names to get started—and then segment these broad product-market areas into more "relevant" product-markets which they might pursue. So let's take a closer look at what segmenting involves.

Market segmentation is the process of *naming* product-markets and then *segmenting* these broad product-markets into more homogeneous sub-markets—in order to select target markets and develop suitable marketing mixes. You can see that market segmentation—and "segmenting"—are *not* planning marketing strategies. Segmenting is concerned only with identifying product-markets or sub-markets which might become parts of marketing strategies.

Market segmentation assumes that any product-market usually consists of sub-markets—which may need separate marketing mixes. So target marketers segment product-markets into smaller, more homogeneous product-markets—which they may be able to satisfy better than if they treated everybody alike.

Market grid is a visual aid to segmenting

Assuming that any market may consist of sub-markets, it helps our understanding to picture a market as a rectangle with boxes representing smaller, more homogeneous product-markets. See Figure 3–4.

Think of the whole rectangle as representing a broad product-market—or even a generic market. Now think of each of the boxes as sub-markets. Product-markets usually require several dimensions to describe them. And within a broad product-market, the sub-markets may require very different dimensions. We saw this in Chapter 2 in the British home decorating market example. So don't try to use the same two dimensions to name the markets—or to label the sides of the market grid boxes.

Target Marketers Aim at Specific Targets

Once you accept the idea that broad product-markets may have sub-markets, you can see that target marketers may have a problem choosing among many possible target markets.

There are three basic ways of developing market-oriented strategies for a broad product-market:

■ FIGURE 3–4   Market grid diagram with sub-markets (numbered)

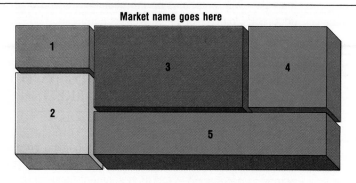

Market name goes here

■ FIGURE 3–5   Target marketers have specific aims

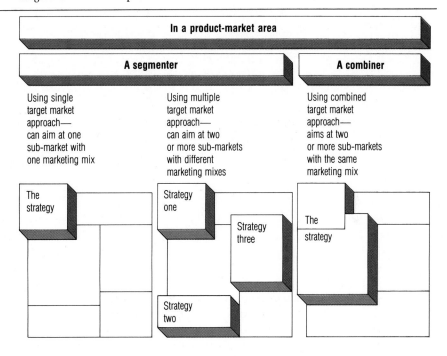

1. The **single target market approach**—segmenting the market and picking one of the homogeneous sub-markets as the firm's target market.
2. The **multiple target market approach**—segmenting the market and choosing two or more sub-markets—each of which will be treated as a separate target market—needing a different marketing mix.
3. The **combined target market approach**—combining two or more sub-markets into one larger target market—as a basis for one strategy.

Note that all three approaches involve target marketing—they are all aiming at specific—and clearly defined—target markets. See Figure 3–5. For convenience, we'll call people who follow the first two approaches the "segmenters" and the people who use the third approach "combiners."

Combiners Try to Satisfy Pretty Well

Combiners try to increase the size of their target markets by combining two or more sub-markets—perhaps to gain some economies of scale, to reduce risk, or just because they don't have enough resources to develop more than one marketing mix. Combiners look at various sub-markets for similarities—rather than differences. Then they try to extend or modify their basic offering to appeal to these "combined" customers—with just one marketing mix. See Figure 3–6. For example, combiners may try a new package, a new brand, or new flavors. But even if physical changes are made, their aim is not at smaller

■ FIGURE 3–6   There may be different demand curves in different market segments

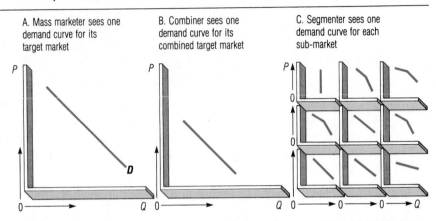

A. Mass marketer sees one demand curve for its target market

B. Combiner sees one demand curve for its combined target market

C. Segmenter sees one demand curve for each sub-market

Note: A familiarity with economic analysis, and especially demand curves and demand elasticity, is assumed in this text. Those desiring a review of these materials should see Appendix A at the end of Chapter 2.

sub-markets. Instead, combiners try to improve the general appeal of their marketing mix—to appeal to a bigger "combined" target market.

Segmenters Try to Satisfy "Very Well"

Segmenters, on the other hand, aim at one or more homogeneous sub-markets and try to develop a different marketing mix for each sub-market. They want to satisfy each one very well.

Segmenters may make more basic changes in marketing mixes—perhaps in the physical product itself—because they are aiming at smaller target markets—each needing a separate marketing mix.

Instead of assuming that the whole market consists of a fairly similar set of customers—like the mass marketer does—or merging various sub-markets together—like the combiner—a segmenter sees sub-markets with their own demand curves—as shown in Figure 3–6. Segmenters believe that aiming at one—or some—of these smaller markets will provide greater satisfaction to the target customers—and greater profit potential for the firm.

Segmenting May Produce Bigger Sales

Note that a segmenter is not settling for a smaller sales potential. Instead, by aiming the firm's efforts at only a part of a larger product-market, the segmenter hopes to get a much larger share of his target market(s). In the process, total sales may be larger. The segmenter may even get almost a monopoly in "his" market(s).

Should You Segment or Combine?

Which approach should be used? This depends on many things, including the firm's resources, the nature of competition, and—most important—the similarity of customer needs, attitudes, and buying behavior.

It is tempting to aim at larger combined markets—instead of smaller segmented markets. If successful, such a strategy can result in economies of scale. Also, offering one marketing mix to two or more sub-markets usually requires less investment—and may appear to involve less risk—than offering different marketing mixes to different sub-markets.

However, a combiner faces the continual risk of segmenters "chipping away" at the various sub-markets of the combined target market—especially if the combined market is quite heterogeneous. In the extreme, a combiner may create a fairly attractive marketing mix, but then watch segmenters capture one after another of its sub-markets with more targeted marketing mixes—until finally the combiner is left with no market at all!

In general, it's safer to be a segmenter—that is, to try to satisfy some customers very well—instead of many just fairly well. That's why many firms use the single or multiple target market approach—instead of the combined target market approach. Procter & Gamble, for example, offers many products which seem to compete directly with each other (e.g., Tide versus Cheer or Crest versus Gleem). However, P&G offers "tailor-made" marketing mixes to each sub-market that is large enough and profitable enough to deserve a separate marketing mix. This approach can be extremely effective—but it may not be possible for a smaller firm with more limited resources. It may have to use the single target market approach—aiming at the one sub-market which looks "best" for it.

TYPES OF OPPORTUNITIES TO PURSUE

Most people have unsatisfied needs—and alert marketers can find opportunities all around them. Starting with the firm's present product-markets is useful. By carefully defining its product-markets, it may see new opportunities. Or it may see opportunities beyond its present activities.

It helps to see the kinds of opportunities which may be found. Figure 3–7 shows the four possibilities: market penetration, market development, product development, and diversification.

■ FIGURE 3–7   Four basic types of opportunities

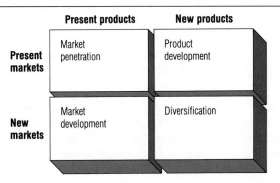

Market Penetration

Market penetration is trying to increase sales of a firm's present products in its present markets—probably with a more aggressive marketing mix. The firm may try to increase customers' rate of use—or attract either the competitors' customers or present non-users. New promotion appeals may be effective. McDonald's may have Ronald McDonald invite the kids in for a special offer. More stores may be added in present areas—for greater convenience. Short-term price cuts or coupon offers may help. Obviously, effective strategy planning is aided by a real understanding of why some people are buying now—and what will motivate them to buy more—or persuade others to shift brands or begin—or resume—buying.

Market Development

Market development is trying to increase sales by selling present products in new markets. This could include, for example, McDonald's adding new stores in new areas—perhaps in downtown locations, in schools or hospital lobbies, or even in foreign countries. Or it may only involve advertising in different media to reach new target customers.

Product Development

Product development is offering new or improved products for present markets. Here, the firm should know each market's needs—and may see ways of adding or modifying product features to satisfy a present market better. For example, McDonald's now offers breakfast for adults—and cookies for kids.

Diversification

Diversification is moving into totally different lines of business—which may include entirely unfamiliar products, markets, or even levels in the production-marketing system. For example, manufacturers may go into wholesaling or retailing—or buy their suppliers.[4]

Diversification offers the most challenging opportunities because both new products *and* new markets are involved. The further the opportunity is from what the firm is already doing, the more attractive it may look—and the harder it will be to evaluate. The firm may have a good understanding of all the problems close to its current operations—that's why it's considering other opportunities! But opportunities which are far from a firm's current operations may involve much higher risks. This is why it is very important to avoid wasteful searches for opportunities—while carefully evaluating those which are finally considered. How this can be done is discussed in the following pages.

COMPANY RESOURCES MAY LIMIT SEARCH FOR OPPORTUNITIES

Every firm has some resources—perhaps some unique strengths—that help in planning good strategies. Attractive opportunities should make use of these strengths. To find its strengths, a firm must analyze its outstanding successes and failures—in relation to its resources—to find patterns which explain why it was successful—or why it failed—in the past.

In businesses which require a large physical plant, managers usually try to use the existing plant as fully as possible.

Resources which should be considered—when looking for possible strengths—are discussed in the following sections.

Financial Strength

Some industries—such as steel and public utilities—need large amounts of capital to get economies of scale. For them, the cost of production per unit goes down as the quantities produced increase. Therefore, smaller producers would have trouble if they tried to compete in these lines. Large companies however, often have difficulties when they enter low-investment businesses. A large producer of plastic sheets tried to make and sell decorated shower curtains. The effort failed, however. The smaller shower curtain manufacturers and middlemen were much more flexible—changing their styles and price policies more quickly. Here, financial strength was a strength in the basic plastic sheet business—but a weakness where style and flexibility in adapting to customer needs were important.

Raw Material Reserves

Firms that own or have dependable sources of basic raw materials have a head start in businesses that need these resources. But companies—large or small—that don't have this advantage may have difficulty even staying in business. Chemical and paper manufacturers, for example, usually try to control timber resources. Metals and petroleum companies control their own resources. Now that we see a growing shortage of raw materials, it probably will be wise for a firm to be sure of supply before building a marketing strategy which depends on raw materials.

Physical Plant

Some lines of business require large physical plants. If these are well located, they are a strength. On the other hand, badly located or out-of-date plants—or wholesale or retail facilities—can be real weaknesses. The existing physical plant can affect marketing strategy planning—because one of the firm's objectives probably will be to use the existing plant as fully as possible.

Patents

Patents are important to manufacturers. A patent owner has a 17-year "monopoly" to develop and use its new product, process, or material as it sees fit. If a firm has a patent on a basic process, competitors will be forced to use second-rate processes—and they may fail. If a firm has such a patent, it is a resource—while if its competitors have it, it may be a weakness which can't be overcome with other parts of a marketing mix.

Brands

If a firm has developed a loyal following of customers who prefer—or insist on—its product, others may have difficulty invading this market. A strong brand is a valuable resource that a marketing manager can use in developing marketing strategies.

Skilled People

Some firms deliberately pay high wages to attract and keep skilled workers—so they can offer high-quality products. A skilled sales force is also a strength—lack of good salespeople can limit strategy planning. Even if skilled employees can produce a new product, the sales force may not have the contacts—or know-how—to sell it. This often happens when a firm moves from consumer products to industrial products—or vice versa.

Management Attitudes

The attitude of top management toward growth is important in strategy planning—especially in developing new products.

The president of a New England manufacturing company was excited about a new product. But after evaluating company attitudes, he dropped his plans for the product. Why? He found that his employees—especially his management people—had no interest in growth.[5]

OBJECTIVES MAY LIMIT THE SEARCH FOR OPPORTUNITIES

A company's objectives should direct the operation of the whole business. If the firm has decided to stay small—so the owner has more time for golf—this objective will obviously limit the firm's opportunities. (Actually, of course, it probably won't even be looking for opportunities!) On the other hand, if a large, aggressive firm seeks sales growth—then the range of opportunities expands quickly.

Objectives Should Set Firm's Course

A company should know where it is going—or it can fall into this trap: "Having lost sight of our objective, we redoubled our efforts." In spite of their importance, objectives are seldom stated clearly. They may not even be stated until *after the strategies are carried out!*

Setting objectives that really guide the present and future development of the company isn't easy. It forces top management to look at the whole business—relate its present objectives and resources to the external environment—and then decide what it wants to do in the future.

Three Basic Objectives Provide Guidelines

The following three objectives provide a useful starting point for setting objectives for a firm. They should be pursued *together* because—in the long run—a failure in even one of the three areas could lead to total failure of the business.

1. Engage in some specific business activity that will be socially and economically useful.
2. Develop an organization to stay in business—and carry out its strategies.
3. Earn enough profit to survive.[6]

Short-Sighted Top Management May Straitjacket Marketing

Setting objectives must be taken seriously—or the objectives may limit marketing strategies—perhaps damaging the whole business.[7] A few examples will help show how the marketing manager may be forced to choose undesirable strategies.

A quick return on investment is sometimes sought by top management. This can force the marketing manager to choose marketing strategies aimed at quick returns in the short run—but kill brand loyalty in the long run.

Some top managements want a large sales volume or a large market share—because they feel this means higher profits. However, more companies are now shifting their objectives toward *profitable* sales growth—as they realize that sales growth doesn't necessarily mean profit growth.[8]

Objectives Should Guide the Whole Management Process

Ideally, the marketing manager should help set objectives—and these objectives should guide the search for and evaluation of opportunities—as well as later planning of marketing strategies. As shown in Figure 3–8, there should

■ FIGURE 3–8   A hierarchy of objectives

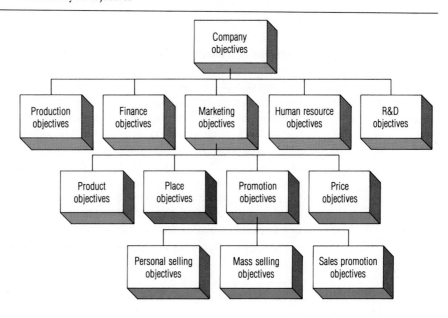

be a hierarchy of objectives—moving from company objectives, to marketing department objectives. For each marketing strategy, there should also be objectives for each of the four Ps—as well as sub-objectives. For example, in the Promotion area, we may need advertising objectives, sales promotion objectives, and personal selling objectives.

HOW TO EVALUATE OPPORTUNITIES

Once some opportunities have been identified, they must be screened and evaluated. A firm can't possibly pursue all of its opportunities. Instead, it must try to match its opportunities to its resources and objectives. The first step is to quickly screen out the obvious mismatches. Then, it can analyze the others more carefully. Let's look at some methods for screening and evaluating opportunities.

Developing and Applying Screening Criteria

First we have to analyze the firm's resources (for strengths and weaknesses), the environmental trends facing the firm (Chapter 4), and the objectives of top management. Then we can combine them into a set of realistic product-market screening criteria. These criteria should include both quantitative and qualitative components. The quantitative components outline the objectives of the firm—sales, profit, and return on investment (ROI) targets for each strategy.* The qualitative components explain what kinds of businesses the firm wants to be in, what businesses it wants to exclude, what weaknesses it should avoid, and what strengths and trends it should build on.[9] Opportunities that pass the screen ought to be able to be turned into strategies which the firm can carry out—with the resources it has.

Figure 3–9 shows the product-market screening criteria for a small sales company (retailer and wholesaler). This whole set would help the firm's managers eliminate unsuitable opportunities—and find attractive ones to turn into strategies and plans.

Profitability of Whole Plans Should Be Evaluated

Forecasts of the probable results of implementing whole strategic plans are needed to apply the quantitative part of the screening criteria—because it is "implemented plans" which produce sales, profits, and return on investment (ROI). For a rough screening, we only need an estimate of the likely profitability of implementing each opportunity over a logical planning period. If a product's life is likely to be five years, for example, then a good strategy may not produce profitable results during the first six months to a year. But evaluate the plan over the projected five-year life, and it might look like a winner. When evaluating the potential of possible opportunities—strategic plans—it's important to evaluate similar things—that is, *whole* plans.[10]

Note that—as shown in Figure 3–10—quite different strategic plans can be

*See Appendix B (following Chapter 17) for definitions of these terms.

■ FIGURE 3–9   An example of product-market screening criteria for a sales company (retail and wholesale—$1 million annual sales)

1. **Quantitative criteria**
   a. Increase sales by $200,000 per year for the next five years.
   b. Earn ROI of *at least* 25 percent before taxes on new ventures.
   c. Break even within one year on new ventures.
   d. Opportunity must be large enough to justify interest (to help meet objectives) but small enough so company can handle with the resources available.
   e. Several opportunities should be needed to reach the objectives—to spread the risks.
2. **Qualitative criteria**
   a. Nature of business preferred.
      (1) Goods and services sold to present customers.
      (2) "Quality" products which can be sold at "high prices" with full margins.
      (3) Competition should be weak and opportunity should be hard to copy for several years.
      (4) Should build on our strong sales skills.
      (5) There should be strongly felt (even unsatisfied) needs—to reduce promotion costs and permit "high" prices.
   b. Constraints
      (1) Nature of businesses to exclude.
         (a) Manufacturing.
         (b) Any requiring large fixed capital investments.
         (c) Any requiring many people who must be "good" all the time and would require much supervision (e.g., "quality" restaurant).
      (2) Geographic
         (a) United States and Canada only.
      (3) General
         (a) Make use of current strengths.
         (b) Attractiveness of market should be reinforced by *more than one* of the following basic trends: technological, demographic, social, economic, political.
         (c) Market should not be bucking *any* of above trends.

■ FIGURE 3–10   Expected sales and cost curves of two strategies over five-year planning periods

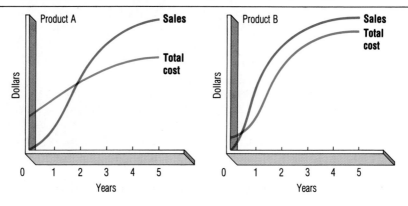

evaluated at the same time. In this case, a much improved product (Product A) is being compared with a "me-too" product for the same target market. In the short run, the "me-too" product would break even sooner and might look like the better choice—if only one year's results were considered. The new product, on the other hand, will take a good deal of pioneering but—over its five-year life—will be much more profitable.

PLANNING GRIDS HELP EVALUATE DIFFERENT KINDS OF OPPORTUNITIES

When a firm has many possibilities to evaluate, it usually has to compare quite different ones. This can present a real problem—but the problem has been reduced by the development of graphical approaches—such as the nine-box strategic planning grid developed by General Electric.

General Electric Looks for Green Positions

General Electric's strategic planning grid—see Figure 3–11—forces company managers to make three-part judgments (high, medium, and low) about the business strengths and industry attractiveness of all proposed or existing products or businesses.

GE feels that opportunities that fall into the green boxes in the upper left-hand corner of the grid are its growth opportunities—the ones that will lead the company to invest and grow with these businesses. The red boxes in the lower right-hand corner of the grid, on the other hand, suggest a no-growth policy. Existing red businesses may continue to generate earnings—but GE

■ FIGURE 3–11   General Electric's strategic planning grid

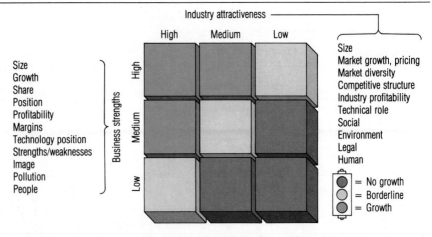

Source: Adapted from M. G. Allen, "Strategic Problems Facing Today's Corporate Planner," speech given at the Academy of Management, 36th Annual Meeting, Kansas City, Missouri, 1976.

figures they no longer deserve much investment. The yellow businesses are the borderline cases—which can go either way. An existing yellow business may be continued and supported—but a proposal for a new yellow business probably would be rejected by top management.

GE's "stop light" evaluation method is very subjective— because GE feels there is too much chance of error if it tries to use over-simplified criteria—like ROI and market share—for judging "attractiveness" or "strength." Instead, top managers review written summaries of about a dozen factors (see Figure 3–11) which help them make summary judgments. Then they make a collective judgment based on the importance they attach to each of the factors. GE reports that the approach generally leads to agreement and, further, a good understanding about why some businesses or new opportunities are supported—while others are not. In addition, it appears that high-high green businesses are uniformly good on almost any quantitative or qualitative measure used. This interaction among the relevant variables makes it practical to boil them all down into a "stop light" framework.[11]

MULTI–PRODUCT FIRMS HAVE A DIFFICULT STRATEGY PLANNING JOB

Firms with many product lines—like General Electric—obviously have a tougher strategic planning job than a firm with only a few products (or product lines) aimed at the same or similar target markets. Firms like GE have to develop strategic plans for very different businesses. And the corporate level must try to balance the plans and needed resources for the various businesses so that the whole corporation reaches its objectives. This requires analysis of the various alternatives—using approaches similar to the General Electric strategic planning grid—and approving strategic plans which make sense for the *whole* corporation.[12]

Details on how to manage such a complicated firm are beyond our scope. But it is important to know (1) that there are such firms and (2) that the principles we will discuss in this text work—they just have to be extended to develop and control many strategic plans.

■ CONCLUSION

Creative strategy planning is needed for survival in our increasingly competitive marketplaces. In this chapter, we discussed ways of finding attractive opportunities—and breakthrough opportunities. And we saw that the firm's own resources and objectives may help limit the search for opportunities. We saw that carefully

defining generic markets and product-markets can help find new opportunities. And segmenting broad product-markets may force target marketers to choose among three approaches to target marketing: (1) the single target market approach, (2) the multiple target market approach, and (3) the combined target market approach. In general, we encourage marketers to be segmenters (single or multiple) rather than combiners.

We discussed an approach for developing screening criteria—from the output of an analysis of the strengths and weaknesses of the company's resources, the environmental trends it faces, and top management's objectives. We also considered ways for evaluating opportunities—including quite different opportunities, using the GE strategic planning grid.

Now—before going on to discuss how to turn opportunities into profitable marketing strategies in the rest of the book—we will look at the uncontrollable variables facing a marketing manager (in Chapter 4). They are important because changes in these variables present new opportunities—as well as problems—a marketing manager must deal with in marketing strategy planning.

■ QUESTIONS AND PROBLEMS

1. Distinguish between an attractive opportunity and a breakthrough opportunity.

2. Explain how new opportunities may be seen by defining a firm's markets more precisely. Illustrate for a situation where you feel there is an opportunity—i.e., an unsatisfied market segment—even if it is not very large.

3. Distinguish between a generic market and a product-market. Illustrate your answer.

4. Explain the major differences among the four basic types of opportunities discussed in the text and cite examples for two of these types of opportunities.

5. Explain why a firm may want to pursue a market penetration opportunity before pursuing one involving product development or diversification.

6. Explain how a firm's resources may limit its search for opportunities. Cite a specific example for a specific resource.

7. Discuss how a company's financial strength may have a bearing on the kinds of products it produces. Will it have an impact on the other three Ps as well? If so, how? Use an example in your answer.

8. Explain how a firm's objectives may affect its search for opportunities.

9. Specifically, how would various company objectives affect the development of a marketing mix for a new type of baby shoe? If this company were just being formed by a former shoe maker with limited financial resources, list the objectives he might have. Then discuss how they would affect the development of his marketing strategy.

10. Explain the components of product-market screening criteria—which can be used to evaluate opportunities.

11. Explain General Electric's strategic planning grid approach to evaluating opportunities.

■ SUGGESTED CASES

4. Uncle Lyle's, Inc.

12. Mason Sport Shop

29. Tower Manufacturing Company

Chapter 4 ■ Uncontrollable environments affecting marketing management

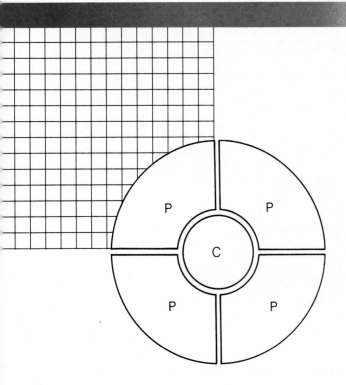

When you finish this chapter, you should:

1. Know the uncontrollable variables the marketing manager must work with.

2. Know about population and income trends.

3. Understand how the economic and technological environment can affect strategy planning.

4. Know the effect of the different kinds of market situations on strategy planning.

5. Know why you can go to prison by ignoring the political and legal environment.

6. Recognize the important new terms (shown in red).

Marketing managers do not plan strategies in a vacuum.

In the early 1980s, IBM's competitors were shocked to find that IBM was no longer going to play the role of "gentle leader"—letting quick followers match its offerings at lower prices—or supply "add-on" equipment. Instead, IBM began aggressive pricing—sometimes dropping prices 20 to 30 percent on a new model within a year—and introducing products in large enough quantities to meet market demand quickly. IBM's more aggressive product-price combinations made it harder for competitors to use lower price to "steal" business away from IBM.

Marketing managers don't plan strategies in a vacuum. Finding attractive opportunities takes a real understanding of what makes customers tick. Managers must be aware of market dimensions that make a difference—in terms of population, income and buying behavior. Marketers also must work with several uncontrollable variables—including competition—when choosing their markets and developing the four Ps. As shown in Figure 4–1—such uncontrollable variables fall into the following areas:

■ FIGURE 4–1   Marketing manager's framework

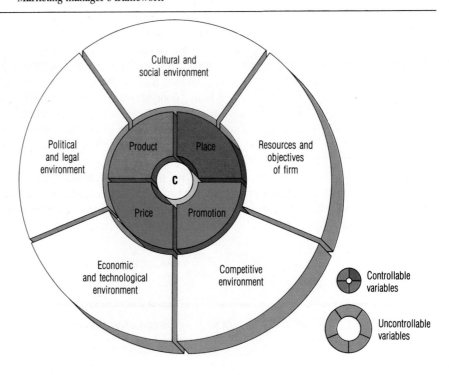

1. Cultural and social environment.
2. Economic and technological environment.
3. Competitive environment.
4. Political and legal environment.
5. Resources and objectives of the firm.

In Chapter 3 we saw how the resources and objectives of a firm affect marketing strategy planning. Now let's look at the first four uncontrollable variables (above)—and see how they add to the challenge of marketing management.

CULTURAL AND SOCIAL ENVIRONMENT

The **cultural and social environment** affects how and why people live and behave as they do. This variable is very important—because it has a direct effect on customer buying behavior in our competitive markets.

Markets consist of real people with money to spend. But the number and location of these people is pretty much set. And many of their attitudes and behavior patterns are fixed—or changing only slowly. In other words, we already know a great deal about our cultural and social environment.

Markets Consist of People

There are already over 225 million people living in the United States. Population experts can estimate how long people in various age groups will live and—at least roughly—where they will live.

Figure 4–2 shows that Americans are not spread out equally across the country. This map of the United States shows the 1984 population for each state. The "high areas" emphasize the concentration of population in different areas. Note that California has the largest population—with New York a distant second. But the heavy concentration in the Northeast makes this market much bigger than the whole West Coast. Also notice the importance of the Midwestern states and the Southern states when taken as a group. These regions are often seen as very good target markets by marketers wanting to avoid the tough competition in the East and West Coast markets. Note, too, the small populations in the Plains and Mountain states. You can see why some "national" marketers pay less attention to these areas. But these states can be an attractive opportunity for an alert marketer looking for less competitive markets.[1]

■ FIGURE 4–2   Map of the United States showing population by state (all figures in thousands)

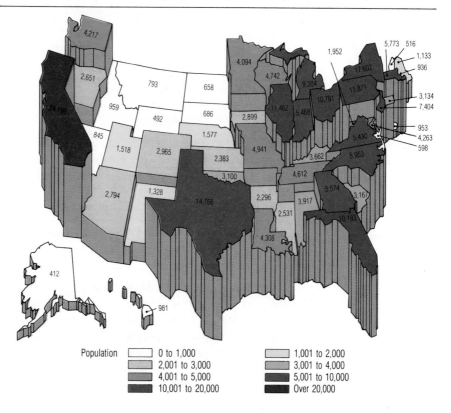

Population
- 0 to 1,000
- 2,001 to 3,000
- 4,001 to 5,000
- 10,001 to 20,000
- 1,001 to 2,000
- 3,001 to 4,000
- 5,001 to 10,000
- Over 20,000

Population Will Keep Growing, but . . .

It seems certain that the U.S. population will continue to grow—at least for another 60 years or so. The big questions are: How much and how fast? The "baby boom" of the 1950s and 1960s turned into the "baby bust" of the 1970s. The **birth rate**—number of babies per 1,000 people—fell from a post-war high of 25.0 in 1957 to 14.8 in 1976. It rose only to 16.2 in 1980. See Figure 4–3. This means there is less need for baby food, toys, teachers, and child-oriented recreation—and more demand for small apartments, travel, and out-of-home entertainment.[2]

Average age will rise

Although our population will continue to grow, there will be a major change in our society because the average age is going to rise. The percentage change—growth or decline—in some key age groups for the decade from 1980 to 1990 is given in Figure 4–4.

The major reason for the rising average age is the baby boom—lasting from about 1947 to 1957—which produced about one fifth of our present population. This large group crowded into the schools in the 1950s and 60s. Then they moved into the job market in the 1970s. In the 1980s and 1990s they will be middle-aged. And early in the 21st century, they will reach retirement—still a large group in the total population. According to one population expert, "It's like a goat passing through a boa constrictor."

■ FIGURE 4–3   Changes in the U.S. birth rate, 1935–1981

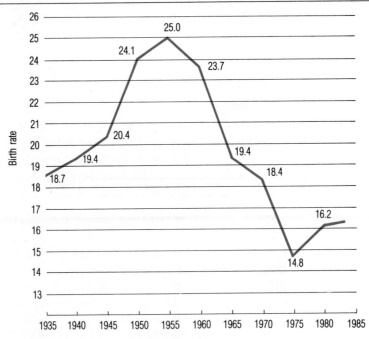

Source: *Statistical Abstract of the United States, 1982–1983.*

■ FIGURE 4–4   Projected changes in size of age groups, 1980–1990

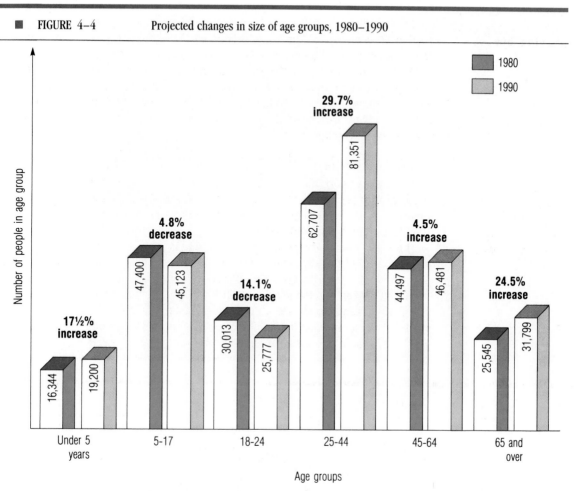

Source: *Statistical Abstract of the United States, 1982–1983.*

Medical advances—that help people live longer—are also adding to the proportion of the population in the senior citizen group. The average age will continue to rise—as there are fewer young people. In the next 20 years, the number of Americans over 65 may increase by 30 percent. This will have obvious effects on many industries—like tourism and health care.

Older people will want a larger share of the resources

Eventually, America's "youth culture" will give way to a new kind of society. In fact, the aging of the population is seriously concerning some planners— because it is possible that the younger people will not be able—or willing—to support all of the older people in the style they now expect. Certainly, the costs will continue to rise—as there are relatively more retired people being supported by fewer young people. Already, the Social Security system is running out of money—forcing higher taxes and later retirement ages.[3]

Sometimes we take our own culture for granted.

Household Composition Is Changing

We often think of the "typical" American household as a married couple with two children—living in the suburbs. This never was true—and it is even less true now. Although almost all Americans marry, they are marrying later—delaying child bearing and having fewer children. Couples with no children under 18 now account for almost half of all families.

And couples don't stay together as long as they used to. The United States has the highest divorce rate in the world—about 38 percent of marriages end in divorce. Almost 80 percent of divorced people remarry—so we see a growing number of "his and hers" families. Still—even with all this shifting around—more than two thirds of all adults are married.[4]

Non-Family Households Are Increasing

Once we get rid of the "couple-with-two-children" image of family life, we should also recognize that many households are not families in the usual sense. *Single-adult households* account for about 20 percent of all households—more than 15 million people! These include young adults who leave home when they finish school—as well as divorced and widowed people who live alone.

These people need smaller apartments, smaller cars, smaller food packages—and in some cases, less expensive household furnishings because they don't have very much money. Other singles have ample discretionary income—and are attractive markets for "top-of-the-line" stereos, clothing, "status" cars, travel, and nice restaurants and bars.

There are also several million unmarried people living together—some in groups but most as couples. Some of these arrangements are temporary—as in college towns or in large cities when recent graduates go to the "big city" for their first "real" job. They're setting up households—without much money—and need to buy or rent cheaper furnishings. But some also have more money than they ever thought they would have—and can be good markets for clothing, recreation, and restaurants.

Marketers should probably pay special attention to these non-family households—because they are growing at a much higher rate than the traditional family households. And they have different needs and attitudes than the "conventional" American family in the TV comedies.

The Shift to Urban and Suburban Areas

Migration from rural to urban areas has continued in the United States since 1800. In 1920, about half the population lived in rural areas. By 1980, it was below 4 percent.

After World War II, there was a race to the suburbs. By 1970, more people were living in the suburbs than in the central cities. Retailers moved, too—following their customers. Lower-income consumers—often with different ethnic backgrounds—moved in—changing the nature of markets in the center of the city.

Some families, however, have become discouraged with the suburban dream. They're tired of commuting, yard and house work, rising local taxes, and gossiping neighbors. These people are reversing the trend to suburbia. The movement back to the city is more common among older—and sometimes wealthier—families. These older families are creating a market for luxury condos and apartments close to downtown or other areas with shopping, recreation, and office facilities.

A New Concept of the Urban Area

These population shifts mean that the usual way of recording population by cities and counties may not be helpful to marketers. They are more interested in the size of homogeneous (similar) *market* areas—than in the number of people within political boundaries. To meet this need, the U.S. Census Bureau publishes data by metropolitan statistical area. Much data is available on the people in these areas.

A **metropolitan statistical area (MSA)** is an economic and social unit having a fairly large population at the center. Usually, a MSA contains one city or urbanized area of at least 50,000 people—and nearby areas which give a combined population of at least 100,000. Some MSAs, of course, are much larger. Figure 4–5 shows the location of the nation's biggest urban areas. This map further emphasizes the concentration of population in urban areas.

The Mobile Ones Are an Attractive Market

Nearly 20 percent of Americans move each year—and about half of them move to a new city. These "mobiles" are an important market. They tend to be younger, better educated people—"on the way up" in their careers. They have money to spend. Many decisions have to be made fairly quickly after they move. They must find new sources of food, clothing, medical and dental care, and household goods. Alert marketers should try to locate these mobile people—and tell them about their products.[5]

■   FIGURE 4–5   Map of major urban areas

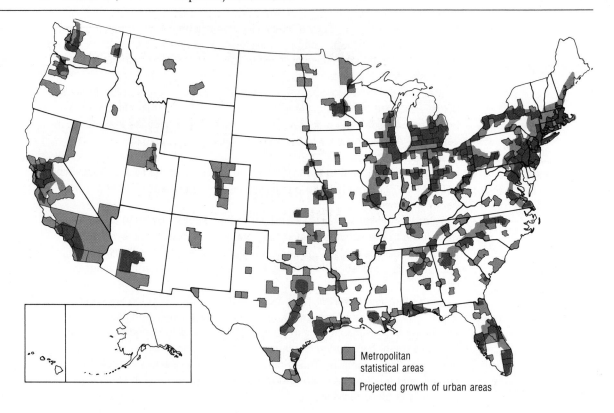

Metropolitan
statistical areas

Projected growth of urban areas

The Income Pyramid Turned Over

Unless people have money to spend—they aren't very attractive customers. The amount they can spend also will affect what they are likely to buy. For this reason, most marketers study income levels, too.

Income comes from producing and selling goods and services. Family incomes in the United States have increased steadily for about 100 years. Even more important to marketers is the change in income distribution. Many more families are now in the middle and upper income levels.

Fifty years ago, the U.S. income distribution looked something like a pyramid. Most families were bunched together at lower income levels. There were fewer families in the middle range—and a relative handful formed an "elite" market at the top. By the 1970s, real income (buying power) had risen so much that the pyramid turned over! See Figure 4–6. This shift is a real revolution—it has created an attractive mass market—and drastically changed our marketing system.

Real incomes may drop

Of course it is hoped that family incomes will keep rising—but this may not happen. See Figure 4–7. Real income stopped rising during the inflation of the

■ FIGURE 4–6   There has been a revolution in the distribution of buying power

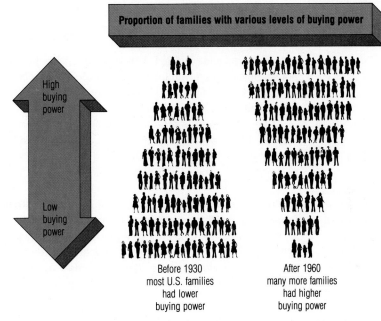

Source: Based on a study in *Business Week,* October 16, 1965, and other income distribution data.

■ FIGURE 4–7   Median household income, 1950–1981 (in 1981 dollars)

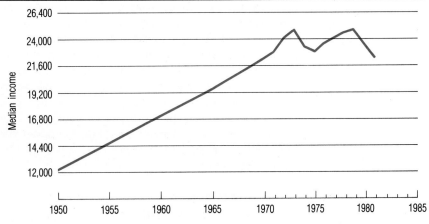

Source: *Statistical Abstract of the United States, 1982–1983,* p. 432.

70s—and actually dropped some. Maybe the peak of real family income in the United States has already passed.

Higher-Income Groups Still Receive a Big Share

Although the income pyramid has turned over, higher-income groups still receive a very large share of the total income and are attractive markets—especially for luxury items. Figure 4–8 shows that although the median income of U.S. households in 1981 was about $22,500, the top 20 percent of the households—those with incomes over $37,485—received more than 40 percent of the total income. This gave them extra buying power—especially for luxury items.

At the lower end, more than 12 million families had less than $11,000 income. These account for 20 percent of the families, but receive about 5 percent of the total income. Even so, they are good markets for some basic commodities—especially food and clothing.

Income Is Not Equally Distributed Geographically

Population is concentrated in some geographic areas—and consumers in urban areas tend to have higher incomes than their country cousins. Figure 4–9 compares the median income by states. The high spots on the map are areas with high median incomes. Companies often map the income of different areas when picking markets. A market area—a city, county, MSA, or state—that has more income will often be more attractive. For example, a chain of

■ FIGURE 4–8   Percent of *total* income going to different income groups in 1981
(based on 1981 dollars)

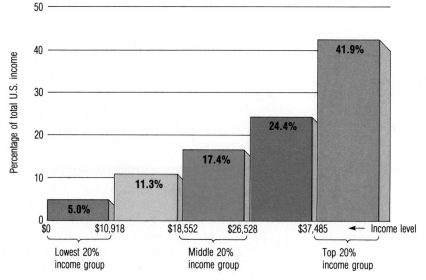

Source: *Statistical Abstract of the United States, 1982–1983*, p. 435.

■ FIGURE 4–9   Median per capita income by state, 1981

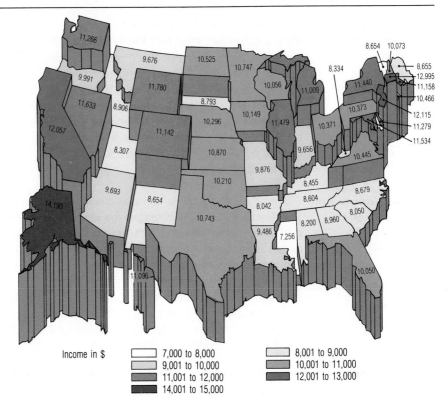

Source: Map prepared by authors based on data from *Statistical Abstract of the United States, 1982–1983.*

retail children's wear stores decided to locate in the suburbs surrounding Washington, D.C.—because there are many high-income people there.

The American "Melting Pot" Is Not Homogenized

There are many differences among Americans. We are called friendly people. But actually this varies by region. People on the West Coast, for example, tend to be more open and friendly. This may be—in part—because many moved West to find a new life. They wanted to leave behind the more tradition-bound social structure of the Midwest and East.

Even eating habits vary in different regions and within urban areas. Biscuits and grits are much more popular in the South, for example. And Mexican food has long been favored in the Southwest. Within the large cities, we still find ethnic and religious groups that are separate markets for some goods and services. Large urban areas often have neighborhoods of Irish, Italians, Poles, Jews, Puerto Ricans, Hispanics, and blacks. Some have newspapers, radio stations, restaurants, grocery stores, and record shops which aim at these culturally defined markets.

Women Are Being Liberated

The last 10 years have seen a change in thinking about women's roles in our culture. Women are now free to seek any kind of job they want—and many are doing so. Greater financial freedom is making many women less dependent on marriage as a career. More women are not marrying at all—or are marrying later. They plan to have fewer children. This is affecting manufacturers of housing, baby foods, convenience foods, clothing, and cosmetics.

This is a big shift in American thinking which must be considered in strategy planning. It will affect not only what is offered to consumers—but also how and by whom. We will see many more women in managerial positions. Others will have responsible selling and advertising jobs. Ineffective and untrained males are in for some real shocks as more women get business training and compete as equals—taking jobs which once might have gone to less able males. This is happening already.

Work and Growth Are Important to Some

Marketers also have to consider changing attitudes toward life and work. The American culture encourages the idea that hard work leads to achievement and material rewards. Most Americans are willing to work—but they also expect rewards and material comforts. This has led us to focus on growth—and producing and distributing goods and services. Much of our study of the U.S. market will be within this cultural framework.

In some other societies, on the other hand, more importance is placed on leisure and the enjoyment of life. More holidays are built into the working year. The output of such economies may not be quite as high—but the people don't feel that they are suffering because of it.[6]

Changes Come Slowly

It's important to see that changes in the cultural and social environment come slowly. An individual firm can't hope to encourage big changes in the short run. Instead, it should understand this environment and plan accordingly.

Attitudes toward materialism vary among different groups in the society.

Sometimes, however, strong outside forces—such as energy shortages, riots, or boycotts—may force more rapid changes in the cultural and social environment. And this can affect the political and economic environments.

ECONOMIC ENVIRONMENT

The **economic and technological environment** refers to the way firms—and the whole economy—use resources. We will treat the economic and technological environments separately—to emphasize that the technological environment provides a base for the economic environment. Technical skills and equipment affect the way resources of an economy are changed into output. The economic environment, on the other hand, is affected by the way all of the parts of our macro-economic system interact. This, then, affects such things as national income, economic growth, and inflation.

National Economic Changes Make a Difference

A well-planned marketing strategy may fail if the country goes through a rapid business decline. As consumers' incomes drop, people have to shift their spending patterns. They may do without some kinds of purchases. The oil-related layoffs during the recession of 1973–75 hurt many producers and retailers—even of lower-priced goods which sometimes sell well in recessions. Finally, the largest retail bankruptcy in U.S. history was announced by the W. T. Grant chain in 1976. And the Robert Hall chain, which sold lower-priced clothing, went bankrupt in 1977. The 1980–83 recession got the Woolco discount chain—as well as many other retailers and manufacturers. Many firms had to cut product lines—and change strategies to avoid similar fates.

Resource Shortages May Limit Opportunities

The growing shortage of some natural resources—in particular, energy resources—may cause continuing problems. Plastic manufacturers—who use oil-based resources—find their costs rising so high that they are priced out of some markets. High gasoline prices have made some consumers less interested in the larger, more profitable (to the auto industry) cars. Further, shifts in auto-buying patterns are affecting the whole economy—because the automobile industry is a major buyer of metals, plastics, fabrics, and tires. Even lower real incomes are possible in the future—because of technological factors. Much of our plant and equipment depends on low-cost energy. Industrial processes that were profitable with low energy prices are now less profitable. This means that U.S. consumers—and industries—will have to adjust their spending patterns.

Inflation Can Change Government Policies and Business Strategies

Inflation is a major factor in many economies. When inflation becomes a way of life, people buy and sell accordingly. Some Latin American countries have had from 25 to 100 percent inflation per year for many years. In contrast, the 6 to 20 percent levels reached in recent years in the United States were "low." Still, inflation must be considered in strategy planning. It can lead to

■ FIGURE 4–10   Rising cost of living in the United States, 1950–1982 (using consumer
                      price index, 1967 = 100)

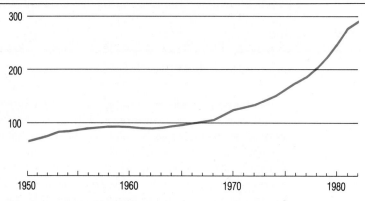

Source: U.S. Bureau of Labor Statistics.

government policies that will reduce income, employment, *and* consumer
spending.

The government-encouraged recession of 1980–83 was the most severe
since the Great Depression of the 1930s. But it was generally agreed that
some pulling back was necessary—to stop inflationary thinking. Figure 4–10
shows how rapidly the cost of living rose in the 1970s—and why the government chose such drastic action in 1980. But even though there was good
reason, the economic hardship was great—especially among the producers
and retailers of major durable goods.

You can see that the marketing manager must watch the economic environment carefully. In contrast to the cultural and social environment, economic
conditions change all the time. And they can move rapidly—up or down—
requiring strategic responses.

TECHNOLOGICAL ENVIRONMENT

**The Technological
Base Affects Opportu-
nities**

Underlying any economic environment is the technological base—the
technical skills and equipment which affect the way the resources of an economy are converted to output. In tradition-bound societies, relatively little technology may be used—and output is small. In modern economies, on the other
hand, aggressive competitors are always looking for better ways of doing
things. They copy the best methods—quickly.

Technological developments certainly affect marketing. The modern automobile, for example, lets farmers come to town—and city people go wherever
they want. This has destroyed the local "monopolies" of some retailers and
wholesalers. Modern trucks and airplanes have opened up national and international markets. Electronic developments have permitted mass promotion via

New technology has replaced vacuum tubes with much smaller transistors and microchips in many products.

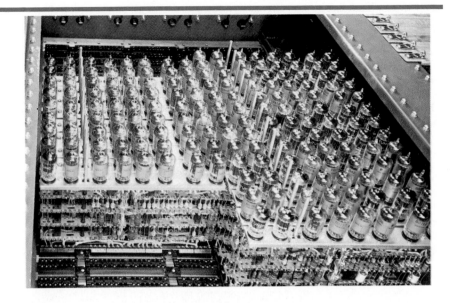

radio, TV, and telephone—reducing the relative importance of other media. Soon, we may be able to shop at home with a combination TV-computer system—eliminating the need for some retailers and wholesalers. Computers also allow more sophisticated planning and control of business.

As we move through the text, you should see that some of the big advances in business have come from early recognition of new ways to do things. Marketers should help their firms see such opportunities by trying to understand the "why" of present methods—and what is keeping their firms from being more effective. Then, as new developments come along, they will be alert to possible uses—and see how opportunities can be turned into profits.

Marketers should also help decide what technical developments will be acceptable to society. With the growing concern about environmental pollution, the quality of life, working conditions, and so on, it's possible that some potentially attractive technological developments will be rejected—because of their long-run effects. Perhaps what is good for the firm and the economy's *economic* growth will not fit with the cultural and social environment—and the political and legal environment. A marketer's closeness to the market should give him a better feel for what people are thinking—and allow him to help his firm avoid serious mistakes.[7]

THE COMPETITIVE ENVIRONMENT

(Note: The following materials assume some familiarity with economic analysis—and especially the nature of demand curves and demand elasticity. For those needing a review of these materials, see Appendix A, which follows Chapter 2.)

The **competitive environment** refers to the number and types of competitors the marketing manager must face—and how they may behave. Although these factors can't be controlled by the marketing manager, he can choose strategies which will avoid head-on competition.

A Manager May Be Able to Avoid Head-On Competition

A marketing manager will operate in one of four kinds of market situations. We will talk about three kinds: pure competition, oligopoly, and monopolistic competition. The fourth kind, monopoly, isn't found very often and is like monopolistic competition.

Understanding these market situations is important—because the freedom of a marketing manager—especially his control over price—is greatly reduced in some situations. The important dimensions of these situations are shown in Figure 4–11.

When Competition Is Pure

Many competitors offer about the same thing

Pure competition is a market situation which develops when a market has:

1. Homogeneous (similar) products.
2. Many buyers and sellers, who have full knowledge of the market.
3. Ease of entry for buyers and sellers; that is, new firms have little difficulty starting in business—and new customers can easily come into the market.

More or less pure competition is found in many agricultural markets. In the

---

■ FIGURE 4–11   Some important dimensions regarding market situations

Important dimensions / Types of situations	Pure competition	Oligopoly	Monopolistic competition	Monopoly
Uniqueness of each firm's product	None	None	Some	Unique
Number of competitors	Many	Few	Few to many	None
Size of competitors (compared to size of market)	Small	Large	Large to small	None
Elasticity of demand facing firm	Completely elastic	Kinked demand curve (elastic and inelastic)	Either	Either
Elasticity of industry demand	Either	Inelastic	Either	Either
Control of price by firm	None	Some (with care)	Some	Complete

■ FIGURE 4–12   Interaction of demand and supply in the potato industry and the resulting
                        demand curve facing individual potato producers

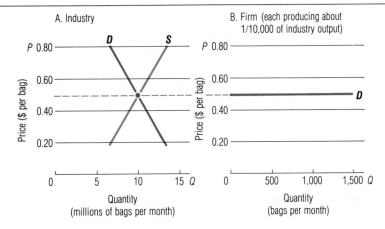

potato industry, for example, there are tens of thousands of producers—and
they are in pure competition. Let's look more closely at these producers.

In pure competition, these many small producers each see an almost perfectly flat demand curve. The relation between the industry demand curve and
the demand curve facing the individual farmer in pure competition is shown in
Figure 4–12. Although the potato industry as a whole has a down-sloping
demand curve, each individual potato producer has a demand curve that is
perfectly flat at the **equilibrium price**—the going market price.

To explain this more clearly, let's look at the demand curve for the individual potato producer. Assume that the equilibrium price for the industry is 50
cents. This means the producer can sell as many potatoes as he chooses at
50 cents. The quantity that all producers choose to sell makes up the supply
curve. But acting alone, a small producer can do almost anything he wants
to do.

If this individual farmer raises 1/10,000th of the quantity offered in the
market, for example, you can see that there will be little effect on the market if
he goes out of business—or doubles his production.

The reason an individual's demand curve is flat in this example is that the
farmer probably could not sell any potatoes above the market price. And there
is no point in selling below 50 cents.

Not many markets are *purely* competitive. But many are close enough to
allow us to talk about "almost" pure competition situations—those in which the
marketing manager has to accept the going price.

Squeeze on the orange growers

Florida orange growers have basically homogeneous products. They have
no control over price. When there is a very large supply, prices drop rapidly.
When supplies are short, the reverse happens. During one year, the crop was

50 percent larger than the previous crop—and most growers sold their oranges below their costs. Oranges "on the tree" which cost 75 cents a box to grow were selling for 35 cents a box. Supply turned around the next year, however, and oranges were selling for $2.40 to $2.60 a box.

Profit squeeze is on in many markets

Such highly competitive situations aren't limited to agriculture. Wherever many competitors sell homogeneous products—such as chemicals, plastics, lumber, coal, printing, and laundry services—the demand curve seen by *each producer* tends to be flat.

Markets tend to become more competitive. In pure competition, prices and profits are pushed down until some competitors are forced out of business. Eventually the price level is only high enough to keep the survivors in business. No one makes much profit. They just cover costs.

When Competition Is Oligopolistic

A few competitors offering similar things

Not all markets move toward pure competition. Some become oligopolies.

Oligopoly situations are special market situations which develop when a market has:

1. Essentially homogeneous products—such as basic industrial chemicals or gasoline.
2. Relatively few sellers—or a few large firms and many smaller ones who follow the lead of the larger ones.
3. Fairly inelastic industry demand curves.

The demand curve facing each firm is unusual in an oligopoly situation. Although the industry demand curve can be inelastic throughout the relevant

■ FIGURE 4–13   Oligopoly—kinked demand curve—situation

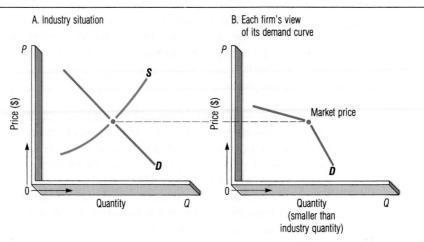

range, the demand curve facing each competitor looks "kinked." See Figure 4–13. The current market price is at the kink.

There is a "market price" because the competing firms watch each other carefully—and know it's wise to be at the kink. Each marketing manager must expect that raising his own price above the market would cause a big loss in sales. Few, if any, competitors would follow his price increase. So his demand curve would be relatively flat above the market price. If he lowers his price, he must expect competitors to follow. Given inelastic industry demand, his own demand curve would be inelastic at lower prices. Since lowering prices along such a curve would drop total revenue, he should leave his price at the kink— the market price.

Actually, however, there are price fluctuations in oligopolistic markets. Sometimes this is caused by firms that don't understand the market situation— and cut their prices to get business. In other cases, big increases in demand or supply change the basic nature of the situation—and lead to price cutting. Sometimes the price cuts are drastic—such as Du Pont's Dacron price cut of 25 percent. This happened when Du Pont decided that industry production capacity already exceeded demand—and more plants were due to start into production.

Price wars are sometimes started

A common example of price fluctuations is in retail gasoline marketing—at a major intersection with several competitors. Apparently enough final consumers think of gasoline as homogeneous to create oligopoly conditions. And oligopoly-type "price wars" are common. These usually start when some gasoline discounter successfully attracts "too much" business—perhaps by cutting his prices one cent a gallon below his usual price. The war proceeds for a time—with everyone losing money—until one of the retailers calls a meeting and suggests that they all "get a little sense." Sometimes these price wars will end immediately after such a meeting—with prices returning to a "reasonable and proper" level.

When Competition Is Monopolistic

A price must be set

You can see why marketing managers want to avoid pure competition or oligopoly situations. They prefer a market in which they have more control.

Monopolistic competition is a market situation which develops when a market has:

1. Different (heterogeneous) products—in the eyes of some customers.
2. Sellers who feel they do have some competition in this market.

The word *monopolistic* means that each firm is trying to get control in its own little market. But the word *competition* means that there are still substitutes. The vigorous competition of a purely competitive market is reduced. Each firm has its own down-sloping demand curve. But the shape of the curve depends on the similarity of competitors' products and marketing mixes. Each monopolistic competitor has freedom—but not complete freedom—in its own market.

Judging elasticity will help set the price

Since a firm in monopolistic competition has its own down-sloping demand curve, it must make a price decision as part of its marketing strategy planning. Here, estimating the elasticity of the firm's own demand curve is helpful. If it is highly inelastic, the firm may decide to raise prices—to increase total revenue. But if demand is highly elastic, this may mean many competitors with acceptable substitutes. Then the price may have to be set near "competition." And the marketing manager probably should try to develop a better marketing mix.

Why Some Products Are Offered in Pure Competition

Why would anyone compete in profitless pure competition? One reason is that the firm was either already in the industry. Or the firm enters without knowing what's happening and must stick it out until it runs out of money.

Production-oriented people seem more likely to make such a mistake than market-oriented managers. Avoiding pure competition seems wise—and certainly fits with our emphasis on target marketing.

POLITICAL ENVIRONMENT

The attitudes and reactions of people, social critics, and governments are becoming more important to the marketing manager. They all affect the political environment.

Consumerism Is Here—And Basic

Consumerism is a social movement seeking to increase the rights and powers of consumers and buyers. Its continued growth is due to a change in thinking which is summarized in President John F. Kennedy's "Consumer Bill of Rights" of 1962. Although they did not become law, they have affected people's thinking—including some in government agencies and courts.

Armstrong Rubber set up a "consumer hotline" to be sure it is meeting customer expectations.

President Kennedy's "Consumer Bill of Rights" includes the following:

The right to safety.

The right to be informed.

The right to choose.

The right to be heard.

Kennedy didn't include "the right to a clean and safe environment"—probably because the environment had not yet become a public concern. But most people are now concerned with such a right. More government pressure is being applied on everyone—including businesses and government units—to improve waste handling and to clean our chimneys and motor exhaust systems. This is probably the outstanding recent example of a rapid change in social attitudes which has been converted into action by the political authorities.

These consumer "rights" aren't as easy to achieve as the antipollution moves. Instead, individual firms and government agencies must change their behavior on a day-to-day basis. This doesn't happen quickly. There will be an ongoing need for consumerists to help make sure the "little guy" isn't ignored by business or government. So the consumerism movement is not likely to die overnight.[8]

Not Meeting Consumer Expectations Could Be Drastic

Generally, the public seems to like what the consumerists are trying to do. Marketers shouldn't forget that the role of businesses is to satisfy consumers. No firm has a God-given right to operate any way it wants to.

This means that the marketing manager—as well as top management—should pay more attention to consumers' attitudes in marketing planning. Ignoring the consumer movement could be fatal. The rules governing business could change. Specific businesses might be told they can't operate. Or they might face fines that—in an "anti-business" environment—could be quite large. Frustrated buyers of auto "lemons" have been awarded up to $75,000. A copier machine dealer was awarded $5 million for injuries resulting from defects in one of the machines he sold. Such an award against a small company could wipe it out. For a large company, it opens the door to additional lawsuits which can be costly—and damage its reputation.[9]

Nationalistic feelings must be considered in planning marketing strategies.

Clearly, more attention must be paid to product design and safety in our social and political environments. The old, production-oriented ways of doing things are no longer acceptable.

Nationalism Can Be Limiting in International Markets

Strong sentiments of **nationalism**—an emphasis on a country's interests before everything else—may also affect the work of some marketing managers. These feelings can reduce sales—or even block all marketing activity—in some international markets. Oil producers and copper mining firms have felt such pressures in recent years—for example, in Latin America, Africa, and the Middle East.

To whom the firms could sell—and how much—have been dictated by national interests. The Arab boycott of firms doing business with Israel is probably the outstanding example in recent years. But the "Buy American" policy in many government contracts reflects similar attitudes in the United States. And there is support for protecting U.S. producers from foreign competition—especially producers of color TVs, footwear, textiles, and cars. Philippine business people have tried to drive out "excessively aggressive" Chinese merchants. Some African countries have driven out Indian merchants.

Nationalistic feelings are important in international business—because often businesses must get permission to operate. In some political environments, this is only a routine formality. In others, a lot of red tape is involved—and personal influence and/or "bribes" are sometimes expected.

UAW PARKING
RESERVED FOR
UNITED STATES AND
CANADIAN VEHICLES
ONLY

PLEASE PARK IMPORTS
ELSEWHERE

Political Environment May Offer New Opportunities

The political environment is not always anti-business. Governments may decide that encouraging business is good for their people. China and Japan are encouraging foreign investors. The U.S. government has special programs and financial incentives to encourage urban redevelopment and minority business. State and local governments also try to attract and hold businesses—sometimes with tax incentives.

Some business managers have become very successful by studying the political environment—and developing strategies which use these political opportunities.

LEGAL ENVIRONMENT

Trying to Encourage Competition

American economic and legislative thinking has been based on the idea that competition among many small firms will make the economy work better. Therefore, attempts by business to limit competition are thought to be against the public interest.

As industries grew larger after the Civil War, some became monopolies controlled by wealthy businessmen—the "robber barons." This made it hard for smaller producers to survive. A movement grew—especially among Midwestern farmers—to control monopolists.

Beginning in 1890, a series of laws were passed that were basically *antimonopoly* or *procompetition*. The names and dates of these laws are shown in Table 4–1.

Antimonopoly Law and Marketing Mix Planning

Specific application of antimonopoly law to the four Ps will be presented in later chapters. To round out our discussion here, you should know what kind of proof the government must have to get a conviction under each of the major laws. You should also know which of the four Ps are most affected by each law. Figure 4–14 provides such a summary—with a phrase following each law to show what must be proved to get a conviction. Note how the wording of the laws is moving to the side of protecting consumers.

Prosecution Is Serious—You Can Go to Jail

Businesses and *business managers* must obey both criminal and civil laws. Penalties for breaking civil laws are limited to blocking or forcing certain actions—along with fines. Where criminal law applies, jail sentences can be imposed. For example, the Sherman Act now provides for fines up to $1 million for corporations—as well as fines of up to $100,000 and/or up to three years in prison for individuals!

Antimonopoly laws are serious business—and jail sentences are a recent development. Some business managers have gone to jail—or received suspended jail sentences—because they violated the criminal law part of these laws. For example, several packaging executives were given prison terms and fines up to $35,000 each.[10] You can see that government is getting more serious about antimonopoly legislation.

Many small businesses have ignored these laws. They felt they were "too small for the government to worry about." But they may be in for a shock. The government's new seriousness should cause marketing managers to pay more attention to the political and legal environment in the future.

Consumer Protection Laws Are Not New

There is more to the legal environment than just the antimonopoly laws. Some consumer protections were built into the English and U.S. common law system. A seller had to tell the truth (if asked a direct question), meet contracts, and stand behind the firm's product (to some reasonable extent).

■ TABLE 4–1   Outline of federal legislation now affecting competition in marketing

Year	Antimonopoly (procompetition)	Anticompetition	Antispecific practices
1890	Sherman Act		
1914	Clayton Act Federal Trade Commission Act		Clayton Act
1936	Robinson-Patman Act	Robinson-Patman Act	Robinson-Patman Act
1938			Wheeler-Lea Amendment
1950	Antimerger Act		Antimerger Act
1975	Magnuson-Moss Act		Magnuson-Moss Act

■ **FIGURE 4–14**   Focus (mostly prohibitions) of federal antimonopoly laws on the four Ps

Law	Product	Place	Promotion	Price
Sherman Act (1890) Monopoly or conspiracy in restraint of trade	Monopoly or conspiracy to control a product	Monopoly or conspiracy to control distribution channels		Monopoly or conspiracy to fix or control prices
Clayton Act (1914) Substantially lessen competition	Forcing sale of some products with others— tying contracts	Exclusive dealing contracts (limiting buyers' sources of supply)		Price discrimination by manufacturers
Federal Trade Commission Act (1914) Unfair methods of competition		Unfair policies	Deceptive ads or selling practices	Deceptive pricing
Robinson-Patman Act (1936) Tends to injure competition		Prohibits paying allowances to "direct" buyers in lieu of middlemen costs (brokerage charges)	Prohibits "fake" advertising allowances or discrimination in help offered	Prohibits price discrimination on goods of "like grade and quality" without cost justification, and quantity discounts limited
Wheeler-Lea Amendment (1938) Unfair or deceptive practices	Deceptive packaging or branding		Deceptive ads or selling claims	Deceptive pricing
Antimerger Act (1950) Lessen competition	Buying competitors	Buying producers or distributors		
Magnuson-Moss Act (1975) Unreasonable practices	Product warranties			

Beyond this, it was expected that vigorous competition in the marketplace would protect consumers—*so long as they were careful.*

Focusing only on competition didn't protect consumers very well in some areas, however. So the government has found it necessary to pass other laws—usually involving specific types of products.

Foods and drugs are controlled

Consumer protection laws go back at least to 1906. The Pure Food and Drug Act was passed then. Colorful stories about unsanitary meat-packing practices in the Chicago stockyards caused consumer interest in this act. After much debate, it was decided to pass a general law to control the quality and labeling of food and drugs in interstate commerce. This was a major victory for consumer protection. Before this, it was assumed that common law and the old warning "let the buyer beware" would take care of consumers.

Some loopholes in the law were corrected in following acts. The law now bans the shipment of unsanitary and poisonous products—and requires much testing of drugs. The Food and Drug Administration (FDA) attempts to control

The government regulates the marketing of many items.

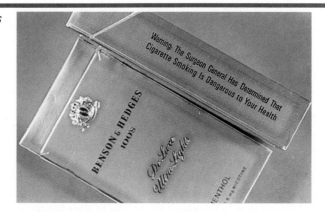

manufacturers of these products. It can *seize* products that violate its rules—including regulations on branding and labeling.

In general, the FDA has done a good job. But complaints over a recent proposal to ban the use of saccharin—commonly used to sweeten "diet" soft drinks—may force the government to rethink how much protection consumers really want. In this case, many users felt that the government should first ban the use of many other products whose bad effects had already been more thoroughly proved—for example, alcohol and cigarettes.

Product safety is controlled

The Consumer Product Safety Act (of 1972) is another important consumer protection law. It set up the Consumer Product Safety Commission to control product safety. This group has broad power to set safety standards—and can impose penalties for failure to meet these standards. Again, there is some question as to how much safety consumers want. The commission found the bicycle the most hazardous product under its control!

But given that the commission has the power to *force* a product off the market, it is obvious that safety must be considered in product design. This is an uncontrollable variable which must be treated seriously by marketing managers.[11]

State and Local Laws Affect Strategy Planning, Too

Besides federal legislation—which affects interstate commerce—marketers must be aware of state and local laws. There are state and city laws regulating minimum prices and the setting of prices; regulations for starting up a business (licenses, examinations, and even tax payments); and in some communities, regulations prohibiting certain activities—such as door-to-door selling or selling on Sundays or during evenings.

Consumerists and the Law Say, "Let the Seller Beware"

The old rule about buyer-seller relations was *let the buyer beware*. Now it seems to be shifting to *let the seller beware*. The number of consumer protection laws is increasing. These "pro-consumer" laws and court decisions suggest that there is more interest now in protecting consumers instead of just protecting competition. This may upset production-oriented managers. But they will just have to adapt to this new political and legal environment. Times have changed.[12]

■ **CONCLUSION**

This chapter was concerned with the variables which—while beyond the marketing manager's control—greatly affect marketing strategy planning. Some uncontrollable variables may change faster than others. But all can change—requiring adjustments in plans. Ideally, likely changes are considered in the strategy planning.

As we have seen, a marketer must develop marketing mixes suited to the culture and attitudes of his target markets.

The economic environment—the chances of recessions or inflation—also will affect the choice of strategies. And the marketer must try to anticipate, understand, and deal with such changes—as well as changes in the technological base underlying the economic environment.

A manager must also study the competitive environment. How well established are competitors? What action might they take? What is the nature of competition: pure, oligopolistic, or monopolistic?

The marketing manager must also be aware of legal restrictions—and be sensitive to changing political climates. The growing acceptance of consumerism may force many changes.

Developing good marketing strategies within all these uncontrollable environments isn't easy. You can see that marketing management is a challenging job which requires much integration of information from many disciplines.

■ **QUESTIONS AND PROBLEMS**

1. Discuss how slower population growth—and especially the smaller number of young people—will affect the businesses in your local community.

2. Discuss the impact of our "aging culture" on marketing strategy planning.

3. Explain how the continuing mobility of consumers—as well as the development of big metropolitan areas—should affect marketing strategy planning in the future. Be sure to consider the impact on the four Ps.

4. Explain how the redistribution of income has affected marketing planning thus far—and its likely impact in the future.

5. Discuss the probable impact on your hometown of a major technological breakthrough in air transportation which would permit foreign producers to ship into any U.S. market for about the same transportation cost that domestic producers incur.

6. If a manufacturer's well-known product is sold at the same price by many retailers in the same community, is this an example of pure competition? When a community has many small grocery stores, are they in pure competition? What characteristics are needed to have a purely competitive market?

7. List three products that are sold in purely competitive markets and three sold in monopolistically competitive markets. Do any of these products have anything in common? Can any generalizations be made about competitive situations and marketing mix planning?

8. Cite a local example of an oligopoly—explaining why it is an oligopoly.

9. Which way does the U.S. political and legal environment seem to be moving (with respect to business-related affairs)?

10. Why is it necessary to have so many laws regulating business? Why hasn't Congress just passed one set of laws to take care of business problems?

11. What and who is the government attempting to protect in its effort to preserve and regulate competition?

12. For each of the *major* laws discussed in the text, indicate whether in the long run this law will promote or restrict competition (see Figure 4–6). As a consumer without any financial interest in business, what is your reaction to each of these laws?

13. Are consumer protection laws really new? Discuss the evolution of consumer protection. Is more such legislation likely?

■ **SUGGESTED CASES**

1. Foodco, Inc.

5. Indian Steel Company

Chapter 5 ■ Getting information for marketing decisions

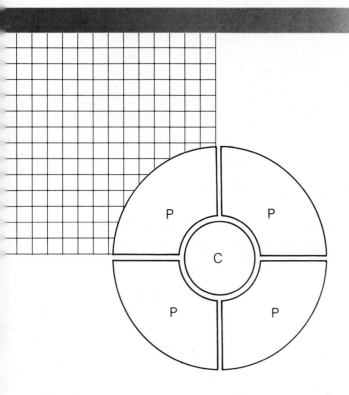

When you finish this chapter, you should:

1. Understand a scientific approach to marketing research.

2. Know how to define and solve marketing problems.

3. Know about getting secondary and primary data.

4. Understand the use of observing, questioning, and experimental methods in marketing research.

5. Know about marketing information systems.

6. Recognize the important new terms (shown in red).

Marketing research doesn't prove that you're right. It gives you a way to find out.

Successful planning of marketing strategies requires information—information about potential target markets and their likely responses to various marketing mixes—and about competition and other uncontrollable variables. Without good marketing information, managers have to use intuition or guesses—and in our fast-changing and competitive economy, this invites failure.

On the other hand, a manager seldom has *all* the information needed to make the best decision. Both customers and competitors are unpredictable. Getting more information may cost too much—or take too long. So a manager often must decide if more information is needed and—if so—how to get it. In this chapter, we'll talk about how a marketing manager can get the information he needs to plan successful strategies.

The marketing manager for a coffee company, for example, wants to know if its discount coupons really work. Do they draw new customers—or do current customers just use the coupons to stock up? If consumers switch from another brand, do they go back to their old brand the next time they buy? The manager needs answers to these questions to plan marketing strategies. Now it's easier for a marketing manager to get these answers. Consumers in some cities are part of a project started by an independent marketing research firm. The grocery check-out clerk keys in each consumer's ID number, and a computer scanner records all of the purchases—including prices and any coupons used. Every food purchase made by each consumer—for over a year—is recorded on the computer. For a fee, a company can use the data and tabulate the actual purchase patterns—and find answers to questions like those worrying our coffee company manager.[1]

Not all marketing research requires computers. A museum director wanted to know which of the many exhibits was most popular. A survey didn't help. Visitors seemed to want to please the interviewer—and generally said that *all* of the exhibits were interesting. Putting observers near exhibits—to record how long visitors spent at each one—didn't help either. The curious visitors stood around to see what was being recorded—and that messed up the measures. Finally, the museum floors were waxed to a glossy shine. Several weeks later, the floors around the exhibits were inspected. It was easy to tell which exhibits were most popular—based on how much wax had worn off the floor!

WHAT IS MARKETING RESEARCH?

Research Provides a Bridge to Customers

The marketing concept says that marketing managers should meet the needs of customers. But today, many marketing managers are isolated in company offices—far from their potential customers.

This means marketing managers have to rely on help from **marketing research**—procedures to gather and analyze information to help marketing managers make decisions. One of the important jobs of a marketing researcher is to get the "facts." This can be done with special projects—or on a continuing basis—depending on the purpose.

Who Does the Work?

Most larger companies have a separate marketing research department to plan and carry out research projects. These departments often use outside specialists—including interviewing and tabulating services—to handle technical assignments.

Small companies—those with less than $3 or $4 million in sales—usually don't have separate marketing research departments. They depend on salespeople or top managers for what research they do.

Effective Research Usually Requires Cooperation

Marketing research is much more than just statistical techniques—or specialists who do computer work. Good marketing researchers keep both marketing research *and* marketing management in mind—to be sure their research focuses on real problems.

Marketing research details can be handled by company or outside specialists. But marketing managers must be able to explain what their problems

Marketing research firms are often called in to do special projects.

are—and what kinds of information they need. They should be able to communicate with specialists in *their* language. They may only be "consumers" of research. But they should be informed consumers—and be able to explain exactly what they want from the research. They should also know about some of the basic decisions made during the research process—so they know the limitations of the findings.

For this reason, our discussion of marketing research won't emphasize mechanics—but rather how to plan and evaluate the work of marketing researchers.[2]

THE SCIENTIFIC METHOD AND MARKETING RESEARCH

Marketing research often has to supply information quickly. But researchers still should use the best methods possible. For this reason, a scientific approach to solving marketing problems makes sense. A scientific approach—combined with the strategy planning framework we discussed in Chapter 2—can help marketing managers make better decisions—even if they have to make them quickly.

The **scientific method** is a decision-making approach that focuses on being objective and orderly in testing ideas before accepting them. With the scientific method, managers don't just *assume* that their intuition is correct. Instead, they use their intuition and observations to develop **hypotheses**—

educated guesses about the relationships between things or what will happen in the future—such as "There is no significant difference between brands A and B in the minds of consumers." Then they test each hypothesis.

The scientific method forces an orderly process. Some managers don't think carefully about what information they need—and blindly move ahead hoping that research will give them "the answer." Other managers may have a clearly defined problem or question, but lose their way in the next steps. These "hit-or-miss" approaches waste both time and money. This waste can be avoided with a scientific approach to solving marketing problems. We'll talk about this approach next.

FIVE–STEP APPROACH TO MARKETING RESEARCH

The **marketing research process** is a five-step application of the scientific method that includes:

1. Definition of the problem.
2. Situation analysis.
3. Obtaining data for the specific problem.
4. Interpretation of data.
5. Problem solution.

Figure 5–1 shows the five steps in the process. Note that the process may lead to a solution before all of the steps are done. Or, as the feedback arrows show, the process may return to an earlier step if needed. For example, the interpretation step may point to a new question—or reveal the need for additional information—before a final decision can be made.

Pepsi and other soft drink companies use consumer taste-tests to find out about consumer preferences.

■ FIGURE 5–1   Five-step scientific approach to marketing research process

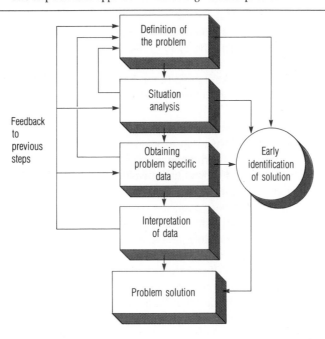

DEFINITION OF THE PROBLEM—STEP ONE

Defining the problem is the most important—and often the most difficult—step in the marketing research process. It's slow work. Sometimes it takes over half the time spent on a research project. But it's time well spent if the objectives of the research are clearly defined. The best research job on the wrong problem is wasted effort.

Finding the Right Problem Level Almost Solves the Problem

The strategy planning framework introduced in Chapter 2 can be useful here. It can help the researcher see where the real problem lies—and what information is needed. Do we really know enough about our target markets to work out all of the four Ps? Do we know enough to decide what background music to use in an ad—or how to handle a price war in New York City or Tokyo? If not, we may want to do research—rather than rely on intuition.

The importance of understanding the nature of the problem—and then trying to solve it—can be seen more clearly in the following example of a manufacturer of a new easy-to-bake cake mix. Top management chose apartment dwellers, younger couples, and the too-busy-to-cook crowd as the target market—a logical market at first glance. A little research on the size of this market indicated that—if these consumers responded as expected—there were enough of them to be a profitable target market. The company decided to aim at this market—and developed a logical marketing mix.

But why didn't this baking mix sell?

During the first few months, sales were disappointing. The manufacturer "guessed" that something was wrong with the product—since the promotion seemed to be adequate. At this point, a consumer survey was run—with surprising results. The taste of the cake was satisfactory—but the target consumers just *weren't interested* in convenience for this kind of product. Instead, the best market turned out to be families who did their own cooking! They liked the convenience of the mix—especially when they needed something in a hurry.

In this case, the original strategy planning was sloppy. The choice of target market was based on executive guesswork. This led to a poor strategy—and wasted promotion money. Some research with consumers—about their needs and attitudes—might have avoided this costly error. Both marketing research and management fumbled the ball—by not studying the target market. Then, when sales were poor, the company fumbled again by assuming that the problem was the product—instead of checking consumers' real attitudes about the product. Fortunately, research finally uncovered the real problem. Then the strategy was changed quickly.

The moral of this story is that our strategy planning framework can be useful for guiding marketing research efforts. First, the marketing managers should understand their target markets—and know that they have unsatisfied needs. Then the managers can focus on lower-level problems—i.e., the sensitivity to change of the marketing mix ingredients. Without such a framework, marketing researchers can waste time—and money—working on the wrong problem.

Carefully planned marketing research can help managers avoid costly errors.

Don't Confuse Problems with Symptoms

Problem definition sounds simple—and that's the danger. It is easy to confuse symptoms with the problem. For example, suppose that a firm's continuing sales analysis shows that the company's sales are decreasing in certain territories—while expenses remain the same—with a resulting decline in profits. Will it help to define the problem by asking: How can we stop the sales decline? Probably not. This would be like asking how to lower a patient's temperature—instead of first trying to find the cause of the fever.

The real problem may be hard to discover. The marketing manager can start with the strategic planning framework—and evaluate what is known about the target market and whether the marketing mix seems to make sense. If there are doubts about one or more of these factors, these problem areas can be explored. But without further evidence, the marketing manager should not assume too quickly that he has defined the real problem. Instead, he should take his list of possible problems and go on to the next step—trying to discover which is the basic cause of the trouble.

SITUATION ANALYSIS—STEP TWO

What Information Do We Already Have?

When the marketing manager feels the real problem has begun to surface, a situation analysis is useful. A **situation analysis** is an informal study of what information is already available in the problem area. It can help define the problem—and specify what additional information—if any—is needed.

Pick the Brains Around You

In a situation analysis, the researchers try to size up the situation. They talk to informed people—in or outside of the firm. They study internal company records. They also search libraries for available material.

Situation Analysis Helps Educate a Researcher

The situation analysis is important since researchers must be sure they understand the problem area—including the nature of the target market, the marketing mix, and what the competition is doing. Otherwise, the researchers may spend time and research dollars to "discover" what is already well known by management.

Secondary Data May Provide the Answers—Or Some Background

A situation analysis should find relevant **secondary data**—information that has been collected or published already. **Primary data** is information specifically collected to solve a current problem. We'll discuss that later. See Figure 5–2. For now, keep in mind that researchers too often rush out to gather primary data when there is already plenty of relevant secondary information. And this data may be available immediately—at little or no cost![3]

One source of good secondary data may be the company's own computer system, files, or reports. Secondary data also is available from libraries, trade associations, and government agencies.

■ FIGURE 5–2   Sources of secondary and primary data

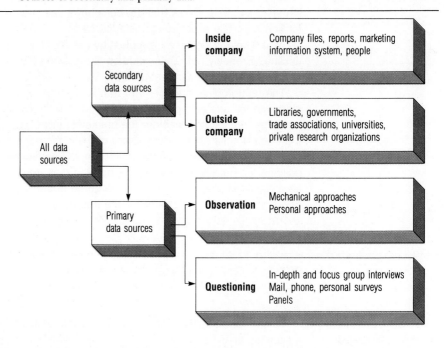

One of the first places a researcher should look for secondary data—after looking within the firm—is in a good library. The *Index of Business Periodicals* helps identify all published references to the topic the firm is concerned about. And some computerized index services are available through libraries, too.

Government sources

The federal and state governments publish data on almost every subject. Government data is often useful in estimating the size of markets. Almost all government data is available in inexpensive publications—and some of it is on computer tapes—ready for further analysis if that is needed.

Sometimes it is more practical to use summary publications—to get leads to more detailed documents. The most useful of these summaries—the *Statistical Abstract of the United States*—is like an almanac. It is issued each year—and lists more than 1,000 summary tables from published sources. References to world markets are included. Detailed footnotes are a guide to more specific information on a topic.

Private sources

Many private research groups—as well as advertising agencies, newspapers, magazines, and trade associations—publish useful data. And a good business library is valuable—for sources such as *Sales & Marketing Management, Industrial Marketing, Advertising Age* and the publications of the National Industrial Conference Board.

Much marketing research information is available in libraries—and a good librarian can help you find it.

Situation Analysis Yields a Lot—For Very Little

A good situation analysis can deliver a lot of information—and takes little time. It's inexpensive compared with more formal research efforts—such as a large-scale survey. If a problem is clear-cut, perhaps it can be solved at this point—with no added expense. The fact that further research *may* not be necessary is important. The situation analyst is really trying to find the exact nature of the situation—*and* the problem. Too-hasty researchers may try to skip this step—perhaps rushing to get out questionnaires. These researchers may see the real problem only when the questionnaires are returned—and they have to start all over. One marketing expert puts it this way: "Some people don't have time to do research right the first time, but they seem to have time to do it over again."

Determine What Else Is Needed

At the end of the situation analysis, you can see which research questions—from the list developed during the problem definition step—remain unanswered. Then you have to decide exactly what information is needed to answer those questions—and what is involved to get it.

GETTING PROBLEM–SPECIFIC DATA—STEP THREE

Gathering Primary Data

The next step is to plan a formal research project to gather data. There are different methods for collecting primary data—and which approach to use depends on how precisely the problem has been defined, the nature of the problem, and how much time and money is available.

Most primary data collection tries to learn what customers think about some topic—or how they behave under some conditions. There are two basic methods for obtaining information about people: *questioning* and *observing*. Questioning can range from qualitative to quantitative research. And many kinds of observing are possible.

Qualitative Questioning—Open-Ended with a Hidden Purpose

Qualitative research seeks in-depth, open-ended answers. The researcher tries to get people to share their thoughts on a topic—without giving them many directions about what to say.

For example, a researcher may ask consumers, "What do you think about when you decide where to shop for food?" One person may talk about convenience of location, another about service in the store, and others about the quality of the fresh produce.

The real advantage of this approach is *depth.* Each person can be asked follow-up questions so that the researcher can really learn what *that* respondent is thinking.

Focus groups focus the discussion

The most widely used form of qualitative questioning in marketing research is the **focus group interview**—which involves interviewing 6 to 10 people in an informal group setting. It uses the open-ended questions we've been discussing, but here the interviewer wants to get group interaction—to stimulate thinking and get immediate reactions.

A trained focus group leader can learn a lot from this approach. A typical session may last an hour—so a lot of ground can be covered. However, conclusions reached from watching a focus group session often vary depending on who watches it! This is typical of qualitative research. It's hard to develop an objective measure of the results. This is a serious criticism because the results seem to depend so much on the point of view of the researcher.[4]

Some researchers use qualitative research to prepare for quantitative research. The qualitative research can provide ideas. But the ideas may need to be tested in some other way.

Structured Questioning Gives More Quantitative Results

With formal questionnaires, many people can be asked questions in the same way. See Figure 5–3. Because the same questions and response choices are used for each respondent, information can be summarized quantitatively. Most survey research is **quantitative research**—which seeks structured responses that can be summarized in numbers—like percentages, averages, or other statistics.

Surveys by Mail, Phone, or in Person

What questions to ask and how to ask them usually depends on how the respondents will be interviewed—by mail, on the phone, or in person.

Mail surveys are the most common and very convenient

The mail questionnaire is useful when much questioning is needed. With a mail questionnaire, respondents can answer the questions at their convenience. But the questions must be simple and easy to follow—since there is no interviewer to help.

A big problem with mail questionnaires is that many people don't complete or return them. The **response rate**—the percent of people contacted who complete the questionnaire—is usually around 25 percent in consumer surveys—and it can be even lower.

■ FIGURE 5–3   Sample questioning methods to measure attitudes and opinions

A. Please check your level of agreement with each of the following statements.

	Strongly agree	Agree	Uncertain	Dis-agree	Strongly disagree
1. In general I prefer frozen pizza to a frozen chicken pot pie	___	___	___	___	___
2. A frozen pizza dinner is more expensive than eating at a fast food restaurant	___	___	___	___	___

B. Please rate how important each of the following is to you in selecting a brand of frozen pizza:

	Not at all important					Very important
1. Price per serving	___	___	___	___	___	___
2. Toppings available	___	___	___	___	___	___
3. Amount of cheese	___	___	___	___	___	___
4. Cooking time	___	___	___	___	___	___

C. Please check the rating which best describes your feelings about the last frozen pizza which you prepared.

	Poor	Fair	Good	Excellent
1. Price per serving	___	___	___	___
2. Toppings available	___	___	___	___
3. Amount of cheese	___	___	___	___
4. Cooking time	___	___	___	___

Mail surveys are economical per questionnaire—if a large number of people respond. But they can be quite expensive if the response rate is poor. In spite of these limits, the convenience and economy of mail surveys makes them a popular approach to collecting primary data.

Telephone surveys—if the information is not too personal

Telephone interviews are growing in popularity. They are effective for getting quick answers to simple questions. Telephone interviews let the interviewer ask several questions to try to understand what the respondent really is thinking. On the other hand, the telephone isn't a good method if you are trying to get confidential personal information—such as details of family income. Respondents are not certain who is calling—or how this personal information might be used.[5]

Personal interview surveys—can be in-depth

It's usually easier to hold a respondent's attention in a face-to-face interview. The interviewer can also explain complicated directions—and perhaps

Telephone interviews are good for getting information quickly.

get more accurate responses. A personal interview survey is usually much more expensive than a mail or telephone survey—but it offers a chance to explore some questions in depth.

Being there also allows the interviewer to change his questions—depending on the respondent's early answers. New problems may be uncovered in a personal interview. The interviewer is often able to judge some characteristics—like socio-economic status. He also can follow up people who weren't available earlier—or who don't usually answer mail questionnaires. For these reasons, personal interviews are commonly used for interviewing industrial customers.

Observing—What You See Is What You Get

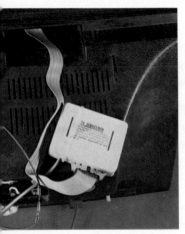

Observing—as a method of collecting data—focuses on a well-defined problem. Here we are not talking about the "casual" observations that may stimulate ideas in the early steps of a research project.

With the observation method, the researcher doesn't talk to the subjects. He watches how they behave—and tries not to influence them at all. For example, a bread manufacturer interested in bread-buying behavior in supermarkets could station an observer near the bread counter. The observer could gather information about the choice of a brand, the amount of label reading that takes place, or multiple purchases.

In some situations, consumers are videotaped. Later, the tape can be analyzed carefully by running the films at very slow speeds—or actually analyzing each frame. This might be useful, for example, in studying product selection in a department store—or studying the routes consumers follow through a supermarket.

Various observation methods are used in advertising research. For example, a device called an "audimeter" adapts the observation method to television audience research. This machine is attached to the TV set in the homes of selected families—and records when the set is on and what station is tuned in.

This method is used by the A.C. Nielsen Company—and the results are widely used for network ratings.[6]

Experimental Method Controls Conditions

A marketing manager can get a different kind of information—with questioning or observing—using the *experimental method.* With the **experimental method** the responses of groups which are similar—except on the characteristic being tested—are compared. The researcher wants to learn if the specific characteristic—which varies among groups—*causes* differences in some *response* among the groups. The "response" might be an observed behavior—like the purchase of a product—or the answer to some question—like "How much do you like the taste of our new product?"

The experimental method isn't used as frequently as surveys and focus groups. This is because in the "real world" it's hard to set up controlled situations where one marketing variable is different—but everything else is the same. But there is probably another reason, too. Many managers don't understand the valuable information they can get from this method. Further, they don't like the idea of some researcher "experimenting" with their business.[7]

INTERPRETATION OF DATA—STEP FOUR

What Does It Really Mean?

When data has been collected it has to be analyzed to decide "what it all means." With quantitative research, this step usually includes the use of statistics. **Statistical packages**—easy-to-use computer programs that analyze data—have opened up many new possibilities. Technical specialists often are involved at this step—and the details are beyond the scope of this book. But a good manager should know at least enough to understand what a research project can—or can't—do.[8]

Is Your Sample Really Representative?

For most marketing research, it's just not possible to collect all the information you might want about *everyone* in a *population.* Here, **population** means the total group in which you are interested. In a marketing research study, only a **sample**—a part of the relevant population—may be surveyed. How well a sample *represents* the total population affects the results. Results from a sample that is not representative may not give a true picture of the whole population.

For example, the manager of a retail store might want a phone survey to learn how consumers feel about the store hours. If interviewers make all of the calls during the day, the sample will not be representative. Consumers who work outside the home during the day won't have an equal chance of being included in the survey. People interviewed might say the limited store hours were "satisfactory." Yet to assume from this that *all* consumers are satisfied would be wrong.[9]

SPSS/Pro is a microcomputer statistical software program that makes it easy to summarize marketing research data.

Research Results Are Not Exact

Remember that an estimate from a sample—even a representative one—usually varies somewhat from the "true value" for a total population. Many managers forget this. They assume that survey results are exact. Instead, when interpreting sample estimates, it is better to think of them as *suggesting* an approximate result.

The nature of the sample—and how it is selected—makes a big difference in how the results of a study can be interpreted. This should be considered as part of planning data collection—to make sure the marketing manager can use the results with confidence.

Even if the sampling is carefully planned, it is also important to evaluate the quality of the research data itself.

Validity Problems Can Destroy Research

Marketers often assume that research data really measures what it is supposed to measure. Managers and researchers should be careful about this—because many of the variables that are of interest to marketing managers are hard to measure accurately. We can create a questionnaire that will let us assign numbers to consumer responses, but that doesn't mean that the result is precise. For example, an interviewer might ask you, "How much did you spend on soft drinks last week?" You might be perfectly willing to cooperate—and be part of a representative sample—but still not be able to remember the right amount. This problem may be increased when trying to assign numbers to consumer attitudes or opinions.

Validity concerns the extent to which data measures what it is intended to measure. Validity problems are important in marketing research because most people want to help and will give an answer—even when they don't know what they're talking about. Sometimes a poorly worded question means different things to different people. Although respondents may not care—a manager should see that he only pays for research results which are representative and valid.

Interpretation of Data Can Destroy Research

Besides sampling and validity problems, a marketing manager should consider whether the analysis of the data supports the conclusions drawn in the interpretation step. Sometimes the technical people pick the right statistical procedure—their calculations are exact—but they offer a wrong interpretation because they don't understand the management problem. In one survey automobile buyers were asked to rank five cars in order—from "most preferred" to "least preferred." One car was ranked first by slightly more respondents than

Results of a marketing research computer analysis may not be very helpful—unless they are correctly interpreted and carefully communicated.

any other car—so the researcher reported it as the "most liked car." That interpretation, however, ignored the fact that most of the other respondents ranked the car last.

Interpretation problems like this can make a big difference. Some people draw misleading conclusions—on purpose—to get the results they want. There's even a book called *How to Lie With Statistics*. A marketing manager must decide whether all of the results support the interpretation—and are relevant to his problem.

Marketing Manager and Researcher Should Work Together

Marketing research involves some technical details. But you can see that the marketing researcher and the marketing manager must work together—to be sure that they really do solve the problems facing the firm. If the whole research process has been a joint effort, then the interpretation step can move quickly to the problem solution—and decision making.

PROBLEM SOLUTION—STEP FIVE

The Last Step Is Solving the Problem

In the problem solution step, the results of the research are used in making marketing decisions.

Some researchers—and inexperienced managers—are fascinated by the interesting tidbits of information that come from the research process. They are satisfied if the research reveals something they didn't know before. But if research doesn't have action applications, it has little value to management—and suggests poor planning by the researcher.

When the research process is finished, the marketing manager should be able to apply the findings to marketing strategy planning—the choice of a target market or the mix of the four Ps. If the research doesn't provide information to help guide these decisions, the research money probably was wasted.

We are emphasizing this step because it is the logical conclusion to the whole research process. This final step must be anticipated at each of the earlier steps. It is the *reason* for these earlier steps.

HOW MUCH RESEARCH SHOULD BE DONE?

Research Is Costly— But Reduces Risk

Dependable research costs money. A large-scale survey can cost from $20,000 to $100,000. The continuing research available from companies such as A. C. Nielsen can cost a company from $25,000 to well over $100,000 a year. And a market test for 6 to 12 months may cost $100,000 to $300,000 per test market! But for companies willing—and able—to pay the cost, marketing research may more than pay for itself. These companies are more likely to select the right target market and marketing mix—or see a potential problem before it becomes a costly crisis.

What Is the Value of Information?

The high cost of good research must be balanced against its probable value to management. You never get all the information you would like to have. Very detailed surveys or experiments may be "too good" or "too expensive" or "too late"—if all that is needed is a rough sampling of retailer attitudes toward a new pricing plan—*by tomorrow.*

Marketing managers must take risks because of incomplete information. That's part of their job—and always will be. They might like more data. But they must weigh the cost of getting it against its likely value. If the risk is not too great, the cost of getting more information may be greater than the potential loss from a poor decision. A decision to expand into a new territory with the present marketing mix, for example, might be made with more confidence after a $25,000 survey. But just sending a sales rep into the territory for a few weeks to try to sell the potential customers would be a lot cheaper—and, if successful, the answer is in *and* so are some sales.

Faced with many risky decisions, the marketing manager should only seek help from research for problems where the risk can be reduced at a reasonable cost.

SOME FIRMS ARE BUILDING MARKETING INFORMATION SYSTEMS

In some companies, marketing researchers have high status—and are deeply involved in major marketing decisions. In other companies, they may be just data collectors. They haven't managed to sell the idea that good information—not just data—will improve decision making.

Once marketing managers learn how a marketing information system can help their decision making, they are eager for more information.

**MIS Makes Available
Data Accessible**

Some companies have set up marketing information systems to improve the quality—and quantity—of information available to their managers. A **marketing information system (MIS)** is an organized way of continually gathering and analyzing data to get information to help marketing managers make decisions. Sometimes this is handled by the marketing research department. In other companies, this information function is separated into a new department—that provides *all* departments in the firm with information.

**Information May
Make Managers
Greedy**

Once marketing managers see how a functioning MIS can help their decision making, they are eager for more information. They see that they can improve all their planning. Further, they can monitor the implementation of current plans—comparing results against plans and making necessary changes more quickly. Figure 5–4 shows all the interacting parts in an MIS. As you can see, it really is an information *system* intended to help managers make better decisions—not just to collect and manipulate data.

■ FIGURE 5–4

A diagram of a marketing information system showing various inputs to a computer and outputs to managers

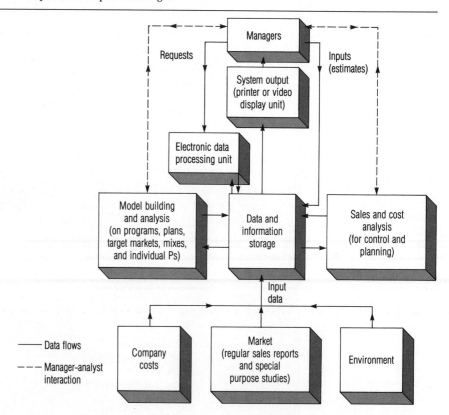

We are now seeing many more marketing information systems—even in small firms. But there is still room in marketing for able students willing to apply advanced techniques to solving real marketing problems.[10]

■ CONCLUSION

In this chapter, we have seen that marketing research is not magic worked by statisticians. It is a management tool that helps the marketing manager make better decisions—based not just on feel and intuition, but on objective information. The manager should understand research procedures—and the researcher should understand management's problems of planning, implementing, and controlling. Without this close cooperation, the output of a marketing research department may be useless.

Marketing researchers should apply the scientific method to solve marketing problems. Some objective and organized approach is needed—because very often a researcher does not have the time or money to complete a whole research project. If the early steps of the research effort have been done effectively, he may be able to "jump" to a solution early in the process. A scientific approach to solving marketing problems involves five steps: definition of the problem, a situation analysis, obtaining data, interpreting data, and solving the problem.

Definition of the problem is obviously the most important step—because good research on the wrong problem is useless. Then a good situation analysis—perhaps using inexpensive secondary data—may help the researcher solve the problem without going on to further steps in the process.

Primary data may be collected—if it is still needed after the situation analysis. Both qualitative and quantitative research may be needed. This step often involves surveys. Surveys can provide helpful information, but often other methods provide better information—at the same or lower cost. Focus groups and observation, for example, may be better when researchers need more ideas about what to study.

Great care must be taken in the interpretation step—to be certain that the research results are properly understood. Marketing managers should not assume results to be more precise than they really are. The interpretation step must be considered when the data collection steps are designed—so there can be enough confidence in the results to take action.

Proper interpretation should lead directly to the problem solution step. Research results should suggest specific action which management might take to solve its problem.

Our strategy planning framework can be helpful in finding the real problem. By focusing on the real problem, the researcher may be able to move quickly to a useful solution—maybe without the cost and risks of a formal research project. If the firm has more time—and an adequate budget—it may be able to enjoy the luxury of more detailed and more sophisticated analysis. And if there is a need for ongoing information, the "answers" may be routinely available in a marketing information system.

■ QUESTIONS AND PROBLEMS

1. Marketing research involves expense—sometimes a considerable expense. Why does the text recommend the use of marketing research even though a highly experienced marketing executive is available?

2. Explain the key characteristics of the scientific method and then show why these are important to managers concerned with research.

3. How is the situation analysis different from the data collection step. Can both these steps be done at the same time to obtain answers sooner? Is this wise?

4. Explain how you might use different types of research (focus groups, observation, survey, and experiment) to forecast market reaction to a new kind of margarine which is to receive no promotion other than what the retailer will give it. Further, assume that the new margarine's name will not be associated with other known products. The product will be offered at competitive prices.

5. Distinguish between primary data and secondary data and illustrate your answer.

6. If a firm were interested in estimating the distribution of income in the state of Ohio, how could it proceed? Be specific.

7. If a firm were interested in estimating sand and clay production in Georgia, how could it proceed? Be specific.

8. Go to the library and find (in some government publication) three marketing-oriented "facts" which you did not know existed or were available. Record on one page and show sources.

9. Distinguish between qualitative and quantitative approaches to research—and give some of the key advantages and limitations of each approach.

10. Discuss the concept that some information may be too expensive to obtain in relation to its value. Illustrate.

11. Discuss the concept of a marketing information system and how its output might differ from the output of a typical marketing research department.

12. Discuss some of the likely problems facing the marketer in a small firm which has just purchased an inexpensive "personal computer" to help develop a marketing information system.

■ SUGGESTED CASES

4. Uncle Lyle's, Inc.

6. The Lido

7. Nite-Time Motel

Chapter 6 ■ Final consumers and their buying behavior

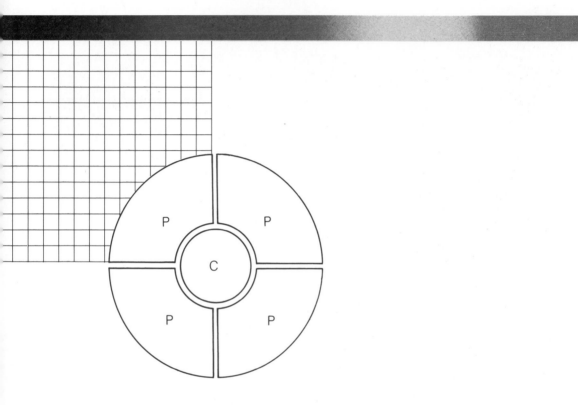

When you finish this chapter, you should:

1. Know how final consumer spending is related to population, income, family life cycle, and other variables.

2. Know how to estimate likely consumer purchases for broad classes of products.

3. Understand how the intra- and inter-personal variables affect an individual's and household's buying behavior.

4. Know how consumers use problem-solving processes.

5. Have some "feel" for how all the behavioral variables and incoming stimuli are handled by a consumer.

6. Recognize the important new terms (shown in red).

Which car will the customer buy—the Ford Mustang or the Audi Fox?

How can marketing managers predict which specific products consumers will buy—and in what quantities? Why does a consumer choose a particular product?

This chapter shows that basic data on consumer spending patterns can help forecast trends in consumer buying. But when many firms sell similar products, this data isn't much help in predicting which *products* and *brands* will be purchased. To find better answers, we need to understand people better. For this reason, many marketers have turned to the behavioral sciences for help. The following example illustrates some of the ideas we'll be discussing in this chapter.

Pam Bowers was very satisfied with the car she had been driving for six years. But a careless driver ran a stop sign—and Pam's dependable old car was "totaled." She needed another one—but what kind? Pam hadn't paid any attention to car ads—she was amazed by all the styles and features offered. She had enjoyed the roominess of her old car—and didn't like the cramped seating in the new compacts. Her husband thought a bigger car would be safer in case of another accident. But Pam didn't want a *really* big car that would be expensive—and harder to drive and park.

Pam went to several car dealers. The salespeople weren't much help. So Pam and her husband studied *Consumer Reports* and asked opinions of friends. Pam really needed a car—so she finally stopped looking—and bought one. Even after buying the car, she kept reading car ads—to be sure she had made the right decision.

Note that Pam's car purchase was *motivated by a need.* Her satisfaction with her old car was a *learning* experience—that shaped her *attitudes* in choosing a new car. *Beliefs* about safety were important, too. Both husband and wife influenced the final decision. A *reference group*—people who weren't directly involved—had some effect too. Pam used *extended* problem solving—including test drives, sales presentations, friends' opinions, and magazine articles. Information that she had *selectively* ignored suddenly was relevant. Even after Pam bought the car, she kept looking for new information to *reinforce* her decision.

Now you'll see how all these ideas fit together—and why they are important. Our discussion will focus on *final consumers,* but keep in mind that many of these behavioral influences apply to industrial and other intermediate buyers, too.

CONSUMER SPENDING PATTERNS RELATED TO POPULATION AND INCOME

Markets are made up of people with money to spend. So consumer spending patterns are related to population *and* income.

Consumer budget studies show that most consumers spend their incomes as part of a family or household unit. The family members usually pool their incomes when planning family purchases. So it makes sense for us to talk about how households or families spend their incomes.

Spending Data Gives Specific Numbers

We have much detailed information on consumer spending patterns. The patterns are more important than the thing—rather than the specific dollar figures—because these patterns stay pretty much the same over time. So even as this data gets older, the relationships will help us see how families spend their incomes. Continuing inflation will, of course, require some adjusting of this data.

Table 6–1 shows the average annual spending by families for major kinds of purchases. These figures should keep you from making wild guesses based only on your own experience. The amount spent on food, housing, clothing, transport, and so on does vary by income level. The relationships make sense when you realize that many of the purchases are for "necessities."

■ TABLE 6–1 Family spending (in dollars and percent of spending) for several family income levels (in 1981 dollars)

Spending Category	$18,000–22,500		$27,000–34,000		$34,000–45,000	
	$	%	$	%	$	%
Food	$ 3,124	18.3	$ 3,928	17.6	$ 4,511	17.0
Housing	4,776	28.0	5,815	26.0	6,794	25.4
Clothing	1,160	6.8	1,553	7.0	1,946	7.3
Transportation	3,191	18.7	4,390	19.7	5,066	18.9
Health care	1,023	6.0	1,140	5.1	1,297	4.8
Personal care	181	1.0	235	1.1	291	1.1
Education	78	.5	166	.7	296	1.1
Reading	80	.5	121	.5	150	.6
Recreation	1,054	6.2	1,533	6.9	2,011	7.5
Alcohol	141	.8	177	.8	237	.9
Tobacco	303	1.8	347	1.5	386	1.4
Insurance	392	2.2	621	2.8	830	3.1
Pensions	879	5.1	1,405	6.3	1,840	6.9
Contributions	698	4.1	904	4.0	1,104	4.1
Total spending	$17,080	100.0%	$22,335	100.0%	$26,759	100.0%

Source: Adapted by authors from data from Bureau of Labor Statistics and U.S. Census Bureau.

Estimating How Potential Customers Spend Their Money

Data such as that in Table 6–1 can help a marketing manager understand how potential target customers spend their money. Let's suppose you are a marketing manager for a swimming pool manufacturer. You're thinking of mailing an ad to households in a neighborhood where most families are in the $27,000–$34,000 income group. Looking at Table 6–1, you can see how families in this category spend their money. The table suggests that such families spend about $1,533 a year on recreation of all kinds. If a particular pool costs at least $1,200 a year—including depreciation and maintenance—the average family in this income category would have to make a big change in life style if it bought the pool.

Data like this won't tell you whether a specific family will buy the pool. But it does supply useful input to help make decisions. If more information is needed—perhaps about the target market's attitudes toward recreation products—then some marketing research may be needed. Perhaps you might want to see a budget study on consumers who already have swimming pools—to see how they adjusted their spending patterns—and how they felt before and after the purchase.

Stage of Family Life Cycle Affects Spending

Two other demographic dimensions—age and number of children—affect spending patterns. Put together, these dimensions tell us about the life-cycle stage of a family. See Figure 6–1 for a summary of life cycle and buying behavior.

Young people and families accept new ideas

Singles and young couples seem to be more open to new products and brands. But they are also careful, price-conscious shoppers. The income of

■ FIGURE 6–1   Stages in the family life cycle

Stage	Characteristics and buying behavior
1. Singles: unmarried people living away from parents	Feel "affluent" and "free." Buy basic household goods. More interested in recreation, cars, vacations, clothes, cosmetics and personal care items.
2. Divorced or separated	May be financially squeezed to pay for alimony or maintaining two households. Buying may be limited to "necessities"—especially for women who have no job skills.
3. Newly married couples: no children	Both may work and so they feel financially well-off. Buy durables: cars, refrigerators, stoves, basic furniture—and recreation equipment and vacations.
4. Full nest I: youngest child under six	Feel squeezed financially because they are buying homes and household durables—furniture, washers, dryers, and TV. Also buying child-related products—food, medicines, clothes, and toys. Really interested in new products.
5. Full nest II: youngest child over five	Financially are better off as husband earns more and/or wife goes to work as last child goes to school. More spent on food, clothing, education, and recreation for growing children.
6. Full nest III: older couples with dependent children	Financially even better off as husband earns more and more wives work. May replace durables and furniture, and buy cars, boats, dental services, and more expensive recreation and travel. May buy bigger houses.
7. Empty nest: older couples, no children living with them, head still working	Feel financially "well-off." Home ownership at peak, and house may be paid for. May make home improvements or move into apartments. And may travel, entertain, go to school, and make gifts and contributions. Not interested in new products.
8. Sole survivor, still working	Income still good. Likely to sell home and continue with previous life style.
9. Senior citizen I: older married couple, no children living with them, head retired	Big drop in income. May keep home but cut back on most buying as purchases of medical care, drugs, and other health-related items go up.
10. Senior citizen II: sole survivor, not working	Same as senior citizen I, except likely to sell home, and has special need for attention, affection, and security.

Source: Adapted from William D. Wells and George Gubar, "Life Cycle Concept in Marketing Research," *Journal of Marketing Research,* August 1968, p. 267.

these younger people is often lower than that of older groups. But they spend a greater proportion of their income on "discretionary" items—because they don't have big expenses for housing, education, and raising a family.[1] Although many are waiting longer to marry—most young people do "tie the knot" eventually. These younger families—especially those with no children—are still buying durable goods, such as automobiles and home furnishings. They need less food. It is only as children begin to arrive and grow that family spending shifts to soft goods and services—such as education, medical, and personal care. This usually happens when the household head reaches the 35–44 age group.

Teenagers mean shifts in spending

Once the children become teenagers, further shifts in spending occur. Teenagers eat more. Their clothing costs more. They develop recreation and education needs that are hard on the family budget. The parents may be forced to change their spending to cover these expenses—by spending less on durable goods, such as appliances, automobiles, household goods, and houses.

Many teenagers do earn much or all of their own spending money—so they are an attractive market. But marketers who have aimed at teenagers are beginning to notice the decline in birth rate. Motorcycle manufacturers, for example, have already been hurt—as teenagers are their heaviest buyers.[2]

Selling to the empty nesters

An important group is the **empty nesters**—people whose children are grown—and who are now able to spend their money in other ways. Usually these people are in the 50–64 age group. It is the empty nesters who move back into the smaller, more luxurious apartments in the city. They may also be more interested in travel, small sports cars, and other things that they couldn't afford before. Much depends on their income, of course. But this is a high-income period for many workers—especially white-collar workers.

Senior citizens are a big new market

Finally, the **senior citizens**—people over 65—should not be neglected. The number of people over 65 is now over 11 percent of the population—and growing.

Although older people generally have reduced incomes, many do have money—and very different needs. Many firms, in fact, are already catering to the senior citizen market. Gerber (in baby foods)—faced with a declining baby market—started producing some products for older people.[3] Some firms have gone into special diet supplements and drug products. Others have designed housing developments to appeal to older people.

The senior citizen segment is a growing market for vacation travel, health care, and retirement housing.

Dark & Lovely...
The Hair Color
For The Woman
Of Color.

Specially Formulated
Because Dark & Lovely Hair Color was specifically formulated for your hair coloring needs, there'll be no surprises. With Dark & Lovely you get true-to-life, natural permanent color from end to end. And built-in protein conditioner will leave your hair soft, alluring and ready for styling.

It's for Real
You can choose Honey Blonde to Jet Black, and Dark & Lovely does all the things a hair color should do for your hair, from covering gray to bringing out radiant highlights.

Dark & Lovely Hair Color covers, softens, heightens, lightens, intensifies, glamorizes, glorifies, satisfies, beautifies, dazzles, brightens, shines, radiates, and glows.

Dark & Lovely Hair Color is rich, lasting, lush, lively, lustrous, manageable, radiant, silky, glowing, elegant, stylish, luxurious, vibrant, and striking.

Dark & Lovely in Jet Black, Black, Dark Brown, Light Brown, Auburn, Bright Auburn, Fiery Auburn and Honey Blonde.

Ahhh, the pleasure of

Separate marketing strategies may be required for ethnically or racially defined markets.

Do Ethnic Groups Buy Differently?

America may be called the "melting pot"—but there are still distinct ethnic groups that require special attention from marketers. Language differences are an obvious example. More than 1 out of 10 families speaks a language other than English at home. Some areas have a much higher rate. In Miami and San Antonio, for example, about one out of three households speaks Spanish.

This is an area where stereotype thinking is common—and where a company may need to do some original marketing research—to reach this varied—and growing—market.[4]

The median age of U.S. blacks and Spanish-speaking people is much lower than that of whites. This means that many more are in earlier stages of the life cycle and, therefore, are a better market for certain goods—especially durable goods.

Some minority groups seem to be striving for what they believe to be white middle-income standards in material goods. Current products may be quite acceptable. Others disregard these objectives in favor of their own traditional values. Clearly, separate strategies may be needed for these ethnically or racially defined markets.[5]

When the Wife Earns, the Family Spends

Another factor that deserves attention is the growing number of married women with paying jobs. In 1950, only 24 percent of wives worked outside the home. This figure is more than 50 percent in the 80s.[6]

In families where the wife works, she contributes about 30 percent of all the family spending power. This is why family income is as high as it is.

When a wife works outside the home, it seems to have little effect on the nutritional value of her family's food. But working wives do *spend more* for food—and choose more expensive types of food.

Families with working wives also spend more on clothing, alcohol and tobacco, home furnishings and equipment, and automobiles. In short, when a wife works, it affects the spending habits of the family. This fact must be considered when planning marketing strategies.

THE BEHAVIORAL SCIENCES HELP US UNDERSTAND BUYING PROCESS

Buying in a Black Box

A simple view of how behavioral scientists see consumer buying behavior is shown in Figure 6–2. Potential customers are exposed to various stimuli—including the marketing mixes of competitors. Somehow, an individual takes in these stimuli and then, for some reason, responds to them. We can't see into the mysterious black box. We can only see resulting behavior—such as whether a purchase is made.

This simple version of the classical **stimulus-response model** says that people respond in some predictable way to a stimulus. The model doesn't explain *why* they behave the way they do—only that there is a predictable response to a stimulus.

■ FIGURE 6–2   Simplified buyer behavior model

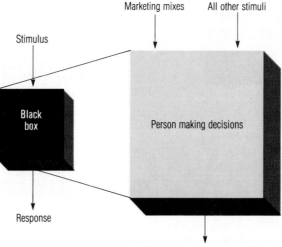

**There Are Many
Black Box Theories**

There are many different opinions about how the black box works. These varying theories lead to different forecasts about how consumers will behave.

Most economists assume that consumers are **economic men**—people who logically compare choices in terms of cost and value received—to get the greatest satisfaction from spending their time, energy, and money. Therefore, the economist analyzes demographic data when trying to predict consumer behavior. It was a logical extension of the economic-man theory which led us to look at consumer spending patterns earlier in the chapter. There is value in this approach. Consumers must at least have income to be in the market. But other behavioral scientists suggest that the black box works in a more complicated way than the economic-man model.

**How We Will View
the Black Box**

Consumers have many dimensions. Let's try to combine these dimensions into a better model of how consumers make decisions. Figure 6–3 presents a more detailed view of the black box model. Here, we see both intra-personal and inter-personal variables affecting the person making decisions.

These topics will be discussed in the next few pages. Then we will look at the consumer's problem-solving process.

■ FIGURE 6–3   More complete buyer behavior model

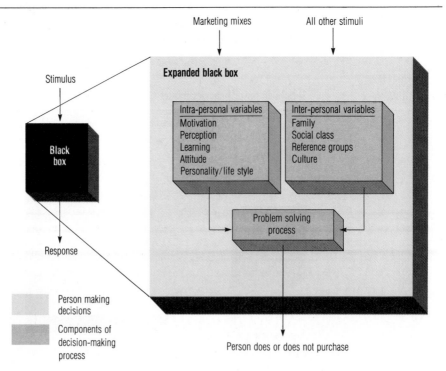

INTRA–PERSONAL VARIABLES FOCUS
ON THE INDIVIDUAL

Motivation Deter-mines What Con-sumers Want

Everybody is motivated by needs and wants. **Needs** are the basic forces which motivate an individual to do something. Some needs are concerned with a person's physical well-being. Other needs are concerned with the individual's view of himself and his relationship with others. Needs are more basic than *wants.* **Wants** are "needs" which are learned during a person's life. For example, we all have a basic need for food—but some people also have learned to want a "Big Mac."

When a need isn't satisfied, it leads to a drive. The food need, for instance, leads to a hunger drive. A **drive** is a strong stimulus that encourages action—to reduce a need. Drives are the reasons behind certain behavior patterns. A product purchase is the result of a drive to satisfy some need.

A Marketing Mix Can't Create a Drive

Marketing managers can't create drives in consumers. Some critics suggest that marketers can somehow make consumers buy products against their will. Most marketing managers realize that trying to get consumers to act against their will just doesn't work. Instead, a good marketing manager studies what consumer drives and needs already exist—and how they can be satisfied better.

We all are a bundle of needs and wants. Figure 6–4 presents a list of some important consumer needs. They can also be thought of as *benefits* which consumers might seek from a marketing mix.

Are There Hierar-chies of Needs?

Some psychologists feel that a person may have several reasons for buying—at the same time. Maslow is well known for his five-level hierarchy of needs. But we will discuss a similar four-level hierarchy which is easier to use—and is supported by more recent research on human motivation.[7] The four levels are illustrated in Figure 6–5. The lowest-level needs are physiological. Then come safety, social, and personal needs. As a study aid, think of the "PSSP needs."

The **physiological needs** are concerned with biological needs—food, drink, rest, and sex. The **safety needs** are concerned with protection and physical well-being (perhaps involving health food, medicine, and exercise). The **social needs** are concerned with love, friendship, status, and esteem—things that involve a person's interaction with others. The **personal needs,** on the other hand, are concerned with an individual's need for personal satisfaction—unrelated to what others think or do. Examples here include self-esteem, accomplishment, fun, freedom, and relaxation.

Motivation theory suggests that we never reach a state of complete satisfaction. As soon as lower-level needs are reasonably satisfied, those at higher levels become more dominant. Further, a particular good or service may sat-

■ FIGURE 6–4   Possible needs motivating a person to some action

Physiological needs

Food	Warmth	Activity
Drink	Coolness	Rest
Sex—tension release	Body elimination	Self-preservation
Sleep		

Psychological needs

Abasement	Deference	Order
Acquisition	Distinctive	Personal fulfillment
Affiliation	Discriminating	Playing—competitive
Aggression	Discriminatory	Playing—relaxing
Beauty	Dominance	Power
Belonging	Emulation	Pride
Being constructive	Exhibition	Security
Being part of a group	Family preservation	Self-expression
Being responsible	Imitation	Self-identification
Being well thought of	Independence	Symmetry
Companionship	Individualism	Tenderness
Conserving	Love	Striving
Curiosity	Nurturing	Understanding (knowledge)
Discovery		

Desire for:

Acceptance	Prestige
Achievement	Recognition
Affection	Respect
Affiliation	Retaliation
Appreciation	Satisfaction with self
Comfort	Security
Contrariness	Self-confidence
Dependence	Sensuous experiences
Distance—"space"	Sexual satisfaction
Distinctiveness	Sociability
Fame	Status
Happiness	Sympathy
Identification	

Freedom from:

Anxiety	Imitation
Depression	Loss of prestige
Discomfort	Pain
Fear	Pressure
Harm—Psychological	Ridicule
Harm—Physical	Sadness

Source: Adapted from C. Glenn Walters, *Consumer Behavior,* 3d ed. (Homewood, Ill.: Richard D. Irwin, 1979); R. M. Liebert and M. D. Spiegler, *Personality,* 3d ed., (Homewood, Ill.: Dorsey Press, 1978), and others. © 1979 by Richard D. Irwin, Inc., and © 1978 by The Dorsey Press.

■ FIGURE 6–5   The PSSP hierarchy of needs

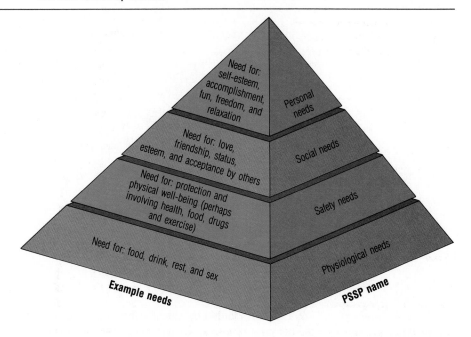

isfy more than one need at the same time. A hamburger in a friendly environment, for example, might satisfy not only the physiological need to satisfy hunger—but also some social need.

Economic Needs Affect How We Satisfy Basic Needs

The need hierarchy idea can help explain *what* we buy. The economic needs help explain *why* we want specific product features.

Economic needs are concerned with making the best use of a consumer's limited resources—as the consumer sees it. Some of us look for the best price. Others want the best quality—almost regardless of price. And others settle for the best value. Some economic needs are:

1. Economy of purchase or use.
2. Convenience.
3. Efficiency in operation or use.
4. Dependability in use.
5. Improvement of earnings.

With economic needs, promotion can emphasize measurable factors—such as specific dollar savings, the length of the guarantee, or how long the product lasts.

Different products meet different needs.

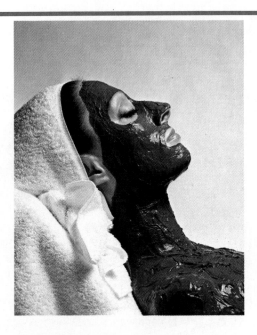

Perception Determines What Is Seen and Felt

We are bombarded by stimuli everywhere—ads, products, stores—but we may not hear or see anything. This is because we apply the following selective processes:

1. **Selective exposure**—our eyes and minds notice only information that interests us.
2. **Selective perception**—we screen out or modify ideas, messages, and information that conflict with previously learned attitudes and beliefs.
3. **Selective retention**—we remember only what we want to remember.

These selective processes help explain why some people aren't affected at all by some advertising—even offensive advertising. They just don't see or remember it!

Our needs affect these selective processes. Decisions that we're currently concerned about affect which stimuli we notice. In our car purchase example, Pam Bowers became interested in available cars, people's attitudes toward them, and car advertising *only* when she had to replace her old car.

Marketers are interested in these selective processes. It helps in strategy planning if they know something about how their target consumers get and retain information. This is also why marketers are interested in how consumers *learn*.

Learning Determines What Response Is Likely

Learning is a change in a person's thought processes caused by experience. A little girl tastes her first ice cream cone—and learning occurs!

There are several steps in the learning process.[8] We have already discussed the idea of a *drive* as a strong stimulus that encourages action. Depending on the **cues**—products, signs, ads, and other stimuli in the environment—an individual chooses some specific response. A **response** is an effort to satisfy a drive. The specific response chosen depends on the cues and the person's past experience.

Reinforcement—of the learning process—occurs when the response is followed by satisfaction—that is, reducing the drive. Reinforcement strengthens the relationship between the cue and the response. And it may lead to a similar response the next time the drive occurs. Repeated reinforcement leads to the development of a habit—making the decision process routine for the individual. The relationships of the important variables in the learning process are shown in Figure 6–6.

The learning process can be illustrated by a thirsty person. The thirst *drive* could be satisfied in a variety of ways. But if our thirsty person happens to walk past a vending machine and sees a 7up sign—a *cue*—then he might satisfy the drive with a *response*—buying a 7up. If the experience is satisfactory, positive *reinforcement* will occur—and our friend may be quicker to satisfy this drive in the same way in the future. This emphasizes the importance of developing good products which live up to the promises of the firm's advertising. People can learn to like or dislike 7up—learning works both ways!

Good experiences can lead to positive attitudes about a firm's product. Bad experiences can lead to negative attitudes—which even good promotion won't be able to change.

Some Needs May Be Learned

Some needs may be culturally (or socially) learned. When babies are born, their needs are simple. But as they grow, they learn different ways to meet needs. The need for food, for instance, may lead to many specific food wants. The people of Western nations like beef—and their children learn to like it. In India, however, Hindus regard the cow as sacred and won't eat beef. Their children learn to eat and like other foods. Many foods, in other words, can satisfy hunger—but in a particular culture, a person may want a steak. And the hunger drive might not be satisfied until he eats one.

Some critics argue that marketing efforts encourage people to spend money on learned wants that satisfy no "basic need" at all. They note, for example, that Europeans are less concerned about body odor—and few buy or use a

■ FIGURE 6–6   The learning process

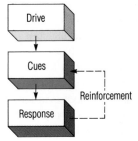

Some needs may be culturally learned.

deodorant. At the same time, millions of dollars are spent on such products in the United States. Advertising implies that the use of deodorants "takes the worry out of being close." But is marketing activity the cause of the difference in the two cultures? Most research says that advertising can't convince buyers of something which is contrary to their basic *attitudes*.

Attitudes Relate to Buying

An **attitude** is a person's point of view toward something. The "something" may be a product, an ad, a firm, or an idea. Attitudes are an important topic for marketers—because attitudes affect the selective processes, learning, and eventually buying decisions.

Attitudes involve liking or disliking—so people are willing to take some action. *Beliefs* are not so action-oriented. A **belief** is a person's conviction about something. Beliefs may help shape attitudes—but don't necessarily involve liking or disliking. It's possible to have a belief—say that Listerine tastes like medicine—without caring what it tastes like.

Attitudes aren't the same thing as buying intentions. A person might have positive attitudes toward a Cadillac without ever intending to buy one. So attitudes must be used with care when trying to predict buying behavior.

Consumers' attitudes—both positive and negative—are learned from experiences with a product, exposure to the attitudes of others, or promotion which affects their own attitudes. If a marketer can learn about the attitudes of the firm's target customers, he has a better idea of what positive attitudes he might appeal to. Or maybe he must change existing attitudes—or create new ones. Each of these jobs requires a slightly different approach.

Marketers generally try to understand the attitudes of their potential customers—and work with them. This is much easier—and more economical—than trying to *change* attitudes. Changing attitudes—especially negative ones—is probably the toughest job that marketers face. If very negative attitudes are held by the target market, it may be more practical to try another strategy.[9]

Personality Affects How People See Things

Much research has been done on how personality affects people's behavior. The results have generally been disappointing to marketers. Certainly, personality traits influence the way people behave. But—so far—we haven't found a way to use personality to help in strategy planning.[10]

Psychographic and Life-Style Analysis May Help

Some marketers try to get help from sets of consumer-related dimensions. **Psychographics** or **life-style analysis** is the analysis of a person's day-to-day living pattern—as expressed in his Activities, Interests, and Opinions—sometimes referred to as "AIOs." A number of variables for each of the AIO dimensions are shown in Table 6–2—along with some demographics which can be used to add detail to the life-style profile of a target market.[11]

Life-style analysis assumes that you can plan better strategies to reach your target market if you know more about them. Understanding the life style of target customers has been especially helpful in providing ideas for advertising themes. Let's see how it adds to a typical demographic description. It may not help a marketer much to know that an average member of the target market for a small station wagon is 30.8 years old, married, lives in a three-bedroom home, and has 2.3 children. Life styles help marketers to paint a more human portrait of the target market. Life-style analysis might show that the 30.8-year-old is also a community-oriented consumer—with a traditional life style—who especially enjoys spectator sports and spends much time in other activities

■ TABLE 6–2   Life-style dimensions

Activities	Interests	Opinions	Demographics
Work	Family	Themselves	Age
Hobbies	Home	Social issues	Education
Social events	Job	Politics	Income
Vacation	Community	Business	Occupation
Entertainment	Recreation	Economics	Family size
Club membership	Fashion	Education	Dwelling
Community	Food	Products	Geography
Shopping	Media	Future	City size
Sports	Achievements	Culture	Stage in life cycle

Source: Joseph T. Plummer, "The Concept and Application of Life-Style Segregation," *Journal of Marketing*, January 1974, pp. 33–37.

with the whole family. An ad might show the station wagon being used by a happy family at a ball game—so the target market could really identify with the ad.[12]

INTER–PERSONAL VARIABLES AFFECT THE INDIVIDUAL'S BUYING BEHAVIOR

We have been discussing how a person's needs, attitudes, and other intra-personal variables influence the buying process. Now we will look at how the individual interacts with family, social class, and other groups who may have influence.

Who Is the Real Decision Maker in Family Purchases?

Although one person in a household usually makes the purchase, in planning strategy it's important to know who is the real decision maker.

Just a short time ago, the wife was "the" family purchasing agent. She had the time to shop—and run errands. So most promotion was aimed at women. But things are changing. As more women work—and as night and weekend shopping become more popular—men are doing more shopping and decision making.

Although one member of the family may go to the store and make a specific purchase, it is important in planning marketing strategy to know who else may be involved. Other family members may have influenced the decision—or really decided what to buy. Still others may use the product.

You don't need to watch much Saturday morning TV to see that the cereal companies know this. Cartoon characters tell kids about the goodies found in certain cereal packages—and urge them to remind Dad or Mom to pick up that brand next time at the store. Studies show that older sons and daughters may even influence big purchases—like cars and television sets.[13]

Family Considerations May Overwhelm Personal Ones

Most decisions are made within a framework developed by experience in a family. A person may think a great deal about his own preferences for various goods or services. But social processes—such as power, domination, and affection—can be involved, too. A wife might want to spend more on the family vacation—while the husband might want a power boat. The actual outcome in such a situation is unpredictable. It depends on the strength of their preferences, degree of dominance in the family, need for affection, or response of other family members.

Social Class Affects Attitudes and Buying

Up to now, we have been concerned with the individual and his relation to his family. Now let's consider how society looks at an individual and the family—in terms of social class. A **social class** is a group of people who have about equal social position—as viewed by others in the society.

Just to mention "social class" upsets some people. But research in sociology shows that a class structure does exist in the United States.

In our discussion of social class, we will use the traditional technical terms:

upper, middle, and lower (see Figure 6–7). These terms seem to imply "superior" and "inferior." But no value judgment is meant. In fact, it is not possible to say that any one class is "better" or "happier" than another. But they do behave differently!

Characteristics of Social Classes in the United States

The U.S. class system is an individual and a family system. A child's social class will depend on the class of his family. But grown children often "join" a different class than their parents. This happens if they reach higher education levels—or take different occupations—than their parents.

Our class system is measured by occupation, education, and housing arrangements. The source of income is related to these variables, of course. *But there is not a direct relation between amount of income and social class.*

The **upper class** (2 percent of the population)—consists of people from old, wealthy families (upper-upper)—and the socially prominent new rich (lower-upper). They have been the traditional leaders in the American community. Most top business executives belong to this class.

The **upper-middle class** (11 percent of the population)—consists of successful professionals, owners of small businesses, or top salespeople. The advertising professional usually is part of this class—reflecting the tastes and attitudes of the first two groups. But note how small a percent of our population these two social class groups represent!

The **lower-middle class** (36 percent of the population)—consists of small business people, office workers, teachers, and technicians—the "white-collar workers." The American moral code and the emphasis on hard work have

■ FIGURE 6–7   Relative sizes of different social class groups

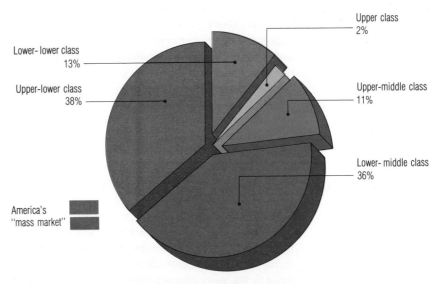

Source: Adapted from Steven L. Diamond, Thomas S. Robertson, and F. Kent Mitchel, "Consumer Motivation and Behavior," in *Marketing Manager's Handbook,* ed. S. H. Britt and N. F. Guess (Chicago: Dartnell, 1983), p. 239.

People from the same social class often have similar values—and even similar preferences for products.

come from this class. This has been the most conforming, church-going, morally serious segment of society. We speak of America as a middle-class society, but the middle-class value system stops here. More than half of our society is *not* middle class.

The **upper-lower class** (38 percent of the population)—consists of factory production line workers, skilled workers, and service people—the "blue-collar workers." Most earn good incomes—but their attitudes are very different from people in the middle class.

The **lower-lower class** (13 percent of the population)—consists of unskilled laborers and people in non-respectable occupations.[14]

What Do These Classes Mean?

Social class studies suggest that an old saying—"A rich man is simply a poor man with more money"—is not true. It appears that a person belonging to the lower classes—given the same income as a middle-class person—handles himself and his money very differently. The various classes shop at different stores. They expect different treatment from salespeople. They buy different brands of products—even though their prices are about the same. And they have different spending-saving attitudes. Some of these differences are shown in Figure 6–8.

The impact on strategy planning is most interesting. Selection of advertising media should be related to social class, for example. Customers in the lower classes have little interest in *Fortune, Vogue,* or *Ladies' Home Journal.* The middle and upper classes probably have little desire to read *True Story, Modern Romances,* or *True Confessions.*

Class should also affect product design—and the kinds of products offered by retailers. Lower-class people seem to like "flashy" home furnishings. Those in the middle and upper classes choose functional or "classic" styles. Further, those in the lower classes may be confused by variety—and have difficulty

■ FIGURE 6–8   Characteristics and attitudes of middle and lower classes

Middle classes	Lower classes
Plan and save for the future ⟷	Live for the present
Analyze alternatives ⟷	"Feel" what is "best"
Understand how the world works ⟷	Have simplistic ideas about how things work
Feel they have opportunities ⟷	Feel controlled by the world
Willing to take risks ⟷	"Play it safe"
Confident about decision making ⟷	Want help with decision making
Want long-run quality or value ⟷	Want short-run satisfaction

making choices. As a result, such buyers look on furniture salespeople as friends and advisors. The middle-class buyers, on the other hand, are more self-confident. They know what they want. They prefer the sales clerk to be an impersonal guide.

Reference Groups Are Important, Too

A **reference group** is the people to whom an individual looks when forming attitudes about a particular topic. We normally have several reference groups—for different topics. Some we meet face-to-face. Others we may just wish to imitate. In either case, we may take our attitudes from these reference groups—and make buying decisions based on what we think they might accept.

The importance of reference groups depends on the product—and whether anyone else will be able to "see" which product and which brand is being used. Figure 6–9 shows products with different degrees of reference group influence.[15]

What we buy is influenced by reference group attitudes.

■ FIGURE 6–9   Examples of different levels of group influence for different types and brands of products

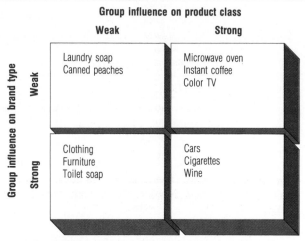

Source: Adapted and updated by authors from H. Kassarjian and Thomas S. Robertson, eds., *Perspectives on Consumer Behavior*, 3rd ed. (Glenview, Ill.: Scott, Foresman, 1981), p. 318; and the work of the Bureau of Applied Social Research, Columbia University, New York.

Reaching the Opinion Leaders Who Are Buyers

Opinion leaders are people who influence others. Opinion leaders aren't necessarily wealthier or better educated. And opinion leaders on one subject are not necessarily opinion leaders on another. Capable homemakers with large families may be consulted for advice on child care. Young women may be opinion leaders for new clothing styles and cosmetics. Each social class tends to have its own opinion leaders. Some marketing mixes are aimed especially at these people—since their opinions affect others.[16]

Culture Surrounds the Whole Decision-Making Process

Culture is the whole set of beliefs, attitudes, and ways of doing things of a similar group of people. We can think of the American culture, the French culture, or the Latin American culture. People in these cultural groupings are similar in outlook and behavior. And sometimes it is useful to think of sub-cultures within such groupings. For example, within the American culture, there are various religious and ethnic sub-cultures.

From a target marketing point of view, if a firm is developing strategies for two cultures, two different marketing plans may be needed.[17]

The attitudes and beliefs within a culture change slowly. So once a manager develops a good understanding of the culture for which he is planning, he can focus on the more dynamic variables discussed above.

CONSUMERS USE PROBLEM–SOLVING PROCESSES

Behavioral scientists agree that people are problem solvers. How an individual solves a particular problem depends on his own intra-personal and inter-personal variables. However, a common problem-solving process seems to be used by most consumers.

The basic problem-solving process consists of five steps:

1. Becoming aware of—or interested in—the problem.
2. Gathering information about possible solutions.
3. Evaluating alternative solutions—perhaps trying some out.
4. Deciding on the appropriate solution.
5. Evaluating the decision.[18]

Marketing managers sometimes offer free samples—to get consumers to try a product.

An expanded version of this process is shown in Figure 6–10. This figure shows the problem-solving process within the buying process we have been discussing.

Three Levels of Problem Solving Are Useful

The basic problem-solving process shows the steps a consumer may go through while trying to find a way to satisfy his needs. But it does not show how long this will take—or how much thought will be given to each step.

It's helpful, therefore, to recognize three levels of problem solving: extensive problem solving, limited problem solving, and routinized response behavior.

■ FIGURE 6–10   Integrated buyer behavior model

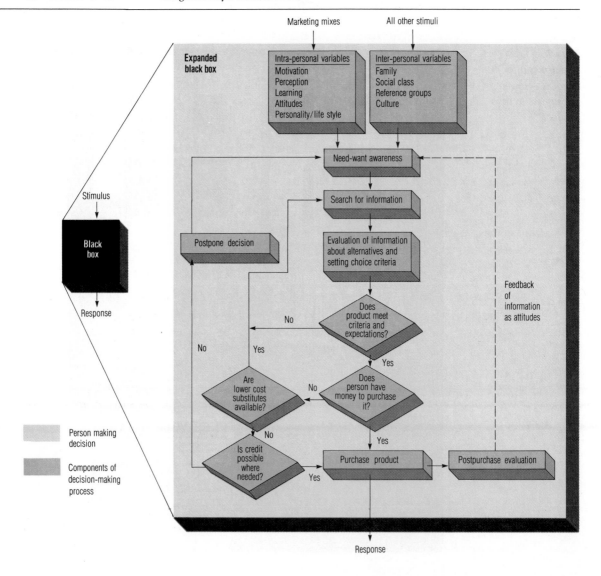

See Figure 6–11. These problem-solving approaches might be used for any kind of good or service.

Extensive problem solving is used when a need is completely new to a person—and much effort is taken to understand the need and how to satisfy it. A new college student, for example, may have feelings of loneliness, a need for company, a need for achievement, and so on. It may take him some time to figure out what he wants to do—and how to do it.

Limited problem solving involves *some* effort to understand a person's need and how best to satisfy it. Our college student, for example, might have tried various ways of satisfying his needs—and come up with several fairly good choices. So limited problem solving means deciding which choice is best at a particular time.

Routinized response behavior means mechanically selecting a particular way of satisfying a need whenever it occurs. When our college student feels the need for company, it might be quickly solved by meeting with friends in familiar surroundings. A daily trip to the local "hangout" might become the answer to this problem.

Routinized response behavior is typical for **low involvement products**—products which do not have high personal importance or relevance for the customer. Let's face it—buying a box of salt is probably not one of the burning issues in your life. Most marketing managers would like their target consumers to always buy their products—in a routinized way.[19]

New Ideas Need an Adoption Process

Really new concepts present a problem solver with a harder job—handling the adoption process. The **adoption process** means the steps which individuals go through on the way to accepting—or rejecting—a new idea. It is similar to the problem-solving process, but the adoption process makes clearer the role of learning. Note how promotion could affect the adoption process.

The adoption process for an individual moves through some definite steps, as follows:

1. Awareness—the potential customer comes to know about the product—but lacks details. He may not even know how it works—or what it will do.
2. Interest—*if* he becomes interested, he gathers general information and facts about the product.

■ FIGURE 6–11   Problem-solving continuum

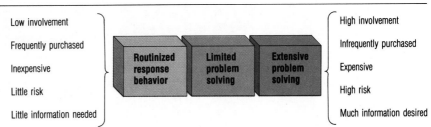

| Low involvement | Routinized response behavior | Limited problem solving | Extensive problem solving | High involvement |

Low involvement / High involvement
Frequently purchased / Infrequently purchased
Inexpensive / Expensive
Little risk / High risk
Little information needed / Much information desired

3. Evaluation—he begins to make a mental trial—applying the product to his own situation.
4. Trial—the customer may buy the product so that he can actually try it. A product that is either too expensive to try—or can't be found for trial—may never be adopted.
5. Decision—the customer decides on either adoption or rejection. A satisfactory experience may lead to adoption of the product and regular use. According to learning theory, reinforcement will lead to adoption.
6. Confirmation—the adopter continues to rethink the decision to support the decision.[20]

Dissonance May Set in after the Decision

After a decision has been made, a buyer may have second thoughts. He may have had to choose from among several attractive choices—weighing the pros and cons and finally making a decision. Later doubts, however, may lead to **dissonance**—tension caused by uncertainty about the rightness of a decision. Dissonance may lead a buyer to search for more information—to confirm the wisdom of the decision—and help reduce tension.[21]

■ FIGURE 6–12 Relation of problem-solving process, adoption process, and learning (given a problem)

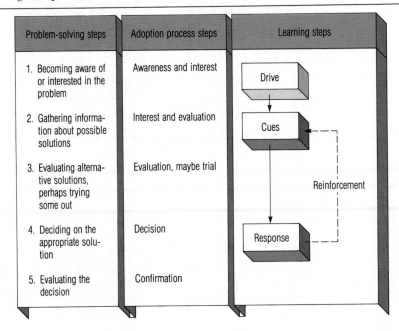

SEVERAL PROCESSES ARE RELATED AND RELEVANT TO STRATEGY PLANNING

The relation between the problem-solving process, the adoption process, and learning can be seen in Figure 6–12. It is important to see that they can be changed by promotion. Also note that the way buyers solve problems will affect the kind of physical distribution system needed. If customers don't want to travel far to shop, then more outlets may be needed to get their business. Also, customer attitudes help determine what price to charge. You can see that knowing how a target market thinks and behaves will aid marketing strategy planning.

■ CONCLUSION

In this chapter, we have analyzed the individual consumer as a problem solver who is influenced by intra- and inter-personal variables. Our "black box" model of buyer behavior helps tie together many variables into one process.

Consumer buying behavior results from the consumer's efforts to satisfy needs and wants. We discussed some reasons why consumers buy—and saw that consumer behavior can't be fully explained by only a list of needs.

We also saw that our society is divided into social classes. The effect of reference groups and opinion leaders was discussed, too.

A buyer behavior model was presented to help you integrate the present findings—and any new data you might obtain from marketing research. As of now, the behavioral sciences can only offer theories—which the marketing manager must blend with intuition and judgment in developing marketing strategies.

Marketing research can be used to answer specific questions. But if there is neither the money—nor the time—for research, marketing managers will have to depend on the available description of present behavior—and "guesstimates" about future behavior.

We have more information on consumer behavior than is generally used by business managers. Applying this information may help you find your breakthrough opportunity.

■ QUESTIONS AND PROBLEMS

1. Discuss the impact of our "aging culture" on marketing strategy planning.

2. Some demographic characteristics are likely to be more important than others in determining market potential. For each of the following characteristics, identify two products for which this characteristic is *most* important: (*a*) size of geographic area, (*b*) population, (*c*) income, (*d*) stage of life cycle.

3. Does the growing homogeneity of the consumer market mean there will be fewer opportunities to segment markets? Do you feel that all consumers of about equal income will probably spend their incomes similarly—and demand similar products?

4. What is the behavioral science concept which underlies the "black box" model of consumer behavior? Does this concept have operational relevance to marketing managers; i.e., if it is a valid concept, can they make use of it?

5. Explain what is meant by a hierarchy of needs and provide examples of one or more products which enable you to satisfy each of the four levels of need.

6. Cut out two recent advertisements: one full-page color ad from a magazine and one large display from a newspaper. Indicate which needs are being appealed to in each case.

7. Explain how an understanding of consumers' learning processes might affect marketing strategy planning.

8. Explain psychographics and life-style analysis. Explain how it might be useful for planning marketing strategies to reach college students as compared to the "average" consumer.

9. How does culture affect purchasing behavior? Give two specific examples.

10. How should the social class structure affect the planning of a new restaurant in a large city? How might the four Ps be adjusted?

11. What social class would you associate with each of the following phrases or items?

a. Sports cars.
b. *True Story, True Romances,* etc.
c. *New Yorker.*
d. *Playboy.*
e. People watching "soap operas."
f. TV bowling shows.
g. Families that serve martinis, especially before dinner.
h. Families who dress formally for dinner regularly.
i. Families who are distrustful of banks (keep money in socks or mattresses).
j. Owners of French poodles.

In each case, choose one class, if you can. If you are not able to choose one class but rather feel that several classes are equally likely, then so indicate. In those cases where you feel that all classes are equally interested or characterized by a particular item, choose all five classes.

12. Illustrate how the reference group concept may apply in practice by explaining how you personally are influenced by some reference group for some product. What are the implications of such behavior for marketing managers?

13. What new status symbols are replacing the piano and automobile? Do these products have any characteristics in common? If they do, what are some possible status symbols of the future?

14. Illustrate the three levels of problem solving with an example from your own personal experience.

15. On the basis of the data and analysis presented in Chapters 4 and 6, what kind of buying behavior would you expect to find for the following products: (*a*) canned peas, (*b*) toothpaste, (*c*) ballpoint pens, (*d*) baseball gloves, (*e*) sport coats, (*f*) dishwashers, (*g*) encyclopedias, (*h*) automobiles, and (*i*) motorboats? Set up a chart for your answer with products along the left-hand margin as the row headings and the following factors as headings for the columns: (*a*) how consumers would shop for these products, (*b*) how far they would go, (*c*) whether they would buy by brand, (*d*) whether they would wish to compare with other products, and (*e*) any other factors they should consider. Insert short answers—words or phrases are satisfactory—in the various boxes. Be prepared to discuss how the answers you put in the chart would affect each product's marketing mix.

■ **SUGGESTED CASES**

7. Nite-Time Motel

9. Barnes Florist Shop

Chapter 7 ■ Industrial and intermediate customers and their buying behavior

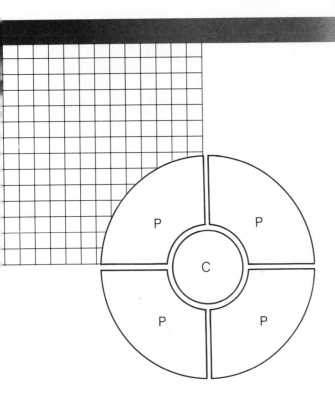

When you finish this chapter, you should:

1. Know who intermediate customers are.

2. Know about the number and distribution of manufacturers.

3. Understand the problem-solving behavior of manufacturers' purchasing agents.

4. Know the basic methods used in industrial buying.

5. Know how buying by retailers, wholesalers, and governments is similar to—and different from—industrial buying.

6. Recognize the important new terms (shown in red).

Intermediate customers buy more than final consumers!

Most of us think *customer* means only the individual final consumer. In fact, more purchases are made by intermediate customers. In this chapter we'll talk about these intermediate consumers—who they are, where they are, and how they buy.

Intermediate customers are any buyers from producers of basic raw materials to final consumers. There are great marketing opportunities in serving intermediate customers—and a student heading toward a business career has a good chance of working with these customers.

Many of the behavioral influences we discussed in the last chapter apply to intermediate customers, too. After all, *people* do the buying. But there are also some important differences—as the following example shows.

General Motors wanted to cut the weight of its cars—to improve gas mileage and be able to compete with imports. Reynolds Aluminum assigned a sales representative—John Biggs—to the account. Reynolds felt its lightweight metals might solve GM's problem. Meetings were arranged with GM engineers, production managers, quality-control and safety experts. Biggs listened to each one and offered advice about which parts could be made of lighter metals—and what technical problems had to be considered.

After more than a year, GM wrote detailed specifications for the lightweight parts it wanted—and asked for bids. In preparing a bid, John Biggs was pleased to see that many of his suggestions appeared in the GM specifications. When Biggs was called by a GM buyer, he was told that the company had picked several suppliers—to make sure of supply and keep suppliers on their toes—but that Reynolds would get a good share of the new business.

The emphasis in this chapter will be on the buying behavior of manufacturers—because we know most about them. Other intermediate customers seem to buy in much the same way.

INTERMEDIATE CUSTOMERS ARE DIFFERENT

There are only about 15 million intermediate customers in the United States—(compare this to the more than 225 million final consumers!). See Figure 7–1. These customers do many different jobs—and many different market dimensions are needed to describe all these different markets.

Even Small Differences Are Important

Understanding how and why intermediate customers buy is important. Competition is often rough in intermediate markets. Even small differences can affect the success of a marketing mix.

Since sellers usually approach each intermediate customer directly—through a sales representative—there is more chance to adjust the marketing mix for each individual customer. It is even possible that a special marketing mix will be developed for each individual customer. This is carrying target marketing to its extreme! But when a customer's purchases are large, it may be worth it.

In such situations, the individual sales rep carries more responsibility for strategy planning. This is relevant to your career planning, since these jobs are very challenging—and pay well.

■ FIGURE 7–1   Kind and number of intermediate customers in 1976–1977

Source: *Statistical Abstract of the United States, 1982–1983.*

■ FIGURE 7–2   Size distribution of manufacturing establishments, 1977

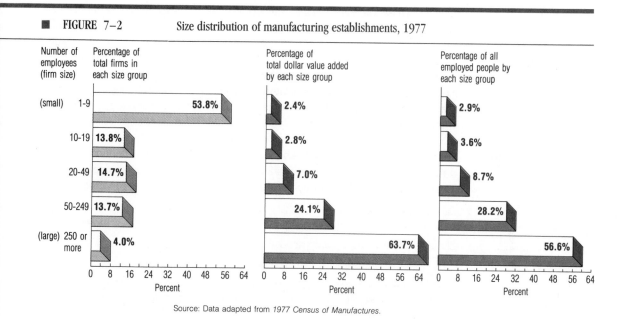

Source: Data adapted from *1977 Census of Manufactures.*

MANUFACTURERS ARE IMPORTANT CUSTOMERS

There Are Not Many Big Ones

There are very few manufacturers compared to final consumers—and most manufacturers are quite small. In the industrial market, there are less than 500,000 manufacturers. In small plants, the owners are often the buyers. They are less formal about the buying process than buyers in the relatively few large plants. Larger plants, however, employ the majority of workers—and produce a large share of the value added by manufacturing. See Figure 7–2. For example, at the last census, plants with 250 or more employees numbered only about 14,000—4 percent of the total—yet they employed nearly 60 percent of the production employees and produced about two thirds of the value added by manufacturers. You can see that these large plants are important markets.

Customers Cluster in Geographic Areas

In addition to concentration by size, industrial markets are concentrated in big metropolitan areas—especially in the Midwest, Middle Atlantic states, and California.

The buyers for some of these larger manufacturers are even further concentrated in home offices—often in big cities. One of the large building materials manufacturers, for example, does most of its buying for more than 50 plants from its Chicago office. In such a case, a sales rep may be able to sell to plants all over the country without leaving his home city. This makes selling easier for competitors, too—and the market may be very competitive. The importance of these big buyers has led some companies to set up "national account" sales forces—specially trained to cater to these needs. A geographically bound salesperson can be at a real disadvantage against such competitors.

Concentration by Industry

Manufacturers also concentrate by industry. Manufacturers of advanced electronics systems are concentrated in California's "Silicon Valley" near San Francisco and along Boston's "Route 128." The steel industry is concentrated in the Pittsburgh, Birmingham (Alabama), and Chicago areas.

Much Data Is Available on Industrial Markets by SIC Codes

In industrial markets, marketing managers can focus their attention on a relatively few clearly defined markets and reach most of the business. Their efforts can be aided by very detailed census information reported by

FIGURE 7–3   Illustrative SIC breakdown for apparel industries

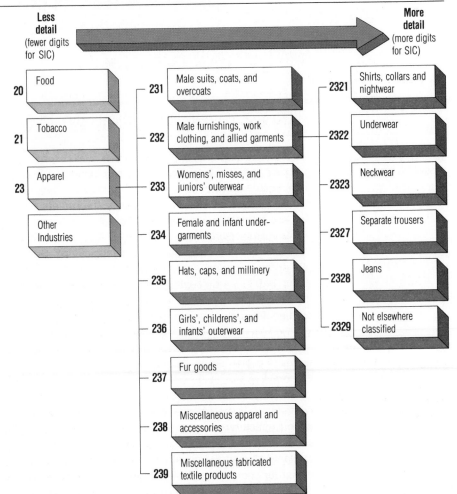

Standard Industrial Classification (SIC) Codes—groups of firms in similar lines of business. The data shows the number of firms, their sales volumes, and number of employees—broken down by industry, county, and MSA. These codes are a real help in market research—for those who can relate their own customers to SIC codes.[1]

SIC code breakdowns start with broad industry categories—such as food and related products (code 20), tobacco products (code 21), textile mill products (code 22), apparel (code 23), and so on.

Within each two-digit industry breakdown, much more detailed data may be available for three-digit and four-digit industries (that is, sub-industries of the two- or three-digit industries). Figure 7–3 shows the apparel industry breakdown.

INDUSTRIAL BUYERS ARE PROBLEM SOLVERS

Some people think of industrial buying as entirely different from consumer buying. But there are many similarities. In fact, the problem-solving framework introduced in Chapter 6 can be applied here.

Three Buying Processes Are Useful

In Chapter 6, we discussed three kinds of buying by consumers: extensive, limited, and routine buying. In industrial markets, it is useful to adapt these ideas a little—and work with *new-task buying,* a *modified rebuy,* or a *straight rebuy.*[2]

New-task buying occurs when a firm has a new need and the buyer wants a great deal of information. New-task buying can include setting product specifications and sources of supply.

A **modified rebuy** is the in-between process where some review of the buying situation is done—though not as much as in new-task buying.

A **straight rebuy** is a routine repurchase which may have been made many times before. Buyers probably would not bother looking for new information—or new sources of supply. Most of a company's small purchases are of this type. They take only a small part of a good buyer's time.

Note that a particular product might be bought in any of the three ways. Careful market analysis is needed to learn how the firm's products are bought—and by whom. A new-task buy will take much longer than a straight rebuy—and give much more chance for promotion impact by the seller. This can be seen in Figure 7–4—which shows the time—and many influences—involved in buying a special drill.

Industrial Buyers Are Becoming Specialists

The large size of some manufacturers has led to a need for buying specialists. **Purchasing agents** are buying specialists for manufacturers.

The purchasing agent usually must be seen first—before any other employee is contacted. Purchasing agents have a lot of power—and take a dim view of sales reps who try to go around them. In large companies, purchasing agents usually specialize by product area—and are real experts.

■ **FIGURE 7–4**   Decision network of the buying situations: Special drill

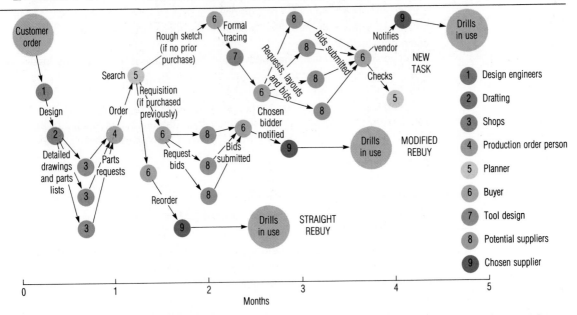

Source: Patrick J. Robinson and Charles W. Faris, *Industrial Buying and Creative Marketing* (Boston: Allyn & Bacon, 1967), p. 33. Reprinted by permission of the publisher.

Rather than being "sold," these buyers expect accurate information that will help them buy wisely. They need information on new goods and services—as well as tips on possible price changes, strikes, and other changes in business conditions. Most industrial buyers are serious and well educated. A sales rep should treat them accordingly.

Basic Purchasing Needs Are Economic

Industrial buyers are usually less emotional in their buying than final consumers. Buyers look for certain product characteristics—including economy, productivity, uniformity, purity, and ability to make the buyer's final product better.

In addition to product characteristics, buyers consider the reliability of the seller, general cooperativeness, ability to provide speedy maintenance and repair—as well as dependable and fast delivery.

Many buyers use **vendor analysis**—formal rating of suppliers on all areas of performance. Evaluating suppliers—and how they are working out—can result in better buying decisions.

Emotional Needs Are Relevant, Too

Vendor analysis emphasizes economic factors—but industrial purchasing does have an emotional side. Buyers are human—and want friendly relationships with suppliers. Some buyers are eager to imitate progressive competitors—or be the first to try new products. Such "innovators" might deserve special attention—especially when new products are being introduced.

Industrial buyers' basic purchasing needs are economic.

Buyers also want to protect their own position in the company. "Looking good" isn't easy for purchasing agents. They have to buy a wide variety of products from many sources—and make decisions involving many factors beyond their control. If a new source delivers low-quality materials—for example—you can guess who will be blamed. Poor service—or late delivery—also will reflect on the buyer's ability. Therefore, anyone or anything that helps the buyer look good to higher-ups has a definite appeal. In fact, this one factor may make the difference between a successful and an unsuccessful marketing mix.

Supply Sources Must Be Dependable

The matter of dependability is very important. There is nothing worse to a purchasing agent and a production manager than shutting down a production line because sellers haven't delivered the goods. Product quality is important, too. The cost of a small item may have little to do with its importance. If it causes the breakdown of a larger unit, it may result in a large loss—much greater than its own value.

A seller's marketing mix should satisfy both the needs of the buyer's company as well as the buyer's individual needs. Therefore, it helps to find some common area where both can be satisfied. (See Figure 7–5.)

Multiple Buying Influences in a Buying Center

Much of the work of the typical purchasing agent consists of straight rebuys. But in some cases—especially in new-task buying—a multiple buying influence may be important. **Multiple buying influence** means the buyer shares the purchasing decision with several people—perhaps even top management. Each of these "influences" may have very different interests.

It is helpful to think of a **buying center** that consists of all the people who participate in or influence a purchase. A salesperson must study each case carefully. Just finding out who to talk with may be hard—but thinking about the various roles in the buying center can help.

A sales rep might have to talk to every member of the buying center—stressing different topics for each. This not only complicates the promotion job—but also lengthens it. Approval of a routine order may take anywhere from a week to several months. On very important purchases—a new computer system, a new plant, or major equipment—the selling period may stretch out to a year or more.[3]

BASIC METHODS AND PRACTICES IN INDUSTRIAL BUYING

Should You Inspect, Sample, Describe, or Negotiate?

Industrial buyers—really, buyers of all types, including final consumers—can use four basic approaches to evaluating and buying products: (1) *inspection,* (2) *sampling,* (3) *description,* and (4) *negotiated contracts.* Understanding

■   FIGURE 7–5   A model of individual industrial buyer behavior—showing overlapping needs

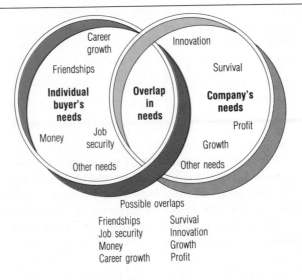

Multiple buying influence is often involved in industrial purchase decisions.

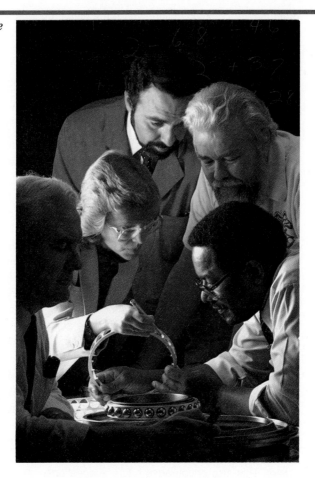

the differences in these buying methods is important in strategy planning—so let's look at each approach now.

Inspection Looks at Everything

Inspection buying means looking at every item. It is used for products that are not standardized—for example: livestock, used buildings, or used cars. These products are often sold in open markets—or at auction. Buyers inspect the goods and either bargain with the seller—or bid against competitors.

Sampling Looks at Some

Sampling buying means looking at only part of a potential purchase. As products become more standardized—perhaps because of more careful grading or quality control—buying by sample becomes possible. For example, a power company might buy miles of heavy electric cable. A sample section might be heated to the melting point—to be certain it is safe.

Prices may be based on a sample. The general price level may be set by demand and supply factors—but the actual price level may be adjusted, depending on the quality of a specific sample. This kind of buying is used in grain markets, for example—where the actual price is based on an analysis of a sample taken from a carload of corn or wheat.

Description Just Describes Accurately

Description (specification) buying means buying from a written (or verbal) description of the product. The goods are not inspected. This method is used when quality can be controlled and described—as with many branded products.

Today, most buyers of fruits and vegetables accept government grading standards for these products. They are packed in the fields and sold without further inspection or sampling. This, of course, reduces the cost of buying and is used by buyers whenever practical.

Negotiated Contracts Explain How to Handle Relationships

Negotiated contract buying means agreeing to a contract that allows for changing the purchase arrangements.

Sometimes, the buyer knows roughly what is needed—but can't fix all the details in advance. The specifications—or total requirements—may change as the job progresses. This is found, for example, in research and development work—and in the building of special-purpose machinery or buildings. In such cases, the general project is described. Then a basic price may be agreed on—with guidelines for changes and price adjustments up or down. The whole contract may even be subject to bargaining as the work proceeds.

Buyers May Favor Loyal, Helpful Suppliers

To be sure of dependable quality, a buyer may develop loyalty to certain suppliers. This is especially important when buying non-standardized products. When a friendly relationship is developed over the years, the supplier almost becomes a part of the buyer's organization.

Most buyers have a sense of fair play. When a seller suggests a new idea that saves the buyer's company money, the seller is usually rewarded with orders. This also encourages future suggestions.

In contrast, buyers who use a bid system exclusively may not be offered much beyond the basic goods or services. They are interested mainly in price. Marketing managers who have developed better marketing mixes may not seek such business—at least with their better marketing mixes.

But Buyers Must Spread Their Risk— By Seeking Several Sources

Even if a firm has developed the best marketing mix possible, it probably won't get all the business of its industrial customers. Purchasing agents usually look for several dependable sources of supply. They must protect themselves from unpredictable events—such as strikes, fires, or other problems in one of their suppliers' plants. Still, a good marketing mix is likely to win a larger share of the total business.

Most Buyers Try to Routinize Buying

Most firms use a buying procedure that tries to routinize the process. When someone wants to buy something, a **requisition**—a request to buy something—is filled out. After approval by a supervisor, the requisition is forwarded to the buyer—for placement with the "best" seller. Now the buyer is responsible for placing a purchase order—and getting delivery by the date requested.

Borden Chemical knows that industrial buyers want dependable sources of supply.

ZERO DEFECTS. In service, in delivery. That's our goal.

At Borden Graphics, our service, delivery and production systems interact with each other. This chain of systems improves performance and enables us to achieve the same standard for each one. The very highest.

Our staff of quality control, R&D and sales professionals are dedicated to delivering the best inks, pigments and flushes. Their expertise, aided by the most sophisticated testing equipment in the business, enables them to respond to any problem, however complex.

If there's a pressroom problem, they can rectify it immediately. And if, for any reason, you have an unexpected customer request, they can help you respond to it without delay.

Zero defects is our goal. Our chain of systems and our people make sure we reach it.

ZERO DEFECTS. That's our goal.

For more information on these or any ink subject, call toll-free*. K. Fritz, 1-800-543-1670. *In Ohio call 1-800-582-1621.
Or write Borden Chemical, Graphics Division, 630 Glendale-Milford Road, Cincinnati, Ohio 45215.   *Borden Inc 1983

BORDEN CHEMICAL

Ordering May Be Routine after Requisitioning

Requisitions are converted to purchase orders as quickly as possible. Straight rebuys are usually made the day the requisition is received. New-task and modified rebuys take longer. If time is important, the buyer may place the order by telephone—and then a confirming purchase order is typed and sent out.

It Pays to Know the Buyer

Notice the importance of being one of the regular sources of supply. The buyers don't even call potential suppliers for straight rebuys.

You can see that having a good image is an advantage for a sales rep. It is likely that he will get a slightly larger share of the orders. Moving from a 20 percent to a 30 percent share may not seem like much from a buyer's point of view, but for the seller it is a 50 percent increase in sales!

Industrial buyers favor helpful suppliers who offer solutions to their problems.

Some Buy by Computer

Some buyers have turned over a large part of their routine order-placing to computers. They program decision rules that tell the computer how to order—and leave the details of following through to the machine. When economic conditions change, the buyers modify the computer instructions. When nothing unusual happens, however, the computer system continues to routinely rebuy as needs develop—printing out new purchase orders to the regular suppliers.

Obviously, it's a big "sale" to be selected as a supplier—and routinely called up by the computer. It is also obvious that such a buyer will be more impressed by an attractive marketing mix for a whole *line* of products—not just a lower price for a particular order. It's too expensive—and too much trouble—to change a whole buying system just because somebody is offering a low price on a particular day.

**Tax Rules Affect
Spending Decisions**

How the cost of a particular purchase is handled on a firm's profit and loss statement has a big effect on a buyer. Internal Revenue rules—and accepted accounting practice—recognize two types of purchases: capital and expense items.

Capital items are durable goods—such as large machinery or buildings—which are charged off over many years, that is, depreciated. The depreciation period could be from 2 to 50 years—depending on the particular item. Capital purchases are important—and tie up much of the firm's money for a long period. So managers avoid quick decisions. New-task buying and multiple buying influence are common.[4]

In contrast to capital items, **expense items** are short-lived goods and services which are charged off as they are used—usually in the year of purchase. A company isn't spending against future profits when it buys these items—and so is less concerned about costs—especially if business is good. Multiple buying influence is less here. Straight rebuys are more common.

**Inventory Policy May
Determine Purchases**

Industrial firms generally try to maintain an adequate inventory—at least enough to keep production lines moving. There is nothing worse than to have a production line close down.

Adequate inventory is often stated in terms of number of days' supply—for example, 60- or 90-days' supply. But what a 60- or 90-days' supply is depends on the level of demand for the company's products. If the demand rises sharply—say by 10 percent—then total purchases will expand by more than 10 percent to maintain inventory levels *and* meet the new needs. On the other hand, if sales drop 10 percent, actual needs and inventory requirements drop, too. Buying may even stop while inventory is being "worked off." During such

A printing press is a capital item, but the paper is an expense item.

a cutback, a seller probably couldn't stimulate sales—even by reducing price. The buyer is just "not in the market."

Reciprocity Helps Sales, but . . .

Reciprocity means trading sales for sales—that is, "If you buy from me, I'll buy from you." If a company's customers also can supply products which the firm buys, then the sales departments of both buyer and seller may try to "trade" sales for sales. Purchasing agents generally resist reciprocity. But often it is forced on them by their sales departments.

When both prices and quality are competitive, it's hard to ignore pressure from the sales department. An outside supplier can only hope to become an alternate source of supply—and wait for the "insiders" to let their quality slip or prices rise.

The U.S. Justice Department frowns on reciprocity. It tries to block reciprocal buying on the grounds that it injures competition. This has forced some firms that have depended on reciprocity to rethink their marketing strategies.[5]

RETAILERS AND WHOLESALERS ARE PROBLEM SOLVERS, TOO

They Must Buy for Their Customers

Most retail and wholesale buyers see themselves as purchasing agents for their target customers. They believe the old saying: "Goods well bought are half sold." They do *not* see themselves as sales agents for manufacturers. They buy what they think they can sell. They don't try to make value judgments about the desirability of what they are selling. Instead, they focus on the needs and attitudes of *their* target customers.

They Must Buy Too Many Items

Most retailers carry a large number of items—drug stores up to 12,000 items, hardware stores from 3,000 to 25,000, and grocery stores up to 20,000 items. They just don't have the time to pay close attention to every item.

Wholesalers, too, handle so many items that they can't give constant attention to each one. A drug wholesaler may stock up to 125,000 items—and a dry-goods (textiles and sewing supplies) wholesaler up to 250,000 items.

You can see why retailers and wholesalers buy most of their products as straight rebuys. Many buyers are annoyed by the number of sales reps who call on them with little to say about one or a few items. Sellers to these markets must understand the size of the buyer's job—and have something useful to say and do when they call. For example, besides just improving relations, they might take inventory, set up displays, or arrange shelves—while looking for a chance to talk about specific products.

In larger firms, buyers spend more time on individual items. They may specialize in certain lines. Some large chains even expect buyers to seek out additional and lower-cost sources of supply.[6]

This wholesaler uses a computer-to-telephone hookup to place orders and control inventory.

They Must Watch Inventories and Computer Output

The large number of items bought and stocked by wholesalers and retailers means that inventories must be watched carefully. Smart retailers and wholesalers try to maintain a selling stock and *some* reserve stock—and then depend on a continual flow through the channel.

Most larger firms now use computer-controlled inventory control systems. Even small firms are using automated control systems. Now, for relatively low cost, electronic cash registers and countertop microcomputers can keep a count of items sold. Such systems can print daily unit control reports—which show sales of every product on the shelves. Buyers with this kind of information know their needs. They become more demanding about dependability of delivery. They also know how goods move—and what promotion help might be needed.

Automatic computer ordering is a natural outgrowth of such systems. For example, some wholesale drug companies give retail pharmacists a microcomputer to maintain all inventory records. At the end of the day, the druggist types in a command—and the computer automatically dials the wholesaler's computer—and places an order which arrives the next morning.

Some Are Not Always "Open to Buy"

Just as manufacturers sometimes try to reduce their inventory—and are "not in the market"—retailers and wholesalers may stop buying for similar reasons. No special promotions or price cuts will make them buy.

In retailing, another factor affects buying. A buyer may be controlled by a strict budget. This is really a miniature profit and loss statement for each department or merchandise line. In an effort to make a profit, the buyer tries to forecast sales, merchandise costs, and expenses. The figure for "cost of merchandise" is the amount the buyer has to spend during the budget period. If the money hasn't been spent, the buyer is **open to buy**—that is, the buyer has budgeted funds which he can spend during the current time period.

Owners or Professional Buyers May Buy

The buyers in small stores—and for many wholesalers—are the owners or managers. There is a very close relationship between buying and selling. In larger operations, buyers may specialize in certain lines—and supervise the salespeople who sell what they buy. These buyers are in close contact with their customers—*and* with their salespeople. The salespeople are sensitive to the effectiveness of the buyer's efforts—especially when they are on commission. A buyer may even buy some items to satisfy the preferences of his salespeople. These salespeople can't be ignored in a promotion effort. The multiple buying influence may make the difference.

As sales volumes rise, a buyer may specialize in buying only—and have no responsibility for sales. Sears is an extreme case. But it has a buying department of more than 3,000—supported by a staff department of over 1,400. These are professional buyers—who often know more about prices, quality, and trends in the market than their suppliers. Obviously, they are big potential customers—and should be approached differently than the typical small retailer.

Resident Buyers May Help a Firm's Buyers

Resident buyers are independent buying agents who work—in central markets—for several retailer or wholesaler customers in outlying areas. They work in cities like New York, Chicago, Los Angeles, and San Francisco. They buy new styles and fashions—and fill-in items—as their customers run out of stock during the year. Some resident buyers have hundreds of employees—and buy more than $1 billion worth of goods a year.

Resident buying organizations fill a need—helping small channel members (producers and middlemen) who can't afford large sales forces. Resident buyers usually are paid an annual fee—based on the amount they buy.

Committee Buying Happens, Too

In some large companies—especially chains selling foods and drugs—the major buying decisions may be made by a *buying committee.* The seller still calls and gives a "pitch" to a buyer—but the buyer does not have final responsibility. The buyer prepares a form summarizing the proposal for a new product. The seller may help complete this form—but probably won't get to present his story to the buying committee in person.

This rational, almost cold-blooded approach reduces the impact of the persuasive salesperson. It has become necessary because of the flood of new products. Consider the problem facing grocery chains. In an average week, up to 250 new items are offered to the buying offices of the larger food chains. If all were accepted, 10,000 new items would be added during a single year! Obviously, buyers must be hard-headed and impersonal. About 90 percent of the new items presented to food stores are rejected.

Marketing managers for wholesalers and manufacturers must develop good marketing mixes when buying becomes this organized and competitive.

Armstrong Rubber knows that government agencies are big customers.

THE GOVERNMENT MARKET

Size and Variety

Some marketers avoid the government market because they think that government "red tape" is "more trouble than it's worth." This is a mistake because government is the largest customer group in the United States. About 21 percent of the U.S. gross national product is spent by various government units. Government buyers spend more than $500 *billion* a year—to buy almost every kind of product. They run schools, police departments, and military organizations. They also run supermarkets, public utilities, research laboratories, offices, hospitals, and even liquor stores. Government buying cannot be ignored by an aggressive marketing manager.

Bid Buying Is Common

Many government buyers buy by description—using a required bidding policy which is open to public review. Often the government buyer is required to accept the lowest bid. You can see how important it is for the buyer to accurately describe his need—so he can write a specification that is precise and complete. Otherwise, sellers may submit a bid that fits the "specs" but doesn't really match what is needed. By law, the buyer might have to accept the low bid—for an unwanted product. Writing specifications is not easy—and buyers usually appreciate the help of well-informed salespeople.

Specification and bidding difficulties aren't problems in all government orders. Some items which are bought frequently—or for which there are widely accepted standards—are purchased routinely by simply placing an order at a previously approved price. To share in this business, a supplier may need to be on the list of "approved suppliers."

Negotiated Contracts Are Common, Too	Negotiation (bargaining) is often necessary when products are not standardized. Unfortunately, this is exactly where "favoritism" and "influence" can slip in. Nevertheless, negotiation is an important buying method in government sales. Here, a marketing mix must emphasize more than just low price.[7]
Learning What Government Wants	There are more than 80,000 local government units—school districts, cities, counties, and states—as well as many federal agencies that make purchases. Since most government contracts are advertised, potential suppliers should focus on the government units they want to sell to—and learn their bidding methods.
	A marketer can learn a lot about potential government target markets from various government publications. The Federal Government's *Commerce Business Daily* lists most current purchase bid requests. Similarly, the Small Business Administration's *U.S. Purchasing, Specifications, and Sales Directory* explains government procedures—since it wants to encourage competition for its business. State and local governments also offer guidance. There are trade magazines and trade associations providing information on how to reach schools, hospitals, highway departments, park departments, and so on. These are unique target markets—and must be treated as such when developing marketing strategies.

■ CONCLUSION

In this chapter, we have considered the number, size, location, and buying habits of various intermediate customers—to try to identify logical dimensions for segmenting markets. We saw that the nature of the buyer and the buying situation are important. We also learned that the problem-solving models of buyer behavior introduced in Chapter 6 apply here—with modifications.

The chapter emphasized buying in the industrial market—because more is known about

manufacturers' buying behavior. Some differences in buying by retailers and wholesalers were discussed. The government market was described as an extremely large, complex set of markets that offer opportunities for target marketers.

A clear understanding of intermediate customer buying behavior can aid marketing strategy planning. And since there are fewer intermediate customers than final consumers, it may even be possible to develop a unique strategy for each potential customer.

■ QUESTIONS AND PROBLEMS

1. Discuss the importance of thinking "target marketing" when analyzing intermediate customer markets. How easy is it to isolate homogeneous market segments in these markets?

2. Explain how SIC codes might be helpful in evaluating and understanding industrial markets.

3. Compare and contrast the problem-solving approaches used by final consumers and by industrial buyers.

4. Describe the situations which would lead to the use of the three different buying processes for a particular product—such as computer tapes.

5. Compare and contrast the buying processes of final consumers and industrial buyers.

6. Distinguish among the four methods of evaluating and buying (inspection, sampling, etc.) and indicate which would probably be most suitable for furniture, baseball gloves, coal, and pencils—assuming that some intermediate customer is the buyer.

7. Discuss the advantages and disadvantages of reciprocity from the industrial buyer's point of view. Are the advantages and disadvantages merely reversed from the seller's point of view?

8. Is it always advisable to buy the highest-quality product?

9. Discuss how much latitude an industrial buyer has in selecting the specific brand and the specific source of supply for that product, once a product has been requisitioned by some produc-tion department. Consider this question with specific reference to pencils, paint for the offices, plastic materials for the production line, a new factory, and a large printing press. How should the buyer's attitudes affect the seller's marketing mix?

10. How does the kind of industrial good affect manufacturers' buying habits and prac-tices? Consider lumber for furniture, a lathe, nails for a box factory, and a floor cleaner.

11. Considering the nature of retail buying, outline the basic ingredients of promotion to retail buyers. Does it make any difference what kinds of products are involved? Are any other factors relevant?

12. The government market is obviously an extremely large one, yet it is often slighted or even ignored by many firms. "Red tape" is cer-tainly one reason, but there are others. Discuss the situation and be sure to include the possibility of segmenting in your analysis.

13. Based on your understanding of buying by manufacturers and governments, outline the basic ingredients of promotion to each type of customer. Use two products as examples for each type. Is the promotion job the same for each pair?

■ **SUGGESTED CASES**

---

3. Apex Chemical Company

5. Indian Steel Company

Chapter 8 ■ Segmenting markets and forecasting their potential

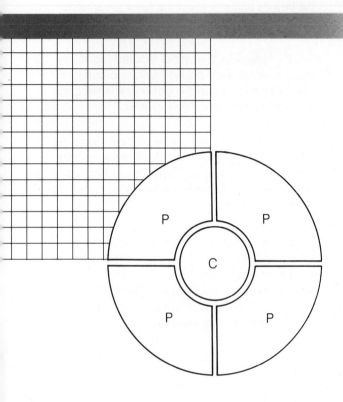

When you finish this chapter, you should:

1. Know what market segmentation is.

2. Know dimensions which may be useful for segmenting markets.

3. Understand how to segment markets into sub-markets.

4. Know a seven-step approach to segmenting which you can do yourself.

5. Understand several forecasting approaches which extend past behavior.

6. Understand several forecasting approaches which do not rely on extending past behavior.

7. Recognize the important new terms (shown in red).

You have to aim at somebody—not just everybody—to make a profit.

Aiming at specific "somebodies" is the big difference between production-oriented managers and target marketers.

Production-oriented managers think of their markets in terms of *products*—and aim at everybody. They think of the "women's clothing" market or the "car" market.

Target marketers think of markets in terms of *customers' needs*. They segment these product-markets into sub-markets—as they look for attractive opportunities. A computer manufacturer, for example, might aim only at the government market or the large Fortune 500 companies. And a restaurant owner might choose to aim only at people seeking gourmet dining—rather than everyone who "eats out."

In Chapter 3, we began to talk about market segmentation—including *naming* generic markets and broad product-markets. Now we'll go into more depth—to see if it's practical to segment broad product-markets into sub-markets. We'll also talk about forecasting sales in these product-markets. Segmenting markets isn't just a classroom exercise—if a product isn't aimed at a specific target market big enough to support the effort, all the effort will be wasted.

MARKET SEGMENTATION REQUIRES JUDGMENT

Effective market segmentation is a two-step process: (1) *naming* broad product-markets and then (2) *segmenting* these broad product-markets into more homogeneous sub-markets—also called product-markets—to select target markets and develop suitable marketing mixes.

This two-step process isn't well understood. First-time market segmentation efforts often fail because beginners start with the whole "mass market" and

One of E. F. Hutton's target markets is the growing segment of professional women.

Are a woman's financial requirements different from a man's?

Some are astonishingly similar, others vastly different.

Financial requirements are as diverse as individuals. But the need for wise investing is common to all.

That is why for over 78 years, people have been listening to E.F. Hutton.

When EF Hutton talks, people listen.

then try to find one or two demographic characteristics to explain differences. But customer behavior is too complex to be explained in terms of just one or two demographic characteristics. For example, not all old men or all young women buy the same products or brands. Other dimensions usually must be considered—starting with customer needs.

Sometimes, many different dimensions are needed to describe sub-markets. We saw this in the home-decorating market example in Chapter 2. Recall that the British paint manufacturer finally settled on the "cost-conscious couple" as its target market. In that case, four possible target markets with very different dimensions were placed in the four corners of a market diagram. This is the kind of market segmentation we want to do.

Naming Markets Is Dis-Aggregating	The first step in effective market segmentation is to name the broad product-market of interest to the firm. This was discussed in Chapter 3. Recall, that a product-market name should consist of four parts: product type, customer (user) functional needs, customer type, and geographic area. Such a four-part definition can be clumsy, so it's practical to reduce it to a "nickname"—as long as everyone understands what the nickname stands for.

This product-market naming approach helps get us in the "right ballpark," but it usually does *not* provide the detailed product-market names which segmenters want. The naming step is just a narrowing-down process—a dis-aggregating process. It emphasizes functional needs.

Now let's talk about *segmenting.* This focuses on the needs of different customer types in the geographic area we named in our broad product-market.

Segmenting in an Aggregating Process	Marketing-oriented managers think of **segmenting** as an aggregating (gathering) process. They start with the idea that each person is "one of a kind"—and can be described by a special set of dimensions. This is shown in Figure 8–1. Here the many dots show each person's position in a product-market with two dimensions—need for status and need for dependability. While each person's position is unique, you can see that many of them are similar in terms of how much status and dependability they want. So a segmenter can aggregate (gather) these people into three (an arbitrary number) relatively homogeneous sub-markets—A, B, and C. Group A might be called "Status Oriented" and group C "Dependability Oriented." Members of group B want both—and might be called the "Demanders."

One of the difficult things about segmenting is that some potential customers just don't fit neatly into market segments. For example, not everyone in Figure 8–1 was put into one of the three groups. They could be *forced* into one of the groups—but this wouldn't really be segmenting. Additional segments could be created—but they might be small and hard to please. These people are just too "unique." Marketers may have to ignore these customers—unless they are willing to pay a high price for special treatment.

How Far Should the Aggregating Go?	Segmenters have basically three choices: they can treat everyone alike; they can treat everyone differently; or they can try to aggregate people into

■ FIGURE 8–1

Every individual has his or her own position in a market—those with similar positions can be aggregated into potential target markets

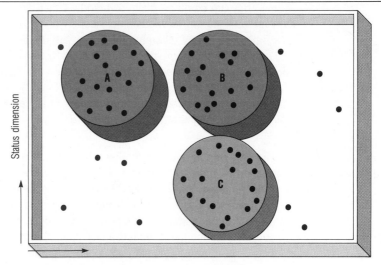

Dependability dimension

some workable number of relatively homogeneous sub-markets—and treat each sub-market differently.

Looking at Figure 8–1, remember we said that there were three sub-markets. This was an arbitrary number, however. As Figure 8–2 shows, there may really be *six* sub-markets. What do you think—does this product-market consist of three segments or six segments?

It's a Matter of Judgment

The number of sub-markets that should be formed depends more on judgment than on some scientific rule. There is no point in trying to segment a market if customer needs are all basically the same. Usually, however, there are some important differences—and segmenting is helpful. In fact, in very competitive markets, even small variations can make a big difference in how well a firm does against competitors.

Basically, a profit-oriented firm will probably want to continue aggregating potential customers into a larger market as long as its marketing mix could satisfy those customers—at a profit.

Criteria for Segmenting Product-Markets

Ideally, "good" product-market segments meet the following criteria:

1. *Homogeneous (similar) within*—the people in a market segment should be as similar as possible with respect to their segmenting dimensions—*and* their likely responses to marketing mix variables.
2. *Heterogeneous (different) between*—the people in different market segments should be as different as possible with respect to the segmenting dimensions—*and* their likely responses to marketing mix variables.

■ FIGURE 8–2   How many segments are there?

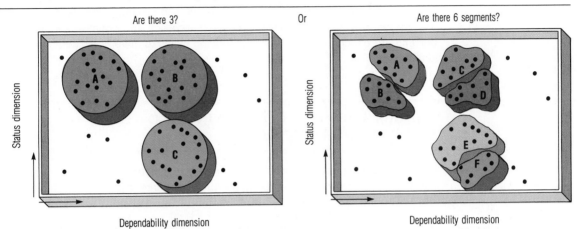

Are there 3?   Or   Are there 6 segments?

3. *Substantial*—the product-market segments should be big enough to be profitable.
4. *Operational*—their dimensions should be useful for identifying customers and deciding on marketing mix variables.

There is no point in having a dimension that isn't usable.

Number 4 is especially important—because it is possible to find dimensions which are useless. A personality trait such as moodiness, for example, might be found among the traits of heavy buyers of a product—but how could you use this fact? Personal salespeople would have to give a personality test to each buyer—an impossible task. Similarly, advertising media buyers or copywriters couldn't make much use of this information. So although moodiness might be related in some way to previous purchases, it would not be a useful dimension for segmenting.

Criterion 4 may lead to including readily available dimensions—such as demographics—to aid marketing mix planning. Dimensions such as age, income, location, and family size may be very useful—at least for Place and Promotion planning. In fact, it is difficult to make some Place and Promotion decisions without such information.

Profit Is the Balancing Point

Target marketers develop whole strategies—they don't just segment markets. As a practical matter, this means that cost considerations probably encourage *more aggregating*—to obtain economies of scale—while demand considerations suggest less aggregating—to satisfy needs more exactly.

Profit is the balancing point. It determines how unique a marketing mix the firm can afford to offer to a particular group.

Too Much Aggregating Is Risky

Segmenters must be careful not to aggregate too far in search of profit. As sub-markets are made larger, they become less homogeneous—and individual differences within each sub-market may begin to outweigh the similarities. This makes it harder to develop marketing mixes which can do an effective job of satisfying potential customers within each of the sub-markets. This also leaves the firm more open to competitive efforts—especially from innovative segmenters who are offering more attractive marketing mixes to more homogeneous sub-markets.[1]

THERE MAY BE BOTH QUALIFYING AND DETERMINING DIMENSIONS

We know that marketers must consider several dimensions when segmenting potential customers. Some dimensions may be more important than others,

The 4-wheel drive benefits of this car meet the needs of some consumers— who have been aggregated into a target market.

■ FIGURE 8–3   Finding the relevant segmenting dimensions

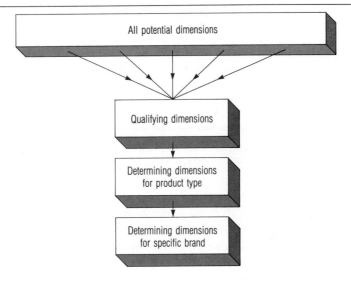

however, so it is useful to talk about **qualifying dimensions**--the dimensions which are relevant to a product-market—and **determining dimensions**—the dimensions which actually affect the purchase of a specific product or specific brand in a product-market. These are the segmenting dimensions we are seeking.

A prospective car buyer, for example, has to have enough money—or credit—to buy a car. He also must have—or be able to get—a driver's license. This still doesn't guarantee that he'll buy a car. He may just rent one—or continue borrowing his parents' or friends' cars—or hitchhike. He may not get around to actually buying a car until his status with his buddies is falling because he doesn't have "wheels." This need may lead him to buy *some* car. But it is not determining with respect to a specific brand or a specific model.

Determining Dimensions May Have to Be Very Specific

How specific the determining dimensions have to get depends on whether we are concerned with a general product type or a specific brand. See Figure 8–3. The more specific we want to be, the more particular the determining dimensions may have to be. In a particular case, the determining dimensions may seem minor. But they are important because they *are* the determining dimensions. In the car–status-seekers market, for example, paint colors—or the brand name—may determine which cars people buy.

Qualifying Dimensions Are Important, Too

The qualifying dimensions help identify the "core features" which must be offered to everyone in the broad product-market. Qualifying and determining dimensions work together to affect marketing strategy planning.

Different Dimensions May Be Needed for Different Segments in a Market

Each different product-market *within* the same broad product-market may be motivated by a different set of dimensions. In the "snack food" market, for example, health food enthusiasts might be interested in nutrition—dieters might care only about calories—and economical shoppers with lots of kids might be interested in volume to "fill them up." The related product-markets might be called: "health-conscious snack food market," "dieters' snack food market," and "kids' snack food market."

WHAT DIMENSIONS ARE USED TO SEGMENT MARKETS?

Segmenting forces the marketing manager to decide which product-market dimensions might be useful for planning marketing mixes. The dimensions should help guide marketing mix planning. Table 8–1 shows some of the kinds of dimensions we have been talking about in the last several chapters—and their probable effect on the four Ps. Ideally, we would like to describe any potential product-market in terms of all three types of customer-related dimensions—plus a product type description—because these dimensions will help us develop better marketing mixes.

Consumers have many dimensions—and several may be useful for segmenting a broad product-market. Table 8–2 shows some possible consumer market segmenting dimensions—and their typical breakdowns. As Table 8–2 shows, there are customer-related dimensions and situation-related dimensions—which may be more important in some cases.[2]

Table 8–3 shows some possible dimensions for segmenting industrial goods markets and typical breakdowns.

■ TABLE 8–1   Relation of potential target market dimensions to marketing mix decision areas

Potential target market dimensions	Effects on decision areas
1. Geographic location and other demographic characteristics of potential customers	Affects size of *Target Markets* (economic potential) and *Place* (where products should be made available) and *Promotion* (where and to whom to advertise)
2. Behavioral needs, attitudes, and how present and potential goods or services fit into customer's consumption patterns	Affects *Product* (design, packaging, length or width of product line) and *Promotion* (what potential customers need and want to know about the product offering, and what appeals should be used)
3. Urgency to get need satisfied and desire and willingness to compare and shop	Affects *Place* (how directly products are distributed from producer to consumer, how extensively they are made available, and the level of service needed) and *Price* (how much potential customers are willing to pay)

■ TABLE 8–2   Possible segmenting dimensions and typical breakdowns for consumer markets

Dimensions	Typical breakdowns
Customer related	
Geographic	
Region	Pacific, Mountain, West North Central, West South Central, East North Central, East South Central, South Atlantic, Middle Atlantic, New England
City, county,	
SMSA size	Under 5,000; 5,000–19,999; 20,000–49,999; 50,000–99,999; 100,000–249,999; 250,000–499,999; 500,000–999,999; 1,000,000–3,999,999; 4,000,000 or over
Demographic	
Age	Infant, under 6; 6–11; 12–17; 18–24; 25–34; 35–49; 50–64; 65 and over
Sex	Male, female
Family size	1–2, 3–4, 5+
Family life cycle	Young, single; young, married, no children; young, married, youngest child under 6; young, married, youngest child 6 or over; older, married, with children; older, married, no children under 18; older, single; other
Income	Under $5,000; $5,000–$7,999; $8,000–$9,999; $10,000–$14,999; $15,000–$24,999; $25,000 or over
Occupation	Professional and technical; managers, officials, and proprietors; clerical, sales; craftsmen, foremen; operatives; farmers; retired; students; housewives; unemployed
Education	Grade school or less, some high school, graduated high school, some college, college graduate
Religion	Catholic, Protestant, Jewish, other
Race	White, Black, Oriental, other
Nationality	American, British, French, German, etc.
Social class	Lower-lower, upper-lower, lower-middle, upper-middle, lower-upper, upper-upper
Situation related	
Benefits offered	
Need satisfiers	PSSP, economic, and more detailed needs
Product features..............	Situation specific, but to satisfy specific or general needs
Consumption or use patterns	
Rate of use	Heavy, medium, light, non-users
Use with other	
products	Situation specific, e.g., gas with a traveling vacation
Brand familiarity	Insistence, preference, recognition, non-recognition, rejection
Buying situation	
Kind of store	Convenience, shopping, specialty
Kind of shopping	Serious versus browsing, rushed versus leisurely
Depth of assortment	Out of stock, shallow, deep
Type of good	Convenience, shopping, specialty, unsought

| ■ TABLE 8–3 | Possible segmenting dimensions for industrial markets |

Type of organization—Manufacturing, institutional, government, public utility, military, farm, etc.

Demographics—Size
        Employees
        Sales volume
        SIC code
        Number of plants
        Geographic location:
          East, Southeast, South, Midwest, Mountains, Southwest, West
          Large city ⟶ rural

Type of good—Installations, accessories, components, raw materials, supplies, services

Type of buying situation—Decentralized ⟶ centralized
                Buyer ⟶ multiple buying influence
                Straight rebuy ⟶ modified rebuy ⟶ new buy

Source loyalty—Weak ⟶ strong loyalty
          Last resort ⟶ second source ⟶ first source

Kinds of commitments—Contracts, agreements, financial aids

Reciprocity—None ⟶ complete

With so many possible dimensions—and knowing that several dimensions may be needed to show what is determining in specific product-markets, how should we proceed?

Basically, we start with the assumption that potential customers are reasonably sensible problem solvers who have needs they want to satisfy. This doesn't mean they always solve their problems in a strictly economic way—or the way the marketer might solve them. But we assume that they do follow a somewhat logical process. Further, research seems to suggest that most customers only have a few really important determining dimensions—so the task is to try to understand the "few" determining dimensions of groups of customers.

A SEVEN–STEP APPROACH TO SEGMENTING CONSUMER PRODUCT–MARKETS

We have talked about the ideas behind segmenting. Now let's look at a seven-step approach which can be used without expensive marketing research—or computer analyses. More sophisticated methods are discussed later—but this one works and has led to successful strategies.

To be sure you understand this approach, we'll list each step separately, explain its importance, and provide a common example to show how each step works. The example is rental housing—in particular, the apartment market in a big urban area.

1. Name the broad product-market area to be segmented

After the firm has defined its objectives, it must decide what market it wants to be in. If it is already in some product-market, this might be a good starting point. If it is just starting out, then many more choices are open—although the available resources, both human and financial, will limit the possibilities. Remember—it is better to build on the firm's strengths—while trying to avoid its weaknesses and competitors' strengths.

Example: The firm might be building small utility apartments for low-income families—basically just satisfying physiological needs. A narrow view of the product-market—that is, considering only products now being produced—might lead the firm to think *only* in terms of more low-income housing. A bigger view might see these compact apartments as only a small part of the total apartment market—or total rental housing market—or even the total housing market—in the firm's geographic area. Taking an even bigger view, it could consider expanding to other geographic areas—or moving into other construction markets.

There has to be some balance between naming the product-market too narrowly (same old product, same old market) and naming it too broadly (the whole world and all its needs). Here the firm looked at the whole apartment renters' market in one urban area—because this is where the firm had some experience and wanted to work.

2. List all needs that all potential customers may have in this broad product-market

This is a "brain-storming" step. Write down as many needs as you can—as quickly as possible. The list doesn't have to be complete. The idea here is to have enough input to stimulate thinking in the next several steps. Some need dimension which is just "thrown in" now may be *the* determining dimension for some market segment. If that need is not included at this step, that market segment might be missed.

Possible need dimensions can be identified by starting with the PSSP hierarchy of basic needs—see Chapter 6—to be sure that all potential dimensions are being considered. You can expand these four basic needs by thinking about why some people buy the present offerings in this product-market.

Example: In the apartment renters' market, it is fairly easy to list the following needs—which start with but move beyond the four basic needs: basic shelter, parking, play space, safety and security, distinctiveness, economy, privacy, convenience (to something), enough living area, attractive interiors, and good supervision and maintenance to assure trouble-free and comfortable living.

3. Form possible product-markets using determining dimensions

Assuming that some market segments will have different needs than others, select from the above list the most important ones for yourself, then for a friend, then for several acquaintances from widely different demographic groups. Form one segment around yourself or an obvious user—and then go on aggregating others into other segments until three or more market segments emerge. Be sure you know the customer-related characteristics of the segments—so you can name them later. For example, if the people in one segment tend to be college students looking for a "party environment," then this will help you understand what they want and why—and will help you name or nickname the segment (perhaps as the "partyers").

Obviously some judgment is needed here—but you should have some thoughts about how you behave. Given that you are unique, you can see that others have different needs and attitudes. Once this is accepted, it is surprising how good your judgment becomes about how others behave. We all may have different preferences, but experienced observers do tend to agree—at least roughly—on how and why people behave. Market-related experience and judgment are needed to screen all the possible dimensions. But at least the geographic, demographic, and behavioral topics discussed in earlier chapters should be considered when forming these possible product-market segments.

Example: A college student living off campus probably wants an apartment to provide basic shelter, parking, economy, convenience to school and work, and enough room somewhere to have parties. An older married couple, on the other hand, may have quite different needs—perhaps for basic shelter and parking but *also* privacy and good supervision—so they don't have to put up with the rowdy parties which appeal to the student. A couple with a family is also interested in shelter and parking—but may not have much money. So they also want economy—while getting enough room for the children to live and play.

4. Remove qualifying dimensions

Review the list of dimensions in each possible product-market segment and remove any that appear in all segments. They may be important qualifying dimensions—reflecting "core needs"—but they are not the determining dimensions we are seeking now.

A potential dimension—such as low price or good value—may be important to *all* potential customers. It may be an extremely important qualifying dimension—which will have to be satisfied in *any* marketing mix. But for segmenting purposes, it should be removed *at this step.*

Example: With our "apartment renters," the need for basic shelter, parking, and safety and security appear to be *common* needs. Therefore—in this step—remove them from your list of possible segmenting dimensions.

5. Name the possible product-market segments

Review the remaining dimensions—segment by segment—and name (or nickname) each segment—based on the relative importance of the determining dimensions (and aided by their customer-related characteristics, as explained in Step 3). To visualize what this market looks like, draw a picture of the market and put these segments in it.

Example: We can identify the following "apartment renter" segments at this time: swingers, sophisticates, family, job-centered, and urban-centered. See Figure 8–4. Each segment has a different set of determining benefits sought—product features—which follow directly from customer types and their needs. (See the legend at the bottom of Figure 8–4.)

6. Seek better understanding of possible product-market segments

After naming the segments as we did in Step 5, you need to think about what is already known about each segment—to help you understand how and why these markets behave the way they do. This can explain why some competitive offerings are more successful than others. It also can lead to splitting and renaming some segments.

Example: Newly married couples might have been treated as "swingers" in

■   FIGURE 8–4   Market for apartment renters in a metropolitan area

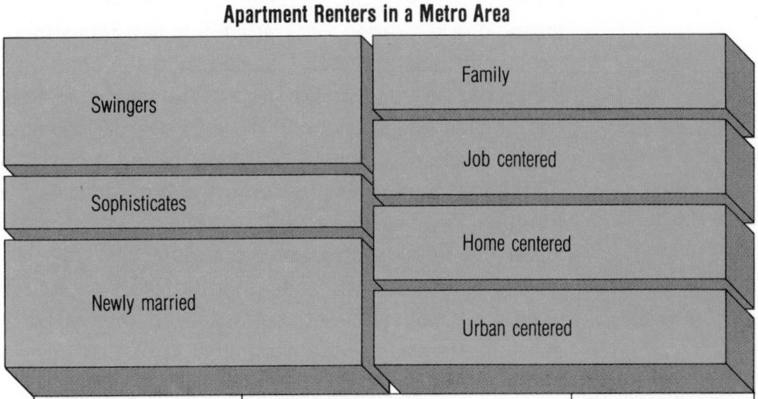

Apartment Renters in a Metro Area

Swingers	Family
Sophisticates	Job centered
	Home centered
Newly married	Urban centered

Name of market segment	People types and needs characteristics	Determining benefits sought (Product features)
Swingers	Young, unmarried, active, fun-loving, party-going	Economy Common facilities Close-in location
Sophisticates	Young, but older than swingers, more mature than swingers, more income and education than swingers, more desire for comfort and individuality	Distinctive design Privacy Interior variety Strong management
Newly married	No longer swingers, want a home but do not yet have enough money, wife works so economy not necessary	Privacy Strong management
Job centered	Single adults, widows, or divorcees, not much discretionary income and want to be near job	Economy Close-in location Strong management
Family	Young families with children and not enough income to afford own home	Economy Common facilities Room size
Home centered	Former homeowners who still want some aspects of suburban life	Privacy Room size Interior variety
Urban centered	Former homeowners in the suburbs, who now want to be close to attractions of city	Distinctive design Close-in location Strong management

Source: Adapted from *House and Home,* April 1965, pp. 94–99.

Step 5—because the "married" dimension was not seen as determining. But with more thought, we see that while some newly married couples are still swingers at heart, others have begun to shift their focus to buying a home. For these "newly married," the apartment is a temporary place. Further, they are not like the sophisticates—as shown at the bottom of Figure 8–4—and probably should be treated as a separate segment. The point here is that these market differences might only be discovered in Step 6. It is at this step that the "newly married" segment would be named.

7. Tie each segment to demographic and other customer-related characteristics, if possible, and then draw a new picture of the whole market to show the relative sizes of the segments

Remember, we are looking for profitable opportunities. So now we must try to tie our product-market segments to demographic data—to make it easier to estimate the sizes of the segments. We *aren't* trying to estimate market potential here. Now we only want to provide the basis for later forecasting and marketing mix planning. The more we know about possible target markets, the easier those jobs will be.

Fortunately, much demographic data is available. And bringing in demographics adds a note of economic reality. It is possible that some market segments will have almost no market potential. Without some hard facts, the risks of aiming at such markets are great.

To help understand the broad product-market—and explain it to others—draw a picture of the market—with boxes that give some idea of the size of the various market segments. This will help you see the larger—and perhaps more attractive—opportunities.

Example: It is possible to tie the swingers to demographic data. Most of them are young—in their 20s. The U.S. Census Bureau has very detailed information related to age. Given age data—and an estimate of what percentage are swingers—it's easy to estimate the number of swingers in a metropolitan area.

Market Dimensions Suggest a Good Mix

Once we have followed all seven steps, we should be able to see the outlines—at least—of the kinds of marketing mixes that would appeal to the various market segments. Let's take a look.

We know that "swingers" are active, young, unmarried, fun-loving, and party-going. The product benefits (features) shown at the bottom of Figure 8–4 show what the swingers want in an apartment. (It's interesting to note what they do *not* want—strong management. Most college students will probably understand why!)

A very successful appeal to the swingers in the Dallas, Texas, area includes an apartment complex with a swimming pool, a tennis court, a night club that offers bands and other entertainment, poolside parties, receptions for new tenants, and so on. And to maintain their image, management insists that tenants who get married move out shortly—so that new swingers can move in.

As a result, apartment occupancy rates have been extremely high. At the same time, other builders often have difficulty filling their apartments—mostly because their units are just "little boxes" with few unique and appealing features.

SEVEN–STEP APPROACH APPLIES IN INDUSTRIAL MARKETS, TOO

A similar seven-step approach can be used for industrial markets, too. The major change is in the first step—selecting the broad product-market area. It is the functional needs which are different.

Industrial buyers are especially interested in accomplishing "basic" functions. Their demands are derived from final consumer demands—so the industrial market is concerned with finding or producing raw materials and converting them into finished goods and services. The functions which industrial buyers are concerned about include, but are not limited to: forming, bending, grading, digging, cutting, heating, cooling, conducting, transmitting, containing, filling, cleaning, analyzing, sorting, training, insuring, feeding employees, and so on.

Defining the relevant product-market—using both geographic dimensions and functional needs—will usually ensure that the focus is broad enough—that is, not exclusively on the product now being supplied to present customers. But it also keeps the focus from expanding to "all the industrial needs in the world."

It is better to focus on functional needs—not product characteristics. New ways of satisfying the functional need may be found—and completely surprise and upset current producers—if the product-market is defined too narrowly. For example, aluminum wire now competes in what some copper wire producers thought was the "copper wire market." And plastic products are taking more of this business. Perhaps this product-market should be called the "components for transmitting" or "components for conducting" market. Certainly, the "copper" view was too narrow. Market-oriented strategy planners attempt to avoid surprises which result from such tunnel vision.

Understanding how products are used helps to segment industrial markets.

After the first step—in the seven-step approach—the other steps would be similar to segmenting consumer markets—only the dimensions discussed in Chapter 7 would be used here. For example, the size of the buyer's company, the nature of the buying situation, and the importance of multiple buying influence should be considered in identifying the qualifying and determining dimensions. When it comes to estimating the size of the markets, SIC-coded information can be quite helpful. In fact, given all of the data which is available—and the relative ease of tying it to market segments—there is no excuse for ignorance about the size of industrial markets.

MORE SOPHISTICATED TECHNIQUES MAY HELP IN SEGMENTING

The seven-step approach is logical, practical—and it works. But a marketing manager no longer is limited to such an intuitive approach. Some computer-aided methods can help. Called "clustering" techniques, they seek to do—mechanically—some of what used to require much intuition and judgment.

Clustering Usually Requires a Computer

Clustering techniques try to find similar patterns within sets of data. This data could include demographic characteristics, attitudes toward the product or life in general, and past buying behavior. The computer searches among all the data for homogeneous groups of people. When they are found, the dimensions of the people in the groups must be studied—to see why the computer clustered them together. If the results make some sense, they may suggest new, or at least better, marketing strategies.[3]

A cluster analysis of the toothpaste market, for example, might show that some people buy toothpaste because it tastes good (the sensory segment), while others are concerned with the effect of clean teeth on their social image (the sociables). Others are worried about decay (the worriers), and some are just interested in the best value for their money (the economic men). See Figure 8–5. Each of these market segments calls for a different marketing mix—although some of the four Ps may be similar. Finally, a marketing manager has to decide which one (or more) of these segments will be the firm's target market(s).

You can see that these techniques only aid the manager. Judgment is still needed to develop an original list of possible dimensions—and then to name the resulting clusters.[4]

Clustering Works for Services, Too

These clustering techniques can be useful for both goods and services—and consumer goods and industrial goods.

In a study of the commercial banking market, for example, six different groups were found. These groups were called the "non-borrowers," "value seekers," "non-saving convenience seekers," "loan seekers," "one-stop bankers," and an "other" group (which was not particularly different on any dimensions). Because of this study, changes were made in the bank's whole

■ **FIGURE 8–5**   Toothpaste market segment description

Segment name	The sensory segment	The sociables	The worriers	The independent segment
Principal benefit sought	Flavor, product appearance	Brightness of teeth	Decay prevention	Price
Demographic strengths	Children	Teens, young people	Large families	Men
Special behavioral characteristics	Users of spearmint flavored toothpaste	Smokers	Heavy users	Heavy users
Brands disproportionately favored:	Colgate, Stripe	Macleans, Plus White, Ultra Brite	Crest	Brands on sale
Personality characteristics	High self-involvement	High sociability	High hypochon-driasis	High autonomy
Life-style characteristics	Hedonistic	Active	Conservative	Value-oriented

Source: Russell I. Haley, "Benefit Segmentation: A Decision-Oriented Research Tool," *Journal of Marketing,* July 1968, p. 33.

program—aiming at each of the markets and treating them as the basis for separate strategies. Instead of its "we are friendly people" advertising campaign, the bank decided to appeal to the different markets. The non-borrowers were appealed to with messages about the bank's checking account, bank charge card, insurance, and investment counseling. For the convenience seekers, on the other hand, stress was placed on faster teller service, express drive-in windows, overnight drop boxes, and deposit-by-mail accounts. To reach the loan seekers, promotion stressed auto-loan checking accounts, mail-loan request forms, and loan programs through automobile dealers.[5]

FORECASTING TARGET MARKET POTENTIAL AND SALES

Estimates of target market potential and likely sales volumes are necessary for effective strategy planning. But a manager can't forecast *sales* without some possible plans. Sales are *not* just "out there for the taking." Market opportunities may be there—but whether a firm can change these opportunities into sales depends on the strategy it selects.

Much of our discussion in the rest of the chapter will be concerned with estimating **market potential**—what a whole market segment might buy—rather than a sales forecast. A **sales forecast** is an estimate of how much an industry or firm hopes to sell to a market segment. We must first try to judge market potential before we can estimate what share a particular firm may be able to win.

TWO APPROACHES TO FORECASTING

Many methods are used in forecasting market potential and sales—but they can be grouped under two basic approaches: (1) extending past behavior and (2) predicting future behavior. The large number of methods may seem confusing at first—but this variety is an advantage. Forecasts are so important that management often prefers to develop forecasts in two or three different ways—and then compare the differences before preparing a final forecast.

Extending Past Behavior

Trend extension can miss important turning points

When we forecast for existing products, we usually have some past data to go on. The basic approach—called **trend extension**—extends past experience into the future. See Figure 8–6.

Ideally—when extending past sales behavior—we should decide why sales vary. This is the difficult and time-consuming part of sales forecasting. Usually we can gather a lot of data about the product or market—or about the economic environment. But unless the *reason* for past sales variations is known, it's hard to predict in what direction—and by how much—sales will move. Graphing the data and statistical techniques—including correlation and regression analysis—can be useful here. These techniques are beyond our scope. They are discussed in beginning statistics courses.

Once we know why sales vary, we usually can develop a specific forecast. Sales may be moving directly up as population grows, for example. So we can just get an estimate of how population is expected to grow—and project the impact on sales.

The weakness of the trend extension method is that it assumes past conditions will continue unchanged into the future. In fact, the future isn't always like the past. And, unfortunately, trend extension will be wrong whenever there are big changes. For this reason—although they may extend past behavior for one

■ FIGURE 8–6   Straight-line trend projection—extends past sales into the future

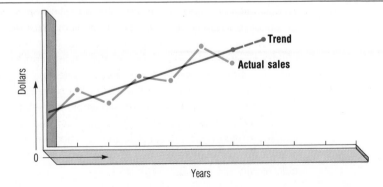

estimate—most managers look for another way to help them forecast sharp economic changes.

Predicting Future Behavior Takes Judgment

When we try to predict what will happen in the future—instead of just extending the past—we have to use other methods and add a bit more judgment. Some of these methods—to be discussed later—include juries of executive opinion, salespeople's estimates, surveys, panels, and market tests.

THREE LEVELS OF FORECAST ARE USEFUL

We are interested in forecasting the potential in specific market segments. To do this, it helps to make three levels of forecasts.

Some economic conditions affect the entire economy. Others may influence only one industry. And some may affect only one company or one product's sales potential. For this reason, a common approach to forecasting is to:

1. Develop a *national income forecast* and use this to:
2. Develop an *industry sales forecast,* which then is used to:
3. Develop *specific company* and *product forecasts.*

Generally, a marketing manager doesn't have to make forecasts for the national economy or his industry. This kind of forecasting—basically, trend projecting—is a specialty in itself. These forecasts are available in business and government publications. Managers can just use one source's forecast or combine several together. Unfortunately, however, the more targeted the marketing manager's earlier segmenting effort has been, the less likely that available industry forecasts will match the firm's product-markets. So the managers

Knowing past trends helps in forecasting—but trend projecting can be dangerous.

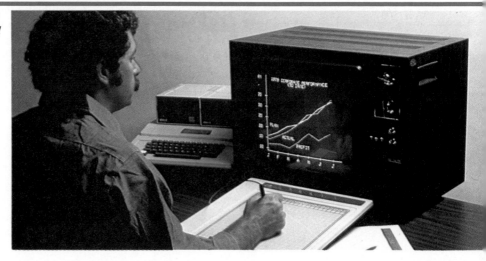

will have to move directly to estimating potential for their own company and specific products. This is the subject of the rest of this chapter.

FORECASTING COMPANY AND PRODUCT SALES BY EXTENDING PAST BEHAVIOR

Past Sales Can Be Extended

At the very least, a marketing manager ought to know what the firm's present markets look like—and what it has sold to them in the past. A detailed sales analysis—for products and geographic areas—helps to project future results.

Just extending past sales into the future may not seem like much of a forecasting method. But it's better than just assuming that next year's *total* sales will be the same as this year's.

Factor Method Includes More Than Time

Simple extension of past sales gives one forecast. But it is usually desirable to tie future sales to something more than the passage of time. The factor method tries to do this.

The **factor method** tries to forecast sales by finding a relation between the company's sales and some other factor (or factors). The basic formula is: something (past sales, industry sales, etc.) *times* some factor *equals* sales forecast. A **factor** is a variable which shows the relation of some variable to the item being forecasted.

A Bread Manufacturer Example

The following example for a bread manufacturer shows how forecasts can be made for many geographic market segments—using the factor method and available data. This general approach can be useful for any firm—manufacturer, wholesaler, or retailer.

Analysis of past sales relationships showed that a particular bread manufacturer regularly sold one half of 1 percent (0.005) of the total retail food sales in its various target markets. This is a single factor. By using this single factor, estimates of the manufacturer's sales for the coming period could be obtained by multiplying a forecast of expected retail food sales by 0.005.

Retail food sales estimates are made each year by *Sales & Marketing Management* magazine. Figure 8–7 shows the kind of geographically detailed data available.

Let's carry this bread example further—using the data in Figure 8–7 for Evanston, Illinois. Evanston's food sales were $96,309,000 for the last year. By simply accepting last year's food sales as an estimate of next year's sales—and multiplying the food sales estimate for Evanston by the 0.005 factor (the firm's usual share in such markets)—the manager would have an estimate of his next year's bread sales in Evanston. That is, last year's food sales estimate ($96,309,000) times 0.005 equals this year's bread sales estimate of $481,545.

■ FIGURE 8–7   Sample of pages from *Sales & Marketing Management's* "Survey of Buying Power"

ILL. (cont.) SMM ESTIMATES	POPULATION—12/31/83								RETAIL SALES BY STORE GROUP 1983						
METRO AREA / County / City	Total Population (Thousands)	% Of U.S.	Median Age of Pop.	18–24 Years	25–34 Years	35–49 Years	50 & Over	House-holds (Thousands)	Total Retail Sales ($000)	Food ($000)	Eating & Drinking Places ($000)	General Mdse. ($000)	Furniture/ Furnish./ Appliance ($000)	Auto-motive ($000)	Drug ($000)
CHAMPAIGN - URBANA - RANTOUL .	168.8	.0716	25.5	27.8	19.2	14.3	17.5	61.0	929,801	201,576	129,664	129,396	36,967	114,452	30,613
Champaign	168.8	.0716	25.5	27.8	19.2	14.3	17.5	61.0	929,801	201,576	129,664	129,396	36,967	114,452	30,613
• Champaign	58.5	.0248	24.7	34.8	18.4	12.2	17.7	22.3	490,086	75,754	65,922	78,631	27,379	67,829	20,202
• Rantoul	19.2	.0082	23.2	31.0	18.9	12.7	10.3	5.6	96,116	16,647	17,520	9,374	2,525	26,918	2,588
• Urbana	36.7	.0156	24.7	37.0	20.3	10.8	17.1	12.9	106,249	18,914	22,999	11,032	5,379	11,525	2,310
SUBURBAN TOTAL	54.4	.0230	29.5	12.8	19.5	19.4	19.9	20.2	237,350	90,261	23,223	30,359	1,684	8,180	5,513
CHICAGO	6,028.5	2.5597	31.5	12.2	17.5	18.2	25.7	2,211.9	31,119,257	6,510,053	3,639,397	3,951,513	1,407,488	4,461,365	1,428,189
Cook	5,148.0	2.1858	31.7	12.3	17.2	17.8	26.6	1,897.9	25,315,759	5,436,685	3,058,523	3,310,542	1,157,285	3,501,170	1,206,119
Arlington Heights	66.7	.0283	33.3	10.0	15.5	23.6	23.8	23.1	421,577	46,685	53,488	38,829	29,208	122,826	16,167
Berwyn	45.4	.0193	42.6	10.1	14.2	15.8	42.7	19.8	210,394	24,557	34,691	24,922	8,945	59,041	12,591
• Chicago	2,938.9	1.2478	31.0	12.8	17.5	16.6	26.4	1,102.6	11,544,385	2,470,279	1,527,715	1,317,930	558,944	1,243,573	653,955
• Chicago Heights	36.1	.0153	29.1	13.0	15.8	15.9	24.8	12.0	261,146	51,761	36,475	23,225	10,206	81,053	7,978
Cicero	59.7	.0253	35.7	11.6	15.8	15.9	34.9	24.3	178,496	69,066	26,850	5,471	2,749	26,760	4,236
Des Plaines	55.2	.0234	34.4	11.2	16.0	20.4	28.7	19.9	491,553	75,302	69,620	57,584	3,231	121,424	19,943
• Evanston	72.2	.0307	32.0	17.5	20.0	16.5	27.6	28.2	476,836	96,309	49,428	21,263	20,741	97,566	26,114

ILL. SMM ESTIMATES EFFECTIVE BUYING INCOME 1983							
METRO AREA / County / City	Total EBI ($000)	Median Hsld. EBI	(A) $10,000–$19,999	(B) $20,000–$34,999	(C) $35,000–$49,999	(D) $50,000 & Over	Buying Power Index
CHAMPAIGN - URBANA - RANTOUL	1,638,851	21,945	25.9	30.6	16.0	8.1	.0731
Champaign	1,638,851	21,945	25.9	30.6	16.0	8.1	.0731
• Champaign	565,417	19,907	25.4	28.2	14.0	7.5	.0295
• Rantoul	161,285	20,108	36.4	30.5	15.3	4.6	.0075
• Urbana	329,445	19,464	27.4	27.0	14.3	7.4	.0129
SUBURBAN TOTAL	582,704	26,093	22.7	35.4	19.5	10.2	.0232
CHICAGO	67,420,753	27,453	18.9	29.4	20.9	14.3	2.7460
Cook	55,083,778	25,805	20.0	29.7	19.5	12.5	2.2598

SMM ESTIMATES EFFECTIVE BUYING INCOME 1983							
METRO AREA / County / City	Total EBI ($000)	Median Hsld. EBI	(A) $10,000–$19,999	(B) $20,000–$34,999	(C) $35,000–$49,999	(D) $50,000 & Over	Buying Power Index
CHICAGO							
Arlington Heights	948,670	39,354	11.1	24.6	30.2	29.2	.0367
Berwyn	532,998	24,355	23.3	31.9	18.4	9.5	.0206
• Chicago	27,082,802	20,910	23.0	28.6	15.1	8.3	1.1229
• Chicago Heights	317,377	24,429	20.7	31.5	20.3	7.8	.0165
Cicero	603,008	22,415	25.9	33.0	16.1	6.6	.0225
Des Plaines	691,497	33,497	15.1	31.0	29.1	17.5	.0320
• Evanston	988,680	28,580	19.9	30.8	19.6	18.3	.0394

Source: *Sales & Marketing Management,* July 23, 1984, pp. c–62ff.

Factor Method Can Use Several Factors

The factor method is not limited to using just one factor. Several factors can be used together. For example, *Sales & Marketing Management* regularly gives a "buying power index" (BPI) as a measure of the potential in different geographic areas. See Figure 8–7. This index includes (1) the population in a market, (2) the market's income, and (3) retail sales in that market. But the same basic approach is used.

PREDICTING FUTURE BEHAVIOR CALLS FOR MORE JUDGMENT AND SOME OPINIONS

The past-extending methods discussed above make use of quantitative data—projecting past experience into the future and assuming that the future will be like the past. But this is risky in competitive markets. Usually, it's desirable to add some judgment to get other forecasts—before making the final forecast.

Jury of Executive Opinion Adds Judgment

One of the oldest and simplest methods of forecasting—the **jury of executive opinion**—combines the opinions of experienced executives—perhaps from marketing, production, finance, purchasing, and top management. Basically, each executive is asked to estimate market potential and sales for the *coming years*. Then they try to work out a consensus.

The main advantage of the jury approach is that it can be done quickly—and easily. On the other hand, the results may not be very good. There may be too much extending of the past. Some of the executives may have little contact with outside market influences. But it could point to major shifts in customer demand or competition.

Estimates from Salespeople Can Help, Too

Using salespeople's estimates to forecast is like the jury approach. But salespeople are more likely than home office managers to be familiar with customer reactions—and what competitors are doing. Their estimates are especially useful in industrial markets—where the limited number of customers may be well known to the salespeople. But this approach is useful in any type of market. Good retail clerks have a "feel" for their markets—their opinions shouldn't be ignored.

However, a manager should keep two points in mind when using estimates. First, salespeople usually don't know about possible changes in the national economic climate—or even about changes in the company's marketing mix.

Second, salespeople may have little to offer if they change jobs often.

Surveys, Panels, and Market Tests

Special surveys of final buyers, retailers, and/or wholesalers can show what's happening in different market segments. Some firms use panels of

Salespeople know their markets and can be helpful in sales forecasting.

stores—or final consumers—to keep track of buying behavior—and to decide when just extending past behavior isn't enough.

Surveys are sometimes combined with market tests—when the company needs to estimate the reaction of customers to possible changes in its marketing mix. A market test might show that a product increased its share of the market by 10 percent when its price was dropped one cent below competition. But this extra business might be quickly lost if the price were increased one cent above competition. Such market experiments help the marketing manager make good estimates of future sales when one or more of the four Ps are changed.

ACCURACY OF FORECASTS

The accuracy of forecasts varies a lot. The more general the number being forecast, the more accurate the forecast is likely to be. This is because small errors in various components of the estimate tend to offset each other—and make the whole estimate more accurate. Annual forecasts of national totals—such as GNP—may be accurate within 5 percent. When style and innovation are important in an industry, forecast errors of 10 to 20 percent for *established products* are common. The accuracy of specific *new-product* forecasts is even lower. Many new products fail completely.[6]

■ CONCLUSION

This chapter discussed market segmentation—the process of naming and segmenting broad product-markets—to find potentially attractive target markets. Some people try to segment markets by breaking them down into smaller sub-markets. But this can lead to poor results. Instead, segmenting should be seen as an aggregating process. The more similar the potential customers are, the larger the sub-markets can be. Four criteria for evaluating possible market segments were presented.

Even "rough and ready" segmenting can add insight about the nature of possible product-markets—and may lead to breakthrough opportunities. Seemingly minor determining dimensions may make a winner out of what appears to be a "me-too" strategy.

We also talked about two basic approaches to forecasting market potential and sales: (1) extending past behavior and (2) predicting future behavior. The most common approach is to extend past behavior into the future. This gives reasonably good results if market conditions are fairly stable. Methods here include extension of past sales data and the factor method. We saw that projecting the past into the future is risky when big market changes are likely. To make up for this possible weakness, marketers predict future behavior using their own experience and judgment. They also may be able to bring in the judgment of others—using the jury of executive opinion method and salespeople's estimates. They may also use surveys, panels, and market tests.

We saw that the accuracy of forecasts depends on how general a forecast is being made. The most error occurs with specific forecasts for products—and especially new products.

Even though forecasts are subject to error, they are still necessary to help the firm choose among possible marketing plans. Sloppy forecasting can lead to poor strategies. No forecasting at all is stupid!

In summary, good marketers should be experts on markets and likely segmenting dimensions. By creatively segmenting markets, they may spot opportunities—even breakthrough opportunities—and help their firms to succeed against aggressive competitors offering similar products. Segmenting is basic to target marketing. And the more you practice segmenting, the more meaningful market segments you will see.

■ QUESTIONS AND PROBLEMS

1. Explain what market segmentation is.

2. List the types of potential segmenting dimensions and explain which you would try to apply first, second, and third in a particular situation. If the nature of the situation would affect your answer, explain how.

3. Explain why "first-time" segmentation efforts may be very disappointing.

4. Illustrate the concept that segmenting is an aggregating process by referring to the apparent admissions policies of your own college and a nearby college or university.

5. (a) Evaluate how "good" the seven markets identified in the market for apartments are (Figure 8–4) with respect to the four criteria for selecting good market segments. (b) Same as (a) but evaluate the four corner markets in the British home decorating market (Figure 2–8).

6. Review the types of segmenting dimensions listed in Tables 8–2 and 8–3, and select the ones which you feel should be combined to fully explain the market segment you personally would be in if you were planning to buy a new automobile today. Do not hesitate to list several dimensions, but when you have done so, try to develop a short-hand name, like "swinger," to describe your own personal market segment.

Then try to estimate what proportion of the total automobile market would be accounted for by your market segment. Next, explain if there are any offerings which come close to meeting the needs of your market. If not, what sort of a marketing mix is needed? Do you feel it would be economically attractive for anyone to try to satisfy your market segment? Why or why not?

7. Identify the determining dimension or dimensions which explain why you bought the specific brand you did in your most recent purchase of a (a) soft drink, (b) pen, (c) shirt or blouse, and a (d) larger, more expensive item, such as a bicycle, camera, boat, and so on. Try to express the determining dimension(s) in terms of your own personal characteristics rather than the product's characteristics. Estimate what share of the market would probably be motivated by the same determining dimension(s).

8. Apply the seven-step approach to segmenting consumer markets to the college-age market for off-campus recreation, which can include eating and drinking. Then evaluate how well the needs in these market segments are being met in your geographic area. Is there an obvious breakthrough opportunity waiting for someone?

9. Explain how the first step in the seven-step approach to segmenting markets would have to be changed to apply it in industrial markets. Illustrate your answer.

10. Explain the difference between a forecast of market potential and a sales forecast.

11. Suggest a plausible explanation for sales fluctuations for (a) bicycles, (b) baby food, (c) motor boats, (d) baseball gloves, (e) wheat, (f) wood-working tools, and (g) latex for rubber-based paint.

12. Explain the factor method. Illustrate your answer.

13. Discuss the relative accuracy of the various forecasting methods. Explain why some are more accurate than others.

14. Given the following annual sales data for

a company which is not planning any spectacular marketing strategy changes, forecast sales for the coming year (7) and explain your method and reasoning.

(a)		(b)	
Year	Sales ($000)	Year	Sales ($000)
1	$200	1	$160
2	230	2	155
3	210	3	165
4	220	4	160
5	200	5	170
6	220	6	165

15. Discuss the relative market potential of Cicero and Evanston, Illinois, for: (a) prepared cereals, (b) automobiles, and (c) furniture.

■ **SUGGESTED CASES**

4. Uncle Lyle's, Inc.

6. The Lido

8. Iceland

Chapter 9 ■ Elements of product planning

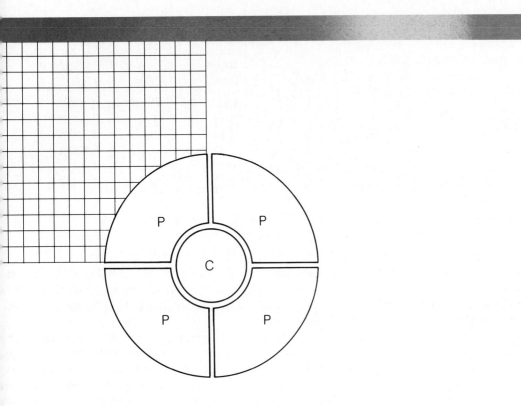

When you finish this chapter, you should:

1. Understand what "Product" really means.

2. Know the differences among the various consumer and industrial goods classes.

3. Understand how the goods classes can help a marketing manager plan marketing strategies.

4. Understand what branding is and how it can be used in strategy planning.

5. Understand the strategic importance of packaging.

6. Recognize the important new terms (shown in red).

The product must satisfy customers—what they want is what they'll get.

Developing the "right" product isn't easy—because customer needs and attitudes keep changing. Further, *most customers want some combination of goods and services in their product.*

A young couple has a new baby—and a new need—getting diapers clean. They decide to buy a washing machine. It's a big purchase, so they shop at several stores for a machine with just the right features. They want a well-known brand—like Whirlpool—to be sure of quality. They also want the washer delivered—so this service is part of the product they're considering. And they want to be sure that the machine will last—so they want a warranty included with the product.

This little story includes many of the topics we'll discuss in this chapter. First, we'll look at how customers see a firm's product. Then, we'll talk about goods classes—to help you understand marketing strategy planning better.

We will also talk about branding and packaging. Most products need some packaging. And both goods and services should be branded. A successful

■ FIGURE 9–1 Strategy planning for Product

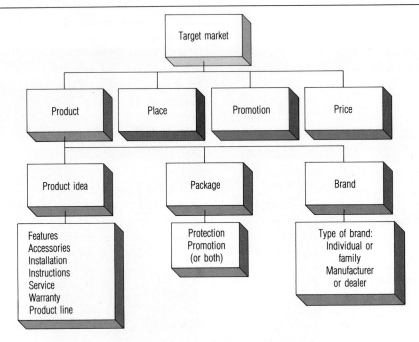

marketer wants to be sure that satisfied customers will know what to ask for the next time.

In summary, we will talk about the strategic decisions of manufacturers—or middlemen—who make these Product decisions. These strategic decisions are shown in Figure 9–1.

WHAT IS A PRODUCT?

Customers Buy Satisfaction, Not Parts

First, we have to define what we mean by a "product."

If we sell an automobile, are we selling a certain number of nuts and bolts, some sheet metal, an engine, and four wheels?

If we sell a laundry detergent, are we just selling a box of chemicals?

If we sell a delivery service, are we selling so much wear and tear on a delivery truck—and so much driver fatigue?

The answer to all these questions is *no.* Instead, what we are really selling is the satisfaction, use, or profit the customer wants.

All customers care about is that their cars look good—and keep running. They want to clean with their detergent—not analyze it. And when they order something, they really don't care how much out of the way the driver had to go—or where he's been. They just want their package.

In the same way, when producers or middlemen buy products, they are interested in the profit they can make from their purchase—through its use or resale—not how the products were made.

Product means the need-satisfying offering of a firm. The idea of "product" as potential customer satisfaction or benefits is very important. Many business managers—trained in the production side of business—get wrapped up in the number of nuts and bolts, variety of transistors and resistors, and other technical details. Middlemen, too, are often concerned with technical details. These are important to *them,* but they have little effect on the way most customers view the product. What matters to customers is how *they* see the product.

Product May Only Be a Service

"Product" may not include a physical good at all! The product of a hair stylist is the trimming or styling of your hair. A doctor may just look at you—giving you nothing but an opinion. An accounting firm may only review the correctness of a firm's records. But each satisfies needs—and provides a product in the sense we will use "product" in this book.

Goods and/or Services Are the Product

Most products are a blend of physical goods *and* services. Figure 9–2 emphasizes this by showing that a "product" can range from 100 percent physical good—such as commodities like common nails or dried beans—to 100 percent service, like a taxi ride.

This bigger view of a product must be understood completely—it's too easy to slip into a *physical product* point of view. We want to think of a product in terms of the *needs it satisfies.* If the objective of a firm is to satisfy customer needs, it must see that service is part of the product—or service may be *the* product—and has to be provided as part of the marketing mix.

Given this view, we won't make a distinction between goods and services—but will call them all *Products.*[1]

"Product" may not include a physical good at all.

■ FIGURE 9–2   Possible blends of goods and services in a product

WHOLE PRODUCT LINES MUST BE DEVELOPED, TOO

We have been talking about a single product. But most businesses have to offer complete lines of products to satisfy their customers. This makes the job of product planning harder. But if this is what customers want, then complete lines must be offered.

To keep our discussion simple, we will focus mainly on developing one marketing strategy at a time. But you should remember that *several* strategies for goods and/or services might have to be planned—to develop an effective marketing program for a whole company.

GOODS CLASSES HELP PLAN MARKETING STRATEGIES

It would be difficult to treat *every* product as unique when planning strategies. It would help to have some goods classes that are related to marketing mixes. Luckily, products can be classified in this way. These goods classes will be a useful starting point for developing marketing mixes for new products—and evaluating present mixes.

Whether a product should be treated as a consumer or industrial good depends on who will use it. **Consumer goods** are products meant for final consumers. **Industrial goods** are products meant for use in making other products. All goods fit into one of these two groups. Market research shows that these goods classes are useful in marketing mix planning.

CONSUMER GOODS CLASSES

Consumer goods classes are based on the way people buy products. Consumer goods are divided into four groups: (1) convenience goods, (2) shopping goods, (3) specialty goods, and (4) unsought goods. See Figure 9–3 for a summary of how these goods classes are related to marketing mixes.[2]

■ FIGURE 9–3   Consumer goods classes and marketing mix planning

1. *Convenience goods.*
   a. Staples—need maximum exposure—need widespread distribution at low cost.
   b. Impulse goods—need maximum exposure—need widespread distribution but with assurance of preferred display or counter position.
   c. Emergency goods—need widespread distribution near probable point of use.
2. *Shopping goods.*
   a. Homogeneous—need enough exposure to facilitate price comparison.
   b. Heterogeneous—need adequate representation in major shopping districts or large shopping centers near other, similar shopping goods.
3. *Specialty goods*—can have limited availability, but in general should be treated as a convenience or shopping good (in whichever category product would normally be included), to reach persons not yet sold on its specialty-goods status.
4. *Unsought goods*—need attention directed to product and aggressive promotion in outlets, or must be available in places where similar products would be sought.

CONVENIENCE GOODS—PURCHASED QUICKLY WITH LITTLE EFFORT

Convenience goods are products a consumer needs but isn't willing to spend much time or effort shopping for. These products are bought often, require little service or selling, don't cost much, and may even be bought by habit. Examples are toothpaste, chewing gum, candy bars, soap, newspapers, magazines, and most grocery products.

Convenience goods are of three types—staples, impulse goods, and emergency goods—again based on *how customers think about products*—not the features of the products themselves.

Staples—Purchased and Used Regularly

Staples are products which are bought often and routinely—without much thought. Examples include most packaged foods used frequently in every household. Here, branding can be important—to help customers cut shopping effort.

Because staples are purchased often, they are sold in convenient places like food stores, discount stores, or vending machines.

Impulse Goods— Bought Immediately on Sight

Impulse goods are products which are bought quickly—as unplanned purchases—because of a strongly felt need. True impulse goods are items that the customer had not planned to buy, decides to buy on sight, may have bought the same way many times before, and wants "right now." An ice cream seller at a beach sells impulse goods. If sun bathers don't buy an ice cream bar, the need goes away, and the purchase won't be made later.[3]

This is important because it affects Place—and the whole marketing mix— for impulse goods. If the buyer doesn't see an impulse item at the "right" time, the sale may be lost. As a result, impulse goods are put where they will be seen and bought—near the check-out counters or in other heavy traffic areas of a store. Gum, candy bars, and magazines are often sold this way in grocery stores.

Emergency Goods—Purchased Only When Urgently Needed

Emergency goods are products which are purchased immediately when the need is great. The customer doesn't have the time to shop around. Price isn't important. Examples are ambulance services, umbrellas or raincoats during a rainstorm, and tire chains during a snowstorm.

Meeting customers' emergency needs may require a different marketing mix—especially regarding Place. Some small neighborhood stores carry "emergency" goods to meet these needs—staying open "7 till 11" and stocking "fill-in" items like milk or bread. Usually, these stores charge higher prices. But customers don't mind because they think of these products as "emergencies."

SHOPPING GOODS—ARE COMPARED

Shopping goods are products that a customer feels are worth the time and effort to compare with competing products.

Shopping goods can be divided into two types—depending on what customers are comparing: (1) homogeneous and (2) heterogeneous shopping goods.

Homogeneous Shopping Goods—The Price Must Be Right

Homogeneous shopping goods are shopping goods that the customer sees as basically the same—and wants at the lowest price. Some consumers feel that certain sizes and types of refrigerators, television sets, washing machines, and even automobiles are very similar. They are shopping for the best price.

Manufacturers may try to emphasize their product differences—and retailers may try to promote their "better service." But if the customers don't believe these differences are real, they will just look at price.

Low-price items are seen this way, too

Even some inexpensive items like butter and coffee may be thought of as homogeneous shopping goods. Some customers carefully read food store advertising for the lowest prices—and then go from store to store getting the items. They wouldn't do this for staples.

Heterogeneous Shopping Goods—The Product Must Be Right

Heterogeneous shopping goods are shopping goods that the customer sees as different—and wants to inspect for quality and suitability. Examples are furniture, clothing, dishes, and some cameras. Quality and style are more important than price.

For non-standardized products, it's harder to compare prices. Once the

These robes seem to be a heterogeneous shopping good for this woman.

customer has found the right product, price may not matter—as long as it's "reasonable."

Branding may be less important for heterogeneous shopping goods. The more consumers want to make their own comparisons of price and quality, the less they rely on brand names and labels. Some retailers carry competing brands so consumers don't need to go to a competitor to compare items.

Often the buyer of heterogeneous shopping goods not only wants—but expects—some kind of help in buying. And if the product is expensive, the buyer may want extra service—such as alteration of clothing or installation of appliances.

SPECIALTY GOODS—NO SUBSTITUTES PLEASE!

Specialty goods are consumer goods that the customer really wants—and is willing to make a special effort to find. Shopping for a specialty good doesn't mean comparing—the buyer wants that special product and is willing to search for it. It is not the extent of searching, but the customer's *willingness* to search—that makes it a specialty good.

Don't Want Substitutes!

Specialty goods don't have to be expensive, once-in-a-lifetime purchases. *Any* branded item that consumers insist on by name is a specialty good. Consumers have been observed asking for a drug product by its brand name and—when offered a chemically identical substitute—actually leaving the store in anger.

A product which is viewed as an unsought good by some consumers may be a shopping good for others.

UNSOUGHT GOODS—NEED PROMOTION

Unsought goods are products that potential customers do not yet want or know they can buy. Therefore, they don't search for them at all. In fact, consumers probably won't buy these products if they see them—unless Promotion can show their value.

There are two types of unsought goods. **New unsought goods** are products offering really new ideas that potential customers don't know about yet. Informative promotion can help convince customers to accept or even seek out the product—ending their unsought status. When microwave ovens first came out, consumers didn't know what the oven could do. Promotion showed the benefits provided by the new product—and now many consumers buy them.

Regularly unsought goods are products—like gravestones, life insurance, and encyclopedias—that stay unsought but not unbought forever. There may be a need—but the potential customers are not motivated to satisfy it. And there probably is little hope that they will move out of the unsought class for most consumers. For this kind of product, personal selling is *very* important.

ONE PRODUCT MAY BE SEEN AS SEVERAL CONSUMER GOODS

We have been looking at product classes *one at a time.* But the same product might be seen in different ways by different target markets—at the same time. Each of these groups might need a different marketing mix.

A Tale of Four Motels

Motels are a good example of a service that can be seen as *four different* kinds of consumer goods. Some tired motorists are satisfied with the first motel they come to—a convenience good. Others shop for just basic facilities at the lowest price—a homogeneous shopping good. Some shop for the kind of place they want at a fair price—a heterogeneous shopping good. And others study tourist guides, talk with traveling friends, and phone ahead to reserve a place in a recommended motel—a specialty good.

How an individual views a motel may vary, too. During a cross-country move, one type of motel may be needed. Another may be needed for a family vacation.

Perhaps one motel could satisfy *all* potential customers. But it would be hard to produce a marketing mix attractive to everyone—easy access for convenience, good facilities at the right price for shopping goods buyers, and qualities special enough to attract the specialty goods travelers. As a result, we see very different kinds of motels seemingly—but not really—competing with each other.

Of course, marketing strategy planners would like to know more about potential customers than how they buy specific products. But these classes are a good place to start strategy planning.

INDUSTRIAL GOODS CLASSES

Industrial goods classes are based on how buyers see products—and how the products are to be used. Expensive and/or long-lasting products are treated differently than inexpensive items. Products that become a part of a firm's own product are seen differently from those which only aid production. Finally, the size of a particular purchase can make a difference. An air compressor might be a small item to a buyer from General Motors—but a very big purchase for a small garage owner.

The classes of industrial goods are: (1) installations, (2) accessory equip-

■ FIGURE 9–4   Industrial goods and marketing mix planning

1. *Installations.*
   a. Buildings (used) and land rights—need widespread and/or knowledgeable contacts, depending upon specialized nature of product.
   b. Buildings (new)—need technical and experienced personal contact, probably at top management level (multiple buying influence).
   c. Major equipment.
      i. Custom-made—need technical (design) contacts by person able to visualize and design applications, and present to high-level and technical management.
      ii. Standard—need experienced (not necessarily highly technical) contacts by person able to visualize applications and present to high-level and technical management.
2. *Accessory equipment*—need fairly widespread and numerous contacts by experienced and sometimes technically trained personnel.
3. *Raw materials.*
   a. Farm products—need contacts with many small farmer producers and fairly widespread contact with users.
   b. Natural products—need fairly widespread contacts with users.
4. *Component parts and materials*—need technical contacts to determine specifications required—widespread contacts usually not necessary.
5. *Supplies.*
   a. Maintenance—need very widespread distribution for prompt delivery.
   b. Repairs—need widespread distribution for some, and prompt service from factory for others (depends on customers' preferences).
   c. Operating supplies—need fair to widespread distribution for prompt delivery.
6. *Services*—most need very widespread availability.

ment, (3) raw materials, (4) component parts and materials, (5) supplies, and (6) services. See Figure 9–4 for a summary of how these goods classes are related to what is needed in a marketing mix.

INSTALLATIONS—MAJOR CAPITAL ITEMS

Installations are important long-lived capital items—durable products which are depreciated over many years. They include buildings, land rights, and major equipment. One-of-a-kind installations—like buildings and custom-made equipment—generally require special negotiations for each sale. Standard major equipment is more homogeneous—and is treated more routinely. All installations, however, are important enough to require high-level—and even top-management—consideration.

Size of Market Small at Any Time

Installations are long-lasting products—so they aren't bought very often. The number of potential buyers *at any particular time* usually is small. For custom-made machines, there may be only a half-dozen potential customers— compared to a thousand or more potential buyers for similar standard machines.

Potential customers are generally in the same industry. Their plants are likely to be near each other—which makes personal selling easier. The auto-

To meet customers' needs, installations may have to be leased or rented.

mobile industry, for example, is heavily concentrated in and around Michigan. The aircraft industry—from a world view—is in the United States.

Buying Needs Basically Economic

Buying needs are basically economic—and concerned with the performance of the installation over its expected life. After comparing expected performance to present costs and figuring interest, the expected return on capital can be determined. Yet emotional needs—such as a desire for industry leadership and status—also may be involved.

Installations May Have to Be Leased or Rented

Since installations are relatively expensive, the producer will often lease or rent the product—rather than sell it. For example, many firms lease computers so they can expand to bigger systems as the firm grows. Leasing also shifts a capital item to an expense.

Specialized Services Are Needed as Part of the Product

Since the expected return on an installation is based on efficient operation, the sales contract may require regular service visits. Service people may even be permanently assigned to a company. Computer manufacturers sometimes station service people with the machine. The cost is included in the price.

ACCESSORY EQUIPMENT—IMPORTANT BUT SHORT–LIVED CAPITAL ITEMS

Accessory equipment consists of short-lived capital items. They are the tools and equipment used in production or office activities. Examples include portable drills, sanding machines, electric lift trucks, typewriters, and filing cabinets.

Since these products cost less—and last a shorter time—than installations, multiple buying influence is less important. Operating people and purchasing agents—rather than top managers—may do the buying.

More Target Markets Requiring Different Marketing Mixes	Accessories are more standardized than installations. And they are usually needed by more customers! A large, special-purpose belt sanding machine, for example, may be produced as a custom-made installation for wood-working firms. But small portable sanding machines would be considered as accessory equipment. There are many more possible customers. And they are likely to be spread out geographically. Therefore, different marketing mixes are needed for accessory equipment than for installations.
Might Want to Lease or Rent	Some target markets prefer to lease or rent accessories because the cost can be treated as an expense. A producer of electric lift trucks, for example, was able to expand sales by selling the basic truck—and then charging for the expensive battery system by the amount of time it was used. This increased sales because, as one manager said: "Nobody worries about costs that are buried as an operating expense."

RAW MATERIALS—FARM PRODUCTS AND NATURAL PRODUCTS ARE EXPENSE ITEMS

Become Part of a Physical Good	**Raw materials** are unprocessed goods—such as logs, iron ore, wheat, and cotton—that are handled as little as is needed to move them to the next production process. Unlike installations and accessories, *raw materials become part of a physical good*—and are expense items.
	We can divide raw materials into two types: (1) farm products and (2) natural products. **Farm products** are grown by farmers—examples are oranges, wheat, strawberries, sugar cane, cattle, hogs, poultry, eggs, and milk. **Natural products** are products which occur in nature—such as fish and game, lumber, copper, zinc, iron ore, oil, and coal.

FARM PRODUCTS VARY IN QUALITY AND QUANTITY

Involve Grading, Storing, and Transporting	The need for grading is one of the important differences between farm products and other industrial goods. Nature produces what it will—and someone must sort and grade farm products to satisfy various market segments. Some of the top grades of fruits and vegetables find their way into the consumer goods market. The lower grades are treated as industrial goods—and used in juices, sauces, and soup.

Most farm products are produced seasonally—yet the demand for them is fairly constant all year. As a result, storing and transporting are important.

Buyers of industrial goods usually don't seek suppliers. This complicates the marketing of farm products. The many small farms usually are widely scattered—sometimes far from potential buyers. Selling direct to final users would be difficult. So Place and Promotion are important in marketing mixes for these products.

NATURAL PRODUCTS—QUANTITIES ARE ADJUSTABLE

In contrast to farm products with their many producers, natural products are usually produced by fewer and larger companies. There are some exceptions—such as in the coal and lumber industries which have almost pure competition—but oligopoly conditions are common for natural products.

The supply of natural products harvested or mined in any one year can be adjusted up or down—at least within limits. And storage is less of a problem—since few are perishable.

As with farm products, buyers of natural products usually need specific grades and dependable supply sources—to be sure of continued production in their own plants. Large buyers, therefore, often try to control—or even buy—their sources of supply. Some control can be gained through contracts—perhaps negotiated by top-level managers—using standard grades and specifications.

Another way to assure supply sources is with **vertical integration** ownership of the natural product source by the user. Examples are paper manufacturers who own timber resources, oil refiners who control crude oil sources, and tire manufacturers who own rubber plantations.

Natural products and farm products vary in quality and usually need to be graded.

COMPONENT PARTS AND MATERIALS—IMPORTANT EXPENSE ITEMS

The Whole Is No Better Than . . .

Component parts and materials are expense items which have had more processing than raw materials. They require different marketing mixes than raw materials—even though they both become part of a finished product.

Component *parts* include those items that are (1) finished and ready for assembly or (2) nearly finished—requiring only minor processing (such as grinding or polishing) before being assembled into the final product. Examples are automobile batteries, small motors, and tires—all of which go directly into a finished product.

Component *materials* are items such as wire, paper, textiles, or cement. They have already been processed—but must be processed further before becoming part of the final product.

Multiple Buying Influences

Some component parts are custom-made. Much negotiation may be needed between the engineering staffs of both buyer and seller to arrive at the right specifications. If the price of the item is high—or if it is extremely important in the final product—top managers may be involved.

Other component parts and materials are produced to commonly accepted standards or specifications—and produced in quantity. Production people in the buying firm may specify quality—but the purchasing agent will do the buying. And he will want several dependable sources of supply.

Since components become part of the firm's own product, quality is extremely important. The buyer's own name and whole marketing mix are at stake. Because of this, a buyer will try to buy from sources that help assure a good product.

SUPPLIES—EVERYBODY WANTS THESE EXPENSE ITEMS, BUT HOW MUCH?

Supplies are expense items that do not become a part of a final product. They may be treated less seriously by buyers.

They Are Called MRO Items

Supplies can be divided into three types: (1) maintenance, (2) repair, and (3) operating supplies—giving them their common name: "MRO items."

Maintenance items include such things as paint, nails, light bulbs, sweeping compounds, brooms, and cleaning equipment. *Repair items* are parts—like filters, bearings, and gears—needed to fix worn or broken equipment. *Operating*

The same bearings may be sold as components to equipment manufacturers—and as repair parts to final users.

supplies include lubricating oils and greases, grinding compounds, typing paper, ink, pencils, and paper clips.

Important Operating Supplies

Some operating supplies are needed regularly—and in large amounts. They receive special treatment from buyers. Some companies buy coal and fuel oil in carload or tankcar quantities. Usually there are several sources for such homogeneous products—and large volumes may be purchased in highly competitive markets. Or contracts may be negotiated—perhaps by high-level managers.

Maintenance and Small Operating Supplies

These items are like convenience goods. They are so numerous that a buyer can't possibly be an expert in buying all of them.

Each requisition for maintenance and small operating supplies may be for relatively few items. A purchase order may amount to only $1 or $2. Although the cost of handling a purchase order may be from $5 to $10, the item will be ordered—because it is needed—but not much time will be spent on it.

Branding may become important for such products. It makes product identi-fication and buying easier for such "nuisance" items. Width of assortment and dependability of the seller are important when buying supplies. Middlemen usually handle the many supply items.

Repair Items

The original supplier of installations or accessory equipment may be the only source of supply for repairs or parts. The cost of repairs in relation to the cost of a production break-down may be so small that buyers are willing to pay the price charged—whatever it is.

SERVICES—YOU EXPENSE THEM

Services are expense items which support the operations of a firm. Engineering or management consulting services can improve the plant layout or the operation of a company. Design services can supply designs for a physical plant, products, and promotion materials. Maintenance services can handle window-cleaning, painting, or general housekeeping. Other companies can supply in-plant lunches—and piped-in music—to improve employee morale and production.

The cost of buying services outside the firm is compared with the cost of having company people do them. For special skills needed only occasionally, an outsider can be the best source. And service specialists are growing in number in our complex economy.

BRANDING IS A STRATEGY DECISION, TOO

There are so many brands—and we're so used to seeing them—that we take them for granted. In the grocery products area alone, there are more than 40,000 brands. Brands are of great importance to their owners—because they help identify the company's marketing mix—and help consumers recognize the firm's products and advertising. Branding is an important decision area which is ignored by many business people. So we will treat it in some detail.

What Is Branding, Brand Name, and Trademark?

Branding means the use of a name, term, symbol, or design—or a combination of these—to identify a product. It includes the use of brand names, trademarks, and practically all other means of product identification.

Brand name has a narrower meaning. A **brand name** is a word, letter, or a group of words or letters.

Trademark is a legal term. A **trademark** includes only those words, symbols, or marks that are legally registered for use by a single company.

The word *Buick* can be used to explain these differences. The Buick car is *branded* under the *brand name* "Buick" (whether it is spoken or printed in any manner). When "Buick" is printed in a certain kind of script, however, it becomes a *trademark*. A trademark need not be attached to the product. It need not even be a word. A symbol can be used. Figure 9–5 shows some common trademarks.

These differences may seem technical. But they are very important to business firms that spend a lot of money to protect and promote their brands.

BRANDING—WHY IT DEVELOPED

Brands Meet Needs

Branding started during the Middle Ages—when craft guilds (similar to labor unions) and merchant guilds formed to control the quantity and quality of pro-

■ FIGURE 9–5   Recognized trademarks and symbols help in promotion

duction. Each producer had to mark his goods—so output could be cut back when necessary. This also meant that poor quality—which might reflect unfavorably on other guild products and discourage future trade—could be traced back to the guilty producer. Early trademarks were also a protection to the buyer—who could now know the source of the product.

Not Restriction but Identification

More recently, brands have been used mainly for identification. The earliest and most aggressive brand promoters in America were the patent medicine companies. They were joined by the food manufacturers—who grew in size after the Civil War. Some of the brands started in the 1860s and 1870s (and still going strong) are Borden's Condensed Milk, Quaker Oats, Pillsbury's Best Flour, and Ivory Soap.

Well-recognized brands make shopping easier. Think of trying to buy groceries, for example, if you had to evaluate the advantages and disadvantages of each of 10,000 items every time you went to a supermarket.

Many customers are willing to buy new things—but having gambled and won, they like to buy a "sure thing" the next time.

CONDITIONS FAVORABLE TO BRANDING

Most marketing managers accept branding—and are concerned with seeing that their brands succeed.

The following conditions are favorable to successful branding:

You have our word on it.

Sunkist brand means quality to its loyal customers.

1. The demand for the general product class should be large.
2. The demand should be strong enough so that the market price can be high enough to make the effort profitable.
3. There should be economies of scale. If the branding is really successful, the cost of production should drop, and profits should increase.
4. The product quality should be the best for the price—that is, the best "value" for the price. And the quality should be easy to maintain.
5. The product should be easy to identify by brand or trademark.
6. Dependable and widespread availability should be possible. When customers start using a brand, they want to be able to continue finding it in their stores.
7. Favorable shelf locations or display space in stores will help.

ACHIEVING BRAND FAMILIARITY IS NOT EASY

Brand acceptance must be earned with a good product and regular promotion. **Brand familiarity** means how well customers recognize and accept a company's brand. The degree of brand familiarity affects the planning for the rest of the marketing mix—especially where the product should be offered and what promotion is needed.

Five Levels of Brand Familiarity

Five levels of brand familiarity are useful for strategy planning: (1) rejection, (2) non-recognition, (3) recognition, (4) preference, and (5) insistence.

Some brands have been tried and found wanting. **Brand rejection** means the potential customers won't buy a brand—unless its image is changed.

■ FIGURE 9–6   Characteristics of a good brand name

Short and simple.
Easy to spell and read.
Easy to recognize and remember.
Pleasing when read or heard—and easy to pronounce.
Pronounceable in only one way.
Pronounceable in all languages (for goods to be exported).
Always timely (does not get out of date).
Adaptable to packaging or labeling needs.
Legally available for use (not in use by another firm).
Not offensive, obscene, or negative.
Suggestive of product benefits.
Adaptable to any advertising medium (especially billboards and television).

Rejection may suggest a change in the product—or perhaps only a shift to target customers who have a better image of the brand. Overcoming negative images is difficult—and can be very expensive.

Some products are seen as basically the same. **Brand non-recognition** means a brand is not recognized by final customers at all—even though middlemen may use the brand name for identification and inventory control. Examples here are school supplies, novelties, inexpensive dinnerware, and similar goods found in discount stores.

Brand recognition means that customers remember the brand. This can be a big advantage if there are many "nothing" brands on the market.

Most branders would like to win **brand preference**—which means target customers will usually choose the brand over other brands—perhaps because of habit or past experience.

Brand insistence means customers insist on a firm's branded product and are willing to search for it. This is an objective of many target marketers.

The Right Brand Name Can Help

A good brand name can help build brand familiarity. It can help tell something important about the company or its product. Figure 9–6 lists some characteristics of a good brand name. Some successful brand names seem to break all these rules. Many of these names, however, got started when there was less competition.

PROTECTING BRAND NAMES AND TRADEMARKS

Common law protects the rights of the owners of trademarks and brand names. And the *Lanham Act* of 1946 spells out the exact method of protecting trademarks—and what kinds of marks (including brand names) can be protected. The law applies to goods shipped in interstate or foreign commerce.

The Lanham Act does not force registration. But a good reason to register under the Lanham Act is to protect a trademark to be used in international markets. Before a trademark can be protected in a foreign country, some nations require that it be registered in its home country.

**You Must Protect
Your Own**

A brand can be a real asset to a company. Each firm should try to see that its brand doesn't become a common descriptive term for its kind of product. When this happens, the brand name or trademark becomes public property. The owner loses all rights to it. This happened with the names cellophane, aspirin, shredded wheat, and kerosene. There was concern that "Teflon" and "Scotch Tape" might become public property—and Miller Brewing Company tried—unsuccessfully—to protect its "Lite" beer by suing other brewers who wanted to use the word "light."[4]

WHAT KIND OF BRAND TO USE?

Keep It in the Family

Branders who manufacture or handle more than one item must decide whether they are going to use a **family brand**—the same brand name for several products—or individual brands for each product. Examples of family brands are the Kraft food products, the three A&P brands (Ann Page, Sultana, and Iona) and Sears' "Craftsman" tools and "Kenmore" appliances.

The use of the same brand for many products makes sense if all are similar in type and quality. The goodwill attached to one or two products may help the others. This cuts promotion costs. It also tends to build loyalty to the family brand—and makes it easier to introduce new products.

A **licensed brand** is a well-known brand which sellers pay a fee to use. For example, the creators of "Sesame Street" allow different sellers to brand their

Kraft sells many different products under its family brand.

products with the Sesame Street name and trademark—for a fee. In this case, many different companies may be in the "family."

Individual Brands for Outside and Inside Competition

Individual brands—separate brand names for each product—are used by a brander when its products are of varying quality or type. If the products are really different—such as motor oil and cooking oil—individual brands are better.

Sometimes firms use individual brands to encourage competition within the company. Each brand is managed by a different group. Management feels that internal competition keeps everyone alert. The theory is that if anyone is going to take business away from them, it ought to be their own brand. This kind of competition is found among General Motors' brands. Chevrolet, Pontiac, Oldsmobile, Buick, and even Cadillac compete with each other in some markets.

Generic Brands for "Commodities"

Products which are seen by consumers as "commodities" may be difficult to brand. Recently, some manufacturers and middlemen have faced this problem and come up with **generic products**—products which have no brand at all other than identification of their contents and the manufacturer or middleman. Generic products are most common for staple goods—especially food products and drug items. For example, many supermarkets offer generic paper towels, macaroni, beans, noodles, and dog food. Typically, these are offered in plain packages at lower prices.

Some generic products have been well accepted by some target markets. These consumers don't see big differences among these products—except in price. When generic products were first introduced, many critics predicted that they wouldn't last. It now appears that some products will continue to be offered in this way.[5]

Many "commodity" products are now sold as generic "brands."

Generics, manufacturer brands, and dealer brands often battle for the consumer's dollar.

WHO SHOULD DO THE BRANDING?

Manufacturer Brands versus Dealer Brands

Manufacturer brands are brands which are created by manufacturers. These are sometimes called "national brands"—because manufacturers often promote these brands all across the country or in large regions. Such brands include Kellogg's, Stokely, Whirlpool, Ford, and IBM.

Dealer brands are brands created by middlemen. These are sometimes called "private brands." Examples of dealer brands include the brands of Kroger, Ace Hardware, Sears, and Radio Shack. Some of these are advertised and distributed more widely than many "national brands."

The Battle of the Brands—Who's Winning?

The **battle of the brands** is the competition between dealer brands and manufacturer brands. The "battle" is just a question of whose brands will be more popular—and who will be in control.

At one time, manufacturer brands were much more popular than dealer brands. But they may be losing the battle. Sales of dealer brands have continued to grow. Now sales are about equal—and rising. Middlemen have some advantages in this battle. They can control shelf space. They often price their own brands lower. Customers can benefit from the "battle." Price differences between manufacturer brands and well-known dealer brands have already narrowed due to the competition.[6]

THE STRATEGIC IMPORTANCE OF PACKAGING

Packaging involves protecting and promoting the product. Packaging can be important to both sellers and customers. Packaging can make a product more convenient to use or store. It can prevent spoiling or damage. Good packaging makes products easier to identify—and promotes the brand at the store and even in use.

Packaging Can Make the Difference

A new package can make *the* important difference in a new marketing strategy—by meeting customers' needs better. A better box, wrapper, can, or bottle may help create a "new" product—or a new market. Frozen vegetables in 1-pound packages served larger families better. The little 10-ounce packages were too small—but two packages held too much.

Multiple packs were the basis of a new marketing strategy, too. Surveys showed that some customers were buying several units at a time of products like soft drinks, beer, and frozen orange juice. Manufacturers tried packaging in 4-, 6-, and 8-packs—and have been very successful.

Sometimes a new package improves a product by making it easier to use. A producer of light-sensitive X-ray films increased sales by packing each sheet in a separate foil pack—making it easier for doctors to handle. Many frozen convenience foods are now packaged in containers that can be used in microwave ovens.

Packaging can improve product safety: shampoo comes in plastic bottles—that won't break if dropped in the shower.

Packaging can tie the product to the rest of the marketing strategy. Expensive perfume may come in a crystal bottle—adding to the prestige image. L'eggs pantyhose—in plastic eggs—make the product stand out in store displays and remind customers of the name.

May Lower Total Distribution Costs

Better protective packaging is very important to manufacturers and wholesalers. They often have to pay the cost of goods damaged in shipment. There are also costs for settling such claims. Goods damaged in shipment also may delay production—or cause lost sales.

Retailers need good packaging, too. Packaging that provides better protection can reduce store costs—by cutting breakage, preventing discoloration, and stopping theft. Packages that are easier to handle can cut costs by speeding price marking, improving handling and display, and saving space.

Promotion-oriented packaging may be better than advertising

A good package sometimes gives a firm more promotion effect than it could possibly afford with advertising. Packaged products are seen regularly in retail stores—where customers are actually buying products. The package may be seen by many more potential customers than the company's advertising. An attractive package may speed turnover so much that total costs will drop as a percentage of sales.

Or . . . May Raise Total Costs

In other cases, total distribution costs may rise because of packaging. But customers may be more satisfied because the packaging improves the product—by offering much greater convenience or reducing waste.

Packaging costs as a percentage of a manufacturer's selling price vary widely—ranging from 1 to 70 percent. Let's look at sugar as an example. In

Packaging can make a new product.

100-pound bags, the cost of packaging sugar is only 1 percent of the selling price. In two- and five-pound cartons, it is 25 to 30 percent. And for individual serving packages, it is 50 percent. Most customers don't want to haul a 100-pound bag home—and are quite willing to pay for more convenient packages. Restaurants use one-serving envelopes of sugar—finding that they reduce the cost of filling and washing sugar bowls—and that customers prefer the more sanitary little packages. In both cases, packaging adds value to the product. Actually, it creates new products—and new marketing strategies.

The Right Packaging Is Just Enough Packaging

A specific package must be designed for each product. The package must safely transport its contents, serve in a specific climate (especially if the product is to be exported), and last for a specific time. Underpackaging costs money—for damage claims or poor sales. But overpackaging also costs money—because dollars are spent for no benefit.

Glassware, for example, needs to be protected from even relatively light blows that might smash it. Heavy-duty machinery doesn't need protection from blows—but may need protection from moisture. To provide such packaging, the manufacturer must know about the product, the target customers, and how the product will be delivered.[7]

WHAT IS SOCIALLY RESPONSIBLE PACKAGING?

Some consumers say that some package designs are misleading—perhaps on purpose. Others feel that the great variety of packages makes it hard to compare values. And some are concerned about whether they are biodegradable—or can be recycled.

Federal Law Tries to Help

Consumer criticism finally led to the passage of the **Federal Fair Packaging and Labeling Act** (of 1966)—which requires that consumer goods be clearly labeled in easy-to-understand terms—to give consumers more information. The law also calls on government agencies and industry to try to reduce the number of package sizes—and to make labels more useful.[8]

Food products must now list nutrition information—as well as weight or volume. But there is some question whether many consumers understand this information—or what to do with it—or even if this is the information they want. At the same time, it is difficult or impossible to provide the kind of information they *do* want—for example, regarding taste and texture.

Unit-Pricing Is a Possible Help

Some retailers—especially large supermarket chains—make it easier for consumers to compare packages with different weights or volumes. They use **unit-pricing**—which involves placing the price per ounce (or some other standard measure) on or near the product. This makes price comparison easier—and some consumers do appreciate this service.[9]

Universal Product Codes Allow More Information

To speed the handling of fast-selling products, government and industry representatives have developed a **universal product code (UPC)**—which identifies each product with marks that can be "read" by electronic scanners. Through a computer, each code is related to the type of product—and its price. Supermarkets and other high-volume retailers have been eager to use these codes. They speed the check-out process—and get rid of the need for marking the price on every item. They also reduce errors by cashiers—and make it easy to control inventory and track sales of specific products. Figure 9–7 shows a universal product code mark.

Some consumers don't like the codes because they can't compare prices—either in the store or at home. To solve this problem, most new systems now include a printed receipt showing the prices of products bought. In the future, the codes probably will become even more widely used—because they do lower operating costs.

■   FIGURE 9–7   An illustration of a universal product code for a ballpoint pen

WARRANTIES ARE IMPORTANT, TOO

**Warranty Should
Mean Something**

Common law says that producers must stand behind their products. And now the federal **Magnuson-Moss Act** of 1975 says that producers must provide a clearly written warranty if they choose to offer any warranty. A **warranty** explains what the seller promises about its product. The warranty does not have to be strong. But Federal Trade Commission (FTC) guidelines do try to make sure that warranties are clear and definite—and not "deceptive" or "unfair." Some firms used to say their products were "fully warranted" or "absolutely guaranteed." The time period wasn't stated. And the meaning of the warranty was not spelled out either.

Now a company has to make clear whether it's offering a "full" or "limited" warranty—and the law defines what "full" means. Also, the warranty must be available for inspection before the purchase. Most firms offer a limited warranty—if they offer one at all. Some firms just guarantee their products against "defects of material or workmanship" for 30 to 90 days. Others are trying to design more quality into their products. They offer longer and stronger warranties. Some companies have gone even further by providing one-year replacement—not just repair—if there is a problem.

Some firms use warranty levels to segment the market. The basic price for a product may include a warranty for a short time period—or cover parts but not labor. Consumers who want more or better protection can pay extra for an extended warranty—or a service contract.

Customers might like a strong warranty, but it can be very expensive—even economically impossible for small firms. Backing up warranties can be a problem, too. Some customers abuse products—and demand a lot of service on warranties. Although manufacturers may be responsible, they may have to depend on reluctant or poorly trained middlemen to do the job. For example, when energy prices began to rise, many consumers bought chain saws to cut their own fire wood. To reach this target market, Homelite and other companies began to distribute their saws through chain stores like K mart. But they had to set up their own service centers, because the retail chains had no repair facilities. In situations like this, it's hard for a small firm to compete with larger firms with many service centers.

Deciding on the warranty is a strategic matter. Specific decisions should be made about what the warranty will cover—and then it should be communicated clearly to the target customers. A warranty can make the difference between success and failure for a whole marketing strategy.[10]

■ **CONCLUSION**

In this chapter, we looked at Product very broadly. A Product may not be a physical good at all. It may be a service. Or it may be some combination of goods and services—like a meal at a restaurant.

A firm's Product is what satisfies the needs of its target market. This *may* be a physical good—but also could include a package, brand, installation, repair service, a warranty—whatever is needed to satisfy target customers.

Consumer goods and industrial goods classes were introduced to simplify your study of marketing—and help in planning marketing mixes. The consumer goods classes are based on consumers' buying behavior. Industrial goods classes are based on how buyers see the products—and how they are used. Knowing these goods classes—and learning how marketers handle specific products within these classes—will speed the development of your "marketing sense."

The fact that different people may see the same product in different goods classes helps explain why seeming competitors may use very different marketing mixes—and succeed.

Packaging and branding can create new and more satisfying products. Variations in packaging can make a product salable in various target markets. A specific package may have to be developed for each strategy. Both under-packaging and over-packaging are expensive.

To customers, the main value of brands is as a guarantee of quality. This leads to repeat purchasing. For marketers, such "routine" buying means lower promotion costs and higher sales.

Should brands be stressed? The decision depends on whether the costs of brand promotion and honoring the brand guarantee can be more than covered by a higher price or more rapid turnover—or both. The cost of branding may reduce other costs—by reducing pressure on the other three Ps.

Branding gives marketing managers choice. They can add brands—and use individual or family brands. In the end, however, customers express their approval or disapproval of the whole Product (including the brand). The degree of brand familiarity is a measure of the marketing manager's ability to carve out a separate market—and affects Place, Price, and Promotion decisions.

Warranties are also important in strategy planning. A warranty need not be strong—it just has to be clearly stated. But some customers find strong warranties attractive.

So it should be clear that Product is concerned with much more than a physical good or service. The marketing manager must also be concerned about packaging, branding, and warranties—if he is to help his firm succeed in our increasingly competitive marketplaces.

■ **QUESTIONS AND PROBLEMS**

1. Define, in your own words, what a Product is.

2. Explain how the addition of warranties, service, and credit can improve a "product." Cite a specific case where this has been done and explain how customers viewed this new "product."

3. What "products" are being offered by an exclusive men's shop? By a nightclub? By a soda fountain? By a supermarket?

4. What kinds of consumer goods are the following: (a) fountain pens, (b) men's shirts, (c) cosmetics? Explain your reasoning and draw a picture of the market in each case to help illustrate your thinking.

5. Some goods seem to be treated perpetually as unsought goods by their producers. Give an example and explain why.

6. How would the marketing mix for a staple convenience good differ from the one for a homogeneous shopping good? How would the mix for a specialty good differ from the mix for a heterogeneous shopping good? Use examples.

7. Which of the Ps would receive the greatest emphasis in the marketing mix for a new unsought good? Explain why, using an example.

8. In what types of stores would you expect to find: (a) convenience goods, (b) shopping goods, (c) specialty goods, and (d) unsought goods?

9. Cite two examples of industrial goods which require a substantial amount of service in order to make them useful "products."

10. Would you expect to find any wholesalers selling the various types of industrial goods? Are retail stores required (or something like retail stores)?

11. What kinds of industrial goods are the following: (a) nails and screws, (b) paint, (c) dust-collecting and ventilating systems, (d) an electric lift truck? Explain your reasoning?

12. How do farm product raw materials differ from other raw materials or other industrial goods? Do the differences have any impact on their marketing mixes? If so, what specifically?

13. For the kinds of industrial goods described in this chapter, complete the following table (use one or a few well-chosen words).

Goods	1	2	3
Installations			
Buildings and			
land rights			
Major equipment			
Standard			
Custom made			
Accessory equipment			
Raw materials			
Farm products			
Natural products			
Components			
Parts			
Materials			
Supplies			
Operating supplies			
Maintenance and			
small operating			
supplies			
Services			

1—Kind of distribution facility(ies) needed and functions they will provide.
2—Caliber of salespeople required.
3—Kind of advertising required.

14. Is there any difference between a brand name and a trademark? If so, why is this difference important?

15. Is a well-known brand valuable only to the owner of the brand?

16. Would it be profitable for a firm to spend large sums of money to establish a brand for any type product in any competitive situation? Why or why not? If the answer is no, suggest examples.

17. Evaluate the suitability of the following brand names: (*a*) Star (sausage), (*b*) Pleasing (books), (*c*) Rugged (shoes), (*d*) Shiny (shoe polish), (*e*) Lord Jim (ties).

18. Explain family brands. Sears, Roebuck and A&P use family brands, but they have several different family brands. If the idea is a good one, why don't they have just one brand?

19. What is the "battle of the brands?" Who do you think will win and why?

20. What does the degree of brand familiarity

imply about previous promotion efforts and the future promotion task? Also, how does the degree of brand familiarity affect the Place and Price variables?

21. If you have been operating a small supermarket with emphasis on manufacturers' brands and have barely been breaking even, how should you evaluate the proposal of a large wholesaler who offers a full line of dealer-branded groceries at substantially lower prices? Specify any assumptions necessary to obtain a definite answer.

22. Suggest an example where packaging costs probably: (*a*) lower total distribution costs and (*b*) raise total distribution costs.

■ SUGGESTED CASES

9. Barnes Florist Shop

10. Revon Company

Chapter 10 ■ Product management and new-product development

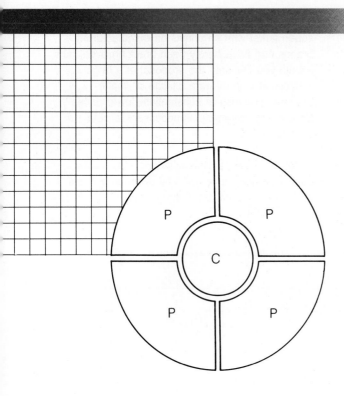

When you finish this chapter, you should:

1. Understand how product life cycles affect strategy planning.

2. Know what is involved in designing new products and what "new products" really are.

3. Know about a new-product development process.

4. Know about product positioning.

5. Understand the need for product or brand managers.

6. Recognize the important new terms (shown in red).

Product management is a dynamic, full-time job for product managers.

Just 15 years ago, almost every engineer in the country owned a slide rule. Now slide rules have been replaced by pocket calculators. Once-popular fountain pens have lost out to disposable ballpoint and felt-tip pens. Wood stoves all but disappeared for 40 years, but the recent energy crunch brought them back again. Electric cars and solar-powered water heaters haven't caught on yet—but may be common in another 20 years.

The point of these examples is simple. Products, markets, and competition change over time. This makes marketing management difficult—but exciting. Developing new products and managing existing products in changing conditions is necessary for the success of every firm. In this chapter, we'll look at some important ideas in these areas.

MANAGEMENT OF PRODUCTS OVER THEIR LIFE CYCLES

Industry Sales and Profits Don't Move Together

Products—like consumers—have life cycles. So product and marketing mix planning are important. Competitors are always developing and copying ideas and products—making existing products out-of-date more quickly than ever.

The **product life cycle**—is the stages a new idea goes through from beginning to end. It is divided into four major stages: (1) market introduction, (2) market growth, (3) market maturity, and (4) sales decline.

A particular firm's marketing mix for a product should change during these stages—for several reasons. Customers' attitudes and needs may change through the course of the product's life cycle. Entirely different target markets may be appealed to at different stages of the product's life cycle. And the nature of competition moves toward pure competition or oligopoly.

Further, total sales of the product—by all competitors in the industry—vary in each of its four stages. More importantly, the profit picture changes, too. These relationships can be seen in Figure 10–1. Note that sales and profits do not move together over time. *Industry profits start to decline while industry sales are still rising.*[1]

Market Introduction— Investing in the Future

In the **market introduction** stage, sales are low as a new idea is first introduced to a market. Customers aren't looking for the product. They don't even know about it. Informative promotion is needed to tell potential customers about the advantages and uses of the new product.

Even though a firm promotes its new product, it takes time for customers to learn about it. The introduction stage usually shows losses—with much money spent for Promotion, Product, and Place development. Money is being invested in the hope of future profits.

■ **FIGURE 10–1** Life cycle of a typical product

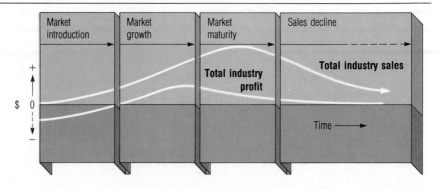

Microwave ovens have been selling well—and probably haven't reached the market maturity stage.

Market Growth—Profits and Then Competition

In the **market growth** stage, industry sales are growing fast—but industry profits rise and then start falling. The innovator begins to make big profits. But competitors enter the market—each trying to improve on the product design. This results in much product variety. But some competitors just copy the most successful products.

This is the time of biggest profits—*for the industry. But it is also when industry profits begin to decline*—as competition increases. See Figure 10–1.

Some firms make big strategy planning mistakes at this stage—by not understanding the product life cycle. They see the big sales and profit opportunities of the early market growth stage—but ignore the competition that will soon follow. When they realize their mistake, it may be too late.

Market Maturity—Sales Level Off, Profits Go Down

The **market maturity** stage is when industry sales level off—and competition gets tougher. Many competitors have entered the race for profits—except in oligopoly. Industry profits go down during the market maturity stage—because promotion costs rise and some competitors cut prices to attract business. Less efficient firms can't compete with this pressure—and they drop out of the market. Even in oligopoly situations, there is a long-run downward pressure on prices. Note, however, that good strategies may be profitable all through this stage—even as weak competitors drop out of the market.

New firms may still enter the market at this stage—increasing competition even more. Note that late entries skip the early life-cycle stages—including the profitable market growth stage.

Promotion becomes more important during the market maturity stage. Products may differ only slightly—if at all. Most competitors have discovered the most effective appeals—or copied the leaders. Although each firm may still have its own demand curve, the curves become more elastic—as the various products appear almost the same in the minds of potential consumers.

In the United States, the markets for most automobiles, boats, many household appliances, most groceries, and television sets are in market maturity.[2] This stage may continue for many years—until a basically new product idea comes along. This is true even though individual brands or models may come and go.

Sales Decline—A Time of Replacement

The **sales decline** stage occurs as new products replace the old. Price competition from dying products increases—but firms with strong brands may make profits almost until the end. These firms have down-sloping demand curves—because they have been able to differentiate their products.

As the new products go through their introduction stage, the old ones may keep some sales—by appealing to the most loyal target customers or those who are slow to try new ideas. These conservative buyers might switch later—smoothing the sales decline.

Product Life Cycles Are Getting Shorter

The length of a product life cycle may vary from 90 days—in the case of a toy like Rubic's cube—to possibly 90 years for gas-powered cars. In general, however, product life cycles are getting shorter.

In the highly competitive grocery products industry, they are down to 12–18 months for really new ideas. Simple variations of a new idea may have even shorter cycles. Competitors can copy flavor or packaging changes in months . . . or even weeks.

Fast copying is also common in industrial goods markets. A top Du Pont manager said: "Lead time is gone . . . there's no company so outstanding today that it can expect a long lead time on a new discovery." Du Pont had nylon to itself for 15 years. But in just two years, a major competitor—Celanese Corporation—came out with a product very similar to Delrin—another synthetic fiber discovery that Du Pont hoped would be as important as nylon.

Patents may not be much protection for a new product. The product's life may be over before the case can get through the courts. The copy-cat competitor may be out of business by then. Or competitors may find other ways to make the product.

Improved products can push existing products into the sales decline stage.

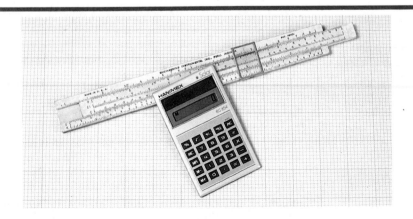

The Early Bird Makes the Profits	The increasing speed of product life cycles means that a successful firm must be developing new products all the time. It must try to have marketing mixes that will make the most of the market growth stage—when profits are highest.

PRODUCT LIFE CYCLES SHOULD BE RELATED TO SPECIFIC MARKETS

Each Market Should Be Carefully Defined	To fully understand the *why* of a product life cycle, we should carefully define the market area we are considering. The way we define a market makes a difference in the way we see product life cycles—and who the competitors are. If a market is defined too generally, there may be many competitors—and the market may appear to be in market maturity. On the other hand, if we look at a narrow area—and a particular way of satisfying specific needs—then we may see much shorter product life cycles—as improved product ideas come along to replace the old. For example, the general market demand for power lawnmowers appears to be in the market maturity stage—where only minor product changes are expected. If we think of lawnmowers using different technical principles, however, we get a different view. "Air-cushion" mowers for very uneven lawns were introduced recently and may take some of the "wheeled" mower business. Power lawnmower producers who defined their market too generally may miss this opportunity.
Each Market Segment Has Its Own Product Life Cycle	Too narrow a view of a market segment can lead to misreading the nature of competition—and the speed of the relevant product life cycle. A firm producing exercise machines, for example, may focus on only the "exercise machine" market. But this narrow view can lead it to compete only with other exercise machine producers—when it might make more sense to compete in the "fitness" market. Of course, it can't ignore competitors' machines, but even tougher competition may come from health clubs—and suppliers of jogging suits, athletic shoes, and other fitness-related goods. In other words, there may be two markets—and two life cycles—to work with: the exercise machine market and the fitness market. Each may require a different strategy.
Individual Products Don't Have Product Life Cycles	Notice that product life cycles describe *industry* sales and profits within a particular product-market—*not* the sales and profits of an *individual* product or brand. Individual products or brands may be introduced—or withdrawn—during any stage of the product life cycle. Further, their sales and profits may vary up and down throughout the life cycle—sometimes moving in the opposite direction of industry sales and profits.
	A "me-too" product introduced during the market growth stage, for example, may reach its peak and start to decline even before market maturity—or it may never get any sales at all—and suffer a quick death. Market leaders may enjoy high profits during the market maturity stage—even though industry prof-

its are declining. Weaker products, on the other hand, may not earn a profit during any stage of the product life cycle.

What this discussion means, therefore, is that sales of *individual* products often do not follow the product life cycle curve shown in Figure 10–1—and studying a specific product's past sales patterns can be misleading for strategy planning purposes. It's the life cycle for the whole product-market—including all current or potential competitors—that marketing managers must study when planning their strategies. In fact, it might be more sensible to think in terms of "market life cycles" or "product-market life cycles" rather than product life cycles—but we will use the term *product life cycle* because it is commonly accepted and widely used.

PLANNING FOR DIFFERENT STAGES OF THE PRODUCT LIFE CYCLE

Length of Cycle Affects Strategy Planning

The probable length of the cycle affects strategy planning—realistic plans must be made for the later stages. In fact, where a product is in its life cycle—and how fast it's moving to the next stage—should affect strategy planning. Figure 10–2 shows the relation of the product life cycle to the marketing mix variables. The new technical terms in this figure are discussed later in the book.

Introducing New Products

Figure 10–2 shows that a marketing manager has a tough job introducing a really new product. Even if the product is unique—this doesn't mean that everyone will immediately come running to the producer's door. The firm will have to build channels of distribution—perhaps offering special incentives to win cooperation. Promotion will have to build demand *for the whole idea*—not just try to sell a specific brand. All of this costs money—so losses can be expected in the market introduction stage of the product life cycle. The marketing manager may try to "skim" the market—charging a relatively high price to help pay for these costs.

The best strategy, however, depends on how fast the product life cycle is likely to move—that is, how quickly the idea will be accepted by customers—and how quickly competitors will follow with their own versions of the product.

Also relevant is how quickly the firm can change its strategy as the life cycle moves on. Some firms are very flexible—and are able to compete effectively with larger, less adaptable competitors.

Managing Maturing Products

Whether a firm has developed some competitive advantage is important as its products move into market maturity. Even a small advantage can make a big difference—and some firms do very well by careful management of maturing products. They are able to take advantage of a slightly better product—or perhaps lower production and/or marketing costs. Or they are more successful

■ FIGURE 10–2   Typical changes in marketing variables over the course of the product life cycle

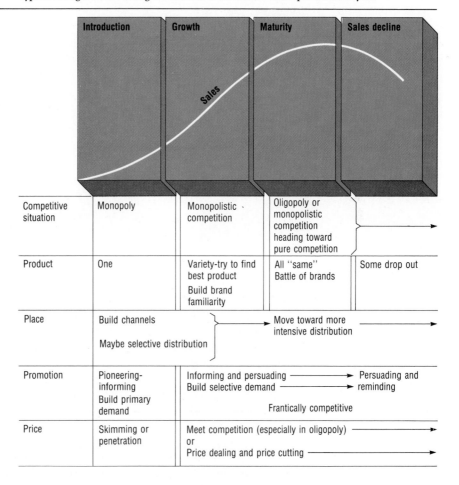

	Introduction	Growth	Maturity	Sales decline
Competitive situation	Monopoly	Monopolistic competition	Oligopoly or monopolistic competition heading toward pure competition	
Product	One	Variety-try to find best product Build brand familiarity	All "same" Battle of brands	Some drop out
Place	Build channels Maybe selective distribution		Move toward more intensive distribution	
Promotion	Pioneering-informing Build primary demand	Informing and persuading ——————→ Persuading and Build selective demand ——————→ reminding Frantically competitive		
Price	Skimming or penetration	Meet competition (especially in oligopoly) ——————→ or Price dealing and price cutting ——————→		

at promotion—allowing them to differentiate their more-or-less homogeneous product from competitors.

An important point to remember here, however, is that industry profits are declining in market maturity. Financially oriented top management must see this—or they will continue to expect the attractive profits of the market growth stage—profits that may no longer be possible. If top managers don't understand this, they may place impossible burdens on the marketing department—causing marketing managers to think about collusion with competitors, deceptive advertising, or some other desperate way of reaching impossible objectives.

Top management must see that there is an upper limit in any product-market. The product life cycle concept has been very useful in communicating this unhappy message. It is one of the powerful tools of marketing which is

■ FIGURE 10–3   Significantly improved product starts a new cycle, but maybe with short introductory stage

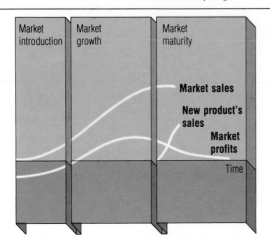

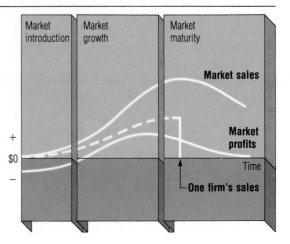

turning up in finance and top management literature—because it is useful for overall corporate planning and objective setting.

Product life cycles keep moving. But if a company doesn't have any competitive advantage, it doesn't have to sit by and watch its products go through a complete product life cycle. It has choices. It can improve the product—for the same or a different market—and let it start on a different cycle. Or it can withdraw the product before it completes the cycle. These two choices are shown in Figure 10–3.

Product Life Cycles Can Be Extended

When a firm's product wins the position of "*the* product that meets my needs," its life will last as long as it continues to meet these needs. If the needs change, the product may have to change—but the target consumers will continue to buy it if it still meets their needs. An outstanding example is Procter & Gamble's Tide. Introduced in 1947, this synthetic detergent gave consumers a much cleaner wash than they were able to get before—because it did away with soap film. Tide led to a whole new generation of laundry products—because it produced better cleaning with fewer suds. Since 1947, consumers' needs have changed, washing machines have changed, and fabrics have changed—so the Tide sold today is much different than the one sold in 1947. In fact, there were 55 modifications during its first 29 years of life. But the product continues to sell well—because it continues to meet consumers' needs.[3]

Do the kinds of product changes made with Tide create a new product which should have its own product life cycle—or are they just technical changes in the original product idea? We will take the second view—focusing on the product *idea* rather than technical changes. Detergents did permit a new standard of cleanliness. Consumers who wanted this feature shifted quite rapidly to detergents—causing sales to drop for the traditional soaps. As detergents gained acceptance, they went through the early stages of the product life cycle—and now may continue in market maturity until a new cleaning idea comes along. Note that for strategy planning purposes, new brands of similar detergents must be seen as immediately entering the *market maturity* stage—*not* market introduction.

Phasing Out Dying Products

Not all strategies have to be growth strategies. If prospects are poor in some product-market, then a "phase-out" strategy may be needed. The need for phasing out becomes more obvious as the sales decline stage arrives. But even in market maturity, it may be clear that a particular product is not going to be profitable enough to reach the company's objectives. Then, the wisest move is to develop a strategy which helps the firm get out of the product-market as quickly as possible—even before the sales decline stage sets in—while minimizing possible losses.

Marketing plans are carried out as "ongoing" strategies—with salespeople making calls, inventory moving in the channel, advertising planned for several months ahead, and so on. So usually it isn't possible to avoid losses if a plan is ended abruptly. Sometimes it's better to phase out the product gradually. This can involve selective materials ordering—so that production can end with a minimum of unused inventory. Salespeople can be shifted to other jobs—or laid off. The advertising and other promotion efforts should be cancelled or phased out quickly—since there is no point in promoting for the long run anymore. These various actions obviously affect morale within the company—and may cause channel members to pull back too. So the company may have to offer price incentives in the channels.

Obviously, there are some difficult problems here, but it should be clear that a phase-out is also a *strategy*—and it must be market-oriented to cut losses. In fact, it is even possible to "milk out" a dying product for some time if competitors move out more quickly. There is still ongoing demand—although it is declining—and some customers may be willing to pay attractive prices to get their "old favorite." Further, there may be an ongoing need for repair parts and service—which adds to the overall profitability of the phase-out strategy. Or a new strategy could handle just the repairs and service—even as the basic product is being phased out. You can see that whole product life cycles should be planned—for each strategy.

NEW—PRODUCT PLANNING

Competition is so fierce in most markets that a firm has to keep developing new products—as well as modifying its current products—to meet changing customer needs and competitors' actions. Not having an active new-product development process means that consciously—or subconsciously—the firm has decided to "milk" its current products and go out of business. New-product planning *must* be done—just to survive in our dynamic marketplaces.

Eggs are not new—but this frozen egg roll is a new product with many possibilities.

How to take advantage of Gourm-egg.®
FROZEN HARD-COOKED EGG ROLL PRODUCT.

What Is a New Product?

A **new product** is one that is new *in any way* for the company concerned. A product can become "new" in many ways. A fresh idea can be turned into a new good or service. Small changes in an existing product also can make it "new." Or an existing product can be offered to new markets—as new products. Lemons are a good example. In the marketing of Sunkist lemons, no physical changes were made—but promotion created many "new" products. The same old lemons were promoted successfully for lemonade, mixed drinks, diet supplements, cold remedies, lemon cream pies, a salad dressing, sauce for fish, and many other uses.[4] For each of these markets, each product idea had to go through the early stages of the product life cycle.

FTC Says Product Is "New" Only Six Months

A product can be called "new" for only six months—according to the **Federal Trade Commission (FTC)**—the federal government agency which polices antimonopoly laws. To be called new—says the FTC—a product must be entirely new or changed in a "functionally significant or substantial respect." While six months may seem a very short time for production-oriented managers, it may be reasonable, given the short life cycles of many products.

AN ORGANIZED NEW–PRODUCT DEVELOPMENT PROCESS IS CRITICAL

Identifying and developing new-product ideas—and effective strategies to go with them—is often the key to a firm's success and survival. But this isn't easy. New-product development demands effort, time, and talent—and still the risks and costs of failure are high. (The failure rate on new products actually placed in the market may be as high as 50 percent.)[5]

To improve this effort, it is useful to follow an organized new-product development process. Figure 10–4 shows such a process—moving logically through

■ FIGURE 10–4   New product development process

Industrial markets	Consumer markets
1. Idea generation	1. Idea generation
2. Screening	2. Screening
Rough ROI estimate	*Rough ROI estimate*
3. Idea evaluation	3. Idea evaluation
Exploratory	Concept testing
Rough ROI verification	*Rough ROI verification*
Qualitative	
Quantitative	
ROI estimate	
4. Development	4. Development
R&D	R&D
Build model	Engineering
Engineering test	Build model(s)
Test in market	Test in market
ROI estimate	*ROI estimate*
	Revise product specifications
	Pilot production
	Production and quality
	control test
	Market testing
	Product variations
	Variations of marketing mix
	ROI estimates
5. Commercialization	5. Commercialization
Finalize production model	Finalize product
Finalize marketing mix (plan)	Finalize market mix (plan)
Final ROI estimate	*Final ROI estimate*
Start full-scale production	Start full-scale production
and marketing plan	and marketing plan

Source: Adapted from Frank R. Bacon, Jr. and Thomas W. Butler, Jr., *Planned Innovation*, rev. ed. (The University of Michigan, Ann Arbor: Institute of Science and Technology, 1980).

five steps: (1) idea generation, (2) screening, (3) idea evaluation, (4) development (of product and marketing mix), and (5) commercialization.[6]

Process Tries to Kill New Ideas— Economically

An important element in this new-product development process is continued evaluation of the likely profitability and return on investment of new ideas. In fact, it's desirable to apply the hypothesis-testing approach discussed in Chapter 5 to new-product development. The hypothesis which is tested is that the new idea will *not* be profitable. This puts the burden on the new idea to prove itself—or be rejected. This may seem harsh, but experience shows that most new ideas have some flaw which can lead to problems—and even large losses. Marketers try to discover those flaws early—and either find a remedy or reject the idea completely. Applying this process requires much analysis of the idea—both within and outside the firm—*before* any money is spent by research and development (R&D) or engineering to develop a physical item. This is a major departure from the usual production-oriented approach—which develops a product first and then asks sales to "get rid of it."

The value of an organized new-product development process can be seen in Figure 10–5. It shows how few ideas survive when they are carefully evaluated—from the screening stage to commercialization. It is estimated that out of 40 new ideas, only one is left after the ideas have passed through an organized development process. The rate of rejection varies among industries and companies—but the general shape of the decay curve seems to be typical. An especially conservative company may have even more rejects, of course. In summary, it is important to see that if a firm doesn't use this sort of organized process, it probably will bring many poor or weak ideas to market—at a big loss.

■ FIGURE 10–5   Decay of new-product ideas during an organized new-product development process

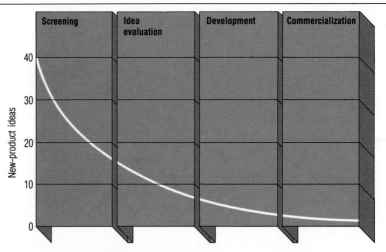

Source: Adapted from Management Research Department, Booz, Allen, and Hamilton, Inc.

Cracker Jack Extra Fresh Popping Corn. It's everything it's popped up to be.

It's packed up fresh. So it pops up perfect.
Our gourmet-quality popping corn is vacuum-packed in glass jars while it's fresh. So you always get popcorn that's big, tender, fluffy and delicious.

It's packed with experience.
Since 1871, we've popped more popcorn than anyone. With our Cracker Jack® Extra Fresh Popping Corn, you can be sure you're popping with the one—and only—real Cracker Jack.

It's packed with value.
Cracker Jack Extra Fresh Popping Corn comes in big 1, 2 and 3-pound easy-grip jars. It's just pennies for every serving, too—so you can enjoy it every day.

CRACKER JACK.
Since 1871, we've popped more popcorn than anyone.

© Borden Inc 1983

Consumers saw Cracker Jack as makers of good caramel-coated popcorn—so Cracker Jack introduced a plain popping corn, too.

Remember Customers—And Middlemen

When looking for new ideas, the consumer's viewpoint is very important. It is helpful to consider the image that potential customers have of the firm. For example, the makers of Cracker Jack had a familiar brand of caramel-coated popcorn—so they introduced a line of plain popping corn—because consumers saw them as makers of "good" popcorn.

New-product planners must consider not only the consumers, however—but the middlemen who will handle or sell the product. There may be special handling or packaging needs. The shelf height in supermarkets, for example, may limit package size. Shipping or handling problems in the warehouse—or on carriers—might call for different types of packaging to keep damage down—or make handling easier.

Social Responsibility Important, Too

The firm's final choice in product design should fit with the company's overall objectives—and make good use of the firm's resources. But it's also desirable to create a need-satisfying product which will appeal to consumers—in the long run as well as the short run. Different kinds of new-product opportunities

■ FIGURE 10–6   Types of new-product opportunities

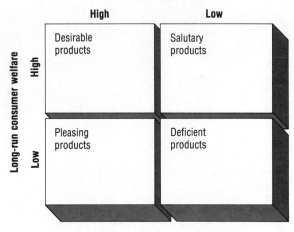

Source: Adapted from Philip Kotler, "What Consumerism Means for Marketers," *Harvard Business Review,* May–June 1972, pp. 55–56.

are shown in Figure 10–6. Obviously, a socially responsible firm tries to find "desirable" opportunities—rather than "deficient" ones. This may not be as easy as it sounds, however. Some consumers want "pleasing products"—instead of "desirable products." And some competitors are quite willing to offer what consumers want. Creating "socially responsible" new-product ideas is a challenge for new-product planners.

Safety Should Be Considered, Too

Real acceptance of the marketing concept should lead to the design of safe products.

The **Consumer Product Safety Act** of 1972 calls for more awareness of safety in product design—and better quality control. The commission can set safety standards for products—and it can order costly repairs or return of

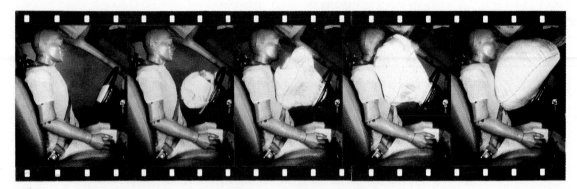

Real acceptance of the marketing concept should lead to the design of safe products.

"unsafe products." And it can back up its orders with fines and jail sentences. The Food and Drug Administration has similar powers for foods and drugs.

Product liability must be taken seriously

Product liability means the legal obligation of sellers to pay damages to individuals who are injured by defective products—or unsafely designed products. Some firms find their product liability insurance costs rising to the point where they have to "self-insure"—take the risk themselves—or go out of business. For example, Nissen Corporation, a maker of gym equipment, recently was offered a product liability insurance policy costing about $400,000 to cover $300,000 worth of protection (because of uncertainty about the size of court settlements). The major reason for these rising premiums is a growing number of claims, lawsuits, *and* settlements. And the potential for more suits is great. Recently, users of two paper-making presses sued the manufacturer for damages from industrial accidents. One of the presses was built in 1895 and the other in 1897!

Obviously, the uncontrollable environments have changed. And it's more important than ever to take new-product planning—and especially product safety—seriously. Managers who ignore these issues may be forced out of business.[7]

PRODUCT POSITIONING AIDS PRODUCT MANAGEMENT

A new aid to marketing management—**product positioning**—shows where proposed and/or present brands are located in a market—*as seen by customers*. It requires some formal marketing research. The results are usually plotted on graphs to help show where the products are "positioned" in relation to competitors. Usually, the products' positions are related to two product features which are important to the target customers.[8]

We won't discuss product positioning techniques here, but the results of one such analysis—for different brands of bar soap—shows the possibilities. In this case—besides plotting the customers' view of several brands of soap in relation to two product features—the respondents were asked about their "ideal" soap.

Figure 10–7 shows the "product space" for different brands of bar soap using two dimensions—the extent to which consumers think the soaps moisturize and deodorize their skin. For example, consumers see Dial as quite low on moisturizing—but high on deodorizing. Lifebuoy and Dial are close together—apparently consumers think of them as similar on these features. Dove is viewed as different—and is further away on the graph. Remember that positioning maps are based on customers' perceptions—the actual characteristics of the products (as determined by a chemical test) might be different!

The circles on Figure 10–7 show sets of consumers clustered near their "ideal" soap preferences. These clusters were obtained by asking consumers

■ FIGURE 10–7   "Product space" representing consumers' perceptions for different brands of soap

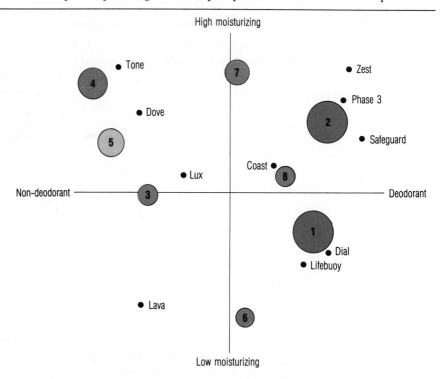

to rate their ideal soap, plotting the results, and then drawing circles around concentrations of consumers.

Note that some ideal clusters are not near any of the present brands. This might be a chance to introduce a new product—a strong moisturizer with some deodorizers. You can see that product positioning can help show how customers see markets.

NEW–PRODUCT DEVELOPMENT: A TOTAL COMPANY EFFORT

Top-Level Support Is Needed

New-product development should be a total company effort—with the enthusiastic support of top management. New products tend to upset old routines. So someone—or a department or group—has to be in charge of new-product development.[9]

Some Organization Helps

What specific organization is used may not be too important—as long as there is top management support. A new-product development department or committee can help make sure that new ideas are studied carefully—and good ones profitably marketed. Delays lead to late introduction—and give competitors a head start. A delay of even six months can make the difference between a product's success or failure.

A well-organized development process even makes it possible for a firm to copy others' successful ideas—quickly and profitably. This possibility should not be overlooked. No one company can always be first with the best new ideas.[10]

NEED FOR PRODUCT MANAGERS

Product Variety Leads to Product Managers

When a firm has only one or a few related products, everyone is interested in them. But when many new products are being developed, someone should be in charge of new-product planning—to be sure it is not neglected. Also, when a firm has several different kinds of products, management may decide to put someone in charge of each kind—or even each brand—to be sure they are not lost in the rush of everyday business. **Product managers** or **brand managers** manage specific products—often taking over the jobs once handled by an advertising manager. That gives a clue to what is often their major responsibility—Promotion—since the products have already been developed by the "new-product" people.

Product managers are especially common in large companies that produce many kinds of products. Several product managers may work under a marketing manager. Sometimes these product managers are responsible for the profitable operation of the whole marketing effort for a particular product. They must coordinate their efforts with others—including the sales manager, advertising agencies, and production and research people.

New products tend to upset old routines—for both customers and marketers.

In some companies, the product manager has a lot of power—and profit responsibility. In other firms, the product manager may be a "product champion"—concerned with planning and getting the promotion done.

The activities of product managers vary a lot—depending on their experience and aggressiveness—and the company's organizational philosophy. Today, companies are emphasizing marketing *experience*—as it becomes clear that this important job takes more than academic training and enthusiasm.[11]

■ CONCLUSION

Product planning is an increasingly important activity in a modern economy—because it is no longer very profitable to sell just "commodities."

The product life-cycle concept is especially important to marketing strategy planning. It shows that different marketing mixes—and even strategies—are needed as a product moves through its cycle. This is an important point, because profits change during the life cycle—with most of the profits going to the innovators or fast copiers.

We pointed out that a new product is not limited to physical newness. We will call a product "new" if it is new in any way—to any target market.

Product positioning was described as an aid to product planning—helping to see where products and brands are positioned in a market.

New products are so important to the survival of firms that some organized process for developing them is needed. Such a process was discussed—and we stressed that it must be a total company effort to be successful.

The failure rate of new products is high—but it is lower for larger and better-managed firms that recognize product development and management as vital processes. Some firms appoint product managers to manage individual products—and new-product committees to assure that the process is carried out successfully.

■ QUESTIONS AND PROBLEMS

1. Explain how industry sales and industry profits behave over the product life cycle.

2. Cite two examples of products which you feel are currently in each of the product life cycle stages.

3. Explain how different conclusions might be reached with respect to the correct product life cycle stage(s) in the automobile market—especially if different views of the market are held.

4. Can product life cycles be extended? Illustrate your answer for a specific product.

5. Discuss the life cycle of a product in terms of its probable impact on a manufacturer's marketing mix. Illustrate using battery-operated toothbrushes.

6. Explain how product positioning differs from segmenting markets. Is target marketing involved in product positioning?

7. What is a new product? Illustrate your answer.

8. Explain the importance of an organized new-product development process and illustrate how it might be used for (a) an improved phonograph, (b) new frozen-food items, (c) a new children's toy.

9. Explain the role of product or brand managers. Are they usually put in charge of new-product development?

10. Discuss the social value of new-product development activities which seem to encourage people to discard products that are not "all worn out." Is this an economic waste? How worn out is "all worn out?" Must a shirt have holes in it? How big?

■ **SUGGESTED CASES**

11. Pang Corporation

18. Gray Sports Company

Chapter 11 ■ Place and physical distribution

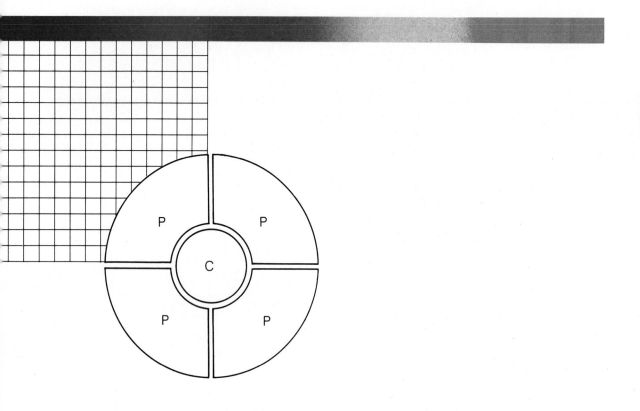

When you finish this chapter, you should:

1. Understand how and why marketing specialists adjust discrepancies of quantity and assortment.

2. Know why physical distribution is such an important part of Place *and* marketing.

3. Know about the transporting and storing possibilities a marketing manager can use.

4. Know about the different kinds of channel systems.

5. Understand how much market exposure would be "ideal."

6. Recognize the important new terms (shown in red).

You may build a "better mousetrap," but if it's not in the right place at the right time, it won't do anyone any good.

Offering customers a good product at a reasonable price is important for a successful marketing strategy—but it isn't enough. Managers must also think about **Place**—getting the product to the customer's place—in the right quantities and when the customer wants it. Place often requires marketing specialists—middlemen, transporting and storing companies, and facilitators—to provide target customers with time, place, and possession utilities.

There are many ways to provide Place—so many decisions are needed. Magnavox televisions are sold by a selected group of stores—while Zenith televisions are sold by many more retailers. Many industrial goods are sold by the producer directly to the customer—and delivered in the producer's own trucks. But most consumer goods are sold to middlemen—who later sell to the final consumer.

Place decisions are important strategic decisions. See Figure 11–1 for a picture of the strategic areas we will discuss in the next three chapters.

■ FIGURE 11–1   Strategic decision areas in Place

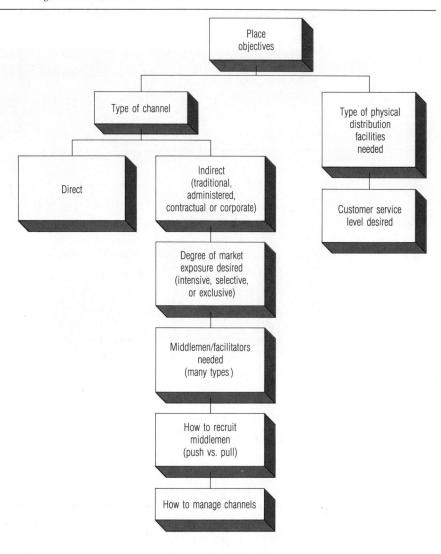

"IDEAL" PLACE OBJECTIVES SUGGESTED BY GOODS CLASSES

Obviously, the needs and attitudes of potential target markets have to be considered when developing Place. People in a particular target market should have similar needs and attitudes—and therefore should be satisfied with a similar Place system. Their attitudes about urgency to have needs satisfied—and willingness to shop—have already been summarized in the goods classes. Now we should be able to use these goods classes to suggest how Place should be handled—that is, some logical place objectives.

The relationship between goods classes and *ideal place objectives* was shown in Figure 9–3 for consumer goods and Figure 9–4 for industrial goods. These figures should be studied carefully—since they set the framework for solving the whole Place problem.

Place System Is Not Automatic

Just as goods classes are not automatic, we can't automatically decide on the best Place arrangement. If there are two or three market segments with different views of a product, then different Place arrangements may be needed as well. Further, Place depends on both (1) what customers would like best and (2) what channel members can provide profitably.

DIRECT CHANNEL SYSTEMS MAY BE BEST, SOMETIMES

Many producers like to handle the whole distribution job themselves. There are advantages in selling directly to the final user or consumer. Marketing research is easier—because the producer's sales reps are in direct contact with the target customers. If any special selling effort or technical services are needed, the marketing manager can be sure that the sales force will receive the necessary training and motivation.

Some products typically have short channels of distribution—and a *direct-to-user channel* is not uncommon. It is not always necessary to use middlemen. On the other hand, it isn't always best to "go direct" either.

Some consumer goods companies—like Avon and Fuller Brush—have been very successful with direct-to-user channels.

SPECIALISTS AND CHANNEL SYSTEMS DEVELOP TO ADJUST DISCREPANCIES

Discrepancies Require Channel Specialists

All producers want to be sure that their products reach the final customer. But the assortment and quantity of goods wanted by customers may be different than the assortment and quantity of goods normally produced. Specialists develop to adjust these discrepancies.[1]

Discrepancy of quantity means the difference between the quantity of goods it is economical for a producer to make and the quantity normally wanted by final users or consumers. For example, most manufacturers of golf balls produce large quantities—perhaps 200,000 to 500,000 in a given time period. The average golfer, however, wants only a few balls at a time. Adjusting for this discrepancy usually requires middlemen—wholesalers and retailers.

Producers typically specialize by product—and therefore another discrepancy develops. **Discrepancy of assortment** means the difference between the lines the typical producer makes and the assortment wanted by final consumers or users. Most golfers, for example, need more than golf balls. They want golf shoes, gloves, clubs, a bag, and so forth. And probably they would prefer not to shop around for each item. So, again, there is a need for middlemen to adjust these discrepancies.

Channel Specialists Adjust Discrepancies with Regrouping Activities

Regrouping activities adjust the quantities and/or assortments of goods handled at each level in a channel of distribution.

There are four regrouping activities: accumulating, bulk breaking, sorting, and assorting. When one or more of these activities is required, a marketing specialist might develop to fill this need.

Adjusting quantity discrepancies by accumulating and bulk-breaking

Accumulating involves collecting products from many small producers. This is common for agricultural products. It is a way of getting the lowest transporting rate—by combining small quantities which then can be shipped in truckload or carload quantities.

Bulk-breaking involves dividing larger quantities into smaller quantities as goods get closer to the final market. This may involve several middlemen. Wholesalers may sell smaller quantities to other wholesalers—or directly to retailers. Retailers continue the bulk-breaking as they sell to their customers.

Adjusting assortment discrepancies by sorting and assorting

Different types of specialists are needed to adjust assortment discrepancies. Two types of regrouping activities may be needed: sorting and assorting.

Sorting means separating products into grades and qualities desired by different target markets. This is a common process for agricultural products. Nature produces what it will—and then these products must be sorted to meet the needs of different target markets.

Assorting means putting together a variety of products to give a target

Channel specialists sort products—in this case, eggs—according to grades and sizes desired by different target markets.

market what it wants. Here, instead of nature producing a mixed assortment which must be sorted, marketing specialists put together an assortment to satisfy some target market. This usually is done by those close to the final consumer or user—retailers or wholesalers who try to supply a wide assortment of products for the convenience of their customers. An electrical goods wholesaler, for example, may take on a line of lawnmowers or garden products for the convenience of hardware retailer-customers.

Rapid shifts in buying habits or preferences can result in discrepancies of assortment—and new marketing opportunities.

Channel Systems Can Be Complex

Adjusting discrepancies can lead to complex channels of distribution. The possibility for competition among different channels is shown in Figure 11–2. This figure shows the many channels used by manufacturers of paperback books. These can be both consumer goods and industrial goods. This helps explain why some channels develop. But note that the books go through wholesalers and retailers—independent and chain bookstores, schools, drug stores, supermarkets, and convenience stores. This can cause problems—because these wholesalers supply retailers who are used to different markups. Among such channels, there is a lot of competition—including price competition. And the different markups may lead to open price wars—especially on well-known and branded products.

Dual distribution occurs when a manufacturer uses several competing channels to reach the same target market—perhaps using several middlemen and selling directly itself. This is resented by some established middlemen because they don't like *any* competition—especially competition set up by their own suppliers. But manufacturers often are forced to use dual distribution—because their present channels are doing a poor job—or aren't reaching some potential customers.

■ FIGURE 11–2   Sales of paperback books are made through many kinds of wholesalers and retailers

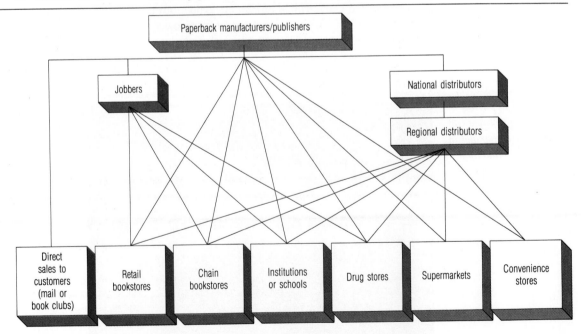

Source: Neil Suits, Suits News Company, Lansing, Michigan.

Sometimes There's Not Much Choice

The paperback example seems to suggest that there are plenty of middlemen around to form almost any kind of channel system. But this isn't true. Sometimes there is only one good middleman serving a market. To reach this market, producers may have no choice but to use this one middleman.

In other cases, there are no middlemen at all! Then a producer may try to go directly to target customers. If this isn't possible, the product may die—because it can't be distributed economically. Some products aren't wanted in big enough volume and/or at high enough prices to justify any middlemen providing the regrouping activities needed to reach the potential customers.

PHYSICAL DISTRIBUTION IS AN IMPORTANT PART OF PLACE PLANNING

Physical distribution (PD) is the transporting and storing of physical goods within individual firms and along channel systems. Nearly half of the costs of marketing are spent on physical distribution. These PD activities are very important to a firm—and the macro-marketing system. Goods that remain in a factory or on a farm really have no "use" at all. And possession utility is not possible until time and place utility have been provided. This requires the transporting and storing functions that are a part of physical distribution.

Deciding Who Will Haul and Store Is Strategic

As a marketing manager develops the Place part of a strategy, it is important to decide who will store and transport the goods—and who will pay for these services. A wholesaler may use its own trucks to haul goods from a producer to its warehouse—and from there to retailers—but only because the manufacturer gives a transporting allowance. Another wholesaler may want the goods delivered.

When developing a marketing strategy, the marketing manager must decide how these functions are to be shared—since this will affect the other three Ps—and especially Price.

These are important strategic decisions—because they can make or break a strategy. The case of a small producer of "rabbit ear" TV antennas illustrates these ideas. The growth of cable TV was hurting the firm's sales. So the firm developed a new product—a dish-like antenna used by motels to receive satellite TV signals—that looked like it could be a real success. Because it couldn't finance a lot of inventory, the firm decided to work only with wholesalers who were willing to buy and stock several units—to be used for demonstrations and to make sure that buyers got immediate delivery. In a few months, the firm had $2 million in sales to its wholesalers—and recovered its development costs before any products were sold to users. Here, the wholesalers helped share the risk of the new venture—but it was a good decision for them, too. They won many sales from a competing channel that didn't offer such fast delivery—because it didn't do any storing and used higher cost transporting. So they easily got back the interest cost of their inventory investment—and more.

THE TRANSPORTING FUNCTION

Transporting is the marketing function of moving goods. It provides time and place utilities.

Modern transporting facilities—including railroads, pipe lines, trucks, barges and ships, and airplanes—have changed marketing. Without these transporting facilities, there could be no mass distribution—with its regrouping activities—or any urban life as we know it today. Producers in small towns and rural areas can now reach customers all over the world.

Trucks are fast and flexible—which helps explain why they are so important in bringing goods to market.

How a video game from California ended up in a Boston pizza parlor.

Trucks brought it.

And trucks brought the pizza ingredients and the beer. And all those paper napkins. Trucks make possible the electricity to run the game, and the telephone to call your order in.

It's impossible to say how many trucks have to roll to feed, clothe, and shelter you—and keep you on the job. But you can easily see that trucking is

America's lifeline—essential to the essentials and luxuries alike.

Efficiency is essential, too—but the super-efficient over-the-road trucks are being harried and hampered by unnecessary nuisance taxes. They don't raise much revenue, but they sure raise our costs.

Fair taxes we'll pay—no complaint here. Unfair taxes

place an unfair burden on the entire trucking system. It's a burden every American winds up paying for.

TRUCK STOPPER #1:

57% of America's manufactured goods, and 90% of fresh fruits and vegetables, are moved totally by truck.

For 100 "Truck Stoppers", write:
TRUCK STOPPERS, Room 503, 1616 P Street, N.W., Washington, D.C. 20036

IF YOU'VE GOT IT, TRUCKS BROUGHT IT. **ATA** FOUNDATION INC.
AMERICAN TRUCKING INDUSTRY

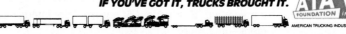

■ FIGURE 11–3   Intercity freight movement in the United States, 1955 and 1980

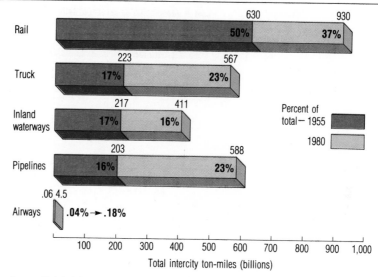

Source: *Statistical Abstract of the United States, 1982–1983.*

Seventy-five percent of all U.S. freight moves by trucks—at least part of the way. Railroads carry goods for long distances, but trucks have the bulk of the short-haul business. The trucking industry slogan, "If you have it, it came by truck," is true for consumer goods. However, many industrial goods are delivered by railroads—or by other transporting methods. See Figure 11–3.

Can You Afford to Hit the Target?

The cost of shipping varies a lot by product. Transporting bulky and low-value products like sand and gravel, for example, costs about 55 percent of their value. At the other extreme, lighter or more valuable items like office machines are transported for 3 percent of their selling price. See Figure 11–4.

Different Kinds of Carriers Fill Different Roles

Public carriers—such as the railroads and truckers—are transporters which usually maintain regular schedules—and accept goods from any shipper. Some public carriers, however, are willing to work for individual shippers for an agreed sum—and for any length of time. Public carriers provide a dependable transporting service for the many producers and middlemen who do not make enough shipments to do it themselves.

Private carriers are company-owned transporting facilities. "Do-it-yourself" transporting is always a possibility. But it often isn't economical—because the public carriers can make fuller use of their facilities and therefore charge less.

Marketing Manager Can Affect Rates

Until recently, the government controlled transporting rates, routes, and schedules. This made it harder for transporting firms to compete with each other. But deregulation has changed this.

■ FIGURE 11–4   Transporting costs as a percent of selling price for different products

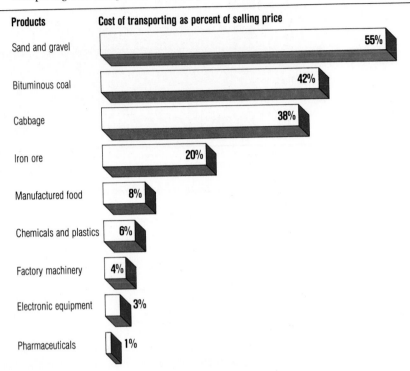

Products   **Cost of transporting as percent of selling price**

Sand and gravel — 55%

Bituminous coal — 42%

Cabbage — 38%

Iron ore — 20%

Manufactured food — 8%

Chemicals and plastics — 6%

Factory machinery — 4%

Electronic equipment — 3%

Pharmaceuticals — 1%

Source: Adapted from B. J. LaLonde and P. H. Zinzer, *Customer Service: Meaning and Measurement* (Chicago: National Council of Physical Distribution Management, 1976); and D. Phillip Locklin, *Transportation for Management* (Homewood, Ill.: Richard D. Irwin, 1972).

Creative marketing managers—by bargaining for better transporting rates—can help their channel system members with the transporting function. In fact, some manufacturers and middlemen maintain *traffic departments* to deal with carriers. These departments can be a great help—not only to their own firms but also to their suppliers and customers—finding the best carriers and bargaining for the lowest rates.

Which Transporting Alternative Is Best?

The best transporting choice should not only be as low in cost as possible—but also provide the level of service (e.g., speed and dependability) required. See Figure 11–5. Sometimes this means using one of the special services offered by railroads. In other cases, air freight might be the best choice. Or it might be best to "do it yourself" if the transporting specialists don't have any advantage.[2]

Railroads—workhorse of the nation

The railroads have been the workhorses of U.S. transporting—carrying heavy, bulky freight such as coal, sand, and steel. By handling large quantities

■ FIGURE 11–5   Relative benefits of different transport modes

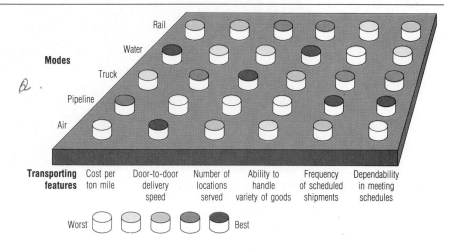

of such products, the railroads are able to charge relatively low rates for these products. But railroads have had profit problems in recent years, in part because trucks have set their rates low enough to get some of the more profitable business that railroads counted on to make up for the low rates on the bulky products.

Truck competition has forced the railroads to offer faster and more flexible services. A "fast freight" service for perishable or high-value items, for example, can be competitive with trucks if the shippers and receivers are located near rail lines. And a **piggy-back service** loads truck trailers on rail cars to provide both speed and flexibility. On some routes it may even cost less. A loaded truck trailer can be shipped piggy-back from the Midwest to the West Coast for about half the cost of sending it over highways.

Trucks are flexible, fast and dependable

The flexibility of trucks makes them especially good for moving small loads for short distances. They can travel on almost any road. They can give extremely fast service. Also, trucks cause less breakage and handling than rails—an important factor because it may allow lower packaging costs. For short distances and for higher-value products, trucks may charge rates that are the same as (or lower than) railroad rates—yet provide much faster service.

Ships and barges—slow and seasonal, but inexpensive

Water transporting is the lowest-cost method—but it is also the slowest. Where speed is not as important, however, barges or ships are important methods of transporting. Barges on internal waterways are used for bulky, nonperishable products—such as iron ore, grain, steel, oil, cement, gravel, sand, and coal. By a combination of rivers, canals, and locks, it is possible to ship goods from industrial and agricultural regions of inland United States all

Federal Express provides overnight transporting—and is especially good for high-value, low-weight products.

over the world. Foreign ships regularly move on the Great Lakes. Ocean-going barges can reach as far north as Minneapolis-St. Paul—and deep into Arkansas.

More manufactured goods are being shipped by water—as large standard-sized containers are being loaded at factories and then shipped as a unit all the way to their destination. Now ships combined with trucks offer a **fishy-back service**—similar to rail piggy-back—but using ships and trucks. Door-to-door service is now offered between the United States and European cities!

Airplanes may cut the total cost of distribution

The most expensive means of cargo transporting is air freight—but it also is fast! Air freight rates normally are at least twice as high as trucking rates—but the greater speed may be worth the added cost. Most air freight—so far—has been fashions, high-value industrial parts for the electronics and metal-working industries, and perishable items. California's strawberries, for example, are flown to the Midwest and East all through the year.

A big advantage of air transport is that the cost of packing, unpacking, and preparing goods for sale may be reduced—or eliminated—when goods are shipped by air. Some women's fashions are shipped on racks which eventually are moved right into the store!

Air freight can help a producer reduce inventory costs by eliminating outlying warehouses. The greater speed may also reduce spoilage, theft, and damage. So, although the *transporting cost* may be higher, the *total cost of distribution* may be lower.

STORING MAY BE NEEDED IN SOME CHANNELS

Storing is the marketing function of holding goods. It provides time utility. Storing is necessary because production does not always match consumption. Some products—such as farm produce—are produced seasonally although they are in demand year-round. And some products—such as suntan products—have a big demand for short periods.

Storing can be done by both manufacturers and middlemen. It can balance supply and demand—keeping stocks at convenient locations, ready to meet customers' needs. Storing is one of the major activities of some middlemen.

Specialized Storing Facilities Can Be Very Helpful

Private warehouses are storing facilities owned by companies for their own use. Most manufacturers, wholesalers, and retailers have some storing facilities in their own main buildings—or in a warehouse district.

Private warehouses are used when a large volume of goods must be stored regularly. Owning warehouse space can be expensive, however. If the need changes, the extra space may be hard—or impossible—to rent to others.

Public warehouses are independent storing facilities. They can provide all the services that a company's own warehouse can provide. A company might choose to use a public warehouse if it didn't have a regular need for warehouse space. With a public warehouse, the customer pays only for space used—and may buy a variety of other services. Public warehouses are useful to manufacturers who must maintain stocks in many locations—including foreign countries. Public warehouses are found in all major urban areas—and many smaller cities. Rural towns also have public warehouses for locally produced agricultural products.

Warehousing Facilities Have Modernized

The cost of physical handling is a major storing cost. The goods must be handled once when put into storage—and again when they come out. Further—in the typical old "downtown" warehouse districts—traffic congestion, crowded storage areas, and slow freight elevators slow the process. This increases the cost.

Today, modern one-story buildings are replacing the old multi-story buildings. They are located away from downtown traffic. They eliminate the need for elevators—and permit the use of power-operated lift trucks, battery-operated motor scooters, roller-skating order-pickers, electric hoists for heavy items, and hydraulic ramps to aid loading and unloading. Some even have computer controlled order picking systems.[3]

Distribution Center Is a Different Kind of Warehouse

A **distribution center** is a special kind of warehouse designed to speed the flow of goods—and avoid unnecessary storing costs. Basically, it is a bulk-breaking operation. Turnover is increased—and the cost of carrying inventory is reduced. This is important—these costs may run as high as 35 percent of the value of the average inventory each year.

The idea behind the distribution center is that reducing costs—and increasing turnover—will lead to bigger profits. Storing is sensible only if it helps obtain time utility.

Some large food manufacturers and supermarket operators run their own distribution centers. For example, the Pillsbury Company—a large manufacturer of baking mixes and flour—ships products in rail carloads from its many manufacturing plants (which each specialize in a few product lines) directly to distribution centers. Almost no goods are stored at the factories. These distri-

Modern distribution centers help to speed the flow of goods from producers to consumers.

bution centers are able to quickly ship any combination of goods by the most economical transporting route. This lets Pillsbury offer faster service—at lower cost.

PHYSICAL DISTRIBUTION CONCEPT FOCUSES ON WHOLE DISTRIBUTION SYSTEM

We have been looking at the transporting and storing functions as separate activities—partly because it's the usual approach. Recently, however, attention has turned to the *whole* physical distribution function—not just storing or transporting. Focusing only on one function at a time may actually increase a firm's—and channel's—total distribution costs.

"Physical distribution" people usually study the total cost of possible PD systems—because there may be attractive trade-offs. For example, higher transporting costs may be more than offset by lower storing costs—as with air freight.

Total Cost Approach Helps

The **total cost approach**—to selecting a PD system—evaluates *all* the costs of possible PD systems. This means that all costs—including some which are sometimes ignored—should be considered. Inventory costs, for example, are often ignored in marketing decisions—because these costs are buried in "overhead costs." But inventory costs can be very high. In fact, including them may lead to a different decision.[4]

The tools of cost accounting and economics are used with this approach. Sometimes, total cost analyses show that unconventional PD methods will provide service as good as—or better than—usual methods—and at lower cost, as the following example shows.

Evaluating Rail/Warehouse versus Air freight

The Good Earth Vegetable Company had been shipping produce to distant markets by train. The cost of shipping a ton of vegetables by train averaged less than half the cost of air freight. But when a competitor began using air freight, the Good Earth managers were forced to rethink their PD system. To their surprise, they found the air freight system was not only faster—but cheaper. See Figure 11–6.

Figure 11–6 compares the costs for the two distribution systems—airplane and railroad. Because shipping by train was slow, Good Earth had to store a large inventory in a warehouse—to fill orders on time. And the company was also surprised at the extra cost of carrying the inventory "in transit." Good Earth's managers also found that the cost of spoiled vegetables—during shipping and in the warehouse—was much higher when rail shipment was used. By using air freight, Good Earth could offer better service—at lower total cost.

■   FIGURE 11–6   Comparative costs of airplane versus rail and warehouse

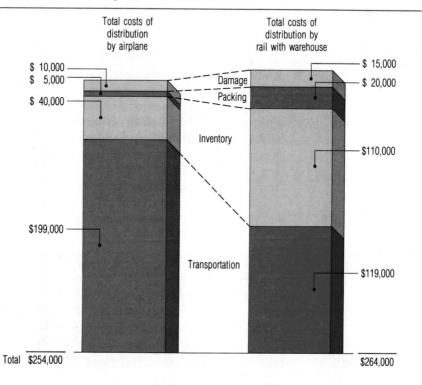

■ FIGURE 11–7   High customer service levels are obtained at a cost

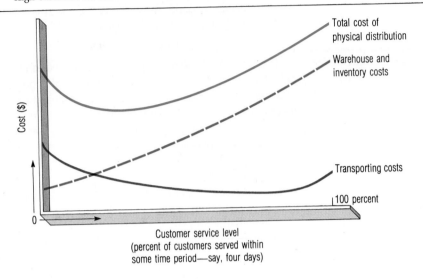

Customer service level
(percent of customers served within
some time period—say, four days)

**Decide What Service
Level to Offer**

Early physical distribution efforts emphasized lowering costs—to increase profits. Now there is more emphasis on making physical distribution planning a part of the company's strategy planning. Sometimes, by increasing physical distribution cost a little, the customer service level can be increased so much that, in effect, a new and better marketing mix is created.[5]

Customer service level is a measure of how rapidly and dependably a firm can deliver what customers want. Figure 11–7 shows the typical relation between physical distribution costs and customer service level. When a firm decides to lower total cost, it may also be settling for a lower customer service level. By increasing the number of distribution points, the firm might be able to serve more customers—better—within a specified time period. Transporting costs would be reduced—but warehousing and inventory costs would be increased. The higher service level, however, might greatly improve the company's strategy. Increased sales might more than make up for increased costs. Clearly, a marketing manager has a strategic decision to make about what service level to offer. Minimizing cost is not always the right answer. Similarly, a marketing manager has a strategic decision about going direct or being part of an indirect channel system.

INDIRECT CHANNELS MAY BE BEST, SOMETIMES

Although a producer might prefer to handle the whole distribution job, this is just not economical for many kinds of products—unless the firm integrates and forms its own "vertical marketing system." But typically, producers have to use

■ FIGURE 11–8   Types of indirect channel systems

		Vertical marketing systems		
	Traditional	Administered	Contractual	Corporate
Amount of cooperation	Little or none	Some to good	Fairly good to good	Complete
Control maintained by	None	Economic power and leadership	Contracts	Ownership by one company
Examples	Typical channel of "independents"	General Electric, Miller's Beer, O.M. Scott & Sons (lawn products)	McDonald's, Holiday Inn, IGA, Ace Hardware, Super Valu, Coca-Cola, Chevrolet	Florsheim Shoes, Firestone Tire

middlemen—like it or not. They join—or develop—one of the indirect channel systems described below—and summarized in Figure 11–8.

Traditional Channel Systems Are Common

In a **traditional channel system**—the various channel members make little or no effort to cooperate with each other. They buy and sell from each other—and that's all. In some very independent channels, buyers may even wait until sellers desperately need to sell—hoping to force the price down. This leads to erratic production, inventory, and employment patterns—that can only increase total costs. Traditional channel members may have their independence—but they may pay for it, too. As we will see, such channels are declining in importance—with good reason. But they are still typical in some industries.

Vertical Marketing Systems Focus on Final Customers

In contrast to traditional channel systems are **vertical marketing systems**—channel systems in which the whole channel shares a common focus on the same target market at the end of the channel. Such systems make sense—and are growing in importance—because if the final customer doesn't buy the product, the whole channel suffers. We'll talk about the three types of vertical marketing systems next.

Corporate Channel Systems—Shorten Channels

Some firms develop their own vertical marketing systems by internal expansion and/or buying other firms. With **corporate channel systems**—corporate ownership all along the channel—we might say the firm is going "direct." But actually it may be handling manufacturing, wholesaling, *and* retailing—and it is more accurate to think of it as running a vertical marketing system.

Vertical integration is at different levels

Corporate channel systems are often developed by **vertical integration**—acquiring firms at different levels of channel activity. Firestone, for example,

has rubber plantations in Liberia, tire plants in Ohio, and Firestone wholesale and retail outlets all over the United States.

Corporate channel systems are not always started by manufacturers. A retailer might integrate into wholesaling—and perhaps even manufacturing. A&P has fish canning plants. Genesco and Florsheim make their own shoes. J. C. Penney controls textile plants.

There are many advantages to vertical integration—stability of operations, assurance of materials and supplies, better control of distribution, better quality control, larger research facilities, greater buying power, and lower executive overhead. The economies of vertical integration benefit the consumer, too, through lower prices and better products.

Provided that discrepancies of quantity and assortment aren't too great at each level in a channel—that is, the firms fit together well—vertical integration can be very efficient and profitable.

Administered and Contractual Systems May Work Well

Although a company's managers might prefer to handle the whole distribution job, this just isn't economically practical for many products. So instead of integrating corporately, they may develop an administered or contractual channel system. In **administered channel systems,** the various channel members informally agree to cooperate with each other. This can include agreements to routinize ordering, standardize accounting, and coordinate promotion efforts. In **contractual channel systems,** the various channel members agree by contract to cooperate with each other. With both of these systems, the members get some of the advantages of corporate integration—but have some of the flexibility of a traditional channel system.

An appliance manufacturer, for example, developed an informal arrangement with the independent wholesalers in its administered channel system—agreeing to keep production and inventory levels in the system balanced—using sales data from the wholesalers. Every week, its managers make an item-by-item analysis of up to 130,000 major appliance units located in the many warehouses operated by its 87 wholesalers throughout the country. This helps the manufacturer plan production and shipments to maintain adequate inventory levels—and also helps the wholesalers manage their inventories. The wholesalers are guaranteed enough inventory—without the expense of too much. And the manufacturer has better information to plan its manufacturing and marketing efforts.

Similar systems are run by middlemen in the grocery, hardware, and drug industries. Electronic cash registers keep track of sales. This information is sent to the wholesaler's computer, and an order is entered—automatically. This reduces buying and selling costs, inventory investment, and customer frustration with "out-of-stock" items.

Vertical Marketing Systems—New Wave in the Marketplace

Besides their other advantages, smoothly operating channel systems are competitively superior.

In the consumer goods field, corporate chains that are at least partially vertically integrated account for about 26 percent of total retail sales. Firms linked with other vertical systems account for an additional 37.5 percent. This gives vertical systems in the consumer goods area much more than half of retail sales. It appears that such systems will continue to increase their share in the future. Vertical marketing systems are becoming the key units in the U.S. distribution system.[6]

THE BEST CHANNEL SYSTEM SHOULD ACHIEVE IDEAL MARKET EXPOSURE

Although it might seem that all marketing managers would want their products to have maximum exposure to potential customers, this isn't true. Some goods classes require much less market exposure than others.

Ideal market exposure makes a product widely enough available to satisfy target customers' needs—but not exceed them. Too much exposure only increases the total marketing cost.

Three Degrees of Market Exposure May Be Ideal

Intensive distribution is selling a product through all responsible and suitable wholesalers or retailers who will stock and/or sell the product. **Selective distribution** is selling through only those middlemen who will give the product special attention. **Exclusive distribution** is selling through only one middleman in each geographic area.

In practice, this means that cigarettes are handled—through intensive distribution—by at least a million U.S. outlets, while Rolls Royces or expensive chinaware are handled—through exclusive distribution—by only a limited number of middlemen across the country.

Intensive Distribution—Sell It Where They Buy It

Intensive distribution is commonly needed for convenience goods and for industrial supplies—such as pencils, paper clips, and typing paper—used by all plants and offices. Customers want such products nearby.

The seller's *intent* is important here. Intensive distribution refers to the *desire* to sell through *all* responsible and suitable outlets. What this means depends on customer habits and preferences. If target customers normally buy a certain product at a certain type of outlet, ideally you would specify this type of outlet in your Place policies. If customers prefer to buy certain hardware items only at hardware stores, you would try to sell all hardware stores to achieve intensive distribution.

Selective Distribution—Sell It Where It Sells Best

Selective distribution covers the area between intensive and exclusive distribution. It can be suitable for all products. Only the better middlemen are used. Here, a firm hopes to get some of the advantages of exclusive distribution—while still getting fairly widespread coverage.

A selective policy might be used to avoid selling to wholesalers or retailers who (1) have a poor credit rating, (2) have a reputation for making too many returns or wanting too much service, (3) place orders that are too small to justify making calls or providing service, or (4) are not in a position to do a good job.

Selective distribution is growing in popularity—as firms see that it isn't necessary to have 100 percent coverage of a market. Often, most of the sales come from relatively few customers—and the others buy too little compared to the cost of working with them. This is called the "80/20 rule"—because 80 percent of a company's sales often come from only 20 percent of its customers—*until it becomes more selective in choosing customers.*

Exclusive Distribution Sometimes Makes Sense

Exclusive distribution means that only one middleman is selected in each geographic area. Manufacturers might want to use exclusive distribution to help control prices—and the service offered in a channel.

But Is Limiting Market Exposure Legal?

Exclusive distribution is not specifically illegal under the antimonopoly laws. But current interpretation of these laws by the courts gives the impression that almost any exclusive distribution arrangement *could be* interpreted as an injury to some competitor—somewhere.

The Supreme Court has consistently ruled that horizontal arrangements—among competing retailers, wholesalers, or manufacturers—to limit sales by customer or territory are illegal. This is seen as collusion—reducing competition and harming customers!

The legality of vertical arrangements—between producers and middlemen—is not as clear. A 1977 Supreme Court decision reversed its 1967 ruling that vertical relationships limiting territories or customers were always illegal. Now possible good effects can be weighed against possible harm to competition. Under the previous rule, the price-cutting "maverick" who came in after the introductory work had been done could not be controlled. Now that may be changed, as long as some good reason can be shown for limiting distribution—such as building stronger retailers who can offer advertising and sales support and better repair services.[7]

Caution is suggested

In spite of the recent Supreme Court ruling, firms should be very careful about entering into *any* exclusive distribution arrangements. The antimonopoly rules still apply. The courts can force a change in expensively developed relationships. And—even worse—triple damages can be imposed if the courts rule that competition has been hurt. Apparently, the law will allow some exclusive arrangements—to permit the introduction of a new product or to help a new company enter a market—but these arrangements probably should be short term.

The same cautions apply to selective distribution. Here, however, less formal arrangements are typical—and the possible impact on competition is less likely. It's now more acceptable to carefully select channel members when building a channel system. Refusing to sell to some middlemen, however, should be part of a logical marketing plan which has long-term benefits.

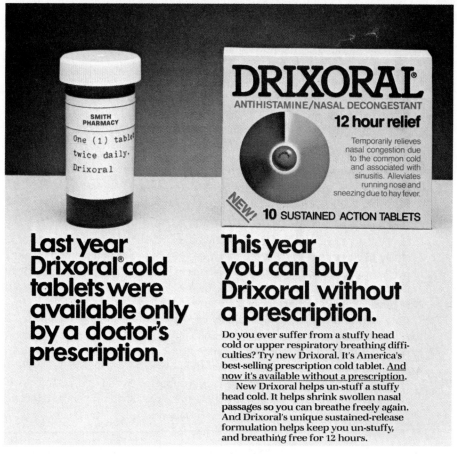

When the channel system for this product changed, the package and other elements of the marketing mix changed, too.

HOW TO RECRUIT MIDDLEMEN

A producer has a special challenge—making sure its product reaches the end of the channel. To reach the target market, a producer may have to recruit middlemen.

The two basic methods of recruiting middlemen are pushing and pulling.

Pushing Policy—Get a Hand from the Firms in the Channel

Pushing (a product through a channel) means using normal promotion effort—personal selling and advertising—to help sell the whole marketing mix to possible channel members. The approach emphasizes the importance of building a channel—and getting the cooperation of channel members. The producer—in effect—tries to develop a team that will work well—to "push" the product down the channel to the final user.

Pulling Policy—Make Them Reach for It Out There

By contrast, **pulling** means getting consumers to ask middlemen for the product. This usually involves very aggressive promotion to final consumers—perhaps using coupons or samples—and temporary bypassing of middlemen. If the promotion works, the middlemen are forced to carry the product—to satisfy customer requests.

This method may be used if many products are already competing in all desired outlets. But channel members should be told about the planned pulling effort—so they can be ready if the promotion is successful.

CHANNEL CAPTAIN NEEDED TO GUIDE CHANNEL PLANNING

Until now, we have considered an individual marketing manager as the strategy planner. But now we see that there may be several firms and managers in a single distribution channel. It is logical that each channel have a **channel captain**—a manager who helps guide the activities of the whole channel. The question is: Which marketing manager should be the captain?[8]

The idea of a single channel captain makes sense—but some channels don't have such a captain. The various firms may not be acting as a system—because of lack of leadership. Or the members of a channel system may not understand that they are part of a channel.

But even if they don't know it, firms *are* connected by their policies. It makes sense to try to avoid channel conflicts by planning for channel relationships.

Manufacturer or Middlemen?

In the United States, manufacturers frequently are the leaders in channel relations. Middlemen wait and see what the manufacturer intends to do—and what it wants done. Then they decide whether their roles will be profitable—and whether they want to join in the manufacturer's plans.

Some middlemen do take the lead—especially in foreign markets where there are fewer large manufacturers. Such middlemen may decide what their customers want and seek out manufacturers—perhaps small ones—who can provide these products at reasonable prices.

Large middlemen are closer to the final user or consumer—and in an ideal position to assume the channel captain role. It is even possible that middlemen—especially retailers—may dominate the marketing systems of the future.

The Captain Guides the Channel

The job of a channel captain is to arrange for the necessary marketing activities in the best way. This might be done as shown in Figure 11–9 in a manufacturer-dominated channel system. Here, the manufacturer has picked a target market—and developed a product, set the price structure, done some promotion, and developed the place setup. Middlemen are then expected to finish the promotion job—at their own places.

■ FIGURE 11-9   How channel strategy might be handled in a manufacturer-dominated system

Manufacturer's part of the job   Middleman's part of the job

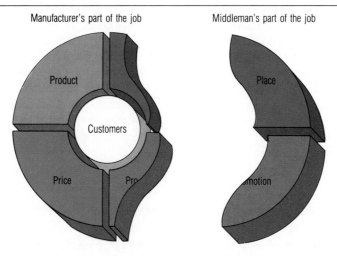

Source: Adapted from D. J. Bowersox and E. J. McCarthy, "Strategic Development of Planned Vertical Marketing Systems," in *Vertical Marketing Systems*, ed. Louis Bucklin (Glenview, Ill.: Scott, Foresman, 1970).

If a middleman is the channel captain, we would see quite a different picture. In the extreme—in a channel like that dominated by Sears, Roebuck—the middleman's part of the job would be large. Manufacturers would be mainly concerned with manufacturing the product to meet Sears' requirements.

A Coordinated Channel System May Help Everyone

A channel system in which the members have accepted the leadership of a channel captain can work very well—even though not everyone in the channel system is strongly market-oriented. As long as the channel captain is market-oriented, it is possible to win the confidence and support of production-oriented firms—and make the whole channel work well. Small production-oriented producers in Japan or Hong Kong, for example, become part of an effective channel reaching the U.S. market—if there is a middleman who correctly understands market needs and explains them clearly to the producers. The producers may not even know where their products are going—but the system will compete with other systems and be profitable for all the members.[9]

■ CONCLUSION

This chapter has discussed the role of Place. Place decisions are especially important because they may be hard to change.

Marketing specialists and channel systems develop to adjust discrepancies of quantity and assortment. Their regrouping activities are basic in any economic system—and adjusting discrepancies provides opportunities for creative marketers.

Physical distribution functions—transporting

and storing—were discussed. These activities are needed to provide time, place, and possession utilities. And by using the total cost approach, the lowest-cost PD alternative—or the cost of various customer service levels—can be found.

The importance of planning channel systems was discussed—along with the role of a channel captain. It was stressed that channel systems compete with each other—and that smoothly operating vertical marketing systems seem to be winning out in the marketplace.

Channel planning also requires deciding on the degree of market exposure desired. The legality of limiting market exposure should also be considered—to avoid jail or having to undo an expensively developed channel system.

Finally, it was emphasized that producers aren't necessarily channel captains. Often, middlemen control or even dominate channels of distribution. The degree of this control must be considered by producers when they decide whether they should try to push or pull products through a channel system.

■ QUESTIONS AND PROBLEMS

1. Explain "discrepancies of quantity and assortment" using the clothing business as an example. How does the application of these concepts change when selling coal to the steel industry? What impact does this have on the number and kinds of marketing specialists required?

2. Explain the four regrouping activities with an example from the building supply industry (nails, paint, flooring, plumbing fixtures, etc.). Do you think that many specialists develop in this industry, or do manufacturers handle the job themselves? What kinds of marketing channels would you expect to find in this industry, and what functions would various channel members provide?

3. If a manufacturer has five different markets to reach, how many channels is he likely to use? If only one, why? If more than one, what problems may this cause?

4. Discuss the relative advantages and disadvantages of railroads, trucks, and airlines as transporting methods.

5. Discuss some of the ways that air transportation can change other aspects of a Place system.

6. Explain which transportation mode would probably be most suitable for shipping the following goods to a large Chicago department store:
a. A 10,000-pound shipment of dishes from Japan.
b. 15 pounds of screwdrivers from New York.
c. Three couches from High Point, North Carolina.
d. 500 high-fashion dresses from the garment district in New York City.
e. 300 pounds of Maine lobsters.
f. 600,000 pounds of various appliances from Evansville, Indiana.
How would your answers change if this department store were the only one in a large factory town in Ohio?

7. Indicate the nearest location where you would expect to find substantial storage facilities. What kinds of products would be stored there, and why are they stored there instead of some other place?

8. Indicate when a producer or middleman would find it desirable to use a public warehouse rather than a private warehouse. Illustrate, using a specific product or situation.

9. Discuss the distribution center concept. Is

this likely to eliminate the storing function of conventional wholesalers? Is it applicable to all products? If not, cite several examples.

10. Clearly differentiate between a warehouse and a distribution center. Explain how a specific product would be handled differently by these marketing institutions.

11. Explain the total cost approach and why it may be controversial in some firms. Give examples of where conflicts might occur.

12. Explain how adjusting the customer service level could improve a marketing mix. Illustrate.

13. Explain how a "channel captain" could help traditional independent firms compete with a corporate (integrated) channel system.

14. Relate the nature of the product to the degree of market exposure desired.

15. Why would middlemen want to be exclusive distributors for a product? Why would producers want exclusive distribution? Would middlemen be equally anxious to get exclusive distribution for any type of product? Why or why

not? Explain with reference to the following products: cornflakes, razor blades, golf clubs, golf balls, steak knives, stereo equipment, and industrial wood-working machinery.

16. Explain the present legal status of exclusive distribution. Describe a situation where exclusive distribution is almost sure to be legal. Describe the nature and size of competitors and the industry, as well as the nature of the exclusive arrangement. Would this exclusive arrangement be of any value to the producer or middleman?

17. Discuss the promotion a grocery products manufacturer would need in order to develop appropriate channels and move goods through those channels. Would the nature of this job change at all for a dress manufacturer? How about for a small producer of installations?

18. Discuss the advantages and disadvantages of either a pushing or pulling policy for a very small manufacturer just entering into the candy business with a line of inexpensive candy bars. Which policy would probably be most appropriate? State any assumptions you need to obtain a definite answer.

■ **SUGGESTED CASES**

14. Miller Company

15. Cooper Lumber Company

Chapter 12 ■ Retailing

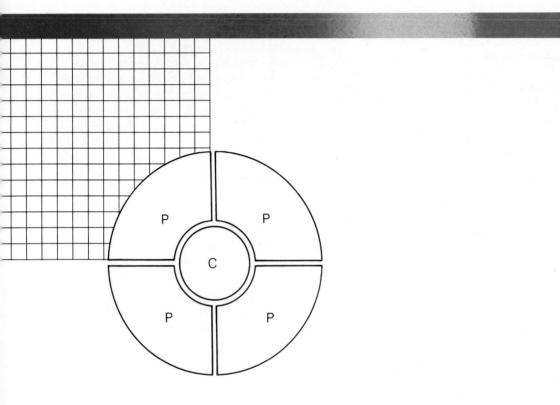

When you finish this chapter, you should:

1. Understand about retailers planning their own marketing strategies.

2. Know about the many kinds of retailers which might become members of producers' or wholesalers' channel systems.

3. Understand the differences among conventional and non-conventional retailers—including those who accept the mass-merchandising concept.

4. Understand "scrambled merchandising" and the "wheel of retailing."

5. Recognize the important new terms (shown in red).

If the goods aren't sold, nobody makes any money.

Retailing covers all of the activities involved in the sale of goods and/or services to final consumers. It is *not* concerned with industrial goods—or the sale of consumer goods in the channels. Retailing is important to all of us. As consumers, we spend a *trillion* dollars (that's $1,000,000,000,000!) a year buying goods and services from retailers. If the retailing effort fails, everyone in the channel suffers—and some products aren't sold at all. So retailing is important to marketing managers of consumer goods at *all* channel levels.

Retailers must choose their own target markets and marketing mixes very carefully. Retailing is very competitive—and always changing. For example, department stores and conventional clothing stores are being challenged by a new kind of discount operation. These "no-frills" stores sell name brand clothing—including "designer" labels—at far below regular retail prices. Stores like Marshall's, Hit or Miss, and Loehmann's are expanding—and attracting more price-conscious customers with their bargain emphasis.

What are the different kinds of retailers—and why did they develop? How do their strategies vary? What does the future look like for retailers? In this

■   FIGURE 12–1   Strategic decision areas for a retailer

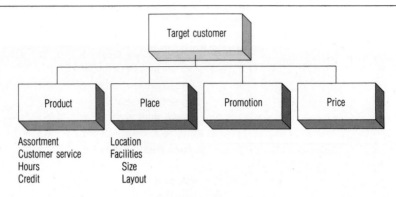

chapter, we'll try to answer these important questions. We will talk about the strategic decision areas shown in Figure 12–1.

PLANNING A RETAILER'S STRATEGY

Retailers are so directly involved with final consumers that their strategy planning must be done well or they won't survive. Because they are so aware that they must satisfy customers, retailers make *buying* an important activity. Successful retailers know the truth of the old rule: Goods well bought are half sold.

A retailer usually sells more than just one item. We will think of the retailer's whole offering—assortment of goods and services, advice from sales clerks, convenient parking, etc.—as its "Product." Let's look at why customers choose particular retailers.

Consumers Have Reasons for Buying from Particular Retailers

We know that different consumers prefer different kinds of retailers—but *why* they do is often ignored by retailers. Just renting a store and assuming that customers will come running is very common among beginning small retailers—and the failure rate is high. More than three fourths of new retailing efforts fail in their first year![1]

To be successful, a new retailer—or one trying to adjust to changing conditions—should try to identify possible target markets and understand why these people buy where they do.

Economic Needs— Which Store Has the Best Value?

There are many things a consumer might consider when choosing a particular retailer. For example:

1. Convenience.
2. Variety of selection.
3. Quality of products—freshness, purity, craftsmanship.

4. Courtesy of salespeople.
5. Integrity—Reputation for fairness in dealings.
6. Services offered—delivery, credit, returned-goods privileges.
7. Value offered.

Emotional Needs— The Importance of Social Class

There may also be important emotional reasons for preferring particular retailers. Some customers may think a certain store has higher social status— and get an ego boost from shopping there.

Different stores do seem to attract customers from different social classes. People like to shop where salespeople and other customers are like them- selves. No one wants to feel "out of place." Some people even go to a partic- ular store hoping they will meet friends there. For them, a trip to the store is also a social event.

The emotional needs that a store fills are related to its target market(s). Family Dollar Stores—a chain of variety stores in the Southeast—has been very successful with a "budget" image that appeals to lower-class shoppers. Saks Fifth Avenue works at its upper-class image. But not all stores have—or want—a particular class image. Some try to avoid creating one—because they want to appeal to a wide audience. Macy's, for example, has departments that carry some very expensive items—and others that handle products for the masses.

There is no one "right" answer as to whom a store should appeal. But ignoring emotional dimensions—including social class appeal—could lead to serious errors in marketing strategy planning.

Goods Classes Help Understand Store Types

We can also use the consumer goods classes idea—convenience goods, shopping goods, and specialty goods (Chapter 9)—to define three types of stores: convenience stores, shopping stores, and specialty stores.

A **convenience store** is a convenient place to shop—either centrally located "downtown" or "in the neighborhood." Such stores attract many cus- tomers because they are so handy. **Shopping stores** attract customers from greater distances because of the width and depth of their assortments. Stores selling furniture, clothing, or household appliances are usually thought of as shopping stores. **Specialty stores** are those for which customers have devel- oped a strong attraction. For whatever reasons—service, selection, or reputa- tion—some customers will regularly buy at these stores. This is like brand insistence for products.

Store Types Based on How Customers See Store

Note that these store types refer to the way *customers think of the store—* not just the kind of products the store carries. Also, different market segments might see or use a particular store differently. Remember this was true with the goods classes, too. So a retailer's strategy planning must consider poten- tial customers' attitudes toward *both* the product and the store. Classifying market segments by how they see both the store and the product—as shown in Figure 12–2—helps to understand this.

A retailer can get a better understanding of a market by estimating the rela- tive size of each of the boxes shown in Figure 12–2. By identifying which

■ FIGURE 12–2   How customers view store-product combinations

Store type / Product class	Convenience	Shopping	Specialty
Convenience	Will buy any brand at most accessible store	Shop around to find better service and/or lower prices	Prefer store. Brand may be important
Shopping	Want some selection but will settle for assortment at most accessible store	Want to compare both products and store mixes	Prefer store but insist on adequate assortment
Specialty	Prefer particular product but like place convenience too	Prefer particular product but still seeking best total product and mix	Prefer both store and product

Source: Adapted from Louis Bucklin, "Retail Strategy and the Classification of Consumer Goods," *Journal of Marketing*, January 1963, pp. 50–55.

competitors are satisfying which market segments, the retailer may see that some boxes are already "filled." He may find that he and his competitors are all charging head-on after the same customers—and completely ignoring others.

For example, house plants used to be sold only by florists and greenhouses. This was fine for those customers who wanted "shopping store" variety. But for others, this was too much trouble—and they just didn't buy plants. When some retailers went after the "convenience store" segment—with small house plant departments or stores in neighborhood shopping centers—they found a new, large market segment willing to buy plants—at convenience stores.

While the way consumers see stores can help guide strategy planning, other dimensions of retailers are useful, too. Let's look at the kinds of retailers already competing in the marketplace—and how they developed.

TYPES OF RETAILERS AND THE NATURE OF THEIR OFFERINGS

There are over 2 million retailers in the United States—and they are always evolving.

Retailers differ in terms of the service they offer, the product assortments they sell, and the width and depth of their product lines. A paint store and a fabric store, for example, both have depth in their different lines. By contrast, a department store might have less depth in any one line—but carry more different lines and more variety in each one. Some stores are strictly "self service"—while others provide helpful sales clerks as well as credit, delivery, trade-ins, gift wrap, special orders, and returns. Some retailers have "status" locations—downtown or at a mall. Others sell from vending machines or directly to a customer's home—without any store at all.

Each retailer's offering is some *mix* of these different characteristics. So we can't classify retailers using only a single characteristic. But it is helpful to describe basic types of retailers—and some differences in their strategies.

Over time, new types of retailers have evolved. Let's look first at some of the conventional retailers and then see how others have modified the conventional offering and survived—because they met the needs of *some* consumers.

CONVENTIONAL RETAILERS—AVOID PRICE COMPETITION

Single-Line, Limited-Line Retailers Specialize by Product

A hundred and fifty years ago, general stores—that carried anything they could sell in reasonable volume—were the main retailers. But after the Civil War, the growing number and variety of consumer goods made it hard for a general store to offer the depth and width customers wanted. So some stores began to specialize in dry goods, apparel, furniture, or groceries.

Now most conventional retailers are single-line stores or limited-line stores specializing in certain lines of related products rather than a wide assortment. Some of these stores specialize not only in a single line—such as clothing—but also in a *limited-line* within the broader line. For example, within the clothing line a store might carry *only* shoes, or formal wear, or men's casual wear, or even neckties—but offer depth in that limited line. This special-

Most conventional retailers are single-line or limited-line stores—like this one which specializes in men's casual wear.

■ FIGURE 12–3   Types of retailers and the nature of their offerings

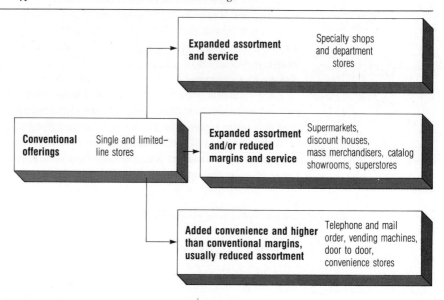

ization will probably continue as long as customer demands are varied—and large enough to support such stores.

Single-Line, Limited-Line Stores Are Being Squeezed

The main advantage of these stores is that they can satisfy some target markets better. Some even win specialty-store status by changing their marketing mix—including store hours, credit, and product assortment—to suit certain customers. But these stores face the costly problem of having to stock some slow-moving items to satisfy their customers. Further, many of these stores are small—with high expenses relative to sales. Stores like these have traditionally followed the retailing rule of "buy low and sell high." If there is much competition, they may expand assortment—specialize further—trying to keep costs down and prices up by avoiding competition on identical products.

These conventional retailers have been around for a long time. They obviously satisfy some needs. But they will continue to be squeezed by newer retailers with more to offer. (See Figure 12–3). Let's take a closer look at these newer types of retailers.

EXPAND ASSORTMENT AND SERVICE—TO COMPETE AT A HIGH PRICE

Specialty Shops Usually Sell Shopping Goods

A **specialty shop**—a type of limited-line store—usually is small, with a distinct "personality." Specialty shops aim at a carefully defined market segment by offering a unique product assortment, good service, and salespeople who

know their products.[2] For example, small specialty shops have developed to satisfy joggers. The clerks are runners themselves. They know the sport—and are eager to explain the advantages of different types of running shoes to their customers. These stores also carry a selection of books on running—as well as clothes for the jogger. Some even offer discounts to customers who are members of local track teams.

A specialty shop's major advantage is that it caters to certain types of customers whom the management and salespeople come to know well. This is important because specialty shops usually offer special types of shopping goods. Knowing their market simplifies buying, speeds turnover, and cuts costs. Specialty shops probably will continue to be a part of the retailing scene as long as customers have varied tastes—and the money to satisfy them.

Do not confuse specialty *shops,* with specialty *stores.* A specialty store is a store that for some reason (service, quality, etc.) has become *the* store for some customers. For example, some customers see Sears as a specialty store and regularly buy their paint, hardware, and major appliances at Sears— without shopping anywhere else.

Department Stores Combine Many Limited-Line Stores and Specialty Shops

Department stores are larger stores—organized into separate departments. Each department is like a separate limited-line store or specialty shop. They usually handle a wide variety of products—such as women's ready-to-wear and accessories, men's and boys' wear, textiles, housewares, and home furnishings.

Department stores are often looked to as the retailing leaders in a community. They usually do lead in customer services—including credit, merchandise return, delivery, fashion shows, and Christmas displays. They also are leaders because of their size. The 1977 *Census of Retail Trade* showed that U.S. department stores had about $9 million in annual sales—compared to about $390,000 for the average retail store. The biggest—Macy's, May Company, and Dayton-Hudson—each top $500 million in sales annually. Although department stores account for less than 1 percent of the total number of retail stores, they had almost 11 percent of total retail sales in 1977.

Department stores generally try to serve customers seeking shopping goods—and probably would be thought of as shopping *stores* by most people. But some department stores have earned specialty-store status. They have a strong hold on their market.

Originally, most department stores were downtown—close to other department stores and convenient for many potential customers. Many downtown stores suffered after World War II, when many of their customers moved to the suburbs. Some department stores opened suburban branches—usually in shopping centers—to serve these customers.[3]

The building of downtown "condos," improved mass transit, and urban renewal are attracting more middle- and upper-income people back to the cities. This may save some department stores. But they still face many challenges—especially price competition from mass-merchandising retailers who operate with lower costs and sell larger volumes. We'll discuss them next.

EVOLUTION OF NEW, MASS–MERCHANDISING RETAILERS

Mass-Merchandising Is Different Than Conventional Retailing

So far we have been describing retailers mainly in terms of the number of lines and their physical facilities. This is the traditional way to think about retailing. We could talk about supermarkets and discount houses in these terms, too. But then we would miss an important difference—just as some conventional retailers did when these stores first appeared.

Conventional retailers believe in a fixed demand for a territory—and have a "buy low and sell high" philosophy. Some modern retailers, however, have accepted the **mass-merchandising concept**—which says that retailers should offer low prices to get faster turnover and greater sales volume—by appealing to larger markets. To understand mass-merchandising better, let's look at its evolution from the development of supermarkets and discounters to the modern mass-merchandisers—like K mart.

Supermarkets Started the Move to Mass-Merchandising

A **supermarket** is a large store specializing in groceries—with self-service and wide assortments. As late as 1930, most food stores were relatively small single- or limited-line operations. In the early Depression years, some creative people felt that they could increase sales by charging lower prices. They introduced self-service, provided a very broad product assortment in large stores, and offered low prices. Their early experiments in vacant warehouses were an immediate success. Profits came from large sales volume—not from traditional "high" markups.[4]

Supermarkets sell convenience goods—but in quantity. Supermarkets typically carry more than 7,000 product items. Stores are large—around 20,000 square feet—with free parking. According to the Food Marketing Institute, $1 million is the minimum annual sales volume for a store to be called a supermarket. In 1982, there were over 37,000 supermarkets—about 23 percent of all food stores—and they handled about 76 percent of total food store sales. Today, there are almost too many supermarkets, but new ones still do well when they are well located.[5]

Supermarkets are planned so goods can be loaded on the shelves easily. The store layout makes it easy for customers to shop. Some stores carefully analyze the sales and profit of each item—and allow more shelf space for faster moving and high profit items. This helps sell more goods in less time, reduces the investment in inventory, makes stocking easier, and reduces the cost of handling goods. Such efficiency is very important—because there is so much competition. Net profits (after taxes) in grocery supermarkets usually run a thin 1 percent of sales—*or less*!

Catalog Showroom Retailers Came before Discount Houses

Catalog showroom retailers sell several lines out of a catalog and display showroom—with backup inventories. Before 1940, these retailers were usually wholesalers who also sold at retail to friends and members of groups—such as labor unions or church groups. In the 1970s, however, these operations

Supermarkets were the first retailers to adopt the mass-merchandising concept.

expanded rapidly—offering big price savings on jewelry, gifts, luggage, and small appliances.[6] Catalog showrooms tend to focus on well-known manufacturers' brands. They offer few services.

The early catalog operations didn't bother the conventional retailers—because they were not well promoted and accounted for only a small part of total retail sales. If these early catalog retailers had moved ahead aggressively—as the current catalog retailers are doing—the retailing scene might be different. But instead, discount houses developed.

Discount Houses Upset Some Conventional Retailers

Right after World War II, some retailers moved beyond offering discounts to selected customers. These **discount houses** offered "hard goods" (cameras, TVs, appliances) with big price cuts—to customers who would go to the discounter's low-rent store, pay cash, and take care of any service or repair problems themselves. These retailers sold at 20 to 30 percent below conventional retailers.

In the early 1950s—with war shortages finally over—well-known brands were more available. The discount houses were able to offer fuller assortments. At this stage, many discounters "turned respectable"—moving to better locations and offering more services and guarantees. They began to act more like regular retailers—but still *kept their prices lower than conventional retailers to keep turnover high.* And they still do today—frustrating conventional retailers!

Mass-Merchandisers Are More Than Discounters

Mass-merchandisers are large, self-service stores with many departments—which emphasize "soft goods" (housewares, clothing, and fabrics) but still follow the discount house's emphasis on lower margins to get faster turnover. Mass-merchandisers—like K mart and Zayre—have check-out counters in the front of the store and little or no sales help on the floor. This is in contrast to more conventional retailers—such as Sears and J. C. Penney—who

still offer some service and have sales stations and cash registers in most departments. The conventional retailer may try to carry complete stocks and reorder popular sizes or items in the lines it carries, while mass-merchandisers do less of this. They want to move merchandise—fast—and are less concerned with continuity of lines and assortment.

The average mass-merchandiser has nearly 60,000 square feet of floor space—three to four times the size of the average supermarket.[7] Mass-merchandisers have grown rapidly. In fact, they expanded so rapidly in some areas that they were no longer taking customers from conventional retailers—but from each other.[8] Profits have dropped—and many mass-merchandisers have gone bankrupt. Seeing fewer opportunities in big cities, K mart has started moving into smaller towns with a smaller K mart. This has really upset some small-town merchants—who felt they were safe from this kind of competition.

Super-Stores Meet All Routine Needs

Super-stores—are very large stores that try to carry not only foods, but all goods and services which the consumer purchases *routinely*. Such a store may *look* like a mass-merchandiser, but it is different. A super-store is trying to meet *all* the customer's routine needs—at a low price.

Super-stores are bigger than supermarkets or mass-merchandisers. The super-store offers not only foods—but also personal care products, alcoholic beverages, some clothing, some lawn and garden products, gasoline—and services such as laundry, dry cleaning, shoe repair, check cashing, and bill paying.[9] Some mass-merchandisers have moved in this direction—and if super-stores spread, the food-oriented supermarkets may suffer. Their present buildings and parking lots are not large enough to convert to super-stores.

SOME RETAILERS FOCUS ON ADDED CONVENIENCE

The supermarkets, discounters, and mass-merchandisers sell many different products "under one roof." But they are inconvenient in some ways. They offer fewer customer services, check-out lines may be longer, and stores may be in less convenient, "low-rent" locations. The savings may justify these inconveniences when a consumer has a lot to buy. But sometimes—for some products—convenience is much more important—even if the price is a little higher. Let's look at some retailers who have met a need by emphasizing convenience.

Convenience (Food) Stores Must Have the Right Assortment

Convenience (food) stores are a convenience-oriented variation of the conventional limited-line food stores. Instead of carrying a big variety, they limit their stock to "fill-in" items like bread, milk, ice cream, or beer. Stores such as 7-Eleven, Majik Market, and White Hen Pantry fill needs between major shopping trips to a supermarket. They are offering *convenience*—not assortment—and often charge prices 10 to 20 percent higher than at nearby supermarkets. Their higher margins—together with faster turnover of a narrow assortment—

Automatic vending may change in the future as machines take credit cards—like with this new system from Exxon.

make them much more profitable than supermarkets. They net about 4 percent on sales—rather than the 1 percent earned by supermarkets. This helps explain why the number of such stores rose from 2,500 in 1960 to over 38,000 in 1982.[10]

Vending Machines Are Convenient

Automatic vending is selling and delivering products through vending machines. Vending machine sales have increased, but still are only about 1.5 percent of total U.S. retail sales. In some lines, however, vending machines are very important. Sixteen percent of all cigarettes sold in the United States, 20 percent of the candy bars, and 25 percent of canned and bottled soft drinks are sold through machines.[11]

The major problem with automatic vending is high cost. The machines are expensive to buy, stock, and repair—relative to the volume they sell. Marketers of similar non-vended products can operate profitably on a margin of about 20 percent—while the vending industry needs about 41 percent to break even. So they must charge higher prices.[12] If costs come down—and consumers continue to want convenience—we may see more growth in this retailing method. "24-hour" bank teller machines—which give a customer cash, using a "money card"—provide a hint of how technology may change automatic vending.

Shop at Home—With Telephone and Mail-Order Retailing

Telephone and mail-order retailing allows consumers to shop at home—placing orders by mail or telephone—and charging the purchase to a credit card. Catalogs let customers "see" the offerings—and purchases are delivered by mail or United Parcel Service (UPS). This method can be useful for reaching widely scattered markets that conventional retailers can't serve.

"Mail-order" retailing has continued to grow—recently at the rapid rate of about 15 percent per year—and now accounts for about 4 percent of retail

Mail and telephone order catalogs are the classic consumer "wish books."

sales. Today, however, mail-order is changing. Many companies offer toll-free telephone numbers for ordering and information. They aim at a narrower target market—with more expensive fashion, gift, and luxury items.

The big mail-order houses started all this—but now department stores and limited-line stores are seeing the profit possibilities and selling by mail, too. Not only can they get additional business this way—but costs may be lower because they can use warehouse-type buildings and limited sales help. After-tax profits for mail-order retailers average 7 percent of sales—more than twice the profit margins for most other types of retailers.[13]

Door-to-Door Retailers—Give More Personal Attention

Door-to-door selling means going directly to the consumer's home. This can be a good method to introduce a new product or sell unsought goods. But it is expensive. Markups range from 30 to 50 percent—often higher.

Door-to-door selling can be successful—although it accounts for less than 1 percent of retail sales. Avon—the largest cosmetics firm in the world—has nearly a million people selling door-to-door.

WHY RETAILERS EVOLVE AND CHANGE

We have been talking about the different kinds of retailers. Figure 12–4 shows the relationship among these different retailers—and their offerings. Now let's look at how retailing is changing.

Scrambled Merchandising—Mixing Product Lines for Higher Profits

Conventional retailers tend to specialize by product line. But most modern retailers have moved toward **scrambled merchandising**—carrying *any* product lines which they feel they can sell profitably. Supermarkets and "drug stores" are selling anything they can move in volume—while mass-merchandisers are selling groceries, cameras, jewelry, and even home computers. Why has scrambled merchandising become so common?

The Wheel of Retailing Keeps Rolling

The **wheel of retailing theory** says that new types of retailers enter the market as low-status, low-margin, low-price operators and then—if they are successful—evolve into more conventional retailers offering more services—with higher operating costs and higher prices. Then they are threatened by new low-status, low-margin, low-price retailers—and the wheel turns again.

Early department stores began this way. Then they became higher priced—and added "bargain basements" to serve the more price-conscious customers. Mail-order houses developed on a price basis. So did the food chains, economy apparel chains, drug chains, and the automotive accessory chains which developed during the 1920s. The supermarket, in turn, was started with low prices and little service.

Some Innovators Start with High Margins

The wheel of retailing theory, however, does not explain all major retailing developments. Vending machines entered as high-cost, high-margin operations. Convenience food stores are high-priced. Suburban shopping centers have not had a low-price emphasis.

■   FIGURE 12-4   A three-dimensional view of the market for retail facilities and the probable position of some present offerings

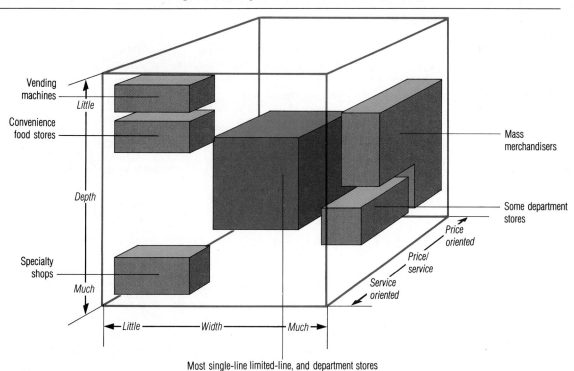

Retailing Types Also Explained by Consumer Needs Filled

Consumer needs also affect the type of retailer that develops. Look at Figure 12–4. It gives a simplified view of the consumer market. It suggests that three consumer-oriented dimensions affect the kinds of retailers customers choose. These dimensions are: (1) width of assortment desired, (2) depth of assortment desired, and (3) price/service combination. It is possible to place most existing retailers within this three-dimensional market. Figure 12–4, for example, suggests the "why" of vending machines. Some customers—in the front upper left-hand corner—have a strong need for a specific item—and are *not* interested in the width of assortment, the depth of assortment, *or* the price.

Product Life Cycle Concept Applies to Retailer Types, Too

We have seen that people's needs help explain why different kinds of retailers developed. But we need to apply the product life-cycle concept to understand this process better. A retailer with a new idea may have big profits—for awhile. But if it's a really good idea, he can count on speedy imitation—and a squeeze on his profits. Other retailers will "scramble" their product mix—to sell products which offer them high margins or faster turnover.

Some conventional retailers are far along in their life cycles—and may be declining. Recent innovators are still in the market growth stage. See Figure 12–5.

■ FIGURE 12–5   Retailer life cycles—timing and years to market maturity

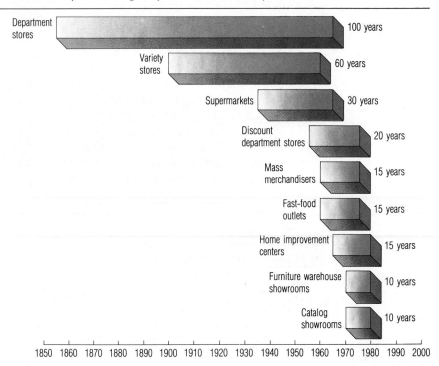

Some retailers are confused by the scrambling going on around them. They don't see this evolutionary process—and don't understand that some of their more successful competitors are aiming at different market segments—instead of just "selling products."

It is not surprising to find that some modern success stories in retailing are among firms which moved into a new market and started another "product life cycle"—by aiming at needs along the edges of the market shown in Figure 12–4. The convenience food stores, for example, don't just sell food. They deliberately sell a particular assortment-service combination to meet a different need. This is also true of specialty shops—and some of the mass-merchandisers and department store chains.[14]

RETAILER SIZE AND PROFITS

We have talked about different types of retailers—and how they have evolved. Now let's look at the size of stores—and how they are owned—because this is related to retailer strategy planning too.

The Number of Retailers Is Very Large

There are lots of retailers—in part because it is easy to enter retailing. Kids can open and close a lemonade stand in one day. A more serious retailer can rent an empty store and be in business without putting up much money (capital). There are about 2.4 million retailers compared to almost 600,000 wholesalers and 500,000 manufacturers.

But a Few Big Ones Do Most of the Business

The large number of retailers might suggest that retailing is a field of small businesses. This is partly true. As shown in Figure 12–6, about half of all the retail stores had annual sales of less than $100,000. The larger retail stores—such as supermarkets and others selling more than $1 million annually—do most of the business. Only about 7 percent of the retail stores are this big, yet they account for over 60 percent of all retail sales.

The many small retailers reach many consumers—and often are valuable channel members. But they cause problems for producers and wholesalers. Their large number—and relatively small sales volume—make working with them expensive. They often require separate marketing mixes.

Small Size May Be Hard to Overcome

A small retailer may satisfy some personal needs—by being his own boss. And he can be very helpful to some target customers—because of more flexibility. But a small store may only *seem* profitable because some of the costs of doing business are ignored. The owner may not be allowing for depreciation—or for family members working without pay. About a half million small retailers sell less than $50,000 per year—which, after expenses, leaves hardly enough to support one person.

Even the average retail store is too small to gain economies of scale. Average annual sales of only $390,000 is not very impressive—especially considering that net profits as a percentage of sales range from 1 to 5 percent.

The disadvantage of small size may even apply to the many departments in a large department store. Its many small departments may not be any larger than independent limited-line stores—and so there is little possibility for volume buying.

Being in a Chain May Help

One way for a retailer to gain economies of scale is with a corporate chain. A **(corporate) chain store** is one of several stores owned and managed by the same corporation. Most chains do at least some central buying for different stores—which allows them to take advantage of quantity discounts. They may also have advantages in promotion and management—spreading the costs to many stores.

Chains grew slowly until after World War I—then spurted ahead during the 1920s. Chains have continued to grow. They now account for about 45 percent of retail sales—and about 15 percent of the retailers.

Chains have done even better in certain lines. They have 95 percent of the department store business. Sears, Montgomery Ward, and J. C. Penney are

■ FIGURE 12–6   Distribution of stores by size and share of total retail sales (United States, 1977)

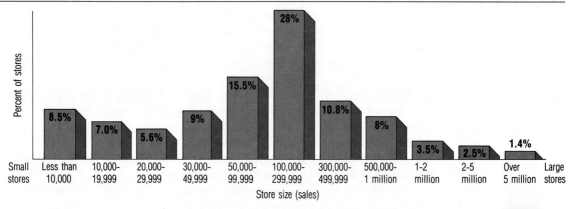

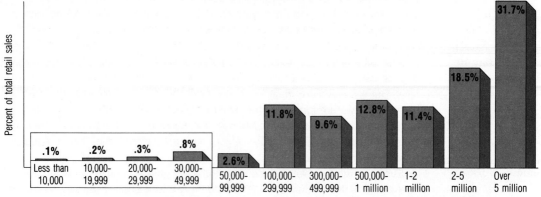

Source: Based on data from 1977 *Census of Retail Trade*, Table 1, pp. 1–8.

Chain stores—like Sears—win a very large share of all retail business.

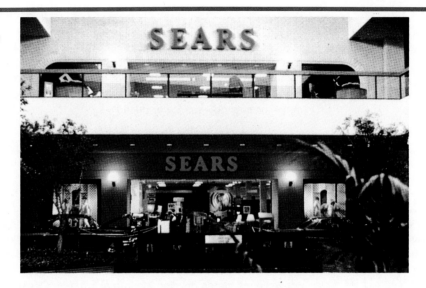

chains. Safeway, Kroger, A&P, and other supermarket chains have 57 percent of the grocery sales.

Independents Form Chains, Too

The growth of corporate chains has encouraged the development of cooperative chains and voluntary chains.

Cooperative chains are retailer-sponsored groups—formed by independent retailers—to run their own buying organization and joint promotion efforts. Sales of cooperative chains have risen as they learned how to meet the corporate chain competition. Examples include Associated Grocers, Certified Grocers, and True Value (in hardware).

Voluntary chains are wholesaler-sponsored groups which work with "independent" retailers. Some are linked by contracts stating common operating procedures—and the use of common storefront designs, store name, and joint promotion efforts. Examples include IGA and Super Valu in groceries, Ace in hardware, and Western Auto in auto supplies.

Franchising Is Similar

In **franchise operations** the franchiser develops a good marketing strategy—and the franchise holders carry out the strategy in their own units. They are like voluntary chains. Examples include McDonald's (fast food), Midas Mufflers (auto repair), Century 21 (real estate), and Baskin-Robbins (ice cream).

The voluntary chains have tended to work with existing retailers, while some franchisers like to work with newcomers—whom they train and get started. Sometimes they will locate the site—as well as supervise building and the opening promotion.

Consumer Co-ops Try—But Usually in Vain

Cooperative and voluntary chains should not be confused with **consumer cooperatives**—which are groups of *consumers* who buy together. These groups usually operate on a non-profit basis—with voluntary or poorly paid management. Consumer cooperatives have never made much of an impact in the United States. Their high point was 1 percent of retail sales in 1954.

Consumer cooperatives have been more successful in Europe—where most retailers have been high-priced and inefficient. Most U.S. markets are so competitive that customers have not been willing to go to the typically out-of-the-way locations for the (sometimes) unknown or co-op dealer brands which may—or may not—be lower priced.

LOCATION OF RETAIL FACILITIES

Downtown and Shopping Strips—Evolve Without a Plan

Most cities have a "central business district"—where many retail stores are found. At first, it may seem that such a district was developed according to some plan. Actually, the location of individual stores is more an accident of time—and what spaces were available. As cities grow, "shopping strips" of convenience stores develop along major roads. Generally, they emphasize convenience goods. But a variety of single-line and limited-line stores may enter too, adding shopping goods to the mix. There may be a lot of turnover—as one goes out of business and another takes its place.

All of these retail areas are more or less unplanned—except that city planners sometimes restrict commercial development. They certainly are not the planned shopping centers which have developed in the last 30 years.

Planned Shopping Centers—Not Just a Group of Stores

A **planned shopping center** is a set of stores planned as a unit—to satisfy some market needs. Free parking is provided. Many centers are enclosed—to make shopping inviting in all kinds of weather. The centers are made up of several independent merchants—who sometimes act together for Promotion purposes.

Many cities are trying to renovate and revitalize downtown shopping areas.

Neighborhood shopping centers consist of several convenience stores. These centers usually include a supermarket, drug store, hardware store, beauty shop, laundry, dry cleaner, gas station, and perhaps others—such as a bakery or appliance shop. They normally must serve 7,500 to 40,000 people living within 6 to 10 minutes driving distance.

Community shopping centers are larger and offer some shopping stores as well as the convenience stores found in neighborhood shopping centers. They usually include a small department store which carries shopping goods (clothing and home furnishings). But most sales in these centers are convenience goods. These centers must serve 40,000 to 150,000 people within a radius of five to six miles.

Regional shopping centers are the largest centers and emphasize shopping stores and shopping goods. They include one or more large department stores—and as many as 200 smaller stores. Stores that feature convenience goods are often placed at the edge of the center—so they won't get in the way of customers mostly interested in shopping.

Regional centers usually serve 150,000 or more persons. They are like downtown shopping districts of larger cities. Regional centers usually are found near suburban areas. They draw customers from a radius of 7 to 10 miles—or even further, from rural areas where shopping facilities are poor. Regional shopping centers are often in the 2 million square foot range—as large as 40 football fields!

WHAT DOES THE FUTURE LOOK LIKE?

Retailing has continued to change over the last 30 years. Scrambled merchandising may become more scrambled. Some people are forecasting larger stores—while others are predicting smaller ones.

More Customer-Oriented Retailing May Be Coming

Forecasting trends is risky—but our three-dimensional picture of the retailing market (Figure 12–4) can be helpful. Those who suggest bigger and bigger stores are looking at the mass market. Those who expect more small stores and specialty shops may be expecting more demanding—but increasingly wealthy—target markets able to afford higher prices for special products.

To serve small but wealthy markets, convenience food stores continue to spread. Sales by vending machines—even with their higher operating costs and prices—may grow. Certainly, some customers are getting tired of the large supermarkets that take so much of their time. Logically, convenience goods should be offered at the customer's—rather than the retailer's—convenience. For example, some retailers still fight night and weekend hours—hours when it is most convenient for many families to shop.

In-Home Shopping Will Become More Popular

Telephone shopping will become more popular, too. The mail-order houses and department stores already find phone business attractive. Telephone supermarkets—now a reality—sell only by phone and deliver all orders. Linking the phone to closed-circuit TV will let the customer see products at home—

while hearing well-prepared sales presentations. The customer could place an order through a home computer system—which would also arrange for billing and delivery.

We now have far greater electronic capabilities than we are using. There seems to be no reason why the customer couldn't shop in the home—saving time and gasoline. Such automated retailing could take over a large share of the convenience goods and homogeneous shopping goods business.[15]

Retailers Becoming Manufacturers, and Vice Versa

We may also see more horizontal and vertical arrangements in channel systems. This would certainly affect present manufacturers—who already see retailers developing their own brands, using manufacturers as production arms.

Large manufacturers themselves may go into retailing—for self-protection. Rexall Corporation, Sherwin-Williams, B. F. Goodrich, Van Heusen, and others already control their own retail outlets.

Retailing will continue to be needed. But the role of individual retailers—and even the concept of a retail store—may have to change. Customers will always have needs. And they will probably want to satisfy these needs with combinations of goods and services. But retail *stores* aren't the only way to do this!

Retailers Must Face the Challenge

One thing is certain—retailing will continue to change. For years, conventional retailers' profits have gone down. Even some of the newer discounters and shopping centers have not done well. Department stores, and food and drug chains have seen profit declines. The conventional "variety stores" have done even worse. Some shifted into mass-merchandising—and, as we saw, even some mass-merchandisers are in trouble, too.

A few firms—especially K mart—have avoided this general profit squeeze. But the future doesn't look bright for retailers who can't—or won't—change.

No Easy Way for More Profit

In fact, it seems that there is no easy way to big profits anymore. Instead, careful strategy planning—and great care in carrying out the plans—will be needed for success in the future. This means more careful market segmenting to find unsatisfied needs which (1) have a long life expectancy and (2) can be satisfied with low levels of investment. This won't be easy. But the imaginative marketing planner will find more profitable opportunities than the conventional retailer who doesn't know that the product life cycle is moving along—and is just "hoping for the best."[16]

■ CONCLUSION

Modern retailing is scrambled—and we will probably see more changes in the future. A producer's marketing manager must choose very carefully among the available retailers. And retail-

ers must plan their marketing mixes with their target customers' needs in mind.

We described many types of retailers—and saw that each has its advantages and disadvantages. We also saw that some modern retailers have left conventional ways behind. The old "buy low and sell high" idea is no longer a safe rule. Lower margins with faster turnover is the modern idea—as retailers move into mass-merchandising. But even this is no guarantee of success—as retailers' product life cycles move on.

Scrambled merchandising will probably continue as the "wheel of retailing continues to roll." But important breakthroughs are still possible—

because consumers may want different retail facilities. Convenience goods, for example, may be made more easily available by some combination of electronic ordering and home delivery or vending.

Our society needs a retailing function—but perhaps not all the present retailers are needed. It is safe to say that retailing will offer the marketing manager new challenges and opportunities.

■ QUESTIONS AND PROBLEMS

1. Identify a specialty store selling convenience goods in your city. Explain why you feel it is that kind of a store and why an awareness of this status would be important to a manufacturer. Does it give the retailer any particular advantage? If so, with whom?

2. What sort of a "product" are specialty shops offering? What are the prospects for organizing a chain of specialty shops?

3. A department store consists of many departments. Is this horizontal integration? Are all of the advantages of horizontal integration achieved in a department store operation?

4. Many department stores have a bargain basement. Does the basement represent just another department, like the hat department or the luggage department, for example, or is some whole new concept involved?

5. Distinguish between discount houses and mass-merchandisers. Forecast the future of low-price selling in food, clothing, and appliances.

6. List five products which seem suitable for automatic vending and yet are not normally sold in this manner. Generally, what characteristics are required?

7. Apply the "wheel of retailing" theory to your local community. What changes seem likely? Does it seem likely that established retailers will see the need for change, or will entirely new firms have to develop?

8. Discuss the kinds of markets served by the three types of shopping centers. Are they directly competitive? Do they contain the same kinds of stores? Is the long-run outlook for all of them similar?

9. Explain the growth and decline of various retailers and shopping centers in your own community. Use the text's three-dimensional drawing (Figure 12–4) and the product life-cycle concept. Also, treat each retailers' whole offering as a "product."

■ SUGGESTED CASES

13. Visual Services, Inc.

16. Meir Company

Chapter 13 ■ Wholesaling

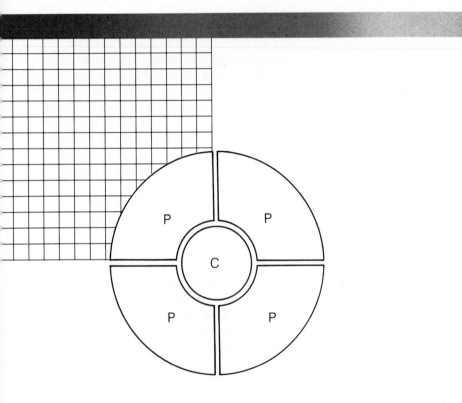

When you finish this chapter, you should:

1. Understand what wholesalers are and the wholesaling functions they *may* provide for others in channel systems.

2. Know the various kinds of merchant wholesalers and agent middlemen.

3. Understand when and where the various kinds of merchant wholesalers and agent middlemen would be most useful to channel planners.

4. Understand why wholesalers have lasted.

5. Recognize the important new terms (shown in red).

"I can get it for you wholesale," the man said. But could he? Would it be a good deal?

George Mims is a heating contractor. His company sells heating systems—and installs them in new buildings. Mr. Mims gets a lot of help from Air Control Company—the wholesaler who supplies this equipment. When Mims isn't sure what type of furnace to install, the experts at the wholesale company give him technical advice. They also keep an inventory of products from different manufacturers. This means that Mr. Mims can order a piece of equipment when he is ready to install it. He doesn't have to tie up his money in a big inventory—or wait for a part to be shipped cross country from the producer. Air Control Company even helps him to finance his business. Mims doesn't have to pay for his purchases until 30 days after he takes delivery. By then, he has finished his work and been paid by his customers. Mr. Mim's whole way of doing business would be different without this wholesaler.

Mr. Mim's story shows that wholesalers can provide many different functions and be an important link in a channel system—helping both suppliers and customers. Although they are separate business firms which must plan their own strategies, you can understand wholesalers better if you look at them as members of a channel of distribution.

In this chapter, you will learn more about wholesalers. You will see how they have evolved, how they fit into various channels, why they are used, and what functions they perform.

WHAT IS A WHOLESALER?

It's not easy to define what a wholesaler is—because there are so many different wholesalers doing different jobs. Some of their activities may even seem like manufacturing. As a result, some wholesalers call themselves "manufacturer and dealer." Others like to identify themselves with such general terms as merchant, dealer, or distributor. Others just use the name which is commonly used in their trade—without really thinking about what it means.

To avoid a long technical discussion on the nature of wholesaling, we will use the U.S. Bureau of the Census definition:

> **Wholesaling** is concerned with the activities of those persons or establishments which sell to retailers and other merchants, and/or to industrial, institutional, and commercial users, but who do not sell in large amounts to final consumers.

So **wholesalers** are firms whose main function is providing wholesaling activities.

Note that producers who take over wholesaling activities are not considered wholesalers. However, if separate middlemen firms—such as branch warehouses—are set up by producers, then these firms are counted as wholesalers by the U.S. Census Bureau. Wholesaling must be understood as a middleman activity.

There is wide variation in the way wholesalers operate, but they do not sell in large amounts to final consumers.

POSSIBLE WHOLESALING FUNCTIONS

Wholesalers may perform certain functions for both their own customers and their suppliers. These *wholesaling functions* are just adaptions of the eight basic marketing functions discussed in Chapter 1. And note that *these functions are provided by some, but not all, wholesalers.*

What a Wholesaler Might Do for Customers

1. *Regroup products*—provide the quantity and assortment wanted by customers at the lowest possible cost.
2. *Anticipate needs*—forecast customers' demands and buy for them.
3. *Carry stocks*—carry inventory so customers don't have to store a large inventory.
4. *Deliver products*—provide prompt delivery at low cost.
5. *Grant credit*—give credit to customers, perhaps supplying their working capital. (Note: This financing function may be *very* important to small customers. It is sometimes the main reason why they use wholesalers—rather than buying directly from manufacturers.)
6. *Provide information and advisory service*—supply price and technical information as well as suggestions on how to install and sell products. (Note: The wholesaler's sales force may be experts in the products they sell.)
7. *Provide part of buying function*—offer products to potential customers so they don't have to hunt for supply sources.
8. *Own and transfer title to products*—permits completing a sale without the need for other middlemen—speeding the whole buying and selling process.

What a Wholesaler Might Do for Producer-Suppliers

1. *Provide part of producer's selling function*—by going to producer-suppliers instead of waiting for their sales reps to call.
2. *Store inventory*—reducing a producer's need to carry large stocks—and cutting his warehousing expenses.
3. *Supply capital*—reducing a producer's need for working capital by buying his output and carrying it in inventory until it is sold.
4. *Reduce credit risk*—by selling to customers the wholesaler knows—and taking the loss if these customers don't pay.
5. *Provide market information*—as an informed buyer and seller closer to the market, the wholesaler reduces the producer's need for market research.[1]

KINDS AND COSTS OF AVAILABLE WHOLESALERS

Figure 13–1 compares the number, sales volume, and operating expenses of some major types of wholesalers. The differences in operating expenses

■ FIGURE 13–1   Wholesale trade by type of operation and cost (as a percent of sales)

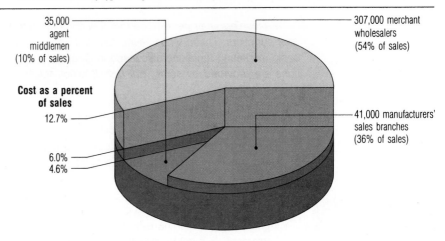

35,000
agent
middlemen
(10% of sales)

307,000 merchant
wholesalers
(54% of sales)

**Cost as a percent
of sales**
12.7%

41,000 manufacturers'
sales branches
(36% of sales)

6.0%
4.6%

Source: Based on data from 1977 *Census of Wholesale Trade.*

suggest that each of these types performs different wholesaling functions. But which ones and why?

Why, for example, do manufacturers use merchant wholesalers—costing 12.7 percent of sales—when manufacturers' sales branches cost only 6.0 percent? Why use either when brokers cost only 4.6 percent?

To answer these questions, we must understand what these wholesalers do—and don't do. Figure 13–2 gives a big-picture view of the wholesalers described in more detail below. Note that a major difference is whether they *own* the products they sell.

**Each Wholesaler
Found a Niche**

We have been talking about the evolution of our marketing system. This also applies to wholesaling. As American output grew, so did the need for middlemen to handle it.

To serve the early retail general stores, wholesalers carried a wide line of merchandise. These wholesalers were called "general merchandise" wholesalers—because their merchandise was so varied. As the general store evolved into a single- or limited-line store, "single-line" wholesalers developed. Those specializing in very narrow lines were called "specialty" wholesalers.

Wholesalers served not only retailers and final consumers—but also manufacturers. Many manufacturers were so small that it was hard for them to contact the growing number of wholesalers or other manufacturer customers. So special wholesalers—called agent middlemen—developed to make these contacts. In general, special needs arose—and specialized wholesalers developed to meet them.[2]

■ FIGURE 13–2   Types of wholesalers

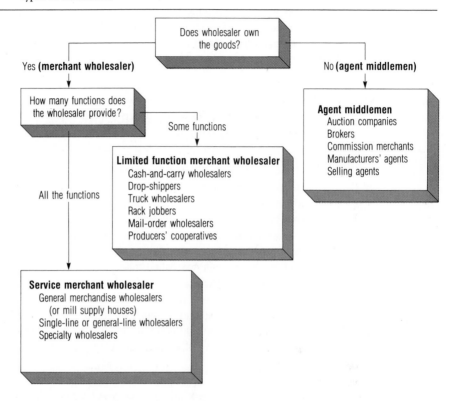

Wholesaler Provides Access to a Target Market

One of the main assets of a wholesaler is its customers. A certain wholesaler may be the only one who reaches some customers. The manufacturer who wants to reach these customers *may have no choice but to use that wholesaler.* "What customers does this wholesaler serve?" should be one of the first questions you ask when planning a channel of distribution.[3]

Learn the Pure to Understand the Real

The next important question would be, "What functions does this particular wholesaler provide?" Wholesalers typically specialize by product line. But they do provide different functions. And they probably will keep doing what they are doing—no matter what others might like them to do!

To help you understand wholesaling better, we will describe "pure types" of wholesalers. In practice, it may be hard to find examples of these pure types—because many wholesalers are mixtures. Further, the names commonly used in a particular industry may be misleading. Some so-called "brokers" actually behave as limited-function merchant wholesalers—and some "manufacturers' agents" operate as full-service wholesalers. This casual use of terms makes it all the more important for you to understand the pure types before trying to understand the blends—and the names given to them in the business world.

In the following pages, we'll discuss the major types of wholesalers identified by the U.S. Census Bureau. Remember, detailed data is available by kind of business, by product line, and by geographic territory. Such detailed data can be valuable in strategy planning—to learn whether potential channel members are serving a target market—as well as the sales volumes achieved by the present middlemen.

MERCHANT WHOLESALERS ARE THE MOST NUMEROUS

Merchant wholesalers own (take title to) the products they sell. For example, a wholesale lumber yard that buys plywood from a producer is a merchant wholesaler. It actually owns—"takes title to"—the lumber for some period of time before selling to its customers.

Besides taking title, merchant wholesalers also provide some—or all—of the wholesaling functions. There are two basic kinds of merchant wholesalers: (1) service—sometimes called full-service—wholesalers and (2) limited-function or limited-service wholesalers. Their names explain their difference.

From Figure 13–1, we can see that about four out of five wholesaling firms are merchant wholesalers—but they handle only about half of wholesale sales. Understanding *why* will help you understand wholesaling. Basically, it's because other kinds of wholesalers play important roles, too.

Service Wholesalers Provide All the Functions

Service wholesalers provide all the wholesaling functions. Within this basic group are three types: (1) *general merchandise,* (2) *single line,* and (3) *specialty.*

General merchandise wholesalers carry a wide variety of non-perishable items such as hardware, electrical supplies, plumbing supplies, furniture, drugs, cosmetics, and automobile equipment. With this broad line of convenience and shopping goods, they serve many kinds of retail stores. In the industrial goods field, the *mill supply house* operates in a similar way. Somewhat like a retail hardware store, the mill supply house carries a broad variety of accessories and supplies for industrial customers.

Single-line (or general-line) wholesalers carry a narrower line of merchandise than general merchandise wholesalers. For example, they might carry only groceries, or wearing apparel, or certain types of industrial tools or supplies.

Specialty wholesalers carry a very narrow range of products. A consumer goods specialty wholesaler might carry only health foods or oriental foods—instead of a full line of groceries.

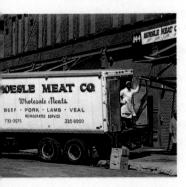

For industrial goods, a specialty wholesaler might limit itself to fields requiring technical knowledge or services. This specialty wholesaler tries to become an expert in selling the product lines it carries. Where there is need for this kind of technical service, the specialty wholesaler usually has little difficulty taking business away from less-specialized wholesalers.

General merchandise wholesalers carry a wide variety of non-perishable staple items.

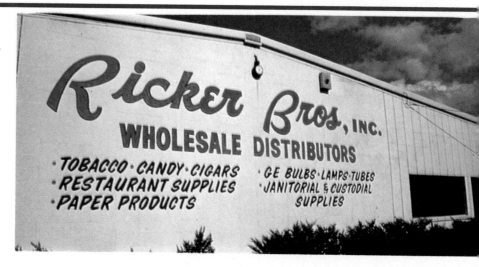

The Cadillac Plastic and Chemical Company in Detroit, for example, became a specialty wholesaler serving the needs of both plastics makers and users. Neither the large plastics manufacturers nor the merchant wholesalers with wide lines were able to give technical advice to each of the many customers (who often have little knowledge of which product would be best for them). Cadillac carries 10,000 items and sells to 25,000 customers—ranging in size from very small firms to General Motors.

Limited-Function Wholesalers Provide Some Functions

Limited-function wholesalers provide only *some* wholesaling functions. Figure 13–3 shows the functions typically provided—and not provided. In the following paragraphs, the main features of these wholesalers will be discussed. Some are not very numerous. In fact, they are not counted separately by the U.S. Census Bureau. Nevertheless, these wholesalers are very important for some products.

Cash-and-Carry Wholesalers Want Cash

Cash-and-carry wholesalers operate like service wholesalers—except that the customer must pay cash.

Many small retailers—especially small grocers and garages—are too small to be served profitably by a service wholesaler. To handle these markets, service wholesalers often set up cash-and-carry operations—to serve these small retailers for cash on the counter. The cash-and-carry wholesaler can operate at lower cost—because the retailers take over many wholesaling functions.

Drop-Shipper Does Not Handle the Products

Drop-shippers own the products they sell—but do not actually handle, stock, or deliver them. These wholesalers are mainly involved in selling. They get orders—from wholesalers, retailers, or industrial users—and pass these products on to producers. Then the orders are shipped directly to the customers. Because drop-shippers do not have to handle the products, their operating costs are lower.

■ FIGURE 13–3 Functions provided by limited-function merchant wholesalers

Functions	Cash-and-carry	Drop-shipper	Truck	Mail-order	Coopera-tives	Rack jobbers
For customers:						
Anticipates needs	X		X	X	X	X
"Regroups" goods (one or more of four steps)	X		X	X	X	X
Carries stocks	X		X	X	X	X
Delivers goods			X		X	X
Grants credit		X	Maybe	Maybe	Maybe	Consignment (in some cases)
Provides information and advisory services		X	Some	Some	X	X
Provides buying function		X	X	X	Some	X
Owns and transfers title to goods	X	X	X	X	X	X
For producers:						
Provides producers' selling function	X	X	X	X	X	X
Stores inventory	X		X	X	X	X
Helps finance by owning stocks	X		X	X	X	X
Reduces credit risk	X	X	X	X	X	X
Provides market information	X	X	Some	X	X	Some

Drop-shippers commonly sell products which are so bulky that additional handling would be expensive—and possibly damaging. Also, the quantities they usually sell are so large that there is little need for regrouping—for example, rail carload shipments of coal, lumber, oil, or chemical products.

Truck Wholesalers Deliver—At a Cost

Truck wholesalers specialize in delivering products which they stock in their own trucks. Handling perishable products in general demand—tobacco, candy, potato chips, and salad dressings—truck wholesalers may provide almost the same functions as full-service wholesalers. Their big advantage is that they deliver perishable products that regular wholesalers prefer not to carry. Others call on many small service stations and "back-alley" garages—providing local delivery of the many small items these customers often forget to pick up from a service wholesaler. Truck wholesalers' operating costs are relatively high—because they provide a lot of service for the little they sell.

Mail-Order Wholesalers Reach Outlying Stores

Mail-order wholesalers sell out of catalogs which may be distributed widely to smaller industrial customers or retailers. These wholesalers operate in the hardware, jewelry, sporting goods, and general merchandise lines. Their best markets are often small industrial or retailer customers who might not be called on by other middlemen. They often take orders by phone and use United Parcel Service (UPS) for fast delivery.

Mail-order wholesalers sell out of catalogs—usually to widely spread customers.

Producers' Cooperatives Do Sorting

Producers' cooperatives operate almost as full-service wholesalers—with the "profits" going to the cooperative's customer-members. The successful producers' cooperatives have emphasized the sorting process—to improve the quality of farm products offered to the market. Some have also branded their products—and then promoted the brands. Farmers' cooperatives have sometimes had success in limiting output and then increasing prices—by taking advantage of the normally inelastic demand for agricultural commodities.

Examples of producers' cooperatives are the California Fruit Growers Exchange (citrus fruits), Sunmaid Raisin Growers Association, The California Almond Exchange, and Land O'Lakes Creameries, Inc.

Rack Jobbers Sell Hard-to-Handle Assortments

Rack jobbers specialize in non-food items which are sold through grocery stores and supermarkets. They often display them on their own wire racks. Most grocers don't want to bother with non-food items (housewares, hardware items, and books and magazines) because they sell only small quantities of so many different kinds of products. So the rack-jobber specializes in these items. Rack jobbers are almost service wholesalers—except that they usually are paid cash for the amount of stock sold or delivered.

This is a relatively expensive service—with operating costs of about 18 percent of sales. The large volume of sales from these racks has encouraged some large food chains to try to handle these items on their own. But they often find that rack jobbers can provide this service as well as—or better than—they can themselves. For example, a rack jobber of paperback books studies which titles are selling in the local area—and applies that knowledge in many stores. The chain may have many stores—but in different areas where preferences vary. It may not be worth trying to study the market in each area.

AGENT MIDDLEMEN ARE STRONG ON SELLING

They Don't Own the Products

Agent middlemen are wholesalers who do not own the products they sell. Their main purpose is to help in buying and selling. They usually provide even fewer functions than the limited-function wholesalers. In some fields, however, they are extremely valuable. They operate at relatively low cost, too— sometimes 2 to 6 percent of their selling price.

In the following paragraphs, only the most important points about each type will be mentioned. See Figure 13–4 for details on the functions provided by

■ FIGURE 13–4   Functions provided by agent middlemen

Functions	Manufacturers' agents	Brokers	Commission merchants	Selling agents	Auction companies
For customers:					
Anticipates needs	Sometimes	Some			
"Regroups" goods (one or more of four steps)	Some		X		X
Carries stocks	Sometimes		X		Sometimes
Delivers goods	Sometimes		X		
Grants credit			Sometimes	X	Some
Provides information and advisory services	X	X	X	X	
Provides buying function	X	Some	X	X	X
Owns and transfers title to goods			Transfers only		Transfers only
For producer:					
Provides selling function	X	Some	X	X	X
Stores inventory	Sometimes		X		X
Helps finance by owning stocks					
Reduces credit risk				X	Some
Provides market information	X	X	X	X	

each. You can see from the number of empty spaces in Figure 13–4 that agent middlemen provide fewer functions than merchant wholesalers.

**Manufacturers'
Agents—Free-
Wheeling Sales
Reps**

A **manufacturers' agent** sells similar products for several non-competing manufacturers—for a commission on what is actually sold. Such agents work almost as members of each company's sales force—but they are really independent middlemen. Manufacturers' agents account for more than half of all agent middlemen.

Their big "plus" is that they already call on a group of customers and can add another product line at relatively low cost—and no cost to the producer until they sell something! If the sales potential in an area is low, a manufacturers' agent may be used instead of a company's own sales rep because the agent can do the job at lower cost. A small producer often has to use agents—because its sales volume is too small to support its own sales force.

Manufacturers' agents are very useful in fields where there are many small manufacturers who need to call on customers. These agents are often used in the sale of machinery and equipment, electrical products, automobile products, clothing and apparel accessories, and some food products. Each may cover one city or several states. So many may be needed to cover a large country like the United States.

The agent's main job is selling. The agent—or his customer—sends the orders to the producer. The agent, of course, gets credit for the sale. Agents seldom have any part in setting prices—or deciding on the producer's policies. Basically, they are independent, aggressive salespeople.

Agents are especially useful in introducing new products. For this service, they may earn 10 to 15 percent commission. (In contrast, their commission on large-volume established products may be quite low—perhaps only 2 percent.) The higher rates for new products often become the agent's major disadvantage for the manufacturer. The 10 to 15 percent commission rate may have seemed small when the product was new—and sales volume was low. Once the product is selling well, the rate seems high. At about this time, the producer often begins using its own sales reps—and the manufacturers' agent must look for other new products to develop. Agents are well aware of this possibility. Most try to work for many manufacturers—so they are not dependent on only one or a few lines.

**Brokers Provide
Information**

Brokers bring buyers and sellers together. Their "product" is information about what buyers need—and what supplies are available. They aid in buyer-seller negotiation. When a deal is completed, they earn a commission from whoever hired them.

Brokers are especially useful for selling seasonal products. For example, they could represent a small food canner during the canning season—then go on to other activities.

Brokers also sell used machinery, real estate, and even ships. These products are not similar, but the needed wholesaling functions *are.* In each case, buyers don't come into the market often. Someone with knowledge of available

Some kind of broker will develop whenever and wherever market information is inadequate.

products is needed to help both buyers and sellers complete the sale quickly—and at a reasonable cost.

Commission Merchants Handle and Sell Products in Distant Markets

Commission merchants handle products shipped to them by sellers, complete the sale, and send the money—minus their commission—to each seller.

Commission merchants are common in farm markets where farmers must ship to big-city central markets. They need someone to handle the products there—as well as to sell them—since the farmer can't go with each shipment. Although commission merchants do not own the products, they generally are allowed to sell them at the market price—or the best price above some stated minimum. Prices in these markets usually are published in newspapers, so the producer-seller has a check on the commission merchant. Costs are usually low because commission merchants handle large volumes of products—and buyers usually come to them.

Commission merchants are sometimes used in other fields—such as textiles. Here, many small producers wish to reach buyers in a central market—without having to maintain their own sales force.

Selling Agents— Almost Marketing Managers

Selling agents take over the whole marketing job of manufacturers—not just the selling function. A selling agent may handle the entire output of one or more producers—even competing producers—with almost complete control of pricing, selling, and advertising. In effect, the agent becomes each producer's marketing manager.

Financial trouble is one of the main reasons a producer calls in a selling agent. The selling agent may provide working capital—while handling the affairs of the business.

Selling agents have been common in highly competitive fields—such as textiles and coal. They also have been used for marketing lumber and some food, clothing, and metal products. Here, marketing is much more important than production for survival. The selling agent provides the necessary financial assistance and marketing know-how.

Auction Companies— Display the Products

Auction companies provide a place where buyers and sellers can come together and complete a transaction. There aren't many of these middlemen, but they are important in certain lines—such as livestock, fur, tobacco, and used cars. For these products, demand and supply conditions change rapidly. Also, these products must be seen to be evaluated. The auction company allows buyers and sellers to get together—and set the price while the products are being inspected.

Facilities can be simple—keeping overhead low. Often, auction companies are close to transportation so that the products can be reshipped quickly. The auction company just charges a set fee or commission for the use of its facilities and services.

International Marketing Is Not So Different

We find agent middlemen in international trade, too. Most operate much like those just described. **Export or import agents** are basically manufacturers' agents. **Export or import commission houses** and **export or import brokers** are really brokers. A **combination export manager** is a blend of manufacturers' agent and selling agent—handling the entire export function for several manufacturers of non-competing lines. Agent middlemen are more common in international trade. Financing is usually needed, but many markets have only a few well-financed merchant wholesalers. The best many manufacturers can do is get local representation through agent middlemen—and arrange financing through banks which specialize in international trade.

MANUFACTURERS' SALES BRANCHES PROVIDE WHOLESALING FUNCTIONS, TOO

Manufacturers' sales branches are separate businesses which manufacturers set up away from their factories. For example, computer manufacturers like IBM set up local branches to provide service, display equipment, and handle sales. About 11 percent of wholesale businesses are owned by manufacturers—but they handle 36 percent of total wholesale sales. One reason the sales per branch are so high is that the branches are usually placed in the best market areas. This also helps explain why their operating costs are often lower. But cost comparisons between various channels can be misleading. Sometimes the cost of selling is not charged to the branch. If all the expenses of the manufacturers' sales branches were charged to them, they probably would turn out to be more costly than they seem now.[4]

WHOLESALERS TEND TO CONCENTRATE TOGETHER

Different Wholesalers Are Found in Different Places

Some wholesalers—such as grain elevator operators—are located close to producers. But most wholesaling is done in or near large cities. Over 40 percent of all wholesale sales are made in the 15 largest metro areas.

This heavy concentration of wholesale sales in large cities is because many large wholesalers and industrial buyers are there. Some large manufacturers buy for many plants through one purchasing department located in the general offices in these cities. Also, merchant wholesalers need the transporting, warehousing, and financing facilities found in these big cities. This is true not only in the United States—but also in world markets.

COMEBACK AND FUTURE OF WHOLESALERS

In the 1800s in the United States, wholesalers dominated marketing. The many small producers and small retailers needed their services. As producers became larger, some bypassed the wholesalers. When retailers also began to grow larger—especially during the 1920s when chain stores began to spread rapidly—many predicted the end of wholesalers.

Not Fat and Lazy, but Enduring

Some people felt the end of wholesalers might be desirable because many wholesalers had grown "fat and lazy"—contributing little more than bulk-breaking. Their salespeople were often only order takers. The selling function was neglected. High-quality management was not attracted to wholesaling.

We have seen, however, that wholesaling functions *are* necessary—and wholesalers have not disappeared. Their sales volume declined in the 1930s. But, by 1954, they had returned to the same importance they had in 1929. And they have continued to hold their own since then.

Producing Profits, Not Chasing Orders

Wholesalers have lasted, in part, because of new management and new techniques. Many are still operating in the old ways. But progressive wholesalers are more concerned with their customers—and with channel systems. Some are offering more services. Others are developing voluntary chains that bind them more closely to their customers. Some ordering is now done routinely by mail or telephone—or directly by telephone to computer.

Some modern wholesalers no longer make all customers pay for all the services offered—simply because some customers use them. This traditional practice had the effect of encouraging limited-function wholesalers and direct channels. Now some wholesalers are making a basic service available at a minimum cost—then charging extra fees for any special services required. In the grocery field, for instance, the basic servicing of a store costs the store 3 to 4 percent of wholesale sales. Promotion assistance and other aids are offered at extra cost.

Modern wholesalers also are becoming more selective in picking customers—i.e., choosing a selective distribution policy—as cost analysis shows that many of their smaller customers are unprofitable. By cutting out these customers, wholesalers can give more attention to their better customers. In this way, they are helping to promote healthy retailers—who are able to compete in any market.

Today's progressive wholesalers are no longer just order takers. Some wholesalers have renamed their salespeople "store advisers" or "supervisors" to reflect their new roles. They provide management advisory services—including site selection and store design. They offer legal assistance on new leases or adjustments in old leases. They even provide store-opening services, sales training, and sales promotion and advertising help. Such salespeople—really acting as management consultants—must be more competent than the order takers of the past.

Many wholesalers are now using electronic data processing systems to control inventory. And some are modernizing their warehouses and physical handling facilities.

Some progressive whole-salers are using auto-mated warehouses to pro-vide better service.

Some wholesalers are offering central bookkeeping facilities for their retailers—realizing that their own survival is linked to their customers' survival. In this sense, some wholesalers are becoming more channel system minded—no longer trying to overload retailers' shelves. Now they are trying to clear the merchandise *off* retailers' shelves. They follow the old saying, "Nothing is really sold until it is sold at retail."[5]

Perhaps Good-Bye to Some

Not all wholesalers are progressive, however. Some of the smaller, less efficient ones may fail. While the average operating expense ratio is 12.7 percent for merchant wholesalers, some small wholesalers have expense ratios of 20 to 30 percent.

Low cost, however, is not all that's needed for success. The higher operating expenses of some wholesalers may be a result of the special services they offer to *some* customers. Truck wholesalers are usually small—and have high operating costs—yet *some* customers are willing to pay the higher cost of this service. Although full-service wholesalers may seem expensive, some will continue operating because they offer the wholesaling functions and sales contacts needed by some small manufacturers.

It is clear that—to survive—wholesalers must each carve out a specific market. Profit margins are not large in wholesaling—typically ranging from less than 1 percent to 2 percent—and they have been declining in recent years as the competitive squeeze has tightened.

The function of wholesaling will last—but weaker, less progressive wholesalers may not.

■ CONCLUSION

Wholesalers can provide wholesaling functions for those both above and below them in a channel of distribution. These functions are closely related to the basic marketing functions.

There are many types of wholesalers. Some provide all the wholesaling functions—while others specialize in only a few. Eliminating wholesalers would not eliminate the need for the functions they provide. And we cannot assume that direct channels will be more efficient.

Merchant wholesalers are the most numerous—and account for just over half of wholesale sales. They take title—and often possession—of products. Agent middlemen, on the other hand,

act more like sales representatives for sellers or buyers. They usually *do not* take title or possession.

In spite of various predictions of the end of wholesalers, they're still around. And the more progressive ones have adapted to a changing environment. No such revolutions as we saw in retailing have yet taken place in the wholesaling area—and none seem likely. But it is probable that some smaller—and less progressive—wholesalers will fail, while larger and more market-oriented wholesalers will continue to provide the necessary wholesaling functions.

■ QUESTIONS AND PROBLEMS

1. Discuss the evolution of wholesaling in relation to the evolution of retailing.

2. What risks do merchant wholesalers assume by taking title to goods? Is the size of this risk about constant for all merchant wholesalers?

3. Why would a manufacturer set up its own sales branches if established wholesalers were already available?

4. What is an agent middleman's marketing mix? Why don't manufacturers use their own salespeople instead of agent middlemen?

5. Discuss the future growth and nature of wholesaling if low-margin retailing and scrambled merchandising become more important. How will wholesalers have to adjust their mixes if retailers become larger and the retail managers more professional? Might the wholesalers be eliminated? If not, what wholesaling functions would be most important? Are there any particular lines of trade where wholesalers may have increasing difficulty?

6. Which types of wholesalers would be most appropriate for the following products? If more than one type of wholesaler could be used, provide the specifications for the situation in each case. For example, if size or financial strength of a company has a bearing, then so indicate. If several wholesalers could be used in this same channel, explain this also.
a. Fresh tomatoes.
b. Paper-stapling machines.
c. Auto mechanics' tools.
d. Men's shoes.
e. An industrial accessory machine.
f. Ballpoint pens.
g. Shoelaces.

7. Would a drop-shipper be desirable for the following products: coal, lumber, iron ore, sand and gravel, steel, furniture, or tractors? Why or why not? What channels might be used for each of these products if drop-shippers were not used?

8. Which types of wholesalers are likely to become more important in the next 25 years? Why?

■ SUGGESTED CASES

14. Miller Company

15. Cooper Lumber Company

Chapter 14 ■ Promotion—introduction

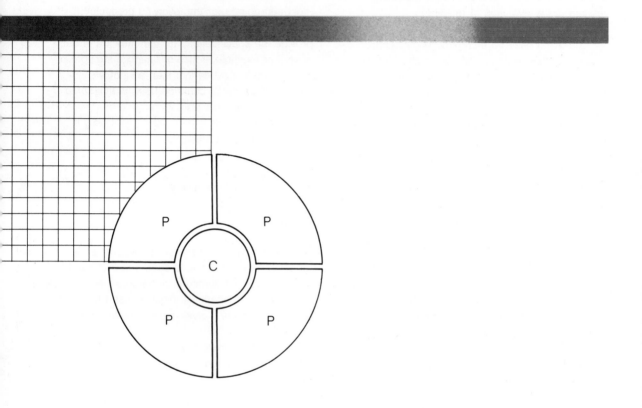

When you finish this chapter, you should:

1. Know the advantages and disadvantages of the promotion methods a marketing manager can use in strategy planning.

2. Understand the importance of promotion objectives.

3. Know how the communication process should affect promotion planning.

4. Know how the adoption processes can guide promotion planning.

5. Understand how promotion blends may have to change along the adoption curve.

6. Know how typical promotion budgets are blended.

7. Know who plans and manages promotion blends.

8. Recognize the important new terms (shown in red).

People won't buy your product if they've never heard of it.

"M*A*S*H" was one of the most popular TV series ever. In fact, the final program attracted the largest audience in TV history. To tell that big audience about their products, companies like General Motors paid almost $15,000 *per second* for advertising time—or nearly a half million dollars for each 30-second ad.

Rent-a-car firms—like Avis, Hertz, and Budget—compete for the attention—and business—of traveling executives. Lower prices alone don't appeal to many executives—since their companies usually pay their travel expenses. To influence the purchase decision, some car rental firms run sales promotions—and give luggage or other "gifts" with a car rental. The executives keep the gifts—even though their companies pay the rental bills.

Promotion is communicating information between seller and buyer—to influence attitudes and behavior. The marketing manager's promotion job is to tell target customers that the right Product is available at the right Place at the right Price.

What the marketing manager communicates is set when the target customers' needs and attitudes are known. *How* the messages are delivered depends on what promotion methods are chosen.

SEVERAL PROMOTION METHODS ARE AVAILABLE

The marketing manager can choose from several promotion methods. These include personal selling, mass selling, and sales promotion (see Figure 14–1).

Personal Selling—Is Flexible

Personal selling involves direct face-to-face communication between sellers and potential customers. It lets the salesperson see—immediately—how a customer is reacting. This allows salespeople to *adapt* the company's marketing mix to the needs of each target market. Salespeople are included in most marketing mixes. However, personal selling is very expensive. It often is necessary to combine personal selling with mass selling and sales promotion.

Mass Selling— Reaching Millions at a Price or Even Free

Mass selling is communicating with large numbers of potential customers at the same time. It isn't as flexible as personal selling. But when the target market is large and spread out—mass selling can be less expensive.

Advertising is the main form of mass selling. **Advertising** is any *paid* form of non-personal presentation of ideas, goods, or services by an identified sponsor. It uses media such as magazines, newspapers, radio and TV, signs, and

■ FIGURE 14–1   Basic promotion methods and strategy planning

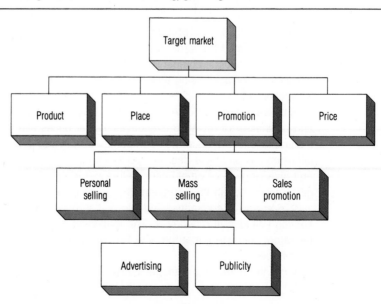

Advertising is the main form of mass selling.

direct mail. While advertising must be paid for, another form of mass selling—publicity—is "free."

Publicity is "free"

Publicity is any *unpaid* form of non-personal presentation of ideas, goods, or services. Although, of course, publicity people get paid, they try to attract attention to the firm and its offerings *without having to pay media costs.* For example, book publishers try to get authors on TV "talk shows" because this generates a lot of interest—and book sales—at no cost to the publisher.

If a firm has a really new message, publicity may be more effective than advertising. Trade magazines, for example, may carry articles featuring the newsworthy products of regular advertisers—in part because they *are* regular advertisers. Often a firm's publicity people write the basic copy—and then try

■ TABLE 14–1   Examples of sales promotion activities

Aimed at final consumers or users	Aimed at middlemen	Aimed at company's own sales force
Banners	Price deals	Contests
Streamers	Promotion allowances	Bonuses
Samples	Sales contests	Meetings
Calendars	Calendars	Portfolios
Point-of-purchase materials	Gifts	Displays
Aisle displays	Trade shows	Sales aids
Contests	Meetings	Training materials
Coupons	Catalogues	
Trade shows	Merchandising aids	
Trading stamps		

to convince magazine editors to print it. Each year, the auto manufacturers send photos and news releases to magazine publishers. They even draft stories about new car models and features. Magazines print many pages based on these materials. This publicity may even raise more interest than the company's paid advertising. A potential customer might not pay any attention to an ad—but might carefully read a trade magazine story with the same information.[1]

Sales Promotion Tries to Spark Immediate Interest

Sales promotion refers to those promotion activities—other than advertising, publicity, and personal selling—which stimulate interest, trial, or purchase by final customers or others in the channel. Sales promotion can be aimed at consumers, at middlemen, or even at a firm's own sales force. Many examples are listed in Table 14–1.

Sales promotion for final consumers or users

Sales promotion aimed at final consumers or users usually is trying to increase demand—or speed up the time of purchase. This might involve devel-

Sales promotions can attract consumer attention—and often spark sales.

oping displays for retailers' stores—including banners and streamers, sample packages, calendars, and various point-of-purchase materials. The sales promotion people also might develop the aisle displays for supermarkets. They might be responsible for "jackpot" and "sweepstakes" contests—as well as coupons designed to get customers to try a product. All of these efforts are aimed at specific promotion objectives.

Sales promotion directed at industrial goods customers might use the same kinds of ideas. In addition, the sales promotion people might set up and staff trade show exhibits. Here, attractive models are often used to try to encourage economically oriented buyers to look over a firm's product—especially when it is displayed near other similar products in a circus-like atmosphere.

Sales promotion for middlemen

Sales promotion aimed at middlemen—sometimes called *trade promotion*— stresses price-related matters—because the objective assigned to sales promotion may be to encourage stocking new items, or buying in larger quantity, or buying early. The tools used here are price and/or merchandise allowances, promotion allowances, and perhaps sales contests—to encourage retailers or wholesalers to sell specific items—or the company's whole line. Offering to send contest winners to Hawaii, for example, may increase sales greatly.

Sales promotion for own sales force

Sales promotion aimed at the company's own sales force might try to encourage getting new customers, selling a new product, or generally stimulating sales of the company's whole line. Depending on the objectives, the tools might be contests, bonuses on sales or number of new accounts, and holding sales meetings at fancy resorts to raise everyone's spirits.

Ongoing sales promotion work might also be aimed at the sales force—to help sales management. Sales promotion people might be responsible for preparing sales portfolios, displays, and other sales aids. They might develop the sales training material which the sales force uses in working with customers—and other channel members. They might develop special racks for product displays—which the sales rep sells or gives to retailers. In other words, rather than expecting each individual salesperson—or the sales manager—to develop these sales aids, sales promotion managers might be given this job.

This Neglected Method Is Bigger Than Advertising

Sales promotion—like publicity—is a weak spot in marketing. Sales promotion includes a wide variety of activities—each of which may be custom-designed and used only once. Few companies develop their own experts in sales promotion. Many companies—even large ones—don't have a separate budget for sales promotion. Few even know what it costs in total.

This neglect of sales promotion is a mistake, however. In total, sales promotion costs *much more than advertising*. This means it deserves more attention—and perhaps separate status—within the marketing organization.

The spending on sales promotion is large and growing—sometimes at the expense of other promotion methods. There are several reasons for this. Sales

Coupons have become a big part of promotion—because they encourage action.

promotion has proved successful in an increasingly competitive markets. Sales promotion can usually be implemented quickly—and get results sooner than advertising. Sales promotion activities can help the product manager win support from an already overworked sales force. Salespeople welcome sales promotion—including promotion in the channels—because it makes their job easier.

Creative sales promotion can be very effective, but making it work is a learned skill—not a sideline for amateurs. It can't be delegated to a sales trainee. In fact, sales promotion specialists have developed—both inside firms and as outside consultants. Some are very creative—and might be willing to take over the whole promotion job. But it's the marketing manager's job to set promotion objectives and policies which fit in with the rest of a marketing strategy.

We've been talking about sales promotion—and how it can be used by a marketing manager. Now let's look at the whole promotion blend—personal selling, mass selling, and sales promotion combined—to see how promotion fits into the rest of the marketing mix.

WHICH METHODS TO USE DEPENDS ON PROMOTION OBJECTIVES

Overall Objective Is to Affect Behavior

The different promotion methods can all be seen as different forms of communication. But good marketers don't want to just "communicate." They want to communicate information which will lead target customers to choose *their* product. They know that if they have a better offering, informed customers are more likely to buy. Therefore, they are interested in (1) reinforcing present attitudes that might lead to favorable behavior or (2) actually changing the attitudes and behavior of the firm's target market.

Informing, Persuading, and Reminding Are Basic Promotion Objectives

For a firm's promotion to work, it's necessary to clearly define the firm's promotion objectives. The right promotion blend depends on what the firm wants to accomplish. It's helpful to think of three basic *promotion objectives*: to *inform, persuade,* and *remind* target customers about the company and its marketing mix. All aim to affect behavior—by providing more information.

A more specific set of promotion objectives—that states *exactly who* you want to inform, persuade, or remind, and *why*—is even more useful. But this is unique to each company's strategy—and too detailed to discuss here. Instead, we will limit ourselves to the three basic promotion objectives—and how you might reach them.

Informing Is Educating

We know that potential customers must know something about a product if they are to buy at all. Therefore, *informing* may be the most important objective. For example, a cable TV company found that whenever it offered service to a new area, most families subscribed. So the main promotion job was to inform prospects that cable was available.

Persuading Usually Becomes Necessary

When competitors are offering similar products, the firm must not only inform the customers that its product is available—but also persuade them to buy it. A *persuading* objective means the firm will try to develop or reinforce a favorable set of attitudes—hoping to affect buying behavior.

Reminding May Be Enough, Sometimes

If target customers already have positive attitudes about the firm's product, then a *reminding* objective might be used. This objective can be extremely

Trade show promotions inform and persuade intermediate buyers.

important. Even though customers have been attracted and sold once, they are still targets for competitors' promotion. Reminding them of their past satisfaction may keep them from shifting to a competitor. Coca-Cola realizes that people already know about Coke—so much of its advertising is intended to remind.

PROMOTION REQUIRES EFFECTIVE COMMUNICATION

Promotion obviously must get the attention of the target audience—and communicate effectively—or it's wasted. What is obvious, however, isn't always easy to do. Much promotion doesn't really communicate. For example, you might listen to the radio for several hours—but never really be aware of any of the ads. There are many ways in which promotional communication can break down.

The Same Message May Be Interpreted Differently

Different people may see the same message in different ways. They may interpret the same words differently. Such differences are common in international marketing—where translation is a problem. General Motors, for example, had trouble in Puerto Rico with its Nova automobile. Then it discovered that—while Nova means "star" in Spanish—when it is spoken it sounds like "no va," which means "it doesn't go." The company quickly changed the car's name to "Caribe"—and it sold well.[2]

Such problems in the same language may not be so obvious—but can cause trouble for marketers. For example, a new children's cough syrup was advertised as "extra strength." The advertising people thought that would assure parents that the product worked well. But worried mothers avoided the product because they were afraid it might be too strong for their children. Marketing research can help avoid such problems.

■ FIGURE 14–2   The communication process

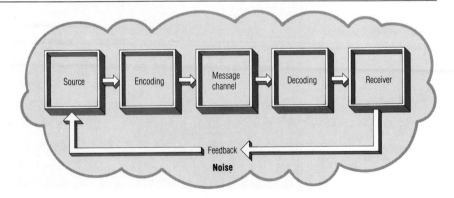

Personal selling allows immediate feedback in the communication process.

Feedback Leads to Better Communication

The **communication process** shows how a source tries to reach a receiver with a message. Figure 14–2 shows this process. Here we see that a **source**—the sender of a message—is trying to deliver a message to a **receiver**—a potential customer. A source can deliver a message by many message channels. The personal salesperson does it with voice and actions. Advertising must do it with mass media—magazines, newspapers, radio, and TV.

A major advantage of personal selling is that the source—the seller—can get immediate feedback from the receiver. It's easier to judge how the message is being received—and change it if necessary. Mass sellers must depend on marketing research or total sales figures for feedback—which can take too long.

The **noise**—shown in Figure 14–2—is any factor which reduces the effectiveness of the communication process. Perhaps the source can't agree on what should be said—or how—and settles for a very general message. Or the receiver—perhaps a parent—may be distracted by children when the message is on the radio. Or other advertisers may be saying the same things—and the receiver becomes confused and ignores *all* the messages.[3]

Encoding and Decoding Depend on Common Frame of Reference

The big difficulty in the communication process occurs during encoding and decoding. **Encoding** is the source deciding what it wants to say and translating it in a way that will have the same meaning to the receiver. **Decoding** is the receiver translating the message. This process can be very tricky. The meanings of various words and symbols may differ—depending on the attitudes and experiences of the two groups. A common frame of reference is needed to communicate effectively. See Figure 14–3.

■ FIGURE 14–3   Encoding and decoding depend on common frame of reference

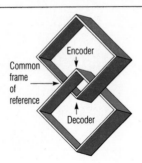

Average car drivers, for example, might think of the Ford Mustang as a sports car. If they are the target market, they want to hear about ease of handling, acceleration, and racing symbols—such as wide tires. Auto engineers and sports car fanatics, however, don't consider the Mustang a real sports car. So, if they are writing—or approving—copy, they might encode the message in regular "small-car" terms.

Message Channel Is Important, Too

The communication process is complicated even more because the receiver is aware that the message is not only coming from a source but also coming through some **message channel**—the carrier of the message. The receiver may give more value to a firm's product if the message comes in a well-respected newspaper or magazine—rather than over the radio.

ADOPTION PROCESSES CAN GUIDE PROMOTION PLANNING

The adoption process discussed in Chapter 6 is related to effective communication—and promotion planning. You learned that there are six steps in the adoption process: awareness, interest, evaluation, trial, decision, and confirmation. Further, in Chapter 6 we saw consumer buying as a problem-solving process in which buyers go through these several steps on the way to adopting (or rejecting) an idea or product. Now we will see that the three basic promotion objectives can be related to these various steps—to show what is needed to achieve the objectives. See Figure 14–4.

Informing and *persuading* may be needed to affect the potential customer's knowledge and attitudes about a product—and then bring about its adoption. Later, promotion can simply remind the customer about that favorable experience—aiming to confirm the adoption decision.

The AIDA Model Is a Practical Approach

The basic adoption process fits very neatly with another action-oriented model—called AIDA—which we will use in this and the next two chapters to guide some of our discussion.

■ FIGURE 14–4   Relation of promotion objectives, adoption process, and AIDA model

Promotion objectives	Adoption process (Chapter 6)	AIDA model
Informing	⎧ ⎧ Awareness	Attention
	⎨ Interest	Interest
	⎨ ⎩ Evaluation ⎫	
Persuading	Trial ⎬	Desire
	⎩ Decision ⎫	
Reminding	Confirmation ⎬	Action

The **AIDA model** consists of four promotion jobs—(1) to get *Attention,* (2) to hold *Interest,* (3) to arouse *Desire,* and (4) to obtain *Action.* (As a memory aid, note that the first letters of the four key words spell AIDA—the well-known opera.)

The relation of the adoption process to the AIDA jobs can be seen in Figure 14–4. *Getting attention* is necessary if the potential customer is to become aware of the company's offering. *Holding interest* gives the communication a chance to really build the prospect's interest in the product. *Arousing desire* affects the evaluation process—perhaps building preference. And *obtaining action* includes obtaining trial—which may lead to a purchase decision. Continuing promotion is needed to confirm the decision—and encourage continuing action.

GOOD COMMUNICATION VARIES PROMOTION BLENDS ALONG ADOPTION CURVE

The AIDA and adoption processes discussed above look at individuals. This emphasis on individuals helps us understand how people behave. But it's also useful to look at markets as a whole. Different customers within a market may behave differently—with some taking the lead in trying new products and, in turn, influencing others.

Getting attention does not always lead to interest, desire, or action.

Adoption Curve Focuses on Market Segments, Not Individuals

Research on how markets accept new ideas has led to the adoption curve idea. The **adoption curve** shows when different groups within a market accept ideas. It shows the need to change the promotion effort as time passes. It also shows that some groups act as leaders in accepting new ideas.

Promotion Must Vary for Different Adopter Groups

The adoption curve for a typical successful product is shown in Figure 14–5. Some of the important characteristics of each of these customer groups are discussed below. Which one are you?

Innovators don't mind taking some risk

The **innovators** are the first to adopt. They are eager to try a new idea— and willing to take risks. Innovators tend to be young and well educated. They are likely to be mobile and sophisticated—with many contacts outside their local social group and community. Business firms in the innovator group usually are large and rather specialized.

An important characteristic of innovators is that they rely on impersonal and scientific information sources—or other innovators—instead of personal salespeople. They often read articles in technical publications—or informative advertisements in special interest magazines or newspapers.

Early adopters are often opinion leaders

Early adopters are well respected by their peers—and often are opinion leaders. They are younger, more mobile, and more creative than later adopters. But they have fewer contacts than innovators outside their own social group or community. Business firms in this category also tend to be specialized.

Of all the groups, this group tends to have the greatest contact with sales-

---

■ FIGURE 14–5   The adoption curve

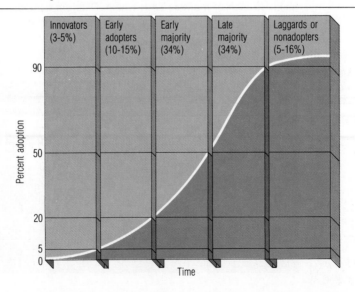

people. Mass media are important information sources, too. Marketers should be very concerned with attracting and selling the early adopter group. Their acceptance is really important in reaching the next group—because the early majority look to the early adopters.

Early majority group is deliberate

The **early majority** avoid risk and wait to consider a new idea until many early adopters have tried it—and liked it.

Average-sized business firms with less specialization often fit in this category. If successful companies in their industry adopt the new idea, they will, too.

The early majority have a great deal of contact with mass media, salespeople, *and* early adopter opinion leaders. They usually are not opinion leaders.

Late majority may react to social pressure

The **late majority** are cautious about new ideas. Often they are older than the early majority group—and more set in their ways. So they are less likely to follow opinion leaders and early adopters. In fact, some social pressure from their own peer group may be needed before they adopt a new product.

Business firms in this group tend to be conservative, smaller-sized firms with little specialization.

The late majority make little use of marketing sources of information—mass media and salespeople. They are influenced more by other late adopters—rather than by outside sources of information.

Laggards or non-adopters hang on to tradition

The **laggards** or **non-adopters** prefer to do things the way they have been done in the past—and are suspicious of new ideas. They tend to be older and less well educated. They may also be low in social status and income.

The smallest businesses with the least specialization are often in this category. They cling to the status quo—and think it's the safe way.

The main source of information for laggards is other laggards. This certainly is bad news for marketers who want to reach a whole market quickly—or who want to use only one promotion method. In fact, it may not pay to bother with this group.[4]

Opinion Leaders Help Spread the Word

Adoption curve research supports our earlier discussion (in Chapter 6) of the importance of *opinion leaders.* It shows the importance of early adopters. They influence the early majority—and help spread the word to many others.

Marketers know the importance of these personal conversations and recommendations by opinion leaders. If early groups reject the product, it may never get off the ground.[5] But if they accept a product, then what the opinion leaders in each social group say about it can be very important. The "web-of-word-of-mouth" may do the real selling job—long before the customer ever walks into the retail store. You can see the importance of trying to reach the opinion leaders in various social groups. But because they are hard to identify—recall from Chapter 6 that different kinds of people may be opinion leaders for different products—mass media can play an important role in getting the message to them.[6]

MAY NEED A DIFFERENT BLEND
FOR EACH MARKET SEGMENT

Each market segment needs a separate marketing mix—and a different promotion blend. Some mass selling specialists have missed this point. They think in "mass marketing"—rather than "target marketing"—terms. Aiming at large markets may be all right sometimes, but unfortunately, promotion aimed at everyone can end up hitting no one. In the Promotion area, we should be careful about using a "shotgun" approach when what is really needed is a "rifle" approach—with more careful aiming.[7]

A promotion blend may include advertising, contests, and coupons.

SUCCESSFUL PROMOTION MAY BE
AN ECONOMICAL BLEND

Once promotion objectives for a product-market have been set, a marketing manager may decide to use a blend of promotion methods. Certain jobs can be done more cheaply one way than another. This can be seen most clearly in the industrial goods market. While personal selling dominates most industrial goods promotion budgets, mass selling is necessary, too. Personal salespeople nearly always have to complete the sale. But it is usually too expensive for them to do the whole promotion job. The cost of an industrial sales call is over $150. This relatively high cost is because salespeople have only limited time

■ FIGURE 14–6   McGraw-Hill magazine ad

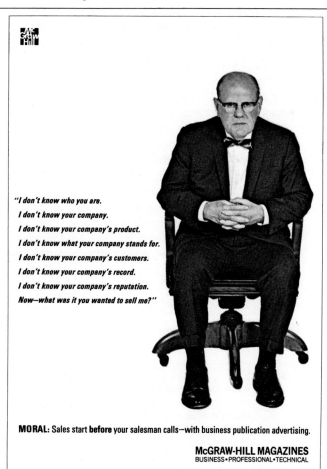

"*I don't know who you are.*
I don't know your company.
I don't know your company's product.
I don't know what your company stands for.
I don't know your company's customers.
I don't know your company's record.
I don't know your company's reputation.
Now—what was it you wanted to sell me?"

MORAL: Sales start **before** your salesman calls—with business publication advertising.

McGRAW-HILL MAGAZINES
BUSINESS•PROFESSIONAL•TECHNICAL

Courtesy: McGraw-Hill Publications Company

and much of it is spent on non-selling activities—traveling, paper work, sales meetings, and service calls. Less than half of their time is available for actual selling.

The job of reaching all the buying influences is made more costly and difficult by the constant turnover of buyers and influencers. An industrial salesperson may be responsible for several hundred customers and prospects—with many buying influences per company. They don't have enough time to get the company's whole message across to every possible contact. The problem is shown in the classic McGraw-Hill advertisement shown in Figure 14–6. As the ad suggests, too much is invested in a salesperson to use his time and skill to answer questions that could be handled better by mass selling. Mass selling "sales calls" can be made at a small fraction of the cost of a personal call. It may cost an industrial advertiser less than a dollar per reader to advertise in a trade magazine. After mass selling does the ground work, a salesperson can answer specific questions—and close the sale.

HOW TYPICAL PROMOTION BUDGETS ARE BLENDED

There Is No One Right Blend

There is no one *right* promotion blend. Each must be developed as part of a marketing mix. We can, however, make some general statements about how manufacturers have divided their promotion budgets. They do vary a lot. Retailers' blends vary widely also. Wholesalers—on the other hand—use personal selling almost exclusively.

Figure 14–7 shows how manufacturers divide their promotion budgets. It shows the relationship of advertising costs to personal selling which can be expected in various situations.

Figure 14–7 shows that manufacturers of well-branded consumer goods—(such as cars, breakfast cereals, and non-prescription drugs)—and especially those trying to build brand familiarity—tend to emphasize advertising. This emphasis might be even stronger if the firm has already built its channel of distribution.

■ FIGURE 14–7   Typical promotion blends of manufacturers (ratio of advertising to personal selling)

10:1	5:1	1:1	1:5	1:10
←——— Advertising emphasis ———→		←——— Personal selling emphasis ———→		
Firms with well-branded consumer goods (with established channels)		Blend of consumer and industrial goods	Smaller companies and any firms offering relatively undifferentiated consumer goods or industrial goods	

This magazine is for marketers who use direct mail promotion to get their message to their target market.

At the other extreme, small companies use more personal selling—especially if competing products are similar. Middlemen and industrial buyers want several sources of supply. So personal selling is quite important to assure that the seller continues to satisfy—and remain on the supplier list.

Personal Selling Usually Is Dominant

The heavier emphasis on personal selling which you might have assumed from Figure 14–7 is correct. The many ads you see in magazines and newspapers—and on television—are impressive and costly. But most retail sales are completed by sales clerks. And much personal selling goes on in the channels. In total, personal selling is several times more expensive than advertising.

SOMEONE MUST PLAN AND MANAGE THE PROMOTION BLEND

Good Blending Calls for a Marketing Manager

Choosing a promotion blend is a strategic decision which should fit with the rest of a marketing strategy. This is the job of the marketing manager. Then, more detailed plans must be developed and implemented by specialists—such as the sales and advertising managers.

Sales managers are concerned with managing personal selling. Often the sales manager is responsible for building good distribution channels and implementing Place policies.

Promotion planning must consider the whole channel. This ad encourages McDonald's franchisees or managers to participate in a promotion.

Kids mean big business for your store. That's why your McDonald's Playland™ gives you such a strong competitive edge.

Now, *make the most* of this unique advantage with the new McDonald's Playland™ B.O.G. card.

These new B.O.G. cards will help bring kids, fun and sales together all year long in your store.

Use your McDonald's Playland™ B.O.G. cards to do these important things:

- Give greater impact to your McDonald's Playland™ Grand Openings
- Build awareness of your existing McDonald's Playland™
- Take advantage of the President's proclamation that August 8, 1982 is National Children's Day

- Help pay off McDonald's promise of fun
- Enhance your LSM kid promotions and McDonald's Playland™ special events
- Bring in add-on sales

ORDER YOUR McDONALD'S PLAYLAND B.O.G. CARDS TODAY!

Advertising managers manage their company's mass selling effort—in television, newspapers, magazines, and other media. Their job is choosing the right media for each purpose—and developing the ads. They may use advertising departments within their own firms—especially if they're in retailing. Or they may use outside advertising agencies. They—or their agencies—may handle publicity too.

Sales promotion managers manage their company's sales promotion effort. Nearly everything the sales promotion department does *could* be done by the sales or advertising departments. But sales promotion activities are so varied that specialists tend to develop. In some companies, the sales promotion managers work for the sales managers. In others, they are moving toward independent status—and report directly to the marketing manager.[8]

Marketing Manager Puts the Parts Together

Because of differences in outlook and experience—the advertising, sales, and sales promotion managers may have a hard time working together. It is the marketing manager's job to develop an effective promotion blend—fitting the various departments and personalities into it.[9]

■ CONCLUSION

Promotion is an important part of any marketing mix. Most consumers and intermediate customers can choose from among many products. To be successful, a manufacturer must do more than offer a good product at a reasonable price. It must also inform potential customers about the product—and where they can buy it. Producers must also tell wholesalers and retailers in the channel about their product—and their marketing mix. These middlemen, in turn, must use promotion to reach *their* customers.

A firm's promotion blend should fit into the strategy which is being developed to satisfy some target market. *What* should be communicated to them—and *how*—should be stated as part of the strategy planning.

The overall promotion objective is to affect buying behavior—but basic promotion objectives include informing, persuading, and reminding.

Various promotion methods can be used to reach these objectives. How the promotion methods are combined can be guided by behavioral science findings. In particular, we know something about the communications process—and how individuals and groups adopt new products.

An action-oriented framework—called AIDA—can help guide planning of promotion blends. But the marketing manager has the final responsibility for blending the promotion methods into one promotion effort—for each marketing mix.

In this chapter, we have studied some basic ideas. In the next two chapters, we will treat personal and mass selling in more detail. We won't discuss sales promotion again—because it is difficult to generalize about all the possibilities. Further, the fact that most sales promotion activities are short-run efforts—which must be specially tailored—means that sales promotion will probably continue to be a "stepchild"—even though sales promotion costs more than advertising. Marketers must find a better way of handling this important decision area.

■ QUESTIONS AND PROBLEMS

1. Briefly explain the nature of the three basic promotion methods which are available to a marketing manager. Explain why sales promotion is currently a "weak spot" in marketing and suggest what might be done.

2. Relate the three basic promotion objectives to the four tasks (AIDA) of the promotion job, using a specific example.

3. Discuss the communication process in relation to a manufacturer's promotion of an accessory good, say, a portable air hammer used for breaking up concrete pavement.

4. Explain how an understanding of the way individuals adopt new ideas or products (the adoption process) would be helpful in developing a promotion blend. In particular, explain how it might be desirable to change a promotion blend during the course of the adoption process. To make this more concrete, discuss it in relation to the acceptance of a new men's sportcoat style.

5. Explain how opinion leaders should affect a firm's promotion planning.

6. Discuss how our understanding of the adoption curve should be applied to planning the promotion blend(s) for a new, small (personal) electric car.

7. Promotion has been the target of considerable criticism. What specific types of promotion are probably the object of this criticism?

8. Might promotion be successful in expanding the general demand for: (*a*) oranges, (*b*) automobiles, (*c*) tennis rackets, (*d*) cashmere sweaters, (*e*) iron ore, (*f*) steel, (*g*) cement? Explain why or why not in each case.

9. Indicate the promotion blend which might be most appropriate for manufacturers of the following established products (assume average- to large-sized firms in each case) and support your answer:
a. Candy bars.
b. Men's T-shirts
c. Castings for automobile engines.
d. Car batteries.
e. Industrial fire insurance.
f. Inexpensive plastic raincoats.
g. A camera which has achieved a specialty-goods status.

10. Discuss the potential conflict among the various promotion managers. How might this be reduced?

■ SUGGESTED CASES

17. Dewitt National Bank

18. Gray Sports Company

Chapter 15 ■ Personal selling

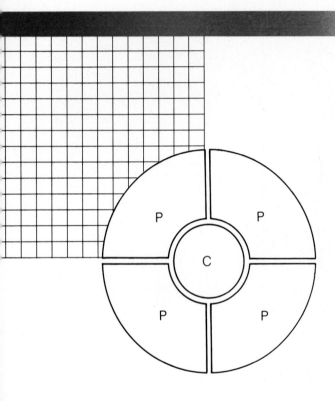

When you finish this chapter, you should:

1. Understand the importance and nature of personal selling.

2. Know the three basic sales tasks and what the various kinds of salespeople can be expected to do.

3. Know what a sales manager must do to carry out the job assigned to personal selling.

4. Understand when and where the three types of sales presentations should be used.

5. Recognize the important new terms (shown in red).

Today, many salespeople are problem-solving professionals.

Promotion is communicating with potential customers. Personal selling is often the best way to do it. While face-to-face with prospects, salespeople can get more attention than an ad or a display. Also, they can adjust the presentation as they move along—and adapt to a prospect's feedback. If—and when—the prospect says that "this might be a good idea," the salesperson is there to close the sale—and take the order. An example shows the importance of personal selling.

A manufacturer of allergy tablets wanted to switch to tamper-proof packages for its products. Some of the firm's managers had been impressed by Carol Wilson—a sales rep for a supplier of specialty packaging. So they helped her meet with different departments to learn about their needs and concerns. Then Carol made a presentation—describing the types of packaging that could be used—as well as the probable cost. The company liked her ideas and wanted the packages in a hurry—faster than Wilson's company could usually fill an order. To win the sale, she had to coordinate schedules with her company's

■ FIGURE 15–1   Strategy planning for personal selling

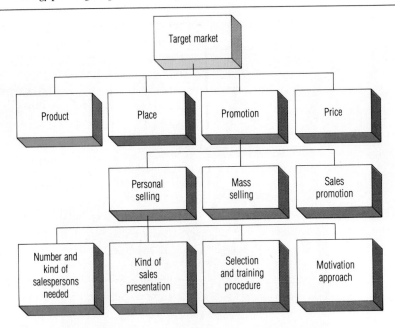

design, production, and distribution departments—to get the packages to the customer on time. Then she even held a training session for the customer's sales force—to explain the details of the new package. Now working with this customer is easy. Carol Wilson simply visits occasionally—to write the routine order—and be certain that the customer is still happy. Successful selling isn't just "pushing the goods out the door." Often it means finding creative ways to solve a customer's problems.

Marketing managers must decide how much—and what kind of—personal selling effort is needed in each marketing mix. As part of their strategy planning, they must decide: (1) how many salespeople will be needed, (2) what kind of salespeople are needed, (3) what kind of sales presentation should be used, (4) how salespeople should be selected and trained, and (5) how they should be motivated. These strategic decisions can be seen more clearly in Figure 15–1.

The sales manager provides inputs to these strategic decisions. And once they are made, it's the sales manager's job to carry out the personal selling part of a marketing strategy.

In this chapter, we'll talk about the importance and nature of personal selling—so you will understand the strategic decisions that face sales managers and marketing managers.

THE IMPORTANCE AND ROLE OF PERSONAL SELLING

We have already seen that personal selling is important in some promotion blends—and essential in others. Some of its supporters feel that personal selling is the dynamic element which keeps our economy going. You could better appreciate the importance of personal selling if you regularly had to meet payrolls, and somehow—almost like magic—your salespeople kept coming in with orders just in time to keep your business from closing.

Our economy does need and use many salespeople. Census Bureau statistics show that about 1 person out of every 10 in the labor force is in sales work. That's about 15 times more people than in advertising! Any activity that employs so many people—and is so important to the economy—deserves study.

Helping to Buy Is Good Selling

Today, good salespeople don't just try to *sell* the customer. Rather, they try to *help the customer buy*—by presenting both the advantages and disadvantages of their products—and showing how they will satisfy needs and solve problems. Such helpfulness results in satisfied customers—and long-term relationships. "Old-time" salesmen with nothing to offer but a funny story, a big expense account, and a nice smile are being replaced by real professionals—who solve problems and help bring in sales.

Salespeople Represent the Whole Company—And Customers, Too

The salesperson is coming to be seen as a representative of the whole company—responsible for explaining its total effort to target customers—rather than just "getting rid of products." The sales force is often the only link between the firm and its customers—especially if customers are far away. A salesperson may provide information about products, explain company policies, and even negotiate prices.

In some cases, the salesperson represents his *customers* back inside his own firm, too. For example, the sales rep is the likely one to explain to the production manager why a customer is unhappy with product performance or

A salesperson represents the company to the customer—and the customer to the company.

quality—or to show the physical distribution manager why slow shipments are causing problems.

As evidence of these changing roles, some companies now give their salespeople such titles as field manager, market specialist, account representative, or sales engineer.

Sales Force Provides Marketing Research Information as Well

The sales force can aid in the marketing research process. The sales rep may be the first to hear about a new competitor—or a competitor's new product or strategy. It's important that this information get back to the firm—as the following example shows.

A salesman for Scripto (ballpoint pens) wondered why sales were dropping off in his California stores—and asked why. He learned that a new Japanese product—a felt-tip writer—was taking sales from ballpoint pens. But the salesman didn't report this to management—until months later. By then, it was too late. The new felt-tip pens were sweeping the country—and Scripto had none in its product line.

Salespeople Can Be Strategy Planners, Too

Some salespeople are expected to be marketing managers in their own geographic territories. Or some may become "marketing managers" by default—because top management hasn't provided clear guidelines. Then the salespeople may have to develop their own marketing mixes—or even their own strategies. A sales rep may be given a geographic territory—with no specific description of the target customers. He may have to start from scratch with strategy planning—the only limits being the general product line to sell and probably the price structure. The salesperson may have choices about (1) what target customers to aim at, (2) which products in the line to push most aggressively, (3) which middlemen to work with, (4) how to use any promotion money available, and (5) how to adjust prices.

A salesperson who can put together profitable strategies—and carry them out—can rise very rapidly. The opportunity is there—for those who are prepared and willing to work.

Even the starting job may offer great opportunities. Some beginning salespeople—especially those working for manufacturers or wholesalers—are responsible for larger sales volumes than are achieved by many retail stores. This is a responsibility which must be taken seriously—and should be prepared for.

Further, the sales job is often used as an entry-level position—to find out what a new employee can do. Success in this job can lead to rapid promotion to higher-level sales and marketing jobs—and more money and job security.

WHAT TYPES OF PERSONAL SELLING TASKS ARE NEEDED?

If a firm has too few salespeople—or the wrong kind—some important personal selling tasks may not be done. But having too many salespeople—or the wrong kind—wastes money. A sales manager has to find a good balance—to have the right number of the right kind of salespeople.

One of the difficulties of setting the right number and kind of salespeople is that every sales job is different. While the engineer or accountant can look forward to fairly specific duties, the salesperson's job is constantly changing. We can, however, describe three basic types of sales tasks.

Personal Selling Is Divided into Three Tasks

The three **basic sales tasks** are *order getting, order taking,* and *supporting.* For convenience, we will describe salespeople by these terms—referring to their main task—although one person might do all three tasks in some situations.

As the names imply, order getters and order takers are interested in obtaining orders for their company. In contrast, supporting salespeople are not directly interested in orders. Their job is to help the order-oriented salespeople. With this variety, you can see that there is a place in personal selling for nearly everyone.[1]

ORDER GETTERS DEVELOP NEW BUSINESS

Order getters are concerned with getting new business. **Order getting** means aggressively seeking out possible buyers with a well-organized sales presentation designed to sell a product.

Order-getting salespeople work for manufacturers, wholesalers, and retailers. They normally are well paid. Many earn more than $60,000 per year.

Manufacturers' Order Getters—Find New Opportunities

Manufacturers of all kinds of products—but especially industrial goods—have a great need for order getters. They are needed to locate new prospects, open new accounts, see new opportunities, and help set up and build channel relationships.

Firms often give special technical training to marketing graduates to make them competent order getters.

Industrial order getters need the "know-how" to help solve their customers' problems. Often they need to understand customers' general business concerns—as well as technical details about the product and how it can be used. To be sure of technically competent order getters, firms often give special technical training to business-trained college graduates. Such salespeople can be a real help to their customers. In fact, they may be more technically able—in their narrow specialty—than anyone in the customer's firm. They can provide a unique service.

Wholesalers' Order Getters—Hand It to the Customer, Almost

Progressive wholesalers are becoming counselors and store advisors—rather than just order takers. Such order getters are almost "partners" of retailers in the job of moving products from the wholesale warehouse through the retail store to consumers. These order getters almost become a part of the retailer's staff—helping to plan stock levels, write orders, conduct demonstrations—as well as planning advertising and special promotions.

Retail Order Getters—Visionaries at the Storm Window

Order getters are needed for unsought goods—and are desirable for some shopping goods.

Unsought goods need order getters

Convincing customers of the value of products they haven't seriously considered takes a high degree of personal selling ability. Order getters must help customers see how a new product can satisfy needs now being filled by something else. For example, early order getters for aluminum storm windows faced a tough job: convincing skeptical customers that this new kind of storm window not only was durable—but would need less maintenance in the long run. Without order getters, many of the products we now accept as part of our standard of living—such as refrigerators and window air-conditioners—might have died in the market introduction stage. It is the order getter who helps bring products out of the introduction stage—into the market growth stage. Without sales and profits in the early stages, the product may fail—and never be offered again.

They help sell shopping goods

Order getters are helpful for selling *heterogeneous* shopping goods. Consumers shop for many of these items on the basis of price *and* quality. They welcome useful information. Automobiles, furniture and furnishings, cameras, and fashion items can be sold effectively by an order getter. Helpful advice—based on knowledge of the product and its alternatives—may help consumers—and bring profits to the salesperson and retailer.

ORDER TAKERS—KEEP THE BUSINESS COMING

Order takers sell the regular or typical customers. Order takers complete most sales transactions. After a customer becomes interested in the products of a specific firm—from an order getter or a supporting salesperson—or through advertising or sales promotion—an order taker usually is needed to answer any final questions and complete the sale. **Order taking** is the routine completion of sales made regularly to the target customers.

Sometimes sales managers or customers will use the term "order taker" as a "put down" when referring to unaggressive salespeople. While a particular salesperson may perform so poorly that criticism is called for, it is a mistake to downgrade the function of order taking. Order taking is extremely important—whether handled by human hands or machines. Many sales are lost just because no one ever *asks* for the order—and closes the sale.

Manufacturers' Order Takers—Train and Explain	After order getters open up industrial, wholesale, or retail accounts, regular follow-up is necessary. Someone has to explain details, make adjustments, handle complaints, and keep customers informed about new developments. Customers' employees may need training to use the product. In sales to middlemen, it may be necessary to train wholesalers' or retailers' salespeople. All these activities are part of the order taker's job.

Usually these salespeople have a regular route with many calls. To handle these calls well, they must have energy, persistence, enthusiasm, and a friendly personality that wears well over time. They sometimes have to "take the heat" when something goes wrong with some other element of the marketing mix.

Sometimes jobs that are basically order taking are used to train potential order getters and managers—since they offer order-getting possibilities.

George Turpin worked for a manufacturer of supplies for automotive body shops—basically an order-taking job. He discovered, however, that one of the biggest body shops in his territory was splitting its orders between a number of suppliers. George spent more time at this shop—studying the business. He found ways to speed up their repairs by suggesting new products they didn't know about. This increased the shop's profits. The owners were impressed—and it helped George convince them that they could save even more if they let him coordinate *all* of their purchases. They agreed to give it a try. Since the body shop scheduled all repairs a week ahead, George could study the work list in advance, figure out what supplies and paints were needed, and write up the order. The shop found that this approach meant fewer delays due to supplies that hadn't been ordered or didn't arrive. And it saved them the time of working up orders. George used the same approach with other customers—and increased sales in his territory by 50 percent.

Wholesalers' Order Takers—Not Getting Orders but Keeping Them	While manufacturers' order takers handle relatively few items—and sometimes only a single item—wholesalers' order takers may sell 125,000 items or more. Most of these order takers just sell out of their catalogs. They have so many items that they can't possibly give aggressive sales effort to many—except perhaps newer or more profitable items. The strength of this type of order taker is a wide assortment—rather than detailed knowledge of individual products.

The wholesale order taker's main job is to maintain close contact with customers—perhaps once a week—and fill any needs that develop. Some retailers let the sales rep take inventory—and then write the order. Obviously, this position of trust can't be abused. After writing up the order, the order taker normally checks to be sure his company fills the order promptly—and accurately. He also handles any adjustments or complaints—and generally acts as a link between the company and customers.

Such salespeople are usually the low-pressure type—friendly and easy going. Usually these jobs aren't as high paying as the order-getting variety—but are attractive to many because they aren't as demanding. Relatively little traveling is required. There is little or no pressure to get new accounts. And some social needs may be satisfied, too. Some order takers become good friends with their customers.

Retail Order Takers— Often They Are Poor Sales Clerks

Order taking may be almost mechanical at the retail level—say at the supermarket check-out counter. Some retail clerks seem to be annoyed by having to complete sales. Many are just plain rude. This is too bad—because order taking is important. They may be poor orders takers, however, because they aren't paid much—often only the minimum wage. But—they may be paid little because they do little. In any case, order taking at the retail level appears to be declining in quality. Probably there will be far fewer such jobs in the future—as more retailers turn to self-service selling.

SUPPORTING SALES FORCE—INFORMS AND PROMOTES IN THE CHANNEL

Supporting salespeople help the order-oriented salespeople—but don't try to get orders themselves. Their activities are aimed at getting sales in the long run. For the short run, however, they are ambassadors of goodwill—who provide specialized services. Almost all supporting salespeople work for manufacturers—or middlemen who do this supporting work for manufacturers. There are two types of supporting salespeople: *missionary salespeople* and *technical specialists.*

Missionary Salespeople Can Increase Sales

Missionary salespeople work for manufacturers—calling on their middlemen and their customers. They try to develop goodwill and stimulate demand, help the middlemen train their salespeople, and often take orders for delivery by the middlemen. Missionary salespeople are sometimes called *merchandisers* or *detailers.*

They may be needed if a manufacturer uses the typical merchant wholesaler to obtain widespread distribution—but knows that the retailers will need promotion help that the merchant wholesaler won't provide. These salespeople may be able to give an occasional "shot in the arm" to the company's regular wholesalers and retailers. Or they may work regularly with these middlemen—setting up displays, arranging special promotions, and, in general, carrying out the sales promotion plans the firm's own specialists have developed.

Missionary salespeople call on middlemen and give constant attention to retail distribution and display.

An imaginative missionary salesperson may double or triple sales. Naturally, this doesn't go unnoticed—and missionary sales jobs are often a route to order-oriented jobs. In fact, this position is often used as a training ground for new salespeople.

Technical Specialists Are Experts Who Know Product Applications

Technical specialists provide technical assistance to order-oriented salespeople. They usually are scientists or engineers with the know-how to explain the advantages of the company's product—but little interest in sales. Instead, they have technical know-how—plus the ability to explain the advantages of their firm's product. Since they usually talk with the customer's technical people, there is little need for much sales ability. Before the specialist's call, an order getter probably has stimulated interest. The technical specialist provides the details. Some technical specialists do become fine order getters. But most are more interested in explaining the technical fine points of their product—than in actual sales work.

MOST SELLING REQUIRES A BLEND OF ALL THREE TASKS

We have described three sales tasks—order getting, order taking, and supporting. Remember, however, that a particular salesperson might have to do any—or all—of these tasks. Ten percent of a particular job may be order getting, 80 percent order taking, and the remaining 10 percent supporting.

Strategy planners should consider all the different types of selling tasks to be handled by a sales force. Once the tasks are identified, the sales manager has to assign responsibility for individual sales jobs.

THE RIGHT STRUCTURE HELPS
ASSIGN RESPONSIBILITY

A sales manager must organize the sales force so that all the necessary tasks are done well and the personal selling objectives achieved. A large organization might have different salespeople who specialize by different selling tasks *and* by the target markets they serve.

Different Target Markets Need Different Selling Tasks

Sales force responsibilities often are divided based on the type of customer involved. For example, a company that sells upholstery fabrics might have one sales group that calls on furniture manufacturers and another that calls on wholesalers who sell to small upholstery shops. They may buy the same products—but the marketing mixes are very different.

Very large customers often require special selling tasks—and are treated differently. A company that makes plumbing fixtures might have a "regular"

Sales reps can't be successful unless the whole marketing mix meets customers' needs.

If a lift truck salesman promises you fast parts delivery, get it in writing.

That's why we have a CAT PLUS Parts Policy:

1. Caterpillar Lift Truck Dealers can hand you most parts in five minutes—right off the shelf.

2. If he doesn't have a part in stock, he can use his computer hook-up to locate the nearest one and get it overnight from one of our

15 regional warehouses. It takes less than one minute to locate the part and *automatically* begin shipment.

3. If he can't get a part you need for your Cat Lift Truck in 48 hours, you get the part free*

But see for yourself. Challenge us with a part number. Ask your Cat Lift Truck Dealer for a sample

of his CAT PLUS Parts Policy. For his name and phone number, look in the Yellow Pages or call toll-free 800-528-6050. Ext. 795.
(In Arizona call 800-352-0458. Ext. 795.)

*Applies to new Cat Lift Trucks sold by participating Cat Lift Truck Dealers in the U.S.A. Specific items included may vary

C CATERPILLAR

Caterpillar Lift Trucks produced in U.S.A. are manufactured by Towmotor Corporation, subsidiary of Caterpillar Tractor Co. Caterpillar, Cat and C are Trademarks of Caterpillar Tractor Co. Towmotor is a Trademark of Towmotor Corporation. 7111 Tyler Blvd., Mentor, OH 44060

sales force to call on building material wholesalers and an "elite" **national accounts sales force** that sells direct to large accounts—like Sears or other major retail chain stores that carry plumbing fixtures.

Sales Tasks Are Done in Sales Territories

Often companies organize selling tasks on the basis of **sales territory**—a geographic area which is the responsibility of one salesperson or several working in a coordinated effort. A territory might be a region of the country, a state, or part of a city—depending on the market potential. Companies like Lockheed Aircraft Corporation often consider a whole country as *part* of a sales territory for one salesperson.[2]

Size of Sales Force Depends on Work-load

Once all the important selling tasks have been identified—and the responsibilities have been divided—the sales manager must decide how many salespeople are needed. The first step is estimating how much work can be done by one person in some time period. Then he can make an "educated guess" about how many people are required in total—as the following example shows.

The Parker Jewelry Company had been successful in selling its silver jewelry to department and jewelry stores in the Southwest. But management decided to expand into the big urban markets of the Northeast. They realized that most of the work for the first few years would require order getters. They felt that a salesperson would have to call on each account at least once a month to get a share of this competitive business. They estimated that a salesperson could make only four calls a day on prospective buyers—and still allow time for travel, waiting, and follow-up on orders that came in. This meant that a sales rep who made calls 20 days a month could handle about 80 stores (4 a day × 20 days).

The managers looked at telephone Yellow Pages for their target cities—and estimated the total number of jewelry departments and stores. Then they simply divided the total number of stores by 80 to estimate the number of salespeople needed. This helped them set up territories, too—defining areas that included about 80 stores for each salesperson.

When a company is starting a new sales force, managers are concerned about its size. But, in many on-going businesses, this strategic decision is often ignored. Some managers forget that over time the "right" number of salespeople may change—as selling tasks change. Then, when a problem becomes obvious, they try to change everything in a hurry—a big mistake. Finding and training effective salespeople takes time.

SOUND SELECTION AND TRAINING TO BUILD A SALES FORCE

Selecting Good Salespeople Takes Judgment, Plus

It is important to hire *good, well-qualified* salespeople. But the selection in many companies is a hit-or-miss affair—done without serious thought about exactly what kind of person is needed. Friends and relations—or whoever is available—may be hired. This often leads to poor sales—and costly sales force turnover.

Progressive companies try to be more careful—updating lists of possible candidates, and using multiple interviews with various executives as well as psychological tests. Unfortunately, these techniques can't guarantee success—but using some selection method results in a better sales force than using no selection aids at all.

One problem in selecting salespeople is that two different sales jobs with identical titles may involve very different selling tasks—and require different skills. One way to avoid this problem is with a carefully prepared *job description.*[3]

Job Descriptions Should Be in Writing and Specific

A **job description** is a written statement of what a salesperson is expected to do. It might list 10 to 20 specific tasks—as well as routine prospecting and sales report writing. Each company must write its own job specifications. And when they are written, they should provide clear guidelines about what selling tasks are involved in the job. This is necessary to decide what kind of salespeople should be selected—and how they should be motivated. A job description also affects the kind of training needed. Later, it can provide a basis for evaluating sales performance.

Good Salespeople Are Trained, Not Born

The idea that good salespeople are born may have some truth in it—but it isn't the whole story. Studies show that any alert person can be trained to be a good salesperson.

What a salesperson needs to be taught—about the company and its products, about planning and making sales presentations, and following up after the sale—may seem obvious. But though they seem obvious—managers often ignore these topics. Many salespeople fail—or do a poor job—because they haven't had good training. New salespeople often are hired and sent out on the road—or retail selling floor—with no training in the basic selling steps and no information about the product or the customer—just a price list and a pat on the back. This isn't enough!

Many sales are lost because the salesperson fails to ask for the order.

All Salespeople Need Some Training

It's up to sales and marketing management to be sure that the salespeople know what they're supposed to do—and how to do it. The kind of initial sales training should depend on the experience and skills of the group involved. But the company's sales training program should cover at least: (1) company policies and practices, (2) product information, and (3) selling techniques.

COMPENSATING AND MOTIVATING SALESPEOPLE

Public recognition, sales contests, or just personal recognition for a job well done may help stimulate greater sales effort.[4] But most companies emphasize cash incentives to attract and motivate their salespeople.[5]

Two basic decisions must be made in developing a compensation plan: (1) the level of compensation and (2) the method of payment.

Level of Compensation Depends on Needed Skills—And Job

To attract—and keep—good people, most companies must pay at least the going market wage for different kinds of sales people. Order getters are paid more than order takers, for example.

The job description explains the salesperson's role in the marketing mix. It should show whether any special skills or responsibilities are needed—requiring higher pay levels. To be sure it can afford a specific type of salesperson, the company should estimate—when the job description is written—how valuable such a salesperson will be. A good order getter may be worth $50,000–$100,000 to one company, but only $5,000–$10,000 to another—just because the second firm doesn't have enough to sell! In such a case, the second company must rethink its job specifications—or completely change its promotion plans—because the "going rate" for order getters is much higher than $5,000 a year.

If a job will require extensive traveling, aggressive pioneering, or contacts with difficult customers—the pay may have to be increased. It must be kept in mind, however, that the salesperson's compensation level should compare—at least roughly—with the pay scale of the rest of the firm. Normally, salespeople are paid more than the office or production force, but less than top management.

Payment Methods Vary

Once the general level of compensation has been decided, the method of payment must be set. There are three basic methods of payment: (1) *straight salary,* (2) *straight commission,* or (3) a *combination plan.*

Straight salary gives the salesperson the most security—and straight commission the most incentive. Most companies want to offer their salespeople some balance between incentive and security. Therefore, the most popular method of payment is a combination plan—which includes some salary and some commission. Bonuses, profit sharing, and fringe benefits may be included, too.

A sales manager's control over a sales rep depends on the compensation

■   FIGURE 15–2   Relation between personal selling expenses and sales volume—for basic personal
selling compensation alternatives

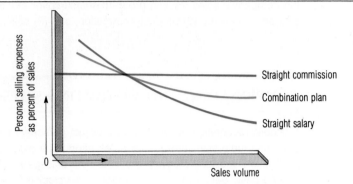

Source: This figure suggested by Professor A. A. Brogowicz, Western Michigan University.

plan. A straight salary plan permits the greatest amount of supervision. A person on commission tends to be his own boss.

The marketing manager should probably try to avoid very complicated compensation plans—or plans that change frequently. Complicated plans are hard for salespeople to understand—and costly for the accounting department to handle. Also, low morale may result if salespeople can't see a direct relationship between their effort and their income.

Simplicity is probably best achieved with straight commission. But, in practice, it is usually better to give up some simplicity to have some control over salespeople—while still providing flexibility and incentive. Figure 15–2 shows the general relation between personal selling expenses and sales volume—for the various alternatives.

There are, unfortunately, no easy answers to the compensation problem. It's up to the sales manager—working with the marketing manager—to develop a good compensation plan. The sales manager's efforts have to be part of the whole marketing program—because he can't accomplish his objectives if enough money isn't allocated for the personal selling job.[6]

PERSONAL SELLING TECHNIQUES—PROSPECTING AND PRESENTING

When we talked about sales training, we mentioned training in selling techniques. Now let's discuss these ideas in more detail—including the basic steps which each salesperson should follow—prospecting, planning sales presentations, making sales presentations, and following up after the sale. Figure 15–3 shows the steps we will consider. From the figure, you can see that the personal salesperson is just carrying out the communication process discussed in the last chapter.[7]

■ **FIGURE 15–3** Personal selling is a communication process

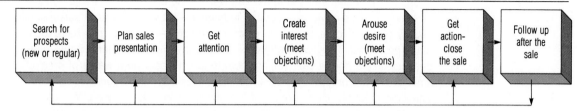

Search for prospects (new or regular) → Plan sales presentation → Get attention → Create interest (meet objections) → Arouse desire (meet objections) → Get action–close the sale → Follow up after the sale

**Finding Prospects—
The Big Buyer Who
Wasn't There**

Finding "live" prospects isn't as easy as it sounds. Although the marketing strategy should specify the target market, we have already seen that some people within a target market may be innovators, while others are late adopters.

Basically, **prospecting** involves following down all the "leads" in the target market. But which ones are currently "live" and will help make the buying decision? In the industrial goods area, for example, about two thirds of industrial calls are made on the wrong person—because of multiple buying influences and the fact that companies often change their organization structures. This means that constant, detailed customer analysis is needed. This requires many personal calls and telephone calls.

Telephone selling—using the telephone to find out about a prospect's interest in the company's marketing mix—and even to make a sales presentation or take an order—is becoming more common as an aid in prospecting. A telephone call has many of the benefits of a personal visit—including the chance to adjust the message as feedback is received. And it is often more efficient. It can cut the number of costly personal visits—and may even sell "hot" prospects on the phone. At the very least, it provides information which can be used in a follow-up sales call.

Telephone selling is often used to find out about a prospect's interest in the company's marketing mix.

How Long to Spend with Whom?

Another part of prospecting is deciding how much time to spend on which prospects. The problem is to "qualify" prospects—to see if they deserve more effort. The potential sales volume—as well as the likelihood of a sale—must be weighed. This obviously requires judgment—but well-organized salespeople usually develop some system to guide prospecting—because they have too many prospects. They can't afford to "wine and dine" all of them. Some may deserve only a phone call. Taking them to lunch would be a waste of precious time. There are only a few hours each business day for personal sales calls. This time must be used carefully if the salesperson is to succeed. You can see that effective prospecting is important to success. In fact, it may be more important than making a good sales presentation—especially if the company's marketing mix is basically strong.[8]

Three Kinds of Sales Presentations May Be Useful

Once a promising prospect has been found, it's necessary to make a **sales presentation**—a salesperson's effort to make a sale. But someone has to plan the kind of sales presentation to be made. This is a strategic matter. The kind of presentation should be set before the sales rep is sent prospecting. And in situations where the customer comes to the salesperson—for example, in a retail store—the planners have to make sure that prospects do come to the salespeople. (This may be the job of advertising or sales promotion.) Then the sales presentation must be made.

The marketing manager can choose two basically different approaches to making sales presentations: The *prepared* approach or the *need-satisfaction* approach. Another approach—the *selling formula approach*—is a combination of the two. Each of these has its place.

The Prepared Sales Presentation

The **prepared sales presentation** approach uses a memorized presentation which is not adapted to each individual customer. A prepared ("canned") presentation builds on the black box (stimulus-response) model discussed in Chapter 6. This model says that a customer faced with a particular stimulus will give the desired response—say, a "yes" answer to the salesperson's request for an order.

The use of prepared sales presentations is shown in Figure 15–4. Basically, the salesperson does most of the talking—see Figure 15–4—only occasionally

■ FIGURE 15–4   Prepared approach to sales presentations

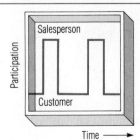

■ **FIGURE 15–5** Need-satisfaction approach to sales presentations

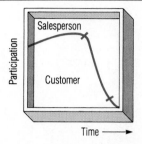

letting the customer talk when the salesperson attempts to close. If one "trial close" doesn't work, another prepared presentation is tried—with another attempt at closing. This can go on until the salesperson runs out of material— or the customer either buys or decides to leave.

This approach can be effective—and practical—when the possible sale is low in value—and only a short time can be spent on selling. It also makes sense with less skilled salespeople. The company can control what is said— and in what order. This approach has the obvious weakness of treating all potential customers alike. It may work for some and not for others—and the salespeople won't know why. They don't improve their selling skills with more experience—because they're just mechanically trying standard presentations. This approach may be suitable for simple order taking. But it is no longer considered good selling for complicated situations.

Need-Satisfaction Approach—Builds on the Marketing Concept

The **need-satisfaction approach** involves developing a good understanding of the individual customer's needs before trying to close the sale. Here, after making some general "benefit" statements—to get the customer's attention and interest—the salesperson leads the customer to do most of the talking—to help him understand the customer's needs. Then the salesperson begins to enter into the conversation more—trying to help the customer understand his own needs better. Once they agree, the seller tries to show how his product fills the customer's special needs—and close the sale. See Figure 15–5. This is a problem-solving approach—in which the customer and salesperson work together to solve the problem.

The need-satisfaction approach is most useful if there are many differences among the various customers in a target market. With this approach, the salesperson is much more on his own. He should have a good grounding in the company's product and policies—and an understanding of people and situations. This kind of selling obviously takes more skill. The salesperson must be able to analyze what motivates a particular customer—and show how the company's offering will help satisfy that customer's needs.

Selling Formula Approach—Some of Both

The **selling formula approach** starts with a prepared presentation outline— much like the prepared approach—and leads the customer through some logical steps to a final close. The steps are logical because we assume that we know something about the target customers' needs and attitudes.

Which sales presentation is best depends on the situation.

The selling formula approach is shown in Figure 15–6. The salesperson does most of the talking at the beginning of the presentation—to be sure the basic points are communicated early. This part of the presentation may even have been prepared for him. Then the salesperson brings the customer into the discussion—to see what special needs this customer has. Next, the salesperson tries to show how his product satisfies this specific customer's needs. Finally, he tries to close the sale.

This approach can be useful for both order-getting and order-taking situations—where potential customers are similar, and relatively untrained salespeople must be used. Some of the office equipment and computer manufacturers, for example, have used this approach—because they know the kinds of situations their salespeople meet—and roughly what they want them to say. Using this approach speeds training—and makes the sales force productive sooner.

■ FIGURE 15–6   Selling-formula approach to sales presentations

**AIDA Helps Plan
Sales Presentations**

AIDA—Attention, Interest, Desire, Action. Each sales presentation—except some very simple "canned" types—follows this AIDA sequence. The "how-to-do-it" might even be set as part of the marketing strategy. The time spent with each of the steps can vary, depending on the situation—and the selling approach used. But it is still necessary to begin a presentation by getting the prospect's *attention* and, of course, moving him to *action* through a close.[9]

Each sales manager—and salesperson—must think through this sequence in deciding what sales approach to use—and in evaluating a possible presentation. Does the presentation do a good job of quickly getting the prospect's attention. Will the presentation hold the prospect's interest? Finally—does the presentation result in action—does the salesperson ask for the order and persuade the customer to buy? It might surprise you to learn that the most common reason for losing a sale is that the seller *never asks for the order*! These ideas may seem very obvious to you. But too often they are overlooked—or ignored—and the sale is lost.

■ CONCLUSION

In this chapter, we have discussed the importance and nature of personal selling. Selling is much more than just "getting rid of the product." In fact, a salesperson who is not provided with a strategy may have to become his own strategy planner. Ideally, however, the sales manager and marketing manger should work together to set some strategic guidelines: the kind and number of salespersons needed, the kind of sales presentation, and selection, training, and motivation approaches.

Three *basic* sales tasks were discussed: (1) order getting, (2) order taking, and (3) supporting. Most sales jobs are a combination of at least two of these three tasks. Once the important tasks have been identified, the structure of the sales organization and the number of salespeople needed to accomplish the tasks can be decided. The nature of the job—and the level and method of compensation—also depend on the blend of these tasks. A job description should be written for each sales job. This, in turn, provides guidelines for selecting, training, and compensating salespeople.

Once the sales manager's basic plan and budget have been set, the job is to implement the plan—including directing and controlling the sales force. This includes assigning sales territories and controlling performance. You can see that a sales manager is deeply involved with the basic management tasks of planning and control—as well as ongoing implementing of the personal selling effort.

Three kinds of sales presentations were discussed. Each has its place—but the need-satisfaction approach seems best for higher-level sales jobs. In jobs like these, personal selling is achieving a new, professional status—because of the ability and personal responsibility required of the salesperson. The old-time "glad-hander" is being replaced by the specialist who is creative, hard working, persuasive, and highly trained—and therefore able to help the buyer. This type of salesperson always has been—and probably always will be—in short supply. And the demand for high-level salespeople is growing.

■ QUESTIONS AND PROBLEMS

1. Identify the strategic decisions which are needed in the personal selling area and explain why they should be treated as strategic decisions to be made by the marketing manager.

2. What kind of salesperson (or what blend of the basic sales tasks) is required to sell the following products? If there are several selling jobs in the channel for each product, then indicate the kinds of salespeople required. (Specify any assumptions necessary to give definite answers.)
a. Soy bean oil.
b. Costume jewelry.
c. Nuts and bolts.
d. Handkerchiefs.
e. Mattresses.
f. Corn.
g. Cigarettes.

3. Distinguish among the jobs of manufacturers', wholesalers', and retailers' order-getting salespeople. If one order getter is needed, must all the salespeople in a channel be order getters? Illustrate.

4. Discuss the role of the manufacturers' agent in the marketing manager's promotion plans. What kind of salesperson is a manufacturers' agent?

5. Discuss the future of the specialty shop if manufacturers place greater emphasis on mass selling because of the inadequacy of retail order taking.

6. Compare and contrast missionary salespeople and technical specialists.

7. Explain how a straight commission system might provide flexibility in the sale of a line of women's clothing products which continually vary in profitability.

8. Explain how a compensation system could be developed to provide incentives for older salespeople and yet make some provision for trainees who have not yet learned their job.

9. Cite an actual local example of each of the three kinds of sales presentations discussed in the chapter. For each situation, explain whether a different type of presentation would have been better.

10. Describe a need-satisfaction sales presentation which you have experienced recently and explain how it might have been improved by fuller use of the AIDA framework.

11. Describe the operation of our economy if personal salespeople were outlawed. Could the economy work? If so, how; if not, what is the minimum personal selling effort necessary? Could this minimum personal selling effort be controlled effectively by law?

■ SUGGESTED CASES

19. Cabco, Inc.

20. York Furniture Company

27. Perry Manufacturing Company

Chapter 16 ■ Mass selling

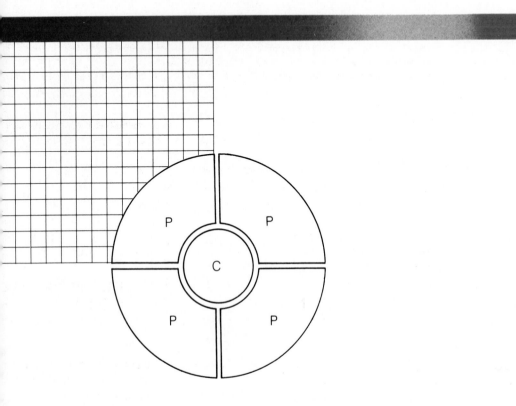

When you finish this chapter, you should:

1. Understand when the various kinds of advertising are needed.

2. Understand how to go about choosing the "best" media.

3. Understand how to plan the "best" message—that is, the copy thrust.

4. Understand what advertising agencies do—and how they are paid.

5. Understand how to advertise legally.

6. Recognize the important new terms (shown in red).

To reach a lot of people quickly and cheaply—use mass selling.

Mass selling makes widespread distribution possible. Although a marketing manager may prefer to use only personal selling, it can be expensive. Mass selling can be cheaper. It is not as pinpointed as personal selling, but it can reach large numbers of potential customers at the same time. Today, most promotion blends contain both personal and mass selling.

Mass selling contacts vary in cost, too—so more strategic decisions are needed. Carol Kidd is an account manager for a large ad agency. She buys time and space for her advertiser clients—and is studying the proposal of a cable TV salesman. He claims that his cable TV programs are a "better buy" than the "Big Three" network programs—because the "cost per thousand viewers" is usually much lower. He claims this is because cable is new and trying to attract customers—so it's a real bargain for her clients. She feels his "cost-cutting" ideas are too simple, but thinks cable might be good for one of her clients.

Barb McKinley is a feature writer for a newspaper in a resort town in North-ern Michigan. She just got the job of promoting the Indian Pow-Wow to be

■ FIGURE 16–1   Strategy planning for advertising

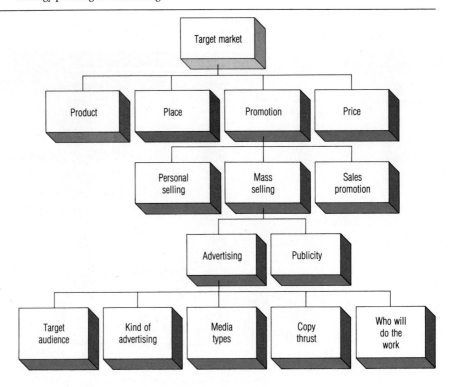

held in two months. Barb is trying to decide what to do. Should she write copy about the Indian people, their history, their dances, or their craftwork? All would be interesting, but Barb finally decides that she needs to know more about the objective(s) of her assignment. So she decides to discuss this with the man organizing the event.

Marketing managers have strategic decisions to make about mass selling. Working with advertising managers, they must decide: (1) who is the target, (2) what kind of advertising to use, (3) how customers are to be reached (via which types of media), (4) what is to be said to them (the copy thrust), and (5) by whom (the firm's own advertising department or by advertising agencies). See Figure 16–1. We'll talk about these questions in this chapter.

THE IMPORTANCE OF ADVERTISING

$75 Billion in Ads

Advertising can get results in a promotion blend. But good advertising results cost money. In the United States, spending for advertising has grown continuously since World War II. And more growth is expected. In 1946, advertising spending was slightly more than $3 billion—it topped $75 billion in 1983.[1]

It's All Done by Less Than Half a Million People

While total advertising expenditures are large, the advertising industry itself employs relatively few people. The major expense is for media time and space. And in the United States, the largest share of this—27 percent—goes for newspaper space. Television takes about 21 percent of the total, and direct mail, about 16 percent.[2]

Fewer than 500,000 people work directly in the U.S. advertising industry. This includes all people who help create or sell advertising—advertising people in radio and television stations, newspapers, and magazines—as well as those in advertising agencies—and those working for retailers, wholesalers, and manufacturers. The sometimes glamorous—and often criticized—4,800 U.S. advertising agencies employ only about 200,000 of those workers. Most agencies are small—employing less than 10 people. Many of these agencies are located in New York and Chicago.[3]

Advertisers Aren't Really Spending That Much

U.S. corporations spend only about 1.5 percent of their sales dollar on advertising. This is relatively small compared to the total cost of marketing—which is about 50 percent of the consumer's dollar.

Some Spend More Than Others

Some industries spend a much larger percentage of sales for advertising than the average of 1.5 percent. Soap and drug manufacturers may spend in the 5 to 10 percent range. At the other extreme, some industrial goods companies—those who depend on personal selling—may spend less than $\frac{1}{10}$ of 1 percent. And wholesalers and retailers may spend about 1 percent. (See Table 16–1 for the top 10 national advertisers in 1983.)

You can see that advertising is important in certain markets—especially the consumer goods markets. Remember, however, that—in total—it costs much less than personal selling—and less than sales promotion.

■ TABLE 16–1   Top 10 U.S. national advertisers in 1983

Rank	Company	Total advertising dollars—1983 ($ million)
1	Procter & Gamble	$773.6
2	Sears, Roebuck & Co.	732.5
3	Beatrice Cos.	602.8
4	General Motors Corp.	595.1
5	R. J. Reynolds Industries	593.4
6	Philip Morris Inc.	527.5
7	Ford Motor Co.	479.1
8	AT&T	463.1
9	K mart Corp.	400.0
10	General Foods Corp.	386.1

Source: *Advertising Age*, September 14, 1984, p. 1.

ADVERTISING OBJECTIVES ARE SET BY MARKETING STRATEGY

Every advertisement—and every advertising campaign—should have clearly defined objectives. These should grow out of the overall marketing strategy—and the jobs assigned to advertising. It's not enough for the marketing manager just to say—"Promote the product."

If You Want Half the Market, Say So!

A marketing manager should spell out exactly what is wanted. A general objective—"To help in the expansion of market share"—could be stated more specifically—"To increase traffic in our cooperating retail outlets by 25 percent during the next three months."

Such specific objectives would obviously affect the kind of promotion used. Advertising that might be right for building a good image among opinion leaders might be all wrong for getting customers into the retailers' stores.

Even more specific objectives might be needed in some cases. For new products, for example, most of the target market may have to be brought through the early stages of the adoption process. General Foods recently developed a sugar-free Kool Aid—sweetened with a new, natural sweetener instead of saccharin. The company included samples of the new drink mix in a free coupon offer mailed to consumers' homes. For more established products,

---

■ **FIGURE 16–2**   Advertising should vary for adoption process stages

Adoption process	Advertising that might be relevant to various stages
Awareness	Teaser campaigns Skywriting Jingles and slogans Classified ads Announcements
↓	
Interest	Informative or descriptive ads Status or glamour appeals Image ads
↓	
Evaluation and trial	Competitive ads Persuasive copy
↓	
Decision	Testimonials Price deal offers "Last-chance" offers "Direct-action" retail ads Point-of-purchase ads
↓	
Confirmation	Informative "why" ads Reminder ads

Source: Adapted from R. J. Lavidge and G. A. Steiner, "A Model for Predictive Measurements of Advertising Effectiveness," *Journal of Marketing*, October 1961, p. 61.

advertising's job might be to build brand preference—as well as help purchasers confirm their decisions. This, too, leads to different kinds of advertising—as shown in Figure 16–2.

Advertising objectives should be very specific—much more than personal selling objectives. One of the advantages of personal selling is that salespeople can shift their presentations to meet customers' needs. Each advertisement, however, is a specific communication that has to work, not just for one customer, but for thousands—or millions—of target customers. This means that specific objectives should be set for each advertisement—as well as a whole advertising campaign. If this isn't done, a creative advertising staff may set some reasonable objective—like "selling the product." Then it will create ads that may win artistic awards within the advertising industry—but fail to do the advertising job management hoped for.

OBJECTIVES DETERMINE THE KINDS OF ADVERTISING NEEDED

The advertising objectives will determine which of two basic types of advertising to use—*product or institutional.*

Product advertising tries to sell a product. It may be aimed at final users or channel members.

Institutional advertising tries to develop good will for a company or even an industry—instead of a specific product.

Product Advertising— Meet Us, Like Us, Remember Us

Product advertising falls into three categories: pioneering, competitive, and reminder advertising.

Pioneering advertising—builds primary demand

Pioneering advertising tries to develop **primary demand**—demand for a product category rather than a specific brand. It's needed in the early stages of the adoption process—to inform potential customers about a new product. Its basic job is to inform—not persuade. It is also needed in the introduction stage of the product life cycle.

Pioneering advertising doesn't have to mention the brand or specific company at all. The California olive industry promoted olives as olives—not certain brands. This was so successful that after only five years of promotion, the industry's surpluses became shortages.

Competitive advertising—emphasizes selective demand

Competitive advertising tries to develop **selective demand**—demand for a specific brand rather than a product category. A firm can be forced into competitive advertising—as the product life cycle moves along—to hold its

Pioneering advertising tries to develop primary demand for a product category—and may not even mention a specific brand.

own against competitors. The United Fruit Company gave up a 20-year pioneering effort to promote bananas—in favor of advertising its own "Chiquita" brand. The reason was simple. While United Fruit was promoting "bananas," it slowly lost market share to competitors. The competitive advertising campaign tried to stop further losses.

Competitive advertising may be either direct or indirect. The **direct type** aims for immediate buying action. The **indirect type** points out product advantages—to affect future buying decisions.

Airline advertising uses both types of competitive advertising. *Direct*-action ads use price, timetables, and phone numbers to call for reservations. *Indirect*-action ads suggest that you mention the airline's name when talking to your travel agent.

Competitive advertising tries to develop selective demand for a specific brand rather than a product category.

Comparative advertising is even rougher competitive advertising. **Comparative advertising** means making specific brand comparisons—using actual product names. Ban Roll-On deodorant ran ads claiming to be more effective than Right Guard, Secret, Sure, Arrid Extra Dry, Soft & Dri, Body All, and Dial products.

The Federal Trade Commission encouraged these kinds of ads. But this approach caused legal as well as ethical problems—and some advertisers and their agencies have backed away from it. Research is supposed to support superiority claims, but the rules aren't clear here. Some firms just do small tests until they get the results they want. Others talk about minor differences that don't reflect the overall benefits of a product. This may make consumers less—rather than more—informed. Some comparative ads leave consumers confused—or even angry—if the product they are using has been criticized. And, in at least one case, comparative ads appear to have helped the competitive product (Tylenol) more than the advertisers' products (Datril, Anacin, and Bayer aspirin).[4]

Many advertisers don't like comparative advertising. But it is likely that the approach will be continued by some advertisers—and encouraged by the government—as long as the ad copy is not actually false.[5]

■ FIGURE 16–3 Example of a reminder ad

Reminder advertising—reinforces early promotion

Reminder advertising tries to keep the product's name before the public. It may be useful when the product has won brand preference or insistence—perhaps in the market maturity or sales decline stages. Here, the advertiser may use "soft-sell" ads that just mention or show the name—as a reminder. Many Chanel perfume ads have been of this type. See Figure 16–3.

Institutional Advertising—Remember Our Name in Dallas, Seattle, Boston

Institutional advertising focuses on the name and prestige of a company or industry. It tries to inform, persuade, or remind.

This kind of promotion is sometimes used by large companies with several divisions. AT&T, for example, does institutional advertising of the AT&T name—emphasizing the quality and research behind *all* AT&T products. See Figure 16–4.

Sometimes an advertising campaign may have both product and institutional aspects—because the federal government has limited tax deductions on some institutional advertising—claiming it had no "business purpose." Defense contractors are specifically barred from including advertising expenditures as a cost of doing business with the government.

■ **FIGURE** 16–4   Example of an institutional ad

MORE THAN A NEW LOOK, A NEW OUTLOOK.

AT&T

We're the new AT&T. A new company with a new symbol. But we're not exactly a newcomer. We have more than a hundred years' experience and a worldwide reputation. With the breakup of the Bell System, we know we must earn your confidence all over again—under new circumstances.

As we compete for your business, we'll stand out from the crowd by giving you better service than anyone. That's a commitment.

And we'll offer you the most advanced technology from our world-renowned Bell Laboratories. That's a guarantee.

We'll be the brand name that means dependable, state-of-the-art phones for your home, the best information systems for your business and the one and only long distance service that lets you reach out and touch anyone, any time—across the nation and around the world.

We'll use our research, development and marketing talents to keep American communications technology the best in the world.

We're the new AT&T. Our new outlook is also our competitive strategy and our goal: to give you every reason, every day, to choose us.

COOPERATIVE ADVERTISING MAY BUY MORE

Vertical Cooperation— Advertising Allowances, Cooperative Advertising

So far, our discussion might suggest that only producers do product or institutional advertising. This isn't true, of course. But producers can affect the advertising done by others. Sometimes a manufacturer knows what he wants advertising to do—but finds that it can be done better or cheaper by someone further along in the channel. In this case, the manufacturer may offer **advertising allowances**—price reductions to firms further along in the channel to encourage them to advertise or otherwise promote the firm's products locally.

Cooperative advertising may get more cooperation

Cooperative advertising involves middlemen and producers sharing in the cost of ads. It helps a manufacturer get more promotion for the advertising dollar—since media rate structures usually give local advertisers lower rates than national firms. Also, a retailer is more likely to follow through when he is paying part of the cost.

Cooperative advertising and advertising allowances can be abused. Allowances can be given to retailers without really expecting that they will be used for ads. This may become a hidden price cut—or even price discrimination. The Federal Trade Commission has become more interested in this problem—and some manufacturers have pulled back from cooperative advertising. To avoid legal problems, wise producers insist on proof of use.

CHOOSING THE "BEST" MEDIUM—HOW TO DELIVER THE MESSAGE

For effective promotion, ads have to reach specific target customers. Unfortunately, not all potential customers read all newspapers and magazines—or listen to all radio and television programs. So not all media are equally effective.

What is the best medium? There is no simple answer to this question. Effectiveness depends on how well it fits with the rest of a marketing strategy—that is, it depends on (1) your promotion objectives, (2) your target markets, (3) the funds available for advertising, and (4) the nature of the media—including who they *reach,* with what *frequency,* with what *impact,* at what *cost.* Table 16–2 shows some of the pros and cons of major kinds of media—and some typical costs.

Billboards are especially good for simple messages and reminder advertising.

■ **TABLE 16–2**   Relative size and costs, and advantages and disadvantages of major kinds of media

Kinds of media	Sales volume—1983 ($ billions)	Typical costs— 1983	Advantages	Disadvantages
Newspaper $20.6		$15,000 for one page weekday, Cleveland (ADI Network)	Flexible Timely Local market Credible source	May be expensive Short life No "pass-along"
Television...... 16.1		$2,800 for a 30-second spot, prime time, Cleveland	Offers sight, sound, and motion Good attention Wide reach	Expensive in total "Clutter" Short exposure Less selective audience
Direct mail..... 11.8		$25/1,000 for listing of 103,000 engineers	Selected audience Flexible Can personalize	Relatively expensive per contact "Junk mail"—hard to retain attention
Radio 5.2		$150 for one minute drive time, Cleveland	Wide reach Segmented audiences Inexpensive	Offers audio only Weak attention Many different rates Short exposure
Magazine...... 4.2		$45,915 for one page, 4-color in *U.S. News & World Report*	Very segmented audiences Credible source Good reproduction Long life Good "pass-along"	Inflexible Long lead times
Outdoor 0.8		$4,159 (painted) for prime billboard, 30–60-day showings, Cleveland	Flexible Repeat exposure Inexpensive	"Mass market" Very short exposure

Source: Data from Standard Rate and Data Service and estimates from May 14, 1984 *Advertising Age*, p. 63.

Specify Promotion Objectives

Before you can choose the best medium, you must decide on your promotion objectives. For example, if the objective is to inform—telling a long story with a lot of detail and pictures—then magazines and newspapers may be best. Jockey switched its annual budget of more than $1 million to magazines from television when it decided to show the variety of colors, patterns, and styles that Jockey briefs offer. They felt it was too hard to show this in a 30-second TV spot. Jockey ads were run in men's magazines—such as *Sports Illustrated, Outdoor Life, Field and Stream, Esquire,* and *Playboy.* But aware that women buy over 80 percent of men's ordinary underwear—and 50 percent of fashion styles—they also placed the ads in *TV Guide, New Yorker, People, Money, Time,* and *Newsweek.* And a page of scantily clad males was run in *Cosmopolitan.*[6]

Match Your Market with the Media

To guarantee good media selection, the advertiser first must *clearly* specify its target market—a step necessary for all marketing strategy planning. Then media can be chosen that will reach *those* target customers.

Matching target customers and media is the major problem in effective media selection. It's hard to be sure who sees or hears what. Most of the major media use marketing research to develop profiles of the people who buy their publications—or live in their broadcasting area. But they cannot be as sure about who actually reads each page—or sees or hears each show.

The difficulty of evaluating alternative media has led some media buyers to select media based only on lowest "cost per thousand" figures. But too great concern with numbers of "bodies" may lead to ignoring the target market's dimensions—and slipping into "mass marketing." The media buyer may look only at the relatively low cost (per 1,000 people) of "mass media"—such as national network radio or TV—when a more specialized medium might be a much better buy. Its audience might have more interest in the product—or more money to spend—or more willingness to buy. An opera on public television, for example, or a tennis show on ESPN (cable television's Entertainment Sports Programming Network) may be "better buys" for some advertisers than some network TV shows aimed at "everyone."

Specialized Media Help Zero in on Target Markets

Media are now trying to reach smaller, more defined target markets. Some national media offer regional editions. *Time* magazine, for example, offers not only several regional and metropolitan editions, but also special editions for college students, educators, doctors, and business managers.

Many magazines serve only special-interest groups—such as fishermen, radio and television fans, homemakers, religious, or professional groups. In fact, the most profitable magazines seem to be those aimed at clearly defined markets—such as *Penthouse, Car Craft, Skiing, Bride's Magazine,* and *Southern Living.*

There are trade magazines in many fields—such as chemical engineering, electrical wholesaling, farming, and the defense market. *Standard Rate and Data* provides a guide to the thousands of magazines now available.

Radio suffered at first from TV competition. But now—like some magazines and newspapers—it has become more specialized. Some stations aim at nationality, racial, or religious groups—such as Puerto Ricans, blacks, and Catholics—while others appeal to country, rock, or classical music fans.

Perhaps the most specific medium is **direct-mail advertising**—selling directly to customers via their mailboxes. With this method, a specific message is sent to a carefully selected list of names. Some firms specialize in providing mailing lists—ranging in number from hundreds to millions of names. The variety of these lists (Table 16–3) shows the importance of knowing your target market.

"Must Buys" May Use up Available Money

Selecting which media to use is still pretty much an art. The media buyer may start with a budgeted amount and try to buy the best blend to reach the target audience. There may be some media that are obvious "must buys"—such as *the* local newspaper for a retailer in a small or medium-sized town. Such "must buys" may even use up the available money. If not, then the media buyer must begin to think of the relative advantages and disadvantages of the alternatives. The buyer might want to select a media blend which includes some "expensive" media—like TV—as well as cheaper ones which might reach additional customers.

■ TABLE 16–3   Examples of available mailing lists

Quantity of names	Name of list
425	Small Business Advisors
40,000	Social Register of Canada
5,000	Society of American Bacteriologists
500	South Carolina Engineering Society
2,000	South Dakota State Pharmaceutical Association
250	Southern California Academy of Science
12,000	Texas Manufacturing Executives
720	Trailer Coach Association
1,200	United Community Funds of America
50,000	University of Utah Alumni
19,000	Veterinarians

PLANNING THE "BEST" MESSAGE—WHAT IS TO BE COMMUNICATED

Specifying the Copy Thrust

Once it has been decided *how* the messages are to reach the target audience, then it is necessary to decide on the **copy thrust**—*what* is to be communicated by the written copy and illustrations. This should flow from the promotion objectives—and the specific jobs assigned to advertising.

Carrying out the copy thrust is the job of advertising specialists. But the advertising manager and the marketing manager should have an understanding of the process—to be sure that the job is done well.

Let AIDA Help Guide Message Planning

There are few set rules in message planning. Basically, the overall marketing strategy should determine *what* should be said in the message. Then management judgment—with the help of marketing research—can decide how this message can be encoded so it will be decoded as the advertiser intended.

As a guide to message planning, we can make use of the AIDA concept: getting *Attention,* holding *Interest,* arousing *Desire,* and obtaining *Action.*

Getting attention

Getting attention is the first job of an ad. If this isn't done, it doesn't matter how many people "see" it. Many readers leaf through magazines and newspapers without paying attention to any of the ads. Many listeners or viewers do chores—or get snacks—during commercials on radio and TV.

There are many ways to catch a customer's attention. A large headline, newsy or shocking statements, pictures of pretty girls, babies, cartoon characters—or anything that is "different" or eye-catching—may do the trick. But . . . the attention-getting device must not take away from the next step—holding interest.

An attention-getting picture can help attract readers to an ad.

Holding interest

Holding interest is another matter. A pretty girl may get attention. But once you've seen her, then what? A man may pause to admire her. Women may evaluate her. But if there is no relation between the girl and the product, observers of both sexes will move on.

More is known about holding interest than getting attention. The tone and language of the ad must fit with the experience and attitudes of target customers. A food ad featuring fox hunters in riding coats, for example, might be noted but passed over by many potential customers who don't "ride to the hounds."

The advertising layouts should also look "right" to the customer. Print illustrations and copy should be arranged so that the eye moves smoothly through the ad—i.e., encouraging *gaze motion.*

Arousing desire

Arousing desire for a particular product is one of the most difficult jobs for an ad. The advertiser must communicate with the customer. This means that the advertiser should understand how the target customers think, behave, and make decisions—and then give them a reason to buy. A successful ad must convince customers that the product can meet their needs. Although products may satisfy certain emotional needs, many consumers find it necessary to justify their purchases on an economic or even moral basis. Desire may develop around emotional needs, but economic reasons must also be reinforced.

Telephone directory publishers say that 84 percent of Yellow Pages references are followed by action—a visit, a phone call, or a letter.

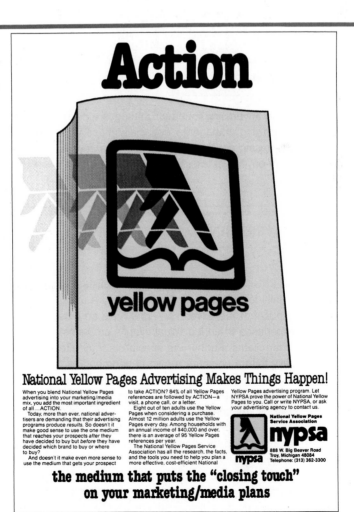

Obtaining action

Getting action is the final requirement—and not an easy one. The potential customers should be encouraged to try the product. They should be led beyond considering how the product *might* fit into their lives—to actually trying it or letting the company's sales rep come in and demonstrate it.

For better communication—strongly felt customer needs might be featured in the ads. Careful research on the attitudes in the target market may help uncover such strongly felt unsatisfied needs.

Appealing to these needs can get more action—and also provide the kind of information the buyers need to confirm their decisions. Doubts may set in after the purchase—so providing reassurance may be one of the important advertising objectives. Some customers seem to read more advertising *after* the purchase than before. What is communicated to them may be very important if satisfied customers are to start—or keep—the web-of-word-of-mouth going. The ad may reassure them about the correctness of their decision—and also supply the words they use to tell others about the product.

ADVERTISING MANAGER DIRECTS MASS SELLING

An advertising manager manages a company's mass selling effort. Many advertising managers—especially those working for retailers—have their own advertising departments that plan the specific advertising campaigns—and carry out the details. Others use advertising agencies.

ADVERTISING AGENCIES OFTEN DO THE WORK

Ad Agencies Are Specialists

Advertising agencies are specialists in planning and handling mass selling details for advertisers. Agencies play a useful role—because they are independent of the advertiser—and have an outside viewpoint. They bring wide experience to an individual client's problems, because they work for many other clients. Further, as specialists they often can do the job more economically than a company's own department.

One of the ad agency's advantages is that the advertiser is free to cancel the arrangement at any time. This provides extreme flexibility for the advertiser. Some companies even use their advertising agency as a scapegoat. Whenever anything goes wrong, it's the agency's fault—and the advertiser shops around for a new one.

Are They Paid Too Much?

The major users of advertising agencies are manufacturers or national middlemen—because of the media rate structure. Normally, media have two prices: one for national advertisers—and a lower rate for local advertisers,

Advertising agencies work with marketing managers to plan ad campaigns.

such as retailers. The advertising agency gets a 15 percent commission on national rates (only). This makes it worthwhile for national advertisers to use agencies. The national advertiser would have to pay the full media rate, anyway. So it makes sense to let the agency experts do the work—and earn their commission. Local retailers—allowed the lower media rate—seldom use agencies.

There is a growing resistance to the traditional method of paying agencies. The chief complaints are (1) that the agencies receive the flat 15 percent commission—regardless of work performed—and (2) that this makes it hard for the agencies to be completely objective about lower cost media—or promotion campaigns that use little space or time.

The fixed commission system is most favored by accounts—such as producers of industrial goods—that need a lot of service but buy relatively little advertising. These are the firms the agencies would like to—and sometimes do—charge additional fees.

The fixed commission system is generally opposed by very large consumer goods advertisers who do much of their own advertising research and planning. They need only basic services from their agencies.

Fifteen percent is not required

The Federal Trade Commission worked for many years to change the way advertising agencies are compensated. Finally, in 1956, the American Association of Advertising Agencies agreed they would no longer require the 15 percent commission system. This opened the way to fee increases and decreases.

Du Pont recently reported that it was paying agencies an average of 21 percent of billings on industrial accounts—and 14 percent on consumer goods accounts. Other companies report very different arrangements with their agencies—but most start from the 15 percent base.[7]

MEASURING ADVERTISING EFFECTIVENESS IS NOT EASY

Success Depends on the Total Marketing Mix

It would be convenient if we could measure the results of advertising just by looking at sales. Unfortunately, we can't—although the advertising literature is filled with success stories that "prove" advertising has increased sales. The total marketing mix—not just promotion—is responsible for the sales result. The one exception to this rule is direct mail advertising. If it doesn't produce immediate results, it's considered a failure.

Research and Testing Can Improve the Odds

Ideally, advertisers should test advertising before it's run—rather than *just* relying on creative people or advertising "experts."

Some progressive advertisers now demand laboratory or market tests to check the effectiveness of ads. Sometimes, opinion and attitude research is used before ads are run generally. And split runs on cable TV are being used to experiment with possible ads.

While advertising research techniques aren't foolproof, they are probably far better than just trusting the judgment of advertising "experts." Until better advertising research tools are developed, the present methods seem safest. This means carefully defining specific advertising objectives, choosing media and messages to accomplish these objectives, testing plans, and then evaluating the results of actual ads.

HOW TO AVOID DECEPTIVE ADVERTISING

FTC Is Getting Tougher about Unfair Practices

The Federal Trade Commission now has the power to control unfair or deceptive business practices—including "deceptive advertising." Both advertising agencies and advertisers must share equal responsibility for false, misleading, or unfair ads. The possibility of large financial penalties and/or the need to pay for new ads—to correct past "mistakes"—has caused more agencies and advertisers to stay well within the law.

The FTC would like to move more aggressively against what it feels are "unfair" practices—since it now finds few outright deceptive ads in national campaigns. For example, some in the FTC feel it is unfair for children to be a target for advertising. The FTC is also concerned about effective energy use. An FTC lawyer recently created a stir by criticizing electric hair dryers. His feeling was "that if you wait 15 minutes, your hair gets dry anyway." There is also concern about whether food and drug advertising should be controlled to protect "vulnerable" groups—such as the aged, poor, non-English-speaking, or less-educated adults. For example, some wonder whether obesity among low-income women might be caused by ads for high-calorie foods.[8]

What Is Unfair or Deceptive Is Changing

What is unfair and deceptive is a difficult topic—which marketing managers have to deal with. Clearly, the social and political environment has changed. Practices that were acceptable some years ago are now questioned—or actually considered deceptive. Saying—or even implying—that your product is "best"—even in fun—is now deceptive, unless you have proof.

This is a serious matter, because if the FTC decides that a particular practice is unfair or deceptive, it has the power to require *affirmative disclosures*—such as the health warnings on cigarettes and diet soft drinks—or **corrective advertising**—ads to correct deceptive advertising. Industry groups have made some efforts at self-regulation. But the offenders usually aren't members of such groups. So the need for some government regulation will probably continue.[9]

In the long run, however, the safest way to avoid "unfair" and "deceptive" criticisms will be to stop trying to advertise the typical "me-too" products as "really new" or "better." Already, some advertising agencies are refusing such jobs.

■ CONCLUSION

It may seem simple to develop a mass selling campaign. Just pick the media and develop a message. But it's not that easy. Effectiveness depends on using the "best" medium and the "best" message—considering: (1) promotion objectives, (2) the target markets, and (3) the money available for advertising.

Specific advertising objectives will determine what kind of advertising to use—product or institutional. If product advertising is needed, then the particular type must be decided—pioneering, competitive (direct or indirect), or reminder. And advertising allowances and cooperative advertising may be helpful.

Many technical details are involved in mass selling. Specialists—advertising agencies—handle some of these jobs. But specific objectives must be set for them—or their advertising may have little direction and be almost impossible to evaluate.

Effective advertising should affect sales. But the whole marketing mix affects sales. The results of advertising can't be measured by sales changes alone. Advertising is only a part of promotion. And promotion is only a part of a total marketing mix that the marketing manager must develop to satisfy target customers.

■ QUESTIONS AND PROBLEMS

1. Identify the strategic decisions a marketing manager must make in the mass selling area.

2. Discuss the relation of advertising objectives to marketing strategy planning and the kinds of advertising actually needed. Illustrate.

3. Present three examples where advertising to middlemen might be necessary. What are the objective(s) of such advertising?

4. What does it mean to say that "money is invested in advertising?" Is all advertising an investment? Illustrate.

5. Find advertisements to final consumers which illustrate the following types of advertising: (a) institutional, (b) pioneering, (c) competitive, (d) reminder. What objective(s) does each of these ads have? List the needs appealed to in each of these advertisements.

6. Describe the type of media which might be most suitable for promoting: (a) tomato soup, (b) greeting cards, (c) an industrial component material, (d) playground equipment. Specify any assumptions necessary to obtain a definite answer.

7. Discuss the use of testimonials in advertising. Which of the four AIDA steps might testimonials accomplish? Are they suitable for all types of products? If not, for which types are they most suitable?

8. Find an advertisement which seeks to accomplish all four AIDA steps—and explain how you feel this advertisement is accomplishing each of these steps.

9. Discuss the future of independent advertising agencies now that the 15 percent commission system is not required.

10. Does mass selling cost too much? How can this be measured?

11. How would retailing promotion be affected if all local advertising via mass media, such as radio, television, and newspapers, were prohibited? Would there be any impact on total sales? If so, would it affect all goods and stores equally?

12. Is it "unfair" to advertise to children? Is it "unfair" to advertise to less-educated or less-experienced people of any age? Is it "unfair" to advertise for "unnecessary" products?

■ SUGGESTED CASES

17. Dewitt National Bank

18. Gray Sports Company

Chapter 17 ■ Pricing objectives and policies

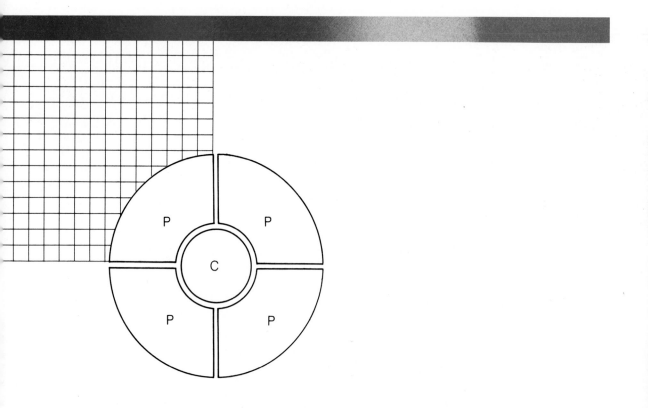

When you finish this chapter, you should:

1. Understand how pricing objectives should guide pricing decisions.

2. Understand choices the marketing manager must make about price flexibility, and price levels over the product life cycle.

3. Understand the legality of price level and price flexibility policies.

4. Understand the many possible variations of a price structure, including discounts, allowances, and who pays transporting costs.

5. Recognize the important new terms (shown in red).

Deciding what price to charge can be agonizing.

Price is one of the four major variables a marketing manager controls. Price decisions affect both sales and profit.

A little example shows how pricing is complicated by different views of cost, benefits (value), and price. A Hollywood starlet rushed into a famous hat designer demanding a new hat—at once—for a party. The designer took a few yards of ribbon, twisted it cleverly, arranged it on her head, and said "There's your hat, madam." The starlet looked in the mirror and said "Marvelous!" The designer bowed and said, "That will be $50." "But," complained the starlet, "that's a lot of money for a couple yards of ribbon." Indignant, the designer unwound the ribbon and handed it to her saying, "Madam, the ribbon is *free.*"

Guided by the company's objectives, marketing managers must develop a set of pricing objectives and policies. These policies should explain: (1) how flexible prices will be, (2) at what level they will be set—over the product life cycle, (3) how transporting costs will be handled, and (4) to whom—and when—discounts and allowances will be given. These strategic pricing decision areas are shown in Figure 17–1.

■ FIGURE 17–1   Strategy planning for Price

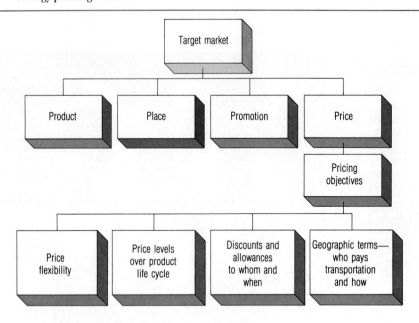

PRICE HAS MANY DIMENSIONS

It's not easy to define price in real-life situations. This is because price has many dimensions. If a catalog offered—at $175—a pair of stereo speakers sold by local retailers for $300—this might look like a real bargain. However, your view of this "deal" might change if you found that the speakers came in a kit for you to assemble—and that there was no warranty because you were assembling the parts. The price might look even less attractive if you learned that you had to pay $35 for insurance and shipping from the factory. Further, how would you feel if you ordered the speakers anyway and then found that delivery takes two months!

The Price Equation: Price Equals Something

This example shows that a price should be related to *some* assortment of goods and/or services. So **Price** is what is charged for "something." *Any business transaction can be thought of as an exchange of money—the money being the Price—for Something.*

The *Something* can be a physical product in various stages of completion, with or without the services usually provided, with or without quality guarantees, and so on. The Something may not include a physical good at all. It may be a play in a theater, a medical check-up, or a taxi ride.

How much is charged for this Something depends on what is included.

■ **FIGURE 17–2**   Price as seen by consumers or users

Price	equals	Something
List price Less: *Discounts* Quantity Seasonal Cash Less: *Allowances:* Trade-ins Damaged goods	equals	*Product* Physical product Service Assurance of quality Repair facilities Packaging Credit Trading stamps or coupons *Place of delivery or availability*

■ **FIGURE 17–3**   Price as seen by channel members

Price	equals	Something
List price Less: *Discounts:* Quantity Seasonal Cash Trade or functional Less: *Allowances:* Damaged goods Advertising Push money	equals	*Product:* Branded—well known Guaranteed Warranted Service—repair facilities Convenient packaging for handling *Place:* Availability—when and where *Price:* Price-level guarantee Sufficient margin to allow chance for profit *Promotion:* Promotion aimed at customers

Some consumers will pay list price—while others will get discounts or allowances because something is not included. The possible variations are shown in Figure 17–2—for consumers or users—and in Figure 17–3—for channel members. We'll discuss some of these variations more fully below—but you can see that Price has many dimensions.

PRICING OBJECTIVES SHOULD GUIDE PRICING

Pricing objectives should flow from company-level objectives. Pricing objectives should be *clearly stated*—because they have a direct effect on pricing policies and on the methods used to set prices.

Possible pricing objectives are shown in Figure 17–4.

■   FIGURE 17-4   Possible pricing objectives

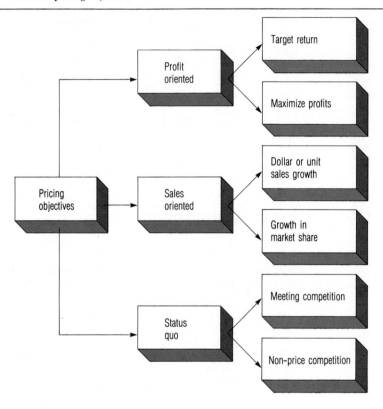

PROFIT-ORIENTED OBJECTIVES

Target Returns Provide Specific Guidelines

A **target return objective** sets a specific level of profit as an objective. Often this amount is stated as a percentage of sales—or of capital investment. For example, a large manufacturer might aim for a 25 percent return on investment—while the target for a grocery chain might be a 1 percent return on sales.

A target return objective has advantages for a large company. Performance can be compared against the target. Some companies will cut out divisions— or drop products—that don't earn the target rate of return on investment.

Some Just Want Satisfactory Profits

Some managers aim for only "satisfactory" returns. They just want to make enough to be sure the firm stays in business—and convince stockholders that they're "doing a good job." Similarly, some small family run businesses aim for a profit that will provide a "comfortable life style."[1]

Companies which are leaders in their industries—like Alcoa, Du Pont, and General Motors—sometimes pursue only "satisfactory" long-run targets. They know that the public—and the government—expect them to follow policies that are "in the public interest" when they play the role of price leader or wage setter. Too large a return might invite government action.[2]

But this kind of situation can lead to decisions which are not in the public interest. A large company afraid of making "too much" profit may not be motivated to keep costs and prices low.

Profit Maximization Can Be Socially Responsible

A **profit maximization objective** seeks to get as much profit as possible. It might be stated as a desire to earn a rapid return on investment. Or—more bluntly—to charge "all the traffic will bear."

Some people believe that anyone seeking a profit maximization objective will charge *high* prices. Economic theory doesn't support this idea. *Profit maximization doesn't always lead to high prices.* Demand and supply *may* bring extremely high prices—if competition can't offer good substitutes. But this happens *if and only if* demand is highly inelastic. The oil producers were able to raise prices because of this. But if demand is very elastic, it can be in a monopolist's interest to charge relatively low prices—so sales will increase. When prices for electronic calculators were very high, few people bought them. When prices dropped, nearly everyone bought calculators. Contrary to popular belief, a profit maximization objective can be socially desirable.

SALES—ORIENTED OBJECTIVES

A **sales-oriented objective** seeks some level of unit sales, dollar sales, or share of market—without referring to profit.

Sales Growth Doesn't Mean Big Profits

Some managers are more concerned with sales growth than profits.[3] They think sales growth always leads to big profits. This kind of thinking causes problems when a firm's costs are growing faster than sales—or when managers don't keep track of their costs. Recently, some major corporations have faced declining profits even though their sales were growing. More attention is now being paid to profits—not just sales.

Market share objectives are popular

Many firms seek a specific share (percent) of a market. One advantage of a market share objective is that it forces a manager to pay attention to what competitors are doing in the market. Also, it's easier to measure a firm's market share than to determine if profits are being maximized. Large consumer package goods firms—such as Procter & Gamble, Coca-Cola, and General Foods—often use market share objectives.

Aggressive companies often aim to increase market share—or even to control a market. In some businesses, economies of scale encourage a firm to seek increased market share—and probably greater profits.

Cutting prices to sell more units may reduce profits.

Sometimes, however, firms blindly follow market growth objectives—setting low prices to get more of the market. This can lead to profitless "success."

Remember: *larger sales volume, by itself, doesn't necessarily lead to higher profits.*

STATUS QUO PRICING OBJECTIVES

Don't-Rock-the-Boat Objectives

Managers who are satisfied with their current situation and want to reduce risk sometimes adopt status quo objectives—"don't-rock-the-*pricing*-boat" objectives. They may be stated as "stabilizing prices," "meeting competition," or "avoiding competition." Maintaining stable prices may discourage price competition—and avoid the need for hard decisions. The managers may have more time for golf!

Or Stress Non-Price Competition Instead

On the other hand, a status quo *pricing objective* can be part of an aggressive marketing strategy focusing on non-price competition—aggressive action on one or more of the Ps other than Price. Fast-food chains like McDonald's and Hardee's prefer non-price competition.

MOST FIRMS SET SPECIFIC PRICING POLICIES—TO REACH OBJECTIVES

Specific pricing policies are important for any firm. Otherwise, the marketing manager has to rethink his strategy every time a customer asks for a price.

Some channel members don't charge the suggested list price.

If you paid full price you didn't buy it at CROWN ♛ BOOKS

Administered Prices Help Achieve Objectives

Price policies usually lead to **administered prices**—consciously set prices. In other words, instead of letting daily market forces decide their prices, most firms set their own prices.

Some firms do their pricing without much thought—just "meeting competition." They act as if they have no choice. Managers *do* have many choices. They *should* administer their prices. And they should consider price setting carefully. If customers won't pay the price set—the whole marketing mix fails. In the rest of this chapter, we'll talk about policies a marketing manager must set to do an effective job of administering Price.

PRICE FLEXIBILITY POLICIES

One of the first decisions a marketing manager has to make is about price flexibility. Should he have a one-price—or a flexible-price—policy?

One-Price Policy— The Same Price for Everyone

A **one-price policy** means offering the *same price to all customers* who purchase goods under the same basic conditions—and in the same quantities. Most U.S. firms use a one-price policy. This is mainly for convenience—and to maintain goodwill among customers.

A one-price policy makes pricing easier. But a marketing manager must be careful to avoid a rigid one-price policy. This can amount to broadcasting a price which competitors can undercut—especially if the price is high. One reason for the growth of discount houses is that conventional retailers used traditional margins—and stuck to them.

Flexible-Price Policy— Different Prices for Different Customers

A **flexible-price policy** means offering the same product and quantities to different customers at different prices.

Flexible pricing was more common when businesses were small—products weren't standardized—and most customers expected to bargain for a price. These conditions still exist in many foreign countries.

Flexible pricing is most common in the channels, in direct sales of industrial goods, and at retail for more expensive items. The advantage of flexible pricing is that the sales rep can make adjustments for market conditions—instead of having to turn down an order.[4]

Flexible pricing has disadvantages, however. Customers are unhappy if they find that others are getting lower prices. And if customers know that prices are flexible, they may want to bargain. The cost of selling may rise—as buyers become aware that bargaining could save them money. Also, some sales reps let price cutting become a habit. This could make price useless as a competitive tool—and lead to a lower price level.

PRICE LEVEL POLICIES—OVER THE PRODUCT LIFE CYCLE

When marketing managers administer prices—as most do—they must decide on a price level policy. They must decide if their prices should be above the market, at the same level as competition, or below the market price.

The product life cycle should be considered when the original price level for a new product is set. The price will affect how fast the product moves through the cycle. A high price, for example, may lead to attractive profits—but also to competition and a faster cycle. With this in mind, should the firm's original price be a skimming—or a penetration price?

Skimming Pricing— Feeling out Demand at a High Price

A **skimming price policy** tries to sell the top ("skim the cream") of a market—the top of the demand curve—at a high price before aiming at more price-sensitive customers.

When Polaroid first introduced its "instant picture" camera, it set a high price. This high-priced camera was sold mainly to professional photographers and serious amateurs—at camera stores. Soon Polaroid introduced other models with fewer features. These sold at lower prices—to different market segments. Finally, before its patents ran out, Polaroid introduced a low-cost camera—sold through department, drug, and discount stores.

Skimming is useful for getting a better understanding of the shape of the demand curve. It's easier to start with a high price and lower it—than to start with a low price and then try to raise it.

Penetration Pricing— Get Volume at a Low Price

A **penetration pricing policy** tries to sell the whole market at one low price. This approach might be used where there is no "elite" market—where the whole demand curve is fairly elastic.

A penetration policy is more attractive if selling larger quantities lowers costs—because of economies of scale. And it may be a good idea if the firm expects strong competition *very* soon after introduction. A *low* penetration price is a "stay out" price. It discourages competitors from entering the market.

Price-off promotions are a way of lowering prices—temporarily.

Introductory Price Dealing—Temporary Price Cuts

Price cuts do attract customers. Therefore, marketers often use **introductory price dealing**—temporary price cuts—to speed new products into a market. These *temporary* price cuts should not be confused with low penetration prices, however. The plan here is to raise prices as soon as the introductory offer is over.

Established competitors often choose not to meet introductory price dealing—as long as the introductory period is not too long or too successful.[5]

"Meeting Competition" May Be Wise Sometimes

Regardless of their introductory pricing policy, most firms face competition sooner or later in the product life cycle. When that happens, how high or low a price is may be relative not only to the market demand curve, but also to the prices charged by competitors.

The nature of competition will usually affect whether prices are set below, at, or above competition. The clearest case is in pure competition. The decision is really made by the market. To set a price above or below the market price is foolish.

Similarly, there is little choice in oligopoly situations. Pricing "at the market"—that is, meeting competition—may be the only sensible policy. To raise prices might lead to a big loss in sales. And cutting prices would probably cause competitors to cut prices, too. This can only lead to a drop in total revenue for the industry—and probably for each firm. Therefore, a meeting-competition policy makes sense for each firm. And price stability often develops—without any price fixing in the industry.

Is It Above or Below the Market?

Some firms emphasize "below-the-market" prices in their marketing mixes. Prices offered by discounters and mass-merchandisers—such as K mart—are below the prices charged by conventional retailers. At the other extreme, some firms price "above-the-market"—they may even brag about it. Tiffany's is well known as one of the most expensive jewelry stores in the world. Curtis Mathes advertises that it makes "the most expensive TV you can buy."

The question is: Do these various strategies contain prices which are "above" or "below" the market—or are they really different prices *for different*

"Low prices" may really be different prices for different market segments.

market segments? Perhaps *some* target customers *do* see important differences in the physical product or the whole marketing mix. Then what we are talking about is different marketing strategies—not just different price levels.

K mart may have lower TV prices than conventional television retailers, but it offers less help in the store. K mart may be appealing to budget-oriented shoppers who are comparing prices among different mass-merchandisers. If so, we should think of K mart's price as part of a different marketing mix for a different target market—not as a "below-the-conventional-retailers'-market" price.[6]

MOST PRICES ARE BUILT AROUND LIST PRICES

Prices Start with a List Price

Most prices are built around list prices. **Basic list prices** are the prices that final customers or users are normally asked to pay for products. Unless noted otherwise, "list price" refers to "basic list price" in this book.

How these list prices are set is discussed in the next chapter. Now, however, we will consider when adjustments are made to list price.

DISCOUNT POLICIES—REDUCTIONS FROM LIST PRICES

Discounts are reductions from list price that are given by a seller to a buyer who either gives up some marketing function or provides the function himself. Discounts can be useful in marketing strategy planning. In the following discussion, think about what function the buyers are giving up—or providing—when they get each of these discounts.

Quantity Discounts Encourage Volume Buying

Quantity discounts are discounts offered to encourage customers to buy in larger amounts. This lets a seller get more of a buyer's business, shifts some of the storing function to the buyer, reduces shipping and selling costs—or all of these. These discounts are of two kinds: cumulative and non-cumulative.

Cumulative quantity discounts apply to purchases over a given period— such as a year. The discount usually increases as the amount purchased increases. Cumulative discounts are intended to encourage buying from one company—by reducing the price for additional purchases.

Non-cumulative quantity discounts apply only to *individual orders.* Such

Non-cumulative quantity discounts encourage buyers to purchase in larger quantities—which in this case are more economical for the printer.

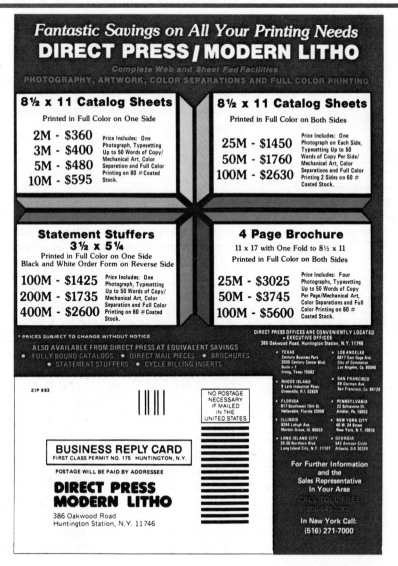

discounts encourage larger orders but don't tie a buyer to the seller after that one purchase.

Quantity discounts may be based on the dollar value of the entire order, or on the number of units purchased, or on the size of the package purchased. While quantity discounts are usually given as price cuts, sometimes they are given as "free" or "bonus" goods.

Quantity discounts can be a very useful tool for the marketing manager. Some customers are eager to get them. But marketing managers must use quantity discounts carefully—offering them to all customers on equal terms—to avoid price discrimination.

Seasonal Discounts—Buy Sooner and Store

Seasonal discounts are discounts offered to encourage buyers to stock earlier than present demand requires. If used by producers, this discount tends to shift the storing function further along in the channel. It also tends to even out sales over the year—permitting year-round operation. If seasonal discounts are large, channel members may pass them along to their customers. For example, a manufacturer of lawnmowers might offer its wholesalers a seasonal discount in the fall—when the lawnmower market is slow. The wholesalers can then offer a discount to retailers—who may then sell the mowers during a special "fall sale."

Payment Terms and Cash Discounts Set Payment Dates

Most sales to channel members and other intermediate customers are made on credit. The seller sends a bill (invoice)—and the buyer sends it through for payment. Many channel members depend on other channel members for temporary working capital (credit). Therefore, it's very important for both sides to clearly state the terms of payment—including the availability of cash discounts. The following terms of payment are commonly used.

Net means that payment for the face value of the invoice is due immediately. These terms are sometimes changed to "net 10" or "net 30"—which means payment is due within 10 or 30 days of the date on the invoice.

2/10, net 30 means that a 2 percent discount off the face value of the invoice is allowed if the invoice is paid within 10 days. Otherwise, the full face value is due within 30 days. And it usually is understood that an interest charge will be made after the 30-day free credit period.

Why cash discounts are given and should be taken

Cash discounts are reductions in the price to encourage buyers to pay their bills quickly. Smart buyers take advantage of them. A discount of 2/10, net 30 may not look like very much, but any company that passes it up is missing a good chance to save money. In this case, a 2 percent discount would be earned just for paying 20 days before the full amount is due anyway. This would amount to an annual interest rate of about 36 percent. The company would be better off to borrow at a bank—if necessary—to pay such invoices by the earlier date.

An invoice shows the terms of a sale.

SERVCO, INC.		INVOICE NO.		**4238**
SERVCO, INC.		ORDER NO. 179642	INVOICE DATE 1/8/85	
1475 LAKE LANSING ROAD		DATE SHIPPED 1/30/85	SHIPPED VIA Truck	
LANSING, MI 48912		NO. PCS. 5	WT. 300	FOB Lansing, MI	TERMS Net 30

SOLD TO	SHIPPED TO
Jones Supply Co.	Jones Supply Co.
220 Commercial Ave.	623 Kensington
South Gate, CA 94087	Portland, OR 90722

QUANTITY	UNIT	DESCRIPTION	UNIT PRICE	TOTAL PRICE
200	263-A	Smoke alarms	12.00	2400.00
		Thank You.		

While the marketing manager can often use the cash discount as a marketing variable, a specific cash discount may be so firmly set in his industry that he can't change it. He must give the usual terms—even if he has no need for cash. Purchasing agents are well aware of the value of cash discounts and will insist that the marketing manager offer the same terms offered by competitors. In fact, some buyers automatically deduct the accepted cash discount from their invoices—regardless of the seller's invoice terms.

Trade Discounts Often Are Set by Tradition

A **trade (functional) discount** is a list price reduction given to channel members for the job they are going to do.

A manufacturer, for example, might allow retailers a 30 percent trade discount from the suggested retail list price—to cover the cost of the retailing function and their profit. Similarly, the manufacturer might allow wholesalers a chain discount of 30 percent and 10 percent off the suggested retail price. In this case, the wholesalers would be expected to pass the 30 percent discount on to retailers.

Trade discounts might seem to offer a manufacturer's or wholesaler's marketing manager great flexibility in varying a marketing mix. In fact, they may limit him greatly. The customary trade discount can be so well established that a manager has to accept it when setting prices.

ALLOWANCE POLICIES—OFF LIST PRICES

Allowances—like discounts—are given to final consumers, customers, or channel members for doing "something" or accepting less of "something."

Bring in the Old, Ring up the New— With Trade-Ins

A **trade-in allowance** is a price reduction given for used goods when similar new goods are bought.

Trade-ins give the marketing manager an easy way to lower the price without reducing list price. Proper handling of trade-ins is important when selling durable goods. Customers buying machinery or buildings, for example, buy long-term satisfaction—in terms of more manufacturing capacity. If the list price less the trade-in allowance doesn't offer greater satisfaction—as the customer sees it—then no sales will be made.

Many firms replace machinery slowly—perhaps too slowly—because they value their old equipment above market value. This also applies to cars. Customers want higher trade-ins for their old cars than the current market value. This encourages the use of high, perhaps "phony," list prices so that high trade-in allowances can be given.

Advertising Allowances—Something for Something

Advertising allowances are price reductions given to firms in the channel to encourage them to advertise or otherwise promote the supplier's products locally. General Electric gave an allowance (1.5 percent of sales) to its wholesalers of housewares and radios. They, in turn, were expected to provide something—in this case, local advertising.

PMs—Push for Cash

Push money (or prize money) allowances—are given to retailers by manufacturers or wholesalers to pass on to the retailers' salespeople—for aggressively selling certain items. PM allowances are used for new merchandise, slower-moving items, or higher-margin items. They are especially common in the furniture and clothing industries. A salesperson, for example, might earn an additional $5 for each of a new-type mattress sold.

SOME CUSTOMERS GET EXTRA SOMETHINGS

Trading Stamps— Something for Nothing?

Trading stamps are free stamps (such as "Green Stamps") given by some retailers with each purchase.

Retailers buy trading stamps from trading-stamp companies—or set up their own plans. In either case, customers trade the stamps for merchandise premiums or cash.

Some retailers offer trading stamps to their customers to try to get a "competitive advantage." Some customers think they are getting something for nothing. And sometimes they are—if the retailer doesn't pass the cost of the stamps (2 to 3 percent of sales) along to customers. This can occur when lower promotion costs—or a large increase in sales—make up for the cost of the stamps.

There was much interest in trading stamps in the 1950s and 60s. The early users of stamps in a community seemed to gain a competitive advantage. But this soon disappeared as competitors started offering stamps. Now their use has declined—especially in grocery retailing.

Clipping Coupons Brings Other Extras

Many manufacturers and retailers offer discounts—or free items—through the use of coupons distributed in packages, mailings, newspapers ads—or at the store. By presenting a coupon to a retailer, the consumer is given "10 cents off" the product. This is especially common in the grocery business. Coupons have become so popular that special firms have been set up to help repay retailers for redeeming manufacturers' coupons.[7]

LIST PRICE MAY DEPEND ON GEOGRAPHIC PRICING POLICIES

Retail list prices often include free delivery—because the cost may be small. But producers and middlemen must take the matter of who pays for transporting seriously. Much money may be involved. Usually, purchase orders spell out these matters—because transporting costs might be as much as half of the delivered cost of goods! There are many possible variations open to a creative marketing manager. Some special terms have developed. A few are discussed in the following paragraphs.

F.O.B. Pricing Is Easy

A commonly used transporting term is F.O.B.—which means "free on board" some vehicle at some place. Typically, it is used with the place named—often the location of the seller's factory or warehouse—as in "F.O.B. Detroit" or "F.O.B. mill." This means that the seller pays the cost of loading the goods onto some vehicle—usually a truck, railroad car, or ship. At the point of loading, title to the goods passes to the buyer. Then the buyer pays the freight and takes responsibility for damage in transit—except as covered by the transporting company.

Variations are made easily—by changing the place part of the term. If the marketing manager wants to pay the freight—for the convenience of custom-ers—he can use: "F.O.B. delivered" or "F.O.B. buyer's factory" (or ware-house). In this case, title does not pass until the goods are delivered. If the seller wants title to pass immediately—but is willing to pay the freight (and then include it in the invoice)—he can use "F.O.B. seller's factory–freight pre-paid."

F.O.B. "shipping point" pricing simplifies the seller's pricing—but it may narrow the market. Since the delivered cost of goods varies depending on the buyer's location, a customer located farther from the seller must pay more—and might buy from closer suppliers.

Different geographic pricing policies may be needed to expand into new territories.

Zone Pricing Smoothes Delivered Prices

Zone pricing means making an average freight charge to all buyers within specific geographic areas. The seller pays the actual freight charges and bills each customer for an average charge. A company might divide the United States into seven zones, for example. All customers in the same zone pay the same amount for freight.

Zone pricing reduces the wide variation in delivered prices which results from an F.O.B. shipping point pricing policy. It also simplifies charging for transporting.

This approach often is used by manufacturers of hardware and food items—both to lower the chance of price competition in the channels and to simplify figuring transporting charges for the thousands of wholesalers and retailers they serve.

Uniform Delivered Pricing—One Price to All

Uniform delivered pricing means making an average freight charge to all buyers. It is like zone pricing. The whole market is considered as one zone—and the average cost of delivery is included in the price. It is most often used when (1) transporting costs are relatively low and (2) the seller wishes to sell in all geographic areas at one price—perhaps a nationally advertised price.

Freight-Absorption Pricing—Competing on Equal Grounds in Another Territory

When all firms in an industry use F.O.B. shipping point pricing, a firm usually does well near its shipping point—but not farther away. As sales reps look for business farther away, delivered prices rise. The firm finds itself priced out of the market.

This problem can be reduced with **freight absorption pricing**—which means absorbing freight cost so that a firm's delivered price meets the nearest competitor's. This amounts to cutting list price to appeal to new market segments.

With freight absorption pricing, the only limit on the size of a firm's territory is the amount of freight cost it is willing to absorb. These absorbed costs cut net return on each sale, but the new business may raise total profit.

LEGALITY OF PRICING POLICIES

Generally speaking, companies can charge any price they wish for their products. Governments do put some restrictions on pricing, however.

Unfair Trade Practice Acts Control Some Minimum Prices

Unfair trade practice acts put a lower limit on prices, especially at the wholesale and retail levels. They have been passed in more than half the states. Selling below cost in these states is illegal. Wholesalers and retailers are usually required to take a certain minimum percentage markup over their merchandise-plus-transportation costs. The most common markup figures are 6 percent at retail and 2 percent at wholesale.

Most retailers know enough about their costs to set markups larger than these minimums. The practical effect of these laws is to protect certain limited-line food retailers—such as dairy stores—from the kind of "ruinous" competition that full-line stores might offer if they sold milk as a "leader"—offering it below cost—for a long time.

Even Very High Prices Are OK—If You Don't Lie

A firm can charge high prices—even "outrageously high" prices—as long as they aren't fixed with competitors. Also, a firm can't lie about prices.

Phony list prices are prices that customers are shown to suggest that the price they are to pay has been discounted from "list." Some customers seem more interested in the supposed discount than in the actual price. Most businesses, Better Business Bureaus, and government agencies consider the use of phony list prices unethical. And the FTC tries to stop such pricing—using the **Wheeler Lea Amendment**—which bans "unfair or deceptive acts in commerce."[8]

Price Fixing Is Illegal—You Can Go to Jail

Difficulties with pricing—and violations of price legislation—usually occur when competing marketing mixes are quite similar. When the success of an entire marketing strategy depends on price, there is pressure (and temptation) to make agreements with competitors (conspire). And **price fixing**—competitors getting together to raise, lower, or stabilize prices—is common and relatively easy. *But it is also completely illegal.* It is "conspiracy" under the Sherman Act and the Federal Trade Commission Act. To discourage price fixing, both companies and individual managers are held responsible. Some executives have already gone to jail! And governments are getting tougher on price fixing.[9]

Antimonopoly Legislation Bans Price Discrimination Unless . . .

Price level and price flexibility policies can lead to price discrimination. The **Robinson-Patman Act** (of 1936) makes illegal any **price discrimination**— selling the same products to different buyers at different prices—which injures competition. This law does permit some price differences—but they must be based on (1) cost differences or (2) the need to meet competition. Both buyers and sellers are guilty if they know they are entering into discriminatory agreements. This is a serious matter—and price discrimination suits are common.

What Does "Like Grade and Quality" Mean?

The Robinson-Patman Act lets a marketing manager charge different prices for *similar* products if they are *not* of "like grade and quality." But how similar can they be? The FTC position is that if the physical characteristics of a product are similar, then they are of like grade and quality. The FTC's view was upheld in a 1966 U.S. Supreme Court ruling against the Borden Company. The Court held that a well-known label *alone* does not make a product different from the one with an unknown label. The issue was rather clear-cut in the Borden case. The company agreed that the physical characteristics of the canned milk it sold at different prices under different labels were basically the same.

The FTC's "victory" in the *Borden* case was not complete, however. Although the U.S. Supreme Court agreed with the FTC in the *Borden* case—with respect to like grade and quality—it sent the case back to the U.S. Court of Appeals to determine whether the price difference actually injured competition—which is also required by the law. In 1967, this court found no evidence of injury and further noted that there could be no injury unless Borden's price difference was more than the "recognized consumer appeal of the Borden label." How "consumer appeal" is to be measured was not spelled out—and may lead to more court cases.[10]

Eventually, what the consumer thinks about the product may be the deciding factor. For now, however, it's safer for producers who want to sell several brands at lower prices than their main brand to offer physical differences—and differences that are really useful, not just decorative.[11]

Can Cost Analysis Justify Price Differences?

The Robinson-Patman Act allows price differences if there are cost differences—perhaps for larger quantity shipments.

Justifying cost differences is difficult. Costs usually must be charged to several products—perhaps using logical assumptions. It's easy—then—for the FTC to raise objections to whatever method is used. And such objections are often raised—because the FTC is concerned about the impact of price differences on competition—and especially on small competitors.[12]

Can You Legally Meet Price Cuts?

Meeting competition is permitted as a defense in price discrimination cases—although the FTC normally has taken a negative view of this argument.

A major aim of antimonopoly legislation is to protect competition—not competitors—and "meeting competition" in "good faith" still seems to be legal.

Special Promotion Allowances Might Not Be Allowed

Some firms have violated the Robinson-Patman Act by providing PMs (push money), demonstrations, advertising allowances, or other promotion allowances to some customers and not others. The act bans such allowances—*unless they are made available to all customers on "proportionately equal" terms.* No proof of injury to competition is necessary. The FTC has been fairly successful in prosecuting such cases.

The need for such a rule is clear—once price regulation begins. Allowances for promotion could be granted to retailers or wholesalers without expecting

A retail chain may get a special functional discount.

that any promotion would be done. This plainly is price discrimination in disguise.

The law does cause hardships, however. It is hard to provide allowances on "proportionately equal" terms to both large and small customers. The Robinson-Patman Act does not say clearly whether a small store should be allowed the same dollar allowance as a large one or in proportion to sales. But the latter probably would not buy the same promotion impact.

It may also be difficult to decide which customers are competitors. The FTC might define competitors much more broadly than either the seller or the competing buyers. Supermarket operators might only be concerned about other supermarkets and the food discounters. But the FTC might feel small drug stores were also competitors for health and beauty aids.[13]

How to Avoid Discriminating

Because the price discrimination laws are complicated—and penalties heavy—many business managers play down price as a marketing variable. They have decided that it is safer to offer the same cost-based prices to *all* customers.

■ CONCLUSION

The Price variable offers an alert marketing manager many possibilities for varying marketing mixes. What pricing policies should be used depends on the pricing objectives. We looked at profit-oriented, sales-oriented, and status quo-oriented objectives.

A marketing manager must set policies about price flexibility, price levels over the product life cycle, who will pay the transporting costs, and who will get discounts and allowances. The

manager also should be aware of pricing legislation affecting these policies.

In most cases, a marketing manager must set prices—that is, administer prices. Starting with a list price, a variety of discounts and allowances may be offered to adjust for the "Something" being offered in the marketing mix.

Throughout this chapter, we have assumed that a list price has already been set. We have talked about what may be included (or excluded) in the "Something"—and what objectives a firm might set to guide its pricing policies. Price setting itself was not discussed. It will be covered in the next chapter—showing ways of carrying out the various pricing objectives and policies.

■ QUESTIONS AND PROBLEMS

1. Identify the strategic decisions a marketing manager must make in the Price area. Illustrate your answer for a local retailer.

2. How should the acceptance of a profit-oriented, a sales-oriented, or a status quo-oriented pricing objective affect the development of a company's marketing strategy? Illustrate for each.

3. Distinguish between one-price and flexible-price policies. Which is most appropriate for a supermarket? Why?

4. Cite two examples of continuously selling above the market price. Describe the situations.

5. Explain the types of competitive situations which might lead to a "meeting competition" pricing policy.

6. What pricing objective(s) is a skimming pricing policy most likely implementing? Is the same true for a penetration pricing policy? Which policy is probably most appropriate for each of the following products: (a) a new type of home lawn-sprinkling system, (b) a new low-cost meat substitute, (c) a new type of children's toy, (d) a faster computer?

7. Discuss unfair trade practices acts. To whom are they "unfair"?

8. Is price discrimination involved if a large oil company sells gasoline to taxicab associations for resale to individual taxicab operators for 2½ cents a gallon less than the price charged to retail service stations? What happens if the cab associations resell gasoline not only to taxicab operators, but to the general public as well?

9. Indicate what the final consumer really obtains when paying the list price for the following "products": (a) an automobile, (b) a radio, (c) a package of frozen peas, and (d) a lipstick in a jeweled case.

10. Are seasonal discounts appropriate in agricultural businesses (which are certainly seasonal)?

11. Explain how a marketing manager might change his F.O.B. terms to make his otherwise competitive marketing mix more attractive.

12. What type of geographic pricing policy is most appropriate for the following products (specify any assumptions necessary to obtain a definite answer): (a) a chemical by-product, (b) nationally advertised candy bars, (c) rebuilt auto parts, (d) tricycles?

13. Explain how the prohibition of freight absorption (that is, requiring F.O.B factory pricing) might affect a producer with substantial economies of scale in production.

■ **SUGGESTED CASES**

23. Speedy Photo Company

24. Westco Machinery Company

Appendix B ■ Marketing arithmetic

When you finish this appendix, you should:

1. Understand the components of an operating statement (profit and loss statement).

2. Know how to compute the stockturn rate.

3. Understand how operating ratios can help analyze a business.

4. Understand how to calculate markups and markdowns.

5. Understand how to calculate return on investment (ROI) and return on assets (ROA).

6. Recognize the important new terms (shown in red).

Business students must become familiar with the essentials of the "language of business." Business people commonly use accounting terms when talking about costs, prices, and profit. So you need to understand these terms. Using accounting data is a practical tool in analyzing marketing problems.

The following discussion introduces the basic ideas underlying the operating statement, some commonly used ratios related to the operating statement, markups, the markdown ratio, and ROI and ROA ratios. Other analytical techniques are discussed in various parts of the text—and are not treated separately here.

THE OPERATING STATEMENT

An operating statement for a wholesale or retail business—commonly referred to as a profit and loss statement—is presented in Figure B–1. A complete and detailed statement is shown so you will see the framework

■ FIGURE B–1   An operating statement (profit and loss statement)

XYZ COMPANY
Operating Statement
For the Year Ended December 31, 198X

Gross sales			$54,000
Less: Returns and allowances			4,000
Net sales			$50,000
Cost of goods sold:			
Beginning inventory at cost		$ 8,000	
Purchases at billed cost	$31,000		
Less: Purchase discounts	4,000		
Purchases at net cost	27,000		
Plus freight-in	2,000		
Net cost of delivered purchases		29,000	
Cost of goods available for sale		37,000	
Less: Ending inventory at cost		7,000	
Cost of goods sold			30,000
Gross margin (gross profit)			20,000
Expenses:			
Selling expenses:			
Sales salaries	6,000		
Advertising expense	2,000		
Delivery expense	2,000		
Total selling expense		10,000	
Administrative expense:			
Office salaries	3,000		
Office supplies	1,000		
Miscellaneous administrative expense	500		
Total administrative expense		4,500	
General expense:			
Rent expense	1,000		
Miscellaneous general expenses	500		
Total general expense		1,500	
Total expenses			16,000
Net profit from operation			$ 4,000

throughout the discussion—but the amount of detail on an operating statement is not standardized. Many companies use financial statements with much less detail than this one. Their emphasis is on clarity and readability—rather than detail. To understand an operating statement, however, you must know about its parts.

The **operating statement** is a simple summary of the financial results of the operations of a company over a specified period of time. Some beginning students may feel that the operating statement is complex—but as we shall see, this really isn't true. *The main purpose of the operating statement is determining the net profit figure—and presenting data to support that figure.*

Only Three Basic Components

The basic components of an operating statement are *sales*—which come from the sale of goods or services; *costs*—which come from the making and selling process; and the balance—called *profit or loss*—which is just the difference between sales and costs. So there are only three basic components in the statement: *sales, costs,* and *profit (or loss).*

Time Period Covered May Vary

There is no one time period which an operating statement covers. Rather, statements are prepared to satisfy the needs of a particular business. This may be at the end of each day—or at the end of each week. Usually, however, an operating statement summarizes results for one month, three months, six months, or a full year. Since the time period does vary, this information is included in the heading of the statement as follows:

XYZ COMPANY
Operating Statement
For the (Period) Ended (Date)

Also, see Figure B–1.

Management Uses of Operating Statements

Before going on to a more detailed discussion of the components of our operating statement, let's think about some of the uses for such a statement. A glance at Figure B–1 shows that a lot of information is presented in a clear and concise manner. With this information, a manager can easily find the relation of net sales to the cost of goods sold, the gross margin, expenses, and net profit. Opening and closing inventory figures are available—as is the amount spent during the period for the purchase of goods for resale. The total expenses are listed to make it easier to compare them with previous statements—and to help control these expenses.

All of this information is important to the managers of a company. Assume that a particular company prepares monthly operating statements. Obviously, a series of these statements is a valuable tool for directing and controlling the business. By comparing results from one month to the next, managers can uncover unfavorable trends in the sales, expense, or profit areas of the business—and take the needed action.

A Skeleton Statement Gets Down to Essential Details

Let's refer to Figure B–1 and begin to analyze this seemingly detailed statement. The intention at this point is to get first-hand knowledge of the components of the operating statement.

As a first step, suppose we take all the items that have dollar amounts extended to the third, or right-hand, column. Using these items only, the operating statement looks like this:

Gross sales	$54,000
Less: Returns and allowances	4,000
Net sales	$50,000
Less: Cost of goods sold	30,000
Gross margin	$20,000
Less: Total expenses	16,000
Net profit (loss)	$ 4,000

Is this a complete operating statement? The answer is yes. This skeleton statement differs from Figure B–1 only in supporting detail. All the basic components are included. In fact, the only items we *must* list to have a *complete* operating statement are:

Net sales $50,000
    Less: Costs   46,000
Net profit (loss) . . . . $ 4,000

These three items are the *essentials* of an operating statement. All other subdivisions or details are just useful additions.

Meaning of "Sales"

Now let's define the meaning of the terms in the skeleton statement.

The first item is "sales." What do we mean by sales? The term **gross sales** is the total amount charged to all customers during some time period. It is certain, however, that there will be some customer dissatisfaction—or just plain errors in ordering and shipping goods. This results in returns and allowances—which reduce gross sales.

A **return** occurs when a customer sends back purchased products. The company either refunds the purchase price or allows the customer dollar credit on other purchases.

An **allowance** occurs when a customer is not satisfied with a purchase for some reason. The company gives a price reduction on the original invoice (bill), but the customer keeps the goods.

These refunds and price reductions must be considered when the net sales figure for the period is computed. Really, we are only interested in the revenue which the company manages to keep. This is **net sales**—the actual sales dollars the company will receive. Therefore, all reductions, refunds, cancellations, and so forth—made because of returns and allowances—are deducted from the original total (gross sales) to get net sales. This is shown below:

Gross sales $54,000
    Less: Returns and allowances . .   4,000
Net sales $50,000

Meaning of "Cost of Goods Sold"

The next item in the operating statement—**cost of goods sold**—is the total value (at cost) of all the goods sold during the period. We will discuss this computation later. Meanwhile, note that after the cost of goods sold figure is obtained, it is subtracted from the net sales figure to get the gross margin.

Meaning of "Gross Margin" and "Expenses"

Gross margin (gross profit) is the money left to cover the cost of selling the products and managing the business. The hope is that a profit will be left after subtracting these expenses.

Selling expense commonly is the major expense below the gross margin. Note that in Figure B–1, **expenses** are all the remaining costs which are subtracted from the gross margin to get the net profit. The expenses in this case are the selling, administrative, and general expenses. (Note that the cost of purchases and cost of goods sold are not included in this total expense figure—they were subtracted from net sales earlier to get the gross margin.)

Net profit—at the bottom of the statement—is what the company has earned from its operations during a particular period. It is the amount left after the cost of goods sold and the expenses have been subtracted from net sales. Note: *Net sales and net profit are not the same.* Many firms have large sales and no profits—they may even have losses!

DETAILED ANALYSIS OF SECTIONS OF THE OPERATING STATEMENT

Cost of Goods Sold for a Wholesale or Retail Company

The cost of goods sold section includes details which are used to find the "cost of goods sold" ($30,000 in our example).

In Figure B–1, it is obvious that beginning and ending inventory, purchases, purchase discounts, and freight-in are all necessary in calculating costs of goods sold. If we pull the cost of goods sold section from the operating statement, it looks like this:

Cost of goods sold

Beginning inventory at cost		$ 8,000
Purchases at billed cost	$31,000	
Less: Purchase discounts	4,000	
Purchases at net cost.	$27,000	
Plus: Freight-in	2,000	
Net cost of delivered purchases . . .	29,000	
Cost of goods available for sale. . .	$37,000	
Less: Ending inventory at cost . .	7,000	
Cost of goods sold		$30,000

"Cost of goods sold" is the cost value of goods *sold*—that is, actually removed from the company's control—and not the cost value of goods on hand at any given time.

The inventory figures merely show the cost of merchandise on hand at the beginning and end of the period the statement covers. These figures may be obtained by a physical count of the merchandise on hand on these dates—or they may be estimated through a system of perpetual inventory bookkeeping which shows the inventory balance at any given time. The methods used in determining the inventory should be as accurate as possible—since these figures affect the cost of goods sold during the period, and net profit.

The net cost of delivered purchases must include freight charges and purchase discounts received—since these items affect the money actually spent to buy goods and bring them to the place of business. A **purchase discount** is a reduction of the original invoice amount for some business reason. For example, a cash discount may be given for prompt payment of the amount due. The total of such discounts is subtracted from the original invoice cost of purchases to get the *net* cost of purchases. To this figure we add the freight charges for bringing the goods to the place of business. This gives the net cost of *delivered* purchases. When the net cost of delivered purchases is added to the beginning inventory at cost, we have the total cost of goods available for sale during the period. If we now subtract the ending inventory at cost from the cost of the goods available for sale, we finally get the cost of goods sold.

One important point should be noted about cost of goods sold. The way the value of inventory is calculated varies from one company to another—and different methods can cause big differences on the operating statement. See any basic accounting textbook for how the various inventory valuation methods work.

Cost of Goods Sold for a Manufacturing Company

Figure B–1 shows the way the manager of a wholesale or retail business arrives at his cost of goods sold. Such a business *purchases* finished goods and resells them. In a manufacturing company, the "purchases" section of this operating statement is replaced by a section called "cost of goods manufactured." This section includes purchases of raw materials and parts, direct and indirect labor costs, and factory overhead charges (such as heat, light, and power)—which are necessary to produce finished goods. The cost of goods manufactured is added to the beginning finished-goods inventory to arrive at the cost of goods available for sale. Often, a separate cost of goods manufactured statement is prepared—and only the total cost of production is shown in the operating statement. See Figure B–2 for an illustration of the cost of goods sold section of an operating statement for a manufacturing company.

Expenses

"Expenses" go below the gross margin. They usually include the costs of selling and the costs of administering the business. They do not include the cost of goods—either purchased or produced.

There is no "right" method for classifying the expense accounts or arranging them on the operating statement. They can just as easily be arranged alphabetically—or according to amount, with the largest placed at the top and so on down the line. In a business of any size, though, it is desirable to group the expenses in some way—and to use subtotals by groups for analysis and control purposes. This was done in Figure B–1.

Summary on Operating Statements

The statement presented in Figure B–1 contains all the major categories in an operating statement—together with a normal amount of supporting detail. Further detail can be added to the statement under any of the major categories—without changing the nature of the statement. The amount of detail normally is determined by how the statement will be used. A stockholder may be given a sketchy operating statement—while the one prepared for internal company use may have a lot of detail.

■ FIGURE B–2   Cost of goods sold section of an operating statement for a manufacturing firm

Cost of goods sold:

Finished goods inventory (beginning)...............	$ 20,000
Cost of goods manufactured (Schedule 1)	100,000
Total cost of finished goods available for sale	120,000
Less: Finished goods inventory (ending)	30,000
Cost of goods sold	$ 90,000

Schedule 1, Schedule of cost of goods manufactured

Beginning work in process inventory		15,000
Raw materials		
Beginning raw materials inventory..................	10,000	
Net cost of delivered purchases	80,000	
Total cost of materials available for use..............	90,000	
Less: Ending raw materials inventory	15,000	
Cost of materials placed in production	75,000	
Direct labor	20,000	
Manufacturing expenses		
Indirect labor $4,000		
Maintenance and repairs.......................... 3,000		
Factory supplies.................................. 1,000		
Heat, light, and power 2,000		
Total manufacturing expenses	10,000	
Total manufacturing costs		105,000
Total work in process during period		120,000
Less: Ending work in process inventory.............		20,000
Cost of goods manufactured		$100,000

Note: The last item, cost of goods manufactured, is used in the operating statement to determine the cost of goods sold, as above.

COMPUTING THE STOCKTURN RATE

A detailed operating statement can provide the data needed to compute the **stockturn rate**—a measure of the number of times the average inventory is sold during a year. Note that the stockturn rate is related to the *turnover during a year*—not the length of time covered by a particular operating statement.

The stockturn rate is a very important measure—because it shows how rapidly the firm's inventory is moving. Some businesses typically have slower turnover than others—but a drop in the rate of turnover in a particular business can be very alarming. For one thing, it may mean that the firm's assortment of products is no longer as attractive as it was. Also, it may mean that more working capital will be needed to handle the same volume of sales. Most businesses pay a lot of attention to the stockturn rate—trying to get faster turnover.

Three methods—all basically similar—can be used to compute the stockturn rate. Which method is used depends on the data available. These three methods are shown below—and usually give approximately the same results.*

$$\frac{\text{Cost of goods sold}}{\text{Average inventory at cost}} \qquad (1)$$

$$\frac{\text{Net sales}}{\text{Average inventory at selling price}} \qquad (2)$$

$$\frac{\text{Sales in units}}{\text{Average inventory in units}} \qquad (3)$$

Computing the stockturn rate will be illustrated only for Formula 1—since all are similar. The only difference is that the cost figures used in Formula 1 are changed to a selling price or numerical count basis in Formulas 2 and 3. Note: It is necessary—regardless of the method used—to have both the numerator and denominator of the formula in the same terms.

Using Formula 1, the average inventory at cost is computed by adding the beginning and ending inventories at cost—and dividing by 2. This average inventory figure is then divided *into* the cost of goods sold (in cost terms) to get the stockturn rate.

For example, suppose that the cost of goods sold for one year was $100,000. Beginning inventory was $25,000 and ending inventory, $15,000. Adding the two inventory figures and dividing by 2, we get an average inventory of $20,000. We next divide the cost of goods sold by the average inventory ($100,000 divided by $20,000) and get a stockturn rate of 5.

Further discussion of the use of the stockturn rate is found in Chapter 18.

OPERATING RATIOS HELP ANALYZE THE BUSINESS

Many business people use the operating statement to calculate **operating ratios**—the ratio of items on the operating statement to net sales—and compare these ratios from one time period to another. They can also compare their own operating ratios with those of competitors. Such competitive data is often available through trade associations. Each firm may report its results to the trade association—and then summary results are distributed to the members. These ratios help management to control their operations. If some expense ratios are rising, for example, those particular costs are singled out for special attention.

Operating ratios are computed by dividing net sales into the various operating statement items which appear below the net sales level in the operating statement. Net sales is used as the denominator in the operating ratio—because this figure shows the sales actually won by the firm.

---

*Differences will occur because of varied markups and non-homogeneous product assortments. In an assortment of tires, for example, those with high markups might have sold much better than those with small markups—but with Formula 3, all tires would be treated equally.

We can see the relation of operating ratios to the operating statement if we think of there being another column to the right of the dollar figures in an operating statement. This column contains percentage figures—using net sales as 100 percent. This can be seen below:

Gross sales	$540.00	
Less: Returns and allowances	40.00	
Net sales	$500.00	100%
Cost of goods sold	350.00	70
Gross margin	$150.00	30%
Expenses	100.00	20
Net profit	$ 50.00	10%

The 30 percent ratio of gross margin to net sales in the above example shows that 30 percent of the net sales dollar is available to cover sales expenses and administering the business—and provide a profit. Note that the ratio of expenses to sales added to the ratio of profit to sales equals the 30 percent gross margin ratio. The net profit ratio of 10 percent shows that 10 percent of the net sales dollar is left for profit.

The value of percentage ratios should be obvious. The percentages are easily figured—and much easier to compare than large dollar figures.

Note that because these various categories are interrelated, only a few pieces of information are needed to figure the others. In this case, for example, knowing the gross margin percent and net profit percent makes it possible to figure the expense and cost of goods sold percentages. Further, knowing just one dollar amount lets you figure all the other dollar amounts.

MARKUPS

A **markup** is the dollar amount added to the cost of goods to get the selling price. The markup is similar to the gross margin. Gross margin and the idea of markups are related because the amount added onto the unit cost of a product by a retailer or wholesaler is expected to cover the selling and administrative expenses—and to provide a profit.

The markup approach to pricing is discussed in Chapter 18—so it will not be discussed at length here. A simple example will illustrate the idea, however. If a retailer buys an article which cost $1 when delivered to his store, then obviously he must sell it for more than this cost if he hopes to make a profit. So he might add 50 cents onto the cost of the article to cover his selling and other costs and, hopefully, to provide a profit. The 50 cents would be the markup.

It would also be the gross margin or gross profit on that item *if* it is sold— but note that it is *not* the net profit. His selling expenses may amount to 35 cents, 45 cents, or even 55 cents. In other words, there is no assurance that the markup will cover his costs. Further, there is no assurance that the customers will buy at the marked-up price. This may require markdowns—which are discussed later in this appendix.

<table>
<tr><td>**Markup Conversions**</td><td>

Sometimes it is convenient to talk in terms of markups on cost, while at other times markups on selling price are useful. To have some agreement, *markup* (without any explanation) will mean percentage of selling price. By this definition, the 50 cents markup on the $1.50 selling price is a markup of 33⅓ percent.

</td></tr>
</table>

Some retailers and wholesalers have developed markup conversion tables—so they can easily convert from cost to selling price—depending on the markup on selling price they want. To see the interrelation, look at the two formulas below. They can be used to convert either type of markup to the other.

$$\frac{\text{Percentage markup}}{\text{on selling price}} = \frac{\text{Percent markup on cost}}{100\% + \text{Percentage markup on cost}} \quad (4)$$

$$\frac{\text{Percentage markup}}{\text{on cost}} = \frac{\text{Percent markup on selling price}}{100\% - \text{Percentage markup on selling price}} \quad (5)$$

In the previous example, we had a cost of $1, a markup of 50 cents, and a selling price of $1.50. We saw that the markup on selling price was 33⅓ percent—and on cost, it was 50 percent. Let's substitute these percentage figures—in Formulas 4 and 5—to see how to convert from one basis to the other. Assume first of all that we only know the markup on selling price—and want to convert to markup on cost. Using Formula 5, we get:

$$\text{Percentage markup on cost} = \frac{33\frac{1}{3}\%}{100\% - 33\frac{1}{3}\%} = \frac{33\frac{1}{3}}{66\frac{2}{3}} = 50\%$$

If we know, on the other hand, only the percentage markup on cost, we can convert to markup on selling price as follows:

$$\text{Percentage markup on selling price} = \frac{50\%}{100\% + 50\%} = \frac{50\% = 33\frac{1}{3}\%}{150\%}$$

These results can be proved and summarized as follows:

$$\begin{array}{l}
\text{Markup } \$0.50 = 50\% \text{ of cost, or } 33\frac{1}{3}\% \text{ of selling price} \\
\underline{+ \ \text{Cost } \$1.00 = 100\% \text{ of cost, or } 66\frac{2}{3}\% \text{ of selling price}} \\
\text{Selling price } \$1.50 = 150\% \text{ of cost, or } 100\% \text{ of selling price}
\end{array}$$

It is important to see that only the percentage figures change—while the money amounts of cost, markup, and selling price stay the same. Note, too, that when selling price is the base for the calculation (100 percent), then the cost percentage plus the markup percentage equal 100 percent. But when the cost of the product is used as the base figure (100 percent), it is obvious that the selling price percentage must be greater than 100 percent—by the markup on cost.

MARKDOWN RATIOS HELP CONTROL
RETAIL OPERATIONS

The ratios we discussed above were concerned with figures on the operating statement. Another important ratio, the **markdown ratio**—is a tool used by many retailers to measure the efficiency of various departments and their whole business. But note—it is *not directly related to the operating statement.* It requires special calculations.

A **markdown** is a retail price reduction which is required because the customers will not buy some item at the originally marked-up price. This refusal to buy may be due to a variety of reasons—soiling, style changes, fading, damage caused by handling, or an original markup that was too high. To get rid of these products, the retailer offers them at a lower price.

Markdowns are generally considered to be due to "business errors"— perhaps because of poor buying, too high original markups, and other reasons. Regardless of the cause, however, markdowns are reductions in the original price—and are important to managers who want to measure the effectiveness of their operations.

Markdowns are similar to allowances—because price reductions are made. Thus, in computing a markdown ratio, markdowns and allowances are usually added together and then divided by net sales. The markdown ratio is computed as follows:

$$\text{Markdown \%} = \frac{\$ \text{ Markdowns} + \$ \text{ Allowances} \times 100}{\$ \text{ Net sales}}$$

The 100 is multiplied by the fraction to get rid of decimal points.

Returns are *not* included when figuring the markdown ratio. Returns are treated as "consumer errors"—not business errors—and therefore are *not* included in this measure of business efficiency.

Retailers who use markdown ratios keep a record of the amount of markdowns and allowances in each department—and then divide the total by the net sales in each department. Over a period of time, these ratios give management a measure of the efficiency of the buyers and salespeople in the various departments.

It should be stressed again that the markdown ratio is not calculated directly from data on the operating statement—since the markdowns take place before the products are sold. In fact, some products may be marked down and still not sold. Even if the marked-down items are not sold, the markdowns—that is, the reevaluations of their value—are included in the calculations in the time period when they are taken.

The markdown ratio is calculated for a whole department (or profit center)— *not* for individual items. What we are seeking is a measure of the effectiveness of a whole department—not how well the department did on individual items.

RETURN ON INVESTMENT (ROI) REFLECTS ASSET USE

Another "off the operating statement" ratio is **return on investment (ROI)**—the ratio of net profit (after taxes) to the investment used to make the net profit—multiplied by 100 to get rid of decimals. "Investment" is not shown on the operating statement—but it is on the **balance sheet** (statement of financial condition)—another accounting statement—which shows the assets, liabilities, and net worth of a company. It may take some "digging" or special analysis, however, to find the right investment number.

"Investment" means the dollar resources the firm has "invested" in a project or business. For example, a new product may require $400,000 in new money—for inventory, accounts receivable, promotion, and so on—and its attractiveness may be judged by its likely ROI. If the net profit (after taxes) for this new product is expected to be $100,000 in the first year, then the ROI is 25 percent—that is, ($100,000 ÷ $400,000) × 100.

There are two ways to figure ROI. The *direct* way is:

$$\text{ROI (in \%)} = \frac{\text{Net profit (after taxes)} \times 100}{\text{Investment}}$$

The *indirect* way is:

$$\text{ROI (in \%)} = \frac{\text{Net profit (after taxes)}}{\text{Sales}} \times \frac{\text{Sales}}{\text{Investment}} \times 100$$

This way is concerned with net profit margin and turnover—that is:

$$\text{ROI (in \%)} = \text{Net profit margin} \times \text{Turnover} \times 100$$

This indirect way makes it clearer how to *increase* ROI. There are three ways:

1. Increase profit margin.
2. Increase sales.
3. Decrease investment.

Effective marketing strategy planning and implementation are ways of increasing profit margin and/or sales. And careful asset management can decrease investment.

ROI is a revealing measure of how good a job management is doing. Most companies have alternative uses for their funds. If the returns in the business aren't at least as high as outside uses, then the money probably should be shifted to the more profitable uses. Further, many companies must borrow to finance some of their operation. So the ROI should be higher than the cost of money—or the company should cut back until it can operate more profitably.

Some firms borrow more than others to make "investments." In other words, they invest less of their own money to acquire assets—what we have called "investments." If ROI calculations use only the firm's own "investment," this gives higher ROI figures to those who borrow a lot—which is called leveraging. To adjust for different borrowing proportions—to make comparisons among projects, departments, divisions, and companies easier—another ratio (ROA) has come into use. **Return on assets (ROA)** is the ratio of net profit (after taxes) to the assets used to make the net profit—times 100.

Both ROI and ROA measures are trying to get at the same thing—how effectively the company is using resources. These measures have become increasingly popular as profit rates have dropped and it becomes more obvious that increasing sales volume does not necessarily lead to higher profits—or ROI—or ROA. Further, inflation and higher costs for borrowed funds force more concern for ROI and ROA. Marketers must include these measures in their thinking—or top managers are likely to ignore their plans—and requests for financial resources.

■ QUESTIONS AND PROBLEMS

1. Distinguish between the following pairs of items which appear on operating statements: (*a*) gross sales and net sales, (*b*) purchases at billed cost and purchases at net cost, and (*c*) cost of goods available for sale and cost of goods sold.

2. How does gross margin differ from gross profit? From net profit?

3. Explain the similarity between markups and gross margin. What connection do markdowns have with the operating statement?

4. Compute the net profit for a company with the following data:

Beginning inventory (cost)	$ 15,000
Purchases at billed cost	33,000
Sales returns and allowances	25,000
Rent	6,000
Salaries	40,000
Heat and light	18,000
Ending inventory (cost)	25,000
Freight cost (inbound)	9,000
Gross sales	130,000

5. Construct an operating statement from the following data:

Returns and allowances	$ 15,000
Expenses	20%
Closing inventory at cost	60,000
Markdowns	2%
Inward transportation	3,000
Purchases	100,000
Net profit (5%)	30,000

6. Data given:

Markdowns	$ 10,000
Gross sales	100,000
Returns	8,000
Allowances	12,000

Compute net sales and percent of markdowns.

7. (*a*) What percentage markups on cost are equivalent to the following percentage markups on selling price: 20, 37½, 50, and 66⅔? (*b*) What percentage markups on selling price are equivalent to the following percentage markups on cost: 33⅓, 20, 40, and 50?

8. What net sales volume is required to secure a stockturn rate of 20 times a year on an average inventory at cost of $100,000, with a gross margin of 30 percent?

9. Explain how the general manager of a department store might use the markdown ratios computed for his various departments? Is this a fair measure? Of what?

10. Compare and contrast return on investment (ROI) and return on assets (ROA) measures. Which would be best for a retailer with no bank borrowing or other outside sources of funds; i.e., the retailer has put up all the money that is needed in the business?

Chapter 18 ■ Price setting in the real world

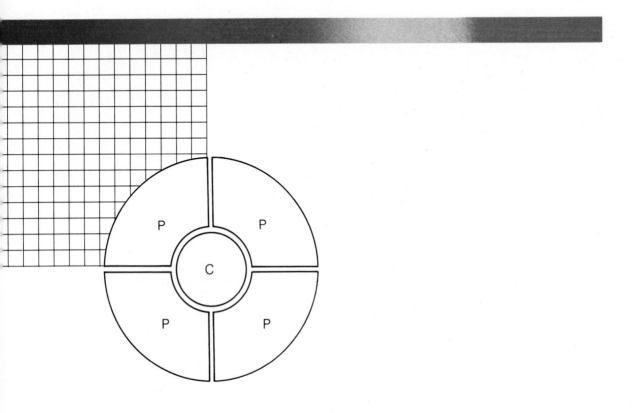

When you finish this chapter, you should:

1. Understand how most wholesalers and retailers set their prices—using markups.

2. Understand why turnover is so important in pricing.

3. Understand the advantages and disadvantages of average-cost pricing.

4. Know how to find the most profitable price and quantity.

5. Know the many ways that price setters use demand estimates in their pricing.

6. Recognize the important new terms (shown in red).

*"How should I price this product?" is a common problem
facing marketing managers.*

In the last chapter, we talked about variations from list price. Now, let's see
how the basic list price might be set in the first place.

Think about how a paint and wallpaper store might price a new item—a
paint sprayer that costs the store $80. The store may get the list price by add-
ing the same dollar amount it adds to paint that costs $80. Or the manager
may just use a list price suggested by the sprayer's manufacturer. Or he may
use estimates of demand . . . estimating how many sprayers might be sold at
various price levels.

There are many ways to set list prices. But—for simplicity—we'll talk about
two basic approaches: *cost-oriented* and *demand-oriented* price setting. We'll
look at cost-oriented approaches first.

Cost-oriented pricing is typical in business. As we will see, however, cost-
oriented pricing isn't as easy—or foolproof—as some people think. Ideally, the
marketing manager should consider potential demand—as well as his own
costs—when setting prices. Let's begin by looking at how most retailers and
wholesalers set cost-oriented prices.

PRICING BY WHOLESALERS AND RETAILERS

Markups Guide Pricing by Middlemen

Most retailers and wholesalers set prices by using a **markup**—a dollar amount added to the cost of goods to get the selling price. For example, suppose that a drug store buys a case of shampoo at $1 a bottle. To make a profit, the drug store obviously must sell each bottle for more than $1. If 50 cents is added to cover operating costs—and provide a profit—we say that the store is marking up the item 50 cents.

Markups, however, usually are stated as percentages—rather than dollar amounts. And this is where the confusion begins. Is a markup of 50 cents on a cost of $1 a markup of 50 percent? Or should the markup be figured as a percentage of the selling price—$1.50—and therefore be 33⅓ percent? A clear definition is necessary.

Markup Percent Is Based on Selling Price—A Convenient Rule

Unless otherwise stated, **markup (percent)** means "percentage of selling price." So the 50-cent markup on the $1.50 selling price is a markup of 33⅓ percent. Markups are related to selling price for convenience.

There is nothing wrong, however, with the idea of markup on cost. The important thing is to state clearly which markup percent we are using—to avoid confusion.

Managers often need to change a markup on cost to one based on selling price—or vice versa.[1] The calculations to do this are simple. (See the section on markup conversion in Appendix B on Marketing Arithmetic.)

Many Use a "Standard" Markup Percent

It's very common for a middleman to set prices on all of his products by applying the same markup percent. This makes pricing easier! When you think of the large number of items the average retailer and wholesaler carry—and the small sales volume of any one item—this approach makes sense. Spending the time to find the "best" price to charge on every item in stock (day-to-day or week-to-week) just wouldn't pay.

Markups Are Related to Gross Margins

How do managers decide on a standard markup in the first place? It is usually based on information about the firm's *gross margin*. Managers regularly see gross margins on their profit and loss statements. (See Appendix B on Marketing Arithmetic if you are not familiar with these ideas.) They know that unless there is a large enough gross margin, there won't be any profit. For this reason, they accept a markup percent that is close to their usual gross margin (percent).

Smart manufacturers pay attention to the gross margins and standard markups of middlemen in their channel. They usually allow trade (functional) discounts that are very similar to the standard markups expected by these middlemen.

Markup Chain May Be Used in Channel Pricing

The markup used by different firms in a channel often varies. A **markup chain**—the sequence of markups used by firms at different levels in a channel—sets the price structure in the whole channel. A markup is figured on the *selling price* at each level of the channel. The producer's selling price becomes the wholesaler's cost—the wholesaler's selling price becomes the retailer's cost—and this cost plus a retail markup becomes the retail selling price. Each markup should cover the costs of selling and running the business—and leave a profit.

Figure 18–1 shows how a markup chain might work for an electric drill. The production (factory) cost of the drill is $21.60. In this case, the producer is taking a 10 percent markup and sells the drill for $24. The markup is 10 percent of $24 or $2.40. The producer's selling price now becomes the wholesaler's cost—$24. If the wholesaler is used to taking a 20 percent markup on selling price, the markup is $6—and the wholesaler's selling price becomes $30. $30 now becomes the cost for a hardware retailer. And if the retailer is used to a 40 percent markup, $20 is added, and the retail selling price becomes $50.

High Markups Don't Always Mean Big Profits

Some people—including many retailers—think high markups mean high profits. But this often is not true. Some kinds of business just have high operating costs—and need high markups. In other cases, a high markup may result in a price that's too high—and few customers will buy. The key to profits is turnover. You can't earn much if you don't sell much—no matter how high your markup. But many retailers and wholesalers seem more concerned with the size of their markup than with their total profit.

Lower Markups Can Speed Turnover— And the Stockturn Rate

Some retailers and wholesalers, however, try to speed turnover to increase profit—even if this means reducing the markup. They know that the business is running up costs over time. If they can sell a much greater amount in the same time period, they may be able to take a lower markup—and still have a higher profit at the end of the period.

An important idea here is the **stockturn rate**—the number of times the average inventory is sold in a year. Various methods of figuring stockturn rates can be used. (See "Computing the Stockturn Rate" in Appendix B.) If the stockturn rate is low, this can be bad for profits.

At the very least, a low stockturn will increase costs by tying up working capital. If a firm with a stockturn of 1 (once per year) sells goods which cost it

■   FIGURE 18–1   Example of a markup chain and channel pricing

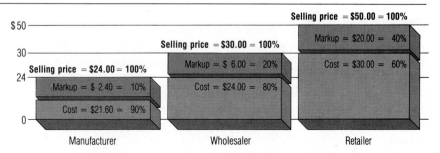

Items with a high stockturn rate may have a lower markup.

$100,000, that much money is tied up in inventory all the time. But a stockturn of 5 requires only $20,000 worth of inventory ($100,000 cost divided by 5 turn-overs a year).

Whether a stockturn rate is high or low depends on the industry. An annual rate of 1 or 2 may be expected in the retail jewelry business—while 40 to 50 would be typical for fresh fruits and vegetables.

Supermarkets and Mass-Merchandisers Run in Fast Company

Supermarkets and mass-merchandisers know the importance of fast turn-over. They put low markups on fast-selling items—and higher markups on items which sell less frequently. For example, a mass-merchandiser may put a small margin (like 20 percent) on fast-selling health and beauty aids (tooth-paste or shampoo) but higher margins on appliances and clothing. Super-market operators put low markups on fast-selling items like milk, sugar, and detergents. (Sugar, for example, may have a markup of only 9 percent.) Since supermarket expenses are 18–22 percent of sales—it looks as if many of these items are carried at a loss. But this need not be true. A small profit per unit is earned more often. Fast-moving goods are less expensive to sell. They take up valuable space for shorter periods, are damaged less, and tie up less working capital.

PRICING BY PRODUCERS

It's up to the Pro-ducer to Set the List Price

Some markups eventually become customary in a trade. Most of the chan-nel members tend to follow a similar process—adding a certain percentage to the previous price. Who sets price in the first place?

The basic list price usually is decided by the producer and/or brander of the product—a large retailer, a large wholesaler, or, most often, the producer. Now we'll look at the pricing approaches of such firms. For convenience, we will call them "producers."

AVERAGE–COST PRICING IS COMMON AND DANGEROUS

Average-cost pricing is adding a "reasonable" markup to the average cost of a product. The average cost per unit is usually found by studying past records. The total cost for the last year is divided by all the units produced and sold in that period—to get the "expected" average cost per unit for the next year. If the total cost was $5,000 for labor and materials and $5,000 for fixed overhead expenses—such as selling expenses, rent, and manager salaries—then "expected" total cost is $10,000. If the company produced 10,000 items in that time period, the "expected" average cost is $1 per unit. To get the price, the producer decides how much profit per unit seems "reasonable." This is added to the average cost per unit. If 10 cents is considered a reasonable profit for each unit, then the new price is set at $1.10. See Figure 18–2.

It Does Not Make Allowances for Cost Variations as Output Changes

This approach is simple. But it can also be dangerous. It's easy to lose money with average-cost pricing. To see why, let's follow this example further.

First, remember that the price of $1.10 per unit was based on output of 10,000 units. But, if only 5,000 units are produced and sold in the next year, the firm may be in trouble. Five thousand units sold at $1.10 each ($1.00 cost

■ **FIGURE 18–2**   Results of average-cost pricing

Calculation of planned profit if 10,000 items are sold	Calculation of actual profit if only 5,000 items are sold
Calculation of costs:	Calculation of costs:
Fixed overhead expenses .... $ 5,000	Fixed overhead expenses $5,000
Labor and materials 5,000	Labor and materials 2,500
Total costs......................... 10,000	Total costs $7,500
"Reasonable" profit.................... 1,000	
Total costs and planned profit $11,000	

Calculation of "reasonable" price for both possibilities:

$$\frac{\text{Total costs and planned profit}}{\text{Planned number of items to be sold}} = \frac{\$11,000}{10,000} = \$1.10 = \text{"Reasonable" price}$$

Calculation of profit or (loss):	Calculation of profit or (loss):
Actual unit sales (10,000) times price ($1.10) = ... $11,000	Actual unit sales (5,000) times price ($1.10) = ... $5,500
Minus: Total costs 10,000	Minus: Total costs 7,500
Profit (loss) .... $ 1,000	Profit (loss)........................ ($2,000)
Therefore: Planned ("reasonable") profit of $1,000 is earned if 10,000 items are sold at $1.10 each.	Therefore: Planned ("reasonable") profit of $1,000 is not earned. Instead, $2,000 loss results if 5,000 items are sold at $1.10 each.

■   FIGURE 18–3   Typical shape of average cost curve

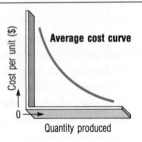

plus $.10 for "profit") yields a total revenue of only $5,500. The overhead is still fixed at $5,000. And the variable material and labor cost drops in half to $2,500—for a total cost of $7,500. This means a loss of $2,000—or 40 cents a unit. The method that was supposed to allow a profit of 10 cents a unit actually causes a loss of 40 cents a unit! See Figure 18–2.

The basic problem is that this method does not allow for cost variations at different levels of output. In a typical situation, economies of scale set in. The average costs per unit are high when only a few units are produced. Average costs drop as the quantity produced increases. (See Figure 18–3 for the typical shape of the average cost curve.) This is why mass production and mass distribution often make sense. This behavior of costs must be considered when setting prices.

MARKETING MANAGER MUST CONSIDER VARIOUS KINDS OF COSTS

Average-cost pricing may fail because total cost includes a variety of costs. And each of these costs changes in a *different* way as output changes. Any pricing method that uses cost must consider these changes. To understand why, however, we need to define *six types of costs*. Differences among these costs help explain why many companies have problems with pricing.

There Are Three Kinds of Total Cost

1. **Total fixed cost** is the sum of those costs that are fixed in total—no matter how much is produced. Among these fixed costs are rent, depreciation, managers' salaries, property taxes, and insurance. Such costs stay the same even if production stops temporarily.

2. **Total variable cost,** on the other hand, is the sum of those changing expenses that are closely related to output—expenses for parts, wages, packaging materials, outgoing freight, and sales commissions.

At zero output, total variable cost is zero. As output increases, so do variable costs. If a dress manufacturer doubles its output of dresses in a year, the total cost of cloth also (roughly) doubles.

3. **Total cost** is the sum of total fixed and total variable costs. Changes in

Fixed costs must be covered even if little is being produced.

total cost depend upon changes in total variable cost—since total fixed cost stays the same.

There Are Three Kinds of Average Cost

The pricing manager usually is more interested in cost per unit than total cost—because prices are usually quoted per unit. Costs per unit are called "average costs."

1. **Average cost** (per unit) is obtained by dividing total cost by the related quantity (that is, the total quantity which causes the total cost). See Table 18–1.

■ TABLE 18–1   Cost structure of a firm

Quantity (Q)	Total fixed costs (TFC)	Average fixed costs (AFC)	Average variable costs (AVC)	Total variable costs (TVC)	Total cost (TC)	Average cost (AC)
0	$30,000	—	—	—	$ 30,000	—
10,000	30,000	$3.00	$0.80	$ 8,000	38,000	$3.80
20,000	30,000	1.50	0.80	16,000	46,000	2.30
30,000	30,000	1.00	0.80	24,000	54,000	1.80
40,000	30,000	0.75	0.80	32,000	62,000	1.51
50,000	30,000	0.60	0.80	40,000	70,000	1.40
60,000	30,000	0.50	0.80	48,000	78,000	1.30
70,000	30,000	0.43	0.80	56,000	86,000	1.23
80,000	30,000	0.38	0.80	64,000	94,000	1.18
90,000	30,000	0.33	0.80	72,000	102,000	1.13
100,000	30,000	0.30	0.80	80,000	110,000	1.10

$$\begin{bmatrix} 110{,}000 \text{ (TC)} \\ -80{,}000 \text{ (TVC)} \\ \hline 30{,}000 \text{ (TFC)} \end{bmatrix}$$ (Q) 100,000 $\overline{)\,30{,}000 \text{ (TFC)}}$ $\dfrac{0.30 \text{ (AFC)}}{}$ $\begin{bmatrix} 100{,}000 \text{ (Q)} \\ \times 0.80 \text{ (AVC)} \\ \hline 80{,}000 \text{ (TVC)} \end{bmatrix}$ $\begin{bmatrix} 30{,}000 \text{ (TFC)} \\ +80{,}000 \text{ (TVC)} \\ \hline 110{,}000 \text{ (TC)} \end{bmatrix}$ (Q) 100,000 $\overline{)\,110{,}000 \text{ (TC)}}$ $\dfrac{1.10 \text{ (AC)}}{}$

$\dfrac{0.80 \text{ (AVC)}}{}$

2. **Average fixed cost** (per unit) is obtained by dividing total fixed cost by the related quantity. See Table 18–1.

3. **Average variable cost** (per unit) is obtained by dividing total variable cost by the related quantity. See Table 18–1.

An Example Illustrates Cost Relations

Table 18–1 shows typical cost data for one firm. Here we assume that average variable cost is the same for each unit. Note how average fixed cost goes down steadily as the quantity increases. Note also how total variable cost increases when quantity increases, although the average variable cost stays the same. Average cost decreases continually, too. This is because average variable cost is the same—and average fixed cost is decreasing. Figure 18–4 shows the three "average" curves.

Ignoring Demand Is the Major Weakness of Average-Cost Pricing

Average-cost pricing works well if the firm actually sells the quantity which was used in setting the average cost price. Losses may result, however, if actual sales are *much lower* than expected. On the other hand, if sales are much higher than expected, then profits may be very good. But this will only happen by accident—because the firm's demand is much larger than expected.

To use average-cost pricing, a marketing manager must make *some* estimate of the quantity to be sold in the coming period. But unless this quantity is related to price—that is, unless the firm's demand curve is considered—the marketing manager may set a price that doesn't even cover a firm's total cost! This can be seen in a simple example for a firm with the cost curves shown in Figure 18–4. This firm's demand curve is shown in Figure 18–5. You can see that customers' demands (and their demand curve) are still important—whether management takes time to analyze the demand curve or not.

In this example, whether management sets the price at a high $3—or a low $1.25—it will have a loss. At $3, only 10,000 units will be sold for a total revenue of $30,000. But total cost will be $38,000—for a loss of $8,000. At the

■ FIGURE 18–4   Typical shape of cost (per unit) curves when AVC is assumed constant per unit

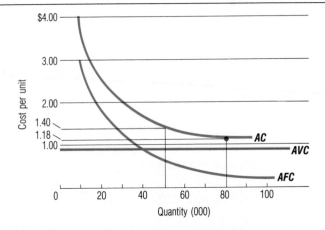

■ FIGURE 18–5   Evaluation of various prices along a firm's demand curve

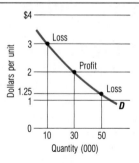

$1.25 price, 50,000 units will be sold—for a loss of $7,500. If management tries to estimate the demand curve—however roughly—the price probably will be set in the middle of the range—say at $2—where a profit of $6,000 will be earned. See Figure 18–5.

In short, average-cost pricing is simple in theory—but often fails in practice. In stable situations, prices set by this method may yield profits—but not necessarily maximum profits. And note that such cost-based prices might be higher than a price that would be more profitable for the firm—as shown in Figure 18–5. When demand conditions are changing, average-cost pricing is even more risky.

Figure 18–6 shows the relationships discussed above. Cost-oriented pricing suggests that the total number of units to be sold determines the *average* fixed

■ FIGURE 18–6   Summary of relationships among quantity, cost, and price using cost-oriented pricing

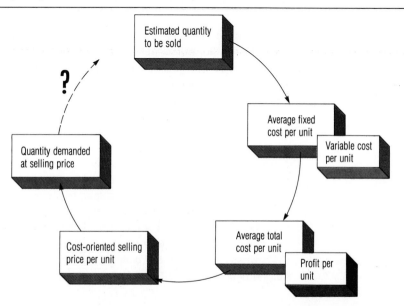

Marketing managers know that the price which is set will affect the quantities that will be sold.

cost per unit—and thus the average total cost. Then some amount of profit per unit is added to average total cost to get the cost-oriented selling price. But we are back where we started—when demand is considered—because the number of units sold will depend on the selling price—and the quantity sold (times price) determines total revenue (and total profit or loss). This figure emphasizes that a decision made in one area affects each of the others—directly or indirectly.[2] A manager who forgets this can make bad pricing decisions.

FINDING THE MOST PROFITABLE PRICE AND QUANTITY TO PRODUCE

A marketing manager facing the typical down-sloping demand curve must pick *one* price (for a time period). His problem is which price to choose. This price, of course, will set the quantity that will be sold.

To maximize profit, the marketing manager should choose the price which will lead to the greatest difference between total revenue and total cost. Finding this best price and quantity requires an estimate of the firm's demand curve. This should be seen as an "iffy" curve—*if* price A is set, then quantity A will be sold—*if* price B is set, then quantity B will be sold—and so on. By multiplying all these possible prices by their related quantities, you can find the possible total revenues. Then, by estimating the firm's likely costs—at various quantities—it is possible to figure a total cost curve. The difference between these two curves shows possible total profits. You can see that the best price would be the one which has the greatest distance between the total revenue and total cost curves. These ideas are shown in Table 18–2 and in Figure 18–7, where these data are plotted on a graph. In this example, you can see that the best price is $79—and the best quantity is six units.[3]

■ TABLE 18–2   Revenue, cost, and profit for an individual firm

(1) Quantity Q	(2) Price P	(3) Total revenue TR	(4) Total cost TC	(5) Profit TR–TC
0	$150	$ 0	$200	$–200
1	140	140	296	–156
2	130	260	316	– 56
3	117	351	331	+ 20
4	105	420	344	+ 76
5	92	460	355	+105
6	79	474	368	+106
7	66	462	383	+ 79
8	53	424	423	+ 1
9	42	378	507	–129
10	31	310	710	–400

A Profit Range Is Reassuring

Estimating demand curves isn't easy. But some estimate of demand is needed to set prices. This is just one of the tough jobs facing a marketing manager. Ignoring demand curves doesn't make them go away! So some estimates must be made. This shows again how very important it is to understand the needs and attitudes of your target market.

■ FIGURE 18–7   Graphic determination of the output giving the greatest total profit for a firm

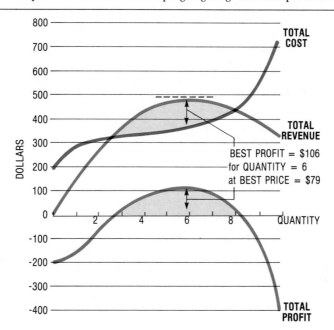

■ FIGURE 18–8 Range of profitable prices for illustrative data in Table 18–2 and Figure 18–7

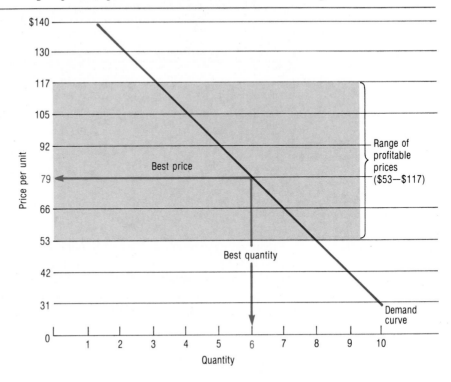

Note that the demand estimates don't have to be exact. Figure 18–8 shows that there is a *range* of profitable prices. This strategy would be profitable all the way from a price of $53 to $117. $79 is just the "best" price.

The marketing manager probably would want to try to estimate the price which would lead to the middle of the profit range. But a slight "miss" would not mean failure. And at least trying to estimate demand would probably lead to being some place in the profitable range. In contrast, mechanical use of average-cost pricing could lead to much too high—or much too low—prices. This is why estimating demand isn't just desirable—it's necessary.

SOME PRICE SETTERS DO ESTIMATE DEMAND

Full use of demand curves isn't very common in business. But we do find marketers setting prices as though they believe demand curves are there. The following sections discuss examples of demand-related pricing.

Value-in-use pricing considers what a customer will save by buying a product.

Value-in-Use Pricing—How Much Will the Customer Save?

Industrial and commercial buyers are very aware of costs. Some marketers who aim at industrial markets keep this in mind in setting prices. They use **value-in-use pricing**—setting prices that will capture some of what customers will save by substituting the firm's product for the one being used. For example, a manufacturer of a word processor knows that his machine doesn't just replace a standard office typewriter, but also reduces secretarial costs. He can estimate the labor cost that will be saved—and set a price for the word processor that will lead to lower clerical costs.[4]

Leader Pricing—Make It Low to Attract Customers

Leader pricing is setting some very low prices—real bargains—to attract customers—not to sell large quantities of the leader items.[5] Certain products are picked for their promotion value and priced low—but above cost. In food stores, the leader prices are the "specials" that are advertised regularly—to give an image of low prices. Leader items usually are well-known, widely used items which customers don't stock heavily—milk, butter, eggs, or coffee—but on which they will recognize a real price cut.

Leader pricing may try to appeal to customers who normally shop elsewhere. But it can backfire—if they buy only the low-price leaders. To avoid hurting profits, managers may select items that aren't directly competitive with major lines—as when bargain-priced recording tape is the leader for a stereo equipment store.

Bait Pricing—Offer a "Steal" but Sell under Protest

Bait pricing is setting some very low prices to attract customers—and then trying to sell more expensive models or brands once the customer is in the store. For example, a furniture store may advertise a color TV for $199. But, when bargain hunters come to buy it, sales clerks point out the disadvantages of the low-price TV—and try to convince them to "trade-up" to a better (and more expensive) set. It's something like leader pricing. But here the seller *doesn't* plan to sell much at the low price. Some stores even make it very difficult to buy the "bait" item.

If bait pricing is successful—the demand for higher-quality products expands. But extremely aggressive—and sometimes dishonest—bait-pricing advertising has given this method a bad reputation. The Federal Trade Commission considers bait pricing a deceptive act—and has banned its use in interstate commerce. But some retailers who operate only within one state continue to advertise bait prices.

Psychological Pricing—Some Prices Just Seem Right

Psychological pricing is setting prices which have special appeal to target customers. Some marketers feel there are whole ranges of prices which potential customers see as the same. So price cuts in these ranges do not increase the quantity sold. But just below this range, customers may buy more. Then, at even lower prices, the quantity demanded stays the same again. And so on.

The kind of demand curve that leads to psychological pricing is shown in Figure 18–9. Vertical drops mark the price ranges which customers see as the same. Pricing research shows that there are such demand curves.[6]

Odd-even pricing is setting prices which end in certain numbers. For example, products selling below $50 often end in the number 5 or the number 9—such as $.49 or $24.95.

Some marketers use odd-even pricing because they feel that consumers react better to these prices. They seem to assume that they have a rather jagged demand curve—that slightly higher prices will greatly reduce the quantity demanded. Odd-even prices were used long ago by some retailers to force their clerks to make change. Then they had to record the sale and couldn't pocket the money. Today, however, it isn't always clear why these prices are used—or whether they really work. Perhaps it is done just because "everyone else does it."[7]

Prestige Pricing: Make It High—But Not Cheap

Prestige pricing is setting a rather high price to suggest high quality or high status. Some target customers want the "best." If prices are dropped a little below this "high" level, they may see a bargain. But if the price seems "cheap," they worry about quality and don't buy.[8]

■ FIGURE 18–9   Demand curve when psychological pricing is appropriate

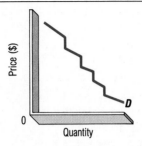

Prestige pricing is most common for luxury products—such as furs and jewelry. It is also used in service industries—where customers can't see the product in advance and rely on price to judge the quality that will be supplied. Target customers who respond to prestige pricing give the marketing manager an unusual demand curve. Instead of a normal down-sloping curve, the curve goes down for a while and then bends back to the left again. See Figure 18–10.

Price Lining—A Few Prices Cover the Field

Price lining is setting a few price levels for a product class and then marking all items at these prices. This approach assumes that customers have in mind a certain price that they expect to pay for a product. For example, most neckties are priced between $10 and $25. In price lining, there will not be many prices in this range. There will be only a few. Ties will not be priced at $10, $10.50, $11, and so on. They might be priced at four levels—$10, $12.50, $15, and $25.

The main advantage of price lining is simplicity—for both clerks and customers. It is less confusing than having many prices. Some customers may consider items at only one price level. Their big decision, then, is which item(s) to choose at that price. Price is no longer a question—unless the products at that price are not satisfactory. Then the customer can be "traded-up" to the next price level.

■ FIGURE 18–10   Demand curve showing a prestige pricing situation

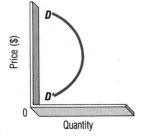

Prestige pricing is common for luxury products.

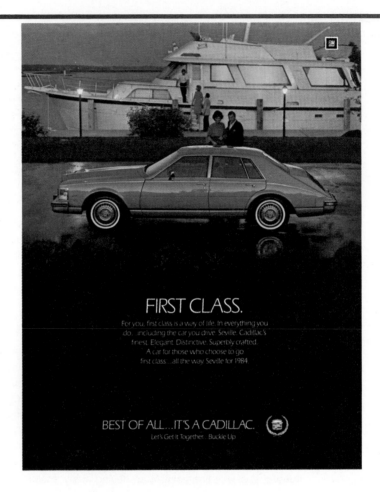

FIRST CLASS.

For you, first class is a way of life. In everything you do...including the car you drive. Seville, Cadillac's finest. Elegant. Distinctive. Superbly crafted. A car for those who choose to go first class...all the way. Seville for 1984.

BEST OF ALL...IT'S A CADILLAC.

Let's Get It Together...Buckle Up

For retailers, price lining has several advantages. Sales may increase because (1) they can offer a bigger variety in each price line and (2) it's easier to get customers to make decisions within one price line. Stock planning is simpler—because demand is larger at the relatively few prices. Price lining also can reduce costs because inventory needs are lower—even though large stocks are carried in each line. In summary, price lining results in faster turnover, fewer markdowns, quicker sales, and simplified buying.[9]

Demand-Backward Pricing Aids Price Lining

Demand-backward pricing is setting an acceptable final consumer price and working backward to what a producer can charge. It is commonly used by producers of final consumer products—especially shopping goods, such as women's and children's clothing and shoes. It is also used for toys or gifts for which customers will spend a specific amount—because they are seeking a "five-dollar" or a "ten-dollar" gift. Here, a reverse cost-plus pricing process is used. This method has been called "market-minus" pricing.

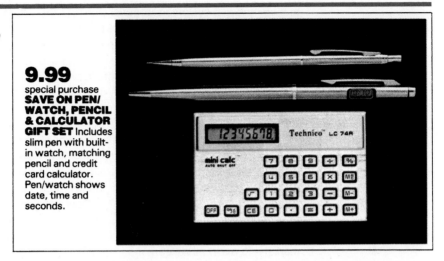

Demand-backward pricing is often used with "gift" items.

The producer starts with the retail price for a particular item and then works backward—subtracting the typical margins which channel members expect. This gives the approximate price that he can charge. Then the average or planned marketing expenses are subtracted from this price to find how much can be spent producing the item.

Demand estimates are needed if demand-backward pricing is to be successful. The quantity which will be demanded affects production costs—that is, where the firm will be on its average cost curve. Also, since competitors can be expected to make the best product possible, it is important to know customer needs—to set the best amount to be spent on manufacturing costs. By increasing costs a little, the product may be so improved in consumers' eyes that the firm will sell many more units. But if consumers only want novelty, additional quality may not increase the quantity demanded—and shouldn't be offered.

PRICING A FULL LINE

Our emphasis has been—and will continue to be—on the problem of pricing a single item—mainly because this makes our discussion clearer. But most marketing managers are responsible for more than one product. In fact, their "product" may be the whole company line!

Full-Line Pricing—Market- or Firm-Oriented?

Full-line pricing is setting prices for a whole line of products. How to do this depends on which of two basic strategies a firm is using.

In one case, all products in the company's line are aimed at the same general target market—which makes it important for all prices to be related to one another. A TV manufacturer could offer several price and quality levels—

to give its target customers some choice. But the different prices should appear "reasonable" to the target customers.

In the other case, the different products in the line are aimed at entirely different target markets—and so there doesn't have to be any relation between the various prices. A chemical manufacturer of a wide variety of products for several target markets, for example, probably should price each product separately.

Cost Is Not Much Help in Full-Line Pricing

The marketing manager must try to recover all costs on the whole line—perhaps by pricing quite low on competitive items and much higher on less competitive items. But costs are not much help in full-line pricing. There is no one "right" way to assign a company's fixed costs to each of the products. And if any method is carried through without considering demand, it may lead to very unrealistic prices. The marketing manager should judge demand for the whole line—as well as demand for each individual product in each target market—to avoid mistakes.

Complementary Product Pricing

Complementary product pricing is setting prices on several products as a group. One product may be priced very low—so that the profits from another product will increase—and increase the product group's total profits. A new razor, for example, may be priced low to sell the blades—which must be replaced regularly.

Complementary product pricing differs from full-line pricing because quite different products and production facilities may be involved. So there's no cost allocation problem. Instead, the problem is really understanding the target market and the demand curves for each of the complementary products.

BID PRICING DEPENDS HEAVILY ON COSTS

A New Price for Every Job

Bid pricing is offering a specific price for each possible job—rather than setting a price that applies for all potential customers. Building contractors, for example, must bid on possible projects. And many companies selling services (such as cleaning or data processing) must submit bids for jobs they would like to have.

The big problem in bid pricing is estimating all the costs that will apply to each job. This may sound easy, but thousands of cost components may have to go into a complicated bid. Further, management must include an overhead charge and a charge for profit.

Demand Must Be Considered, Too

Competition must be considered when adding in overhead and profit. Usually, the customer will get several bids and accept the lowest one. So mechanical rules for adding overhead and profit should be avoided. Some bidders use the same overhead and profit rates on all jobs—regardless of competition—and then are surprised when they don't get some jobs.

Bidding can be expensive. So a marketing manager may want to be selective about which jobs to bid on—and select those where he feels he has the greatest chance of success. Thousands—or even millions—of dollars have been spent just developing bids for large industrial or government orders.[10]

Sometimes Bids Are Bargained

Some buying situations (including much government buying) require the use of bids—and the purchasing agent must take the lowest bid. In other cases, however, bids may be called for, and then the company submitting the *most attractive* bid—not necessarily the lowest—will be singled out for further bargaining. This may include price adjustments—but it also may be concerned with how additions to the job will be priced, what guarantees will be provided, and the quality of labor and supervisors who will do the job. Some projects—such as construction projects—are hard to define exactly. So it is important that the buyer be satisfied about the whole marketing mix—not just the price. Obviously, effective personal selling is important here.

■ CONCLUSION

In this chapter, we discussed various approaches to price setting. Generally, retailers and wholesalers use traditional markups. Some use the same markups for all their items. Others have found that varying the markups may increase turnover and profit. In other words, demand is considered!

Cost-oriented pricing seems to make sense for middlemen—because they handle small quantities of many items. Producers must take price setting more seriously. They are the ones that set the "list price" to which others apply markups.

Producers commonly use average cost curves to help set their prices. But this approach sometimes ignores demand completely. A more realistic approach to average-cost pricing requires a sales forecast. This may just mean assuming that sales in the next period will be roughly the same as in the last period. This *will* enable the marketing manager to set a price—but this price *may or may not* cover all costs and earn the desired profit.

We discussed how demand could be brought into pricing. And it appears that some marketers do consider demand in their pricing. We saw this with value-in-use pricing, leader pricing, bait pricing, odd-even pricing, psychological pricing, prestige pricing, price lining, demand-backward pricing, full-line pricing, complementary product pricing, and bid pricing.

We have stressed throughout the book that the customer should be considered before anything is done. This certainly applies to pricing. It means that when managers are setting a price, they should consider what customers will be willing to pay. This isn't always easy, but it is nice to know that there is a profit range around the "best" price. Therefore, even "guesstimates" about what potential customers will buy at various prices will probably lead to a better price than mechanical use of traditional markups or average-cost pricing.[11]

■ QUESTIONS AND PROBLEMS

1. Why do department stores seek a markup of about 40 percent when some discount houses operate on a 20 percent markup?

2. A manufacturer of household appliances distributed its products through wholesalers and retailers. The retail selling price was $250, and the manufacturing cost to the company was $100. The retail markup was 40 percent and the wholesale markup 25 percent. (a) What was the cost to the wholesaler? To the retailer? (b) What percentage markup did the manufacturer take?

3. Relate the concept of stock turnover to the rise of discounters. Use a simple example in your answer.

4. If total fixed costs are $100,000 and total variable costs are $200,000 at the output of 10,000 units, what are the probable total fixed costs and total variable costs at an output of 20,000 units? What are the average fixed costs, average variable costs, and average costs at these two output levels? Determine the price which should be charged. (Make any simplifying assumptions necessary to obtain a definite answer.)

5. Construct an example showing that mechanical use of very large or very small markup might still lead to unprofitable opera-

tion while some intermediate price would be profitable.

6. Discuss the idea of drawing separate demand curves for different market segments. It seems logical because each target market should have its own marketing mix. But won't this lead to a considerable number of demand curves and possible prices? And what will this mean with respect to functional discounts and varying prices in the marketplace? Will this be legal? Will it be practical?

7. How does a prestige pricing policy fit into a marketing mix? Would exclusive distribution be necessary?

8. Cite a local example of the use of odd-even pricing and then evaluate whether you feel it makes sense.

9. Cite a local example of the use of psychological pricing and then evaluate whether you feel it makes sense.

10. Distinguish between leader pricing and bait pricing. What do they have in common? How can their use affect a marketing mix?

11. Is a full-line pricing policy available only to producers? Cite local examples of full-line pricing. Why is full-line pricing important?

■ SUGGESTED CASES

21. Newman Dance Studio

22. Acme Wire Inc.

26. Custom Manufacturing Company

Chapter 19 ■ Marketing strategy planning for international markets

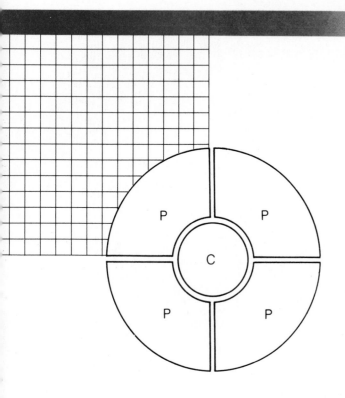

When you finish this chapter, you should:

1. Understand the various ways that businesses can get into international marketing.

2. Understand what multinational corporations are.

3. Understand the kinds of opportunities in international markets.

4. Understand the market dimensions which may be useful in segmenting international markets.

5. Recognize the important new terms (shown in red).

Did you know that more packaged spaghetti is eaten in Germany than in Italy?

Planning strategies for international markets can be even harder than for domestic markets—because cultural differences are more important. Each foreign market must be treated as a separate market—with its own sub-markets. Lumping together all people outside the United States as "foreigners"—or assuming they are just like U.S. customers—is almost a guarantee of failure.

There has been too much narrow thinking about international marketing: "We wouldn't want to risk putting a plant over there and then having it nationalized," or "Fighting all that 'red tape'" would be too much trouble," or "It sold here—it'll sell there" or "Just have the ad put into Spanish (or French, or German or—) and run it in all their papers."

This chapter tries to get rid of some of these wrong ideas—and to suggest how strategy planning has to be changed when a firm enters international markets. We will see that a marketing manager must make several strategic decisions about international marketing: (1) whether the firm even wants to work in international markets at all and, if so, its degree of involvement, (2) in which

■ FIGURE 19–1   Strategic decisions about international marketing

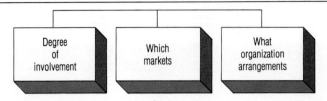

markets, and (3) what organization arrangements should be made when it moves beyond its domestic activities. See Figure 19–1.

THE IMPORTANCE OF INTERNATIONAL MARKETS TO THE UNITED STATES

**As a Nation Grows,
Its Trade Grows**

All countries trade to some extent—we live in an interdependent world. But you may be surprised to know that the United States is the largest exporter and importer of goods in the world. Our share of the world's foreign trade is about 12 percent. Even the United Kingdom and Japan—which have built their growth on exports and imports—are below the United States. Most of the largest traders are highly developed nations. Trade seems to expand as a country develops and industrializes.

But while the United States is the biggest trading nation in the world, foreign trade does not control our economy. This is because of the large size of our national income. Our foreign trade makes up a relatively small part of our income—about 10 percent—but this is still greater in total dollars than in other major trading countries.

DEGREES OF INVOLVEMENT IN INTERNATIONAL MARKETING

Opportunities in foreign countries have led many companies into world-wide operations. The marketing concept is less understood in some foreign markets. So there are exciting opportunities for those who apply it abroad—from just exporting to joint ventures to investment in foreign operations. See Figure 19–2. Many companies are very interested in foreign market opportunities— because they find their foreign operations becoming more profitable than domestic activities.

■ FIGURE 19–2   Kinds of involvement in international marketing that a marketing manager can choose

| Exporting | Licensing | Contract manufacturing | Management contracting | Joint venturing | Wholly-owned subsidiaries |

Exporting Often Comes First

Some companies get into international marketing by just selling the products they are already producing. Sometimes this is just a way of "getting rid of" surplus output. For others, it comes from a real effort to look for new opportunities.

Exporting is selling some of what the firm is producing to foreign markets. Often this is tried without changing the physical product—or even the service or instruction manuals! As a result, some early efforts are not very satisfying—to buyers or sellers.

Exporting gets a firm involved in a lot of government "red tape." Beginning exporters build their own staffs—or depend on specialized middlemen to handle these details. Export agents can handle the paper work as the goods are shipped outside the country. Then agents or merchant wholesalers can handle the importing details. Even large manufacturers with many foreign operations use international middlemen for some products or markets. These specialists know how to handle the sometimes confusing formalities and specialized functions. Even a small mistake can tie goods up at national borders for days—or months.

Exporting means selling present products in foreign markets.

Some relationships get a firm more involved

Exporting doesn't have to involve permanent relationships. Of course, channel relationships take time to build—and shouldn't be treated lightly. Sales reps' contacts in foreign countries are "investments." But it is relatively easy to cut back on these relationships—or even drop them.

Some firms, on the other hand, develop more formal and permanent relationships with nationals in foreign countries—including licensing, contract manufacturing, management contracting, and joint venturing.

Licensing Is an Easy Way

Licensing is a relatively easy way to enter foreign markets. **Licensing** means selling the right to use some process, trademark, patent, or other right—for a fee or royalty. The licensee takes most of the risk—because it must invest some capital to use the right.

This can be an effective way of entering a market if good partners are available. (Gerber entered the Japanese baby food market in this way, but Gerber still exports to other countries.)

Contract Manufacturing Takes Care of the Production Problems

Contract manufacturing means turning over production to others while retaining the marketing process. Sears used this approach as it opened stores in Latin America and Spain.

This approach can be especially good where labor relations are difficult—or there are problems getting supplies and "buying" government cooperation. Growing nationalistic feelings may make this approach more attractive in the future.

Management Contracting Sells Know-How

Management contracting means the seller provides only management skills—the production facilities are owned by others. Some mines and oil refineries are operated this way. And Hilton operates hotels all over the world for local owners. This is a relatively low-risk approach to international marketing. No commitment is made to fixed facilities—which can be taken over or damaged in riots or wars. If conditions get too bad, the key management people can fly off on the next plane—and leave the nationals to manage the operation.

Joint Venturing Is More Involved

Joint venturing means a domestic firm entering into a partnership with a foreign firm. As with any partnership, there can be honest disagreements over objectives—for example, about how much profit is desired—how fast it should be paid out—and operating policies. Where a close working relationship can be developed—perhaps based on a U.S. firm's technical and marketing know-how, and the foreign partner's knowledge of the market and political connections—this approach can be very attractive to both parties. At its worst, it can be a nightmare—and cause the U.S. firm to want to go into a wholly-owned operation. But the terms of the joint venture may block this for years—or the foreign partners may acquire enough "know-how" to be tough competitors.

Clorox managers review plans for a Saudi Arabia liquid bleach plant with the general manager of the joint venture.

Wholly-Owned Subsidiaries Give More Control

When a firm feels that a foreign market looks really promising, it may want to go the final step. A **wholly-owned subsidiary** is a separate firm—owned by a parent company. This gives complete control—and helps a foreign branch work more easily with the rest of the company.

Some multinational companies have gone this way. It gives them a great deal of freedom to move goods from one country to another. If a firm has too much capacity in a country with low production costs, for example, some production may be moved there from other plants—and then exported to countries with higher production costs. This is the same way that large firms in the United States ship goods from one area to another—depending on costs and local needs.

MULTINATIONAL CORPORATIONS EVOLVE TO MEET INTERNATIONAL CHALLENGE

Multinational corporations have a direct investment in several countries and run their businesses depending on the choices available anywhere in the world. Well-known U.S.-based multinational firms include Coca-Cola, Eastman Kodak, Warner-Lambert, Pfizer, Anaconda, Goodyear, Ford, IBM, ITT, Corn Products, 3M, National Cash Register, H. J. Heinz, and Gillette. They regularly earn over a third of their total sales or profits abroad.[1]

Many multinational companies are American. But there are also many well-known foreign-based companies—such as Nestle's, Shell (Royal Dutch Shell), Lever Brothers (Unilever), Sony, and Honda. They have well-accepted "foreign" brands—not only in the United States, but around the world.

Gerber makes different marketing arrangements around the world.

Multinational Operations Make Sense to More Firms

As firms become more involved in international marketing, some reach the point where the firm sees itself as a worldwide business. As a chief executive of Abbott Laboratories—a pharmaceutical company with plants in 22 countries—said, "We are no longer just a U.S. company with interests abroad. Abbott is a world-wide enterprise, and many major fundamental decisions must be made on a global basis."

A Texas Instruments manager had a similar view: "When we consider new opportunities and one is abroad and the other domestic, we can't afford to look upon the alternative here as an inherently superior business opportunity simply because it is in the United States. We view an overseas market just as we do our market, say, in Arizona, as one more market in the world."

A General Motors manager sees this trend as "the emergence of the modern industrial corporation as an institution that is transcending national boundaries."[2]

Much of the multinational activity of the 1960s and early 1970s was U.S.-based firms expanding to other countries. As these opportunities became less attractive in the mid-1970s—due to the energy crisis, inflation, currency devaluations, labor unrest, and unstable governments—foreign multinational companies began moving into the United States. The United States is, after all, one of the richest markets in the world.

Foreign firms are beginning to see that it may be attractive to operate in this large—if competitive—market. The Japanese "invasion" with all kinds of electronic products is well known. Now they are building plants here, too. For example, Sony has a TV assembly plant and a TV tube plant in southern California. And Honda makes cars in Ohio.

Multinational Companies Overcome National Boundaries

From an international view, multinational firms do—as the GM manager said—"transcend national boundaries." They see world market opportunities—and locate their production and distribution facilities for greatest effectiveness. This has upset some nationalistic business managers and politicians. But these multinational operations may be hard to stop. They are no longer just exporting or importing. They hire local residents—and build local plants. They have busi-

Multinational companies have to view the world objectively to run their companies profitably.

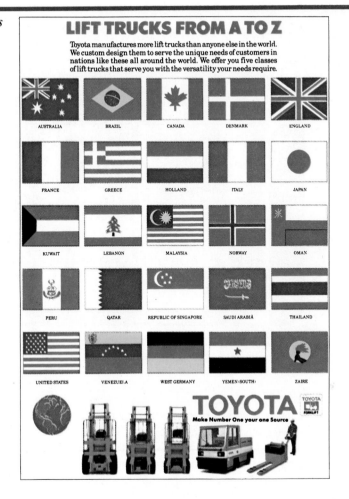

ness relationships with local business managers and politicians. These are powerful organizations which have learned to deal with nationalistic feelings and typical border barriers—treating them simply as uncontrollable variables.

We do not have "one world" politically as yet—but business is moving in that direction. We may have to develop new kinds of corporations and laws to govern multinational operations. The limitations of national boundaries on business and politics will make less and less sense in the future.

IDENTIFYING DIFFERENT KINDS OF INTERNATIONAL OPPORTUNITIES

Firms Usually Start from Where They Are

A multinational firm which has accepted the marketing concept will look for opportunities in the same way that we have been discussing throughout the

■ **FIGURE 19–3**   International marketing opportunities as seen by a U.S. firm from the viewpoint of its usual product-market in the United States

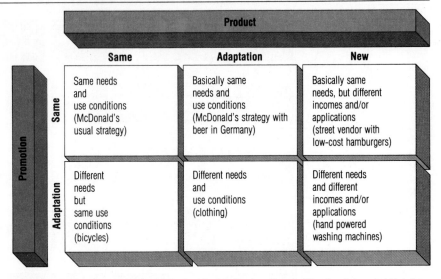

		Product	
	Same	**Adaptation**	**New**
Same	Same needs and use conditions (McDonald's usual strategy)	Basically same needs and use conditions (McDonald's strategy with beer in Germany)	Basically same needs, but different incomes and/or applications (street vendor with low-cost hamburgers)
Adaptation	Different needs but same use conditions (bicycles)	Different needs and use conditions (clothing)	Different needs and different incomes and/or applications (hand powered washing machines)

(left axis label: **Promotion**)

Source: Adapted from Warren Keegan, "Multinational Product Planning: Strategic Alternatives," *Journal of Marketing,* January 1969, p. 59.

text, that is, looking for unsatisfied needs—anywhere—that it might be able to satisfy—given its resources and objectives.

The typical approach, however, is to start with the firm's current products—and the needs it knows how to satisfy—and try to find new markets—wherever they may be—with the same or similar unsatisfied needs. Next, the firm might adapt its Product—and perhaps its Promotion. Later, the firm might develop new products and new promotion policies. Some of these possibilities are shown in Figure 19–3. Here, we only look at Product and Promotion—because Place would obviously have to be changed in new markets—and Price adjustments probably would be needed, too.

The "Same-Same" box in Figure 19–3 can be illustrated with McDonald's (fast-food chain) entry into European markets. Its director of international marketing says, "Ronald McDonald speaks eight languages. Our target audience is the same world-wide—young families with children—and our advertising is designed to appeal to them." The basic promotion messages must be translated, of course, but the same strategy decisions which were made in the U.S. market apply. McDonald's has adapted its Product in Germany, however, by adding beer to appeal to adults who prefer beer to soft drinks. Its efforts have been extremely successful so far. Some stores are selling over $1 million per year—something that took many more years to do in the United States.[3]

McDonald's and other firms expanding into international markets usually move first into markets with good economic potential—such as Western Europe and Japan. But if McDonald's or some other fast-food company wanted to move into much lower-income areas, it might have to develop a whole new Product—perhaps a traveling street vendor with "hamburgers" made from soybean products. This kind of opportunity is in the upper right-hand corner of Figure 19–3.

The lower left-hand box in this figure is illustrated by the different kind of Promotion that is needed for just a simple bicycle. In some parts of the world, a bicycle provides basic transportation—while in the United States, it is mainly for recreation. So a different Promotion emphasis is needed in these different target markets.

Both Product and Promotion changes will be needed as one moves to the right along the bottom row of Figure 19–3. Such moves obviously require more market knowledge—and increase the risk.

The Risk of Opportunities Varies by Environmental Sensitivity

International marketing means going into unfamiliar markets. This can increase risk. The farther you go from familiar territory, the greater the chance of making big mistakes. But not all products offer the same risk. It is useful to think of the risks running along a "range of environmental sensitivity." See Figure 19–4. Some products are relatively insensitive to the economic or cultural environment. These products may be accepted "as is"—or may need just a little change to make them suitable for local use. Most industrial goods are near the insensitive end of this range.

At the other end of the range, we find highly sensitive products which may be difficult or impossible to adapt to all international situations. At this end, we find "faddy" or high-style consumer goods. It is sometimes difficult to understand why a particular product is well accepted in a home market—which makes it even harder to know how it might be received in a different environment.

This range of sensitivity helps explain why many of the early successes in international marketing were basic commodities such as gasoline, soap, transporting vehicles, mining equipment, and agricultural machinery. It also suggests that firms producing and/or selling highly sensitive products should carefully study how their products will be seen and used in new environments—and plan their strategies accordingly.[4] American-made blue jeans, for example, have become "status symbols" in Western Europe and Latin America—and producers have been able to sell them at premium prices through the "best" middlemen.

■ FIGURE 19–4   Range of environmental sensitivity

Insensitive		Sensitive
Industrial goods	Basic commodity-type consumer goods	Faddy or high-style consumer goods

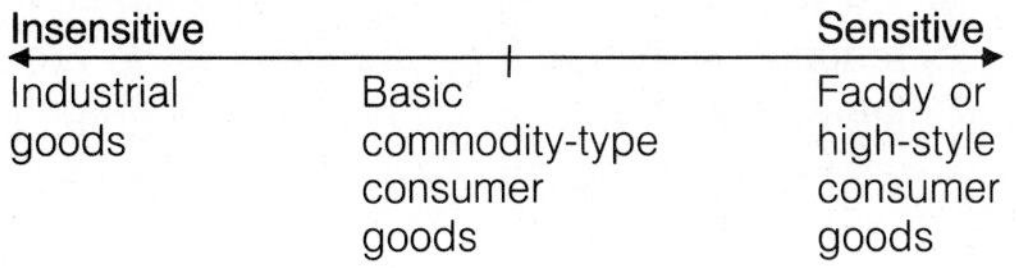

Evaluating Opportunities in Possible International Markets

Judging opportunities in international markets uses the same principles we have been discussing. Basically, each opportunity must be evaluated—within the limits of the uncontrollable variables. But there may be more of these variables—and they may be harder to evaluate—in international markets. Estimating the risk in some opportunities may be very difficult. Some countries are not as politically stable as the United States. Their governments and constitutions come and go. An investment that was safe under one government might become the target for a take-over under another. Further, the possibility of foreign exchange controls—and tax rate changes—can reduce the chance of getting profits and capital back to the home country.

Because the risks are hard to judge, it may be wise to enter international marketing by exporting first—building know-how and confidence over time. Experience and judgment are needed even more in unfamiliar areas. Allowing time to develop these skills among a firm's top management—as well as its international managers—makes sense. Then the firm will be in a better position to estimate the prospects—and risks—of going further into international marketing.

INTERNATIONAL MARKETING REQUIRES EVEN MORE SEGMENTING

Success in international marketing requires even more attention to segmenting. There are over 140 nations—each with its own unique differences! There can be big differences in language, customs, beliefs, religions, race, and even income distribution patterns from one country to another. This obviously complicates the segmenting process. But what makes it even worse is that there is less good data as one moves into international markets. While the number of variables increases, the quantity and quality of data go down. This is one reason why some multinational firms insist that local operations be handled by natives. They, at least, have a "feel" for their markets.

There Are More Dimensions—But There Is a Way

Segmenting international markets may require more dimensions. But a practical method adds just one step before the seven-step approach discussed in Chapter 8. See Figure 19–5. First, segment by country or region—looking at demographic, cultural, and other characteristics—including stage of economic development. This may help find reasonably similar sub-markets. Then—depending on whether the firm is aiming at final consumers or intermediate customers—it can apply the seven-step approach discussed earlier.

Most of the discussion in the rest of this chapter will emphasize final consumer differences—because they are likely to be greater than intermediate customer differences. Also, we will consider regional groupings and stages of economic development—which can aid your segmenting.

■ FIGURE 19–5   Segmenting in international markets

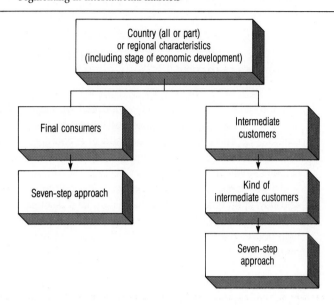

REGIONAL GROUPINGS MAY MEAN MORE THAN NATIONAL BOUNDARIES

While national boundaries are a common and logical dimension for segmenting markets, sometimes it makes more sense to treat several nearby countries with similar cultures as one region—Central America or Latin America, for example. Or if several nations have banded together to have common economic boundaries, then these nations may be treated as a unit. The outstanding example is the European Economic Community (EEC)—or "Common Market." They have dared to discard old ideas and nationalistic prejudices—in favor of cooperative efforts to reduce tariffs and other controls usually applied at national boundaries.

These cooperative arrangements are very important, because the taxes and restrictions at national borders can be not only annoying—but also can greatly reduce marketing opportunities. Tariffs—taxes on imported goods—vary, depending on whether the country is trying to raise revenue or limit trade. Restrictive tariffs often block all movement. But even revenue-producing tariffs cause red tape and discourage free movement of goods. Quotas act like restrictive tariffs. Quotas set the specific quantities of goods which can move in or out of a country. Great market opportunities may exist in a country, but import quotas (or export controls applied against a specific country) may discourage outsiders from entering. The U.S. government, for example, has controlled Japan's export of cars to the United States. (Otherwise, we would have had even more Japanese cars in the U.S. market!)

STAGES OF ECONOMIC DEVELOPMENT HELP DEFINE MARKETS

International markets are so varied that we can't make general rules for all of them. Some markets are more advanced and/or growing more rapidly than others. And some countries—or parts of a country—are at different stages of economic development. This means their demands—and even their marketing systems—will vary.

To get some idea of the many possible differences in potential markets—and how they affect strategy planning—let's discuss six stages of economic development. These stages are over-simplified, of course. But they can help you to understand economic development better—and how it affects marketing.

Stage 1—Agricultural—Self-Supporting

In this stage, most people are subsistence farmers. There may be a simple marketing system—perhaps weekly markets—but most of the people are not even in a money economy. Some parts of Africa and New Guinea are in this stage. In a practical sense, these people are not a market—they have no money to buy products.

Stage 2—Preindustrial or Commercial

Some countries in Sub-Sahara Africa and the Middle East are in this second stage. During this stage, we see more market-oriented activity. Raw materials such as oil, tin, and copper are extracted and exported. Agricultural and forest crops such as sugar, rubber, and timber are grown and exported. Often this is done with the help of foreign technical skills and capital. A commercial economy may develop along with—but not related to—the subsistence economy. These activities may require the beginning of a transporting system—to tie the extracting or growing areas to shipping points. A money economy operates in this stage.

In this stage, industrial machinery and equipment are imported. And huge construction projects may import many special supplies. Buying for these needs may be handled by purchasing agents in industrialized countries. There is also the need for imports—including luxury goods—to meet the living standards of technical and supervisory people. These may be handled by company stores—rather than local retailers.

The relatively few large landowners—and those who benefit by this business activity—may develop expensive tastes. The few natives employed by these larger firms—and the small business managers who serve them—may form a small, middle-income class. But most of the population is still in the first stage. For practical purposes, they are not in the market. This total market may be so small that local importers can easily handle the demand. There is little reason for local manufacturers to try to supply it.

Stage 3—Primary Manufacturing

In this third stage, there is some processing of metal ores or the agricultural products that once were shipped out of the country in raw form. Sugar and rubber, for example, are both produced and processed in Indonesia. The same is true for oil on the Persian Gulf. Multinational companies may set up factories to take advantage of low-cost labor. They may export most of the output—but they do stimulate local development. More local labor becomes involved in this stage. A domestic market develops. Small local businesses start to handle some of the raw material processing.

Even though the local market expands in this third stage, a large part of the population is still at the subsistence level—almost entirely outside the money economy. A large foreign population of professionals and technicians may still be needed to run the developing agricultural-industrial complex. The demands of this group—and the growing number of wealthy natives—are still quite different from the needs of the lower class and the growing middle class. A domestic market among the local people begins to develop. But there may not be enough demand to keep local manufacturers in business.

Stage 4— Non-Durable and Semi-Durable Consumer Goods Manufacturing

At this stage, small local manufacturing begins—especially in those lines that need only a small investment to get started. Often these industries grow out of small firms that developed to supply the processors dominating the last stage. For example, plants making sulfuric acid and explosives for extracting mineral resources might expand into soap manufacturing. And recently, multinational firms have speeded development of countries in this stage by investing in promising opportunities.

Now paint, drug, food and beverage, and textile industries begin to develop. The textile industry is usually one of the first to develop. Clothing is a necessity. This early emphasis on the textile industry in developing nations is one reason the world textile market is so competitive.

Some of the small manufacturers become members of the middle- or even upper-income class. They help to expand the demand for imported goods. As this market grows, local businesses begin to see enough volume to operate profitably. So the need for imports to supply non-durable and semi-durable goods is less. But consumer durables and capital items are still imported.

Stage 5—Capital Goods and Consumer Durable Goods Manufacturing

In this stage, the production of capital goods and consumer durable goods begins. This includes automobiles, refrigerators, and machinery for local industries. Such manufacturing creates other demands—raw materials for the local factories, and food and fibers for clothing for the rural population entering the industrial labor force.

Industrialization has begun. But the economy still depends on exports of raw materials—either unprocessed or slightly processed.

It still may be necessary to import special heavy machinery and equipment in this stage. Imports of consumer durable goods may still compete with local products. The foreign community and the status-conscious wealthy may prefer these imports.

Japan—like the United States—is at the stage of economic development where exporting manufactured products is important.

Stage 6—Exporting Manufactured Products

Countries that have not gone beyond the fifth stage are mainly exporters of raw materials. They import manufactured goods and equipment to build their industrial base. In the sixth stage, exporting manufactured goods becomes most important. The country specializes in certain types of manufactured goods—such as iron and steel, watches, cameras, electronic equipment, or processed food.

There are many opportunities for importing and exporting at this stage. These countries have grown richer and have needs—and the purchasing power—for a wide variety of products. In fact, countries in this stage often carry on a great deal of trade with each other. Each trades those goods in which it has production advantages. In this stage, almost all consumers are in the money economy. There may be a large middle-income class. The United States, most of the Western European countries, and Japan are at this last stage.[5]

It is important to see that it is not necessary to label a whole country or geographic region as being in one stage. Certainly, different parts of the United States have developed differently—and could be placed in different stages.

HOW THESE STAGES CAN BE USEFUL IN FINDING MARKET OPPORTUNITIES

A good starting point for estimating present and future market potentials in a country—or part of a country—is to estimate its present stage of economic development and how fast it is moving to another stage. Actually, the speed of movement, if any—and the possibility that stages may be skipped—may suggest whether market opportunities are there—or are likely to open. But just naming the present stage can be very useful in deciding what to look at—and whether there are prospects for a firm's products.

Fitting the Firm to Market Needs

Manufacturers of automobiles, expensive cameras, or other consumer durable goods, for example, should not plan to set up a mass distribution system in an area that is in Stage 2 (the preindustrial stage) or even Stage 3 (the primary manufacturing stage). To sell these consumer goods profitably requires a large base of cash or credit customers—but as yet, too few are part of the money economy.

On the other hand, a market in the non-durable goods manufacturing stage (Stage 4) has more potential—especially for durable goods producers. Incomes and the number of potential customers are growing. There is no local competition yet.

Opportunities might still be good for durable goods imports in Stage 5— even though domestic producers are trying to get started. But more likely, the local government would raise some controls to aid local industry. Then the foreign producer might have to license local producers—or build a local plant.

Coke has successfully used similar strategies around the world—but most companies need to adjust their marketing mixes for different countries.

Pursuing That Tempting Inverted Pyramid

Areas or countries in the final stage often are the biggest and most profitable markets. While there may be more competition, many more customers have higher incomes. We have already seen how income distribution shifted in the United States from a pyramid to more families with middle and upper incomes. This can be expected during the latter stages—when a "mass market" develops.

OTHER MARKET DIMENSIONS MAY SUGGEST OPPORTUNITIES, TOO

Considering country or regional differences—including stages of economic development—can be useful as a first step in segmenting international markets. After finding some possible areas (and eliminating less attractive ones), we must look at more specific market characteristics.

We discussed many potential dimensions in the U.S. market. It's impossible to cover all possible dimensions in all world markets. But some of the ideas discussed for the United States certainly apply in other countries. So here we will just outline some dimensions of international markets—and show some examples to emphasize that depending on half-truths about "foreigners" won't work in increasingly competitive international markets.

The Number of People in Our World Is Staggering

Although our cities may seem crowded with people, the over 225 million population of the United States is less than 5 percent of the world's population—which is over 4 billion.

Numbers are important

Instead of a boring breakdown of population statistics, let's look at a map showing area in proportion to population. Figure 19–6 makes the United States look unimportant—because of our small population. This is also true of Latin America and Africa. In contrast, Western Europe is much larger—and the Far Eastern countries are even bigger.

But people are not spread out evenly

People everywhere are moving off the farm and into industrial and urban areas. Shifts in population—combined with already dense populations—have led to extreme crowding in some parts of the world.

Figure 19–7 shows a map of the world emphasizing density of population. The darkest shading shows areas with more than 250 persons per square mile.

The urban areas in the United States show up clearly as densely populated areas. Similar areas are found in Western Europe, along the Nile River Valley in Egypt, and in many parts of Asia. In contrast, many parts of the world (like our western plains and mountain states) have few people.

Population densities are likely to increase in the near future. Birth rates in most parts of the world are high—higher in Africa, Latin America, and Asia

■ FIGURE 19–6   Map of the world showing area in proportion to population

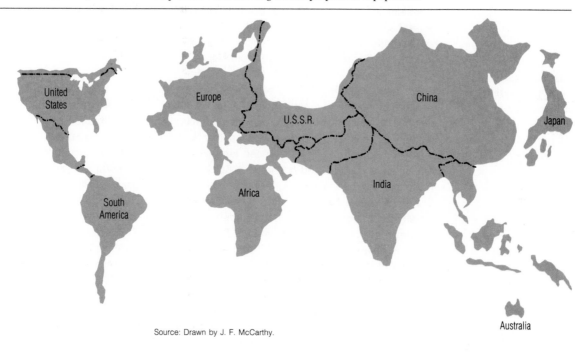

Source: Drawn by J. F. McCarthy.

■ FIGURE 19–7   Map of the world emphasizing density of population

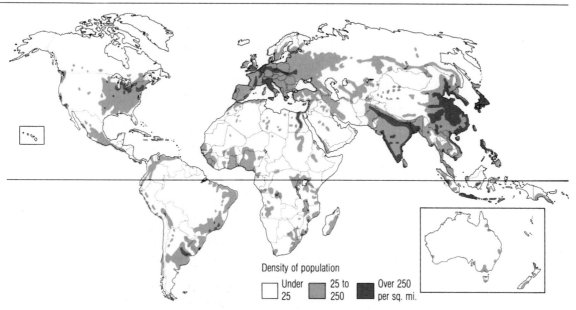

Density of population

Under 25 | 25 to 250 | Over 250 per sq. mi.

Source: Adapted from Norton Ginsberg, *Atlas of Economic Development,* by permission of the University of Chicago Press. Copyright 1961 by the University of Chicago.

than in the United States—and death rates are declining as modern medicine is more widely accepted. Generally, population growth is expected in most countries. But the big questions are: How rapidly?—and—Will output increase faster than population? This is important to marketers—because it affects how rapidly these countries move to higher stages of development and become new markets for different kinds of products.

You Must Sell Where the Income Is

Profitable markets require income—as well as people. The best available measure of income in most countries is **gross national product (GNP)**—the total market value of goods and services produced in a year. Unfortunately, this may not give a true picture of consumer well-being in many countries—because the method commonly used for figuring GNP may not be accurate for very different cultures and economies. For instance, do-it-yourself activities, household services, and the growing of produce or meat by family members for their own use are not usually figured as part of GNP. Since the activities of self-sufficient family units are not included, GNP can give a false picture of economic well-being in less-developed countries.

Gross national product, though, is useful—and sometimes the only available measure of market potential in many countries. Figure 19–8 shows the population and GNP of major regions of the world—except the USSR and mainland China. You can see that the more developed industrial regions have the biggest share of the world's GNP. This is why so much trade takes place between these countries—and why many companies see them as the more important markets.

Income per Person Can Be More Helpful

GNP per person is a commonly available figure—but it can be a misleading estimate of market potential. When GNP per person is used for comparison,

■ FIGURE 19–8   Population (1982) and gross national product (1979) of major geographic regions of the world

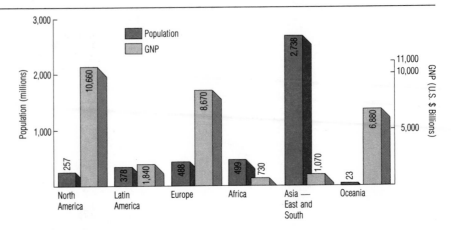

Source: *Statistical Abstract of the United States, 1982–1983*, p. 856, and *Yearbook of National Accounts Statistics, 1980*, vol. II (New York, United Nations, 1982), pp. 3–9.

we assume that the wealth of each country is distributed evenly among all consumers. This is seldom true. In a developing economy, 75 percent of the population may be on farms and receive 25 percent or less of the income. And there may be unequal distribution along class or racial lines.

To provide some examples, the GNP per person for several countries is shown in Figure 19–9. The range is wide, from $241 (in U.S. dollars) per person per year in India to $40,587 in the United Arab Emirates.

A business, and a human opportunity

Much of the world's population lives in extreme poverty. Many countries are in the early stages of economic development. Most of their people work on farms—and live barely within the money economy.

These people, however, have needs. And many are eager to improve themselves. But they may not be able to raise their living standards without outside

---

■ FIGURE 19–9   Gross national product per capita for major regions of the world and selected countries (in 1980 U.S. dollars)

	GNP per capita for countries	GNP per capita for regions
North America		$11,340
United States	$11,416	
Canada	10,585	
Latin America		2,320
Brazil	2,021	
Mexico	2,591	
Venezuela	4,315	
Haiti	283	
Europe		9,860
United Kingdom	9,351	
France	12,137	
West Germany	13,304	
Italy	6,907	
Sweden	14,882	
Portugal	2,474	
Middle East		3,160
Israel	5,431	
United Arab Emirates	40,587	
Africa		900
Algeria (1979)	1,724	
Egypt (1979)	435	
Kenya	426	
Nigeria (1977)	717	
South Africa	2,639	
Zambia	649	
East and South Asia		1,150
India	241	
Pakistan	339	
Japan	8,873	
Indonesia	472	
Oceania		7,850
Australia	10,210	
New Zealand	7,578	

Source: *Yearbook of National Statistics, 1981* Vol. II, (New York: United Nations, 1983) pp. 3–9.

help. This presents a challenge—and an opportunity—to the developed nations—and to their business firms.

Some companies—including American firms—are trying to help the people of developing countries. Corporations such as Pillsbury, Corn Products, Monsanto, and Coca-Cola have developed nutritious foods that can be sold cheaply—but still profitably—in poorer countries. One firm sells a milk-based drink (Samson)—with 10 grams of protein—to the Middle East and the Caribbean areas. Such a drink can make an important addition to diets. Poor people in developing nations usually get only 8 to 12 grams of protein per day in their normal diet (60 to 75 grams are considered necessary for an adult.)[6]

Reading, Writing, and Marketing Problems

The ability of a country's people to read and write has a direct influence on the development of the economy—and on marketing strategy planning. Certainly, the degree of literacy affects the way information is delivered—which in marketing means promotion. Literacy studies show that only about two thirds of the world's population can read and write.

Low literacy sometimes causes difficulties with product labels and instructions—for which we normally use words. In countries with high illiteracy, some manufacturers found that placing a baby's picture on food packages was unwise. Some illiterate natives believed that the product was just that—a ground-up baby! Singer Sewing Machine Company met this lack of literacy with an instruction book that used no words.

Even in Latin America—which has generally higher literacy than Africa or Asia—large numbers of people cannot read or write. Marketers have to use symbols, colors, and other non-verbal means of communication if they want to reach the masses.

CAREFUL MARKET ANALYSIS IS BASIC

The opportunities in international marketing are exciting. But market differences present a real challenge to target marketers. Careful market analysis is especially important—since there often are subtle differences that are easy to miss.

What Are You Drinking?

Tastes do differ across national boundaries. French Burgundy wine going to Belgium must have a higher sugar content than the Burgundy staying in France. Burgundy going to Sweden must have still higher sugar content to be sold successfully there.

Milk-drinking habits also differ greatly. Scandinavians consider milk a daily staple—while Latins feel that milk is only for children. A former French premier was able to get his picture on the front page of every Paris newspaper just by drinking a glass of milk in public.

ORGANIZING FOR INTERNATIONAL MARKETING

Until a firm develops a truly world-wide view of its operations, it usually is desirable to have someone in charge of international matters. The basic concern should be to see that the firm transfers its domestic know-how into international operations.

Organization Should Transfer Know-How

As the firm moves beyond just a few international locations, the managers may develop regional groupings of similar kinds of countries. It is important to develop an organization that transfers know-how—allowing local managers to control matters that require "local feel," while sharing their larger experience with others in the firm.

Top management may delegate a great deal of responsibility for strategy planning to these local managers. These managers may be given a lot of freedom in planning—but still be tightly controlled against their own plans. When the firm reaches this stage, it is being managed like a well-organized domestic corporation—which insists that its managers (of divisions and territories) meet their own plans, so that the whole company's program works out as intended.[7]

■ CONCLUSION

The international market is large—and keeps growing in population and income. Many American companies are becoming aware of the opportunities for alert and aggressive businesses.

The great variations in stages of economic development, income, population, literacy, and other factors, however, mean that foreign markets must be treated as many separate target markets—and studied carefully. Lumping foreign nations together under the common and vague heading of "foreigners"—or, at the other extreme, assuming that they are just like U.S. customers—almost guarantees failure.

Involvement in international marketing usually begins with exporting. Then a firm may become involved in joint ventures or wholly-owned subsidiaries in several countries. Companies that become this involved are called multinational corporations. Some of these corporations have a global outlook—and are willing to move across national boundaries as easily as our national firms move across state boundaries.

Much of what we have said about marketing strategy planning throughout the text applies directly in international marketing. Sometimes Product adaptions or changes are needed. Promotion messages must be translated into the local languages. And, of course, new Place arrangements and Prices are needed. But blending the four Ps still requires a knowledge of the all-important customer.

The major "roadblock" to success in international marketing is an unwillingness to learn about—and adjust to—different peoples and cultures. To those who are willing to make these adjustments, the returns can be great.

■ QUESTIONS AND PROBLEMS

1. Discuss the "typical" evolution of corporate involvement in international marketing. What impact would a whole-hearted acceptance of the marketing concept have on the evolutionary process?

2. Distinguish between licensing and contract manufacturing in a foreign country.

3. Distinguish between joint ventures and wholly-owned subsidiaries.

4. Discuss the long-run prospects for (*a*) multinational marketing by U.S. firms producing in the United States only and (*b*) multinational firms willing to operate anywhere.

5. Discuss how a manufacturer interested in finding new international marketing opportunities might organize its search process. What kinds of opportunities would it look for first, second, and so on?

6. Discuss how the approaches to market segmentation (which were described in Chapters 3 and 8) might have to be modified when moving into international markets.

7. Evaluate the growth of "common markets" in relation to the phases of economic development of the members. Is this basically a movement among the developing countries which are seeking to "catch up"?

8. Discuss the prospects for a Latin American entrepreneur who is considering building a factory to produce machines which would manufacture cans for the food industry. His country happens to be in Stage 4—the non-durable and semi-durable consumer goods manufacturing stage. The country's population is approximately 20 million, and there is some possibility of establishing sales contacts in a few nearby countries.

9. Discuss the value of gross national product per capita as a measure of market potential. Refer to specific data in your answer.

10. Discuss the possibility of a multinational marketer using essentially the same promotion campaign in the United States and in many international markets.

11. Discuss the kinds of products which you feel may become popular in Europe in the near future. Does the material on U.S. consumption behavior—discussed earlier in the text—have any relevance here?

12. Discuss the importance of careful target marketing within the European Common Market.

13. Discuss how a multinational firm might organize to develop an effective organization.

■ SUGGESTED CASES

30. Multi Foods, Limited

33. Mayfair Detergent Company

Chapter 20 ■ Marketing in a consumer-oriented society: Appraisal and challenges

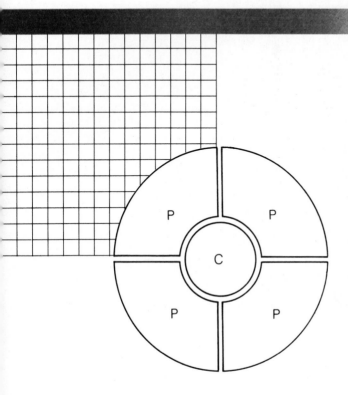

When you finish this chapter, you should:

1. Understand why marketing must be evaluated differently at the micro and macro levels.

2. Understand why the text argues that micro-marketing costs too much.

3. Understand why the text argues that macro-marketing does not cost too much.

4. Know some of the challenges facing marketers in the future.

Does marketing cost too much?

Does marketing cost too much? This is a very basic question. Many people feel strongly that marketing does cost too much—that it is a waste of resources which would be better used elsewhere. Now that you have a better understanding of what the marketing manager does—and how he contributes to the *macro*-marketing process—you should be able to consider whether marketing costs too much. That's what this chapter is about.

Your answer is very important. Your own business career and the economy in which you will live will be affected by your answer.

Do auto manufacturers, for example, produce as high quality cars as they could—or did in the "good old days?" Do producers of food and drug products spend too much advertising their own brands instead of offering more generics—at lower prices? Do we have too many retailers and wholesalers—all taking "too big" markups? Some critics of marketing would answer Yes! to *all* these important questions. Such critics probably want to change our political and legal environments—and the world in which you'll live and work. Do you agree with these critics? Or are you fairly satisfied with the way our system works? How will you "vote" on your consumer ballot?

MARKETING MUST BE EVALUATED AT TWO LEVELS

As we saw in Chapter 1, it is useful to talk about marketing at two levels: the *micro* level (how individual firms run) and the *macro* level (how the whole system works). Some complaints against marketing are aimed at only one of these levels. In other cases, the criticism *seems* to be directed to one level— but actually is aimed at the other. Some critics of specific ads, for example, probably would not be satisfied with *any* advertising. When evaluating marketing, we must treat each of these levels separately.

HOW SHOULD MARKETING BE EVALUATED?

Different nations have different social and economic objectives. Dictatorships, for example, may be concerned mainly with satisfying the needs of the people at the top. In a socialist state, the objective is to satisfy the needs of the people—as defined by government planners.

Consumer Satisfaction Is the Objective in the United States

In the United States, *the aim of our economic system has been to satisfy consumer needs as they—the consumers—see them.* This is no place for a long discussion of whether this objective is right or wrong. Our democratic political process is where such matters are decided.

Therefore, let's try to evaluate the operation of marketing in the American economy—where the objective is to satisfy consumer needs *as consumers*

In the United States, the customer is assumed to be right—usually.

see them. This is the basis of our system. The business firm that ignores this fact is in for trouble.

CAN CONSUMER SATISFACTION BE MEASURED?

Since consumer satisfaction is our objective, marketing effectiveness must be measured by how *well* it satisfies consumers. Unfortunately, consumer satisfaction is hard to define—and harder to measure.

Measuring Macro-Marketing Isn't Easy

Economists believe that consumer satisfaction comes from economic utility—remember form, time, place, and possession utility. However, no practical method of measuring utility has been developed yet. This is partly because satisfaction seems to depend on each person's own view of things. Further, products that were satisfactory one day may not be satisfactory the next day—or vice versa. Most of us now expect cars to work—almost without maintenance! For early car owners (in the 1910s and 20s), breakdowns and flat tires were common. A "Sunday drive" often included fixing several flats—on a dusty road—with no helpful AAA on call! So you can see that consumer satisfaction is a very personal concept which doesn't provide a very good standard for evaluating marketing effectiveness.[1]

The final measure, probably, is whether the macro-marketing system satisfies enough individual consumer/citizens so that they vote—at the ballot box—to keep it running. So far, we have done so in the United States.

There Are Ways to Measure Micro-Marketing

Measuring micro-marketing effectiveness is also difficult. But there are ways that individual business firms can measure how well their products satisfy their customers. These methods include attitude studies, analysis of consumer complaints, opinions of middlemen and salespeople, market test results—and profits.[2]

Since every company uses slightly different marketing strategies, it's up to each customer to decide how well individual firms satisfy his or her needs. Usually, customers are willing to pay higher prices for—or buy more of—products which satisfy them. So profits can be used as a rough measure of a firm's success in satisfying customers. In this sense, a firm's own interests and society's are the same.

Evaluating Marketing Effectiveness Is Difficult—But Not Impossible

Because it's hard to measure consumer satisfaction—and therefore the effectiveness marketing—it's easy to see why there are different views on the subject. If the objective of the economy is clearly defined, however, the quessions about marketing effectiveness probably *can* be answered.

In this chapter, we will argue that micro-marketing (how individual firms and channels operate) frequently *does* cost too much but that macro-marketing (how the whole marketing system operates) *does not* cost too much, *given the present objective of the American economy—consumer satisfaction.* In the end, you will have to make your own decision.[3]

MICRO—MARKETING OFTEN *DOES* COST TOO MUCH

Throughout the text, we talked about what marketing managers could or should do to help their firms do a better job of satisfying customers—while achieving company objectives. While many firms carry out very successful marketing programs, many more firms are still too production-oriented and inefficient. It is clear that many consumers are not happy with the marketing efforts of some firms. "Helping consumers get a fair deal when shopping" ranks very high among public concerns. Only inflation, unemployment, government spending, welfare, and taxes rank higher.[4]

The Failure Rate Is High

Further evidence that most firms are too production-oriented—and not nearly as efficient as they could be—is the fact that many new products fail. New and old businesses fail regularly, too.

These failures are caused by one or more of three reasons:

1. Lack of interest in—or understanding of—the customer.
2. Poor blending of the four Ps—because of a lack of a customer orientation.
3. Lack of understanding of—or failure to adjust to—uncontrollable variables.

The Company Can Get in the Way of the Customer

Serving the customer should be the role of business—but some producers seem to feel that customers are eagerly waiting for any product they turn out. They don't see a business as a "total system" responsible for satisfying customer needs.

Middlemen, too, often get tied up in their own internal problems. Goods may be stocked where it is easy for the retailer to handle them—rather than for

There would be fewer failures of new and old businesses if managers did a better job of marketing strategy planning.

consumers to find them. And fast-moving, hard-to-handle goods may not be stocked at all—"They are too much trouble," or "We're always running out."

In the same way, accounting and finance departments try to cut costs by encouraging the production of standardized, "me-too" products—even though they aren't what customers want.

Company Objectives May Force Higher-Cost Operation

Top-management decisions on company objectives may increase the cost of marketing. A decision to aim for growth for growth's sake, for example, might lead to too much spending for Promotion. Diversification for diversification's sake could require costly new arrangements for Place.

For these reasons, the marketing manager should take a big part in shaping the firm's objectives. Recognizing the importance of marketing, progressive firms have given marketing management more control in setting company objectives. Unfortunately, though, in many more firms, marketing is still looked on as the department that "gets rid of" the product.

Micro-Marketing Does Cost Too Much—But Things Are Changing

Marketing *does* cost too much in many firms. The marketing concept has not *really* been applied in many places. Sometimes, the sales manager is renamed "marketing manager"—and the vice president of sales is called "vice president of marketing"—but nothing else changes. Marketing mixes are still put together by production-oriented managers in the same old ways.

But not all business firms are so old-fashioned. More firms *are* becoming customer-oriented. And some are paying more attention to market-oriented strategic planning—to better carry out the marketing concept.

One hopeful sign is the end of the idea that anybody can run a business successfully. This never was true. Today the growing complexity of business is drawing more and more professionals into the field. This includes not only professional business managers but psychologists, sociologists, statisticians, and economists.

Managers who adopt the marketing concept as a way of business life do a better job. As more of these professionals enter business, micro-marketing costs will go down.

MACRO–MARKETING DOES *NOT* COST TOO MUCH

Many critics of marketing take aim at the operation of the macro-marketing system. They suggest that (1) advertising—and promotion in general—are socially undesirable and (2) that the macro-marketing system causes a poor distribution of resources, limits income and employment, and leads to unfair distribution of income. Most of these complaints imply that some micro-marketing activities should not be allowed—and because of them, our macro-marketing system does a poor job.

Many of these critics have their own version of the ideal way to run an economy. Some of the most severe critics of our marketing system are economists who use pure competition as their ideal. They will give consumers and producers free choice in the market—but they are critical of the way the present market operates. Meanwhile, other critics would scrap our market-directed system and substitute the decisions of central planners for those of individual producers and consumers—reducing freedom of choice in the marketplace. These different views should be kept in mind when evaluating criticisms of marketing.

Is Pure Competition the Ideal?

One criticism of our macro-marketing system is that it permits—or even encourages—the use of too many resources for marketing activities—and that this may actually reduce consumer "welfare." This argument is concerned with how the economy's resources (land, labor, and capital) are used for producing and distributing goods. These critics usually argue that scarce resources should be spent on producing goods—not on marketing them. The basis for this view is the idea that marketing activities are unnecessary and do not create value. These critics feel that pure competition would result in the greatest consumer benefit.

In pure competition, you remember, we assume that consumers are "economic men," that is, that they know all about all the homogeneous offerings and will make "wise" choices. Economic analysis can be made to prove that pure competition will provide greater consumer welfare than monopolistic competition—*if all the conditions of pure competition are met.* But are they?

Different people want different things

Our present knowledge of consumer behavior and people's desire for different products pretty well destroys the economists' "economic man" idea—and therefore the pure-competition ideal.[5] People, in fact, are different—and they want different products. With this type of demand (down-sloping demand curves), monopoly elements naturally develop. A pioneer in this kind of analysis concluded that "monopoly is necessarily a part of the welfare ideal . . ."[6]

Once we admit that not all consumers know everything—and that they have

People are different and they want different things.

many different demands—the need for a variety of micro-marketing activities becomes clear.

New Ideas Help the Economy Grow

Some critics feel that marketing helps create monopolistic competition—and that this leads to higher prices, limits production, and reduces national income and employment.

It is true that firms in a market-directed economy try to carve out separate monopolistic markets for themselves with new products. But customers don't *have* to buy a new product unless they feel it is a better value. The old products are still available. The prices may even be lower on the old products to meet the new competition.

Over several years, the profits of the innovator may rise—but the rising profits also encourage more innovation by competitors. This leads to new investments—which contribute to economic growth and raise the level of national income and employment.

Does Marketing Make People Buy Things They Don't Need?

From our discussion so far, it seems that the individual firm's efforts to satisfy consumer needs would lead to a better division of national income. Giving customers what they want, after all, is the purpose of our market-directed economic system. However, some critics feel that most firms—especially large corporations—do not really try to satisfy consumers. Instead—these critics argue—they use clever ads to persuade consumers to buy whatever the firms want to sell.

Historian Arnold Toynbee, for example, felt that American consumers have been manipulated into buying products which are not necessary to satisfy "the minimum material requirements of life." Toynbee saw American firms as mainly trying to fulfill *unwanted demand*—demand created by advertising—rather than genuine wants. He defined genuine wants as "wants that we become aware of spontaneously, without having to be told by Madison Avenue that we want something that we should never have thought of wanting if we had been left in peace to find out our wants for ourselves."[7]

What are the minimum requirements of life?

One problem with this kind of thinking is how to decide what *are* "the minimum material requirements of life." Which products that we use today are unnecessary—and should be taken off the market? One critic suggested, for example, that Americans could and *should* do without items such as pets, newspaper comic strips, second family automobiles, motorcycles, snowmobiles, campers, recreational boats and planes, cigarettes, pop and beer cans, and hats.[8] You may agree with some of those. But who should decide "minimum material requirements of life"—consumers or critics?

Consumers are not puppets

The idea that firms can persuade consumers to buy anything the company wants to produce simply isn't true. A consumer who buys a can of soda pop that tastes terrible won't buy another can of that brand—regardless of how much it's advertised. In fact, many new products fail the test of the marketplace. Not even large corporations can be sure of success every time they

Advertising is often criticized—but it can result in lower prices and stimulate economic growth.

market a new product. Consider, for example, the sad fate of products such as Ford's Edsel, Du Pont's Corfam, Campbell's Red Kettle Soups, and RCA's computers.

Needs and wants change

Consumer needs and wants are constantly changing. Few of us would care to live the way our grandparents lived—let alone like the pioneers who traveled west in covered wagons. Marketing's job is not just to satisfy consumer wants just for today. Rather, marketing must always *keep* looking for new—and better—ways to serve customers.[9]

Does Marketing Make People Materialistic?

There is no doubt that marketing caters to materialistic values. But there is a lot of disagreement as to whether marketing creates these values—or just appeals to values that are already there.

Anthropologists tell us that even in the most primitive societies people decorate themselves with trinkets—and want to accumulate possessions. In fact, in some tribal villages, social status is measured by how many goats or sheep a person owns. Surely the desire of ancient pharaohs and kings to surround themselves with wealth and treasures can hardly be blamed on the persuasive powers of the advertising agencies!

The idea that marketers create and serve "false tastes"—as defined by individual critics—has been answered by a well-known economist—George Stigler—who said:

> The marketplace responds to the tastes of consumers with the goods and services that are salable, whether the tastes are elevated or depraved. It is unfair to criticize the marketplace for fulfilling these desires, when clearly the defects lie in the popular tastes themselves. I consider it a cowardly concession to a false extension of the idea of democracy to make sub rosa attacks on public tastes by denouncing the people who serve them. It is like blaming waiters in restaurants for obesity.[10]

Marketing reflects our own values

Experts who have studied the issue of materialism seem to agree that—in the short run—marketing reflects social values, while—in the long run—it reinforces them. One expert pointed out that consumers vote for what they want in the marketplace *and* in the polling place. To say that what they choose is *wrong* is to criticize the basic idea of free choice and democracy![11]

Products do improve the quality of life

More is not always better. The quality of life can't be measured just in terms of quantities of products. But when goods and services are seen as the means to an end—rather than the end itself—we can see that products do make it possible to satisfy higher-level needs. Modern appliances, for example, have greatly reduced the amount of time and effort that must be spent on household duties—leaving homemakers with time for other interests. And more dependable cars have expanded people's geographic horizons—affecting where they can live, work and play. Not having "wheels" would drastically change many people's life styles—and even their self images.

Consumers Ask for It, Consumers Pay for It

The monopolistic competition typical of our economy is the result of customer preferences—*not* control of markets by business. Monopolistic competition may seem expensive at times—when we look at individual firms—but it seems to work fairly well at the macro level—in serving the many needs and wants of consumers.

All these demands add to the cost of satisfying consumers. Certainly the total cost is larger than it would be if simple, homogeneous products were offered at the factory door to long lines of customers on a take-it-or-leave-it basis.

But if the role of the marketing system is to serve consumers, then the cost

*Marketing reflects
people's values.*

THE NOVA™

**Style, beauty, and whirlpool pleasure—
all at an affordable price.**

Presenting the Nova whirlpool bath, an ideal combination of distinctive styling, luxurious comfort, and the whirlpool bathing pleasure that only a genuine Jacuzzi Whirlpool Bath can create. But the beauty of the Nova goes beyond what meets the eye, and beyond the convenient features and built-in quality for which we're famous. Because, with all the Nova has to offer, its very moderate price also makes it a stunning value.

The Real One. The Only One.

Jacuzzi

W H I R L P O O L   B A T H

JACUZZI WHIRLPOOL BATH
Subsidiary of Kidde, Inc.
KIDDE

For more product information and dealer locations, call toll free: (800) 227-0710. In California: (800) 227-0991. Or write: P.O. Drawer J, Walnut Creek, CA 94596.

of whatever services they demand cannot be considered too expensive. It's just the cost of serving consumers the way they want to be served.

Does Macro-Marketing Cost Enough?

The question, Does marketing cost too much? has been answered by one well-known financial expert with another question, Does distribution cost enough?[12] What he meant was that marketing is such an important part of our economic system that perhaps even more should be spent on marketing—since "distribution is the delivery of a standard of living"—that is, the satisfaction of consumers' basic needs and wants. In this sense, then, macro-marketing does *not* cost too much. Some of the activities of individual business firms may cost too much—and if these micro-level activities are improved, the performance of the macro system probably will improve. But regardless, our macro-marketing system performs a vital role in our economic system—and *does not cost too much.*

CHALLENGES FACING MARKETERS

We have said that our macro-marketing system does *not* cost too much—given the present objective of our economy—while admitting that the performance of many business firms leaves a lot to be desired. This presents a challenge to serious-minded students and marketers. What needs to be done—if anything?

We Need Better Performance at the Micro Level

Some business executives seem to feel that—in a market-directed economy—they should be completely "free." They don't understand that ours is a market-directed system—and that the needs of consumer/citizens must be met. Instead, they focus on their own internal problems—and don't satisfy consumers very well.

We need better planning

Most firms are still production-oriented. Some hardly plan at all. Others just extend this year's plans into next year. Progressive firms are beginning to realize that this doesn't work in our fast-changing marketplaces. Market-oriented strategy planning is becoming more important in many companies. More attention is being given to the product life cycle—because marketing variables should change through the product's life cycle.

Figure 20–1 shows some of the typical changes in marketing variables which might be needed over the course of a product life cycle. This figure should be a good review—but it also should emphasize why much better planning is needed. As the product life cycle moves on, the marketing manager should *expect* to find more products entering "his" market—and pushing the market closer to pure competition or oligopoly. This means that as the cycle moves along, he might want to shift from a selective to an intensive distribution policy *and* move from a skimming to a penetration pricing policy. The original marketing plan might include these adjustments—and the probable timing.

May Need More Social Responsiveness

A good business manager should put himself in the consumer's place. This means developing more satisfying marketing mixes for specific target markets. It may mean building in more quality or more safety. The consumers' long-run satisfaction should be considered, too. How will the product hold up in use? What about service guarantees?

Note, however, that this doesn't always mean producing the "highest quality" that can be produced. Low-quality, short-lived products may be "right" sometimes—as long as the target market understands what it is getting. (Recall our cost-conscious couple in the home-decorating market in Chapter 2.) Low-cost products—such as the paint in that example—might be seen as a "good value" by some market segments. In other markets, an entirely different product and/or marketing mix might be needed.

It seems doubtful that production-oriented methods will work in the future. Tougher competition—and more watchful government agencies—may force the typical production-oriented business managers to change. Many of the con-

■ FIGURE 20–1   Typical changes in marketing variables over the course of the product life cycle

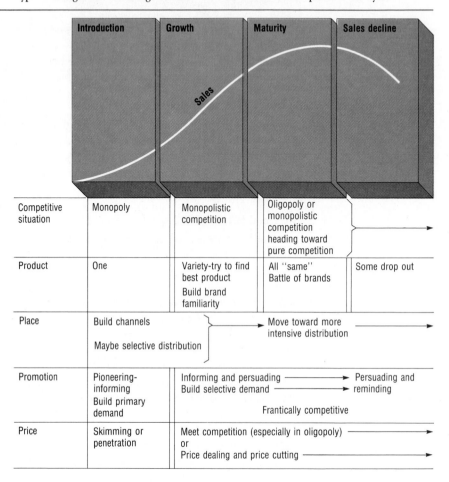

	Introduction	Growth	Maturity	Sales decline
Competitive situation	Monopoly	Monopolistic competition	Oligopoly or monopolistic competition heading toward pure competition	
Product	One	Variety-try to find best product Build brand familiarity	All "same" Battle of brands	Some drop out
Place	Build channels Maybe selective distribution		Move toward more intensive distribution	
Promotion	Pioneering-informing Build primary demand	Informing and persuading ⟶ Persuading and Build selective demand ⟶ reminding Frantically competitive		
Price	Skimming or penetration	Meet competition (especially in oligopoly) ⟶ or Price dealing and price cutting ⟶		

cerns of the consumer movement are caused by the failure of businesses to apply the marketing concept. This has to change.

May Need More Environmental Concern

Besides satisfying consumers' needs, marketers must be aware of environmental problems. A lack of understanding of uncontrollable variables—and a failure to recognize new environmental trends—could be major causes of business failure in the future. Conditions around the world are changing rapidly. Marketing managers must try to see new opportunities, yet be aware of the social and political problems that are part of every new opportunity. They can no longer afford to conduct "business as usual."

We May Need New Laws

One of the advantages of a market-directed economic system is that its operation is relatively automatic—but in our version of this system, consumer/

Marketing managers must be aware of environmental concerns.

citizens provide certain limits (laws). These laws can be strengthened—or modified—at any time.

Need tougher enforcement of present laws

Before piling on too many new laws, however, we should enforce the ones we have. The antimonopoly laws, for example, have often been used to protect competitors from each other—when they really were intended to protect competition.

Laws should affect top management

The results of strict enforcement of present laws could be far reaching if more price fixers, dishonest advertisers, and others who are obviously breaking laws were sent to jail or given heavy fines. A quick change in attitudes might occur if top managers—those who plan overall business strategy—were prosecuted, rather than the salespeople or advertisers who are expected to "deliver" on weak strategies.

In other words, if the government made it clear that it was serious about improving the performance of our economic system, much could be achieved within the present system—*without* adding new laws or trying to "patch up" the present ones.

Need Better-Informed Consumers

We also may need some changes to help potential customers become better informed about the many goods and services on the market. Laws to assure consumers that they will have ways of comparing products (for example, life expectancy of light bulbs and appliances) would be useful. Consumer education designed to teach people how to buy more wisely could be helpful too.

People behave differently as consumers and citizens.

Need Socially Responsible Consumers

We have been stressing the obligation of producers to act responsibly—but consumers have responsibilities, too. This is usually ignored by consumer advocates.[13] Some consumers abuse returned-goods policies, change price tags in self-service stores, and expect attractive surroundings and courteous, well-trained sales and service people—but want discount prices. Others think nothing of "ripping off" businesses.

Americans tend to perform their dual role of consumer/citizens with something of a split personality. We often behave one way as consumers—and then take the opposite stand at the ballot box. For example, while our beaches and parks are covered with garbage and litter, we call for stiff action to curb pollution. We protest sex and violence in the media—and then flock to see *Friday the 13th,* and other R- or X-rated movies. We complain about high energy costs—and then buy low-efficiency appliances.

Let's face it. There is a lot of information already available to aid consumer decision making. The consumerism movement has encouraged nutritional labeling, unit pricing, truth-in-lending, plain-language contracts and warranties, and so on. And government agencies publish many consumer buying guides— as do groups such as Consumers Union. Yet most consumers ignore this information!

We May Need to Modify Our Macro-Marketing System

Our macro-marketing system is built on the idea that we are trying to satisfy consumers. But with resource shortages and high energy costs, how far should the marketing concept be allowed to go?

Should marketing managers limit consumers' freedom of choice?

A "better" macro-marketing system is certainly a good idea. But an important question is what should marketers do—in their roles as producers. Should they, for example, deliberately refuse to produce "energy-gobbling" appliances or cars—even though there is strong demand? Or should they be expected to install safety devices which will increase costs—and which are *not* wanted by potential customers?

Consumer/citizens should vote on the changes

Marketing managers should be expected to improve and expand the range of goods and services they make available to consumers—always trying to better satisfy the needs and wants of potential customers. This is the job we have assigned to business.

If this objective makes "excessive" demands on scarce resources—or causes an "intolerable" level of ecological damage—then consumer/citizens have every right to vote for laws to limit individual firms. These firms can't be expected to fully understand the impact of all their actions. This is the role which we as consumers have assigned to the government—to make sure that the macro-marketing system works effectively.

It is important to see that some critics of marketing are really interested in *basic* changes in our macro-marketing system. And some major changes *might* be accomplished by *seemingly minor* modifications in our present system. Allowing some government agency (for example, the FDA or Consumer Product Safety Commission) to prohibit the sale of products for seemingly good reasons may severely limit our choices in ways we never intended. (Bicycles, for example, are very dangerous consumer products—should they continue to be sold?) Clearly, such government actions could seriously reduce consumers' present "right" to freedom of choice—including "bad" choices.[14]

Consumer/citizens must be careful to see the difference between changes designed just to modify our system and those designed to change it—perhaps completely. In either case, the consumer/citizen should make the decision (through elected representatives). This decision should not be left in the hands of a few well-placed managers—or government planners.

Marketing People May Be Even More Necessary in the Future

No matter what changes might be voted by consumer/citizens, some kind of a marketing system will be needed in the future. If satisfying more subtle needs—such as for the "good life"—becomes our objective, it could be even more important to have market-oriented firms. It may be necessary, for example, not only to define individuals' needs, but also society's needs—perhaps for a "better neighborhood" or "more enriching social experiences," and so on. As we go beyond physical goods—into more sophisticated need-satisfying blends of goods and services—the trial-and-error approach of the typical production-oriented manager becomes even less acceptable.

■ CONCLUSION

Macro-marketing does *not* cost too much. Business has been assigned the role—by consumers—of satisfying their needs as they (the consumers) see them. Customers find it satisfactory—and even desirable—to permit businesses to cater to them. As long as consumers are satis-

fied, macro-marketing will not cost too much—and business firms will be permitted to continue as profit-making organizations.

It must always be remembered that business exists at the consumers' approval. It is only by satisfying consumers that a particular business firm—and our economic system—can justify its existence and hope to keep operating.

In carrying out this role granted by consumers, the activities of business firms are not always as effective as they might be. Many business managers do not understand the marketing concept— or the role that marketing plays in our way of life. They seem to feel that business has a God-given right to operate as it chooses. And they proceed in their typical production-oriented ways. Further, many managers have had little or no training in business management—and are not as competent as they should be. In this sense, micro-marketing *does* cost too much. The situation is being improved, however, as training for business expands—and as more competent people are attracted to marketing and business. Clearly, *you* have a role to play in improving marketing in the future.

Marketing has new challenges to face in the future. All consumers may have to settle for a lower standard of living. Resource shortages, high energy costs, and slowing population growth all combine to reduce income growth. This will force consumers to shift their consumption patterns—and politicians to change some of the rules governing business. Even our present market-directed system may be threatened.

To keep our system working well, individual business firms should try to be more efficient and socially responsible as they carry out the marketing concept. At the same time, individual consumers have the responsibility to use goods and services in an intelligent and socially responsible way. Further, they have the responsibility to vote and make sure that they get the kind of macro-marketing system they want. What kind do you want? What can—and should—you do to see that fellow consumer/citizens will vote for your system? Is your system likely to satisfy you, personally, as well as another macro-marketing system? You don't have to answer these questions right now. But your answers will affect the future you will live in—as well as how satisfied you will be.

■ QUESTIONS AND PROBLEMS

1. Explain why marketing must be evaluated at two levels. Also, explain what criteria you feel should be used for evaluating each level of marketing, and defend your answer. Explain why your criteria are "better" than alternative criteria.

2. Discuss the merits of various economic system objectives. Is the objective of the American economic system sensible? Do you feel more consumer satisfaction might be achieved by permitting some sociologists—or some public officials—to determine how the needs of the lower-income or less-educated members of the society should be satisfied? If you approve of this latter suggestion, what education or income level should be required before an individual is granted free choice by the social planners?

3. Should the objective of our economy be maximum efficiency? If your answer is yes, efficiency in what? If not, what should the objective be?

4. Cite an example of a critic using his own value system when evaluating marketing.

5. Discuss the conflict of interests among production, finance, accounting, and marketing executives. How does this conflict contribute to the operation of an individual business? Of the economic system? Why does this conflict exist?

6. Why does the text indicate that the adoption of the marketing concept will encourage more efficient operation of an individual business? Be specific about the impact of the marketing concept on the various departments of a firm.

7. It appears that competition sometimes leads to inefficiency in the operation of the economic system in the short run. Many people argue for monopoly in order to eliminate this inefficiency. Discuss this solution to the problem of inefficiency.

8. How would officially granted monopolies affect the operation of our economic system? Specifically, consider the effect on allocation of resources, the level of income and employment, and the distribution of income. Is the effect any different than if a monopoly were obtained through winning out in a competitive market?

9. Is there any possibility of a pure-competition economy evolving naturally? Could legislation force a pure-competition economy?

10. Comment on the following statement: Ultimately, the high cost of marketing is due only to consumers.

11. Should marketing managers, or business managers in general, be expected to refrain from producing profitable products which some target customers want but which may not be in their long-run interest? Or should firms be expected to produce "good" products which offer a lower rate of profitability than usual? What if only a break-even level is obtainable? What if the products are likely to be unprofitable, but the company is also producing other products which are profitable so that on balance it will still make some profit? What criteria are you using for each of your answers?

12. Should a marketing manager or a business refuse to produce an "energy-gobbling" appliance which some consumers are demanding? Similarly, should it install an expensive safety device which does not appear to be desired by potential customers and inevitably will increase costs? Are the same principles involved in both of these questions? Explain.

13. Discuss how much slower economic growth or even no economic growth would affect your college community—and in particular its marketing institutions.

■ **SUGGESTED CASES**

Appendix C ■ Career planning in marketing

When you finish this appendix, you should:

1. Know that there is a job—or a career—for you in marketing.

2. Know that marketing jobs can pay well.

3. Understand the difference between "people-oriented" and "thing-oriented" jobs.

4. Know about the many marketing jobs from which you can choose.

One of the hardest jobs facing most college students is the choice of a career. Of course, we can't make this decision for you. You must be the judge of your own objectives, interests, and abilities. Only you can decide what career *you* should pursue. However, you probably owe it to yourself to at least consider the possibility of a career in marketing.

THERE'S A PLACE IN MARKETING FOR YOU

We're happy to tell you that many opportunities are available in marketing. Regardless of your abilities or training, there's a place in marketing for everyone—from a supermarket bagger to a vice president of marketing in a large consumer goods company such as Procter & Gamble or General Foods. The opportunities range widely—so it will be helpful to be a little more specific. In the following pages, we will discuss (1) the financial returns in marketing jobs, (2) setting your own objectives—and evaluating your interests and abilities, and (3) the kinds of jobs available in marketing.

MARKETING JOBS CAN PAY WELL

The supermarket bagger may earn only the minimum wage, but there are many more challenging jobs for those with marketing training.

Fortunately, marketing jobs open to college-level students do pay well! At the time this went to press, marketing undergraduates were being offered starting salaries ranging from $13,000 to $25,000 a year. Of course, these figures are the extremes. Starting salaries can vary considerably—depending on your background, experience, and location.

As shown in Table C–1, starting salaries in sales-marketing compare favorably with many other fields—although they are lower than those for fields such as engineering, for which college graduates are currently in very high demand. How far and fast your income rises above the starting level, however, depends on many factors—including your willingness to work, how well you get along with people, and your individual abilities. But most of all, it depends on *getting results*—individually and through other people. And this is where many marketing jobs offer the newcomer great opportunities. It is possible to show initiative, ability, and judgment in marketing jobs. And some young people move up very rapidly in marketing. Some even end up at the top in large companies—or as owners of their own businesses.

Marketing Can Be the Route to the Top

Marketing is where the action is! In the final analysis, the success or failure of a firm depends on the effectiveness of its marketing program. This doesn't mean the other functional areas aren't important. It merely reflects the fact that a firm will have little need for accountants, finance people, production managers, and so on if it cannot successfully market its products.

Because marketing is so vital to the survival of a firm, many companies look for people with training and experience in marketing when filling key exec-

■ TABLE C–1   Average starting salaries of 1984 college graduates (with bachelor's degrees) in selected fields

Field	Average starting salary (per month)
Engineering	$2,237
Computer	2,072
Chemistry	2,016
Mathematics or statistics	1,868
Accounting	1,681
Sales—marketing	1,635
Business administration	1,618

Source: Victor R. Lindquist, *Northwestern Endicott Report 1984* (Evanston, Ill.: Northwestern University, The Placement Center).

■ FIGURE C–1   Main career emphasis of corporate chief executive officers*

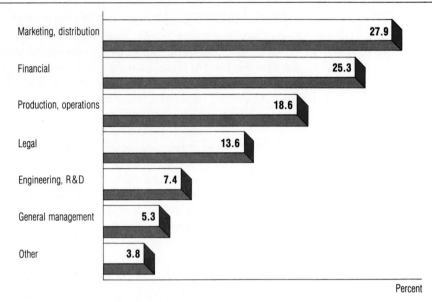

Marketing, distribution — 27.9
Financial — 25.3
Production, operations — 18.6
Legal — 13.6
Engineering, R&D — 7.4
General management — 5.3
Other — 3.8

Percent

*Based on a survey of the chief executive officers of the nation's 500 largest industrial corporations and 300 non-industrial corporations (including commercial banks, life insurance firms, retailers, transportation companies, utilities, and diversified financial enterprises).

Source: Adapted from Charles G. Burck, "A Group Profile of the Fortune 500 Chief Executive," *Fortune*, May 1976, p. 172.

utive positions. A recent survey of the nation's largest corporations showed that the greatest proportion of chief executive officers had backgrounds in marketing and distribution (see Figure C–1).

DEVELOP YOUR OWN PERSONAL MARKETING STRATEGY

Now that you know there are many opportunities in marketing, your problem is matching the opportunities which are available to your own personal objectives and strengths. Basically the problem is a marketing problem: developing a marketing strategy to "sell" a product—yourself—to potential employers. Just as in planning strategies for products, developing your own strategy takes careful thought. Figure C–2 shows how you can organize your own strategy planning. This figure shows that you should evaluate yourself first—a personal analysis—and then analyze the environment—for opportunities. This will help you sharpen your personal long-run and short-run objectives—which will lead to developing a strategy. And, finally, you will start implementing your own personal marketing strategy. These ideas are explained more fully below.

■ FIGURE C–2   Organizing your own personal marketing strategy planning

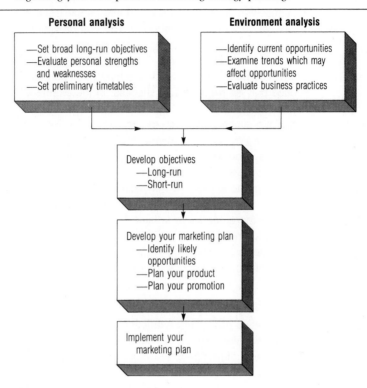

CONDUCT YOUR OWN PERSONAL ANALYSIS

You are the "Product" which you are going to include in your own marketing plan. So first you have to decide what your long-run objectives are—what you want to do, how hard you want to work, and how quickly you want to reach your objective. Be honest with yourself—or you will face eventual frustration. It's helpful to evaluate your own personal strengths and weaknesses—and decide what factors may become the key to your success. Finally, as part of your personal analysis, set some preliminary timetables—to guide your strategy planning and implementation efforts. Let's spell this out in detail.

Set Broad Long-Run Objectives

Strategy planning requires much "trial-and-error" decision making. But at the very beginning, you should make some tentative decisions about your own objectives—what you want out of a job—and out of life. At the very least, you should decide whether you are just looking for a "job"—or whether you want to build a "career." And beyond this, do you want the position to be personally satisfying—or is the financial return enough? And just how much financial return do you need—or are you willing to work for? Some people work only to support themselves and their leisure-time activities. Others work to support themselves and their families. These people seek only financial rewards from a job—and try to find job opportunities that provide adequate financial returns while not being too demanding of their time or effort. Other people, however, look first for satisfaction in their job—and seek opportunities for career advancement. Financial rewards may be important, too, but these may be used only as measures of success. In the extreme, the career-oriented individual may be willing to sacrifice much—including leisure and social activities—to achieve success in a career.

Once you have tentatively decided on these matters, then you can get more serious about whether you should seek a job—or a career—in marketing. If you have decided to pursue a career, you should set your broad long-run objectives to achieve it. For example, one long-run objective might simply be to pursue a career in marketing management (or marketing research). This might require more academic training than you had been planning for—as well as a different kind of training. If your objective is to get a "job" that pays well, on the other hand, then this would call for a different kind of training and different kinds of job experiences before completing your academic work.

Evaluate Personal Strengths and Weaknesses

What kind of a job is right for you?

Because of the great variety of marketing jobs, it's hard to generalize about what aptitudes you should have, ideally, to pursue a career in marketing. Different jobs attract people with various interests and abilities. Here, we will provide some guidelines about what kinds of interests and abilities marketers should have. Note: If you are completely "lost" about your own interests and abilities, you probably should see your campus career counselor and take some vocational aptitude and interest tests. These tests will help you to compare yourself with people who are now working in various career positions. They will *not* tell you what you should do, but they can help—especially in eliminating things you are less interested in and/or less able to do well.

Are You "People-Oriented" or "Thing-Oriented?"

One of the first things you should try to decide for yourself is whether you are basically "people-oriented" or "thing-oriented." This is a very important decision. A "people-oriented" person probably would not be very happy in a bookkeeping job, for example, while a "thing-oriented" person might be miserable in a personal selling job which involves a lot of customer contact.

Marketing has both "people-oriented" and "thing-oriented" jobs. People-oriented jobs are primarily in the promotion area—where company representatives must make contact with potential customers. This may be direct personal selling or customer service activities—for example, in technical service or installation and repair. Thing-oriented jobs focus more on creative activities and analyzing data—as in advertising and marketing research—or on organizing and scheduling work—as in operating warehouses, transportation agencies, or the "back-end" of retailers.

People-oriented jobs tend to pay more, in part because such jobs are more likely to affect sales—the life blood of any business. Thing-oriented jobs, on the other hand, are often seen as "cost-generators" rather than "sales-generators." Taking a big view of the whole company's operations, the thing-oriented jobs are certainly necessary, but without sales no one is needed to do them.

Thing-oriented jobs are usually done at the company's facilities. Further, especially in lower-level jobs, the amount of work that needs to be done—and even the nature of the work—may be spelled out quite clearly. The time it takes to design questionnaires and tabulate results, for example, can be estimated with reasonable accuracy. Similarly, running a warehouse, totaling inventories, packaging outgoing shipments, and so on are more like production operations. It's fairly easy to measure an employee's effectiveness and productivity in a thing-oriented job. At the least, time put in is a measure of the employee's contribution.

A sales representative, on the other hand, might spend all weekend thinking and planning how to make a half-hour sales presentation on Monday. For what should the sales rep be compensated—the half-hour presentation, all of the planning and thinking that went into it, or the results? Typically, sales reps are rewarded for their sales results—and this helps account for the sometimes extremely high salaries paid to effective order getters. At the same time, some people-oriented jobs can be routinized and are lower paid. For example, sales clerks in some retail stores are paid at or near the minimum wage.

Managers Needed for Both Kinds of Jobs

We have oversimplified deliberately to emphasize the differences among types of jobs. Actually, of course, there are many variations between the two extremes. Some sales reps must do a great deal of analytical work before they make a presentation. Similarly, some marketing researchers must be extremely people-sensitive to get potential customers to reveal their true feelings. But the division is still useful—because it focuses on the primary emphasis in different kinds of jobs.

Managers are needed for the people in both kinds of jobs. Managing others generally requires a blend of both people and analytical skills—but people skills may be the more important of the two. Therefore, we often see people-oriented persons being promoted as managers of other people.

What Will Differentiate Your "Product"?

After deciding whether you are generally "people-oriented" or "thing-oriented," you are ready for the next step—to try to identify your specific strengths (to be built upon) and weaknesses (to be avoided or remedied). It is important to become as specific as possible so you can develop a better marketing plan. For example, if you decide you are more people-oriented, are you more skilled in verbal *or* in written communication? Or if you are more thing-oriented, what specific analytical or technical skills do you have? Are you good at working with numbers, solving complex problems, or coming to the root of a problem? Other possible strengths include past experience (career-related or otherwise), academic performance, an outgoing personality, enthusiasm, drive, motivation, and so on.

It is important to see that your plan should build on your strengths—after all, an employer will be hiring you to do something. And you probably should "promote" yourself as someone who is able to do something *well*. In other words, you should have some "competitive advantage" over other prospective employees—and this will be built on the unique things about *you* and what you can do.

While trying to identify strengths, you also must realize that you may have some important weaknesses—depending on your objectives. If you are seeking a career which requires technical skills, for example, then you need to get these skills. Or if you are seeking a career which requires much self-motivation and drive, then you should seek to develop these characteristics in yourself—or change your objectives.

Set Some Timetables

At this point in your strategy planning process, you ought to set some timetables—to organize your thinking and the rest of your planning. You need to make some decisions at this point—to be sure you see where you are going. You might simply focus on getting your "first job," or you might decide to work on two marketing plans: (1) a short-run plan to get your first job and (2) a longer-run plan—perhaps a five-year plan—to show how you're going to accomplish your long-run objectives. People who are basically job-oriented may "get away with" only a short-run plan—just drifting from one opportunity to another as their own objectives and opportunities change. Those interested in "careers," however, need a longer-run plan. Otherwise, they may find themselves pursuing attractive first job opportunities which satisfy short-run objectives—but leave them quickly frustrated when they realize that they can't achieve their long-run objectives without additional training or other experiences.

ENVIRONMENT ANALYSIS

Strategy planning is a matching process—and for your own strategy planning, this means matching yourself to career opportunities. So now let's look at opportunities available in the marketing area. (The same approach applies, of course, in the whole business area.) Some of the possibilities and salary ranges are shown in Figure C–3.

An environment analysis looks at the kinds of business opportunities which are available—and current business practices and attitudes in areas which you might feel are opportunities for you.

Identifying Current Opportunities in Marketing

Because of the wide range of opportunities in marketing, it will be helpful to try to narrow your possibilities. After deciding on your own objectives, and strengths and weaknesses, think about where in the marketing system you might like to work. Would you like to work for manufacturers, or wholesalers, or retailers? Or doesn't it really matter? And do you want to be involved with consumer goods or industrial goods? By analyzing your feelings about these possibilities, you can begin to zero in on the kind of job and the functional area which might interest you most.

■ FIGURE C–3   Some career paths and salary ranges

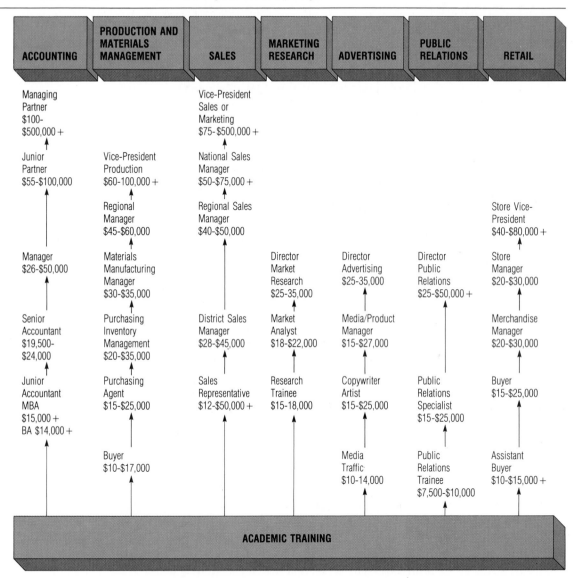

Source: Adapted from Lila B. Stair, *Careers in Business: Selecting and Planning Your Career Path* (Homewood, Ill.: Richard D. Irwin, 1980) and other sources.

One simple way to get a better idea of the kinds of jobs available in marketing is to review the chapters of this text—this time with an eye for job opportunities rather than new concepts. The following paragraphs contain brief descriptions of job areas that are often of interest to marketing graduates—with references to specific chapters in the text. Some, as noted below, offer good starting opportunities, while others do not. While reading these paragraphs, keep your own objectives, interests, and strengths in mind.

Marketing manager (Chapter 2)

This is usually not an entry-level job, although aggressive students may move quickly into this role in smaller companies.

Marketing research opportunities (Chapter 5)

There are entry-level opportunities at all levels in the channel (but especially in large firms where more formal marketing research is done) and in advertising agencies and marketing research firms. Quantitative and behavioral science skills are extremely important in marketing research. So many firms prefer to hire statistics or psychology graduates rather than business graduates. But there still are many opportunities in marketing research for marketing graduates. A recent graduate might begin in a training program—conducting interviews or coding questionnaires—before being promoted to assistant project manager and subsequent management positions.

Consumer researcher (Chapters 3 and 5)

Opportunities as consumer analysts and market analysts are commonly found in large companies, marketing research organizations, and advertising agencies. Beginners start in "thing-oriented" jobs until their judgment and people-oriented skills have been tested. Because knowledge of statistics and/or behavioral sciences is very important, marketing graduates will find themselves competing with majors in fields such as psychology, sociology, statistics, and computer science.

Purchasing agent/buyer (Chapter 7)

Opportunities are commonly found in large companies, with beginners starting as trainees or assistant buyers under the supervision of experienced buyers.

Market analyst (Chapters 3, 5, and 9)

See consumer researcher.

Product planner (Chapter 10)

This probably would not be an entry-level position. Instead, people with experience on the technical side of the business and/or in sales might be moved into new product development as they demonstrate judgment and analytical skills.

Product/brand manager (Chapters 9 and 10)

Many multi-product firms have brand or product managers handling individual products—in effect, managing each product as a separate business. Some firms hire marketing graduates as assistant brand or product managers, although typically only MBAs are considered. Most firms prefer that recent college graduates spend some time in the field doing sales work before moving into brand or product management positions.

Packaging specialists (Chapter 9)

Packaging manufacturers tend to hire and train interested people from various backgrounds—because there is little formal academic training in packaging. There are many sales opportunities in this field—and the manufacturers train interested people to be specialists fairly quickly in this growing area.

Distribution channel management (Chapter 11)

This work is typically handled or directed by sales managers—and therefore is not an entry-level position.

Retailing opportunities (Chapter 12)

Most entry-level marketing positions in retailing involve some kind of sales work. Retailing positions tend to offer lower-than-average starting salaries—but often provide opportunities for very rapid advancement. Most retailers require new employees to have some selling experience before managing others—or buying. A typical marketing graduate can expect to do some sales work and manage one or several departments before advancing to a store management position—or to a staff position which might involve buying, advertising, marketing research, and so on.

Physical distribution opportunities (Chapter 11)

There are many sales opportunities with physical distribution specialists— but there are also many "thing-oriented" jobs involving traffic management, warehousing, and materials handling. Here, training in accounting, finance, and quantitative methods could be quite useful. These kinds of jobs are available at all levels in the channels of distribution—remember that about half of the cost of marketing is caused by physical distribution activities.

Sales promotion opportunities (Chapter 14)

There are not many entry-level positions in this area. Creativity and judgment are required—and it is difficult for an inexperienced person to demonstrate these skills. A beginner would probably move from sales or advertising jobs into sales promotion.

Personal sales opportunities (Chapter 15)

Most of the job opportunities—and especially entry-level jobs—are in personal selling. This might be order getting, order taking, or missionary selling. Many students are reluctant to get into personal selling—but this field offers benefits that are hard to match in any other field. These include the opportunity to earn extremely high salaries and commissions—quickly—a chance to develop your self-confidence and resourcefulness, an opportunity to work with minimal supervision—almost to the point of being your own boss—and a chance to acquire product and customer knowledge that many firms consider necessary for a successful career in product/brand management, sales management, and marketing management. Note, however, that many salespersons spend their entire careers in selling—preferring the freedom and earning potential that go with the job over the headaches and sometimes lower salaries of sales management positions.

Advertising opportunities (Chapter 16)

Job opportunities are varied in this area—and highly competitive. And because the ability to communicate and knowledge of the behavioral sciences are important, marketing graduates will often find themselves competing with majors from fields such as English, journalism, psychology, and sociology. There are "thing-oriented" jobs such as copywriting, media buying, art, and so on. And there are "people-oriented" positions involving sales—which are probably of more interest to marketing graduates. This is a glamorous, but small and extremely competitive industry where young people can rise very rapidly—but can also be as easily displaced by new "bright young people."

Pricing opportunities (Chapters 17 and 18)

Pricing is generally handled by experienced executives, so there are no entry-level opportunities here. In fact, in some companies pricing is not even handled by the sales or marketing people, as explained in the text.

Credit management opportunities

Specialists in credit have a continuing need for employees who are interested in evaluating customers' credit ratings and ensuring that money gets collected. Both people skills and "thing" skills can be useful here. Entry positions normally involve a training program—and then working under the supervision of others, until your judgment and abilities are tested.

International marketing opportunities (Chapter 19)

Many marketing students are intrigued with the adventure and foreign travel promised by careers in international marketing. However, very few firms hire recent college graduates for positions in international marketing—except some MBA graduates from schools that specialize in international trade. Graduates aiming for a career in international marketing usually must spend time mastering the firm's domestic marketing operations before being sent abroad.

Marketing cost and revenue analysis opportunities

Only progressive large firms use these kinds of techniques—usually as analytical tools in sales or marketing management. Some larger firms have staff departments to do these kinds of analyses, but more typically they are simply tools applied by more analytical researchers and managers in their respective jobs. A MBA degree probably would be needed to go directly into a staff position requiring this sort of work.

Customer relations/consumer affairs opportunities (Chapters 16 and 20)

Some firms are becoming more concerned about their relations with customers and the general public. Employees in this kind of work, however, usually have held various positions with the firm before doing customer relations.

**Study Trends Which
May Affect Your
Opportunities**

A strategy planner should always be evaluating the future—because it is easier to go along with trends than to buck them. This means you should watch for political, technical, or economic changes which might open—or close—career opportunities. If you can spot a trend early, you may be able to prepare yourself to take advantage of it as part of your long-run strategy planning. Other trends might mean you should avoid certain career options. For example, rapid technological changes in computers and communications are likely to lead to major changes in retailing and advertising—as well as in personal selling. Cable television, telephone selling, and direct-mail selling may reduce the need for routine order takers—while increasing the need for higher level order getters. More targeted and imaginative sales presentations—to be delivered by mail—and through the telephone or television screen—may be needed. The retailers who survive may need to have a better understanding of their target markets—and be supported by wholesalers and manufacturers who can plan more targeted promotions which make economic sense. This will require a better understanding of the production and physical distribution side of business—as well as of the financial sector. This means better training in accounting, finance, inventory control, and so on. So plan your personal strategy with such trends in mind.

**Evaluate Business
Practices**

Finally, you should know how businesses really operate—and the kind of training required for various jobs. We've already seen that there are many opportunities in marketing—but not all jobs are open to everyone, and not all jobs are entry jobs. Positions such as marketing manager, brand manager, and sales manager are higher rungs on the marketing career ladder. They become available only when you have a few years of experience—and have shown leadership and judgment. Some positions require more education than others. So take a hard look at your long-run objectives—and then see what business expects for the kinds of opportunities you might like. Will a two-year degree get you where you want to go? Or will you need a four-year degree, or even a graduate degree? Is a degree really necessary, or will it only be "helpful"—perhaps to make up for lack of experience or to speed your progress toward your objective?

Women may want to look at whether there are many women in the kinds of positions or kinds of firms they are considering. Some firms and industries are more progressive than others. You should try to find attractive opportunities which match with what you can offer. And if no women are in the positions or firms you are considering, you should decide whether you want to be one of the first to "pioneer" in this area—or whether you want to pursue opportunities with easier entry.

Fortunately, marketing positions are generally concerned with "getting results," and who is doing it is less important than the fact that it gets done. Nevertheless, it is desirable for anyone planning a career to be realistic about the business practices in firms with likely opportunities. Remember, it is usually better to go *with* trends than to buck them.

DEVELOP OBJECTIVES

Once you have done a personal analysis and environment analysis—identifying your personal interests, strengths and weaknesses, and opportunities in the environment—you must define your objectives more specifically—both long-run and short-run.

Develop Long-Run Objectives

Your long-run objectives should clearly state what *you* want to do—and what you will do for potential employers. You might want to be as specific as indicating the exact career area you will pursue over the next 5 to 10 years. For example, your long-run objective might be to apply a set of marketing research and marketing management tools to the food manufacturing industry—with the objective of becoming director of marketing research in a small food manufacturing company.

Your long-run objectives should be realistic and attainable. They should be objectives you have thought about and for which you feel you have the necessary skills (or the capabilities to develop those skills) as well as the motivation to reach the objectives.

Develop Short-Run Objectives

To achieve your long-run objective(s), you need to develop one or more short-run objectives. These should spell out the five-year objectives that are related in some way to reaching your long-run objective(s). For example, you might begin to develop a variety of marketing research skills *and* marketing management skills—because both are needed to reach the longer-run objective. Or you might obtain an entry-level position in marketing research in a large food manufacturer—to gain experience and background. An even shorter-run objective might be to take the academic courses which are necessary to get that desired entry-level job. In this example, you would probably need a minimum of an undergraduate degree in marketing—with an emphasis on marketing research. (Note that given the longer-run objective of managerial responsibility, it probably would be desirable to have a business degree rather than a statistics or psychology degree.)

DEVELOPING YOUR MARKETING PLAN

Now that you have developed your objectives, you can move on to developing your own personal marketing plan. This means zeroing in on likely opportunities and developing a specific marketing strategy for these opportunities. Let's talk about that now.

Identify Likely Opportunities

An important step in strategy planning is to identify potentially attractive opportunities. Depending on where you are in your academic training, this can vary all the way from preliminary exploration to making detailed lists of compa-

When Mr. Donald confronted Jack Kenny—the vice president of marketing—with this charge, his reply was, "It's not our fault. I think the company made a key mistake after World War II. It expanded horizontally—by increasing its number of product offerings—while major competitors were expanding vertically, growing their own raw materials and making all of their packing materials. They can control quality and make profits in manufacturing which can be used in marketing. I lost some of my best people from frustration. We just aren't competitive enough to reach the market the way we should with a comparable product and price."

In further conversation with Kenny, Mr. Donald learned more about the nature of Foodco's market. Although all the firms in the food-processing industry advertise widely to the consumer market, there has been no real increase in the size of the market for processed foods. Further, consumers aren't very selective. If they can't find the brand of food they are looking for, they'll pick up another brand rather than go without a basic part of their diet. No company in the industry has much effect on the price at which its products are sold. Chain store buyers are used to paying about the same price per case for any competitor's product—and won't exceed it. They will, however, charge any price they wish on a given brand sold at retail. (That is, a 48-can case of sweet peas might be purchased from any supplier for $17.28, no matter whose product it is. Generally, the shelf price for each is no more than a few pennies different, but chain stores occasionally attract customers by placing a well-known brand on "sale.")

At this point, Mr. Donald is wondering why Foodco isn't as profitable as it once was. Also, he is puzzled as to why the competition is putting products on the market with low potential sales volume. For example, one major competitor recently introduced a line of dietary fruits and vegetables.

Discuss Foodco's policies and what it might do to improve its situation.

■ 2. BORMAN CLEANING COMPANY

Tom Borman is a 26-year-old ex-Navy frogman and a native of Traverse City, Michigan—a beautiful summer resort area along the eastern shore of Lake Michigan. The area's permanent population is about 50,000—and this more than triples in the summer months.

Tom spent seven years in the Navy after high school graduation, returning home in June 1981. Tom decided to go into business for himself because he couldn't find a good job in the Traverse City area. He set up Borman Cleaning Company. Tom felt that his savings would allow him to start the business without borrowing any money. His estimates of required expenditures were: $4,600 for a used panel truck, $525 for a steam-cleaning machine adaptable to carpets and furniture, $375 for a heavy-duty commercial vacuum cleaner, $50 for special brushes and attachments, $75 for the initial supply of cleaning fluids and compounds, and $200 for insurance and other incidental expenses. This total of $5,825 still left Tom with about $2,800 in savings to cover living expenses while getting started.

One of the reasons Tom chose this kind of business is his previous work experience. From the time he was 16, Tom had worked part-time for Joe Bullard. Mr. Bullard operated the only other successful carpet-cleaning company in Traverse City. There is one other company in Traverse City, but rumors suggest it is near bankruptcy.

Mr. Bullard prides himself on quality work and has a loyal clientele. Specializing in residential carpet cleaning, Bullard has built a strong customer franchise. For 35 years, Bullard's major source of new business, besides retailer recommendations, has been satisfied customers who tell friends about the quality service received from Mr. Bullard. He is so highly thought of that the leading carpet and furniture stores in Traverse City always recommend Bullard's for preventive maintenance in quality carpet and furniture care. Often Bullard is trusted with the keys to Traverse City's finest homes for months at a time—when owners are out of town and want his services. Bullard's customers are so loyal, in fact, that a Vita-Clean national household carpet-cleaning franchise found it impossible to compete with him. Even price cutting was not an effective weapon against Mr. Bullard.

Tom Borman felt that he knew the business as well as Mr. Bullard—having worked for him many years. Tom was anxious to reach his $40,000-per-year sales objective because he thought this would provide him with a comfortable living in Traverse City. While aware of opportunities for carpet cleaning in businesses, such as office buildings and motels, Tom felt that the sales volume available there was only about $16,000 because most businesses had their own cleaning staffs. As he saw it, his only opportunity was direct competition with Bullard.

To get started, he allocated $800 to advertise his business in the local newspaper. With this money he bought two large "announcement" ads and 52 weeks of daily three-line ads in the classified section—listed under Miscellaneous Residential Services. All that was left was to paint a sign on his truck and wait for business to "take off."

Tom had a few customers and was able to gross about $100 a week. He had, of course, expected much more. These customers were usually Bullard regulars who, for one reason or another (usually stains, spills, or house guests), weren't able to wait the two weeks required until Bullard could work them in. While these people did admit that Tom's work was of the same quality as Mr. Bullard's, they preferred Bullard's "quality-care" image. Sometimes, Tom did get more work than he could handle. This happened during April and May—when resort owners were preparing for summer openings and owners of summer homes were ready to "open the cottage." The same rush occurred in September and October—as resorts and homes were being closed for the winter. During these months, Tom was able to gross about $100 to $120 a day—working 10 hours.

Toward the end of his discouraging first year in business, Tom Borman began to think about quitting. While he hated to think of having to leave Traverse City, he couldn't see any way of making a living in the carpet- and furniture-cleaning business in Traverse City. Mr. Bullard had the whole residential market sewed up—except in the rush seasons and for people who needed emergency cleaning.

Why wasn't Tom Borman able to reach his objective of $40,000? Is there any way Tom can stay in business?

■ 3. **APEX CHEMICAL COMPANY**

Apex Chemical Company is a large Texas manufacturer of basic chemicals and polymer resins.

Tom Zang, a bright young engineer, has been working for Apex as a research engineer in the polymer resins laboratory. His job is to do research on established resins—to find new, more profitable applications for resin products.

During the last five years, Tom has been

under heavy pressure from top management to come up with an idea that would open up new markets for the company's foamed polystyrene.

Two years ago, Tom developed the "spiral-dome concept," a method of using the foamed polystyrene to make dome-shaped roofs and other structures. He described the procedure for making domes as follows: The construction of a spiral dome involves the use of a specially designed machine which bends, places, and bonds pieces of plastic foam together into a pre-determined dome shape. In forming a dome, the machine head is mounted on a boom, which swings around a pivot like the hands of a clock, laying and bonding layer upon layer of foam board in a rising spherical form.

According to Tom, polystyrene foamed boards have several advantages:

1. Foam board is stiff—but can be formed or bonded to itself by heat alone.
2. Foam board is extremely lightweight and easy to handle. It has good structural rigidity.
3. Foam board has excellent and permanent insulating characteristics. (In fact, the major use for foamed board is as an insulator.)
4. Foam board provides an excellent base on which to apply a variety of surface finishes.

Using his good selling abilities, Tom had little trouble convincing top management of the soundness of the idea.

According to a preliminary study by the marketing department, the following were areas of construction that could be served by the domes:

1. Bulk storage.
2. Cold storage.
3. Educational construction.
4. Industrial tanks (covers for).
5. Light commercial construction.
6. Planetariums.
7. Recreational construction (such as a golf-course starter house).

The study focused on uses for existing dome structures. Most of the existing domes are made of concrete or some cement base material. It was estimated that large savings would result from using foam boards—due to the reduction of construction time.

Because of the new technology involved, the company decided to do its own contracting (at least for the first four to five years after starting the sales program). It felt this was necessary to make sure that no mistakes were made by inexperienced contractor crews. (For example, if not applied properly, the plastic may burn.)

After building a few domes to demonstrate the concept, the company contacted some leading architects across the country. Reactions were as follows:

> It is very interesting, but you know that the Fire Marshal of Detroit will never give his OK.
>
> Your tests show that foamed domes can be protected against fires, but there are no *good* tests for unconventional building materials as far as I am concerned.
>
> I like the idea, but foam board does not have the impact resistance of cement.
>
> We design a lot of recreational facilities, and kids will find a way of poking holes in the foam.
>
> Building codes in our area are written for wood and cement structures. Maybe when the codes change.

After this unexpected reaction, management didn't know what to do. Tom still thinks the company should go ahead. He feels that a few reports of well-constructed domes in leading newspapers would go a long way toward selling the idea.

What should Apex do? Why did it get into the present situation?

■ 4. UNCLE LYLE'S, INC.

Mr. Lyle Miller is the president and only stockholder of Uncle Lyle's, Inc., a small, successful firm in the restaurant and recreation business in Big Rapids—the site of the state university (population 15,000 plus 20,000 students). Mr. Miller attended the university in the 1950s—and paid most of his college expenses by selling refreshments at all of the school's athletic events. As he expanded his business, he hired local high school students to help him. The business became so profitable that Mr. Miller decided to stay in Big Rapids after graduation—renting a small building near the campus and opening a restaurant.

Over the years, his restaurant business was fairly successful. Mr. Miller earned a $36,000 profit on sales of $1,462,500 in 1981. The restaurant now consists of an attractive 40-table dining room, a large drive-in facility, and free delivery of orders to any point on campus. The only thing that hasn't changed much is Mr. Miller's customers. He estimates that his restaurant business is still over 90 percent students—and that over three fourths of his sales are made between 6 P.M. and 1 A.M. There are several other restaurants with comparable facilities near the campus, but none of these is as popular with the university students as his "Uncle Lyle's."

As a result of the restaurant's success with the student market, Mr. Miller has aimed his whole promotion effort in that direction—by advertising only through the campus newspaper and over the campus and local rock music radio stations. In an attempt to increase his daytime business, from time to time Mr. Miller has used coupon mealbooks priced at 85 percent of face value. And he features daily "lunch specials." Nevertheless, he admits that he hasn't been able to compete with the university cafeterias for daytime business.

In 1972, when Mr. Miller was looking for a new investment opportunity, he contacted a national manufacturer of bowling equipment and supplies about the possibility of opening a bowling alley. Big Rapids didn't have such a facility at the time, and Mr. Miller felt that both the local and university communities would provide a good market. He already owned a large tract of land suitable for construction of the bowling lanes. The land was next to the restaurant—and he felt that this would result in each business stimulating the other.

He went ahead with the bowling venture, and to date the results have been nothing short of outstanding. Several local and university groups have formed bowling leagues. The university's men's and women's physical education departments schedule several bowling classes at Mr. Miller's bowling lanes each term. And the casual bowling in the late afternoons and evenings is such that at least 12 of the 16 lanes are almost always in use. Mr. Miller does some local radio advertising for the bowling lanes, but he doesn't feel that much is necessary. The success of the bowling lanes has encouraged the developer of a small shopping center in the residential part of town to make plans to include a similar facility in his new development. But Mr. Miller believes that competition won't hurt his business because he has more to offer in his recreation center—a restaurant and bowling.

Early in 1982, pleased with the profitability of his bowling investment, Mr. Miller decided to expand his recreational center even further. He noted that both students and local citizens patronized his bowling lanes and concluded that the addition of an attractive, modern billiard parlor would also have a common appeal. There were already two poolrooms in Big Rapids. One was modern—about two miles from campus. The other one was considered to be a "hangout" and was avoided by townspeople and students. Mr. Miller decided that distance and atmosphere were the factors which caused both operations to be only marginally successful. Further, he felt that by offering a billiard parlor operation, he would be able to satisfy yet another recreational demand. He obtained a loan from a local bank and began to build a third building at the back of his land. The billiard parlor was outfitted with 12 tables, a snack bar, wall-to-wall carpeting, and a soft-music background system.

Today, eight months later, Mr. Miller is extremely disappointed with the billiard parlor operation. After the first two or three weeks, business steadily dropped off until now usually only one or two tables are in use—even during the evening hours when business at the bowling lanes is at its peak. Promotion for the billiard parlor has been combined with promotions for the other facilities—which are still doing very well.

In an effort to discover what went wrong, Mr. Miller interviewed several of his restaurant and bowling customers. Some typical responses were:

A *coed:* "I had enough trouble learning how to bowl—but at least it's sociable. Pool looks hard, and everyone is so serious."

A *fraternity man:* "My idea of a good date is dinner at Uncle Lyle's, then the movies or an evening of bowling. You just can't make a good impression by taking a girl to play pool."

A *Big Rapids citizen:* "I've never allowed my children to enter the local pool halls. What's more, as a kid I wasn't allowed either, and so I've never learned the game. It's too late to teach an old dog new tricks!"

Mr. Miller is thinking about selling the billiard equipment and installing pinball and electronic game machines—because he has heard they can be very profitable.

Evaluate Mr. Miller's overall situation and suggest what he should do.

■ 5. INDIAN STEEL COMPANY

Indian Steel Company is one of the two major producers of wide-flange beams in the Chicago area. The other major producer in the area is the U.S. Steel Corporation (USS)—which is several times larger than Indian, as far as production capacity on this particular product is concerned. Bethlehem Steel Company and USS have eastern plants which also produce this product. There are some small competitors, but generally, U.S. Steel and Indian Steel are the major competitors in wide-flange beams in the Chicago area— because typically the mill price charged by all producers is the same and customers must pay freight from the mill. Therefore, the large eastern mills' delivered prices wouldn't be competitive in the Chicago area.

Wide-flange beams are one of the principal steel products used in construction. They are the modern version of what are commonly known as "I-beams." USS rolls a full range of wide flanges from 6 to 36 inches. Indian entered the field about 25 years ago—when it converted an existing mill to produce this product. This mill is limited to flanges up to 24 inches, however. At the time of the conversion, it was estimated that customer usage of sizes over 24 inches was likely to be small. In the past few years, however, there has been a definite trend toward the larger and heavier sections.

The beams produced by the various competitors are almost identical—since customers buy according to standard dimensional and physical-property specifications. In the smaller size range, there are a number of competitors, but above 14 inches, only USS and Indian compete in the Chicago area. Above 24 inches, USS has had no competition.

All the steel companies sell these beams through their own sales forces. The customer for these beams is called a "structural fabricator."

This fabricator typically buys unshaped beams and other steel products from the mills and shapes them according to the specifications of each customer. The fabricator sells to the contractor or owner of a building or structure being built.

The structural fabricator usually sells on a competitive-bid basis. The bidding is done on the plans and specifications prepared by an architectural or structural engineering firm—and forwarded to him by the contractor wanting the bid. Although several hundred structural fabricators compete in the region, relatively few account for the majority of wide-flange tonnage. Since the price is the same from all producers, they typically buy beams on the basis of availability (i.e., availability to meet production schedules) and performance (reliability in meeting the promised delivery schedule).

Several years ago, Indian production schedulers saw that they were going to have an excess of hot-rolled plate capacity in the near future. At the same time, a new production technique was developed which would enable a steel company to weld three plates together into a section with the same dimensional and physical properties and almost the same cross section as a rolled wide-flange beam. This technical development appeared to offer two advantages to Indian: (1) it would enable Indian to use some of the excess plate capacity, and (2) larger sizes of wide-flange beams could be offered. Cost analysts showed that by using a fully depreciated plate mill and the new welding process it would be possible to produce and sell larger wide-flange beams at competitive prices, i.e., at the same price charged by USS.

Indian's managers were excited about the possibilities—because customers usually appreci-

ate having a second source of supply. Also, the new approach would allow the production of up to a 60-inch depth of section and an almost 30-inch width of flange. With a little imagination, these larger sizes could offer a significant breakthrough for the construction industry.

Indian decided to go ahead with the new project. As the production capacity was being converted, the salespeople were kept well informed of the progress. They, in turn, promoted this new capability—emphasizing that soon they would be able to offer a full range of beam products. Several general information letters were sent to the trade, but no advertising was used. Moreover, the market development section of the sales department was very busy explaining the new possibilities of the process—particularly to fabricators at engineering trade associations and shows.

When the new production line was finally ready to go, the market reaction was disappointing. In general, the customers were wary of the new product. The structural fabricators felt they could not use it without the approval of their customers—because it would involve deviating from the specified rolled sections. And as long as they could still get the rolled section, why make the extra effort for something unfamiliar—especially with no price advantage. The salespeople were also bothered with a very common question: How can you take plate which you sell for about $450 per ton and make a product which you can sell for $460? This question came up frequently and tended to divert the whole discussion to the cost of production—rather than to the way the new product might be used.

Evaluate Indian's situation. How could it gain greater acceptance for its new product?

■ 6. THE LIDO

The Lido is a fairly large restaurant—covering about 20,000 square feet of floor space—located in the center of a small shopping center which was completed early in 1981. In addition to this restaurant, other businesses in the shopping center include a bakery, a beauty shop, a liquor store, and a meat market. Ample parking space is available.

The shopping center is located in a residential section of a growing suburb in the East—along a heavily traveled major traffic artery. The nearby population is middle-income families, and although the ethnic background of the residents is fairly heterogeneous, a large proportion are Italian.

The Lido—which sells mostly full-course dinners (no bar)—is operated by Tony DeLuca—a neat-appearing man who was born in the community in 1930, of Italian parentage. He graduated from a local high school and a nearby university and has been living in this town with his wife and two children for many years. He has been in the restaurant business (self-employed) since his graduation from college in 1952. His most recent venture—before opening the Lido—was a large restaurant which he operated successfully with his brother from 1971 to 1977. In 1977, he sold out because of illness. Following his recovery, he was anxious for something to do and opened the present restaurant in April 1981.

Tony felt that his plans for the business and his opening were well thought out. He had even designed his very attractive sign three years before. When he was ready to go into this business, he looked at several possible locations before finally deciding on the present one. He said: "I looked everywhere, and this is one of the areas I inspected. I particularly noticed the heavy traffic when I first looked at it. This is the crossroads from north to south for practically every main artery statewide. So obviously the potential is here."

Having decided upon the location, Tony attacked the problem of the new building with enthusiasm. He tiled the floor; put in walls of surfwood; installed new plumbing and electrical fixtures and an extra washroom; and purchased the necessary restaurant equipment—all brand new. All this cost $52,000—which came from his own cash savings. He then spent an additional $1,200 for glassware, $2,000 for his initial food stock, and $1,525 to advertise his opening in the local newspaper. The local newspaper covered the whole metro area, so the $1,525 purchased only three quarter-page ads. These expenditures also came from his own personal savings. Next, he hired five waitresses at $100 a week and one chef at $250 a week. Then, with $12,000 cash reserve for the business, he was ready to open. (His wife was a high school teacher and could support the family—until the restaurant caught on.) Reflecting his "sound business sense," Tony felt that he would need a substantial cash reserve to fall back on until the business got on its own feet. He expected this to take about one year. He did not have any expectations about "getting rich overnight."

The business opened in April and by August had a weekly gross revenue of only $1,500. Tony was a little discouraged with this, but he was still able to meet all his operating expenses without investing any "new money" in the business. However, he was concerned that he might have to do so if business didn't pick up in the next couple of months. It had not by September, and Tony did have to invest an additional $1,500 in the business "for survival purposes."

Business had not improved in November, and Tony was still insisting that it would take at least a year to build up a business of this type. In view of this slow start, Tony stepped up his advertising to see if this would help the business any. In the last few weeks, he had spent $500 of his cash reserve for radio advertising—10 late evening spots on a news program at a station which aims at "middle-income America." Moreover, he was planning to spend even more during the next several weeks for some newspaper ads.

By April 1982, the situation had begun to improve, and by June his weekly gross was up to between $2,000 and $2,100. By March of 1983, the weekly gross had risen to about $2,500. Tony increased the working hours of his staff six to seven hours a week—and added another cook to handle the increasing number of customers. Tony was more optimistic for the future because he was finally doing a little better than "breaking even." His full-time involvement seemed to be paying off. He had not put any new money into the business since the summer of 1982 and expected business to continue to rise. He had not yet taken any salary for himself, even though he

had built up a small "surplus" of about $7,000. Instead, he planned to put in an air-conditioning system at a cost of $5,000—and was also planning to use what salary he might have taken for himself to hire two new waitresses to handle the growing volume of business. And he saw that if business increased much more he would have to add another cook.

In explaining the survival and growth of his business, Tony said: "I had a lot of cash on hand, a well-planned program, and the patience to wait it out."

Evaluate Tony's marketing strategy. How could he have improved his chances for success and achieved more rapid growth?

■ 7. NITE-TIME MOTEL

After several years as a partner responsible for sales in a medium-sized manufacturer, in 1979 Ben Baker sold his interest at a nice profit. Then, looking for an interesting opportunity that would be less demanding, he spent a lot of time studying alternatives. He decided to buy the Nite-Time Motel—a recently completed 60-room motel at the edge of a small town in a relatively exclusive but rapidly expanding resort area—because he saw a strong market potential for public accommodations. The location was about one-half mile off an interstate highway—and on the road (15 miles away) to a tourist area with several nationally franchised full-service resort motels suitable for "destination" vacations.

He was able to hire the necessary staff—which initially consisted of four maids and a handyman—to care for general maintenance. Mr. Baker and his wife looked after registration and office duties. Since he had traveled a lot himself and had stayed at many different hotels and motels, he had some definite ideas about what vacationers wanted in accommodations. He felt that a relatively plain but modern room with a comfortable bed, standard bath facilities, and air conditioning would appeal to most people.

He felt a swimming pool or any other non-revenue-producing additions were not worthwhile—and considered a restaurant to be a greater management problem than the benefits it would offer. However, after many customers commented, he arranged to serve a free continental breakfast of coffee and rolls from a service counter in a room next to the registration desk.

During the first year of operation, occupancy began to stabilize around 50 to 60 percent of capacity. According to figures which Mr. Baker obtained from *Trends in the Hotel-Motel Business,* published by the accounting firm of Harriss, Kerr, Forster & Company, this was far below the average of 78 percent for his classification—motels without restaurants.

Comparison with these results after two years of operation began to disturb Mr. Baker. He decided to evaluate his operation and look for ways of increasing both occupancy rate and profitability. He did not want to give up his independence—and was trying not to compete directly with the resort areas offering much more complete services. Mr. Baker stressed a price appeal in his signs and brochures. He was quite proud of the fact that he had been able to avoid all the "unnecessary expenses" of the resorts and was able to offer lodging at a very modest price—30 percent below that of even the lowest-priced resort area motels. The customers who stayed at his motel said they found it quite acceptable, but he was troubled by what seemed to be a large number of people driving into his parking lot, looking around, but not coming in to register.

Mr. Baker was particularly interested in the results of a recent study by the regional tourist bureau. This study revealed the following information about area vacationers:

1. 68 percent of the visitors to the area are young couples and older couples without children.
2. 40 percent of the visitors plan their vacations and reserve rooms more than 60 days in advance.
3. 66 percent of the visitors stay more than three days in the area and at the same location.
4. 78 percent of the visitors indicated that recreational facilities were important in their choice of accommodations.
5. 13 percent of the visitors had family incomes of less than $10,000 per year.
6. 38 percent of the visitors indicated that it was their first visit to the area.

Evaluate Mr. Baker's strategy. What should he do to improve the occupancy rate and profitability of the motel?

■ **8. ICELAND**

Fred Born is the manager of Iceland—an ice-skating rink with a conventional hockey rink surface (85 feet × 200 feet). He has a successful hockey program and is almost breaking even—which is about all he can expect if he emphasizes hockey. To try to improve his financial condition, Fred is trying to develop a public skating program. With such a program, it would be possible to have as many as 700 people in a public session at one time, instead of limiting the use of the ice to 12 to 24 people per hour. While the receipts from hockey might be $100 an hour (plus concessions), the receipts from a two-hour public skating session—charging $2 per person—could generate as much as $1,400 for a two-hour period (plus much higher concession revenue). Clearly, the potential revenue from large public skating sessions could add significantly to total receipts and make Iceland a profitable operation.

Fred has put several public skating sessions into his ice schedule, but so far they have not attracted as many people as he hoped. In fact, on the average, they don't generate any more revenue than if the times were sold for hockey use. Even worse, more staff people are needed to handle a public skating session—guards, a ticket seller, skate rental, and more concession help.

The Sunday afternoon public skating sessions have been the most successful—with an average of 300 people attending during the winter season. Typically, this is a "kid-sitting" session with more than half of the patrons being young children who have been dropped off by their parents for several hours. There are some family groups. In general, the kids and the families do seem to have a good time, and a fairly loyal group comes back Sunday after Sunday during the winter season. In the spring and fall, however, attendance drops about in half, depending on how nice the weather is. (Fred schedules no public sessions in the summer—focusing instead on hockey clinics and figure skating.)

It is the Friday and Saturday evening public sessions which are a big disappointment. The sessions run from 8 until 10—a time when he had hoped to attract couples. At $2 per person, plus 75 cents for skate rental if necessary, this could be a more economical date than going to the movies. In fact, Fred has seen quite a few young couples—and some keep coming back.

But he also sees a surprising number of 8- to 12-year-olds who have been dropped off by their parents. In other words, there is some similarity to the Sunday afternoon kid-sitting session. The younger kids tend to race around the rink, playing tag. This affects the whole atmosphere—making it less appealing for dating couples.

Fred feels that it should be possible to develop a teenage and young-adult market—adapting the format used by roller-skating rinks. Their public skating sessions feature a variety of "couples-only" and "group games" as well as individual skating to dance music. This is not the format offered at the usual public ice skating session, however. The idea of making them social activities has not been common, although industry "rumors" suggest that a few operators have had success with the roller-skating format.

Fred installed some soft lights to try to change the evening atmosphere. The music was designed to encourage couples to skate together. For a few sessions, Fred even tried to have some "couples-only" skates, but this was strongly resisted by the young boys who felt that they had paid their money and there was no reason why they should be "kicked off the ice." Fred also tried to attract more young couples by bringing in a local disk jockey to broadcast from Iceland—playing music and advertising the public sessions. But all this has had little effect on attendance—which varies from 50 to 100 per two-hour session.

Fred seriously considered the possibility of limiting the weekend evening sessions to people over 13—to try to change the environment. But when he counted the patrons, he realized that this would be risky. More than half of the patrons on an average weekend night are 12 or under. This means that he would have to make a serious commitment to building the teenage and young-adult market. And, so far, his efforts have not been successful. He has already invested over $2,000 in lighting changes, and over $6,000 promoting the sessions over the rock music radio station—with disappointing results.

Some days, Fred feels it is hopeless. Maybe he should accept that a public skating session is a "mixed-bag." Or maybe he should just sell the time to hockey groups.

What should Fred Born do? Why?

■ 9. BARNES FLORIST SHOP

Barnes Florist Shop is owned and operated by Harold and Anne Barnes (a husband-and-wife team). Offering hundreds of varieties and arrangements of flowers, Barnes' also carries small gift items to complement a floral arrangement. Mr. Barnes serves as manager and sales clerk, while Mrs. Barnes uses her artistic talents to select and arrange flowers. Since opening in 1977, sales have been good. Mr. Barnes, however, is concerned about the failure of a recent addition to the gift line.

The Barneses bought the present operation in 1977 from Jack Boyd—who had been in the location for 20 years. Called Boyd's Florists, the shop was then grossing about $100,000 a year. Harold and Anne were confident that their previous 12 years' experience owning a smaller floral shop in a tiny (population 6,500) resort town less than 20 miles south would help them become a success in their new location.

Harold Barnes feels their new store is in an excellent location. Located in a residential area of a northeast Indiana community of 130,000 population, the new Barnes Florist Shop is somewhat isolated from other neighborhood stores. It is eight blocks to the nearest store—a drug store—and 3½ miles to the closest shopping center. But it is near the intersection of the major north-south and east-west streets.

The Barneses feel they understand their primary customers' characteristics. This helps them direct their efforts more efficiently. As a result, sales increased steadily from $150,000 at the end of 1977 to $300,000 in 1982. Most of the regular customers are women—from medium- to high-income families—living in the local middle-class residential areas. Also, the Barneses are pleased to see that some of their old customers from the resort town come to the new shop—probably because a strong customer acceptance had been built on friendly service and quality floral arrangements. Customers who stop in less frequently are assumed to be similar to the "regulars."

The largest part of the shop's business consists of weddings, funerals, parties, dances, and other big, one-time events which need flowers. However, about 15 percent of the purchases are by casual buyers who like to browse and chat with the Barneses. Approximately 65 percent of the sales are telephone orders, while the remaining 35 percent are made in the shop. Almost all of the telephone orders are for special, one-time events, while the walk-in traffic is divided equally between special events and spur-of-the-moment purchases. Almost no one buys flowers on a daily or regular basis. There is some FTD (Florist Telegraph Delivery) business, but Mr. Barnes considers this to be an added service. It is only about 5 percent of their volume.

Mr. Barnes feels that flowers are fairly homogeneous, unbranded products. Therefore, he feels that he must charge competitive prices to meet those of his 14 competitors throughout the community.

The shop was remodeled in 1978—and selling space was doubled. To fill in the increased display area, it was decided to add several complementary gift items—such as a famous brand of candies, high-quality flowerpots and vases, hand-painted jogging suits for women, pen-and-pencil sets, and candles. All the new lines—except the suits—have taken hold and have increased in sales each month since the items were added. Sales of the suits have been very disappointing. In fact, they haven't paid their way on the basis of display area allotted (about 1/50 of the total display area).

When the busiest store traffic occurs (during a three- to four-day period before traditional flower-giving days), additional help is used. When available, Mary and Will Barnes—the high school-aged children of the owners—fill these jobs. (It was the children who suggested that the market for jogging clothes was growing in their high school during the last school year.) At other times, only one of the owners and a full-time sales clerk handle store traffic.

Samples of everything the shop has for sale are on display. The main activity of the sales clerk is to show customers various selections which could be used for a particular occasion—write up the order—and then ring up the sale. Other than store displays, advertising consists only of what is printed on the delivery truck, an ad in the Yellow Pages of the local telephone directory, and an occasional ad (five or six times per year) in the daily newspaper. None of the advertising mentions anything but flowers—because the Barneses wish to maintain their identity as "florists."

The Barneses are wondering if more display area, a lower price, or extra promotion by the sales clerks might move more of the jogging suits. Further, they are thinking of clearing them out, but aren't sure what should replace them if they did.

Evaluate the present operation and why jogging suits don't sell. What strategy or strategies should the Barneses follow?

■ 10. REVON COMPANY

The Revon Company is a well-known manufacturer of high-quality cosmetics and creams. A little over a year ago, Mr. Byron, the president of Revon, was analyzing the income statements for the last three quarters and didn't like what he saw. At the next board meeting, he stated that Revon should be showing a larger profit. It was generally agreed that the reason for the profit decline was that the firm had not developed any new products during the last two years. The top management team was ordered to investigate this problem—and remedy it if possible.

Mr. Byron immediately asked for a report from the product planning group and found that it had been working on a formula for a new toothpaste that might be put into production immediately if a new product were needed. Mr. Emerson, the head of the research department, assured Mr. Byron that the new ingredients in this toothpaste had remarkable qualities. Clinical tests had consistently shown that the new, as yet unnamed, toothpaste cleaned teeth better than the many toothpastes furiously battling for market share. Based on these tests, Mr. Byron concluded that this product was what was needed—and ordered work to proceed quickly to bring it to the market.

The marketing research department was asked to come up with a pleasing name—and a tube and carton design. Several consulting organizations helped speed the process, and the results were reported back within two months. The product was to be called "Smile," and the package would emphasize eye-catching colors.

The marketing department decided to offer Smile along with its other "prestige" products in the drug stores which were carrying the rest of Revon's better-quality, higher-priced products.

Revon's success had been built on selling quality products through these outlets, and management felt that quality-oriented customers would be willing to pay a bit more for a better toothpaste. Revon was already well established with the wholesalers selling to these retailers and had little difficulty obtaining distribution for Smile.

It is now six months after the introduction of Smile, and the sales results have not been good. The regular wholesalers and retailers stocked the product, but little was purchased by final customers. And now retailers are demanding that Revon accept returns of Smile. They feel it is not going to catch on with consumers—despite the extremely large (matching that of competitors) amounts of advertising which have supported Smile.

Mr. Byron has asked the marketing research department to analyze the situation and explain the disappointing results thus far. It immediately designed a focus group interview with people who had tried Smile and a focus group taste test with non-users. An outside survey agency conducted the tests and tabulated the results. These are pretty well summarized in the following quotes:

> The stuff I'm using now tastes good. Smile tastes terrible!
>
> I never saw that brand at the supermarket where I shop.
>
> I like what I'm using . . . why change?
>
> I'm not going to pay that much for any toothpaste . . . it couldn't be *that* much better!

What recommendation would you make to Mr. Byron? Why?

■ 11. PANG CORPORATION

Pang Corporation is one of the larger chemical companies in the United States—making a wide line of organic and inorganic chemicals, plastics, bio-products, and metals. Technical research has played a vital role in the company's growth.

Recently, Pang's research laboratories developed a new product in the antifreeze line—Save-10. Much research was devoted to the technical phase, involving various experiments concerned with the quality of the new product.

The antifreeze commonly used now is ethylene glycol. If it leaks into the crankcase oil, it forms a thick, pasty sludge that can cause bearing damage, cylinder scoring, or a dozen other costly and time-consuming troubles for both the operator and the owner of heavy-duty equipment.

Pang Corporation believed that Save-10 would be very valuable to the owners of heavy-duty diesel and gasoline trucks—as well as other heavy-equipment owners. Chemically, Save-10 uses a propanol product—instead of the conventional glycol and alcohol products. It cannot prevent leakage, but if it does get into the crankcase, it will not cause any problems.

At first, Pang thought it had two attractive markets for this product: (1) the manufacturers of heavy-duty equipment, and (2) the users of heavy-duty equipment. Pang sales reps have made numerous calls, and so far neither type of customer has been very interested. The manufacturers are reluctant to show interest in the product until it has been proven in actual use. The buyers for construction companies and other firms using heavy-duty equipment have also been hesitant. Some said the price was far too high for the advantages offered. Others didn't understand what was wrong with the present antifreeze—and refused to talk any more about paying extra for "just another" antifreeze.

The price of Save-10 is $16 per gallon—more than twice the price of regular antifreeze. The higher price is due to higher costs in producing the product and an increment for making a better type of antifreeze.

Explain what has happened so far. What would you do if you were responsible for this product?

■ 12. MASON SPORTS SHOP

Bob and Mary Mason graduated from a state university in California in 1981. With some family help, they were planning to open a small ski equipment shop in Aspen, Colorado. They were sure that by offering friendly, personal service they would have something unique and be able to compete with the many other ski shops in town. They were well aware that there were already many competitors because many "ski bums" choose the Aspen area as a place to live—and then try to find a way to earn a living there. By keeping the shop small, however, the Masons hoped to be able to manage most of the activities themselves—keeping costs down and

also being sure of good service for their customers.

Now they are trying to decide which line—or lines—of skis they should carry. Almost all the major manufacturers' skis are offered in the competing shops, so Bob and Mary are seriously considering specializing in the King brand—which is not now carried by any local stores. In fact, the King sales rep has assured them that if they are willing to carry the line exclusively, then King will not sell its skis to any other retailers in Colorado. This appeals to Bob and Mary because it would given them something unique—a new kind of American-made skis which are just being introduced into the U.S. market with supporting full-page ads in skiing magazines. The skis have an injected foam core that is anchored to boron and fiberglass layers above and below by a patented process which causes the fiberglass to penetrate the foam. The process is the result of several years of experimenting by a retired space capsule designer—Kurt King. He felt that it should be possible to apply "space technology" to building lighter and more responsive skis. Now his small company—King Manufacturing Company—is ready to sell the new design as "recreational skis" for the large "beginner" and "intermediate" markets. Jim Vane, the King sales rep, is excited about the possibilities and compares the King ski development to the Head ski (first metal ski) and Prince tennis racket (first "outsize" racket) developments which were big successes. Both of these successes were built on the pioneering work of one man—Mr. Head—who Jim feels is very much like Mr. King—a "hard-working genius."

The Masons are interested because they would have a unique story to tell about skis which could satisfy almost every skier's needs. Further, the suggested retail prices and markups were similar to those of other manufacturers, so the Mason Ski Shop could emphasize the unique features of the King skis while keeping their prices competitive.

The only thing that worries the Masons about committing so completely to the King line is that there are many other manufacturers—both domestic and foreign—which claim to offer unique features. In fact, most ski manufacturers regularly come out with new models and features, and the Masons realize that most consumers are confused about the relative merits of all of the offerings. In the past, Bob, himself, has been reluctant to buy "off-brand" skis—preferring instead to stay with major names such as Hart, Head, K2, and Rossignol. So he wonders if a complete commitment to the King line is wise. On the other hand, the Masons do want to offer something unique. They don't want to run just another ski shop carrying lines which are available "everywhere." The King line isn't their only possibility, of course. There are other "off-brands" which are not yet carried in Aspen. But the Masons like the idea that King is planning to give national promotion support to the skis during the introductory campaign. They feel that this might make a big difference in how rapidly the new skis are accepted. And if they provide friendly sales assistance and quick binding-mounting service, perhaps their chances for success will be even greater. Another reason for committing to the King line is that they like the sales rep, Jim Vane, and are sure he would be a big help in their initial stocking and set-up efforts. They talked briefly with some other firms' salespeople at the major trade shows, but had not gotten along nearly so well with any of them. In fact, most of the sales reps didn't seem too interested in helping a newcomer—preferring instead to talk with and entertain buyers from established stores. The major ski shows are over, so any more contacts with manufacturers will mean the Masons must take the initiative. But from their past experience, this doesn't sound too appealing. Therefore, they seem to be drifting fast toward specializing in the King line.

Evaluate the Masons' and Jim Vane's thinking. What should the Masons do?

■ 13.   VISUAL SERVICES, INC.

Visual Services, Inc., is located in a residential area along a major street about two miles from the downtown of a metropolitan area of 450,000. It is also near a large university. It sells high-quality still and movie cameras, accessories, and projection equipment—including 8mm and 16mm movie projectors, 35mm slide projectors, opaque and overhead projectors, and a large assortment of projection screens. Most of the sales of this specialized equipment are made to area school boards for classroom use, to industry for use in research and sales, and to the university for use in research and instruction.

Visual Services (VS) also offers a wide selection of film and a specialized film-processing service. Instead of processing film on a mass production basis, VS gives each roll of film individual attention—to bring out the particular features requested by a customer. This service is used extensively by local firms which need high-quality pictures of lab or manufacturing processes for analytical and sales work.

To encourage the school and industrial trade, VS offers a graphics consultation service. If a customer wants to build a display—whether large or small—professional advice is readily available. Along with this free service, VS carries a full line of graphic arts supplies.

VS employs four full-time store clerks and two outside sales reps. These sales reps make calls on business firms, attend trade shows, make presentations for schools, and help both present and potential customers in their use and choice of visual aids.

The people who make most of the over-the-counter purchases are (1) serious amateur pho-tographers and (2) some professional photographers who buy in small quantities. Price discounts of up to 25 percent of the suggested retail price are given to customers who buy more than $1,000 worth of goods per year. Most regular customers qualify for the discount.

In the last few years, many more "amateurs" have been taking 35mm pictures (slides) using compact automatic and semi-automatic full-frame cameras priced under $150. These cameras are easy to carry and use—and have attracted many people who had never taken 35 mm pictures (slides)—or any pictures (slides)—before. Because of this, Ken Beem, the manager of VS, felt that there ought to be a good opportunity to expand sales during the Christmas "gift-giving" season. Therefore, he planned a special pre-Christmas sale of three of the most popular brands of these compact cameras and discounted the prices to competitive "discount store" levels. To promote the sale, large signs were posted in the store windows—and ads were run in a Christmas-gift-suggestion edition of the local newspaper. This edition appeared each Wednesday during the four weeks before Christmas. At these prices and with this promotion, Ken hoped to sell at least 450 cameras. However, when the Christmas returns were in, total sales were 57 cameras. Ken was most disappointed with these results—especially because trade estimates suggested that sales of compact cameras in this price and quality range were up 300 percent over last year.

Evaluate what happened. What should Ken Beem do to increase sales and profits?

■ 14. MILLER COMPANY

Butch Miller graduated from a large midwestern university in 1979 with a B.S. in business. After a year as a car salesman, he decided to go into business for himself. Looking for new opportunities, Butch placed several ads in his local newspaper, in Columbus, Ohio—explaining that he was interested in becoming a sales representative in the local area. He was quite pleased to receive a number of responses. Eventually, he became the sales representative in the Columbus area for three local manufacturers: The Morgan Drill Company, which manufactures portable drills; the E. F. Wang Company, a manufacturer of portable sanding machines; and the Casey Lathe Company, which manufactures small lathes. All of these companies were relatively small and were represented in other areas by other sales representatives like Butch Miller.

Miller's main job was to call on industrial customers. Once he made a sale, he would send the order to the respective manufacturer, who would in turn ship the goods directly to the customer. The manufacturer would bill the customer, and Miller would receive a commission varying from 5 percent to 10 percent of the dollar value of the sale. Miller was expected to pay his own expenses.

Miller called on anyone in the Columbus area who might use the products he was handling. At first, his job was relatively easy, and sales came quickly because there was little sales competition. There are many national companies making similar products, but at that time, they were not well represented in the Columbus area.

In 1981, Miller sold $150,000 worth of drills, earning a 10 percent commission; $75,000 worth of sanding machines, also earning a 10 percent commission; and $100,000 worth of small lathes, earning a 5 percent commission. He was encouraged with his progress and was looking forward to expanding sales in the future. He was especially optimistic because he had achieved these sales volumes without overtaxing himself. In fact,

he felt he was operating at about 70 percent of his capacity.

Early in 1982, however, a local manufacturer with a very good reputation—the Sen Equipment Company—started making a line of portable drills. By April 1982, Sen had captured approximately one half of Morgan's Columbus drill market by charging a substantially lower price. Sen was using its own sales force locally, and it was likely that it would continue to do so.

The Morgan Company assured Miller that Sen couldn't afford to continue to sell at such a low price and that shortly Morgan's price would be competitive with Sen's. Butch Miller was not nearly as optimistic about the short-run prospects, however. He began looking for other products he could handle in the Columbus area. A manufacturer of hand trucks had recently approached him, but Butch wasn't too enthusiastic about this offer because the commission was only 2 percent on potential annual sales of $150,000.

Now Butch Miller is faced with another decision. The Kenny Paint Company, also in Columbus, has made what looks like an attractive offer. They heard what a fine job he was doing and felt that he could help them solve their present problem. Kenny is having trouble with its whole marketing effort and would like Butch Miller to take over.

The Kenny Paint Company has been selling mainly to industrial customers in the Columbus area and is faced with many competitors selling essentially the same products and charging the same low prices. Kenny Paint is a small manufacturer. Last year's sales were $210,000. They could handle at least four times this sales volume with ease—and are willing to expand to increase sales—their main objective in the short run. They have offered Miller a 12 percent commission on sales if he will take charge of their pricing, advertising, and sales efforts. Butch was flattered by their offer, but he is a little worried because there might be a great deal more traveling than he is doing at present. For one thing, he would have to call on new customers in Columbus, and he might have to travel outside Columbus to expand the paint business. Further, he realizes that he is being asked to do more than just sell. But he did have marketing courses in college and thinks the new opportunity might be challenging.

What should Butch Miller do? Why?

■ 15.   COOPER LUMBER COMPANY

Bill Cooper—now 55 years old—has been a salesman for over 30 years. He started selling in a department store, but gave it up after 10 years to work in a lumberyard because the future looked much better in the building materials industry. After drifting from one job to another, he finally settled down and worked his way up to manager of a large wholesale building materials distribution warehouse in Kansas City, Kansas. In 1962, he decided to go into business for himself, selling carload lots of lumber to large retail yards in the western Missouri and eastern Kansas area.

He made arrangements to work with five large lumber mills on the West Coast. They would notify him when a carload of lumber was available to be shipped, specifying the grade, condition, and number of each size board in the shipment. Bill wasn't the only person selling for these mills, but he was the only one in his area. He was not obligated to take any particular number of carloads per month—but once he told the mill he wanted a particular shipment, title passed to him and he had to sell it to someone. Bill's main function was to buy the lumber from the mill as it was being shipped, find a buyer, and have the railroad divert the car to the buyer.

Bill has been in this business for 20 years, so he knows all of the lumberyard buyers in his area very well—and is on good working terms with them. Most of his business is done over the telephone from his small office, but he tries to see each of the buyers about once a month. He has been marking up the lumber between 4 and 6 percent—the standard markup, depending on the grades and mix in each car—and has been able to make a good living for himself and his family. The "going prices" are widely publicized in trade publications, so the buyers can easily check to be sure Bill's prices are competitive.

In the last few years, however, interest rates have been high for home loans and the building boom slowed down. Bill's profits did too, but he decided to stick it out—figuring that people still needed housing, and that business would pick up again.

Six months ago, an aggressive salesman—much younger than Bill—set up in the same business, covering about the same area but representing different lumber mills. This new salesman charges about the same prices as Bill, but undersells him once or twice a week in order to get the sale. Many lumber buyers—knowing that they are dealing with a homogeneous product—seem to be willing to buy from the lowest-cost source. This has hurt Bill financially and personally—because even some of his "old friends" are willing to buy from the new man if the price is lower. The near-term outlook seems dark, since Bill doubts if there is enough business to support two firms like his, especially if the markup gets shaved any closer. Now, they seem to be splitting the business about equally—as the newcomer keeps shaving his markup. The main reason Bill is getting some orders is because the lumber mills make up different kinds of carloads (varying the number of different sized products) and specific lumberyards want his cars rather than his competitor's cars.

A week ago, Bill was contacted by Mr. Pope, representing the Pope and White particleboard manufacturing plant. Mr. Pope knew that Bill was well acquainted with the local building supply dealers and wanted to know if he would like to be the sole distributor for Pope and White in that area—selling carload lots, just as he did lumber. Mr. Pope gave Bill several brochures on particleboard, a product introduced about 20 years ago, describing how it can be used as a cheaper and better subflooring than the standard lumber usually used. The particleboard is also made with a wood veneer so that it can be used as paneling in homes and offices. He told Bill that the lumberyards could specify the types and grades of particleboard they needed—unlike lumber where they choose from carloads that are already made up. Bill knew that a carload of particleboard cost about 30 percent more than a carload of lumber—and that sales would be less frequent. In fact, he knew that this product has not been as well accepted in his area as many others, be-

cause no one has done much promotion in his area. But the 20 percent average markup looks very tempting—and the particleboard market is expanding.

Bill has three choices:

1. Take Mr. Pope's offer and sell both products.
2. Take the offer and drop lumber sales.
3. Stay strictly with lumber and forget the offer.

Mr. Pope is expecting an answer within another week, so Bill has to decide soon.

Evaluate what Bill Cooper has been doing. What should he do now? Why?

■ 16. **MEIR COMPANY**

The Meir Company is a full-line department store chain operating in and around Portland, Oregon. The company began in the 1920s in the downtown business district of Portland, and has now expanded until it operates not only the downtown store but also branches in eight major shopping centers around Portland.

One of the more successful departments in the Meir stores is the cosmetic and drug sundries department. This department sells a wide variety of products—ranging from face powder to vitamins. But it has not been in the prescription business—and does not have a registered pharmacist in the department. Its focus in the drug area has been on "proprietary" items—packaged and branded items which are sold without professional advice or supervision—rather than on the "ethical" drugs—which are normally sold only with a doctor's prescription which is filled by a registered pharmacist.

The Meir Company is now considering a proposal of Butler Drug Company. Butler wants to introduce a wholesale prescription service into Meir cosmetic and drug sundries departments. Butler is a well-established drug wholesaler which

is trying to expand its business by serving retailers such as the Meir Company.

Basically, the Butler Drug Company's proposal is as follows:

1. Meir's customers would leave their prescriptions in the drug sundries department one day and then pick up their medicines the following day.
2. A representative of the Butler Drug company would pick up the prescriptions every evening at closing time and return the filled prescriptions before each store opened the following day. The Meir Company would not have to hire a pharmacist or carry any drug inventory.
3. Meir's could offer a savings of from 35 to 40 percent to their customers. This savings would be due to the economies of the operation, including the absence of a pharmacist and the elimination of local inventories.
4. The Meir Company would earn a 40 percent commission on the selling price of each prescription sale.
5. Meir's name could be identified with the

service and be printed on all bags, bottles, and other materials associated with the prescription drug business. In other words, the Butler Drug Company would serve as a wholesaler in the operation, and would not be identified to Meir's customers.

Butler's sales rep, Mary Mackey, pointed out that retail drug sales were expanding and were expected to continue to expand as the average age of the population continues to rise. Further, she noted that prescription drug prices were rising, so Meir would have an opportunity to participate in an expanding business. By offering cost savings to its customers, Meir's would be providing another service—and also building return business

and stimulating store traffic. Also, since Meir's wouldn't need to hire additional personnel or carry inventory, the 40 percent margin would be almost all net profit.

The Butler Drug Company is anxious to begin offering this service to the Portland area and has asked Meir's to make a decision very soon. If Meir agrees to work with Butler, the Butler executives have agreed not to offer the service to any other Portland stores. On the other hand, if Meir decides not to offer the service, Butler does plan to approach other Portland retailers.

Evaluate the Butler proposal. What should the Meir Company do?

■ 17. DEWITT NATIONAL BANK

Bill Dickson was recently appointed director of marketing by his father, Andrew Dickson, president of the Dewitt National Bank. Bill is a recent graduate of a marketing program at the nearby state college. He has worked in the bank during summer vacations—but this is his first full-time job.

The Dewitt National Bank is a profitable, family-run business located in Dewitt—the county seat. The town itself has only about 10,000 population, but it serves farmers as far away as 20 miles. About 20 miles south is a metropolitan area of 350,000. Banking competition is quite strong in the metropolitan area. But in Dewitt, there is only one other bank—of about the same size. The Dewitt National Bank has been quite profitable, last year earning about $300,000—or 1 percent of assets—a profit margin that would look very attractive to big-city bankers.

Dewitt National Bank has prospered over the years by emphasizing a friendly, small-town atmosphere. The employees are all local residents and are trained to be friendly with all customers—greeting them on a first-name basis. Even Bill's father tries to know all the customers personally—and often comes out of his office to talk with them. The bank has followed a conservative

policy—for example, insisting on 25 percent downpayments on homes and relatively short maturities on loans. The interest rates charged are competitive or slightly higher than in the nearby city, but they are similar to those charged by the other bank in town. In fact, the two local banks seem to be following more or less the same approach—friendly, small-town service. Since they both have fairly convenient downtown locations, Bill feels that the two banks will continue to share the business equally unless some change is made.

Bill has developed an idea which he feels might attract a greater share of the local business. At a recent luncheon meeting with his father, he presented his plan and was disappointed that it was not enthusiastically received. Nevertheless, he has continued to push the idea.

Basically, Bill wants to try to differentiate the bank by promoting a new image. In particular, his proposal is to try to get all the people in town to think of the bank as the "Contemporary Bank." Bill wants to paint the inside and outside of the bank in pastel colors and have all the bank's advertising and printed materials refer to the "Contemporary Bank" campaign. The bank would give away pastel shopping bags, offer pastel deposit slips, mail out pastel interest checks, advertise on pastel billboards, and have pastel stationery for the bank's correspondence. Bill realizes that his proposal is "far-out" for a conservative bank. But that is exactly why he thinks it will work. He wants people to notice the Dewitt National Bank, instead of just assuming that both banks are alike. He feels that after the initial surprise, the local citizens will think even more positively about the Dewitt National Bank. Its reputation is very good now, but he would like it to be recognized as "different." Bill feels that this would help attract a larger share of new residents and businesses. Further, he hopes that his "Contemporary Bank" campaign would cause people to talk about the Dewitt National Bank—and given that word-of-mouth comments are likely to be positive, the bank might win a bigger share of the present business.

Bill's father is less excited about his son's proposal. He feels the bank has done very well under his direction, and he is concerned about changing a "good thing." He worries that some of the older farmers who are loyal customers might question the integrity of the bank—or even wonder if it had gone "big city." Further, he feels that Bill is talking about an important change which would be hard to undo once the decision has been made. His initial suggestion to Bill was to come up with some other way of differentiating the bank without running the risk of offending present customers. At the same time, he liked the idea of making the bank appear quite different from its competitor. People are continuing to move into Dewitt, and he would like to get an increasing share of this business. But he is having trouble with the "Contemporary Bank" idea.

Evaluate Bill's proposal. Should it be accepted?

■ 18. GRAY SPORTS COMPANY

Two years ago, Tom Gray bought the inventory, supplies, equipment, and business of Western Sport Sales—located in one of the suburbs of Seattle, Washington. The business was in an older building along a major highway leading out of town, but it was several miles from any body of water. The previous owner had achieved sales volumes of about $250,000 a year—just breaking even. For this reason—plus the desire to retire in southern California—the owner had been willing to sell everything to Tom for roughly the value of the inventory. Western Sport Sales had been selling two well-known brands of small pleasure boats, a leading outboard motor, two brands of snowmobiles, and a line of trailer and pickup-truck campers. The total inventory was valued at about $78,000, and Tom used all of his own savings and borrowed some from two friends to buy the inventory. At the same time, he took over the lease on the building—so he was able to begin operations immediately.

Tom had never operated a business of his own before, but he was sure that he would be able to do well. He had worked in a variety of jobs as an auto repair man, service man, and generally a jack-of-all-trades in the maintenance departments of several local businesses.

Soon after opening his business, Tom hired a friend who had had a similar background. Together, they handled all selling and set-up work on new sales, and performed maintenance work as necessary. Sometimes they were extremely busy—at the peaks of each sport season. Then, both sales and maintenance kept them going up to 16 hours a day. At these times it was difficult to have both new and repaired equipment available as soon as desired by customers. At other times, however, Tom and his friend, Bud, had almost nothing to do.

Tom usually charged the prices suggested by the various manufacturers—except at the end of a weather season when he was willing to make deals to minimize his inventory. Tom was a little annoyed that some of his competitors sold mainly on a price basis—offering 10 to 30 percent off the manufacturer's suggested list prices. Tom didn't want to get into that kind of business, however, because he hoped to build a loyal following based on friendship and personal service. He didn't feel he really had to cut price, because all of the lines he carried were "exclusive" for him in the area. No stores within a 10-mile radius carried any of his brands.

To try to build a favorable image for his company, Tom occasionally placed ads in local papers and bought some radio spots. The basic theme of this advertising was that the Gray Sports Company was a good place to buy the equipment needed for that season of the year. Sometimes he mentioned the brand names he carried, but generally Tom was trying to build his own image. He decided in favor of this approach because, although he had exclusives on the brands he carried, there generally were 10 to 15 different manufacturers' goods being sold in each product category at any one time—and most of the products were quite similar. Tom felt that this similarity among competing products almost forced him to try to differentiate himself on the basis of his own store's services.

The first year's operation was not profitable. In fact, after paying minimal salaries to Bud and himself, the business just about broke even. And this was without making any provision for return on his investment. In hopes of improving his profitability, Tom jumped at a chance to add a line of lawn mowers, tractors, and trimmers as he was starting into his second year of business. This line was offered by a well-known equipment manufacturer who was expanding into Tom's market.

The equipment was similar to that offered by other lawn equipment manufacturers. The manufacturer's willingness to do some local advertising and to provide some point-of-purchase displays appealed to Tom. And he also liked the idea that customers probably would be wanting this equipment sometime earlier than boats and other summer items. So, he would be able to handle this business without interfering with his other peak selling seasons.

Now it is two years since Tom started the Gray Sports Company, and it is still only breaking even. Sales have increased a little, but costs have gone up too because he has had to hire some part-time help. The lawn equipment did help to expand sales as he had expected, but unfortunately, it did not appear to increase profits. The part-time helpers were needed to handle this business—in part because the manufacturer's advertising had generated a lot of sales inquiries. Relatively few of these resulted in sales, however, because many seemed to be shopping for "deals." So it is possible that Tom may have even lost money handling the new line. He hesitates to give up on it, however, because he has no other attractive choices right now, and he doesn't want to lose that sales volume. Further, the manufacturer's sales rep has been most encouraging—assuring Tom that things will get better and that they will be glad to continue their promotion support during the coming year.

Evaluate Gray's overall strategy. What should he do in the future, especially regarding the lawn equipment line?

■ 19. CABCO INC.

Cabco Inc. produces wire cable—ranging from one-half inch to four inches in diameter. The plant is in Chicago, Illinois, and Cabco sells throughout the United States. Principal users of the products are manufacturing firms using cranes and various other overhead lifts in their operations. Ski resorts and amusement parks, for

example, are customers because cables are used in the various lifts. The main customers, however, are cement plants, railroad and boat yards, heavy-equipment manufacturers, mining operations, construction companies, and steel manufacturers.

Cabco employs its own sales specialists to call

on the purchasing agents of potential users. All the sales reps are engineers who go through an extensive training program covering the different applications, strengths, and other technical details concerning rope and cable. Then they are assigned a region or district—the size depending on the number of customers. They are paid a good salary plus generous travel expenses— with small bonuses and prizes to reward special efforts.

Phil Weeks went to work for Cabco in 1952, immediately after receiving a civil engineering degree from the University of Minnesota. After going through the training program, he was assigned, along with one other representative, to the West Virginia, Ohio, and Indiana region. His job was to service and give technical help to present customers of wire and cable. He was expected to call on new customers when inquiries came in. But his primary duties were to: (1) supply the technical assistance needed to use cable in the most efficient and safe manner, (2) handle complaints, and (3) provide evaluation reports to customers' management regarding their use of cabling.

Phil Weeks became one of Cabco's most successful representatives. His exceptional ability to handle customer complaints and provide technical assistance was noted by many of the firm's customers. He also brought in a great deal of new business—mostly from heavy equipment manufacturers in Ohio.

Weeks's success established Ohio as Cabco's largest-volume state. As a result, Ohio became a separate district, and Phil Weeks was assigned as the representative for the district in 1959.

Although the company's sales in Ohio have not continued to grow in the past few years, the replacement market has been steady and profitable. This fact is mainly due to the ability and reputation of Phil Weeks. As one of the purchasing agents for a large machinery manufacturer mentioned, "When Phil Weeks makes a recommendation regarding use of our equipment and cabling, even if it is a competitor's cable we are using, we are sure it is for the best of our company. Last week, for example, a cable of one of his competitors broke, and we were going to give him a contract. He told us it was not a defective cable that caused the break, but rather the way we were using it. He told us how it should be used and what we needed to do to correct our operation. We took his advice and gave him the contract as well!"

Four years ago, Cabco introduced a unique and newly patented wire sling device for holding cable groupings together. The sling makes operations around the cable much safer—and its use could reduce hospital and lost-time costs due to accidents. The slings are expensive, and the profit margin is high. Cabco urged all its representatives to push the sling, but the only sales rep to sell the sling with any success was Phil Weeks. Eighty percent of his customers are currently using the wire sling. In other areas, sling sales are disappointing.

As a result of his success, Cabco is now considering forming a separate department for sling sales and putting Phil Weeks in charge. His duties would include traveling to the various sales districts and training other representatives in how to sell the sling. The Ohio district would be handled by a new person.

Evaluate Cabco's strategy(ies). What would you advise? Why?

■ 20. YORK FURNITURE COMPANY

Mrs. Carol King has been operating the York Furniture Company for 10 years and has slowly built the sales to $900,000 a year. Her store is located in the downtown shopping area of a city of 150,000 population. This is basically a factory town, and she has deliberately selected "blue-collar" workers as her target market. She carries some higher-priced furniture lines, but puts great emphasis on budget combinations and easy credit terms.

Mrs. King is most concerned because she feels she may have reached the limit of her sales growth—because sales have not been increasing during the last two years. Her newspaper advertising seems to attract her target customers, but many of these people come in, shop around, and then leave. Some of them come back, but most do not. She feels her product selections are very suitable for her target market and is concerned that her salespeople do not close more sales with potential customers. She has discussed this matter several times with her salespeople. They say they feel they ought to treat all customers alike—the way they personally want to be treated. They feel their role is just to answer questions when asked—not to make suggestions or help customers arrive at their selections. They feel this would be too much of a "hard sell."

Mrs. King argues that this behavior is interpreted as indifference by the customers who are attracted to the store by her advertising. She feels that customers must be treated on an individual basis—and that some customers need more encouragement and suggestion than others. Moreover, she feels that some customers will actually appreciate more help and suggestion than the salespeople themselves might. To support her views, she showed her salespeople the data from a study about furniture store customers (Tables 1 and 2). She tried to explain to them about the differences in demographic groups and pointed out that her store was definitely trying to aim at specific groups. She argued that they (the salespeople) should cater to the needs and attitudes of their customers—and think less about how they would like to be treated themselves. Further, she suggested that she may have to consider changing the sales compensation plan if they don't "do a better job." Now they are paid a salary of $13,000 to $20,000 per year (depending on years of service) plus a 1 percent commission on sales.

Evaluate Mrs. King's thinking. What would you advise her to do?

TABLE 1

In shopping for furniture I found (find) that	Demographic groups				Marital status	
	Group A	Group B	Group C	Group D	Newly-weds	Married 3–10 yrs.
I looked at furniture in many stores before I made a purchase	78%	57%	52%	50%	66%	71%
I went (am going) to only one store and bought (buy) what I found (find) there	2	9	10	11	9	12
To make my purchase I went (am going) back to one of the stores I shopped in previously	48	45	39	34	51	49
I looked (am looking) at furniture in no more than three stores and made (will make) my purchase in one of these ..	20	25	24	45	37	30
No answer	10	18	27	27	6	4

TABLE 2:   The sample design

Demographic status

Upper class (group A); 13% of sample
This group consisted of managers, proprietors, or executives of large businesses. Professionals, including doctors, lawyers, engineers, college professors and school administrators, research personnel. Sales personnel, including managers, executives, and upper-income sales people above level of clerks.
Family income over $30,000.

Middle class (group B); 37% of sample
Group B consists of white-collar workers including clerical, secretarial, sales clerks, bookkeepers, etc. It also includes school teachers, social workers, semiprofessionals, proprietors or managers of small businesses; industrial foremen and other supervisory personnel.
Family income between $20,000 and $40,000.

Lower middle class (group C); 36% of sample
Skilled workers and semiskilled technicians were in this category along with custodians, elevator operators, telephone linemen, factory operatives, construction workers, and some domestic and personal service employees.
Family income between $10,000 and $40,000.
No one in this group had above a high school education.

Lower class (group D); 14% of sample
Nonskilled employees, day laborers. It also includes some factory operatives, domestic and service people.
Family income under $15,000.
None had completed high school; some had only grade school education.

■ 21. NEWMAN DANCE STUDIO

Anne Newman has been operating the Newman Dance Studio for five years—in a suburban community of about 50,000. Slowly, she has built a clientele—mostly young girls whose mothers want them to have some ballet experience.

The studio is conveniently located downtown—within walking distance of two grade schools (grades one to five) and one middle school (grades six to eight). Some of Anne's customers come from these schools, but even more come from more remote schools. Most are driven and picked up by their mothers.

A few competitors are offering classes in their homes to neighborhood children, but none of them has facilities or quality of instruction comparable to Anne's. The school district offers some classes at lower prices on Saturday and during the summer, but Anne has not considered them to be real competition.

Most of Anne's students come only one hour a week, and slowly make enough progress so that Anne can hold spring recitals to show off the girls' accomplishments to their parents and friends. Even first-year students are able to make a reasonable showing—and "success" in the spring recital tends to encourage mothers to re-

enroll their daughters in the fall classes. Anne has not had much luck developing an interest in summer classes—and last year she stopped trying. She decided that her students associated ballet with the nine-month school year. So Anne took off for a three-month summer vacation. Fortunately, there had been enough business in the previous nine months so she could afford to do this.

Now it is February 1983, and Anne is very much concerned about her financial prospects for the future. Declining school enrollments (which cut state educational support payments) and rising costs (including rising heating gas costs) have forced the school board to take some drastic measures. One of these was changing the school schedule to start later so the students are getting up later and going to school later—thereby saving energy during the dark morning hours. There is some doubt whether this really did accomplish its purpose, but the school system has decided that the new schedule will be continued indefinitely.

The schools now open at 8:40 A.M. and close at 3:40 P.M. instead of 3 P.M. This has drastically cut into Anne's after-school business.

At first Anne did not see the implications when the change was announced for January 1983. But it quickly became clear that her 3:30–4:20 class was at the wrong time when no one signed up for the class during the first week of January. Not only did she lose many of the girls who were formerly enrolled in her 3:30 class, but enrollment in the later classes dropped almost in half. Some of the 3:30 girls did move to the 4:30 and 5:30 classes, but probably only about 20 percent of them. It is hard to get exact figures on enrollment because there's usually at least a 20 percent turnover from fall to winter to spring terms. Anne has become used to a continual flow of new girls. Few girls stay more than a couple of years—because the program is not designed to build serious ballet students, but rather to cater to the "recreational" ballet student. But, it is quite clear to Anne that the change in school schedule has drastically cut her business—and she is trying to decide what to do for the spring term and beyond. In fact, the school schedule change just precipitously compounds the problem of fewer young girls coming along—as a result of parents having fewer children. This has been worrying Anne for some time, but now she must face an immediate problem as well as the longer term trend.

Given that most parents seem to need about one-half hour to get their children from school to the studio, she could move the starting time of the first class to about 4:15 (from 4:30) to try to use a little more after school time. But this would still mean that she could only offer two "prime-time" classes after school (instead of the three which she offered before) because classes starting after 6 p.m. seem to be viewed as "too late." Alternately, she could forget about trying to change the after-school schedule and try to fill later times with older, more serious students. Anne has the credentials and training to offer more advanced courses, but so far there hasn't been much demand for them. The local school district does offer some adult education classes at lower prices—and this may take care of the older market.

Another possibility that Anne is considering is to persuade the local school system to allow "early release" of interested students—with a view to filling the 3:40–4:20 or a 3:10–4:00 slot. Anne knows that some children are now being released an hour early for advanced training in ice skating. But few students are involved, and she fears that such an arrangement for ballet is not likely because her students aren't "advanced."

Now that the total amount of time available between the end of school and dinner is almost an hour shorter, some parents may feel that there just isn't enough time for extra recreation activities. This may help account for the substantial drop in business after school. Anne's Saturday business has not been affected by the change in school schedule, but very few of the weekday students have moved to Saturday, either. This concerns her for the long run because total revenue has dropped about one quarter—bringing her studio below the breakeven point. Clearly, the studio needs more students to break even because it cannot cut costs very easily. Rent, light, taxes, insurance, and other fixed costs can't be changed. Further, her two part-time assistants are paid a fixed amount for the five after-school periods and Saturday.

Saturday classes could use some more students—enrollments have declined slightly over the last few years as the "baby boom" has ended. Similarly, the after-school market has dropped some in the last few years. But the immediate problem is the new after-school market. Something must be done after school if the business is to survive. Before and after the school schedule change, the following numbers of students were enrolled in the various classes at approximately $3.50 per class:

Class	Jan. 1982	Jan. 1983
3:30–4:20	20	0
4:30–5:20	20	9
5:30–6:20	18	9
6:30–7:20	10	6

What has happened to the Newman Dance Studio? What would you recommend Anne Newman do?

■ 22. ACME WIRE, INC.

Acme Wire, Inc.—located in Atlanta, Georgia—is a custom producer of industrial wire products. The company has a lot of experience bending wire into many shapes—and also has the facilities to chrome- or gold-plate finished products. The company was started 10 years ago, and has slowly built its sales volume to $1 million a year. Just one year ago, Anne Egon was appointed sales manager of the consumer products division. It was her responsibility to develop this division as a producer and marketer of the company's own branded products—as distinguished from custom orders which the industrial division produces for others.

Miss Egon has been working on a number of different product ideas for almost a year now, and has developed several unique designs for letter holders, flowerpot holders, key and pencil holders, and other novelties. Her most promising product is a phone message holder in the shape of a telephone. It is very similar to one which the industrial division produced for a number of years for another company. In fact, it was experience with the seemingly amazing sales volume of this product which interested the company in the market—and led to the development of the consumer products division.

Anne Egon has sold hundreds of units of her various products to local chain stores and wholesalers on a trial basis, but each time the price has been negotiated, and no firm policy has been set. Now she is faced with the decision of what price to set on the phone-shaped message holder which she plans to push aggressively wherever she can. Actually, she hasn't decided on exactly which channels of distribution to use—but trials in the local area have been encouraging, and, as noted above, the experience in the industrial division suggests that there is a large market for the product.

The manufacturing cost on this product is approximately 20 cents if it is painted black, and 30 cents if it is chromed or gold-plated. Similar products have been selling at retail in the 75 cents to $2.50 range. The sales and administrative overhead to be charged to the division will amount to $50,000 a year. This will include Miss Egon's salary and some office expenses. It is expected that a number of other products will be developed in the near future, but for the coming year, it is hoped that this message holder will account for about half the consumer products division's sales volume.

Evaluate Anne Egon's marketing strategy. What price should be set?

■ 23. SPEEDY PHOTO COMPANY

Speedy Photo Company is one of the four major Colorado-based photo finishers—each with annual sales of about $5 million.

Speedy was started—in 1950—by three people who had a lot of experience in the photo finishing industry—working in Kodak's photo finishing division in Rochester, New York. Speedy started in a small rented warehouse in Boulder, Colorado. Today it has seven company-owned plants in five cities in Colorado and western Kansas.

They are located in Boulder, Pueblo, Denver, and Colorado Springs, Colorado, and Hays, Kansas.

Speedy does all of its own of black-and-white processing. While they do own color-processing capability, Speedy has found it more economical to have most color film processed by the regional Kodak processing plant. The color film processed by Speedy is of the "off-brand" variety—or is special work done for professional photographers. Despite this limitation in color finishing, the company has always given its customers fast, quality service. All pictures—including those processed by Kodak—can be returned within three days of receipt by Speedy.

Speedy started as a wholesale photo finisher— and later developed its own processing plants in a drive for greater profit. Its customers are drug stores, camera stores, department stores, photo-graphic studios, and any other retail outlets where photo finishing is offered to consumers. These retailers insert film rolls, cartridges, nega-tives, and so on, into separate bags—marking on the outside the kind of work to be done. The cus-tomer is handed a receipt, but seldom sees the bag into which the film has been placed. The bag has the retailer's name on it—not Speedy's.

Each processing plant is fronted by a small retail outlet for drop-in customers who live near the plant. This is a minor part of Speedy's business.

The company also does direct-mail photo fin-ishing within the state of Colorado. Each process-ing plant in Colorado is capable of receiving direct-mail orders from consumers. All film re-ceived is handled in the same way as the other retail business.

A breakdown of the dollar volume by type of business is shown in Table 1.

TABLE 1

Type of business	Percent of dollar volume
Sales to retail outlets	80
Direct-mail sales	17
Retail walk-in sales	3
	100

All processing is priced at the level established by local competition—and all major competitors charge the same prices. Speedy sets a retail list price, and each retailer then is offered a trade discount based on the volume of business gener-ated for Speedy. The pricing schedule used by each of the major competitors in the Colorado-Kansas market is shown in Table 2.

All direct-mail processing for final consumers is priced at 33⅓ percent discount off retail price.

TABLE 2

Monthly dollar volume (12-month average)	Discount (2/10 net 30)
$ 0–$ 100	33⅓%
$ 101–$ 500	40
$ 501–$1,000	45
$1,001–above	50

But this is not done under the Speedy name—to avoid antagonizing retailer customers. Retail walk-in accounts are charged the full list price for all services performed.

Retail stores offering photo finishing are served by Speedy's own sales force. Each proc-essing plant has at least three people servicing accounts. Their duties include daily visits to all present accounts to pick up and deliver all photo finishing work. These sales reps also make daily trips to the nearby Greyhound bus terminal to pick up and drop off color film to be processed by Kodak. They are not expected to call on pos-sible new accounts.

Since the consumer does not come in contact with Speedy, the firm has not felt it necessary to advertise its retail business. Similarly, possible retailer accounts are not called on or advertised to—except that Speedy is listed in the Yellow Pages of all telephone books in cities and towns served by its seven plants under "Photo finishing: Wholesale." Any phone inquiries are followed up by the nearest sales rep.

The direct-mail portion of Speedy's business is generated by regular ads in the Sunday pictorial sections of newspapers servicing Pueblo, Denver, Colorado Springs, and Boulder. These ads usu-ally stress low price, fast service, and fine quality. Speedy does not use its own name for these markets. Mailers are provided for consumers to send to the plant. Some people in the company feel this part of the business might have great potential if pursued more aggressively.

Recently, Speedy's president, Mr. Dickson, has become worried over the loss of several re-tail accounts in the $500 to $1,000 discount range. He has been with the company since its beginning—and has always stressed quality and rapid delivery of the finished products. Demanding that all plants produce the finest quality, Mr. Dickson personally conducts periodic quality tests of each plant through the direct-mail service. Plant managers are called on the carpet for any slips in quality.

To find out what is causing the loss in retail accounts, Mr. Dickson is reviewing sales reps' reports and talking to various employees. In their weekly reports, Speedy's sales reps have reported a major threat to the company—price cutting. Fast-Film—a competitor of equal size that offers the same services as Speedy—is offering an additional 5 percent trade discount in each sales volume category. This really makes a difference at some stores—because these retailers feel that all the major processors can do an equally good job. Further, they note, consumers apparently feel that the quality is acceptable because no complaints have been heard so far.

Speedy has faced price cutting before—but never by an equally well-established company. Mr. Dickson cannot understand why these retailer customers would leave Speedy because Speedy is offering higher quality and the price difference is not that large. He feels the sales reps should

sell "quality" a lot harder. He is also considering a direct-mail and newspaper campaign to consumers to persuade them to demand Speedy's quality service from their favorite retailer. Mr. Dickson feels that consumers demanding quality will force retailers to stay with—or return to—Speedy. He says: "If we can't get the business by convincing the retailer of our fine quality, we'll get it by convincing the consumer."

John Jones, the sales manager, disagrees with Mr. Dickson. John feels that they ought to at least meet the price cut or cut prices another 5 percent wherever Fast-Film has taken a Speedy account. This would do two things: (1) get the business back and (2) signal that continued price cutting will be met by still deeper price cuts. Further, he says: "If Fast Film doesn't get the message, we ought to go after a few of their big accounts with the 10 percent discounts. That ought to shape them up."

Evaluate Speedy's strategies and Mr. Dickson's and Mr. Jones' present thinking. What would you do?

■ 24. THE WESTCO MACHINERY COMPANY

The Westco Machinery Company—of Los Angeles, California—is a leading manufacturer in the wire machinery industry. It has patents covering over 200 machine variations, but it is rare for Westco's customers to buy more than 30 different types in a year. The machines are sold to wire and small-tubing manufacturers—when they are increasing production capacity or replacing outdated equipment.

Established in 1895, the company has enjoyed a steady growth to its present position with annual sales of $35 million.

About 10 firms compete in the wire machinery market. Each is about the same size and manufactures basically similar machinery. Each of the competitors has tended to specialize in its own geographic area. Five of the competitors are in

the East, three in the Midwest, and two—including Westco—on the West Coast. All of the competitors offer similar prices and sell F.O.B. their factories. Demand has been fairly strong in recent years. As a result, all of the competitors have been satisfied to sell in their geographic areas and avoid price cutting. In fact, price cutting is not a popular idea because about 20 years ago one firm tried to win additional business and found that others immediately met the price cut but industry sales (in units) did not increase at all. Within a few years, prices returned to their earlier level, and since then competition has tended to focus on promotion.

Westco's promotion has depended largely on six company sales reps, who cover the West Coast. They usually are supported by sales engineers when the company is close to making a sale. Some advertising is done in trade journals. And direct mailings are used occasionally, but the main promotion emphasis is on personal selling. Personal contact outside the West Coast market, however, is through manufacturers' agents.

James Tang, president of Westco is not satisfied with the present situation. Industry sales have leveled off and so have Westco's sales—although the firm has continued to hold its share of the market. Tang would like to find a way to compete more effectively in the other regions because he sees that there is great potential outside of the West Coast—if he can only find a better way of reaching it.

Competitors and buyers agree that Westco is the top-quality producer in the industry. Its machines have generally been somewhat superior to others in terms of reliability, durability, and productive capacity. The difference, however, usually has not been great enough to justify a higher price—because the others are able to do the necessary job—unless Westco's sales rep convinces the buyer (and other influencers) that the extra quality will help improve the buyer's product and lead to fewer production line breakdowns. The sales rep can also try to "sell" the company's better sales engineers and technical service people. But if a buyer is only interested in comparing delivered prices for basic machines, then Westco's price must be at least competitive to get the sale. In short, if such a buyer had a choice between Westco's and another machine *at the same price,* Westco would probably get the business. But it's clear that Westco's price would have to be at least competitive in such cases.

The average wire machine sells for about $125,000, F.O.B. shipping point. Shipping costs within any of the three major regions averages about $1,500—but another $1,000 must be added on shipments from the West Coast to the Midwest (either way) and another $1,000 from the Midwest to the East.

Mr. Tang is thinking about expanding his market by being willing to absorb the extra $1,000 to $2,000 in freight costs which would be incurred if a midwestern or eastern customer were to buy

from his West Coast location. By so doing, he would not be cutting price in those markets, but rather reducing his net return. He feels that his competitors would not see this as price competition—and therefore would not resort to cutting prices themselves. Further, he thinks such a move would be legal—because all the customers in each major region would be offered the same price.

The sales manager, Robert Dixon, feels that the proposed freight absorption plan might actually stimulate price competition in the Midwest and East—and perhaps on the West Coast. He proposes instead that Westco hire some sales reps to work the Midwest and Eastern regions—selling "quality"—rather than relying on the manufacturers' agents. He feels that two additional sales reps in each of these regions would not increase costs too much—and could greatly increase the sales from these markets over that brought in by the agents. With this plan, there would be no need to absorb the freight and risk disrupting the status quo. This is especially important, he argues, because competition in the Midwest and East is somewhat "hotter" than on the West Coast—due to the number of competitors in those regions. Much expensive entertaining, for example, seems to be required just to be considered as a potential supplier. In contrast, the situation has been rather quiet in the West—because only two firms are sharing this market. The "Eastern" competitors don't send any sales reps to the West Coast—and if they have any manufacturers' agents they haven't gotten any business in recent years.

Mr. Tang agrees that Mr. Dixon has a point, but since industry sales are leveling off, he feels that the competitive situation might change drastically in the near future anyway and he would rather be a leader in anything that is likely to happen rather than a follower. He is impressed with Mr. Dixon's comments about the greater competitiveness in the other markets, however, and therefore is unsure about what should be done.

Evaluate Westco's strategy planning in the light of its market situation, and explain what it should do now.

■ 25. MOUNTAIN VIEW COMPANY

The Mountain View Company is a well-established manufacturer in the highly seasonal fruit canning industry. It packs and sells canned raspberries, boysenberries, plums, strawberries, apples, cherries, and "mixed fruit." Sales are made mainly through food brokers to merchant wholesalers, supermarket chains (such as Kroger, Safeway, A&P, and Jewel), cooperatives, and other outlets—mostly in the San Francisco Bay area. Of secondary importance, by volume, are sales in the immediate local market to institutions, grocery stores, and supermarkets—and sales of dented canned goods at low prices to walk-in customers.

Mountain View is a large fruit canner in the Willamette River Valley area in Oregon—with more than $20 million in sales annually (exact sales data is not published by the closely held corporation). Plants are located in strategic places along the valley—with main offices in Eugene. The Mountain View brand is used only on canned goods sold in the immediate local market. Most of the goods are sold and shipped under a retailer's label, or the broker's/wholesaler's label.

Mountain View has an excellent reputation for the consistent quality of its product offerings. And it is always willing to offer competitive prices. Strong channel rapport was built by Mountain View's former chairman of the board and chief executive officer, J. N. Eggleston. Mr. Eggleston—who owns controlling interest in the firm—had "worked" the Bay area as an aggressive company salesman in the firm's earlier years—before he took over from his father as president in 1940. He was an ambitious and hard-working executive, active in community affairs, and the firm prospered under his direction. He became well known within the canned food processing industry for technical/product innovations.

During the off-canning season, Mr. Eggleston traveled widely. In the course of his travels, he arranged several important business deals. His 1968 and 1970 trips resulted in the following two events: (1) inexpensive pineapple was imported from Formosa and marketed on the West Coast through Mountain View—primarily to expand the product line; and (2) a technically advanced continuous process cooker (65 feet high) was imported from England and installed at the Eugene plant in February-March 1975. It was the first of its kind in the United States and cut process time sharply.

Mr. Eggleston retired in 1975 and named his son-in-law, 35-year-old Mr. Story, as his successor. Mr. Story is intelligent and hard-working. He had been concerned primarily with the company's financial matters, and only recently with marketing problems. During his seven-year tenure as financial director, the firm had received its highest credit rating ever—and was able to borrow working capital ($3 million to meet seasonal can and wage requirements) at the lowest rate ever received by the company.

The fact that the firm isn't unionized allows some competitive advantage. However, minimum wage law changes have increased costs. And these and other rising costs have caused profit margins to narrow. This has led to the recent closing of two plants—as they became comparatively less efficient to operate. The remaining two plants were considerably expanded in capacity (especially warehouse facilities) so that they could operate more profitably due to maximum use of existing processing equipment.

Shortly after Mr. Eggleston's retirement, Mr. Story reviewed the company's current situation with his executives. He pointed out narrowing profit margins, debts contracted for new plant and equipment, and an increasingly competitive environment. Even considering the temporary labor-saving competitive advantage of the new cooker system, there seemed to be no way to improve the "status quo" unless the firm could sell direct—as they do in the local market—absorbing the food brokers' 5 percent commission on sales.

This was the plan of action decided on, and Mr. Monty was directed to test the new method for six months.

Mr. Monty is the only full-time salesman for the firm. Other top executives do some selling—but not much. Larry Monty is a relative of Mr. Eggleston and is also a member of the board of directors. He is well qualified in technical matters—he has a college degree in food chemistry. Although Mr. Monty formerly did call on some important customers with the brokers' sales reps, he is not well known in the industry or even by Mountain View's usual customers.

Five months later, after Mr. Monty has made several selling trips and hundreds of telephone calls, he is unwilling to continue sales efforts on his own. He insists that a sales staff be formed if the present way of operating is to continue. Orders are down in comparison both to expectations and to the previous year's operating results. And sales of the pineapple products are very disappointing. Even some regular supermarket chain customers seem reluctant to buy—though basic consumer demand has not changed. Further, some potential new customers have demanded quantity guarantees considerably larger than the firm can supply. Expanding supply would be difficult in the short run—because the firm typically must contract with growers to assure supplies of the type and quality they normally offer.

Evaluate Mr. Story's strategy planning. What should he tell Mr. Eggleston? What should be done next?

■ 26. CUSTOM MANUFACTURING COMPANY

Bob McNair is working as a sales representative for a plastics components manufacturer. He calls mostly on large industrial accounts—such as refrigerator manufacturers—who might need large quantities of custom-made products, like door liners. He is on a straight salary of $20,000 per year, plus expenses and a company car. He expects some salary increases, but doesn't see much long-run opportunity with this company. As a result, he is seriously considering changing jobs and investing $30,000 in the Custom Manufacturing Company—an established Long Island (New York) thermoplastic molder and manufacturer. Carl Weiss, the present owner, is nearing retirement and has not developed anyone to run the business. He has agreed to sell the business to Jim Arkin, a lawyer-entrepreneur, who has invited Bob McNair to invest and become the sales manager. Mr. Arkin has agreed to give Bob his current salary plus expenses, plus a bonus of 1 percent of profits. However, Bob must invest to become part of the new company. He will obtain a 5 percent interest in the business for his $30,000 investment.

The Custom Manufacturing Company is well established—and last year had sales of $1.5 million, but zero profits (after paying Mr. Weiss a salary of $22,500). In terms of sales, cost of materials was 46 percent; direct labor, 13 percent; indirect factory labor, 15 percent; factory overhead, 13 percent; and sales overhead and general expenses, 13 percent. The company has not been making any profit for several years—but has been continually adding new machines to replace those made obsolete by technological developments. The machinery is well maintained and modern, but most of it is similar to that used by its many competitors. Most of the machines in the industry are standard. Special products are made by using specially made dies with these machines.

Sales have been split about two thirds custom-molded products (that is, made to order for other producers or merchandising concerns) and the balance proprietary items (such as housewares and game items, like poker chips and cribbage sets). The housewares are copies of articles developed by others—and indicate neither originality nor style. Carl Weiss is in charge of the proprietary items distributed through any available wholesale channels. The custom-molded products are sold through three full-time sales engineers, who receive a 5 percent commission on sales up to $10,000 and then 3 percent above that level, as well as by three manufacturers' reps getting the same commissions.

Financially, the company seems to be in fairly good condition—at least as far as book value is concerned. The $30,000 investment would buy approximately $40,000 in assets—and ongoing operations should pay off the seven-year note. See Table 1.

Mr. Arkin feels that—with new management—the company has a real opportunity for profit. He expects to make some economies in the production process because he feels most production operations can be improved. He plans to keep custom-molding sales to approximately the present $1 million level. The major new thrust will be to develop the proprietary line from a sales volume of about $500,000 to $2 million a year. Bob McNair is expected to be a real asset here because of his sales experience. This will bring the firm up to about capacity level—but it will mean adding additional employees and costs. The major advantage of expanding sales will be spreading overhead.

Some of the products proposed by Jim Arkin for the expansion of the proprietary line are listed below.

New products for consideration:

Picnic lunch boxes.

Six-bottle soft drink case.

Laminating printed film on housewares—molded.

Short legs for furniture—molded, $0.5 million minimum market.

Home storage box for milk cartons, $0.5 million minimum market.

Step-on garbage can without liner.

Importing and distributing foreign housewares.

Extruded and embossed or formed wall coverings.

Formed butyrate outside house shutters.

Translucent bird houses.

Formed "train terrain" table topography for model trains.

There is heavy competition in these markets from many other companies like Custom. Further, most retailers expect a wide margin—sometimes 40 to 50 percent. Even so, manufacturing costs are low enough so some money can be spent for promotion, while still keeping the price competitive. Apparently, many customers are willing to pay for the novelty of new products—if they see them in their stores.

Evaluate Jim Arkin's strategy planning. How would you advise Bob McNair? Explain your reasoning.

TABLE 1: Custom Manufacturing Company, statement of financial condition, December 31, 198x

Assets			Liabilities and Net Worth		
Cash		$ 13,000	Liabilities:		
Accounts receivable		35,000	Accounts payable		$ 51,000
Building	$ 125,000		Notes payable—		
Less: depreciation	75,000		7 years (machinery)		194,000
		50,000			
Machinery	1,200,000		Net worth:		
Less: depreciation	450,000		Capital stock		600,000
		750,000	Retained earnings		4,000
Total assets		$848,000	Total liabilities and net worth		$848,000

■ 27. PERRY MANUFACTURING COMPANY

Perry Manufacturing Company is a manufacturer of industrial cutting tools. These tools include such items as lathe blades, drill press bits, and various other cutting edges used in the operation of large metal cutting, boring, or stamping machines. The president of the company, Chuck Perry, takes great pride in the fact that his company—whose $2,759,000 sales in 1982 is small by industry standards—is recognized as a producer of the highest-quality line of cutting tools to be found.

Competition in the cutting-tool industry is intense. Perry Manufacturing Company competes not only with the original manufacturers of the machines, but also with many other larger manufacturers offering cutting tools as one of their many different product lines. This has had the effect, over the years, of standardizing the price, specifications, and in turn, the quality of the competing products of all manufacturers.

About a year ago, Mr. Perry was tiring of the financial pressure of competing with companies enjoying economies of scale. At the same time, he noted that more and more potential cutting-tool customers were turning to small, custom, tool-and-die shops because of specialized needs that could not be met by the mass production firms. Mr. Perry felt that perhaps he should consider some basic strategy changes. Although he was unwilling to become strictly a custom producer, Mr. Perry felt that the recent trend toward buying customized cutting edges suggested the development of new markets which might be too small for the large, multi-product line companies to serve profitably. But, he thought, the new markets might be large enough to earn a good profit for a flexible company of Perry's size.

An outside company, Mothison Research Associates, was hired to study the feasibility of serving these potential new markets. The initial results were encouraging. It was estimated that Perry might increase sales by 50 percent and double profits by servicing the emerging market.

Next, Mr. Perry had the sales manager develop a team of three technical specialists to maintain continuous contact with potential cutting-tool customers. They were supposed to identify any present or future needs which might exist in enough cases to make it possible to profitably produce a specialized product. The technical specialists were not to take orders or "sell" Perry to the potential customers. Mr. Perry felt that only through this policy could these representatives easily gain access to the right persons.

The initial feedback from the technical specialists was most encouraging. Many firms (large and small) had special needs—although it often was necessary to talk to the shop foreman or individual machine operators to find these needs. Most operators were "making do" with the tools available. Either they didn't know customizing was possible or doubted that their supervisors would do anything about it if it were suggested that a more specialized tool would increase productivity. But, these operators were encouraging because some felt that it would be easier to get specialized tools ordered if they were already produced and in stock than if they had to be custom-made. The company, therefore, decided to continually add high-quality products to meet the ever-changing, specialized needs of users of cutting tools and edges.

The potential customers of Perry's specialized tools were widely scattered. The average sale per customer is not expected to exceed $300 at a time, but the sale will be repeated several times within a year. Because of the widely dispersed market and low sales volume per customer, Mr. Perry doesn't feel that selling the products direct—as is done by small custom shops—is practical. At the present time, the Perry Manufacturing Company distributes 90 percent of its regular output through a large industrial wholesaler—Borman Supply Company—which serves the entire area east of the Mississippi River. This wholesaler, although very large and well known,

show—and saw immediately that his plant could produce these products. This especially interested him because of the possibility of using excess capacity—now that auto sales are down. Further, he feels that "jacks are jacks," and that the company would merely be broadening its product line by introducing hydraulic jacks. As he became more enthusiastic about the idea, he found that his engineering department already had a design which appeared to be at least comparable to the products now offered on the market—none had any patent protection. Further, he says that the company would be able to produce a product which is better made than the competition (i.e., smoother castings, etc.) although he agrees that customers probably wouldn't notice the differences. The production department's costs for making products comparable to those currently offered by competitors would be about one half the current retail prices.

Mr. Jack Worth, the sales manager, has just received a memo from Bill Harris, the president of the company, explaining about the production department's enthusiasm for broadening its jack line into hydraulic jacks. He seems enthusiastic about the idea, too, noting that it may be a way to make fuller use of the company's resources and increase its sales. Recognizing this enthusiasm, Jack Worth wants to develop a well thought-out explanation of why he can't get very

excited about the proposal. He knows he is already overworked and could not possibly promote this new line himself—and he is the only salesman the company has. So it probably would be necessary to hire someone to promote the line. And this "sales manager" would probably have to recruit manufacturers' agents (who probably will want a 15 percent commission on sales) to sell the automotive wholesalers who will stock the jacks and make the final sales. These wholesalers will expect a trade discount of about 30 percent, trade show exhibits, some national advertising, and sales promotion help (catalog sheets, mailers, and point-of-purchase displays.) Further, Jack Worth sees that the billing and collection system will have to be expanded because many more customers will be involved, and it will be necessary to keep track of agent commissions and accounts receivable. In summary, Jack feels that the proposed hydraulic-jack line is not very closely related to the company's present emphasis. He has already indicated his lack of enthusiasm to Mr. Bob Karpy, but this has made little difference in Bob's thinking. Now, it is clear that Jack will have to convince the president or he will soon be responsible for selling hydraulic jacks.

Evaluate this situation. What would you advise Jack Worth to say and do?

■ 30. MULTI FOODS LIMITED*

Burt Mann has been the marketing director of Multi Foods Limited for the last four years—since he arrived from international headquarters in New York. Multi Foods—headquartered in Toronto—is a subsidiary of a large U.S.-based consumer packaged-food company with world-wide sales of more than $2 billion in 1982. Its Canadian sales were just under $250 million—with the Quebec

and Ontario markets accounting for 65 percent of the company's Canadian sales.

The company's product line includes such items as cake mixes, puddings, pie fillings, pancakes, and prepared foods. The company has successfully introduced at least six new products every year for the last five years. Its most recent new product was a line of frozen dinners successfully launched last year. Products from Multi Foods are known for their high quality and enjoy much brand preference throughout Canada—including the Province of Quebec.

*This case was adapted from one written by Professor Robert Tamilia, University of Windsor, Canada.

Sales of the company's products have risen every year since Mr. Mann has taken over as marketing director. In fact, the company's market share has increased steadily in each of the product categories in which it competes. The Quebec market has closely followed the national trend except that, in the past two years, total sales growth in that market began to lag.

According to Burt Mann, a big advantage of Multi Foods over its competitors is the ability to coordinate all phases of the food business from Toronto. For this reason, Mr. Mann meets at least once a month with his product managers—to discuss developments in local markets that might affect marketing plans. While each manager is free to make suggestions—and even to suggest major departures from current marketing practices—Mr. Mann has the final say.

One of the product managers, Jac Seine, expressed great concern at the last monthly meeting about the weak performance of some of the company's products in the Quebec market. While a broad range of possible reasons—ranging from inflation to politics—were reviewed to try to explain the situation, Mr. Seine maintained it was due to a basic lack of understanding of that market. Not enough managerial time and money has been spent studying the Quebec market. As a result, Seine felt that the current marketing approach to that market needed to be reevaluated. An inappropriate marketing plan may well be responsible for the sales slowdown. After all, "80 percent of the market is French-speaking. It's in the best interest of the company to treat that market as being separate and distinct from the rest of Canada."

Mr. Seine supported his position by showing that per capita consumption in Quebec of many product categories (in which the firm competes) is above the national average (Table 1). Research projects conducted by Multi Foods also support the "separate and distinct" argument. The firm has found—over the years—many French-English differences in brand attitudes, life-styles, usage rates, and so on.

Mr. Seine argued that the company should develop a unique Quebec marketing plan for

TABLE 1: Per capita consumption index, Province of Quebec (Canada = 100)

Cake mixes	103	Pie fillings	115
Pancakes	91	Frozen dinners	84
Puddings	111	Prepared packaged	
Salad dressings	87	foods	89
Molasses	129	Cookies	119
Soft drinks	122		

some or all of its brands. He specifically suggested that the French-language advertising plan for a particular brand be developed independently of the plan for English Canada. Currently, the agency assigned to the brand just translates its English-language ads for the French market. Mr. Mann pointed out that the existing advertising approach assured Multi Foods of a uniform brand image across Canada. However, the discussion that followed suggested that a different brand image might be needed in the French market if the company wanted to stop the brand's decline in sales.

The executives also discussed the food distribution system in Quebec. The major supermarket chains have their lowest market share in that province. Independents are strongest there—the "mom-and-pop" food stores fast disappearing outside Quebec remain alive and well in the province. Traditionally, these stores have stocked a higher proportion (than supermarkets) of their shelf space with national brands—a point of some interest to Multi Foods.

Finally, various issues related to discount policies, pricing structure, sales promotion, and cooperative advertising were discussed. All of this suggested that things were different in Quebec—and that future marketing plans should reflect these differences to a greater extent than they do now.

After the meeting, Burt Mann stayed in his office to think about what had been said. Although he agreed with the basic idea that the Quebec market was in many ways different, he wasn't sure how far his company should go in recognizing this fact. He knew that regional differences in food tastes and brand purchases existed not only in Quebec, but in other parts of Canada as well.

People were people, on the other hand, with far more similarities than differences.

Mr. Mann was afraid that giving special status to one region might conflict with top management's objective of achieving standardization whenever possible. He was also worried about the long-term effect of such a policy change on costs, organizational structure, and brand image. Still, enough product managers had expressed their concern over the years about the Quebec market to make him wonder if he shouldn't modify the current approach. Perhaps they could experiment with a few brands—and just in Quebec. He could cite the "language difference" as the reason for trying Quebec rather than any of the other provinces. But Mr. Mann realizes that any change of policy could be seen as the beginning of more change, and what would New York think? Could he explain it successfully there?

Evaluate this situation. What would you tell Burt Mann? What are the future implications of your recommendations?

■ 31. **VISITING NURSES ASSOCIATION (VNA)**

The Visiting Nurses Association (VNA) is a non-profit organization which has been operating—with varying degrees of success—for 20 years. Some of its funding comes from the local United Way—to provide emergency nursing services for those who can't afford to pay. The balance of the revenues—about 90 percent of the $1.2 million annual budget—comes from charges made directly to the client or to third-party payers—including insurance companies and the federal government—for Medicare or Medicaid services.

Janet Brown has been executive director of the VNA for two years now—and has developed a well-functioning organization—able to meet the requests for service which come to it from some local doctors and from the discharge officers at local hospitals. Some business also comes to the association by self-referral—the client finding the name of the association in the Yellow Pages of the local telephone directory.

The last two years have been a rebuilding time—because the previous director had had personnel problems. This led to a weakening of the association's image with the local referring agencies. Now, the image is more positive. But Janet is not completely satisfied with the situation. By definition, the Visiting Nurses Association is a non-profit organization—but it still has to cover all its costs in order to meet the payroll, rent payments, telephone expenses, and so on—including her own salary. She can see that while the association is growing slightly and now breaking even, it doesn't have much of a cushion to fall back on if (1) people stop needing as many nursing services, (2) the government changes its rules about paying for the association's kind of nursing services—either cutting back on what would be paid for or reducing the amount that would be paid for specific services—or (3) if new competitors enter the market. In fact, the latter possibility is of great concern to Janet. Some hospitals—squeezed for revenue—are expanding into home health care. And "for-profit" organizations (e.g., Kelly Home Care Services) are expanding around the country—to provide home health care services—including nursing services of the kind offered by VNA. These for-profit organizations appear to be efficiently run—offering good service at competitive—and sometimes even lower—prices than some non-profit organizations. And they seem to be doing this at a profit—which suggests that it would be possible for them to lower their prices if the non-profit organizations tried to compete on price.

Janet is trying to decide whether she should ask her board of directors to let her move into the whole home health care market—i.e., move beyond just nursing.

Now, the VNA is primarily concerned with providing professional nursing care in the home. But her nurses are much too expensive for routine health-care activities—such as helping fix meals, bathing and dressing patients, and so on. The "full cost" of a nurse is about $50 per hour. Besides, a registered nurse is not needed for these jobs. All that is required is an ability to get along with all kinds of people—and a willingness to do this kind of work. Generally, any mature person can be fairly quickly trained to do the job—following the instructions and under the general supervision of a physician, a nurse, or family members. The "full costs" of aides are $5 to $10 per hour for short visits—and as low as $50 per 24 hours for a live-in aide who has room and board supplied by the client.

There seems to be a growing demand for home health care services as more women have joined the work force and can't take over home health care when the need arises—either due to emergencies or long-term disabilities. And with older people living longer, there are more single-survivor family situations where there is no one nearby to take care of their needs. Often, however, there are family members—or third-party payers such as the government or insurers—who would be willing to pay for such services. Now, Janet sometimes assigns nurses to this work—because the VNA is not in a position to send home health-care aides. Sometimes she recommends other agencies, or suggests one or another of three people who have been doing this work on their own—part-time. But with growing demand—she is wondering if the VNA should get into this business—hiring aides as needed.

Janet is concerned that a new, competitive, full-service home health care organization—which would provide both nursing services *and* less-skilled home health care services—might be more appealing to the local hospitals and other referers. She can see the possibility of losing nursing service business if the VNA does not begin to offer a more complete service. This would cause real problems for the VNA—because overhead costs are more or less fixed. A loss in revenue of as little as 10 to 20 percent could require laying off some nurses—or perhaps laying off some secretaries, giving up part of the office, and so on.

Another reason for expanding beyond nursing services—using para-professionals and relatively unskilled personnel—is to offer a better service to present customers *and* make more effective use of the organization structure which has been developed over the last two years. Janet estimates that the administrative and office capabilities could handle 50 to 100 percent more clients without straining the system. It would be necessary to add some clerical help—if the expansion were quite large—as well as expanding the hours when the switchboard was open. But these increases in overhead would be minor compared to the present proportion of total revenue which goes to covering overhead. In other words, additional clients could increase revenue and assure the survival of the association—providing a cushion to cover the normal fluctuations in demand—and some security for the administrative personnel.

Further, Janet feels that if the VNA were successful in expanding its services—and therefore could generate some surplus—it would be in a position to extend services to those who aren't now able to pay. One of the worst parts of her job is refusing service to clients whose third-party benefits have run out—or for whatever reason can no longer afford to pay the association. Janet is uncomfortable about having to cut off service, but must schedule her nurses to provide revenue-producing services if she's going to be able to meet the payroll every two weeks. By expanding to provide more services, she might be able to keep serving more of these non-paying clients. This possibility excites her because her nurse's training has instilled a deep desire to serve people—whether they can pay or not. This continual need to cut off service—because people can't pay—has been at the root of many disagreements—and even arguments—between the nurses serving the clients and Janet, as director and representative of the board of directors.

Expanding into home health care services won't be easy. It may require convincing the nurses' union that the nurses should be available on a 24-hour schedule—rather than the eight-to-five schedule six days a week, which is typical now. It would also require some decisions about relative pay levels for nurses, para-professionals, and home health care aides. It would also require setting prices for these different services and telling the present customers and referral agencies about the expanding service.

These problems aren't bothering Janet too much, however, because she thinks she could handle them. She is sure that home health care services are in demand and could be supplied at competitive prices.

Her primary concern is whether this is the right thing for a nurses' association to do. The name of her group is the Visiting Nurses Association, and its whole history has been oriented to supplying *nurses' services.* Nurses are dedicated professionals who bring high standards to any job they undertake. The question is whether the VNA should offer "less professional" services. Inevitably, some of the home health care aides will not be as dedicated as the nurses might like them to be. And this might reflect unfavorably on the nurse image. At the same time, however, Janet is concerned about the future of the Visiting Nurses Association—and her own future.

What should Janet Brown do? Why?

■ 32.   SUNSHINE REALTY*

Sunshine Realty is a small independent real estate firm located in Sun City, Florida. Because of its success, the company recently decided to expand operations from residential real estate to office development. Management felt the decision to move into this area was sound because of the buoyant economy Florida experienced in the 1970s and the fact that all projections for business, population, and construction are very positive for the next decade. Although most of this growth will be in the middle and southern parts of the state, it is felt that considerable spillover will affect Sun City—which is located in northern Florida and had a population of 50,000 in 1980.

Sunshine's accountant has seen some Census figures indicating that Sun City's growth rate has been significantly higher than the U.S. average and even a little higher than the Florida average. And another source indicated that Sun City had an unusually high "Buying Power Index"—almost double what would be expected based on population alone. Sunshine's executives feel this was a result of high retail expenditures per capita and large retail purchases by people from the many smaller communities surrounding Sun City.

Although Sunshine's management was a bit hesitant to move so quickly, they felt that the demand for office space increased in proportion to population, income, and retail expenditures—all variables which were increasing—and they didn't want someone to get ahead of them. The accountant pointed to the fact that home construction in Sun City was going ahead strongly and that it would be an ideal time for Sunshine to enter office development.

As a result, in 1982 Sunshine Realty purchased a site one block from the central business district—with plans to construct an office building containing about 40,000 square feet of office space.

Before going ahead with construction, Sunshine decided to do some research on the type of facilities which prospective tenants would prefer (e.g., underground parking, recreation facilities, restaurant, etc.). They felt that acting on the results of this research would increase their chances of quickly getting an occupancy rate of at least 90 percent, which they were going to require to make the project financially feasible. The research showed:

---

* This case was adapted from one written by Professor D. W. Balderson, who at the time of its preparation was associated with the University of Lethbridge, Canada.

1. The population of Sun City is growing 3.5 times faster than the U.S. as a whole.
2. Confirmation that the "Buying Power Index" of Sun City is twice as high as would be expected based on population.
3. Per capita retail sales for Sun City are about twice the U.S. average.
4. Population projections for Sun City:

   1980 . . . . 50,000 (actual)
   1985 58,000
   1990 66,000

5. Present supply of office space in Sun City (1982) was estimated at 425,000 square feet with a vacancy rate of 20 percent.
6. Averages for other cities in Florida show an average of about 6.5 to 7 square feet per capita in office space at 90 percent occupancy.

7. There does not appear to be a great demand for restaurant or recreation facilities. The major preference was to be close to downtown.

In view of this information, Sunshine Realty is still planning to go ahead with construction of the building—but they are now a bit worried.

Should Sunshine Realty's managers be concerned about the results of their recent research? How should they have gone about assessing the market potential for their new office building? What additional information, if any, is required at this point? What would you advise Sunshine Realty to do at this time? Why?

■ 33. MAYFAIR DETERGENT COMPANY*

Mike Powell is product manager for Protect Deodorant Soap. He was just transferred to the Canadian company from World Headquarters in New York and is anxious to make a good impression. He is working on developing and securing management approval of next year's marketing plan for Protect. His first step involves submitting a draft marketing plan to Gerry Holden who has recently been appointed group product manager.

Mike's marketing plan is the single most important document he will produce on his brand assignment. Written annually, the marketing plan does three main things:

1. It reviews the brand's performance in the past year, assesses the competitive situation, and highlights problems and opportunities for the brand.
2. It spells out marketing, advertising, and sales promotion strategies and plans for the coming year.

*This case was prepared by Mr. Daniel Aronchick, who at the time of its preparation was Marketing Manager at Thomas J. Lipton, Limited.

3. Finally, and most importantly, the marketing plan sets out the brand's sales objectives and advertising/promotion budget requirements.

In preparing this marketing plan, Mike gathered the information in Table 1.

Mike was aware of the regional disparities in the bar soap market and recognized the significant regional skews.

a. The underdevelopment of the deodorant bar segment in Quebec with a corresponding overdevelopment of the beauty bar segment. Research showed this was due to cultural factors. An identical pattern is evident in most European countries where the adoption of deodorant soaps has been slower than in North America. For similar reasons, the development of perfumed soaps is highest in Quebec.
b. The overdevelopment of synthetic bars in the Prairies. These bars, primarily in the deodorant segment, lather better in the hard water of the Prairies. Non-synthetic bars

TABLE 1: Past 12-month share of soap market (percent)

	Maritimes	Quebec	Ontario	Manitoba/ Saskatchewan	Alberta	British Columbia
Deodorant segment						
Zest	21.3%	14.2%	24.5%	31.2%	30.4%	25.5%
Dial	10.4	5.1	12.8	16.1	17.2	14.3
Lifebuoy	4.2	3.1	1.2	6.4	5.8	4.2
Protect	2.1	5.6	1.0	4.2	4.2	2.1
Beauty bar segment						
Camay	6.2	12.3	7.0	4.1	4.0	5.1
Lux	6.1	11.2	7.7	5.0	6.9	5.0
Dove	5.5	8.0	6.6	6.3	6.2	4.2
Lower-priced bars						
Ivory	11.2	6.5	12.4	5.3	5.2	9.0
Sunlight	6.1	3.2	8.2	4.2	4.1	8.0
All others (including stores' own brands)	26.9	30.8	18.6	17.2	16.0	22.6
Total soap market	100.0	100.0	100.0	100.0	100.0	100.0

lather very poorly in hard-water areas and leave a soap film.

c. The overdevelopment of the "all-other" segment in Quebec. This segment, consisting of smaller brands, fares better in Quebec, where 40 percent of the grocery trade is done by independent stores. Conversely, large chain grocery stores predominate in Ontario and the Prairies.

Mike's brand, Protect, is a highly perfumed, deodorant bar. His business is relatively weak in the key Ontario market. To confirm this share data, Mike calculated consumption of Protect per thousand people in each region (see Table 2).

These differences are especially interesting since per capita sales of total bar soap products are roughly equal in all provinces.

A consumer attitude and usage research study had been conducted approximately a year ago. This study revealed that consumer top-of-mind awareness of the Protect brand differed greatly across Canada. This was true despite the even expenditure of advertising funds in past years. Also, trial of Protect was low in the Maritimes, Ontario, and British Columbia. (Table 3).

The attitude portion of the research revealed that consumers who had heard of Protect were aware of its main attribute of deodorant protection via a high fragrance level. This was the main

TABLE 2: Standard cases of three-ounce bars consumed per 1,000 people in 12 months

	Maritimes	Quebec	Ontario	Manitoba/ Saskatchewan	Alberta	British Columbia
Protect	4.1	10.9	1.9	8.1	4.1	6.2
Sales index	66	175	31	131	131	100

TABLE 3: Usage results (in percent)

	Maritimes	Quebec	Ontario	Manitoba/ Saskatchewan	Alberta	British Columbia
Respondents aware of Protect	20%	58%	28%	30%	32%	16%
Respondents ever trying Protect	3	18	2	8	6	4

TABLE 4:   Allocation of marketing budget, by population

	Maritimes	Quebec	Ontario	Manitoba/ Saskatchewan	Alberta	British Columbia	Canada
Percent of population	10%	27%	36%	8%	8%	11%	100%
Possible allocation of budget based on population	$70M	$190M	$253M	$55M	$55M	$77M	$700M
Percent of Protect business at present	7%	51%	12%	11%	11%	8%	100%

selling point in the copy strategy, and it was well communicated through Protect's advertising. The other important finding was that consumers who had tried Protect were satisfied with the product. Some 72 percent of those trying Protect had repurchased the product at least twice.

One last pressing issue for Protect was the pending delisting of the brand by two key Ontario chains. These chains, which controlled about half the grocery volume in Ontario, were dissatisfied with the level at which Protect was moving off the shelves.

With this information before him, Mike now had to resolve the key aspect of the brand's marketing plan for the following year: how to allocate the advertising and sales promotion budget by region.

Protect's total advertising/sales promotion budget was 22 percent of sales. With forecast sales of $3.2 million, this budget amounted to a $700,000 marketing expenditure. Traditionally such funds had been allocated in proportion to population (Table 4).

Mike's inclination is to skew spending even more heavily into Ontario where the grocery chain delisting problem exists. In the previous year, 36 percent of Protect's budget was allocated to Ontario which accounted for only 12 percent of Protect's sales. Mike wants to increase Ontario spending to 45 percent of the total budget by taking funds evenly from all other areas. Mike expects this will increase business in the key Ontario market which has over a third of Canada's population.

Mike then presented this plan to Gerry, his newly appointed group product manager. Gerry strongly disagreed. He had also been reviewing Protect's business and felt that advertising and rally promotion funds had historically been misallocated. It was his firm belief that, to use his words: "A brand should spend where its business is." Gerry believed that the first priority in allocating funds regionally was to support the areas of strength. He went on to suggest to Mike that there was more business to be had in the brand's strong areas, Quebec and the Prairies, than in chasing sales in Ontario. Therefore, Gerry suggested that spending for Protect in the coming year be proportional to the brand's sales by region rather than to regional population.

Mike felt this was wrong, particularly in light of the Ontario situation. He asked Gerry how the Ontario market should be handled. Gerry suggested the conservative way to build business in Ontario was to consider investing incremental marketing funds. However, before these incremental funds are invested, a test of this Ontario investment proposition should be conducted. Gerry recommended that in a small area or town in Ontario an investment-spending test market be conducted for 12 months to see if the incremental spending resulted in higher sales and profits— profits large enough to justify the higher spending. In other words, an investment payout would have to be assured before spending any extra money in Ontario.

Mike felt this approach would be a waste of time and unduly cautious, given the importance of the Ontario market.

Should Protect's advertising and promotion funds be allocated by region in proportion to past sales, by regional population, or in some other fashion? Why?

■ 34. COOK & MORRISON, CPAs

Cook & Morrison, CPAs (C&M) is a large regional certified public accounting firm based in Grand Rapids, Michigan—with branch offices in Lansing and Detroit. C&M has 10 partners and a professional staff of approximately 100 accountants. Gross service billings for the fiscal year ending June 30, 1982, were $6,460,000. Financial data for 1980, 1981, and 1982 are presented in Table 1.

C&M's professional services include: auditing, tax preparation, and bookkeeping. A breakdown of gross service revenue by service area for 1980, 1981, and 1982 is presented in Table 1. C&M's client base includes municipal governments (cities, villages, and townships), manufacturing companies, professional organizations (attorneys, doctors, and dentists), and various other small business concerns.

The majority of revenue is related to the firm's municipal practice. A breakdown of C&M's gross revenue by client industry for 1980, 1981, and 1982 is presented in Table 1.

At the monthly partner's meeting held in July 1982, Lawrence Cook, the firm's managing partner (CEO), expressed his concern about the firm's municipal practice. Mr. Cook's presentation to his partners appears below:

"Although our firm is considered to be a leader in municipal auditing in our geographic area, I am concerned that as municipals attempt to cut their operating costs, they will solicit competitive bids from other public accounting firms to perform their annual audits. Due to the fact that most of the "Big 8" firms[1] in our area concentrate their practice in the manufacturing industry—which typically has December 31 fiscal year ends—they have several "available" staff during the summer months.[2] Therefore, they can afford to "low-ball" competitive bids in an effort to keep their staff busy and benefit from on-the-job training provided through municipal clientele. I am concerned that we may begin to lose clients in our most established and profitable practice area."

Tom Markus, a senior partner in the firm and the partner-in-charge of the firm's municipal prac-

---

[1] The "Big 8" firms are a group of the eight largest public accounting firms in the United States. They maintain offices in almost every major U.S. city.
[2] Organizations with December fiscal year-ends require audit work to be performed during the fall and in January and February. Those with June 30 fiscal year-ends require auditing during the summer months.

TABLE 1

| | Fiscal year ending June 30 | | |
	1982	1981	1980
Gross billings	6,460,000	6,400,000	5,800,000
Gross billings by service area:			
Auditing	3,100,000	3,200,000	2,750,000
Tax preparation	1,850,000	1,830,000	1,780,000
Bookkeeping	890,000	745,000	660,000
Other	620,000	625,000	610,000
Gross billings by client industry:			
Municipal	3,214,000	3,300,000	2,908,000
Manufacturing	1,949,000	1,880,000	1,706,000
Professional	1,215,000	1,140,000	1,108,000
Other	82,000	80,000	78,000

tice, was the first to respond to Mr. Cook's concern.

"Larry, we all recognize the potential threat of being underbid for our municipal work by our "Big 8" competitors. However, C&M is a recognized leader in municipal auditing, and we have much more local experience than our competitors. Furthermore, it is a fact that we offer a superior level of service quality to our clients—which goes beyond the services normally expected during an audit to include consulting on financial and other operating issues. Many of our less sophisticated clients are dependent on our non-audit consulting assistance. Therefore, I believe, we have been successful in differentiating our services from our competitors. In many recent situations, C&M was selected over a field of as many as 10 competitors even though we had proposed prices significantly higher than our competitors."

The partners at the meeting agreed with Tom Markus' comments. However, even though C&M had many success stories to tell regarding their ability to retain their municipal clients—despite being underbid—they had lost three large municipal clients during the past year. Tom Markus was asked to comment on the loss of those clients.

He explained that the clients that were lost are larger municipalities where there is considerable "in-house" financial expertise—and therefore less dependency on C&M's "consulting" assistance. As a result, C&M's service differentiation went largely unnoticed. Mr. Markus explained that the larger, more sophisticated municipals regarded audits as a "necessary evil" and usually selected the low-cost reputable bidder.

Mr. Cook then requested ideas and discussion from the other partners at the meeting. One partner suggested that C&M should protect itself by diversifying. Specifically, he suggested a substantial practice development effort should be directed toward manufacturing industry. He reasoned that since manufacturing work would occur during C&M's "off-season," they could afford to price very low in order to gain new manufacturing clients. This strategy would also help to counter (and possibly discourage) "Big 8" competitors' "low-ball" pricing for municipals.

Evaluate Cook & Morrison, CPAs' overall situation and the comments and ideas discussed at the partners' meeting. How should they price for municipal clients? Should they "diversify?" Why? What strategy(ies) should they implement?

■ 35.   DIAMOND JIM'S PIZZA COMPANY

Diamond Jim's Pizza Company (DJ's) is a small owner-managed pizza take-out and delivery business with three stores located in Ypsilanti, Southfield, and Pontiac, Michigan. DJ's stores obtain their business by telephone or walk-in orders. They prepare their pizzas at each store location. In addition to pizzas, DJ's also sells and delivers a limited selection of soft drinks.

DJ's Ypsilanti store has been very successful. Much of the store's success is attributed to being close to Eastern Michigan University's campus—which enrolls more than 15,000 students. Most of

these students live within five miles of DJ's Ypsilanti store.

The Southfield store has been moderately successful. It serves mostly residential customers in the Southfield area. Recently, the store had advertised—using direct-mail flyers—to several office buildings within three miles of the store. The flyers describe DJ's willingness and ability to cater large orders for office parties, business luncheons, etc. This promotion has been quite successful. With this new program and DJ's solid residential base of customers in Southfield, improved profitability at the Southfield location seems assured.

DJ's Pontiac location has experienced mixed results during the past three years. The Pontiac store receives only about 50 percent of its customer orders from residential delivery requests. The Pontiac store's new manager, Bill Hendricks, believes the problem with residential pizza delivery in Pontiac is due to distribution of residential neighborhoods in the area. Pontiac has several large industrial plants (mostly auto industry related) that are located throughout the city. Small, mostly factory-worker, neighborhoods are distributed in between the various plant sites. As a result, DJ's store location can service only two or three of these small neighborhoods on one delivery run.

Most of the Pontiac store's potential seems to be in serving the large industrial plants. Many of these plants work two or three work shifts—five days a week. During each work shift, workers are allowed one half-hour "lunch" break—which usually occurs at 11:00 A.M., 8:00 P.M., or 2:30 A.M. (depending on the shift).

Generally, a customer will call from a plant about 30 minutes before a scheduled lunch break and order several (5 to 10) pizzas for a work group. DJ's may receive many orders of this size from the same plant (i.e., from different groups of workers). The plant business is very profitable for several reasons. First, a large number of pizzas can be delivered at the same time to the same location, saving transportation costs. Second, plant orders usually involve many different toppings (double cheese, pepperoni, mushrooms, hamburger) on each pizza. This results in $10 to $15 revenue per pizza. The delivery drivers also like delivering plant orders because the tips are usually $1 or $2 per pizza.

Despite the profitability of the plant orders, there are several factors which make it difficult to serve the plant market. DJ's store is located 5 to 8 minutes from most of the plant sites, so DJ's must prepare the orders within 20 to 25 minutes after the telephone order is received. Often, bottlenecks in oven capacity preclude getting all the orders heated at the same time. Further, the current preparation crew often cannot handle peak order loads in the time available.

Generally, plant workers will wait as long as 10 minutes past the start of their lunch break before ordering from various vending trucks which arrive at the plant sites during lunch breaks. (Currently, no other pizza delivery stores can adequately service plant locations.) But, there have been a few instances when workers refused to pay for pizzas that were only five minutes late! Worse yet, if the same work group gets a couple of late orders, they are lost as future customers. Bill Hendricks believes that the inconsistent profitability of the Pontiac store is a result of lost plant customers.

In an effort to rebuild the plant delivery business, Bill is considering various methods to assure prompt customer delivery service. Bill feels that the potential demand during lunch breaks is significantly above DJ's present capacity. Bill also knows that if he tries to satisfy all phone orders on some peak days, he will be unable to provide prompt customer service and may lose additional plant customers.

Bill has outlined three alternatives that may be used to reestablish the Pontiac store's plant business. He has developed these alternatives to discuss with DJ's owner. Each alternative is briefly described below:

Alternative 1: Determine practical capacities during peak volume periods using existing equipment and personnel. Accept orders only up to that capacity and decline orders beyond. This approach will assure prompt customer service and product quality and also minimize or eliminate losses presently incurred resulting from customers' rejection of late deliveries. Financial analysis of this alternative—shown in Table 1—indicates that a potential daily profit of $1,230 could result from the successful implementation of this alternative.

Alternative 2: Add additional equipment (one oven and one delivery car) and hire additional staff to handle peak loads. This approach would assure timely customer delivery and product quality as well as provide additional capacity to service unmet demand. A conservative estimate of

TABLE 1: Practical capacities and sales potential of current equipment and personnel

	11 A.M. break	8 P.M. break	2:30 A.M. break	Daily totals
Current capacity (pizzas)	48	48	48	144
Average selling price per unit.......................	12.50	12.50	12.50	12.50
Sales potential	$600	$600	$600	$1,800
Variable cost (approximately 40 percent of selling price)*	240	240	240	720
Contribution margin of pizzas	360	360	360	1,080
Beverage sales (2 medium-sized beverages per pizza ordered at 75¢ apiece)†	72	72	72	216
Cost of beverages (30% per beverage)	22	22	22	66
Contribution margin of beverages...................	50	50	50	150
Total contribution margin of pizza and beverages................	$410	$410	$410	$1,230

*The variable cost estimate of 40% of sales includes variable costs of delivery to plant locations.
†Amounts shown are not physical capacities (there is almost unlimited physical capacity), but potential sales volume is constrained by number of pizzas that can be sold.

potential daily demand for plant orders compared to current capacity and proposed increased capacity appears in Table 2. The cost of acquiring the additional equipment and relevant information related to depreciation and fixed costs appears in Table 3.

Using this alternative, the following additional pizza preparation and delivery personnel costs would be required:

	Hours required	Cost per hour	Total additional daily cost
Delivery personnel	6	5	$30.00
Preparation personnel..	8	5	40.00
			$70.00

The addition of even more equipment and the personnel that would be needed to service all unmet demand was not considered in this alternative because the current store is not large enough for more ovens and related personnel.

Alternative 3: Add additional equipment and personnel as described in alternative 2, but move to a new location that would reduce delivery lead times to two to five minutes. This move would probably allow DJ's to service all unmet demand. This is possible because the reduction in delivery time will provide for additional "oven" time. In fact, DJ's might have excess capacity using this approach.

A suitable store space is available which is located adjacent to approximately the same number of residential customers (including many of the store's current residential customer neighborhoods). The available site is slightly larger than needed, and the rent is higher. Relevant cost information on the proposed site appears below:

Additional rental expense of
proposed site over current site ..... $ 1,200 per year
Cost of moving to new
site (one-time cost) $10,000

Bill Hendricks presented each of the three alternatives to DJ's owner—Bob Major. Bob was

TABLE 2: Capacity and demand for plant customer market

	Estimated daily demand	Current daily capacity	Proposed daily capacity
Pizza units (1 pizza)..........	280	144	192

TABLE 3: Cost of required additional assets

	Cost	Estimated useful life	Salvage value	Annual depreciation*	Daily depreciation†
Delivery car (equipped with pizza warmer)	$ 8,000	5 years	$1,000	$1,400	$4.00
Pizza oven.............	$20,000	8 years	$2,000	$2,250	$6.43

*Annual depreciation is calculated on a straight-line basis.
†Daily depreciation assumes a 350-day (plant production) year. All variable expenses related to each piece of equipment (e.g., utilities, gas, oil) are included in the variable cost of a pizza.

pleased that Bill had "done his homework" in putting together these alternatives. He concluded that Bill should make the final decision on what to do (being sure that profits increase) and offered the following comments and concerns:

1. He agreed that the plant market was extremely sensitive to delivery timing. Product quality and pricing, although important, were of secondary importance to delivery.
2. He agreed that plant demand estimates were conservative. "In fact they may be 10 to 20 percent low."
3. He was concerned that under alternative 2, and especially under alternative 3, much of the store's capacity would go unused over 80 percent of the day.
4. He was concerned that DJ's had a bad reputation with plant customers because the prior store manager was not sensitive to timely plant delivery.

He suggested that Bill devise a promotion plan to reestablish DJ's reputation with the plants.

Evaluate DJ's present strategies for the Pontiac store. What should Bill do? Why? Suggest possible promotion plans if alternative 3 is chosen.

■ Notes

Chapter 1

1. To see the basis for such estimates, see Reavis Cox, *Distribution in a High-Level Economy* (Englewood Cliffs, N.J.: Prentice-Hall, 1965), p. 149; and Paul W. Stewart and J. Frederick Dewhurst, *Does Distribution Cost Too Much?* (New York: Twentieth Century Fund, 1963), pp. 117–18.

2. Christopher H. Lovelock and Charles B. Weinberg, *Marketing for Public and Nonprofit Managers* (New York: John Wiley & Sons, 1984); Phillip Kotler, "Strategies for Introducing Marketing into Nonprofit Organizations," *Journal of Marketing,* January 1979, pp. 37–44; Shelby D. Hunt, "The Nature and Scope of Marketing," *Journal of Marketing,* July 1976, pp. 17–28; and Paul N. Bloom and William D. Novelli, *Journal of Marketing* 45, no. 2 (Spring 1981), pp. 79–88.

3. Malcolm P. McNair, "Marketing and the Social Challenge of Our Times," in *A New Measure of Responsibility for Marketing,* ed. Keith Cox and Ben M. Enis (Chicago: American Marketing Association, 1968).

4. "The Hot Discounter," *Newsweek,* April 25, 1977, p. 70.

5. Peter F. Drucker, *Management: Tasks, Responsibilities, Practices* (New York: Harper & Row, 1973), pp. 64–65.

6. George Fisk, "Editor's Working Definition of Macromarketing," *Journal of Macromarketing* 2, no. 1 (Spring 1982), pp. 3–4; and Shelby D. Hunt and John J. Burnett, "The Macromarketing/Micromarketing Dichotomy: A Taxonomical Model," *Journal of Marketing* 46, no. 3 (Summer 1982), pp. 11–26.

7. Much of the material on this topic has been adapted from Y. H. Furuhashi and E. J. McCarthy, *Social Issues of Marketing in the American Economy* (Columbus, Ohio: Grid, 1971), pp. 4–6. See also J. F. Grashof and A. Kelman, *Introduction to Macro-Marketing* (Columbus, Ohio: Grid, 1973).

8. For more on this topic, see Thomas V. Greer, *Marketing in the Soviet Union* (New York: Praeger Publishers, 1973); "Free Enterprise Helps to Keep Russians Fed but Creates Problems," *The Wall Street Journal,* May 2, 1983, pp. 1 and 22; Reed Moyer, "Marketing in the Iron Curtain Countries," *Journal of Marketing,* October 1966, pp. 3–9; G. Peter Lauter, "The Changing Role of Marketing in the Eastern European Socialist Economies," *Journal of Marketing,* October 1971, pp. 16–20; Coskun Samli, *Marketing and Distribution Systems in Eastern Europe* (New York: Praeger Publishers, 1978); and John F. Gaski, "Current Russian Marketing Practice: A Report of the 1982 AMA Study Tour of the Soviet Union," in *1983 American Marketing Association Educators' Proceedings,* ed. P. Murphy et al. (Chicago: American Marketing Association, 1983), pp. 74–77.

9. See, for example, Milton Friedman, *Capitalism and Free-*

dom (Chicago: University of Chicago Press, 1962); and Murray L. Weidenbaum, *Business, Government, and the Public* (Englewood Cliffs, N.J.: Prentice-Hall, 1977). For a contrasting point of view, see John Kenneth Galbraith, *Economics and the Public Purpose* (Boston: Houghton-Mifflin, 1973).

10. Wroe Alderson, "Factors Governing the Development of Marketing Channels," in *Marketing Channels for Manufactured Products,* ed. Richard M. Clewett (Homewood, Ill.: Richard D. Irwin, 1954).

11. Ragnar Nurkse, *Problems of Capital Formation in Underdeveloped Countries* (Oxford: Basil Blackwell, 1953), p. 4.

12. Robert W. Nason and Phillip D. White, "The Visions of Charles C. Slater: Social Consequences of Marketing," *Journal of Macromarketing* 1, no. 2 (Fall 1981), pp. 4–18; and D. F. Dixon, "The Role of Marketing in Early Theories of Economic Development," *Journal of Macromarketing* 1, no. 2 (Fall 1981), pp. 19–27.

13. This discussion is based largely on William McInnes, "A Conceptual Approach to Marketing," in *Theory in Marketing,* second series, ed. Reavis Cox, Wroe Alderson, and Stanley J. Shapiro (Homewood, Ill.: Richard D. Irwin, 1964), pp. 51–67. See also Grashof and Kelman, *Introduction to Macro-Marketing,* pp. 69–78.

14. Reed Moyer, *Macro Marketing: A Social Perspective* (New York: John Wiley & Sons, 1972), pp. 3–5.

15. *Forging America's Future: Strategies for National Growth and Development,* Report of the Advisory Committee on National Growth Policy Processes, reprinted in *Challenge,* January/February 1977.

Chapter 2

1. For a review of how the marketing revolution affected one firm, see Robert J. Keith, "The Marketing Revolution," *Journal of Marketing,* January 1960, pp. 35–38.

2. For an overview of some of Procter & Gamble's current marketing effort, see "Procter & Gamble Co. Starts to Reformulate Tried and True Ways," *The Wall Street Journal,* March 30, 1983, p. 1; C. Scott Greene and Paul Miesing, "Public Policy, Technology, and Ethics: Marketing Decisions for NASA's Space Shuttle," *Journal of Marketing* 48, no. 3 (Summer 1984), pp. 56–67.

3. Alan R. Andreasen, "Nonprofits: Check Your Attention to Customers," *Harvard Business Review* 60, no. 3 (May-June 1982), pp. 105–10; Edward G. Michales, "Marketing Muscle," *Business Horizons* 25, no. 3 (May/June 1982), pp. 63–79; Gene R. Laczniak and Jon G. Udell, "Dimensions of Future Marketing," *MSU Business Topics,* Autumn 1979, pp. 33–44; J. N. Green, "Strategy, Structure, and Survival: The Application of Marketing Principles in Higher Education During the 1980s," *Journal of Busi-*

ness 10 (1982), pp. 24–28; and Philip Kotler, "Strategies for Introducing Marketing into Nonprofit Organizations," *Journal of Marketing* 43 (January 1979), pp. 37–44.

4. Barton A. Weitz and Robin Wensley, eds., *Strategic Marketing: Planning, Implementation and Control* (Boston: Kent, 1984); Ravi Singh Achrol and David L. Appel, "New Developments in Corporate Strategy Planning," in *1983 American Marketing Association Educators' Proceedings,* ed. P. Murphy et al. (Chicago: American Marketing Association, 1983), pp. 305–10; Derek F. Abell and John S. Hammond, *Strategic Market Planning: Problems and Analytical Approaches* (Englewood Cliffs, N.J.: Prentice-Hall, 1979); and Subhash C. Jain, *Marketing Planning and Strategy* (Cincinnati, Ohio: South-Western Publishing, 1980).

5. Thomas V. Bonoma, "A Model of Marketing Implementation," *1984 AMA Educators' Proceedings* (Chicago: American Marketing Association, 1984), pp. 185–89; Robert E. Spekman and Kjell Gronhaug, "Insights on Implementation: A Conceptual Framework for Better Understanding the Strategic Marketing Planning Process," in *1983 American Marketing Association Educators' Proceedings,* ed. P. Murphy et al. (Chicago: American Marketing Association, 1983), pp. 311–14.

6. Alfred P. Sloan, Jr., *My Years with General Motors* (New York: MacFadden Books, 1965), Introduction, chaps. 4 and 9; Jack Givens, "Automobile Industry, Heal Thyself," *Advertising Age,* September 29, 1980, pp. 5–32,33; "U.S. Autos Losing a Big Segment of the Market—Forever?" *Business Week,* March 24, 1980, pp. 78; Jack Honomichl, "Consumer Signals: Why U.S. Auto Makers Ignored Them," *Advertising Age,* August 4, 1980, pp. 43–48; "U.S. Auto Makers Reshape the World Competition," *Business Week,* June 21, 1982; and Jean Ross-Skinner, "Global Auto Battle," *Dun's Review,* June 1980.

7. "Japanese Heat on the Watch Industry," *Business Week,* May 5, 1980, pp. 92–106; "A Reclusive Tycoon Takes Over at Timex," *Business Week,* April 14, 1980, p. 32; "Texas Instruments Wrestles with the Consumer Market," *Fortune,* December 3, 1979, pp. 50–57; "The Great Digital Watch Shake-Out," *Business Week,* May 2, 1977, pp. 70–80; "The Digital Watch Becomes the World's Cheapest Timepiece," *The Wall Street Journal,* April 18, 1977, p. 11; "Gruen Industries Asks Chapter 11 Status," *The Wall Street Journal,* April 15, 1977, p. 9; "Why Gillette Stopped Its Digital Watches," *Business Week,* January 31, 1977, pp. 37–38; "Digital Wristwatch Business is Glowing, but Rivalry Winds Down Prices, Profits," *The Wall Street Journal,* August 24, 1976, p. 6; and "The Long-term Damage From TI's Bombshell," *Business Week,* June 15, 1981, p. 36.

Chapter 3

1. F. R. Bacon, Jr., T. W. Butler, Jr., and E. J. McCarthy, *Planned Innovation Procedures* (printed by authors, 1983). See also George S. Day, A. D. Shocker, and R. K. Srivastava, "Customer-Oriented Approaches to Identifying Product-Markets," *Journal of Marketing* 43 (Fall 1979), pp. 8–19.

2. Ibid.

3. Ibid.

4. Igor Ansoff, *Corporate Strategy* (New York: McGraw-Hill, 1965).

5. Based on a classic article by Charles H. Kline, "The Strategy of Product Policy," *Harvard Business Review,* July-August 1955, pp. 91–100.

6. Adapted from Peter F. Drucker, "Business Objectives and

Survival Needs: Notes on a Discipline of Business Enterprise," *Journal of Business,* April 1958, pp. 181–90.

7. This point of view is discussed at much greater length in a classic article by T. Levitt, "Marketing Myopia," *Harvard Business Review,* September-October 1975, 1f.

8. Carolyn Y. Woo and Arnold C. Cooper, "The Surprising Case for Low Market Share," *Harvard Business Review* 60, no. 6 (November-December 1982), pp. 106–13; and "Reichhold Chemicals: Now the Emphasis is on Profits Rather than Volume," *Business Week,* June 20, 1983, pp. 178–79.

9. Frank R. Bacon, Jr., and Thomas W. Butler, Jr., *Planned Innovation,* rev. ed. (Ann Arbor: Institute of Science and Technology, University of Michigan, 1980).

10. Paul F. Anderson, "Marketing, Strategic Planning and the Theory of the Firm," *Journal of Marketing* 46, no. 2 (Spring 1982), pp. 15–26; George S. Day, "Analytical Approaches to Strategic Market Planning," in *Review of Marketing 1981,* ed. Ben M. Enis and Kenneth J. Roering (Chicago: American Marketing Association, 1981), pp. 89–105; and Michael E. Porter, "How Competitive Forces Shape Strategy," *Harvard Business Review,* March/April 1979, pp. 137–45.

11. M. G. Allen, "Strategic Problems Facing Today's Corporate Planner," speech given to the Academy of Management, 36th Annual Meeting, Kansas City, Missouri, 1976.

12. Richard N. Cardozo and David K. Smith, Jr., "Applying Financial Portfolio Theory to Product Portfolio Decisions: An Empirical Study," *Journal of Marketing* 47, no. 2 (Spring 1983), pp. 110–19; Yoram Wind, Vijay Mahajan, and Donald J. Swire, "An Empirical Comparison of Standardized Portfolio Models," *Journal of Marketing* 47, no. 2 (Spring 1983), pp. 89–99; Philippe Haspeslagh, "Portfolio Planning: Uses and Limits," *Harvard Business Review* 60, no. 1 (January-February 1982), pp. 58–73; and H. Kurt Christensen, Arnold C. Cooper, and Cornelius A. DeKluyver, "The Dog Business: A Re-examination," *Business Horizons* 25, no. 6 (November/December 1982), pp. 12–18.

Chapter 4

1. "Second Sunbelt Seen Emerging in the 1980s," *The Wall Street Journal,* October 23, 1981, p. 28; "Where You Live Often Affects the Kinds of Goods You Buy," *The Wall Street Journal,* September 14, 1983, p. 33; Gregory A. Jackson and George S. Masnick, "Take Another Look at Regional U.S. Growth," *Harvard Business Review* 61, no. 2 (March-April 1983), pp. 76–86; "Cities May Flourish in South and West, Decline in Northeast," *The Wall Street Journal,* April 6, 1976, p. 1f; and "Smaller Cities with No End to Suburbanization," *Business Week,* September 3, 1979, p. 204–6.

2. Based on U.S. Census and *Newsweek,* February 28, 1977, p. 52; "The Baby Boom Muddies the Picture," *The Wall Street Journal,* March 27, 1980, p. 22; "Some Think Baby Boom Spending Spree Could Lead to Strong Economic Recovery," *The Wall Street Journal,* January 24, 1982, p. 25; Landon Y. Jones, "The Baby-Boom Consumer," *American Demographics,* February 1981, pp. 28–35; and Landon Jones, *Great Expectations: America and the Baby Boom Generation* (New York: Coward, McCann and Geoghegan, 1980).

3. Rena Bartos, "Over 49: The Invisible Consumer Market," *Harvard Business Review,* January-February 1980, pp. 140–48; H. Lee Meadow, Stephen C. Cosmas, and Andy Plotkin, "The Elderly Consumer: Past, Present and Future," in *Advances in Consumer Research,* ed. Kent B.

Monroe (Ann Arbor, Mich.: Association for Consumer Research, 1980), pp. 742–47; and Betsy Gelb, "Discovering the 65+ Consumer," *Business Horizons,* May-June 1982, pp. 42–46.

4. "Advertisers Take Aim At a Neglected Market: The Working Women," *The Wall Street Journal,* July 5, 1977, p. 1; "A Living-Alone Affects Housing, Cars, and Other Industries," *The Wall Street Journal,* November 15, 1977, p. 1; "New Benefits for New Lifestyles," *Business Week,* February 11, 1980; and Mary Joyce and Joseph Guiltinan, "The Professional Woman: A Potential Marketing Segment for Retailers," *Journal of Retailing,* Summer 1978, pp. 59–70.

5. James E. Bell, Jr., "Mobiles—A Possible Segment for Retailer Cultivation," *Journal of Retailing,* Fall 1970, pp. 3–15; and "Mobile Americans: A Moving Target with Sales Potential," *Sales & Marketing Management,* April 7, 1980, p. 40.

6. Vern Terpstra, *The Cultural Environment of International Business* (Cincinnati, Ohio: South-Western Publishing, 1978).

7. Maxwell R. Morton, "Technology and Strategy: Creating a Successful Partnership," *Business Horizons* 26, no. 1 (January/February 1983), pp. 44–48; Henry R. Norman and Patricia Blair, "The Coming Growth in 'Appropriate' Technology," *Harvard Business Review* 60, no. 6 (November-December 1982), pp. 62–67; and Alan L. Frohman, "Technology as a Competitive Weapon," *Harvard Business Review* 60, no. 1 (January-February 1982), pp. 97–104; "Polaroid Sharpens Its Focus on the Marketplace," *Business Week,* February 13, 1984, pp. 132–36.

8. Louis W. Stern and Thomas L. Eovaldi, *Legal Aspects of Marketing Strategy: Antitrust and Consumer Protection Issues* (Englewood Cliffs, N.J.: Prentice-Hall, 1984); Paul N. Bloom and Stephen A. Greyser, "The Maturing of Consumerism," *Harvard Business Review* 59, no. 6 (November-December 1981), pp. 130–39; and Robert Pitofsky, "Beyond Nader: Consumer Protection and the Regulation of Advertising," *Harvard Law Review* 90 (February 1977), pp. 661–701.

9. "Suits Touted to Ease Pain of Car Repairs," *The Wall Street Journal,* March 4, 1981, p. 25; and "More Punitive Damage Awards," *Business Week,* January 12, 1981, p. 86.

10. "Packaging Firm Is Found Guilty of Price Conspiracy," *The Wall Street Journal,* January 21, 1977, p. 3. See also, T. McAdams and R. C. Milgus, "Growing Criminal Liability of Executives," *Harvard Business Review,* March-April 1977, pp. 36–40.

11. Rachel Dardis and B. F. Smith, "Cost-Benefit Analysis of Consumer Product Safety Standards," *Journal of Consumer Affairs* 11 (Summer 1977), pp. 34–46; and Paul Busch, "A Review and Critical Evaluation of the Consumer Product Safety Commission: Marketing Management Implications," *Journal of Marketing,* October 1976, pp. 41–49.

12. Ray O. Werner, "Marketing and the United States Supreme Court, 1975–1981," *Journal of Marketing* 46, no. 2 (Spring 1982), pp. 73–81.

Chapter 5

1. A. Parasuraman, "Research's Place in the Marketing Budget," *Business Horizons* 26, no. 2 (March/April 1983), pp. 25–29; J. G. Keane, "Some Observations on Marketing Research in Top Management Decision Making," *Journal of Marketing,* October 1969, pp. 10–15; R. J. Small and L. J. Rosenberg, "The Marketing Researcher as a Decision Maker: Myth or Reality?" *Journal of Marketing,* January 1975, pp. 2–7; Danny N. Bellenger, "The Marketing Manager's View of Marketing Research," *Business Horizons,* June 1979, pp. 59–65; and *The Role and Organization of Marketing Research,* Experiences in Marketing Management, No. 20 (New York: National Industrial Conference Board, 1969), 65 pp.

2. For more details on doing marketing research, see *A Basic Bibliography on Marketing Research,* ed. Robert Ferber et al. (Chicago: American Marketing Association, 1972). A good readable discussion is found in Harper W. Boyd, Jr., Ralph Westfall, and Stanley F. Stasch, *Marketing Research: Text and Cases* (Homewood, Ill.: Richard D. Irwin, 1977).

3. An excellent review of commercially available secondary data may be found in Donald R. Lehmann, *Marketing Research and Analysis,* 2d ed. (Homewood, Ill.: Richard D. Irwin, 1985), pp. 231–72. Also see "Everything You Always Wanted to Know May Soon Be On Line," *Fortune,* May 5, 1980, pp. 226–40.

4. For more on focus groups see William Wells, "Group Interviewing," in *Handbook of Marketing Research,* ed. R. Ferber (New York: McGraw-Hill, 1975); and Bobby J. Calder, "Focus Groups and the Nature of Qualitative Marketing Research," *Journal of Marketing Research,* August 1977, pp. 353–64.

5. Tyzoon T. Tyebjee, "Telephone Survey Methods: The State of the Art," *Journal of Marketing* 43, no. 3 (Summer 1979), pp. 68–77.

6. For more detail on some of these observational approaches, see "Market Research by Scanner," *Business Week,* May 5, 1980, pp. 113–16; "License Plates Locate Customers," *The Wall Street Journal,* February 5, 1981, p. 23; and Eugene Webb, Donald Campbell, Richard Swartz, and Lee Secrest, *Unobtrusive Measures: Nonreactive Research in the Social Sciences* (Chicago: Rand McNally, 1966).

7. Alan G. Sawyer, Parker M. Worthing, and Paul E. Fendak, "The Role of Laboratory Experiments to Test Marketing Strategies," *Journal of Marketing,* Summer 1979, pp. 60–67.

8. A number of surveys have been done which reveal which marketing research areas and techniques are most common. See, for example, Dik Warren Twedt, *1978 Survey of Marketing Research* (Chicago: American Marketing Association, 1978); Rohit Deshpande and Gerald Zaltman, "Factors Affecting the Use of Market Research Information: A Path Analysis," *Journal of Marketing Research* 19 (February 1982), pp. 14–31; and Barnett A. Greenberg, Jac L. Goldstucker, and Danny N. Bellenger, "What Techniques Are Used by Marketing Researchers in Business," *Journal of Marketing* 41 (April 1977), pp. 62–68.

9. Detailed treatment of confidence intervals is beyond the scope of this text, but it is covered in most marketing research texts, such as Donald R. Lehmann, *Marketing Research and Analysis,* 2d ed. (Homewood, Ill.: Richard D. Irwin, 1985); also see Alan G. Sawyer and J. Paul Peter, "The Significance of Statistical Significance Tests in Marketing Research," *Journal of Marketing Research* 20 (May 1983), pp. 122–33.

10. Richard H. Brien and James E. Stafford, "Marketing Information Systems: A New Dimension for Marketing Research," *Journal of Marketing,* July 1968, p. 21; David B. Montgomery and Charles B. Weinberg, "Toward Strategic Intelligence Systems," *Journal of Marketing,* Fall 1979, pp. 41–52; Donald F. Cox and Robert E. Good, "How to Build a Marketing Information System," *Harvard Business Review* 45, no. 3 (May-June 1967), pp. 145–56; Allen S. King, "Computer Decision Support Systems Must be Cred-

ible, Consistent, and Provide Timely Data," *Marketing News,* December 12, 1980, p. 11; Robert Hershey, "Commercial Intelligence on a Shoestring," *Harvard Business Review* 43, no. 3 (Summer 1979), pp. 22–48; and Martin D. J. Buss, "Managing International Information Systems," *Harvard Business Review* 60, no. 5 (September-October 1982), pp. 153–62; Martin D. Goslar and Stephen W. Brown, "Decision Support Systems in Marketing Management Settings," *1984 AMA Educators' Proceedings* (Chicago: American Marketing Association, 1984), pp. 217–21.

Chapter 6

1. "Young Market Becoming More Conventional," *Advertising Age,* May 16, 1977, p. 84; "On a Fast Track to the Good Life," *Fortune,* April 7, 1980, pp. 74–84; "Demography's Good News for the 80's," *Fortune,* November 5, 1979, pp. 92–106; and "The Upbeat Outlook for Family Incomes," *Fortune,* February 25, 1980, pp. 122–30.

2. "Motorcycles: The Dip Continues," *Business Week,* May 3, 1976, pp. 80–81.

3. "Why Gerber Makes an Inviting Target," *Business Week,* June 27, 1977, pp. 26–27.

4. Robert Wilkes and Humberto Valencia, "Shopping Orientations of Mexican-Americans," *1984 AMA Educators' Proceedings* (Chicago: American Marketing Association, 1984), pp. 26–31; Danny N. Bellenger and Humberto Valencia, "Understanding the Hispanic Market," *Business Horizons* 25, no. 3 (May/June 1982), pp. 47–50; Reid T. Reynolds, Bryant Robey, and Cheryl Russell, "Demographics of the 1980s," *American Demographics,* January 1980, pp. 11–19 and Supplement to *American Demographics,* April 1981, p. 2. For additional demographic materials, see Roberto Anson, "Hispanics in the United States: Yesterday, Today and Tommorrow," *The Futurist,* August 1980, pp. 25–31; and Stephanie Ventura and Robert Heuser, "Births of Hispanic Parentage," *Monthly Vital Statistics Report,* March 20, 1981; "Hispanic Marketing" (a special section of) *Advertising Age,* April 16, 1981, pp. S-1–S-24; Jim Sondheim, Rodd Rodriguez, Richard Dillon, Richard Paredes, "Hispanic Market—the Invisible Giant," *Advertising Age,* April 16, 1979, p. S-20; and Luiz Diaz-Albertini, "Brand-Loyal Hispanics Need Good Reason for Switching," *Advertising Age,* April 16, 1979, pp. S-22, S-23.

5. Clarence O. Smith, "Black Market? It's Virtually Untapped," *Advertising Age,* April 16, 1979, p. S-14; D. Parke Gibson, "Black Middle Class Emerges as Dominant Consumer Force," *Advertising Age,* April 16, 1979, p. S-27; *Marketing News,* American Marketing Association, September 15, 1973, p. 5; and "The Upbeat Outlook for Family Incomes," *Fortune.*

6. "The Lasting Changes Brought by Women Workers," *Business Week,* March 15, 1982, p. 59–67; Michael D. Reilly, "Working Wives and Convenience Consumption," *Journal of Consumer Research* 8, no. 4 (March 1982), pp. 407–18; Walter Kiechel III, "Two-Income Families Will Reshape the Consumer Markets," *Fortune,* March 10, 1980; Myra Strober and Charles B. Weinberg, "Strategies Used by Working and Nonworking Wives to Reduce Time Pressures," *Journal of Consumer Research,* March 1979, pp. 338–47; Suzanne McCall, "Meet the Workwife," *Journal of Marketing,* July 1977, pp. 55–65; Rena Bartos, "The Moving Target: The Impact of Women's Employment on Consumer Behavior," *Journal of Marketing,* July 1977, pp. 31–37; "More Food Advertisers Woo the Male Shopper as He Shares the Load," *The Wall Street Journal,* August 26, 1980, p. 1; T. F. Bradshaw, and J. F. Stinson, "Trends in Weekly Earnings: An Analysis," *Monthly Labor Review,*

August 1975, pp. 25–26; W. Lazer and J. E. Smallwood, "The Changing Demographics of Women," *Journal of Marketing,* July 1977, pp. 14–30; and Mary Lou Roberts and Lawrence H. Wotzel, "New Life-Style Determinants of Women's Food Shopping Behavior," *Journal of Marketing,* Summer 1979, pp. 29–39.

7. K. H. Chung, *Motivational Theories and Practices* (Columbus, Ohio: Grid, 1977), pp. 40–43; and A. H. Maslow, *Motivation and Personality* (New York: Harper & Brothers, 1954).

8. Walter R. Nord and J. Paul Peter, "A Behavior Modification Perspective on Marketing," *Journal of Marketing,* Spring 1980, pp. 36–47; and James R. Bettman, "Memory Factors in Consumer Choice: A Review," *Journal of Marketing* 43 (Spring 1979), pp. 37–53.

9. For just a few references, see Alvin A. Achenbaum, "Advertising Doesn't Manipulate Consumers," *Journal of Advertising Research* 12 (April 1972), pp. 3–14; and Steven J. Gross and C. Michael Niman, "Attitude-Behavior Consistency: A Review," *Public Opinion Quarterly* 39 (Fall 1975), pp. 358–68; Paul W. Miniard and Joel B. Cohen, "Isolating Attitudinal and Normative Influences in Behavioral Intentions Models," *Journal of Marketing Research,* February 1979, pp. 102–10; Paul R. Warshaw, "A New Model for Predicting Behavioral Intentions: An Alternative to Fishbein," *Journal of Marketing Research,* Spring 1980, pp. 82–95; J. Pavasars and W. D. Wells, "Measures of Brand Attitudes Can Be Used to Predict Buying Behavior," *Marketing News,* April 11, 1975, p. 6; Joel Huber and John McCann, "The Impact of Inferential Beliefs on Product Evaluations," *Journal of Marketing Research* 19 (August 1982), pp. 324–33; and Calvin P. Duncan and Richard W. Olshavsky, "External Search: The Role of Consumer Beliefs," *Journal of Marketing Research* 19 (February 1982), pp. 32–43.

10. H. H. Kassarjian, "Personality and Consumer Behavior: A Review," *Journal of Marketing Research,* November 1971, pp. 409–18; and W. D. Wells and A. D. Beard, "Personality and Consumer Behavior," in *Consumer Behavior: Theoretical Sources,* ed. Scott Ward and T. S. Robinson (Englewood Cliffs, N.J.: Prentice-Hall, 1973); Raymond L. Horton, *Buyer Behavior: A Decision Making Approach* (Columbus, Ohio: Charles E. Merrill, 1984).

11. William D. Wells and Douglas J. Tigert, "Activities, Interests, and Opinions," in *Market Segmentation,* ed. James F. Engel et al. (New York: Holt, Rinehart & Winston, 1972), p. 258.

12. W. D. Wells, "Psychographics: A Critical Review," *Journal of Marketing Research,* May 1975, pp. 196–213; Alvin C. Burns and Mary C. Harrison, "A Test of the Reliability of Psychographics," *Journal of Marketing Research,* February 1979, pp. 32–38; "Information on Values and Lifestyles Needed to Identify Buying Patterns," *Marketing News,* October 5, 1979, p. 1f; and *Marketing News,* December 31, 1976, p. 8. See also "Life Style Research Inappropriate for Some Categories of Products," *Marketing News,* June 17, 1977, p. 9; and M. E. Goldberg, "Identifying Relevant Psychographic Segments: How Specifying Product Functions Can Help," *Journal of Consumer Research,* December 1976, pp. 163–69.

13. W. H. Reynolds and James H. Meyers, "Marketing and the American Family," *Business Topics,* Spring 1966, pp. 58–59. See also, G. M. Munsinger, J. E. Weber, and R. W. Hansen, "Joint Home Purchasing Decisions by Husbands and Wives," *Journal of Consumer Research,* March 1975, pp. 60–66; E. P. Cox III, "Family Purchase Decision Making and the Process of Adjustment," *Journal of Marketing Research,* May 1975, pp. 189–95; I. C. M. Cun-

ningham and R. R. Green, "Purchasing Roles in the U.S. Family, 1955 & 1973," *Journal of Marketing,* October 1974, pp. 61–64; Harry L. Davis, "Decision Making within the Household," *Journal of Consumer Research,* March 1976, pp. 241–60; Patrick E. Murphy and William A. Staples; "A Modernized Family Life Cycle," *Consumer Research,* June 1979, pp. 12–22; and George J. Szybillo et al., "Family Member Influence in Household Decision Making," *Journal of Consumer Research,* December 1979, pp. 312–16.

14. P. Martineau, "The Pattern of Social Classes," in *Marketing's Role in Scientific Management,* ed. R. L. Clewett (Chicago: American Marketing Association, 1957), pp. 246–47. See also James A. Carman, *The Application of Social Class in Market Segmentation* (Berkeley: Institute of Business and Economic Research, University of California, 1965); William H. Peters, "Relative Occupational Class Income: A Significant Variable in the Marketing of Automobiles," *Journal of Marketing,* April 1970, pp. 74–78; and Arun K. Jain; "A Method for Investigating and Representing an Implicit Theory of Social Class," *Journal of Consumer Research,* June 1975, pp. 53–59.

15. David F. Midgley, "Patterns of Interpersonal Information Seeking for the Purchase of a Symbolic Product," *Journal of Marketing Research* 20 (February 1983), pp. 74–83; James H. Donnelly, Jr., "Social Character and Acceptance of New Products," *Journal of Marketing Research,* February 1970, pp. 111–16; Jeffrey D. Ford and Elwood A. Ellis, "A Reexamination of Group Influence on Member Brand Preference," *Journal of Marketing Research,* February 1980, pp. 125–32; William O. Bearden and Jesse E. Teel, "An Investigation of Personal Influences on Consumer Complaining," *Journal of Retailing* 56, no. 3 (Fall 1980), pp. 3–20; and George P. Moschis, "Social Comparison and Informal Group Influence," *Journal of Marketing Research,* August 1976, pp. 237–44.

16. Richard P. Coleman, "The Continuing Significance of Social Class to Marketing," *Journal of Consumer Research* 10 (December 1983), pp. 265–80; Harold H. Kassarjian, "Social Character and Differential Preference for Mass Communication," *Journal of Marketing Research,* May 1965, pp. 146–53; James H. Myers and Thomas S. Robertson, "Dimensions of Opinion Leadership," *Journal of Marketing Research,* February 1972, pp. 41–46; and Charles W. King and John O. Summers, "Overlap of Opinion Leadership Across Consumer Product Categories," *Journal of Marketing Research,* February 1970, pp. 43–50.

17. Walter A. Henry, "Cultural Values Do Correlate with Consumer Behavior," *Journal of Marketing Research,* May 1976, pp. 121–27.

18. Adapted from James H. Myers and William A. Reynolds, *Consumer Behavior and Marketing Management* (Boston: Houghton Mifflin,1967), p. 49; see also, James R. Bettman, *An Information Processing Theory of Consumer Choice* (Reading, Mass.: Addison-Wesley Publishing, 1979); Richard W. Olshavsky and Donald H. Granbois, "Consumer Decision Making—Fact or Fiction?" *Journal of Consumer Research,* September 1979, pp. 93–100; David A. Sheluga, James Jaccard, and Jacob Jacoby, "Preference, Search, and Choice: An Integrative Approach," *Journal of Consumer Research,* September 1979, pp. 166–176; Lawrence X. Tarpey, Sr., and J. Paul Peter, "A Comparative Analysis of Three Consumer Decision Strategies," *Journal of Consumer Research,* June 1975, pp. 29–37; and J. H. Myers and M. I. Alpert, "Determinant Buying Attributes: Meaning and Measurement," *Journal of Marketing* 32 (October 1968), pp. 13–20.

19. John A. Howard and Jagdish N. Sheth, *The Theory of Buyer Behavior* (New York: John Wiley & Sons, 1969), pp. 46–48.

20. Adapted from E. M. Rogers, *The Diffusion of Innovations* (New York: Free Press, 1962); and E. M. Rogers with F. Shoemaker, *Communication of Innovation: A Cross Cultural Approach* (New York: Free Press, 1968).

21. For further discussion on this topic, see James H. Myers and William H. Reynolds, *Consumer Behavior and Marketing Management* (Boston: Houghton Mifflin, 1967); and J. F. Engel and R. D. Blackwell, *Consumer Behavior* (New York: Holt, Reinhart & Winston, 1981).

Chapter 7

1. For more detail, see *Facts for Marketers,* U.S. Department of Commerce.

2. Edward F. Fern and James R. Brown, "The Industrial/Consumer Marketing Dichotomy: A Case of Insufficient Justification," *Journal of Marketing* 48, no. 2 (Spring 1984), pp. 68–77; Patrick J. Robinson and Charles W. Faris, *Industrial Buying and Creative Marketing* (Boston: Allyn & Bacon, 1967), chap. 2. See also Frederick E. Webster, Jr., and Yoram Wind, "A General Model for Understanding Organizational Buying Behavior," *Journal of Marketing,* April 1972, pp. 12–19; Urban B. Ozanne and Gilbert A. Churchill, Jr., "Five Dimensions of the Industrial Adoption Process," *Journal of Marketing Research,* August 1971, pp. 322–28; J. Patrick Kelly and James W. Coaker, "The Importance of Price as a Choice Criterion for Industrial Purchasing Decisions," *Industrial Marketing Management* 5 (1976), pp. 281–93; Lowell E. Crow, Richard W. Olshavsky, and John O. Summers, "Industrial Buyers' Choice Strategies: A Protocol Analysis," *Journal of Marketing Research,* February 1980, pp. 34–44; Robert E. Spekman and Louis W. Stern, "Environmental Uncertainties and Buying Group Structure: An Empirical Investigation," *Journal of Marketing,* Spring 1979, pp. 54–64; and Arch G. Woodside and David M. Samuel, "Decision Systems Analysis of Corporate Purchase Agreements," *Industrial Marketing Management* 10 (1981), pp. 191–205.

3. Michele D. Bunn, "Structure in the Buying Center," *1984 AMA Educators' Proceedings* (Chicago: American Marketing Association, 1984), pp. 32–36; Thomas V. Bonoma, "Major Sales: Who Really Does the Buying?" *Harvard Business Review* 60, no. 3 (May-June 1982), pp. 120–27; Wesley J. Johnston and Thomas V. Bonoma, "The Buying Center: Structure and Interaction Patterns," *Journal of Marketing* 45, no. 3 (Summer 1981), pp. 143–56; and Rowland T. Moriarty and John E. G. Bateson, "Exploring Complex Decision Making Units: A New Approach," *Journal of Marketing Research* 19 (May 1982), pp. 182–91.

4. James D. Edwards, "Investment Decision Making in a Competitive Society," *MSU Business Topics,* Autumn 1970, pp. 53–60.

5. "Federal Suit Charges GE with Reciprocity on Purchasing; Vigorous Defense Is Vowed," *The Wall Street Journal,* May 19, 1972, p. 2. See also Robert E. Weigand, "The Problems of Managing Reciprocity," *California Management Review,* Fall 1973, pp. 40–48; and Reed Moyer, "Reciprocity: Retrospect and Prospect," *Journal of Marketing,* October 1970, pp. 37–54.

6. For a detailed discussion of supermarket chain buying, see J. F. Grashof, *Information Management for Supermarket Chain Product Mix Decisions,* Ph.D. thesis, Michigan State University, 1968.

7. David E. Gumpert and Jeffry A. Timmons, "Penetrating the Government Procurement Maze," *Harvard Business Review* 60, no. 3 (September-October 1982), pp. 14–23.

Chapter 8

1. Terry Elrod and Russell S. Winer, "An Empirical Evaluation of Aggregation Approaches for Developing Market Segments," *Journal of Marketing,* 46, no. 4 (Fall 1982), pp. 32–34.

2. Russell I. Haley, "Benefit Segmentation—20 Years Later," *Journal of Consumer Marketing* 1, no. 2 (1984), pp. 5–14; Peter R. Dickerson, "Person-Situation: Segmentation's Missing Link," *Journal of Marketing,* 46, no. 4, (Fall 1982), pp. 56–64. See also Richard M. Johnson, "Marketing Segmentation: A Strategic Management Tool," *Journal of Marketing Research,* February 1971, pp. 13–18; James H. Myers, "Benefit Structure Analysis: A New Tool for Product Planning," *Journal of Marketing,* October 1976, pp. 23–32; and Roger J. Calantone and Alan G. Sawyer, "The Stability of Benefit Segments," *Journal of Marketing Research,* August 1978, pp. 395–404.

3. Danny N. Bellenger and Pradeep K. Korgaonkar, "Profiling the Recreational Shopper," *Journal of Retailing* 56, no. 3 (Fall 1980), pp. 77–92; Miriam Tatzel, "Skill and Motivation in Clothes Shopping: Fashion-Conscious, Independent, and Apathetic Consumers," *Journal of Retailing* 58, no. 4 (Winter 1982), pp. 90–96; and "The Sky's the Limit in Luring the Frequent Flier," *Business Week,* October 18, 1982, pp. 152–53.

4. Girish Punj and David W. Stewart, "Cluster Analysis in Marketing Research: Review and Suggestions for Application," *Journal of Marketing Research* 20, (May 1983), pp. 134–48; T. D. Klastorin, "Assessing Cluster Analysis Results," *Journal of Marketing Research* 20 (February 1983), pp. 92–98; Rajendra K. Srivastava, Robert P. Leone, and Allen D. Shocker, "Market Structure Analysis: Hierarchical Clustering of Products Based on Substitution-in-Use," *Journal of Marketing* 45, no. 3 (Summer 1981), pp. 38–48; Frederick W. Winter, "A Cost-Benefit Approach to Market Segmentation," *Journal of Marketing,* Fall 1979, pp. 103–11; Phillip E. Downs, "Multidimensional Scaling versus the Hand-Drawn Technique," *Journal of Business Research,* December 1979, pp. 349–58; and Henry Assael, "Segmenting Markets by Response Elasticity," *Journal of Advertising Research,* April 1976, pp. 27–35.

5. S. Arbeit and A. G. Sawyer, "Benefit Segmentation in a Retail Banking Environment," paper presented at the American Marketing Association Fall Conference, Washington D.C., August 1973.

6. Checking the accuracy of forecasts is a difficult subject. See R. Ferber, W. J. Hawkes, Jr., and M. D. Plotkin, "How Reliable Are National Retail Sales Estimates?" *Journal of Marketing,* October 1976, pp. 13–22; D. J. Dalrymple, "Sales Forecasting Methods and Accuracy," *Business Horizons,* December 1975, pp. 69–73; P. R. Wotruba and M. L. Thurlow, "Sales Force Participation in Quota Setting and Sales Forecasting," *Journal of Marketing,* April 1976, pp. 11–16; R. Shoemaker and R. Staelin, "The Effects of Sampling Variation on Sales Forecasts for New Consumer Products," *Journal of Marketing Research,* May 1976, pp. 138–43; and R. Staelin and R. E. Turner, "Error in Judgmental Sales Forecasts: Theory and Results," *Journal of Marketing Research,* February 1973, pp. 10–16; E. Jerome Scott and Stephen K. Keiser, "Forecasting Acceptance of New Industrial Products with Judgment Modeling," *Journal of Marketing* 48, no. 2 (Spring 1984), pp. 54–67.

Chapter 9

1. Stanley C. Hollander, "Is There a Generic Demand for Services?" *MSU Business Topics,* Spring 1979, pp. 41–46; John M. Rathmell, "What Is Meant by Services?"

Journal of Marketing, October 1966, pp. 32–36; T. Levitt, "The Industrialization of Service," *Harvard Business Review,* September-October 1976, pp. 63–74; R. W. Obenberger and S. W. Brown, "A Marketing Alternative: Consumer Leasing and Renting," *Business Horizons,* October 1976, pp. 82–86; Richard B. Chase, "Where Does the Customer Fit in a Service Operation?" *Harvard Business Review,* November-December 1978, pp. 137–42; Dan R. E. Thomas, "Strategy Is Different in Service Industries," *Harvard Business Review,* July-August 1978, pp. 158–65; Paul F. Anderson and William Lazer, "Industrial Lease Marketing," *Journal of Marketing,* January 1978, pp. 71–79; Robert E. Sabath, "How Much Service Do Customers Really Want?" *Business Horizons,* April 1978, pp. 26–32; "Sony's U.S. Operation Goes in for Repairs," *Business Week,* March 13, 1978, pp. 31–32; Bernard Wysocki, Jr., "Branching Out: Major Retailers Offer Varied Services to Lure Customers, Lift Profits," *The Wall Street Journal,* June 12, 1978, pp. 1, 21; and Phillip D. White and Edward W. Cundiff, "Assessing the Quality of Industrial Products," *Journal of Marketing* 42 (January 1978), pp. 80–86.

2. J. B. Mason and M. L. Mayer, "Empirical Observations of Consumer Behavior as Related to Goods Classification and Retail Strategy," *Journal of Retailing,* Fall 1972, pp. 17–31; Arno K. Kleinenhagen, "Shopping, Specialty, or Convenience Goods?" *Journal of Retailing,* Winter 1966–67, pp. 32–39ff; Louis P. Bucklin, "Testing Propensities to Shop," *Journal of Marketing,* January 1966, pp. 22–27; William P. Dommermuth, "The Shopping Matrix and Marketing Strategy," *Journal of Marketing Research,* May 1965, pp. 128–132; Richard H. Holton, "The Distinction Between Convenience Goods, Shopping Goods, and Specialty Goods," *Journal of Marketing,* July 1958, pp. 53–56; Perry Bliss, "Supply Considerations and Shopper Convenience," *Journal of Marketing,* July 1966, pp. 43–45; and S. Kaish, "Cognitive Dissonance and the Classification of Consumer Goods," and W. P. Dommermuth and E. W. Cundiff, "Shopping Goods, Shopping Centers, and Selling Strategies," *Journal of Marketing,* October 1967, pp. 28–36; Edward M. Tauber, "Why Do People Shop?" *Journal of Marketing,* October 1972, pp. 46–49.

3. David T. Kollat and Ronald P. Willett, "Customer Impulse Purchasing Behavior," *Journal of Marketing Research,* February 1967, pp. 21–31. See also David T. Kollat and Ronald P. Willett, "Is Impulse Purchasing Really a Useful Concept for Marketing Decisions?" *Journal of Marketing,* January 1969, pp. 79–83; and Danny N. Bellenger, Dan H. Robertson, and Elizabeth C. Hirschman, "Impulse Buying Varies by Product," *Journal of Advertising Research* 18 (December 1978), pp. 15–18.

4. "DuPont's Teflon Trademark Survives Attack," *Advertising Age,* July 14, 1975, p. 93; and George Miaoulis and Nancy D'Amato, "Consumer Confusion and Trademark Infringement," *Journal of Marketing,* April 1978, pp. 48–55.

5. Martha R. McEnally and Jon M. Hawes, "The Market for Generic Brand Grocery Products: A Review and Extension," *Journal of Marketing* 48, no. 1 (Winter 1984), pp. 75–83; K. L. Granzin, "An Investigation of the Market for Generic Products," *Journal of Retailing* 57 (1981), pp. 39–55; "Checklist Tells If Generic Products 'Threaten' Your Brand," *Marketing News,* October 31, 1980; Patrick E. Murphy and Gene R. Laczniak, "Generic Supermarket Items: A Product and Consumer Analysis," *Journal of Retailing* 55 (Summer 1979), pp. 3–14; "Co-opting Generics," *Advertising Age,* March 31, 1981; "Generic Products Are Winning Noticeable Shares of Market from National Brands, Private Labels," *The Wall Street Journal,* August 10, 1979, p. 6; and Betsy D. Gelb, "'No-Name' Products:

A Step Toward 'No Name' Retailing," *Business Horizons,* June 1980, pp. 9–13.

6. J. A. Bellizzi, H. F. Kruekeberg, J. R. Hamilton, and W. S. Martin, "Consumer Perceptions of National, Private, and Generic Brands," *Journal of Retailing* 57 (1981), pp. 56–70; I. C. M. Cunningham, A. P. Hardy, and G. Imperia, "Generic Brands versus National Brands and Store Brands," *Journal of Advertising Research* 22, no. 5 (October/November 1982), pp. 25–32; "Is the Private Label Battle Heating Up?" *Grey Matter* 44, no. 7 (July 1973); Zarrel V. Lambert, Paul L. Doering, Eric Goldstein, and William C. McCormick, "Predisposition toward Generic Drug Acceptance," *Consumer Research,* June 1980, pp. 14–23; "Private-Label Firms Aided by Inflation, Expected to Post Healthy Growth in 1980," *The Wall Street Journal,* March 31, 1980, p. 20; Victor J. Cook and T. F. Schutte, *Brand Policy Determination* (Boston: Allyn & Bacon, 1967); Arthur I. Cohen and Ana Loud Jones, "Brand Marketing in the New Retail Environment," *Harvard Business Review,* September-October 1978, pp. 141–48; "The Drugmaker's Rx for Living with Generics," *Business Week,* November 6, 1978, pp. 205–8; "No-Name Goods Catching On with Grocers," *Detroit Free Press,* April 9, 1978, p. 16D; and "The Marketing of Licensed Characters for Kids, Or How the Lovable Care Bears Were Conceived," *The Wall Street Journal,* September 24, 1982, p. 44.

7. "Containers and Packaging" (Chap. 7), *U.S. Industrial Outlook 1980,* p. 75; "Bullish '77: Packagers to Fight Price Hikes," *Modern Packaging,* January 1977, pp. 22–28; Scott Silvenis, "Packaging for the Elderly," *Modern Packaging* 52 (October 1979), pp. 38–39; "Is the Bar of Soap Washed Up?" *Business Week,* January 12, 1982, p. 109–16; "Consumers Examine Packages Very Closely Since Tylenol Tragedy," *The Wall Street Journal,* November 5, 1982, p. 1; and "Designing Art Director Focuses on Marketing-Oriented Packages," *Advertising Age,* November 26, 1979, p. 57; "Paper Bottles Are Coming on Strong," *Business Week,* January 16, 1984, pp. 56–57.

8. Dennis L. McNeill and William L. Wilkie, "Public Policy and Consumer Information: Impact of the New Energy Labels," *Journal of Consumer Research* 6 (June 1979), pp. 1–11; W. A. French and L. O. Schroeder, "Package Information Legislation: Trends and Viewpoints," *MSU Business Topics,* Summer 1972, pp. 39–42. See also J. A. Miller, D. G. Topel, and R. E. Rust, "USDA Beef Grading: A Failure in Consumer Information?" *Journal of Marketing,* January 1976, pp. 25–31.

9. J. E. Russo, "The Value of Unit Price Information," *Journal of Marketing Research,* May 1977, pp. 193–201; and K. B. Monroe and P. J. LaPlaca, "What Are the Benefits of Unit Pricing?" *Journal of Marketing,* July 1972, pp. 16–22.

10. Laurence P. Feldman, "New Legislation and the Prospects for Real Warranty Reform," *Journal of Marketing,* July 1976, pp. 41–47; F. K. Shuptrine and Ellen Moore, "Even After the Magnuson-Moss Act of 1975, Warranties Are Not Easy to Understand," *Journal of Consumer Affairs,* Winter 1980, pp. 394–404; C. L. Kendall and Frederick A. Russ, "Warranty and Complaint Policies: An Opportunity for Marketing Management," *Journal of Marketing,* April 1975, pp. 36–43; Fred W. Morgan, "Marketing and Product Liability: A Review and Update," *Journal of Marketing* 46, no. 3 (Summer 1982), pp. 69–78; David L. Malickson, "Are You Ready for a Product Recall?" *Business Horizons* 26, no. 1 (January/February 1983), pp. 31–35; Karl A. Boedecker and Fred W. Morgan, "The Channel Implications of Product Liability Developments," *Journal of Retailing* 56, no. 4 (Winter 1980), pp. 59–72; and Robert H. Malott, "Let's Restore Balance to Product Liability Law,"

Harvard Business Review 61, no. 3 (May-June 1983), pp. 66–74.

Chapter 10

1. George Day, "The Product Life Cycle: Analysis and Applications Issues," *Journal of Marketing* 45, no. 4 (Fall 1981), pp. 60–67; John E. Swan and David R. Rink, "Fitting Marketing Strategy to Varying Product Life Cycles," *Business Horizons* 25, no. 1 (January/February 1982), pp. 72–76; Igal Ayal, "International Product Life Cycle: A Reassessment and Product Policy Implications," *Journal of Marketing* 45, no. 4 (Fall 1981), pp. 91–96; Stephen G. Harrell and Elmer D. Taylor, "Modeling the Product Life Cycle for Consumer Durables," *Journal of Marketing* 45, no. 4 (Fall 1981), pp. 68–75; William Qualls, Richard W. Olshavsky, and Ronald E. Michaels, "Shortening of the PLC—An Empirical Test," *Journal of Marketing* 45, no. 4 (Fall 1981), pp. 76–80; Gerard J. Tellis and C. Merle Crawford, "An Evolutionary Approach to Product Growth Theory," *Journal of Marketing* 45, no. 4 (Fall 1981), pp. 125–32; Hans B. Thorelli and Stephen C. Burnett, "The Nature of Product Life Cycles for Industrial Goods Businesses," *Journal of Marketing* 45, no. 4 (Fall 1981), pp. 97–108; David F. Midgley, "Toward a Theory of the Product Life Cycle: Explaining Diversity," *Journal of Marketing* 45, no. 4 (Fall 1981), pp. 109–15; and Bernard Catry and Michel Chevalier, "Market Share Strategy and the Product Life Cycle," *Journal of Marketing,* October 1974, pp. 29–34.

2. "RCA to Cut Prices on Eight Color TVs in Promotion Effort," *The Wall Street Journal,* December 31, 1976, p. 16; "Sales of Major Appliances, TV Sets Gain; But Profits Fail to Keep Up: Gap May Widen," *The Wall Street Journal,* August 21, 1972, p. 22; "What Do You Do When Snowmobiles Go on a Steep Slide?" *The Wall Street Journal,* March 8, 1978, pp. 1, 33; "After Their Slow Year, Fast-Food Chains Use Ploys to Speed Up Sales," *The Wall Street Journal,* April 4, 1980, p. 1f; "Home Smoke Detectors Fall On Hard Times as Sales Apparently Peaked," *The Wall Street Journal,* April 3, 1980, p. 1; and "As Once Bright Market for CAT Scanners Dims, Smaller Makers of the X-ray Devices Fade Out," *The Wall Street Journal,* May 6, 1980, p. 40.

3. "'Good Products Don't Die,' P&G Chairman Declares," *Advertising Age,* November 1, 1976, p. 8; "Detroit Brings Back the Fast, Flashy Auto to Aid Sluggish Sales," *The Wall Street Journal,* December 9, 1976, p. 1f; and "Ten Ways to Restore Vitality to Old, Worn-Out Products," *The Wall Street Journal,* February 18, 1982, p. 25.

4. Chester R. Wasson, "What is 'New' About New Products?" *Journal of Marketing,* July 1960, pp. 52–56; Patrick M. Dunne, "What Really Are New Products?" *Journal of Business,* December 1974, pp. 20–25; and S. H. Britt and V. M. Nelson, "The Marketing Importance of the 'Just Noticeable Difference,'" *Business Horizons,* August 1976, pp. 38–40.

5. *Marketing News,* February 8, 1980; C. Merle Crawford, "Marketing Research and the New-Product Failure Rate," *Journal of Marketing,* April 1977, pp. 51–61.

6. Adapted from Frank R. Bacon, Jr., and Thomas W. Butler, Jr., *Planned Innovation,* rev. ed. (Ann Arbor: Institute of Science and Technology, University of Michigan, 1980). See also, John R. Rockwell and Marc C. Particelli, "New Product Strategy: How the Pros Do It," *Industrial Marketing,* May 1982, 49ff; G. Urban and J. Hauser, *Design and Marketing of New Products* (Englewood Cliffs, N.J.: Prentice-Hall, 1980); David S. Hopkins, "New Emphasis in Product Planning and Strategy Development," *Industrial*

Marketing Management Journal 6 (1977), pp. 410–19; Richard P. Greenthal and John A. Larson, "Venturing Into Venture Capital," *Business Horizons* 25, no. 5 (September/October 1982), pp. 18–23; Eric von Hippel, "Get New Products from Customers," *Harvard Business Review* 60, no. 2, (March-April 1982), pp. 117–22; Shelby H. McIntyre and Meir Statman, "Managing the Risk of New Product Development," *Business Horizons* 25, no. 3 (May/June 1982), pp. 51–55; and "Listening to the Voice of the Marketplace," *Business Week,* February 21, 1983, p. 90f; G. Lynn Shostack, "Designing Services That Deliver," *Harvard Business Review* 84 (January-February 1984), pp. 133–39.

7. "Inflation in Product Liability," *Business Week,* May 31, 1976, p. 60; Jane Mallor, "In Brief: Recent Products Liability Cases," *Business Horizons,* October 1979, pp. 47–49; and William L. Trombetta, "Products Liability: What New Court Ruling Means for Management," *Business Horizons,* August 1979, pp. 67–72.

8. David A. Aaker and J. Gary Shansby, "Positioning Your Product," *Business Horizons* 25, no. 3 (May/June 1982), pp. 56–62; Al Ries and Jack Trout, *Positioning: The Battle for Your Mind* (New York: McGraw-Hill, 1981), p. 53; and D. W. Cravens, "Marketing Strategy Positioning," *Business Horizons,* December 1975, pp. 47–54.

9. Phillip R. McDonald and Joseph O. Eastlack, Jr., "Top Management Involvement with New Products," *Business Horizons,* December 1971, pp. 23–31; John H. Murphy, "New Products Need Special Management," *Journal of Marketing,* October 1962, pp. 46–49; and E. J. McCarthy, "Organization for New-Product Development?" *Journal of Business of the University of Chicago,* April 1959, pp. 128–32.

10. See T. Levitt, "Innovation Imitation," *Harvard Business Review,* September-October 1966, pp. 63–70; and Shelby H. McIntyre, "Obstacles To Corporate Innovation," *Business Horizons* 25, no. 1 (January/February 1982), pp. 23–28.

11. Richard T. Hise and J. Patrick Kelly, "Product Management on Trial," *Journal of Marketing,* October 1978, pp. 28–33; and Victor P. Buell, "The Changing Role of the Product Manager in Consumer Goods Companies," *Journal of Marketing,* July 1975, pp. 3–11.

Chapter 11

1. For a classic discussion of the discrepancy concepts, see Wroe Alderson, "Factors Governing the Development of Marketing Channels," in *Marketing Channels for Manufactured Goods,* ed. Richard M. Clewett (Homewood, Ill.: Richard D. Irwin, 1954), pp. 7–9. See also Lee Dahringer, "Colloquium on the Role of Marketing in Developing Nations: Public Policy Implications of Reverse Channel Mapping for Lesotho," *Journal of Macromarketing* 3, no. 1 (Spring 1983), pp. 69–75; Louis W. Stern and Adel I. El-Ansary, *Marketing Channels* (Englewood Cliffs, N.J.: Prentice-Hall, 1977); Bruce Mallen, *Principles of Marketing Channel Management* (Lexington, Mass.: D.C. Heath, 1977); and R. D. Michman and S. D. Sibley, *Marketing Channels and Strategies* (Columbus, Ohio: Grid, 1980).

2. For a more detailed comparison of mode characteristics, see D. J. Bowersox, *Logistical Management* (New York: Macmillan, 1978), p. 120; Edward R. Bruning and Peter M. Lynagh, "Carrier Evaluation in Physical Distribution Management," *Journal of Business Logistics* 5, no. 2 (September 1984), pp. 30–47.

3. Kenneth B. Ackerman and Bernard J. LaLonde, "Making Warehousing More Efficient," *Harvard Business Review* 58, no. 2 (April 1980), p. 94–102.

4. Arthur M. Geoffrion, "Better Distribution Planning with Computer Models," *Harvard Business Review,* July-August 1976, pp. 92–99. See also Donald J. Bowersox, *Logistical Management* (New York: Macmillan, 1978); Kenneth B. Ackerman and Bernard J. LaLonde, "Making Warehousing More Efficient," *Harvard Business Review,* March-April 1980, pp. 94–102; David P. Herron, "Managing Physical Distributor for Profit," *Harvard Business Review,* May-June 1979, pp. 121–32; and "'What If' Help for Management," *Business Week,* January 21, 1980, p. 73.

5. For more discussion on this point, see William D. Perreault, Jr., and Frederick A. Russ, "Physical Distribution Service in Industrial Purchase Decisions," *Journal of Marketing,* April 1976, pp. 3–10. See also William D. Perreault, Jr., and Frederick R. Russ, "Physical Distribution Service: A Neglected Aspect of Marketing Management," *MSU Business Topics,* Summer 1974, pp. 37–46; Douglas M. Lambert and James R. Stock, "Physical Distribution and Consumer Demands," *MSU Business Topics,* Spring 1978, pp. 49–56; Harvey N. Shycon and Christopher R. Sprague, "Put a Price Tag on Your Customer Servicing Levels," *Harvard Business Review,* July-August 1979, pp. 71–78; Richard A. Matteis, "The New Back Office Focuses on Customer Service," *Harvard Business Review,* March-April 1979, pp. 146–59; M. Murphy Bird, "Small Industrial Buyers Call Late Delivery Worst Problem," *Marketing News,* April 4, 1980, p. 24; and "Apparel Makers Face Consolidation as Stores Stiffen Delivery Terms," *The Wall Street Journal,* February 6, 1978, p. 1.

6. Robert D. Buzzell, "Is Vertical Integration Profitable?" *Harvard Business Review* 61, no. 1 (January-February 1983), pp. 92–102; Saul Sands and Robert J. Posch, Jr., "A Checklist of Questions for Firms Considering a Vertical Territorial Distribution Plan," *Journal of Marketing* 46, no. 3 (Summer 1982), pp. 38–43; Louis W. Stern and Torger Reve, "Distribution Channels as Political Economies: A Framework for Comparative Analysis," *Journal of Marketing* 44, no. 3 (Summer 1980), pp. 52–64; Bert C. McCammon, Jr., "The Emergence and Growth of Contractually Integrated Channels in the American Economy," paper presented at the Fall Conference of the American Marketing Association, Washington, D.C., September 2, 1965; and "Why Manufacturers are Doubling as Distributors," *Business Week,* January 17, 1983, p. 41.

7. "The Court Switches Franchise Signals," *Business Week,* July 11, 1977, pp. 30–31. See also James R. Burley, "Territorial Restriction and Distribution Systems: Current Legal Developments," *Journal of Marketing,* October 1975, pp. 52–56; Louis W. Stern et al., "Territorial Restrictions and Distribution: A Case Analysis," *Journal of Marketing,* April 1976, pp. 69–75; "Soft-Drink Bottlers Choke on FTC Ruling against Exclusive-Territory Restrictions," *The Wall Street Journal,* April 25, 1978, p. 6; Michael B. Metzger, "Schwinn's Swan Song," *Business Horizons,* April 1978, pp. 52–56; "Justice Takes Aim at Dual Distribution," *Business Week,* July 7, 1980, pp. 24–25; and Joseph P. Guiltinan, Ismail B. Rejab, and William C. Rodgers, "Factors Influencing Coordination in a Franchise Channel," *Journal of Retailing* 56, no. 4 (Fall 1980), pp. 41–58.

8. Robert W. Little, "The Marketing Channel: Who Should Lead This Extra Corporate Organization?" *Journal of Marketing,* January 1970, pp. 31–39; Phillip McVey, "Are Channels of Distribution What the Textbooks Say?" *Journal of Marketing,* January 1960, pp. 61–65; Bruce Mallen, "Functional Spin-Off: A Key to Anticipating Change in Distribution Structure," *Journal of Marketing,* July 1973, pp. 18–25; and Gary L. Frazier, "On the Measurement of Interfirm Power in Channels of Distribution," *Journal of Marketing Research* 20, (May 1983), pp. 158–66.

9. Michael Etgar, "Selection of an Effective Channel Control Mix," *Journal of Marketing,* July 1978, pp. 53–58; Michael Etgar, "Intrachannel Conflict and Use of Power," *Journal of Marketing Research,* May 1978, pp. 273–74; Robert F. Lusch, "Sources of Power: Their Impact on Intrachannel Conflict," *Journal of Marketing Research,* November 1976, pp. 382–90; William P. Dommermuth, "Profiting from Distribution Conflicts," *Business Horizons,* December 1976, pp. 4–13; Shelby D. Hunt and John R. Nevin, "Power in a Channel of Distribution: Sources and Consequences," *Journal of Marketing Research,* May 1974, pp. 186–93; Louis P. Bucklin, "A Theory of Channel Control," *Journal of Marketing,* January 1973, pp. 39–47; Joseph B. Mason, "Power and Channel Conflicts in Shopping Center Development," *Journal of Marketing,* April 1975, pp. 28–35; Stanley D. Sibley and Donald A. Michie, "An Exploratory Investigation of Cooperation in a Franchise Channel," *Journal of Retailing* 58, no. 4 (Winter 1982), pp. 23–45; James R. Brown, "A Cross-Channel Comparison of Supplier-Retailer Relations," *Journal of Retailing* 57, no. 4 (Winter 1981), pp. 3–18; and John E. Robbins, Thomas W. Speh, and Morris L. Mayer, "Retailers' Perceptions of Channel Conflict Issues," *Journal of Retailing* 58, no. 4 (Winter 1982), pp. 46–67; John F. Gaski, "The Theory of Power and Conflict in Channels of Distribution," *Journal of Marketing* 48, no. 3 (Summer 1984), pp. 9–29.

Chapter 12

1. *Client's Monthly Alert,* June 1977, p. 3.

2. "Bonwit's Turns Up the Heat," *Business Week,* October 11, 1976, pp. 120–22.

3. "Why Profits Shrink at a Grand Old Name (Marshall Field)," *Business Week,* April 11, 1977, pp. 66–78; Louis H. Grossman, "Merchandising Strategies of a Department Store Facing Change," *MSU Business Topics,* Winter 1970, pp. 31–42; "Suburban Malls Go Downtown," *Business Week,* November 10, 1973, pp. 90–94; and "Smaller Cities, With No End to Suburbanization," *Business Week,* September 3, 1979, pp. 204–6.

4. David Appel, "The Supermarket: Early Development of an Institutional Innovation," *Journal of Retailing,* Spring 1972, pp. 39–53.

5. *Industry Surveys,* January 26, 1984, p. R1–7; "Supermarkets Eye the Sunbelt," *Business Week,* September 27, 1976, pp. 61–62; "Safeway: Selling Nongrocery Items to Cure the Supermarket Blahs," *Business Week,* March 7, 1977, pp. 52–58; "How a Long Price War Dragged on and Hurt Chicago Food Chains," *The Wall Street Journal,* July 19, 1976, pp. 1f.; and Gilbert D. Harrell and Michael D. Hutt, "Crowding in Retail Stores," *MSU Business Topics,* Winter 1976, pp. 33–39.

6. "Discount Catalogs: A New Way to Sell," *Business Week,* April 29, 1972, pp. 72–74; "Catalog Discounting Is a Small Man's Game," *Business Week,* October 13, 1973, pp. 70–76; and Pradeep K. Korgaonkar, "Consumer Preferences for Catalog Showrooms and Discount Stores," *Journal of Retailing* 58, no. 3 (Fall 1982), pp. 76–88.

7. Claudia Ricci, "Discount Business Burns, Pleasing Buyers, Irking Department Stores," *The Wall Street Journal,* May 3, 1983, p. 31; and "Mass Merchandisers Move toward Stability," *The Nielsen Researcher,* no. 3, 1976, pp. 19–25.

8. "Those 1,215 K's Stand for Kresge, K mart's, and the Key to Success," *The Wall Street Journal,* March 8, 1977, p. 1f.; and "Where K mart Goes Next Now That It's No. 2," *Business Week,* June 2, 1980, p. 109.

9. Walter J. Salmon, Robert D. Buzzell, and Stanton G. Cort, "Today the Shopping Center, Tomorrow the Superstore," *Harvard Business Review,* January-February 1974, pp.

89–98; "Super-Stores May Suit Customers to a T—a T-Shirt or a T-Bone," *The Wall Street Journal,* March 13, 1973, p. 1f.; and *The Super-Store—Strategic Implications For the Seventies* (Cambridge, Mass.: The Marketing Science Institute, 1972).

10. *Industry Surveys,* January 26, 1984, p. R1–7; "Convenience Stores: A $7.4 Billion Mushroom," *Business Week,* March 21, 1977, pp. 61–64; "Convenience Stores Battle Lagging Sales by Adding Items and Cleaning Up Image," *The Wall Street Journal,* March 28, 1980, p. 16; and "Arco Takes on Convenience Stores," *Advertising Age,* December 17, 1979, p. 1f.

11. "Vendors Pull Out All Stops," *Business Week,* August 15, 1970, pp. 52–54.

12. Douglas J. Dalrymple, "Will Automatic Vending Topple Retail Precedence?" *Journal of Retailing,* Spring 1963, pp. 27–31.

13. "Catalogue Cornucopia," *Time,* November 8, 1982, pp. 72–79.

14. For more discussion on segmenting of retail markets, see "Fast-Food Franchisers Invade the City," *Business Week,* April 22, 1974, pp. 92–93; "Korvettes Tries for a Little Chic," *Business Week,* May 12, 1973, pp. 124–26; Phillip D. Cooper, "Will Success Produce Problems for the Convenience Store?" *MSU Business Topics,* Winter 1972, pp. 39–43; "Levitz: The Hot Name in 'Instant' Furniture," *Business Week,* December 4, 1971, pp. 90–93; David L. Appel, "Market Segmentation—A Response to Retail Innovation," *Journal of Marketing,* April 1970, pp. 64–67; Steven R. Flaster, "A Consumer Approach to the Specialty Store," *Journal of Retailing,* Spring 1969, pp. 21–31; and A. Coskun Samli, "Segmentation and Carving a Niche in the Market Place," *Journal of Retailing,* Summer 1968, pp. 35–49.

15. Larry J. Rosenberg and Elizabeth C. Hirschman, "Retailing Without Stores," *Harvard Business Review,* July-August 1980, pp. 103–12.

16. Albert D. Bates, "The Troubled Future of Retailing," *Business Horizons,* August 1976, pp. 22–28; William R. Davidson, Albert D. Bates, and Stephen J. Bass, "Retail Life Cycle," *Harvard Business Review,* November-December 1976, pp. 89–96; "Investigating the Collapse of W. T. Grant," *Business Week,* July 19, 1976, pp. 60–62; "Shopping Center Boom Appears to Be Fading Due to Overbuilding," *The Wall Street Journal,* September 7, 1976, pp. 1f; "Jewel Co. Discloses Operations Review in Search of a More Successful Strategy," *The Wall Street Journal,* March 23, 1977, p. 12; Ronald D. Michman, "Changing Patterns in Retailing," *Business Horizons,* October 1979, pp. 33–38; "The Discount Twist in Suburban Shopping Malls," *Business Week,* July 7, 1980, pp. 95–96; "Sears Mulls Test of Catalog Sales via Warner Cable," *Advertising Age,* February 18, 1980, p. 1f; and J. Patrick Kelly and William R. George, "Strategic Management Issues for the Retailing of Services," *Journal of Retailing* 58, no. 2 (Summer 1982), pp. 26–43; Joel E. Urbany and W. Wayne Talarzyk, "Videotex: Implications for Retailing," *Journal of Retailing* 59 (Fall 1983), pp. 76–92.

Chapter 13

1. For interesting case studies of the activities of different types of wholesalers, see M. P. Brown, William Applebaum, and W. J. Salmon, *Strategy Problems of Mass Retailers and Wholesalers* (Homewood, Ill.: Richard D. Irwin, 1970).

2. P. Ronald Stephenson, "Wholesale Distribution: An Analysis of Structure, Strategy, and Profit Performance," in *Foundations of Marketing Channels,* ed. Arch G. Wood-

side et al. (Austin, Texas: Lone Star Publishers, 1978), pp. 103–7.

3. James D. Hlavacek and Tommy J. McCuistion, "Industrial Distributors—When, Who, and How?" *Harvard Business Review* 61, no. 2 (January-February 1983), pp. 96-101; and Steven Flax, "Wholesalers," *Forbes,* January 4, 1982.

4. "Why Manufacturers are Doubling as Distributors," *Business Week,* January 17, 1983, p. 41.

5. James R. Moore and Kendall A. Adams, "Functional Wholesaler Sales: Trends and Analysis," in *Combined Proceedings of the American Marketing Association,* ed. E. M. Mazze (Chicago: American Marketing Association, 1976), pp. 403–5; Richard S. Lopata, "Faster Pace in Wholesaling," *Harvard Business Review,* July-August 1969, pp. 130–43; and "Napco: Seeking a National Network as a Nonfood Supermarket Supplier," *Business Week,* November 8, 1982, p. 70; Evelyn A. Thomchick and Lisa Rosenbaum, "The Role of U.S. Export Trading Companies in International Logistics," *Journal of Business Logistics* 5, no. 2 (September 1984), pp. 85–105.

Chapter 14

1. "Attention to Public Opinion Helps Firms Avoid Blunders," *The Wall Street Journal,* June 15, 1981, p. 21; Robert S. Mason, "What's a PR Director For, Anyway?" *Harvard Business Review,* September-October 1974, pp. 120–26; "Top Flacks Want Nobodies, Where the Power, Prestige and Big Bucks Are at More Firms," *The Wall Street Journal,* March 4, 1980, p. 1; and Raymond Simon, *Public Relations: Concepts and Practices,* 2d ed. (Columbus, Ohio: Grid, 1980).

2. "More Firms Turn to Translation Experts to Avoid Costly Embarrassing Mistakes," *The Wall Street Journal,* January 13, 1977, p. 32.

3. For interesting perspectives on this issue, see Jacob Jacoby and Wayne D. Hoyer, "Viewer Miscomprehension of Televised Communication: Selected Findings," *Journal of Marketing* 46, no. 4 (Fall 1982), pp. 12–26; Gary T. Ford and Richard Yalch, "Viewer Miscomprehension of Televised Communication—A Comment," *Journal of Marketing* 46, no. 4 (Fall 1982), pp. 27–31; and Richard W. Mizerski, "Viewer Miscomprehension Findings Are Measurement Bound," *Journal of Marketing* 46, no. 4 (Fall 1982), pp. 32–34. Also see Reed Sanderlin, "Information Is Not Communication," *Business Horizons* 25, no. 2 (March/April 1982), pp. 40–42; and Robert E. Smith and William R. Swinyard, "Information Response Models: An Integrated Approach," *Journal of Marketing* 46, no. 1 (Winter 1982), pp. 81–93.

4. For further discussion, see Gerald Zaltman, *Marketing: Contributions from the Behavioral Sciences* (New York: Harcourt Brace Jovanovich, 1965), pp. 45–56 and 23–37; Everett M. Rogers, *The Diffusion of Innovations* (New York: Free Press, 1962); Kenneth Uhl, Roman Andrus, and Lance Poulsen, "How Are Laggards Different? An Empirical Inquiry," *Journal of Marketing Research,* February 1970, pp. 43–50; Joseph R. Mancuso, "Why Not Create Opinion Leaders for New Product Introductions?" *Journal of Marketing,* July 1969, pp. 20–25; Thomas S. Robertson, "The Process of Innovation and the Diffusion of Innovation," *Journal of Marketing,* January 1967, pp. 14–19; Robert A. Westbrook and Claes Fornell, "Patterns of Information Source Usage among Durable Goods Buyers," *Journal of Marketing Research,* August 1979, pp. 303–12; V. Mahajan and E. Muller, "Innovation Diffusion and New Products," *Journal of Marketing,* Fall 1979, pp. 55–68; L. E. Ostlund, "Perceived Innovation Attributes as Predictors of Innovativeness," *Consumer Research,* Sep-

tember 1974, pp. 23–29; Richard W. Olshavsky, "Time and the Rate of Adoption of Innovations," *Consumer Research,* March 1980, pp. 425–28; and Thomas S. Robertson and Yoram Wind, "Organizational Psychographics and Innovativeness," *Consumer Research,* June 1980, pp. 24–31.

5. Marsha L. Richins, "Negative Word-of-Mouth by Dissatisfied Consumers: A Pilot Study," *Journal of Marketing* 47, no. 1 (Winter 1983), pp. 68–78.

6. Everett M. Rogers and F. Floyd Shoemaker, *Communication of Innovations: A Cross-Cultural Approach* (New York: Free Press, 1971), pp. 203–9; Frederick E. Webster, Jr., "Informal Communication in Industrial Markets," *Journal of Marketing Research,* May 1970, pp. 186–90; Leon G. Schiffman and Vincent Gaccione, "Opinion Leaders in Institutional Markets," *Journal of Marketing,* April 1974, pp. 49–53; John A. Czepiel, "Word-of-Mouth Processes in the Diffusion of a Major Technological Innovation," *Journal of Marketing Research,* May 1974, pp. 172–80; and John A. Martilla, "Word-of-Mouth Communication in the Industrial Adoption Process," *Journal of Marketing Research,* May 1971, pp. 173–78.

7. Christopher H. Lovelock and John A. Quelch, "Consumer Promotions in Service Marketing," *Business Horizons* 26, no. 3 (May/June 1983), pp. 66–75; John A. Quelch, "It's Time to Make Trade Promotion More Productive," *Harvard Business Review* 61, no. 3 (May-June 1983), pp. 130–36; and Thomas V. Bonoma, "Get More out of Your Trade Shows," *Harvard Business Review* 61, no. 1 (January-February 1983), pp. 75–83.

8. Roger A. Strang, "Sales Promotion—Fast Growth, Faulty Management," *Harvard Business Review,* July-August 1976, pp. 115–24; "Now the Battling Airlines Try Mass Marketing," *Business Week,* April 18, 1980, p. 104; Michel Chevalier, "Increase in Sales Due to In-Store Display," *Journal of Marketing Research,* November 1975, pp. 426–31; "Retailing May Have Overdosed on Coupons," *Business Week,* June 13, 1983, p. 147.

9. J. F. Engel, M. R. Warshaw, and T. C. Kinnear, *Promotional Strategy,* 5th ed. (Homewood, Ill.: Richard D. Irwin, 1983); and "A New Toothpaste Takes Off, Promoted By Single Employee," *The Wall Street Journal,* May 26, 1983, p. 31.

Chapter 15

1. "Making Sure the Goods Get on the Shelves," *Business Week,* July 22, 1972, pp. 46–47; P. Ronald Stephenson, William L. Cron, and Gary L. Frazier, "Delegating Pricing Authority to the Sales Force: The Effects on Sales and Profit Performance," *Journal of Marketing,* Spring 1979, pp. 21–24; James H. Fouss and Elaine Solomon, "Salespeople as Researchers: Help or Hazard?" *Journal of Marketing* 44, no. 3 (Summer 1980), pp. 36–39; and Gilbert A. Churchill, Jr., Neil M. Ford, and Orville C. Walker, Jr., *Sales Force Management: Planning, Implementation and Control* (Homewood, Ill.: Richard D. Irwin, 1985).

2. F. Doody and W. G. Nickels, "Structuring Organizations for Strategic Selling," *MSU Business Topics,* Autumn 1972, pp. 27–34; Davis Fogg and Josef W. Rokus, "A Quantitative Method for Structuring a Profitable Sales Force," *Journal of Marketing,* July 1973, pp. 8–17; Porter Henry, "Manage Your Sales Force as a System," *Harvard Business Review,* March-April 1975, pp. 85–94; Charles A. Beswick and David W. Cravens, "A Multistage Decision Model for Salesforce Management," *Journal of Marketing,* May 1977, pp. 135–44; Michael S. Herschel, "Effective Sales Territory Development," *Journal of Marketing,* April,

1977, pp. 39–43; Henry C. Lucas, Jr., Charles B. Weinberg, and Kenneth W. Clowes, "Sales Response as a Function of Territorial Potential and Sales Representative Workload," *Journal of Marketing Research,* August 1975, pp. 298–305; and B. Shapiro and R. Moriarty, "National Account Management," *MSI Report,* Marketing Science Institute, 1980.

3. Kenneth Lawyer, *Training Salesmen to Serve Industrial Markets* (Washington, D.C.: Small Business Management Series No. 36, Small Business Administration, 1975); "Retailers Discover an Old Tool: Sales Training," *Business Week,* December 22, 1980; Derek A. Newton, "Get the Most out of Your Salesforce," *Harvard Business Review,* September-October, 1967, pp. 130–43; Wesley J. Johnston and Martha Cooper, "Analyzing the Industrial Salesforce Selection Process," *Industrial Marketing Management* 10 (April 1981), pp. 139–47; J. Michael Munson and W. Austin Spivey, "Salesforce Selection that Meets Federal Regulations and Management Needs," *Industrial Marketing Management* 9 (February 1980), pp. 11–21; and A. J. Dubinsky, "Recruiting College Students for the Salesforce," *Industrial Marketing Management* 9 (February 1980), pp. 37–46.

4. Stephen X. Doyle and Benson P. Shapiro, "What Counts Most in Motivating Your Sales Force," *Harvard Business Review,* May-June, 1980, pp. 133–40; *The Conference Board, Incentives for Salesmen,* Experiences in Marketing Management, no. 14 (New York: National Industrial Conference Board, 1967); Richard C. Smyth, "Financial Incentives for Salesmen," *Harvard Business Review,* January-February 1968, pp. 109–17; H. O. Pruden, W. H. Cunningham, and W. D. English, "Nonfinancial Incentives for Salesmen," *Journal of Marketing,* October 1972, pp. 55–59; O. C. Walker, Jr., G. A. Churchill, and N. M. Ford, "Motivation and Performance in Industrial Selling: Present Knowledge and Needed Research," *Journal of Marketing Research,* May 1977, pp. 156–68; R. Y. Darmon, "Salesmen's Responses to Financial Incentives: An Empirical Study," *Journal of Marketing Research,* November 1974, pp. 418–26; and Thomas N. Ingram and Danny N. Bellenger, "Motivational Segments in the Sales Force," *California Management Review* 24 (Spring 1982), pp. 81–88.

5. For more discussion, see F. E. Webster, Jr., "Rationalizing Salesmen's Compensation Plans," *Journal of Marketing,* January 1966, pp. 55–58; R. L. Day and P. D. Bennett, "Should Salesmen's Compensation Be Geared to Profits?" *Journal of Marketing,* October 1962, pp. 6–9; John P. Steinbrink, "How to Pay Your Sales Force," *Harvard Business Review,* July-August 1978, pp. 111–22; D. Wilson, "Common Characteristics of Compensation Plans for Industrial Salesmen," in *Marketing's Role in Scientific Management,* ed. R. L. Clewitt (Chicago: American Marketing Association, 1957), p. 168; and "Managers on Compensation Plans: There Has to Be a Better Way," *Sales & Marketing Management,* November 12, 1979, pp. 41–43; and Leon Winer, "A Sales Compensation Plan for Maximum Motivation," *Industrial Marketing Management* 5 (1976), pp. 29–36.

6. G. David Hughes, "Computerized Sales Management," *Harvard Business Review* 61, no. 2 (March-April 1983), pp. 102–12; Douglas N. Behrman and William D. Perreault, "Measuring the Performance of Industrial Salespersons," *Journal of Business Research,* September 1982, pp. 350–70; *Measuring Salesmen's Performance,* Business Policy Study, no. 114 (New York: National Industrial Conference Board, 1965); "'BARS' Performance Rating for Sales Force Personnel," *Journal of Marketing,* July 1978, pp. 87–95; William D. Perreault, Jr., and Frederick A. Russ, "Comparing Multiattribute Evaluation Process

Models," *Behavioral Science,* 22 (November, 1977), pp. 423–31; and Nicholas C. Williamson, *A Model for Predicting Sales Performance* (Ann Arbor, Mich: U.M.I. International, 1982).

7. James Holbert and Noel Capon, "Interpersonal Communication in Marketing," *Journal of Marketing Research,* February 1972, pp. 27–32; Paul Busch and David T. Wilson, "An Experimental Analysis of a Salesman's Expert and Referent Bases of Social Power in the Buyer-Seller Dyad," *Journal of Marketing Research,* February 1976, pp. 3–11; Rosann L. Spiro, William D. Perreault, Jr., and Fred D. Reynolds, "The Personal Selling Process: A Critical Review and Model," *Industrial Marketing Management* 5 (December 1977), pp. 351–64; and Rosann L. Spiro and William D. Perreault, Jr., "Influence Used by Industrial Salesmen: Influence Strategy Mixes and Situational Determinants," *Journal of Business* 52 (July 1979), pp. 435–55.

8. Leonard M. Lodish, "Vaguely Right Approach to Sales Force Allocations," *Harvard Business Review,* January-February 1974, pp. 119–24; Gary M. Armstrong, "The SCHEDULE Model and the Salesman's Effort Allocation Problem," *California Management Review,* Summer 1976, pp. 43–51; and "To Computer Salesmen, the 'Big-Ticket' Deal is the One to Look For," *The Wall Street Journal,* January 22, 1974, p. 1.

9. Adapted from Harold C. Cash and W. J. E. Crissy, "Ways of Looking at Selling," *Psychology of Selling,* 1957. See also Barton A. Weitz, "Effectiveness in Sales Interactions: A Contingency Framework," *Journal of Marketing* 45, no. 1 (Winter 1981), pp. 85–103; Marvin A. Jolson, "The Underestimated Potential of the Canned Sales Presentation," *Journal of Marketing,* January 1975, pp. 75–78; and Don Meisel, "Add Sales Power! Ask Questions," *Industrial Distribution,* December 1976, p. 64. For more on sales presentation approaches, see C. A. Pederson, M. D. Wright, and B. A. Weitz, *Selling: Principles and Methods,* 7th ed. (Homewood, Ill.: Richard D. Irwin, 1981), pp. 224–356.

Chapter 16

1. *Advertising Age,* May 14, 1984, p. 63.

2. Ibid.

3. Exact data on this industry are elusive. But see "Showing Ad Agencies How to Grow," *Business Week,* June 1, 1974, p. 50–56; and "How Many People Work in Advertising?" *Printers' Ink,* December 6, 1957, p. 88.

4. "A Pained Bayer Cries 'Foul,'" *Business Week,* July 25, 1977, p. 142.

5. William L. Wilkie and Paul W. Farris, "Comparison Advertising: Problems and Potential," *Journal of Marketing,* October 1975, pp. 7–15; V. K. Prasad, "Communications Effectiveness of Comparative Advertising: A Laboratory Analysis," *Journal of Marketing Research,* May 1976, pp. 128–37; Murphy A. Seawall and Michael H. Goldstein, "The Comparative Advertising Controversy: Consumer Perceptions of Catalog Showroom Reference Prices," *Journal of Marketing,* Summer 1979, pp. 85–92; Linda L. Golden, "Consumer Reactions to Explicit Brand Comparisons in Advertisements," *Journal of Marketing Research,* November 1979, pp. 517–32; Stephen Goodwin and Michael Edgar, "An Experimental Investigation of Comparative Advertising: Impact of Message Appeal, Information Load and Utility of Product Class," *Journal of Marketing Research,* May 1980, pp. 187–202; and "Should an Ad Identify Brand X?" *Business Week,* September 24, 1979, pp. 156–61.

6. "Why Jockey Switched Its Ads from TV to Print," *Business Week,* July 26, 1976, pp. 140–42.

7. "The 15% Media Commission Is on the Way toward Becoming a Relic," *Marketing News,* June 10, 1983, p. 9; and "How Agencies Should Get Paid: Trend Is to 'Managed' Systems," *Advertising Age,* January 17, 1977, pp. 41–42.

8. Dorothy Cohen, "Unfairness in Advertising Revisited," *Journal of Marketing* 46, no. 1 (Winter 1982), pp. 73–80; "Lysol's Maker Keeps Fighting FTC over Advertising Claims," *The Wall Street Journal,* February 24, 1983, p. 29; and J. J. Boddewyn, "Advertising Regulation in the 1980s: The Underlying Global Forces," *Journal of Marketing* 46, no. 1 (Winter 1982), pp. 27–35.

9. Jacob Jacoby, Margaret C. Nelson, and Wayne D. Hoyer, "Corrective Advertising and Affirmative Disclosure Statements: Their Potential for Confusing and Misleading the Consumer," *Journal of Marketing* 46, no. 1 (Winter 1982), pp. 61–72; William L. Wilkie, Dennis L. McNeil, and Michael B. Mazis, "Marketing's Scarlet Letter: The Theory and Practice of Corrective Advertising," *Journal of Marketing* 48, no. 2 (Spring 1984), pp. 11–31.

Chapter 17

1. For more discussion of the behavior of satisfiers, see Herbert A. Simon, *Administrative Behavior,* 2d ed. (New York: Macmillan, 1961).

2. W. Warren Haynes, *Pricing Decisions in Small Business* (Lexington: University of Kentucky Press, 1962); and Alan Reynolds, "A Kind Word for 'Cream Skimming,'" *Harvard Business Review,* November-December 1974, pp. 113–20. See also, Subhash C. Jain and Michael B. Laric, "A Framework for Strategic Industrial Pricing," *Industrial Marketing Management* 8 (1979), pp. 75–80.

3. Joseph W. McGuire, John S. Y. Chiu, and Alvar O. Elving, "Executive Incomes, Sales and Profits," *American Economic Review,* September 1962, pp. 753–61; "For the Chief, Sales Sets the Pay," *Business Week,* September 30, 1967, p. 174; and Alfred Rappaport, "Executive Incentives versus Corporate Growth," *Harvard Business Review,* July-August 1978, pp. 81–88.

4. For an interesting discussion of the many variations from a one-price system in retailing, see Stanley C. Hollander, "The 'One-Price' System—Fact or Fiction?" *Journal of Marketing Research,* February 1972, pp. 35–40. See also, Michael J. Houston, "Minimum Markup Laws: An Empirical Assessment," *Journal of Retailing* 57, no. 4 (Winter 1981), pp. 98–113.

5. For more discussion on price dealing, see Charles L. Hinkle, "The Strategy of Price Deals," *Harvard Business Review,* July-August 1965, pp. 75–85.

6. See, for example, "The Airline that Thrives on Discounting," *Business Week,* July 24, 1971, pp. 68–70. See also Zarrel V. Lambert, "Product Perception: An Important Variable in Pricing Strategy," *Journal of Marketing,* October 1970, pp. 68–76; and "Price and Choice Behavior," *Journal of Marketing Research,* February 1972, pp. 35–40.

7. "Grocery Coupons Are Seen Threatened by Growth of Fraudulent Redemptions," *The Wall Street Journal,* April 12, 1976, p. 26.

8. "Guides against Deceptive Pricing," Federal Trade Commission, October 10, 1958, and January 8, 1964; and *FTC v. Mary Carter Paint Co.* 382 U.S. 46, 1965.

9. "The FTC Redefines Price Fixing," *Business Week* April 18, 1983, p. 37; "Price-Fixing Charges Rise in Paper Industry Despite Convictions," *The Wall Street Journal,* May 4, 1978, p. 2; and "Plywood Makers Agree to Settle Antitrust Suit," *The Wall Street Journal,* December 5, 1982, p. 3. For discussion concerning European countries, see *Market Power and the Law* (Washington, D.C.: Organization for Economic Cooperation and Development Publication Center, 1970), p. 206.

10. Morris L. Mayer, Joseph B. Mason, and E. A. Orbeck, "The Borden Case—A Legal Basis for Private Brand Price Discrimination," *MSU Business Topics,* Winter 1970, pp. 56–63; and Jacky Knopp, Jr., "What Are 'Commodities of Like Grade and Quality'?" *Journal of Marketing,* July 1963, p. 63.

11. T. F. Schutte, V. J. Cook, Jr., and R. Hemsley, "What Management Can Learn from the Borden Case," *Business Horizons,* Winter 1966, pp. 23–30.

12. "Is the Cost Defense Workable," *Journal of Marketing,* January 1965, pp. 37–42; B. J. Linder and Allan H. Savage, "Price Discrimination and Cost Defense—Change Ahead?" *MSU Business Topics,* Summer 1971, pp. 21–26; "Firms Must Prove Injury from Price Bias to Qualify for Damages, High Court Says," *The Wall Street Journal,* May 19, 1981, p. 8.

13. Lawrence X. Tarpey, Sr., "Who Is a Competing Customer?" *Journal of Retailing,* Spring 1969, pp. 46–58; and John R. Davidson, "FTC, Robinson-Patman and Cooperative Promotion Activities," *Journal of Marketing,* January 1968, pp. 14–18.

Chapter 18

1. Marvin A. Jolson, "A Diagrammatic Model for Merchandising Calculations," *Journal of Retailing,* Summer 1975, pp. 3–9.

2. Mary L. Hatten, "Don't Get Caught with Your Prices Down: Pricing in Inflationary Times," *Business Horizons,* March 1982, pp. 23–28; "Why Detroit Can't Cut Prices," *Business Week,* March 1, 1982, p. 110; and Douglas G. Brooks, "Cost Oriented Pricing: A Realistic Solution to a Complicated Problem," *Journal of Marketing,* April 1975, pp. 72–74.

3. Approaches for estimating price-quantity relationships are reviewed in Kent B. Monroe, *Pricing: Making Profitable Decisions* (New York: McGraw-Hill, 1979). For a specific example, see Frank D. Jones, "A Survey Technique to Measure Demand under Various Pricing Strategies," *Journal of Marketing,* July 1975, pp. 75–77 or Gordon A. Wyner, Lois H. Benedetti, and Bart M. Trapp, "Measuring the Quantity and Mix of Product Demand," *Journal of Marketing* 48, no. 1 (Winter 1984), pp. 101–9.

4. Benson P. Shapiro and Barbara P. Jackson, "Industrial Pricing to Meet Customer Needs," *Harvard Business Review* (November-December 1978), pp. 119–27; and "The Race to the $10 Light Bulb," *Business Week,* May 19, 1980, p. 124.

5. For an example applied to a high-price item, see "Sale of Mink Coats Strays a Fur Piece from the Expected," *The Wall Street Journal,* March 21, 1980, p. 30.

6. E. R. Hawkins, "Price Policies and Theory," *Journal of Marketing,* January 1954, p. 236. See also, B. P. Shapiro, "The Psychology of Pricing," *Harvard Business Review,* July-August 1968, pp. 14–24; and C. Davis Fogg and Kent H. Kohnken, "Price-Cost Planning," *Journal of Marketing,* April 1978, pp. 97–106.

7. Dik W. Twedt, "Does the 9 Fixation in Retailing Really Promote Sales?" *Journal of Marketing,* October 1965, pp. 54–55; H. J. Rudolph, "Pricing and Today's Market," *Printers' Ink,* May 29, 1954, pp. 22–24; and "Strategic Mix of Odd, Even Prices Can Lead to Increased Retail Profits," *Marketing News,* March 7, 1980, p. 24.

8. Peter C. Riesz, "Price versus Quality in the Marketplace," *Journal of Retailing,* (Winter 1978), pp. 15–28; John J. Wheatly and John S. Y. Chiu, "The Effects of Price, Store Image, and Product and Respondent Characteristics on

Perceptions of Quality," *Journal of Marketing Research,* May 1977, pp. 181–86; Arthur G. Bedeian, "Consumer Perception of Price as an Indicator of Product Quality," *MSU Business Topics,* Summer 1971, pp. 59–65; David M. Gardner, "An Experimental Investigation of the Price/Quality Relationship," *Journal of Retailing,* Fall 1970, pp. 25–41; N. D. French, J. J. Williams, and W. A. Chance, "A Shopping Experiment on Price-Quality Relationships," *Journal of Retailing,* Fall 1972, pp. 3–16; Michael R. Hagerty, "Model Testing Techniques and Price-Quality Relationships," *Journal of Consumer Research,* December 1978, pp. 194–205; J. Douglas McConnell, "Comment on 'A Major Price-Perceived Quality Study Reexamined,'" *Journal of Marketing Research,* May 1980, pp. 263–64; and K. M. Monroe and S. Petroshius, "Buyers' Subjective Perceptions of Price: An Update of the Evidence," in *Perspectives in Consumer Behavior,* ed. T. Robertson and H. Kassarjian (Glenview, Ill.: Scott Foresman 1981), pp. 43–55.

9. Alfred Oxenfeldt, "Product Line Pricing," *Harvard Business Review,* July-August, 1966, pp. 135–43.

10. Stephen Paranka, "Competitive Bidding Strategy," *Business Horizons,* June 1971, pp. 39–43; Wayne J. Morse, "Probabilistic Bidding Models; A Synthesis," *Business Horizons,* April 1975, pp. 67–74; and Kenneth Simmonds and Stuart Slatter, "The Number of Estimators: A Critical Decision for Marketing under Competitive Bidding," *Journal of Marketing Research,* May 1978, pp. 203–13.

11. For references to additional readings in the pricing area, see Kent B. Monroe, D. Lund, and P. Choudhury, *Pricing Policies and Strategies: An Annotated Bibliography* (Chicago: American Marketing Association, 1983).

Chapter 19

1. Theodore Levitt, "The Globalization of Markets," *Harvard Business Review* 61, no. 3 (May-June 1983), pp. 92–102.

2. Thomas Hout, Michael E. Porter, and Eileen Rudden, "How Global Companies Win Out," *Harvard Business Review* 60, no. 5 (September-October 1982), pp. 98–108; "Multi-national Companies," *Business Week,* April 20, 1963, pp. 62–86; "Multi-national Firms Now Dominate Much of World's Production," *The Wall Street Journal,* April 18, 1973, p. 1f; "Japanese Multinationals Covering the World with Investment," *Business Week,* June 16, 1980, pp. 92–99; and David A. Heenan and Warren J. Keegan, "The Rise of Third World Multinationals," *Harvard Business Review,* January-February 1979, pp. 101–9.

3. "McDonald's Brings Hamburger (with Beer) to Hamburg," *Advertising Age,* May 30, 1977, p. 61.

4. Warren J. Keegan, "A Conceptual Framework for Multinational Marketing," *Columbia Journal of World Business,* November 1972, pp. 67–78.

5. This discussion is based on William Copulsky's, "Forecasting Sales in Underdeveloped Countries," *Journal of Marketing,* July 1959, pp. 36–37. Another set of stages is interesting although less marketing oriented. See W. W. Rostow, *The Stages of Economic Growth—A Non-Communist Manifesto* (New York: Cambridge University Press, 1960).

6. *The Wall Street Journal,* August 8, 1968, p. 1.

7. Christopher A. Bartlett, "MNCs: Get off the Reorganization Merry-Go-Round," *Harvard Business Review* 61, no. 2 (March-April 1983), pp. 138–46; James M. Hulbert, William K. Brant, and Raimar Richers, "Marketing Planning in the Multinational Subsidiary: Practices and Problems," *Journal of Marketing* 44, no. 3 (Summer 1980), pp. 7–16; Pravin Banker, "You're the Best Judge of Foreign Risks," *Harvard Business Review* 61, no. 2 (March-April 1983), pp.

157–65; and Martin D. J. Buss, "Managing International Information Systems," *Harvard Business Review* 60, no. 5 (September-October 1982), pp. 153–62; David A. Ricks, *Big Business Blunders: Mistakes in Multinational Marketing* (Homewood, Ill: Richard D. Irwin, 1983).

Chapter 20

1. This section is based on Jack L. Engledow, "Was Consumer Satisfaction a Pig in a Poke?" *MSU Business Topics,* April 1977, pp. 88–90.

2. James U. McNeal, "Consumer Satisfaction: The Measure of Marketing Effectiveness," *MSU Business Topics,* Summer 1969, p. 33.

3. For an extensive discussion of the problem and mechanics of measuring the efficiency of marketing, see Stanley C. Hollander, "Measuring the Cost and Value of Marketing," *Business Topics,* Summer 1961, pp. 17–26; and Reavis Cox, *Distribution in a High-Level Economy* (Englewood Cliffs, N.J.: Prentice-Hall, 1965).

4. Hiram C. Barksdale and William D. Perreault, Jr., "Can Consumers Be Satisfied?" *MSU Business Topics,* Spring 1980, pp. 19–30.

5. F. M. Nicosia, *Consumer Decision Processes* (Englewood Cliffs, N.J.: Prentice-Hall, 1966), p. 39

6. E. H. Chamberlin, "Product Heterogeneity and Public Policy," *American Economic Review,* May 1950, p. 86.

7. Arnold J. Toynbee, *America and World Revolution* (New York: Oxford University Press, 1966), pp. 144–45. See also, John Kenneth Galbraith, *Economics and the Public Purpose* (Boston: Houghton-Mifflin, 1973), pp. 144–45.

8. Russell J. Tomsen, "Take It Away," *Newsweek,* October 7, 1974, p. 21.

9. Engledow, "Was Consumer Satisfaction a Pig in a Poke," p. 92.

10. "Intellectuals Should Re-Examine the Marketplace; It Supports Them, Helps Keep Them Free; Prof. Stigler," *Advertising Age,* January 28, 1963. See also, E. T. Grether, "Galbraith versus the Market: A Review Article," *Journal of Marketing,* January 1968, pp. 9–14; and E. T. Grether, "Marketing and Public Policy: A Contemporary View," *Journal of Marketing,* July 1974, pp. 2–7; "Deregulating America," *Business Week,* November 28, 1983, pp. 80–82.

11. Frederick Webster, *Social Aspects of Marketing* (Englewood Cliffs, N.J.: Prentice-Hall, 1974), p. 32.

12. Paul M. Mazur, "Does Distribution Cost Enough?" *Fortune,* November 1947.

13. James T. Roth and Lissa Benson, "Intelligent Consumption: An Attractive Alternative to the Marketing Concept," *MSU Business Topics,* Winter 1974, pp. 30–34; and Robert E. Wilkes, "Fraudulent Behavior by Consumers," *Journal of Marketing,* October 1978, pp. 67–75; and "How Shoplifting is Draining the Economy," *Business Week,* October 15, 1979, pp. 119–23.

14. Dan R. Dalton and Richard A. Cosier, "The Four Faces of Social Responsibility," *Business Horizons* 25, no. 3 (May/June 1982), pp. 19–27; Y. Hugh Furuhashi and E. Jerome McCarthy, *Social Issues of Marketing in the American Economy* (Columbus, Ohio: Grid, 1971); James Owens, "Business Ethics: Age-Old Ideal, Now Real," *Business Horizons,* February 1978, pp. 26–30; Steven F. Goodman, "Quality of Life: The Role of Business," *Business Horizons,* June 1978, pp. 36–37; William F. Dwyer, "Smoking: Free Choice," *Business Horizons,* June 1978, pp. 52–56; Stanley J. Shapiro, "Marketing in a Conserver Society," *Business Horizons,* April 1978, pp. 3–13; and Johan Arndt, "How Broad Should the Marketing Concept Be?" *Journal of Marketing,* January 1978, pp. 101–3.

■ Glossary

Accessory equipment short-lived capital items.

Accumulating collecting products from many small producers.

Administered channel systems channel systems in which the various channel members informally agree to cooperate with each other.

Administered prices consciously set prices—aimed at reaching the firm's objectives.

Adoption curve shows when different groups within a market accept ideas.

Adoption process the steps which individuals go through on the way to accepting or rejecting a new idea.

Advertising any paid form of non-personal presentation of ideas, goods, or services by an identified sponsor.

Advertising agencies specialists in planning and handling mass selling details for advertisers.

Advertising allowances price reductions to firms further along in the channel to encourage them to advertise or otherwise promote the supplier's products locally.

Advertising managers manage their company's mass selling effort.

Agent middlemen wholesalers who do not own the products they sell.

AIDA model consists of four promotion jobs: to get attention, to hold interest, to arouse desire, and to obtain action.

Allowance (accounting term) occurs when a customer is not satisfied with a purchase for some reason and the company gives a price reduction on the original invoice (bill) but the customer keeps the goods or services.

Allowances like discounts, are given to final consumers, customers, or channel members for doing "something" or accepting less of "something."

Assorting putting together a variety of products to give a target market what it wants.

Attitude a person's point of view toward something.

Auction companies agent middlemen who provide a place where buyers and sellers can come together and complete a transaction.

Automatic vending selling and delivering products through vending machines.

Average cost obtained by dividing total cost by the related quantity (i.e., the total quantity which causes the total cost).

Average-cost pricing adding a "reasonable" markup to the average cost of a product.

Average fixed cost obtained by dividing total fixed cost by the related quantity.

Average variable cost obtained by dividing total variable cost by the related quantity.

Bait pricing setting some very low prices to attract customers but then trying to sell more expensive models or brands once the customer is in the store.

Balance sheet an accounting statement which shows the assets, liabilities, and net worth of a company.

Basic list prices prices that final customers or users are normally asked to pay for products.

Basic sales tasks order getting, order taking, and supporting.

Battle of the brands the competition between dealer brands and manufacturer brands.

Belief a person's conviction about something.

Bid pricing offering a specific price for each possible job.

Birth rate the number of babies per 1,000 people (per year).

Brand familiarity how well customers recognize and accept a company's brand.

Brand insistence customers insist on a firm's branded product and are willing to search for it.

Brand managers manage specific products.

Brand name a word, letter, or a group of words or letters.

Brand non-recognition a brand is not recognized by final customers at all—even though middlemen may use the brand name for inventory and control.

Brand preference target customers will usually choose the brand over other brands.

Brand recognition customers remember the brand.

Brand rejection potential customers won't buy a brand—unless its image is changed.

Branding the use of a name, term, symbol, or design—or a combination—to identify a product.

Breakthrough opportunities opportunities which help innovators develop hard-to-copy marketing mixes that will be very profitable for a long time.

Brokers agent middlemen who bring buyers and sellers together.

Bulk-breaking dividing larger quantities into smaller quantities as goods get closer to the final market.

Buying center all the people who participate in or influence a purchase.

Buying function looking for and evaluating goods and services.

Capital items durable goods which are charged off over many years, i.e., depreciated.

Cash-and-carry wholesalers merchant wholesalers who operate like service wholesalers—except that the customer must pay cash.

Cash discounts reductions in the price to encourage buyers to pay their bills quickly.

Catalog showroom retailers sell several lines out of a catalog and display showroom—with backup inventories.

Central markets convenient places where buyers and sellers can meet face-to-face to exchange goods and services.

Chain store (corporate) one of several stores owned and managed by the same corporation.

Channel captain a manager who helps guide the activities of the whole channel.

Channel of distribution any series of firms from producer to final user or consumer.

Clustering techniques try to find similar patterns within sets of data.

Combination export manager a blend of manufacturers' agent and selling agent—handling the entire export function for several manufacturers of non-competing lines.

Combined target market approach combining two or more homogeneous sub-markets into one larger target market as a basis for one strategy.

Combiners try to increase the size of their target markets by combining two or more submarkets.

Commission merchants handle products shipped to them by sellers, complete the sale, and send the money—minus their commission—to each seller.

Communication process shows how a source tries to reach a receiver with a message.

Community shopping centers planned shopping centers which offer some shopping stores as well as the convenience stores found in neighborhood shopping centers.

Comparative advertising makes specific brand comparisons—using actual product names.

Competitive advertising tries to develop selective demand.

Competitive environment the number and types of competitors the marketing manager must face—and how they may behave.

Complementary product pricing setting prices on several products as a group.

Component parts and materials expense items

which have had more processing than raw materials.

Consumer cooperative a group of consumers who buy together.

Consumer goods products meant for the final consumer.

Consumer Product Safety Act calls for more awareness of safety in product design and better quality control.

Consumer surplus the difference to consumers between the value of a purchase and the price they pay.

Consumerism a social movement seeking to increase the rights and powers of consumers and buyers.

Contract manufacturing turning over production to others, while retaining the marketing process.

Contractual channel systems channel systems in which the various channel members agree by contract to cooperate with each other.

Convenience (food) stores a convenience-oriented variation of the conventional limited-line food stores.

Convenience goods products a consumer needs but isn't willing to spend much time or effort shopping for.

Convenience store a convenient place to shop—either centrally located "downtown" or "in the neighborhood."

Cooperative advertising middlemen and producers sharing in the cost of ads.

Cooperative chains retailer-sponsored groups formed by independent retailers to run their own buying organization and joint promotion efforts.

Copy thrust what is to be communicated by the written copy and illustrations.

Corporate chain store one of several stores owned and managed by the same corporation.

Corporate channel systems corporate ownership all along a channel.

Corrective advertising ads to correct deceptive advertising.

Cost of goods sold the total value (at cost) of all the goods sold during the period.

Cues products, signs, ads, and other stimuli in the environment.

Cultural and social environment affects how and why people live and behave as they do.

Culture the whole set of beliefs, attitudes, and ways of doing things of a similar group of people.

Cumulative quantity discounts apply to purchases over a given time period—and the discount usually increases as the amount purchased increases.

Customer service level a measure of how rapidly and dependably a firm can deliver what customers want.

Dealer brands brands created by middlemen—sometimes called "private brands."

Decoding the receiver translating the message.

Demand-backward pricing setting an acceptable final consumer price and working backward to what a producer can charge.

Demand curve a "picture" of the relationship between price and quantity demanded in a market—assuming that all other things stay the same.

Department stores larger stores—organized into many separate departments.

Description (specification) buying buying from a written (or verbal) description of the product.

Determining dimensions the dimensions which actually affect the purchase of a specific product type or specific brand in a product-market.

Direct-mail advertising selling directly to customers via their mailboxes.

Direct type advertising competitive advertising which aims for immediate buying action.

Discount houses retailers who offer "hard goods" (cameras, TVs, appliances) at substantial price cuts—to customers who go to the discounter's low-rent store, pay cash, and take care of any service or repair problems themselves.

Discounts reductions from list price that are given by a seller to a buyer who either gives up some marketing function or provides the function himself.

Discrepancy of assortment the difference between the lines the typical producer makes and the assortment wanted by final consumers or users.

Discrepancy of quantity the difference between the quantity of goods it is economical for a producer to make and the quantity normally wanted by final users or consumers.

Dissonance tension caused by uncertainty about the rightness of a decision.

Distribution center a special kind of warehouse designed to speed the flow of goods and avoid unnecessary storing costs.

Diversification a firm moving into totally different lines of business, which may include entirely unfamiliar products, markets, or even levels in the production-marketing system.

Door-to-door selling going directly to the consumer's home.

Drive a strong stimulus that encourages action to reduce a need.

Drop-shippers merchant wholesalers who own the products they sell—but do not actually handle, stock, or deliver them.

Dual distribution occurs when a manufacturer uses several competing channels to reach the same target market—perhaps using several middlemen and selling directly itself.

Early adopters adopters who are well respected by their peers and often are opinion leaders—see *adoption curve*.

Early majority adopters who avoid risk and wait to consider a new idea until many early adopters have tried it and liked it—see *adoption curve*.

Economic and technological environment refers to the way firms—and the whole economy—use resources.

Economic men people who logically compare choices in terms of cost and value received.

Economic needs concerned with making the best use of a consumer's limited resources—as the consumer sees it.

Economic system the way an economy is organized to use scarce productive resources to produce goods and services and distribute them for consumption—now and in the future—among various people and groups in the society.

Economies of scale as a company produces larger numbers of a particular product, the cost for each of these products goes down.

Elastic demand the quantity demanded would increase enough to increase total revenue if price were decreased (and vice versa if price were increased).

Elastic supply the quantity supplied does stretch more if the price is raised.

Emergency goods products which are purchased immediately when the need is great.

Empty nesters people whose children are grown and who are now able to spend their money in other ways.

Encoding the source deciding what it wants to say and translating it into words or symbols that will have the same meaning to the receiver.

Equilibrium point where the quantity and the price sellers are willing to offer are equal to the quantity and price that buyers are willing to accept.

Equilibrium price the going market price.

Exclusive distribution selling through only one middleman in a particular geographic area.

Expense items short-lived goods and services which are charged off as they are used—usually in the year of purchase.

Expenses costs subtracted from the gross margin to get the net profit on an operating statement.

Experimental method the responses of groups which are similar—except on the characteristic being tested—are compared.

Export agents manufacturers' agents in international marketing.

Export brokers brokers in international marketing.

Export commission houses brokers in international marketing.

Exporting selling some of what the firm is producing to foreign markets.

Extensive problem solving when a need is completely new to a person and much effort is taken to understand the need and how to satisfy it.

Facilitators firms which provide one or more of the marketing functions other than buying or selling.

Factor a variable which shows the relation of some variable to the item being forecasted.

Factor method tries to forecast sales by finding a relation between the company's sales and some other factor (or factors).

Family brand the same brand name for several products.

Farm products products grown by farmers.

Federal Fair Packaging and Labeling Act requires that consumer goods be clearly labeled in easy-to-understand terms to give consumers more information.

Federal Trade Commission (FTC) the federal government agency which polices antimonopoly laws.

Financing function provides the necessary cash and credit to manufacture, transport, store, sell, and buy products.

Fishy-back service similar to rail piggy-back—using ships and trucks.

Flexible-price policy offering the same product and quantities to different customers at different prices.

F.O.B. "free on board" some vehicle at some place.

Focus group interview interviewing 6 to 10 people in an informal group setting.

Form utility utility provided when a manufacturer makes something out of other materials.

Franchise operations the franchiser develops a good marketing strategy, and the franchise holders carry out the strategy in their own units.

Freight-absorption pricing absorbing freight cost so that a firm's delivered price meets the nearest competitor's.

Full-line pricing setting prices for a whole line of products.

General-line wholesalers "full" service merchant wholesalers who carry a narrower line of merchandise than general merchandise wholesalers.

General merchandise wholesalers "full" service merchant wholesalers who carry a wide variety of non-perishable items.

General stores retailers who carry anything they can sell in reasonable volume.

Generic market a market with broadly similar needs and sellers offering various (often diverse) ways of satisfying those needs.

Generic products products which have no brand at all other than identification of their contents and the manufacturer or middleman.

Grading function sorting products according to size and quality.

Gross margin (gross profit) the money left to cover the cost of selling the products and managing the business—and hopefully, leaving a profit—after subtracting cost of goods sold from net sales.

Gross national product (GNP) the total market value of goods and services produced in a year.

Gross sales the total amount charged to all customers during some time period.

Heterogeneous shopping goods shopping goods that the customer sees as different—and wants to inspect for quality and suitability.

Homogeneous shopping goods shopping goods that the customer sees as basically the same—and wants at the lowest price.

Hypotheses educated guesses about the relationships between things or what will happen in the future.

Ideal market exposure makes a product widely enough available to satisfy target customers' needs—but not exceed them.

Import agents manufacturers' agents in international marketing.

Import brokers brokers in international marketing.

Import commission houses brokers in international marketing.

Impulse goods products which are bought quickly—because of a strongly felt need.

Indirect type advertising competitive advertising which points out product advantages—to affect future buying decisions.

Individual brands separate brand names for each product.

Industrial goods products meant for use in making other products.

Inelastic demand the quantity demanded would increase if the price were decreased, but the quantity demanded would not increase enough to avoid a decrease in total revenue.

Inelastic supply the quantity supplied does not stretch much (if at all) if the price is raised.

Innovation the development and spread of new ideas and products.

Innovators the first to adopt new ideas and willing to take risks—see *adoption curve*.

Inspection buying looking at every item.

Installations important long-lived capital items—durable products which are depreciated over many years.

Institutional advertising tries to develop goodwill for a company or even an industry—instead of a specific product.

Intensive distribution selling a product through all responsible and suitable wholesalers or retailers who will stock and/or sell the product.

Intermediate customers any buyers from producers of basic raw materials to final consumers.

Introductory price dealing temporary price cuts—to speed new products into a market.

Job description a written statement of what a salesperson is expected to do.

Joint venturing a domestic firm entering into a partnership with a foreign firm.

Jury of executive opinion combines the opinions of experienced executives as a forecasting method.

Laggards prefer to do things the way they have been done in the past and are suspicious of new ideas—see *adoption curve*.

Late majority adopters who are cautious about new ideas—see *adoption curve*.

Law of diminishing demand says that if the price of a product is raised, a smaller quantity will be demanded, and if the price of a product is lowered, a greater quantity will be demanded.

Leader pricing setting some very low prices—real bargains—to attract customers—not to sell large quantities of the leader items.

Learning a change in a person's thought processes caused by experience.

Licensed brand a well-known brand which sellers pay a fee to use.

Licensing selling the right to use some process, trademark, patent, or other right for a fee or royalty.

Life-style analysis the analysis of a person's day-to-day living pattern—as expressed in Activities, Interests, and Opinions—referred to as AIOs.

Limited-function wholesalers merchant wholesalers who provide only some wholesaling functions.

Limited-line stores retailers who specialize in certain lines of related products—rather than a wide assortment.

Limited problem solving involves some effort to understand a person's need and how best to satisfy it.

Lower-lower class unskilled laborers and people in non-respectable occupations.

Lower-middle class small business people, office workers, teachers, and technicians—the "white-collar workers."

Low involvement products products which do not have high personal importance or relevance for the customer.

Macro-marketing a social process which directs an economy's flow of goods and services from producers to consumers in a way which effectively matches supply and demand and accomplishes the objectives of society.

Magnuson-Moss Act (of 1975) producers must provide a clearly written warranty if they choose to offer any warranty.

Mail-order and telephone retailing allows consumers to shop at home—placing orders by mail or telephone and charging the purchase to a credit card.

Mail-order wholesalers limited function wholesalers who sell out of catalogs which may be distributed widely to smaller industrial customers or retailers.

Management contracting the seller provides only management skills—the production facilities are owned by others.

Manufacturer brands brands which are created by manufacturers—sometimes called "national brands."

Manufacturers' agent an agent middleman who sells similar products for several non-competing manufacturers—for a commission on what is actually sold.

Manufacturers' sales branches separate businesses which manufacturers set up away from their factories.

Manufacturing actually producing goods and services.

Markdown a retail price reduction which is required because the customers will not buy some item at the originally marked-up price.

Markdown ratio a tool used by many retailers to measure the efficiency of various departments and their whole business.

Market a group of sellers and buyers bargaining over the terms of exchange for goods and/or services *or* a group of potential customers with similar needs and sellers offering various products—that is, ways of satisfying those needs.

Market development a firm trying to increase sales by selling present products in new markets.

Market-directed economic system economic system in which the individual decisions of the many producers and consumers make the macro-level decisions for the whole economy.

Market growth the stage in the product life cycle when industry sales are growing fast but industry profits rise and then start falling.

Market information function the collection, analysis, and distribution of all the information needed to plan, carry out, and control marketing activities.

Market introduction the stage in the product life cycle when sales are low as a new idea is first introduced to a market.

Market maturity the stage in the product life cycle when industry sales level off—and competition gets tougher.

Market penetration trying to increase sales of a firm's present products in its present markets.

Market potential what a whole market segment might buy—rather than a sales forecast.

Market segmentation the process of naming product-markets and then segmenting these broad product-markets into more homogeneous sub-markets in order to select target markets and develop suitable marketing mixes.

Marketing company era a time when marketing people develop long-range plans and the whole company effort is guided by the marketing concept.

Marketing concept a firm aims all its efforts at satisfying its customers at a profit.

Marketing department era a time when all marketing activities are brought under the control of one department to try to integrate the firm's activities.

Marketing information system (MIS) an organized way of continually gathering and analyzing data to get information to help marketing managers make decisions.

Marketing management process the process of planning marketing activities, directing the implementation of the plans, and controlling these plans.

Marketing mix the controllable variables which the company puts together to satisfy its target market.

Marketing orientation trying to carry out the marketing concept.

Marketing plan a written statement of a marketing strategy and the time-related details for carrying out the strategy.

Marketing program blends all of the firm's marketing plans into one "big plan."

Marketing research procedures to gather and analyze information to help marketing managers make decisions.

Marketing research process a five-step application of the scientific method that includes: definition of the problem, situation analysis, obtaining problem-specific data, interpretation of data, and problem solution.

Marketing strategy a target market and a related marketing mix.

Marketing strategy planning finding attractive opportunities—and developing profitable marketing strategies and plans.

Markup a dollar amount added to the cost of goods to get the selling price.

Markup (percent) percentage of selling price which is added to the cost to get the selling price.

Markup chain the sequence of markups used by firms at different levels in a channel.

Mass marketing the typical production-oriented approach which aims at everyone with the same marketing mix.

Mass-merchandisers large, self-service stores with many departments—which emphasize "soft goods" (housewares, clothing, and fabrics) but still follow the discount house's emphasis on lower margins to get faster turnover.

Mass-merchandising concept retailers should offer lower prices to get faster turnover and greater sales volumes—by appealing to larger markets.

Mass selling communicating with large numbers of potential customers at the same time.

Merchant wholesalers wholesalers who own (take title to) the goods they sell.

Message channel the carrier of the message.

Metropolitan Statistical Area (MSA) an economic and social unit having a fairly large population at the center.

Micro-marketing the performance of activities which seek to accomplish an organization's objectives by anticipating customer or client needs and directing a flow of need-satisfying goods and services from producer to customer or client.

Middleman someone who specializes in trade rather than production.

Missionary salespeople work for manufacturers—calling on their middlemen and their customers.

Modified rebuy in-between process where some review of the buying situation is done—though not as much as in new-task buying or as little as in straight rebuys.

Monopolistic competition a market situation which develops when a market has: (1) different products and (2) sellers who feel they do have some competition in this market.

Multinational corporations have a direct investment in several countries and run their businesses depending on the choices available anywhere in the world.

Multiple buying influence the buyer shares the purchasing decision with several people—perhaps even top management.

Multiple target market approach segmenting the market and choosing two or more submarkets, each of which will be treated as a separate target market needing a different marketing mix.

National accounts sales force sells direct to large accounts.

Nationalism an emphasis on a country's interests before everything else.

Natural products products which occur in nature.

Need-satisfaction approach a sales presentation which involves developing a good understanding of the individual customer's needs before trying to close the sale.

Needs basic forces which motivate an individual to do something.

Negotiated contract buying agreeing to a contract that allows for changing the purchase arrangements.

Neighborhood shopping centers planned shopping centers which consist of several convenience stores.

Net payment for the face value of the invoice is due immediately.

Net profit what the company has earned from its operations during a particular period.

Net sales the actual sales dollars the company will receive.

New product one that is new in any way for the company concerned.

New-task buying the buying process which occurs when a firm has a new need and the buyer wants a great deal of information.

New unsought goods products offering really new ideas that potential customers don't know about yet.

Noise any factor which reduces the effectiveness of the communication process.

Non-adopters prefer to do things the way they have been done in the past and are suspicious of new ideas—see *adoption curve.*

Non-cumulative quantity discounts quantity discounts which apply only to individual orders.

Non-price competition aggressive action on one or more of the Ps other than Price.

Odd-even pricing setting prices which end in certain numbers.

Oligopoly a market situation which develops when a market has: (1) essentially homogeneous products, (2) relatively few sellers, and (3) fairly inelastic industry demand curves.

One-price policy offering the same price to all customers who purchase goods under the same basic conditions—and in the same quantities.

Open to buy the buyer has budgeted funds which he can spend during the current time period.

Operating ratios the ratio of an item on the operating statement to net sales.

Operating statement a summary of the financial results of the operations of a company over a specified period of time.

Opinion leaders people who influence others.

Order getters salespeople who are concerned with getting new business.

Order getting aggressively seeking out possible buyers with a well-organized sales presentation designed to sell a product.

Order takers salespeople who sell the regular or typical customers.

Order taking routine completion of sales made regularly to the target customers.

Packaging protecting and promoting the product.

Penetration pricing policy trying to sell the whole market at one low price.

Personal needs concerned with an individual's need for personal satisfaction.

Personal selling direct face-to-face communication between sellers and potential customers.

Phony list prices prices that customers are shown to suggest that the price they are to pay has been discounted from list.

Physical distribution (PD) transporting and storing of physical goods within individual firms and along channel systems.

Physiological needs concerned with biological needs.

Piggy-back service loads truck trailers—or flat-bed trailers carrying containers—on rail cars to provide both speed and flexibility.

Pioneering advertising product advertising which tries to develop primary demand.

Place involves making products available in the right quantities and locations when customers want them.

Place utility utility provided by having the product available where the customer wants it.

Planned economic system economic system in which government planners decide what and how much is to be produced and distributed by whom, when, and to whom.

Planned shopping center a set of stores planned as a unit to satisfy some market needs.

Population the total group in which you are interested—in a research project.

Possession utility utility obtained by completing a transaction and gaining possession so that one has the right to use a product.

Prepared sales presentation uses a memorized presentation which is not adapted to each individual customer.

Prestige pricing setting a rather high price to suggest high quality or high status.

Price what is charged for "something."

Price discrimination selling the same products to different buyers at different prices—which injures competition.

Price fixing competitors getting together to raise, lower, or stabilize prices.

Price lining setting a few price levels for a product class and then marking all items at these prices.

Primary data information specifically collected to solve a current problem.

Primary demand demand for a product category rather than a specific brand.

Private carriers company-owned transporting facilities.

Private warehouses storing facilities owned by companies for their own use.

Producers' cooperatives operate almost as "full" service wholesalers—with the profits going to the cooperative's customer-members.

Product the need-satisfying offering of a firm.

Product advertising tries to sell a product.

Product development a firm offering new or improved products for present markets.

Product liability the legal obligation of sellers to pay damages to individuals who are injured by defective products or unsafely designed products.

Product life cycle the stages a new idea goes through from beginning to end.

Product managers manage specific products.

Product-market a market with very similar needs and sellers offering various close substitute ways of satisfying those needs.

Product positioning shows where proposed and/or present brands are located in a market—as seen by customers.

Production era a time when a company focuses on production.

Production orientation making products which are easy to produce—and then trying to sell them.

Profit maximization objective seeks to get as much profit as possible.

Promotion communicating information between seller and buyer—to influence attitudes and behavior.

Prospecting following down all the leads in the target market.

Psychographics the analysis of a person's day-to-day living pattern—as expressed in Activities, Interests, and Opinions—referred to as AIOs.

Psychological pricing setting prices which have special appeal to target customers.

Public carriers transporters which usually maintain regular schedules and accept goods from any shipper.

Public warehouses independent storing facilities.

Publicity any unpaid form of non-personal presentation of ideas, goods, or services.

Pulling getting consumers to ask middlemen for the product.

Purchase discount a reduction of the original invoice amount for some business reason.

Purchasing agents buying specialists for manufacturers and other intermediate customers.

Pure competition a market situation which develops when a market has (1) homogeneous products, (2) many buyers and sellers who have full knowledge of the market, and (3) ease of entry for buyers and sellers.

Pure subsistence economy an economy in which each family unit produces all the goods it needs.

Push money (or prize money) allowances allowances given to retailers by manufacturers or wholesalers to pass on to the retailers' salespeople—for aggressively selling certain items.

Pushing using normal promotion effort to help sell the whole marketing mix to possible channel members.

Qualifying dimensions the dimensions which are relevant to a product-market.

Qualitative research seeks in-depth, open-ended answers.

Quantitative research seeks structured

responses that can be summarized in numbers.

Quantity discounts discounts offered to encourage customers to buy in larger amounts.

Quotas set the specific quantities of goods which can move in or out of a country.

Rack jobbers merchant wholesalers who specialize in non-food items which are sold through grocery stores and supermarkets—often displaying them on their own wire racks.

Raw materials unprocessed goods that are handled as little as is needed to move them to the next production process.

Receiver a potential customer.

Reciprocity trading sales for sales.

Reference group the people to whom an individual looks when forming attitudes about a particular topic.

Regional shopping centers the largest planned shopping centers—emphasizing shopping stores and shopping goods.

Regrouping activities adjust the quantities and/or assortments of goods handled at each level in a channel of distribution.

Regularly unsought goods products that stay unsought but not unbought forever.

Reinforcement (of learning) occurs when the response is followed by satisfaction.

Relevant market the market which is suitable for the firm's purpose.

Reminder advertising tries to keep the product's name before the public.

Requisition a request to buy something.

Resident buyers independent buying agents who work in central markets for several retailer or wholesaler customers in outlying areas.

Response an effort to satisfy a drive.

Response rate the percent of people contacted who complete a questionnaire.

Retailing activities involved in the sale of goods and/or services to final consumers.

Return a customer sends back purchased products.

Return on assets (ROA) the ratio of net profit (after taxes) to the assets used to make the net profit, multiplied by 100 to get rid of decimals.

Return on investment (ROI) the ratio of net profit (after taxes) to the investment used to make the net profit, multiplied by 100 to get rid of decimals.

Risk-taking function marketing function concerned with bearing the uncertainties that are a part of the marketing process.

Robinson-Patman Act makes illegal any price discrimination which injures competition.

Routinized response behavior buying process which involves mechanically selecting a particular way of satisfying a need whenever it occurs.

Safety needs concerned with protection and physical well-being.

Sales decline product life cycle stage when new products replace the old.

Sales era a time when a company emphasizes selling—because of increased competition.

Sales forecast an estimate of how much an industry or firm hopes to sell to a market segment.

Sales managers manage personal selling.

Sales-oriented objective the firm seeks some level of unit sales, dollar sales, or share of market—without referring to profit.

Sales presentation a salesperson's effort to make a sale.

Sales promotion promotion activities other than advertising, publicity, and personal selling which stimulate interest, trial, or purchase by final customers or others in the channel.

Sales promotion managers manage their company's sales promotion effort.

Sales territory a geographic area which is the responsibility of one salesperson or several working in a coordinated effort.

Sample part of the relevant population in a research project.

Sampling buying looking at only part of a potential purchase.

Scientific method a decision-making approach

that focuses on being objective and orderly in testing ideas before accepting them.

Scrambled merchandising retailers carrying *any* product lines which they feel they can sell profitably.

Seasonal discounts discounts offered to encourage buyers to stock earlier than present demand requires.

Secondary data information that has been collected or published already.

Segmenters aim at one or more homogeneous sub-markets and try to develop a different marketing mix for each sub-market.

Segmenting an aggregating process.

Selective demand demand for a specific brand rather than a product category.

Selective distribution selling only through those middlemen who will give the product special attention.

Selective exposure our eyes and mind notice only information that interests us.

Selective perception we screen out or modify ideas, messages, and information that conflict with previously learned attitudes and beliefs.

Selective retention we remember only what we want to remember.

Selling agents take over the whole marketing job of manufacturers—not just the selling function.

Selling formula approach a sales presentation which starts with a prepared presentation outline and leads the customer through some logical steps to a final close.

Selling function promoting the product.

Senior citizens people over 65.

Service wholesalers merchant wholesalers who provide all the wholesaling functions.

Services (industrial good) expense items which support the operations of a firm.

Shopping goods products that a customer feels are worth the time and effort to compare with competing products.

Shopping stores stores which attract customers from greater distances because of the width and depth of their assortments.

Simple trade era a time when families traded or sold their surplus output to local middlemen—who then sold these goods to other consumers or distant middlemen.

Single-line stores stores which specialize in certain lines of related products—rather than a wide assortment.

Single-line wholesalers service merchant wholesalers who carry a narrower line of merchandise than general merchandise wholesalers.

Single target market approach segmenting the market and picking one of the homogeneous sub-markets as the firm's target market.

Situation analysis an informal study of what information is already available in the problem area.

Skimming price policy trying to sell the top of a market—the top of the demand curve—at a high price before aiming at more price-sensitive customers.

Social class a group of people who have about equal social position.

Social needs concerned with love, friendship, status, and esteem—things that involve a person's interaction with others.

Sorting separating products into grades and qualities desired by different target markets.

Source the sender of a message.

Specialty goods consumer goods that the customer really wants—and is willing to make a special effort to find.

Specialty shop a type of limited-line store—usually small, with a distinct personality.

Specialty stores stores for which customers have developed a strong attraction.

Specialty wholesalers service merchant wholesalers who carry a very narrow range of products.

Specification buying buying from a written (or verbal) description of the product.

Standard Industrial Classification (SIC) codes groups of firms in similar lines of business.

Standardization function sorting products according to size and quality.

Staples consumer convenience goods which are bought often and routinely—without much thought.

Statistical packages easy-to-use computer programs that analyze data.

Status quo objectives "don't-rock-the-pricing-boat" objectives.

Stimulus-response model people respond in some predictable way to a stimulus.

Stockturn rate the number of times the average inventory is sold in a year.

Storing the marketing function of holding goods until customers need them.

Straight rebuy a routine repurchase which may have been made many times before.

Strategic (management) planning the managerial process of developing and maintaining a match between the resources of an organization and its market opportunities.

Substitutes goods and services that offer a choice to the buyer.

Supermarket a large store specializing in groceries—with self-service and wide assortments.

Super-stores very large stores that try to carry not only foods, but all goods and services which the consumer purchases routinely.

Supplies (industrial goods) expense items that do not become a part of a final product.

Supply curve shows the quantity of goods that will be supplied to a market at various possible prices—by all suppliers together.

Supporting salespeople help the order-oriented salespeople—but don't try to get orders themselves.

Target market a fairly homogeneous (similar) group of customers to whom a company wishes to appeal.

Target marketing aims at some specific target customers.

Target return objective sets a specific level of profit as an objective.

Tariffs taxes on imported goods.

Technical specialists salespeople who provide technical assistance to order-oriented salespeople.

Technological base the technical skills and equipment which affect the way the resources of an economy are converted to output.

Telephone and mail-order retailing allows customers to shop at home—placing orders by mail or telephone and charging the purchase to a credit card.

Telephone selling using the telephone to find out about a prospect's interest in the company's marketing mix—and even to make a sales presentation or take an order.

Time utility utility provided by having the product available when the customer wants it.

Total cost the sum of total fixed and total variable costs.

Total cost approach involves evaluating all the costs of possible PD systems.

Total fixed cost the sum of those costs that are fixed in total—no matter how much is produced.

Total variable cost the sum of those changing expenses that are closely related to output.

Trade (functional) discount list price reduction given to channel members for the job they are going to do.

Trade-in allowance price reduction given for used goods when similar new goods are bought.

Trademark those words, symbols, or marks that are legally registered for use by a single company.

Trading stamps free stamps given by some retailers with each purchase.

Traditional channel system a channel system in which the various channel members make little or no effort to cooperate with each other.

Transporting function the movement of goods.

Trend extension a forecasting method which extends past experience into the future.

Truck wholesalers specialize in delivering products which they stock in their own trucks.

2/10, net 30 2 percent discount off the face

value of the invoice is allowed if the invoice is paid within 10 days.

Unfair trade practice acts laws which put a lower limit on prices, especially at the whole-sale and retail levels.

Uniform delivered pricing making an average freight charge to all buyers.

Unit pricing placing the price per ounce (or some other standard measure) on or near the product.

Universal functions (of marketing) buying, sell-ing, transporting, storing, standardization and grading, financing, risk taking, and market information.

Universal product code (UPC) identifies each product with marks that can be read by elec-tronic scanners.

Unsought goods consumer goods that potential customers do not yet want or know they can buy.

Upper class people from old, wealthy families (upper-upper) and the socially prominent new rich (lower-upper).

Upper-lower class factory production line work-ers, skilled workers, and service people—the "blue-collar workers."

Upper-middle class successful professionals, owners of small businesses, or top sales-people.

Utility the power to satisfy human needs.

Validity concerns the extent to which data measures what it is intended to measure.

Value-in-use pricing setting prices which will capture some of what customers will save by substituting the firm's product for the one being used.

Vendor analysis formal rating of suppliers on all areas of performance.

Vertical integration ownership of the natural product source by the user *or* acquiring firms at different levels of channel activity.

Vertical marketing system channel system in which the whole channel shares a common focus on the same target market at the end of the channel.

Voluntary chains wholesaler-sponsored groups which work with independent retailers.

Wants needs which are learned during a per-son's life.

Warranty explains what the seller promises about its product.

Wheel of retailing theory new types of retailers enter the market as low-status, low-margin, low-price operators and then evolve into more conventional retailers—offering more services, with higher operating costs and higher prices.

Wheeler Lea Amendment bans "unfair or deceptive acts in commerce."

Wholesalers firms whose main function is pro-viding wholesaling activities.

Wholesaling concerned with the activities of those persons or establishments which sell to retailers and other merchants, and/or to indus-trial, institutional, and commercial users—but who do not sell in large amounts to final con-sumers.

Wholly-owned subsidiary a separate firm owned by a parent company.

Zone pricing making an average freight charge to all buyers within specific geographic areas.

Illustration credits

583

■ Author index

■ Subject index

*This book has been set Linotron 202, in 9 point Helvetica,
leaded 3 points. Chapter numbers are 20 point Garamond
Bold Condensed. The size of the type page is 35 picas 9
points by 49 picas.*